The Frank J. Fabozzi Series

Fixed Income Securities, Second Edition by Frank J. Fabozzi
Focus on Value: A Corporate and Investor Guide to Wealth Creation by James L. Grant and James A. Abate
Handbook of Global Fixed Income Calculations by Dragomir Krgin
Managing a Corporate Bond Portfolio by Leland E. Crabbe and Frank J. Fabozzi
Real Options and Option-Embedded Securities by William T. Moore
Capital Budgeting: Theory and Practice by Pamela P. Peterson and Frank J. Fabozzi
The Exchange-Traded Funds Manual by Gary L. Gastineau
Professional Perspectives on Fixed Income Portfolio Management, Volume 3 edited by Frank J. Fabozzi
Investing in Emerging Fixed Income Markets edited by Frank J. Fabozzi and Efstathia Pilarinu
Handbook of Alternative Assets by Mark J. P. Anson
The Global Money Markets by Frank J. Fabozzi, Steven V. Mann, and Moorad Choudhry
The Handbook of Financial Instruments edited by Frank J. Fabozzi
Interest Rate, Term Structure, and Valuation Modeling edited by Frank J. Fabozzi
Investment Performance Measurement by Bruce J. Feibel
The Handbook of Equity Style Management edited by T. Daniel Coggin and Frank J. Fabozzi
The Theory and Practice of Investment Management edited by Frank J. Fabozzi and Harry M. Markowitz
Foundations of Economic Value Added, Second Edition by James L. Grant
Financial Management and Analysis, Second Edition by Frank J. Fabozzi and Pamela P. Peterson
Measuring and Controlling Interest Rate and Credit Risk, Second Edition by Frank J. Fabozzi,
    Steven V. Mann, and Moorad Choudhry
Professional Perspectives on Fixed Income Portfolio Management, Volume 4 edited by Frank J. Fabozzi
The Handbook of European Fixed Income Securities edited by Frank J. Fabozzi and Moorad Choudhry
The Handbook of European Structured Financial Products edited by Frank J. Fabozzi and Moorad Choudhry
The Mathematics of Financial Modeling and Investment Management by Sergio M. Focardi and Frank J. Fabozzi
Short Selling: Strategies, Risks, and Rewards edited by Frank J. Fabozzi
The Real Estate Investment Handbook by G. Timothy Haight and Daniel Singer
Market Neutral Strategies edited by Bruce I. Jacobs and Kenneth N. Levy
Securities Finance: Securities Lending and Repurchase Agreements edited by Frank J. Fabozzi and Steven V. Mann
Fat-Tailed and Skewed Asset Return Distributions by Svetlozar T. Rachev, Christian Menn, and Frank J. Fabozzi
Financial Modeling of the Equity Market: From CAPM to Cointegration by Frank J. Fabozzi, Sergio M.
    Focardi, and Petter N. Kolm
Advanced Bond Portfolio Management: Best Practices in Modeling and Strategies edited by Frank J. Fabozzi,
    Lionel Martellini, and Philippe Priaulet
Analysis of Financial Statements, Second Edition by Pamela P. Peterson and Frank J. Fabozzi
Collateralized Debt Obligations: Structures and Analysis, Second Edition by Douglas J. Lucas, Laurie S.
    Goodman, and Frank J. Fabozzi
Handbook of Alternative Assets, Second Edition by Mark J. P. Anson
Introduction to Structured Finance by Frank J. Fabozzi, Henry A. Davis, and Moorad Choudhry
Financial Econometrics by Svetlozar T. Rachev, Stefan Mittnik, Frank J. Fabozzi, Sergio M. Focardi, and Teo Jasic
Developments in Collateralized Debt Obligations: New Products and Insights by Douglas J. Lucas,
    Laurie S. Goodman, Frank J. Fabozzi, and Rebecca J. Manning
Robust Portfolio Optimization and Management by Frank J. Fabozzi, Peter N. Kolm,
    Dessislava A. Pachamanova, and Sergio M. Focardi
Advanced Stochastic Models, Risk Assessment, and Portfolio Optimizations by Svetlozar T. Rachev,
    Stogan V. Stoyanov, and Frank J. Fabozzi
How to Select Investment Managers and Evaluate Performance by G. Timothy Haight, Stephen O. Morrell,
    and Glenn E. Ross
Bayesian Methods in Finance by Svetlozar T. Rachev, John S. J. Hsu, Biliana S. Bagasheva, and Frank J. Fabozzi
The Handbook of Municipal Bonds edited by Sylvan G. Feldstein and Frank J. Fabozzi
Subprime Mortgage Credit Derivatives by Laurie S. Goodman, Shumin Li, Douglas J. Lucas,
    Thomas A Zimmerman, and Frank J. Fabozzi
Introduction to Securitization by Frank J. Fabozzi and Vinod Kothari
Structured Products and Related Credit Derivatives edited by Brian P. Lancaster, Glenn M. Schultz, and
    Frank J. Fabozzi
Handbook of Finance: Volume I: Financial Markets and Instruments edited by Frank J. Fabozzi
Handbook of Finance: Volume II: Financial Management and Asset Management edited by Frank J. Fabozzi
Handbook of Finance: Volume III: Valuation, Financial Modeling, and Quantitative Tools edited by
    Frank J. Fabozzi

Finance

Finance

Capital Markets,
Financial Management,
and Investment Management

FRANK J. FABOZZI
PAMELA PETERSON DRAKE

WILEY

John Wiley & Sons, Inc.

Library of Congress Cataloging-in-Publication Data

Fabozzi, Frank J.
    Finance : capital markets, financial management, and investment management /
Frank J. Fabozzi, Pamela Peterson Drake.
    p. cm.—(The Frank J. Fabozzi series)
    ISBN 978-0-470-40735-6 (cloth)
    1. Finance. 2. Investments. 3. Business enterprises—Finance. 4. Corporations—Finance. I.
Peterson Drake, Pamela, 1954- II. Title.
HG173.F27 2009
332–dc22
                                    2009005638

FJF
To my wife Donna, and my children
Francesco, Patricia, and Karly

PPD
To my husband Randy

Contents

Preface

Recent financial events have emphasized the need for an understanding of financial decision-making, financing instruments, and strategies used in financial and investment management. In this book, we provide an introduction to these topics in the field of finance.

We begin our introduction to finance in Part One, where we introduce you to financial mathematics and financial analysis. These are the basic tools of finance that span investment and financing decision-making.

In Part Two, we develop the fundamentals of capital market theory and discuss financial markets, financial intermediaries, and regulators of financial activities. Knowledge of capital markets and how assets are priced is essential to decision-making that involves raising capital in the markets or investing capital. In this part, we also cover the basics of interest rates, bond and stock valuation, asset pricing theory, and derivative instruments.

We present the decision-making within a business enterprise in Part Three. These decisions include capital budgeting—that is, whether or not to invest in specific long-lived projects—and capital structure—that is, how to finance the business. In this part, we also discuss the management of current assets and risk management.

In Part Four, we cover the basics of investment decision-making, beginning with the determination of an investment objective and then proceeding to discuss and demonstrate portfolio theory and performance evaluation. In addition, we discuss basic techniques for managing equity and bond portfolios, and the use of futures and options in portfolio management.

We cover a lot of ground in this book, providing a comprehensive overview of finance. We take the reader, who may have little or no familiarity with finance, to a level of understanding that gives the reader a better appreciation for the complex financial issues that companies and investors face today.

The approach in this book is different from the traditional book that is used in an introductory undergraduate or MBA finance course. In such courses, the focus is on financial management (also referred to as *corporate finance* or *business finance*). We believe that a more appropriate course covers capital markets and investment management, and that is the primary motivation for writing this book. Moreover, we believe there are topics that are often neglected in financial management courses that we cover in this book: financial strategy, financial engineering, asset securitization, and financial risk management.

We hope that the reader benefits from our broader perspective of topics.

Frank J. Fabozzi
Pamela Peterson Drake

About the Authors

Frank J. Fabozzi is Professor in the Practice of Finance and Becton Fellow at the Yale School of Management. Prior to joining the Yale faculty, he was a Visiting Professor of Finance in the Sloan School at MIT. Professor Fabozzi is a Fellow of the International Center for Finance at Yale University and on the Advisory Council for the Department of Operations Research and Financial Engineering at Princeton University. He is the editor of the *Journal of Portfolio Management* and an associate editor of the *Journal of Fixed Income* and *Journal of Structured Finance*. He earned a doctorate in economics from the City University of New York in 1972. In 2002, Professor Fabozzi was inducted into the Fixed Income Analysts Society's Hall of Fame and is the 2007 recipient of the C. Stewart Sheppard Award given by the CFA Institute. He earned the designation of Chartered Financial Analyst and Certified Public Accountant. He has authored and edited numerous books on finance.

Pamela Peterson Drake, PhD, CFA, is the J. Gray Ferguson Professor of Finance and Department Head, Department of Finance and Business Law in the College of Business at James Madison University. She received her Ph.D. in finance from the University of North Carolina at Chapel Hill and her B.S. in Accountancy from Miami University. Professor Drake previously taught at Florida State University (1981–2004), and was an Associate Dean at Florida Atlantic University (2004–2007). She has published numerous articles in academic journals, as well as authored and co-authored several books. Professor Drake's expertise is in financial analysis and valuation.

PART
One

Background

CHAPTER 1

What Is Finance?

Finance is the application of economic principles to decision-making that involves the allocation of money under conditions of uncertainty. Investors allocate their funds among financial assets in order to accomplish their objectives, and businesses and governments raise funds by issuing claims against themselves that are invested. Finance provides the framework for making decisions as to how those funds should be obtained and then invested. It is the financial system that provides the platform by which funds are transferred from those entities that have funds to invest to those entities that need funds to invest.

The theoretical foundations for finance draw from the field of economics and, for this reason, finance is often referred to as *financial economics*. The tools used in financial decision-making, however, draw from many areas outside of economics: financial accounting, mathematics, probability theory, statistical theory, and psychology. In Chapters 2 and 3, we cover the mathematics of finance as well as the basics of financial analysis that we use throughout this book. We need to understand the former topic in order to determine the value of an investment, the yield on an investment, and the cost of funds. The key concept is the time value of money, a simple mathematical concept that allows financial decision-makers to translate future cash flows to a value in the present, translate a value today into a value at some future point in time, and calculate the yield on an investment. The time-value-of-money mathematics allows an evaluation and comparison of investments and financing arrangements. Financial analysis involves the selection, evaluation, and interpretation of financial data and other pertinent information to assist in evaluating the operating performance and financial condition of a company. These tools include financial ratio analysis, cash flow analysis, and quantitative analysis.

It is generally agreed that the field of finance has three specialty areas:

- Capital markets and capital market theory
- Financial management
- Investment management

We cover these three areas in this book in Parts Two, Three, and Four of this book. In this chapter, we provide an overview of these three specialty areas and a description of the coverage of the chapters in the three parts of the book.

CAPITAL MARKETS AND CAPITAL MARKET THEORY

The specialty field of capital markets and capital market theory focuses on the study of the financial system, the structure of interest rates, and the pricing of risky assets.

The financial system of an economy consists of three components: (1) financial markets; (2) financial intermediaries; and (3) financial regulators. For this reason, we refer to this specialty area as financial markets and institutions. In Chapter 4, we discuss the three components of the financial system and the role that each plays. We begin the chapter by defining financial assets, their economic function, and the difference between debt and equity financial instruments. We then explain the different ways to classify financial markets: internal versus external markets, capital markets versus money markets, cash versus derivative markets, primary versus secondary markets, private placement versus public markets, order driven versus quote driven markets, and exchange-traded versus over-the-counter markets. We also explain what is meant by market efficiency and the different forms of market efficiency (weak, semi-strong, and strong forms). In the discussion of financial regulators, we discuss changes in the regulatory system in response to the problems in the credit markets in 2008. We discuss the major market players (that is, households, governments, nonfinancial corporations, depository institutions, insurance companies, asset management firms, investment banks, nonprofit organizations, and foreign investors), as well as the importance of financial intermediaries.

We describe the level and structure of interest rates in Chapter 5. We begin this chapter with two economic theories that each seek to explain the determination of the level of interest rates: the *loanable funds theory* and the *liquidity preference theory*. We then review the Federal Reserve System and the role of monetary policy. As we point out, there is not one interest rate in an economy; rather, there is a structure of interest rates. We explain that the factors that affect interest rates in different sectors of the debt market, with a major focus on the *term structure of interest rates* (i.e., the relationship between interest rate and the maturity of debt instrument of the same credit quality).

As we explain in Chapter 6, derivative instruments play an important role in finance because they offer financial managers and investors the opportunity to cost effectively control their exposure to different types of risk. The two basic derivative contracts are futures/forward contracts and options contracts. As we demonstrate, swaps and caps/floors are economically equivalent to a package of these two basic contracts. In this chapter, we explain the basic features of derivative instruments and how they are priced. We detail the well-known Black-Scholes option pricing model in the appendix of this chapter. We wait until later chapters, however, to describe how they are employed in financial management and investment management.

Valuation is the process of determining the fair value of a financial asset. We explain the basics of valuation and illustrate these through examples in Chapter 7. The fundamental principle of valuation is that the value of any financial asset is the present value of the expected cash flows. Thus, the valuation of a financial asset involves (1) estimating the expected cash flows; (2) determining the appropriate interest rate or interest rates that should be used to discount the cash flows; and (3) calculating the present value of the expected cash flows using the interest rate or interest rates. In this chapter, we apply many of the financial mathematics principles that we explained in Chapter 2. We apply the valuation process to the valuation of common stocks and bonds in Chapter 7 given an assumed discount rate.

In Chapter 8, we discuss asset pricing models. The purpose of such models is to provide the appropriate discount rate or required interest rate that should be used in valuation. We present two asset pricing models in this chapter: the capital asset pricing models and the arbitrage pricing theory.

FINANCIAL MANAGEMENT

Financial management, sometimes called *business finance*, is the specialty area of finance concerned with financial decision-making within a business entity. Often, we refer to financial management as corporate finance. However, the principles of financial management also apply to other forms of business and to government entities. Moreover, not all non-government business enterprises are corporations. Financial managers are primarily concerned with investment decisions and financing decisions within business organizations, whether that organization is a sole proprietorship, a partnership, a limited liability company, a corporation, or a governmental entity.

In Chapter 9, we provide an overview of financial management. Investment decisions are concerned with the use of funds—the buying, holding, or selling of all types of assets: Should a business purchase a new machine? Should a business introduce a new product line? Sell the old production facility? Acquire another business? Build a manufacturing plan? Maintain a higher level of inventory? Financing decisions are concerned with the procuring of funds that can be used for long-term investing and financing day-to-day operations. Should financial managers use profits raised through the firms' revenues or distribute those profits to the owners? Should financial managers seek money from outside of the business? A company's operations and investment can be financed from outside the business by incurring debt—such as though bank loans or the sale of bonds—or by selling ownership interests. Because each method of financing obligates the business in different ways, financing decisions are extremely important. The financing decision also involves the dividend decision, which involves how much of a company's profit should be retained and how much to distribute to owners.

A company's financial strategic plan is a framework of achieving its goal of maximizing shareholder wealth. Implementing the strategic plan requires both long-term and short-term financial planning that brings together forecasts of the company's sales with financing and investment decision-making. Budgets are employed to manage the information used in this planning; performance measures, such as the balanced scorecard and economic value added, are used to evaluate progress toward the strategic goals. In Chapter 10, we focus on a company's financial strategy and financial planning.

The capital structure of a firm is the mixture of debt and equity that management elects to raise in funding itself. In Chapter 11, we discuss this capital structure decision. We review different economic theories about how the firm should be financed and whether an optimal capital structure (that is, one that maximizes a firm's value) exists. The first economic theory about firm capital structure was proposed by Franco Modigliani and Merton Miller in the 1960s. We explain this theory in the appendix to Chapter 11.

There are times when financial managers have sought to create financial instruments for financing purposes that cannot be accommodated by traditional products. Doing so involves the restructuring or repacking of cash flows and/or the use of derivative instruments. Chapter 12 explains how this is done through what is referred to as financial engineering or as it is more popularly referred to as structured finance.

In Chapters 11 and 12, we cover the financing side of financial management, whereas in Chapters 13, 14, and 15, we turn to the investment of funds. In Chapters 13 and 14, we discuss decisions involving the long-term commitment of a firm's scarce resources in capital investments. We refer to these decisions as capital budgeting decisions. These decisions play a prominent role in determining the success of a business enterprise. Although there are capital budgeting decisions that are routine and, hence, do not alter the course or risk of a company, there are also strategic capital budgeting decisions that either affect a company's future market position in its current product lines or permit it to expand into a new product lines in the future.

In Chapter 15, we discuss considerations in managing a firm's current assets. Current assets are those assets that could reasonably be converted into cash within one operating cycle or one year, whichever takes longer. Current assets include cash, marketable securities, accounts receivable and inventories, and support the long-term investment decisions of a company.

In Chapter 16 we look at the risk management of a firm. The process of risk management involves determining which risks to accept, which to neutralize, and which to transfer. After providing various ways to define risk, we look at the four key processes in risk management: (1) risk identification, (2) risk assessment, (3) risk mitigation, and (4) risk transferring. The traditional process of risk management focuses on managing the risks of only parts of the business (products, departments, or divisions), ignoring the implications for the value of the firm. Today, some form of enterprise risk management is followed by large corporation. Doing so allows management to align the risk appetite and strategies across the firm, improve the quality of the firm's risk response decisions, identify the risks across the firm, and manage the risks across the firm.

INVESTMENT MANAGEMENT

Investment management is the specialty area within finance dealing with the management of individual or institutional funds. Other terms commonly used to describe this area of finance are *asset management, portfolio management, money management,* and *wealth management.* In industry jargon, an asset manager "runs money."

Investment management involves five activities: (1) setting investment objectives, (2) establishing an investment policy, (3) selecting an investment strategy, (4) selecting the specific assets, and (5) measuring and evaluating investment performance. We describe these activities in Chapter 17. Setting investment objectives starts with a thorough analysis of what the entity wants to accomplish. Given the investment objectives, policy guidelines must be established, taking into consideration any client-imposed investment constraints, legal/regulatory constraints, and tax restrictions. This task begins with the asset allocation decision (i.e., how the funds are to be allocated among the major asset classes). Next, a portfolio strategy that is consistent with the investment objectives and investment policy guidelines must be selected. In general, portfolio strategies are classified as either active or passive. Selecting the specific financial assets to include in the portfolio, which is referred to as the portfolio selection problem, is the next step. The theory of portfolio selection was formulated by Harry Markowitz in 1952. This theory, as we explain in Chapter 17, proposes how investors can construct portfolios based on two parameters: mean return and standard deviation of returns. The latter parameter is a measure of risk. An important task is the evaluation of the performance of the asset manager. This task allows a client to determine answers to questions such as: How did the asset manager perform after adjusting for the risk associated with the active strategy employed? And, how did the asset manager achieve the reported return?

Our discussion in Chapter 17 provides the principles of investment management applied to any asset class (e.g., equities, bonds, real estate, and alternative investments). In Chapters 18 and 19, we focus on equity and bond portfolio management, respectively. In Chapter 18, we describe the different stock market indicators followed by the investment community, the difference between fundamental and technical strategies, the popular stock market active strategies employed by asset managers including equity style management, the types of stock market structures and locations in which an asset manager may trade, and trading mechanics and trading costs. In Chapter 19, we cover bond portfolio management, describing the sectors of the bond market and the instruments traded in those sectors, the features of bonds, yield measures for bonds, the risks associated with investing in bonds and how some of those risks can be quantified (e.g., duration as a measure of interest rate risk), bond indexes, and both active and structured bond portfolio strategies.

We explain and illustrate the use of derivatives in equity and bond portfolios in Chapters 20 and 21. In the absence of derivatives, the implementation of portfolio strategies is more costly. Though the perception of derivatives is that they are instruments for speculating, we demonstrate in these two chapters that they are transactionally efficient instruments to accomplish portfolio objectives. In Chapter 20, we introduce stock index futures and Treasury futures, explaining their basic features and illustrating how they can be employed to control risk in equity and bond portfolios. We also explain how the unique features of these contracts require that the basic pricing model that we explained Chapter 6 necessitates a modification of the pricing model. We focus on options in Chapter 21. In this chapter, we describe contract features and explain the role of these features in controlling risk.

SUMMARY

The three primary areas of finance, namely capital markets, financial management, and investment management, are connected by the fundamental threads of finance: risk and return. In this book, we introduce you to these fundamentals threads and how they are woven throughout the different areas of finance.

Our goal in this book is to provide a comprehensive view of finance, which will enable you to learn about the principles of finance, understand how the different areas of finance are interconnected, and how financial decision-makers manage risk and returns.

CHAPTER 2

Mathematics of Finance

In later chapters of this book, we will see how investment decisions made by financial managers, to acquire capital assets such as plant and equipment, and asset managers, to acquire securities such as stocks and bonds, require the valuation of investments and the determination of yields on investments. In addition, when financial managers must decide on alternative sources for financing the company, they must be able to determine the cost of those funds. The concept that must be understood to determine the value of an investment, the yield on an investment, and the cost of funds is the time value of money. This simple mathematical concepts allows financial and asset managers to translate future cash flows to a value in the present, translate a value today into a value at some future point in time, and calculate the yield on an investment. The time-value-of-money mathematics allows an evaluation and comparison of investments and financing arrangements and is the subject of this chapter. We also introduce the basic principles of valuation.

THE IMPORTANCE OF THE TIME VALUE OF MONEY

Financial mathematics are tools used in the valuation and the determination of yields on investments and costs of financing arrangements. In this chapter, we introduce the mathematical process of translating a value today into a value at some future point in time, and then show how this process can be reversed to determine the value today of some future amount. We then show how to extend the time value of money mathematics to include multiple cash flows and the special cases of annuities and loan amortization. We then show how these mathematics can be used to calculate the yield on an investment.

The notion that money has a time value is one of the most basic concepts in investment analysis. Making decisions today regarding future cash flows requires understanding that the value of money does not remain the same throughout time.

A dollar today is worth less than a dollar some time in the future for two reasons:

Reason 1: Cash flows occurring at different points in time have different values relative to any one point in time. One dollar one year from now is not as valuable as one dollar today. After all, you can invest a dollar today and earn interest so that the value it grows to next year is greater than the one dollar today. This means we have to take into account the *time value of money* to quantify the relation between cash flows at different points in time.

Reason 2: Cash flows are uncertain. Expected cash flows may not materialize. Uncertainty stems from the nature of forecasts of the timing and the amount of cash flows. We do not know for certain when, whether, or how much cash flows will be in the future. This uncertainty regarding future cash flows must somehow be taken into account in assessing the value of an investment.

Translating a current value into its equivalent future value is referred to as *compounding*. Translating a future cash flow or value into its equivalent value in a prior period is referred to as *discounting*. This chapter outlines the basic mathematical techniques used in compounding and discounting.

Suppose someone wants to borrow $100 today and promises to pay back the amount borrowed in one month. Would the repayment of only the $100 be fair? Probably not. There are two things to consider. First, if the lender didn't lend the $100, what could he or she have done with it? Second, is there a chance that the borrower may not pay back the loan? So, when considering lending money, we must consider the opportunity cost (that is, what could have been earned or enjoyed), as well as the uncertainty associated with getting the money back as promised.

Let's say that someone is willing to lend the money, but that they require repayment of the $100 plus some compensation for the opportunity cost and any uncertainty the loan will be repaid as promised. The amount of the loan, the $100, is the principal. The compensation required for allowing someone else to use the $100 is the interest.

Looking at this same situation from the perspective of time and value, the amount that you are willing to lend today is the loan's present value. The amount that you require to be paid at the end of the loan period is the loan's future value. Therefore, the future period's value is comprised of two parts:

Future value = Present value + Interest

The interest is compensation for the use of funds for a specific period. It consists of (1) compensation for the length of time the money is borrowed; and (2) compensation for the risk that the amount borrowed will not be repaid exactly as set forth in the loan agreement.

DETERMINING THE FUTURE VALUE

Suppose you deposit $1,000 into a savings account at the Surety Savings Bank and you are promised 10% interest per period. At the end of one period, you would have $1,100. This $1,100 consists of the return of your principal amount of the investment (the $1,000) and the interest or return on your investment (the $100). Let's label these values:

$1,000 is the value today, the present value, *PV*.
$1,100 is the value at the end of one period, the future value, *FV*.
10% is the rate interest is earned in one period, the interest rate, *i*.

To get to the future value from the present value:

$$FV = \underset{\uparrow}{PV} + (\underset{\uparrow}{PV} \times i)$$
$$\text{Principal} \quad \text{Interest}$$

This is equivalent to

$$FV = PV(1 + i)$$

In terms of our example,

$$FV = \$1,000 + (\$1,000 \times 0.10) = \$1,000(1 + 0.10) = \$1,100$$

If the $100 interest is withdrawn at the end of the period, the principal is left to earn interest at the 10% rate. Whenever you do this, you earn *simple interest*. It is simple because it repeats itself in exactly the same way from one period to the next as long as you take out the interest at the end of each period and the principal remains the same. If, on the other hand, both the principal and the interest are left on deposit at the Surety Savings Bank, the balance earns interest on the previously paid interest, referred to as *compound interest*. Earning interest on interest is called compounding because the balance at any time is a combination of the principal, interest on principal, and *interest on accumulated interest* (or simply, *interest on interest*).

If you compound interest for one more period in our example, the original $1,000 grows to $1,210.00:

FV = Principal + First period interest + Second period interest
        = $1,000.00 + ($1,000.00 × 0.10) + ($1,100.00 × 0.10)
        = $1,210.00

The present value of the investment is $1,000, the interest earned over two years is $210, and the future value of the investment after two years is $1,210.

The relation between the present value and the future value after two periods, breaking out the second period interest into interest on the principal and interest on interest, is

$FV =$	PV	+	$(PV \times i)$	+	$(PV \times i)$	$(PV \times i \times i)$
	Principal		First period's interest on the principal		Second period's interest on the principal	Second period's interest on the first period's interest

or, collecting the PVs from each term and applying a bit of elementary algebra,

$$FV = PV(1 + 2i + i^2) = PV(1 + i)^2$$

The balance in the account two years from now, $1,210, is comprised of three parts:

1. The principal, $1,000.
2. Interest on principal: $100 in the first period plus $100 in the second period.
3. Interest on interest: 10% of the first period's interest, or $10.

To determine the future value with compound interest for more than two periods, we follow along the same lines:

$$FV = PV(1 + i)^N \qquad (2.1)$$

The value of N is the number of compounding periods, where a compounding period is the unit of time after which interest is paid at the rate i. A period may be any length of time: a minute, a day, a month, or a year. The important thing is to make sure the same compounding period is reflected throughout the problem being analyzed. The term "$(1 + i)^N$" is referred to as the compound factor. It is the rate of exchange between present dollars and dollars N compounding periods into the future. Equation (2.1) is the basic valuation equation—the foundation of financial mathematics. It relates a value at one point in time to a value at another point in time, considering the compounding of interest.

The relation between present and future values for a principal of $1,000 and interest of 10% per period through 10 compounding periods is shown graphically in Figure 2.1. For example, the value of $1,000, earning interest at 10% per period, is $2,593.70, which is 10 periods into the future:

$$FV = \$1,000(1 + 0.10)^{10} = \$1,000(2.5937) = \$2,593.70$$

As you can see in Figure 2.1 the $2,593.70 balance in the account at the end of 10 periods is comprised of three parts:

1. The principal, $1,000.
2. Interest on the principal of $1,000: $100 per period for 10 periods or $1,000.
3. Interest on interest totaling $593.70.

FIGURE 2.1 The Value of $1,000 Invested 10 Years in an Account that Pays 10% Compounded Interest per Year

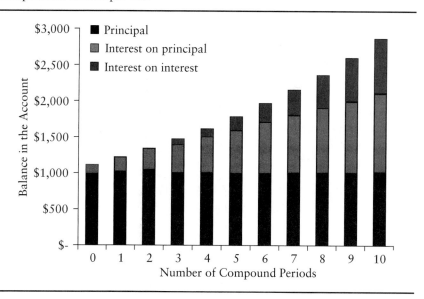

We can express the change in the value of the savings balance (that is, the difference between the ending value and the beginning value) as a growth rate. A *growth rate* is the rate at which a value appreciates (a positive growth) or depreciates (a negative growth) over time. Our $1,000 grew at a rate of 10% per year over the 10-year period to $2,593.70. The average annual growth rate of our investment of $1,000 is 10%—the value of the savings account balance increased 10% per year.

We could also express the appreciation in our savings balance in terms of a return. A *return* is the income on an investment, generally stated as a change in the value of the investment over each period divided by the amount at the investment at the beginning of the period. We could also say that our investment of $1,000 provides an average annual return of 10% per year. The average annual return is not calculated by taking the change in value over the entire 10-year period ($2,593.70 − $1,000) and dividing it by $1,000. This would produce an *arithmetic average return* of 159.37% over the 10-year period, or 15.937% per year. But the arithmetic average ignores the process of compounding. The correct way of calculating the average annual return is to use a *geometric average return*:

$$i = \sqrt[N]{\frac{FV}{PV}} - 1 \qquad\qquad (2.2)$$

which is a rearrangement of equation (2.1). Using the values from the example,

$$i = \sqrt[10]{\frac{\$2,593.70}{\$1,000.00}} - 1 = \left(\frac{\$2,593.70}{\$1,000.00}\right)^{1/10}$$
$$-1 = 1.100 - 1 = 10\%$$

Therefore, the annual return on the investment—sometimes referred to as the *compound average annual return* or the *true return*—is 10% per year.

Here is another example of calculating a future value. A common investment product of a life insurance company is a *guaranteed investment contract* (GIC). With this investment, an insurance company guarantees a specified interest rate for a period of years. Suppose that the life insurance company agrees to pay 6% annually for a five-year GIC and the amount invested by the policyholder is $10 million. The amount of the liability (that is, the amount this life insurance company has agreed to pay the GIC policyholder) is the future value of $10 million when invested at 6% interest for five years. In terms of equation (2.1), $PV = \$10,000,000$, $i = 6\%$, and $N = 5$, so that the future value is

$$FV = \$10,000,000(1 + 0.06)^5 = \$13,382,256$$

Compounding More than One Time per Year

An investment may pay interest more than one time per year. For example, interest may be paid semiannually, quarterly, monthly, weekly, or daily, even though the stated rate is quoted on an annual basis. If the interest is stated as, say, 10% per year, compounded semiannually, the nominal rate—often referred to as the *annual percentage rate* (APR)—is 10%. The basic valuation equation handles situations in which there is compounding more frequently than once a year if we translate the nominal rate into a rate per compounding period. Therefore, an APR of 10% with compounding semiannually is 5% per period—where a period is six months—and the number of periods in one year is 2.

Consider a deposit of $50,000 in an account for five years that pays 8% interest, compounded quarterly. The interest rate per period, i, is 8%/4 = 2% and the number of compounding periods is 5 × 4 = 20. Therefore, the balance in the account at the end of five years is

$$FV = \$50,000(1 + 0.02)^{20} = \$50,000(1.4859474) = \$74,297.37$$

As shown in Figure 2.2, through 50 years with both annual and quarterly compounding, the investment's value increases at a faster rate with the increased frequency of compounding.

FIGURE 2.2 Value of $50,000 Invested in the Account that Pays 8% Interest per Year: Quarterly vs. Annual Compounding

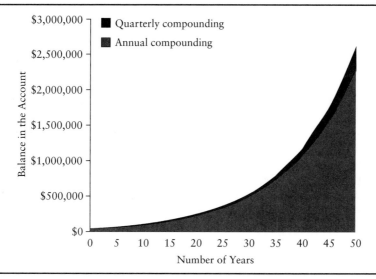

The last example illustrates the need to correctly identify the "period" because this dictates the interest rate per period and the number of compounding periods. Because interest rates are often quoted in terms of an APR, we need to be able to translate the APR into an interest rate per period and to adjust the number of periods. To see how this works, let's use an example of a deposit of $1,000 in an account that pays interest at a rate of 12% per year, with interest compounded for different compounding frequencies. How much is in the account after, say, five years depends on the compounding frequency:

Compounding Frequency	Period	Rate per Compounding Period, i	Number of Periods in Five Years, N	FV at the End of Five Years
Annual	One year	12%	5	$1,762.34
Semiannual	Six months	6%	10	1,790.85
Quarterly	Three months	3%	20	1,806.11
Monthly	One month	1%	60	1,816.70

As you can see, both the rate per period, i, and the number of compounding periods, N, are adjusted and depend on the frequency of compounding. Interest can be compounded for any frequency, such as daily or hourly.

Let's work through another example for compounding with compounding more than once a year. Suppose we invest $200,000 in an investment that pays 4% interest per year, compounded quarterly. What will be the future value of this investment at the end of 10 years?

The given information is $i = 4\%/4 = 1\%$ and $N = 10 \times 4 = 40$ quarters. Therefore,

$$FV = \$200,000(1 + 0.01)40 = \$297,772.75$$

Continuous Compounding

The extreme frequency of compounding is continuous compounding—interest is compounded instantaneously. The factor for compounding continuously for one year is e^{APR}, where e is 2.71828..., the base of the natural logarithm. And the factor for compounding continuously for two years is $e^{APR} e^{APR}$ or e^{2APR}. The future value of an amount that is compounded continuously for N years is

$$FV = PVe^{N(APR)} \tag{2.3}$$

where APR is the annual percentage rate and $e^{N(APR)}$ is the compound factor.

If $1,000 is deposited in an account for five years with interest of 12% per year, compounded continuously,

$$FV = \$1,000e^{5(0.12)} = \$1,000(e^{0.60}) = \$1,000(1.82212) = \$1,822.12$$

Comparing this future value with that if interest is compounded annually at 12% per year for five years, $1,762.34, we see the effects of this extreme frequency of compounding.

Multiple Rates

In our discussion thus far, we have assumed that the investment will earn the same periodic interest rate, i. We can extend the calculation of a future value to allow for different interest rates or growth rates for different periods. Suppose an investment of $10,000 pays 9% during the first year and 10% during the second year. At the end of the first period, the value of the investment is $10,000 $(1 + 0.09)$, or $10,900. During the second period, this $10,900 earns interest at 10%. Therefore, the future value of this $10,000 at the end of the second period is

$$FV = \$10,000(1 + 0.09)(1 + 0.10) = \$11,990$$

We can write this more generally as

$$FV = PV(1 + i_1)(1 + i_2)(1 + i_3)...(1 + i_N) \qquad (2.4)$$

where i_N is the interest rate for period N.

Consider a $50,000 investment in a one-year bank *certificate of deposit* (CD) today and rolled over annually for the next two years into one-year CDs. The future value of the $50,000 investment will depend on the one-year CD rate each time the funds are rolled over. Assuming that the one-year CD rate today is 5% and that it is expected that the one-year CD rate one year from now will be 6%, and the one-year CD rate two years from now will be 6.5%, then we know

$$FV = \$50,000(1 + 0.05)(1 + 0.06)(1 + 0.065) = \$59,267.25$$

Continuing this example, what is the average annual interest rate over this period? We know that the future value is $59,267.25, the present value is $50,000, and $N = 3$

$$i = \sqrt[3]{\frac{\$59,267.25}{\$50,000.00}} - 1 = \sqrt[3]{1.185345} = 5.8315\%$$

which is also

$$i = \sqrt[3]{(1+0.05)+(1+0.06)(1+0.065)} - 1 = 5.8315\%$$

DETERMINING THE PRESENT VALUE

Now that we understand how to compute future values, let's work the process in reverse. Suppose that for borrowing a specific amount of money today, the Yenom Company promises to pay lenders $5,000 two years from today. How much should the lenders be willing to lend Yenom in exchange for this promise? This dilemma is different than figuring out a future value. Here we are given the future value and have to figure out the present value. But we can use the same basic idea from the future value problems to solve present value problems.

If you can earn 10% on other investments that have the same amount of uncertainty as the $5,000 Yenom promises to pay, then:

The future value, FV = $5,000.
The number of compounding periods, N = 2.
The interest rate, i = 10%.

We also know the basic relation between the present and future values:

$$FV = PV(1 + i)^N$$

Substituting the known values into this equation:

$$\$5,000 = PV(1 + 0.10)^2$$

To determine how much you are willing to lend now, PV, to get $5,000 one year from now, FV, requires solving this equation for the unknown present value:

$$PV = \frac{\$5,000}{(1+0.10)^2} = \$5,000\left(\frac{1}{1+0.10}\right)^2$$
$$= \$5,000(0.82645) = \$4,132.25$$

Therefore, you would be willing to lend $4,132.25 to receive $5,000 one year from today if your opportunity cost is 10%. We can check our work by reworking the problem from the reverse perspective. Suppose you invested $4,132.25 for two years and it earned 10% per year. What is the value of this investment at the end of the year?

We know: $PV = \$4,132.25$, $N = 10\%$ or 0.10, and $i = 2$. Therefore, the future value is

$$FV = PV(1 + i)^N = \$4,132.25(1 + 0.10)^2 = \$5,000.00$$

Compounding translates a value in one point in time into a value at some future point in time. The opposite process translates future values into present values: Discounting translates a value back in time. From the basic valuation equation,

$$FV = PV(1 + i)^N$$

we divide both sides by $(1 + i)^N$ band exchange sides to get the present value,

$$PV = \frac{FV}{(1+i)^N} \qquad (2.5)$$

$$\text{or} \quad PV = FV\left(\frac{1}{1+i}\right)^N \quad \text{or} \quad PV = FV\left[\frac{1}{(1+i)^N}\right]$$

The term in square brackets is referred to as the *discount factor* since it is used to translate a future value to its equivalent present value. The present value of $5,000 for discount periods ranging from 0 to 10 is shown in Figure 2.3.

If the frequency of compounding is greater than once a year, we make adjustments to the rate per period and the number of periods as we did in compounding. For example, if the future value five years from today is $100,000 and the interest is 6% per year, compounded semiannually, $i = 6\%/2 = 3\%$ and $N = 5 \times 2 = 10$, and the present value is

$$PV = \$100,000(1 + 0.03)10 = \$100,000(1.34392) = \$134,392$$

Here is an example of calculating a present value. Suppose that the goal is to have $75,000 in an account by the end of four years. And suppose that interest on this account is paid at a rate of 5% per year, compounded semiannually. How much must be deposited in the account today to reach this goal? We are given $FV = \$75,000$, $i = 5\%/2 = 2.5\%$ per six months, and $N = 4 \times 2 = 8$ six-month periods. Therefore, the amount of the required deposit is

FIGURE 2.3   Present Value of $5,000 Discounted at 10%

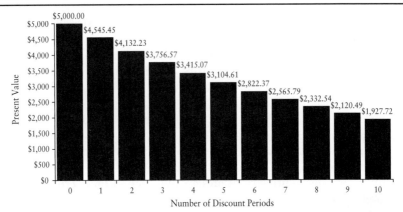

$$PV = \frac{\$75,000}{(1+0.025)^8} = \$61,555.99$$

DETERMINING THE UNKNOWN INTEREST RATE

As we saw earlier in our discussion of growth rates, we can rearrange the basic equation to solve for i:

$$i = \sqrt[N]{\frac{FV}{PV}} - 1 = \left(\frac{FV}{PV}\right)^{1/N} - 1$$

As an example, suppose that the value of an investment today is $100 and the expected value of the investment in five years is expected to be $150. What is the annual rate of appreciation in value of this investment over the five-year period?

$$i = \sqrt[5]{\frac{\$150}{\$100}} - 1$$
$$= \sqrt[5]{1.5} - 1 = 0.0845 \text{ or } 8.45\% \text{ per year}$$

There are many applications in finance where it is necessary to determine the rate of change in values over a period of time. If values are increasing over time, we refer to the rate of change as the growth rate. To make comparisons easier, we usually specify the growth rate as a rate per year.

For example, if we wish to determine the rate of growth in these values, we solve for the unknown interest rate. Consider the growth rate of dividends for General Electric. General Electric pays dividends each year. In 1996, for example, General Electric paid dividends of $0.317 per share of its common stock, whereas in 2006 the company paid $1.03 in dividends per share in 2006. This represents a growth rate of 12.507%:

$$\text{Growth rate of dividends} = \sqrt[10]{\frac{\$1.03}{\$0.317}} - 1$$

$$= \sqrt[10]{3.2492} - 1 = 12.507\%$$

The 12.507% is the average annual rate of the growth during this 10-year span.

DETERMINING THE NUMBER OF COMPOUNDING PERIODS

Given the present and future values, calculating the number of periods when we know the interest rate is a bit more complex than calculating the interest rate when we know the number of periods. Nevertheless, we can develop an equation for determining the number of periods, beginning with the valuation formula given by equation (2.1) and rearranging to solve for N,

$$N = \frac{\ln FV - \ln PV}{\ln(1 + i)} \tag{2.6}$$

where ln indicates the natural logarithm, which is the log of the base e. (e is approximately equal to 2.718. The natural logarithm function can be found on most calculators, usually indicated by "ln".)

Suppose that the present value of an investment is $100 and you wish to determine how long it will take for the investment to double in value if the investment earns 6% per year, compounded annually:

$$N = \frac{\ln 200 - \ln 100}{\ln 1.06} = \frac{5.2983 - 4.6052}{0.0583}$$

$$= 11.8885 \text{ or approximately } 12 \text{ years}$$

You'll notice that we round off to the next whole period. To see why, consider this last example. After 11.8885 years, we have doubled our money if interest were paid 88.85% the way through the 12th year. But, we stated earlier that interest is paid at the and of each period—not part of the way through. At the end of the 11th year, our investment is worth $189.93, and at the end of the 12th year, our investment is worth $201.22. So, our investment's value doubles by the 12th period—with a little extra, $1.22.

THE TIME VALUE OF A SERIES OF CASH FLOWS

Applications in finance may require the determination of the present or future value of a series of cash flows rather than simply a single cash flow. The principles of determining the future value or present value of a series of cash flows are the same as for a single cash flow, yet the math becomes a bit more cumbersome.

Suppose that the following deposits are made in a Thrifty Savings and Loan account paying 5% interest, compounded annually:

Time When Deposit Is Made	Amount of Deposit
Today	$1,000
At the end of the first year	2,000
At the end of the second year	1,500

What is the balance in the savings account at the end of the second year if no withdrawals are made and interest is paid annually?

Let's simplify any problem like this by referring to today as the end of period 0, and identifying the end of the first and each successive period as 1, 2, 3, and so on. Represent each end-of-period cash flow as "CF" with a subscript specifying the period to which it corresponds. Thus, CF_0 is a cash flow today, CF_{10} is a cash flow at the end of period 10, and CF_{25} is a cash flow at the end of period 25, and so on.

Representing the information in our example using cash flow and period notation:

Period	Cash Flow	End-of-Period Cash Flow
0	CF_0	$1,000
1	CF_1	$2,000
2	CF_2	$1,500

The future value of the series of cash flows at the end of the second period is calculated as follows:

Period	End-of-Period Cash Flow	Number of Periods Interest Is Earned	Compounding Factor	Future Value
0	$1,000	2	1.1025	$1,102.50
1	2,000	1	1.0500	2,100.00
2	1,500	0	1.0000	1,500.00
				$4,702.50

The last cash flow, $1,500, was deposited at the very end of the second period—the point of time at which we wish to know the future value of the series. Therefore, this deposit earns no interest. In more formal terms, its future value is precisely equal to its present value.

Today, the end of period 0, the balance in the account is $1,000 since the first deposit is made but no interest has been earned. At the end of period 1, the balance in the account is $3,050, made up of three parts:

1. The first deposit, $1,000.
2. $50 interest on the first deposit.
3. The second deposit, $2,000.

The balance in the account at the end of period 2 is $4,702.50, made up of five parts:

1. The first deposit, $1,000.
2. The second deposit, $2,000.
3. The third deposit, $1,500.
4. $102.50 interest on the first deposit, $50 earned at the end of the first period, $52.50 more earned at the end of the second period.
5. $100 interest earned on the second deposit at the end of the second period.

These cash flows can also be represented in a time line. A time line is used to help graphically depict and sort out each cash flow in a series. The time line for this example is shown in Figure 2.4. From this example, you can see that the future value of the entire series is the sum of each of the compounded cash flows comprising the series. In much the same way, we can determine the future value of a series comprising any number of cash flows. And if we need to, we can determine the future value of a number of cash flows before the end of the series.

FIGURE 2.4 Time Line for the Future Value of a Series of Uneven Cash Flows Deposited to Earn 5% Compounded Interest per Period

End of period	0	1	2
Time			
Cash flows	$CF_0 = \$1,000.00$	$CF_1 = \$2,000.00$	$CF_2 = \$1,500.00$
		➡ $\$2,000.00(1.05) =$	2,100.00
		➡ $\$1,000.00(1.05)2 =$	1,102.50
			$FV = \$4,702.50$

For example, suppose you are planning to deposit $1,000 today and at the end of each year for the next 10 years in a savings account paying 5% interest annually. If you want to know the future value of this series after four years, you compound each cash flow for the number of years it takes to reach four years. That is, you compound the first cash flow over four years, the second cash flow over three years, the third over two years, the fourth over one year, and the fifth you don't compound at all because you will have just deposited it in the bank at the end of the fourth year.

To determine the present value of a series of future cash flows, each cash flow is discounted back to the present, where the beginning of the first period, today, is designated as 0. As an example, consider the Thrifty Savings & Loan problem from a different angle. Instead of calculating what the deposits and the interest on these deposits will be worth in the future, let's calculate the present value of the deposits. The present value is what these future deposits are worth today.

In the series of cash flows of $1,000 today, $2,000 at the $10,000 end of period 1, and $1,500 at the end of period 2, each are discounted to the present, 0, as follows:

Period	End-of-Period Cash Flow	Number of Periods of Discounting	Discount Factor	Present Value
0	$1,000	0	1.00000	$1,000.00
1	$2,000	1	0.95238	1,904.76
2	$1,500	2	0.90703	1,360.54
				FV = $4,265.30

The present value of the series is the sum of the present value of these three cash flows, $4,265.30. For example, the $1,500 cash flow at the end of period 2 is worth $1,428.57 at the end of the first period and is worth $1,360.54 today.

The present value of a series of cash flows can be represented in notation form as

$$PV = CF_0 \left(\frac{1}{1+i} \right)^0 + CF_1 \left(\frac{1}{1+i} \right)^1 + CF_2 \left(\frac{1}{1+i} \right)^2 + \cdots + CF_N \left(\frac{1}{1+i} \right)^N$$

For example, if there are cash flows today and at the end of periods 1 and 2, today's cash flow is not discounted, the first period cash flow is discounted one period, and the second period cash flow is discounted two periods.

We can represent the present value of a series using summation notation as

$$PV = \sum_{t=0}^{N} CF_t \left(\frac{1}{1+i} \right)^t \qquad (2.7)$$

This equation tells us that the present value of a series of cash flows is the sum of the products of each cash flow and its corresponding discount factor.

The Present Value of Cash Flows Using Multiple Interest Rates

In our illustrations thus far, we have used one interest rate to compute the present value of all cash flows in a series. However, there is no reason that one interest rate must be used. For example, suppose that the cash flow is the same as used earlier: $1,000 today, $2,000 at the end of period 1, and $1,500 at the end of period 2. Now, instead of assuming that a 5% interest rate can be earned if a sum is invested today until the end of period 1 and the end of period 2, it is assumed that an amount invested today for one period can earn 5% but an amount invested today for two periods can earn 6%.

In this case, the calculation of the present value of the cash flow in period 1 ($2,000) is obtained in the same way as before: computing the present value using an interest rate of 5%. However, the calculation of the present value for the cash flow for period 2 ($1,500) must be calculated using an interest rate of 6%. The discount factor applicable to the cash flow for period 1 is

$$\frac{1}{(1.06)^2} = 0.89000$$

Notice that the discount factor is less than if the interest rate is 5% (0.89000 versus 0.90703), a fundamental property of the present value. The present value of the cash flow is then as follows:

Period	End-of-Period Cash Flow	Number of Periods of Discounting	Discount Factor	Present Value
0	$1,000	0	1.00000	$1,000.00
1	$2,000	1	0.95238	1,904.76
2	$1,500	2	0.89000	1,335.00
				FV = $4,239.76

As expected, the present value of the cash flows is less then a 5% interest rate is assumed to be earned for two periods ($4,239.76 versus $4,265.39).

Although in many illustrations and applications throughout this book, we will assume a single interest rate for determining the present value of a series of cash flows, in many real-world applications multiple interest rates are used. This is because in real-world financial markets, the interest rate that can be earned depends on the amount of time the investment is expected to be outstanding. Typically, there is a positive relationship between interest rates and the length of time the investment must be held. The relationship between interest rates on investments and the length of time the investment must be held is called the yield curve and is discussed in Chapter 5.

The formula for the present value of a series of cash flows when there is a different interest rate is a simple modification of the single interest rate case. In the formula, i is replaced by i with a subscript to denote the period. That is,

$$PV = CF_0 \left(\frac{1}{1+i_0} \right)^0 + CF_1 \left(\frac{1}{1+i_1} \right)^1 + CF_2 \left(\frac{1}{1+i_2} \right)^2 + \cdots + CF_N \left(\frac{1}{1+i_N} \right)^N$$

Or using summation notation, it can be expressed as

$$PV = \sum_{t=0}^{N} CF_t \left(\frac{1}{1+i_t} \right)^t$$

Shortcuts: Annuities

There are valuation problems that require us to evaluate a series of level cash flows—each cash flow is the same amount as the others—received at regular intervals. Let's suppose you expect to deposit $2,000 at the end of each of the next four years in an account earning 8% compounded interest. How much will you have available at the end of the fourth year?

As we just did for the future value of a series of uneven cash flows, we can calculate the future value (as of the end of the fourth year) of each $2,000 deposit, compounding interest at 8%:

$$FV = \$2,000(1+0.08)^3 + \$2,000(1+0.08)^2 + \$2,000(1+0.08)^3$$
$$+\$2,000(1+0.08)^0$$
$$= \$2,519.40 + \$2,332.80 + \$2,160.00 + \$2,000 = \$9,012.20$$

Figure 2.5 shows the contribution of each deposit and the accumulated interest at the end of each period.

- At the end of year 1, there is $2,000.00 in the account since you have just made your first deposit.
- At the end of year 2, there is $4,160.00 in the account: two deposits of $2,000 each, plus $160 interest (8% of $2,000).

FIGURE 2.5 Balance in an Account in Which Deposits of $2,000 Each Are Made Each Year. (The Balance in the Account Earns 8%)

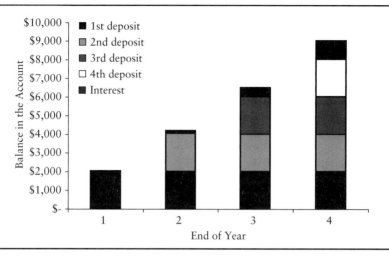

- At the end of year 3, there is $6,492.80 in the account: three deposits of $2,000.00 each, plus accumulated interest of $492.80 [$160.00 + (0.08 × $4,000) + (0.08 × $160)].
- At the end of the fourth year, you would have $9,012.20 available: four deposits of $2,000 each, plus $1,012.20 accumulated interest [$160.00 + $492.80 + (0.08 × $6,000) + (0.08 × ($160.00 + $492.80))].

Notice that in our calculations, each deposit of $2,000 is multiplied by a factor that corresponds to an interest rate of 8% and the number of periods that the deposit has been in the savings account. Since the deposit of $2,000 is common to each multiplication, we can simplify the math a bit by multiplying the $2,000 by the sum of the factors to get the same answer:

$$FV = \$2,000(1.2597) + \$2,000(1.1664) + \$2,000(1.0800)$$
$$+ \$2,000(1.0000) = \$9,012.20$$

A series of cash flows of equal amount, occurring at even intervals is referred to as an annuity. Determining the value of an annuity, whether compounding or discounting, is simpler than valuing uneven cash flows. If each CF_t is equal (that is, all the cash flows are the same value) and the first one occurs at the end of the first period ($t = 1$), we can express the future value of the series as

$$FV = \sum_{t=1}^{N} CF(1+i)^{N-t}$$

N is last and t indicates the time period corresponding to a particular cash flow, starting at 1 for an ordinary annuity. Since CF_t is shorthand for: CF_1, CF_2, CF_3, ..., CF_N, and we know that $CF_1 = CF_2 = CF_3 = ... CF_N$, let's make things simple by using CF to indicate the same value for the periodic cash flows. Rearranging the future value equation we get

$$FV = \sum_{t=1}^{N} CF(1+i)^{N-t} \tag{2.8}$$

This equation tells us that the future value of a level series of cash flows, occurring at regular intervals beginning one period from today (notice that t starts at 1), is equal to the amount of cash flow multiplied by the sum of the compound factors.

In a like manner, the equation for the present value of a series of level cash flows beginning after one period simplifies to

$$PV = \sum_{t=1}^{N} CF_t \left(\frac{1}{1+i} \right)^t = CF \sum_{t=1}^{N} \left(\frac{1}{1+i} \right)^t$$

or

$$PV = CF \sum_{t=1}^{N} \frac{1}{(1+i)^t} \tag{2.9}$$

This equation tells us that the present value of an annuity is equal to the amount of one cash flow multiplied by the sum of the discount factors.

Equations (2.8) and (2.9) are the valuation—future and present value—formulas for an *ordinary annuity*. An ordinary annuity is a special form of annuity, where the first cash flow occurs at the end of the first period.

To calculate the future value of an annuity we multiply the amount of the annuity (that is, the amount of one periodic cash flow) by the sum of the compound factors. The sum of these compounding factors for a given interest rate, i, and number of periods, N, is referred to as the *future value annuity factor*. Likewise, to calculate the present value of an annuity we multiply one cash flow of the annuity by the sum of the discount factors. The sum of the discounting factors for a given i and N is referred to as the *present value annuity factor*.

Suppose you wish to determine the future value of a series of deposits of $1,000, deposited each year in the No Fault Vault Bank for five years, with the first deposit made at the end of the first year. If the NFV Bank pays 5% interest on the balance in the account at the end of each year and no withdrawals are made, what is the balance in the account at the end of the five years?

Each $1,000 is deposited at a different time, so it contributes a different amount to the future value. For example, the first deposit accumulates interest for four periods, contributing $1,215.50 to the future value (at the end of year 5), whereas the last deposit contributes only $1,000 to the future value since it is deposited at exactly the point in time when we are determining the future value, hence there is no interest on this deposit.

The future value of an annuity is the sum of the future value of each deposit:

Year	Amount of Deposit	Number of Periods Interest Is Earned	Compounding Factor	Future Value
1	$1,000	4	1.2155	$1,215.50
2	1,000	3	1.1576	1,157.60
3	1,000	2	1.1025	1,102.50
4	1,000	1	1.0500	1,050.00
5	1,000	0	1.0000	1,000.00
Total			5.5256	$5,525.60

The future value of the series of $1,000 deposits, with interest compounded at 5%, is $5,525.60. Since we know the value of one of the level period flows is $1,000, and the future value of the annuity is $5,525.60, and looking at the sum of the individual compounding factors, 5.5256, we can see that there is an easier way to calculate the future value of an annuity. If the sum of the individual compounding factors for a specific interest rate and a specific number of periods were available, all we would have to do is multiply that sum by the value of one cash flow to get the future value of the entire annuity.

In this example, the shortcut is multiplying the amount of the annuity, $1,000, by the sum of the compounding factors, 5.5256:

$$FV = \$1,000 \times 5.5256 = \$5,525.60$$

For large numbers of periods, summing the individual factors can be a bit clumsy—with possibilities of errors along the way. An alternative formula for the sum of the compound factors—that is, the future value annuity factor—is

$$\text{Future value annuity factor} = \frac{(1+i)^N - 1}{i} \qquad (2.10)$$

In the last example, $N = 5$ and $i = 5\%$:

$$\text{Future value annuity factor} = \frac{(1+0.05)^5 - 1}{0.05}$$

$$= \frac{1.2763 - 1.000}{0.05} = 5.5256$$

Let's use the long method to find the present value of the series of five deposits of $1,000 each, with the first deposit at the end of the first year. Then we'll do it using the shortcut method. The calculations are similar to the future value of an ordinary annuity, except we are taking each deposit back in time, instead of forward:

Year	Amount of Deposit	Discounting Periods	Discounting Factor	Present Value
1	$1,000	1	0.9524	$952.40
2	1,000	2	0.9070	907.00
3	1,000	3	0.8638	863.80
4	1,000	4	0.8227	822.70
5	1,000	5	0.7835	783.50
Total			4.3294	$4,329,40

The present value of this series of five deposits is $4,329.40.

This same value is obtained by multiplying the annuity amount of $1,000 by the sum of the discounting factors, 4.3294:

$$PV = \$1,000 \times 4.3294 = \$4,329.40$$

Another, more convenient way of solving for the present value of an annuity is to rewrite the factor as

$$\text{Present value annuity factor} = \frac{1 - \dfrac{1}{(1+i)^N}}{i} \qquad (2.11)$$

If there are many discount periods and no financial calculator handy, this formula is a bit easier to use. In our last example,

$$\text{Present value annuity factor} = \frac{1 - \dfrac{1}{(1+0.05)^5}}{0.05}$$

$$= \frac{1 - 0.7835}{0.05} = 4.3295$$

which is different from the sum of the factors, 4.3294, due to rounding. We can turn this present value of an annuity problem around to look at it from another angle. Suppose you borrow $4,329.40 at an interest rate of 5% per period and are required to pay back this loan in five installments ($N = 5$): one payment per period for five periods, starting one period from now. The payments are determined by equating the present value with the product of the cash flow and the sum of the discount factors:

$$PV = CF(\text{Sum of discount factors})$$

$$= CF\sum_{t=1}^{5} \frac{1}{(1+0.05)^t}$$

$$= CF(0.9524 + 0.9070 + 0.8638 + 0.8227 + 0.7835)$$

$$= CF(4.3294)$$

substituting the known present value,

$$\$4,329.40 = CF(4.3294)$$

and rearranging to solve for the payment

$$CF = \$4,329.40/4.3290 = \$1,000.00$$

We can convince ourselves that five installments of $1,000 each can pay off the loan of $4,329.40 by carefully stepping through the calculation of interest and the reduction of the principal:

Beginning of Year's Loan Balance	Payment	Reduction in Interest (Principal × 5%)	Loan Balance (Payment – Interest)	End-of-Year Loan Balance
$4,329.40	$1,000.00	$216.47	$783.53	$3,545.87
3,545.87	1,000.00	177.29	822.71	2,723.16
2,723.16	1,000.00	136.16	863.84	1,859.32
1,859.32	1,000.00	92.97	907.03	952.29
952.29	1,000.00	47.61	952.29[a]	0

[a] The small difference between calculated reduction ($952.38) and reported reduction is due to rounding differences.

For example, the first payment of $1,000 is used to: (1) pay interest on the loan at 5% ($4,329.40 × 0.05 = $216.47); and (2) pay down the principal or loan balance ($1,000.00 – 216.47 = $783.53 paid off). Each successive payment pays off a greater amount of the loan—as the principal amount of the loan is reduced, less of each payment goes to paying off interest and more goes to reducing the loan principal. This analysis of the repayment of a loan is referred to as *loan amortization*. Loan amortization is the repayment of a loan with equal payments over a specified period of time. As we can see from the example of borrowing $4,329.40, each payment can be broken down into its interest and principal components.

VALUING CASH FLOWS WITH DIFFERENT TIME PATTERNS

Valuing a Perpetual Stream of Cash Flows

There are some circumstances where cash flows are expected to continue forever. For example, a corporation may promise to pay dividends on preferred stock forever, or, a company may issue a bond that pays interest every six months, forever. How do you value these cash flow streams? Recall that when we calculated the present value of an annuity, we took the amount of one cash flow and multiplied it by the sum of the discount factors that corresponded to the interest rate and number of payments. But what if the number of payments extends forever—into infinity?

A series of cash flows that occur at regular intervals, forever, is a *perpetuity*. Valuing a perpetual cash flow stream is just like valuing an ordinary annuity. It looks like this:

$$PV = CF_1 \left(\frac{1}{1+i} \right)^1 + CF_2 \left(\frac{1}{1+i} \right)^2 + CF_3 \left(\frac{1}{1+i} \right)^3 + \cdots + CF_\infty \left(\frac{1}{1+i} \right)^\infty$$

Simplifying, recognizing that the cash flows CF_t are the same in each period, and using summation notation,

$$PV = CF \sum_{t=1}^{\infty} \left(\frac{1}{1+i} \right)^t$$

As the number of discounting periods approaches infinity, the summation approaches $1/i$. To see why, consider the present value annuity factor for an interest rate of 10%, as the number of payments goes from 1 to 200:

Number of Discounting Periods, N	Present Value Annuity Factor
1	0.9091
10	6.1446
40	9.7791
100	9.9993
200	9.9999

For greater numbers of payments, the factor approaches 10, or 1/0.1. Therefore, the present value of a perpetual annuity is very close to

$$PV = \frac{CF}{i} \qquad (2.12)$$

Suppose you are considering an investment that promises to pay \$100 each period forever, and the interest rate you can earn on alternative investments of similar risk is 5% per period. What are you willing to pay today for this investment?

$$PV = \frac{\$100}{0.05} = \$2,000$$

Therefore, you would be willing to pay \$2,000 today for this investment to receive, in return, the promise of \$100 each period forever.

Let's look at the value of a perpetuity another way. Suppose that you are given the opportunity to purchase an investment for \$5,000 that promises to pay \$50 at the end of every period forever. What is the periodic interest per period—the return—associated with this investment?

We know that the present value is PV = \$5,000 and the periodic, perpetual payment is CF = \$50. Inserting these values into the formula for the present value of a perpetuity,

$$\$5,000 = \frac{\$50}{i}$$

Solving for i, \$50,

$$i = \frac{\$50}{\$5,000} = 0.01 \text{ or } 1\% \text{ per period}$$

Therefore, an investment of \$5,000 that generates \$50 per period provides 1% compounded interest per period.

Valuing an Annuity Due

The ordinary annuity cash flow analysis assumes that cash flows occur at the end of each period. However, there is another fairly common cash flow pattern in which level cash flows occur at regular intervals, but the first cash flow occurs immediately. This pattern of cash flows is called an *annuity due*. For example, if you win the Florida Lottery Lotto grand prize, you will receive your winnings in 20 installments (after taxes, of course). The 20 installments are paid out annually, beginning immediately. The lottery winnings are therefore an annuity due.

Like the cash flows we have considered thus far, the future value of an annuity due can be determined by calculating the future value of each cash flow and summing them. And, the present value of an annuity due is determined in the same way as a present value of any stream of cash flows.

Let's consider first an example of the future value of an annuity due, comparing the values of an ordinary annuity and an annuity due, each comprising three cash flows of $500, compounded at the interest rate of 4% per period. The calculation of the future value of both the ordinary annuity and the annuity due at the end of three periods is

Ordinary annuity:

$$FV = \$500 \sum_{t=1}^{3} (1+0.04)^{3-t}$$

Annuity due:

$$FV_{due} = \$500 \sum_{t=1}^{3} (1+0.04)^{3-t+1}$$

The future value of each of the $500 payments in the annuity due calculation is compounded for one more period than for the ordinary annuity. For example, the first deposit of $500 earns interest for two periods in the ordinary annuity situation [$500 $(1 + 0.04)^2$], whereas the first $500 in the annuity due case earns interest for three periods [$500 $(1 + 0.04)^3$].

In general terms,

$$FV_{due} = CF \sum_{t=1}^{N} (1+i)^{N-t+1} \tag{2.13}$$

which is equal to the future value of an ordinary annuity multiplied by a factor of $1 + i$:

$FV_{due} = CF[\text{Future value annuity factor (ordinary) for } N \text{ and } i](1 + i)$

The present value of the annuity due is calculated in a similar manner, adjusting the ordinary annuity formula for the different number of discount periods:

$$PV_{due} = CF \sum_{t=1}^{N} \frac{1}{(1+i)^{t-1}} \qquad (2.14)$$

Since the cash flows in the annuity due situation are each discounted one less period than the corresponding cash flows in the ordinary annuity, the present value of the annuity due is greater than the present value of the ordinary annuity for an equivalent amount and number of cash flows. Like the future value an annuity due, we can specify the present value in terms of the ordinary annuity factor:

PV_{due} = CF[Present value annuity factor (ordinary) for N and i]$(1 + i)$

Valuing a Deferred Annuity

A *deferred annuity* has a stream of cash flows of equal amounts at regular periods starting at some time after the end of the first period. When we calculated the present value of an annuity, we brought a series of cash flows back to the beginning of the first period—or, equivalently the end of the period 0. With a deferred annuity, we determine the present value of the ordinary annuity and then discount this present value to an earlier period.

To illustrate the calculation of the present value of an annuity due, suppose you deposit $20,000 per year in an account for 10 years, starting today, for a total of 10 deposits. What will be the balance in the account at the end of 10 years if the balance in the account earns 5% per year? The future value of this annuity due is

$$FV_{due,10} = \$20,000 \sum_{t=1}^{10} (1+0.0.5)^{10-t+1}$$

$$= \$20,000 \left(\begin{array}{c} \text{Future value annuity factor (ordinary)} \\ \text{for 10 periods and 5\%} \end{array} \right) \times (1+0.05)$$

$$= \$20,000 \times (12.5779) \times (1+0.05) = \$264,135.74$$

Suppose you want to deposit an amount today in an account such that you can withdraw $5,000 per year for four years, with the first withdrawal occurring five years from today. We can solve this problem in two steps:

Step 1: Solve for the present value of the withdrawals.
Step 2: Discount this present value to the present.

The first step requires determining the present value of a four-cash-flow ordinary annuity of $5,000. This calculation provides the present value as of the end of the fourth year (one period prior to the first withdrawal):

$$PV_4 = \$5,000 \sum_{t=1}^{4} \frac{1}{(1+0.04)^t}$$

$$= \$5,000(\text{Present value annuity factor } N = 4, i = 4\%)$$

$$= \$18,149.48$$

This means that there must be a balance in the account of $18,149.48 at the end of the fourth period to satisfy the withdrawals of $5,000 per year for four years.

The second step requires discounting the $18,149.48—the savings goal—to the present, providing the deposit today that produces the goal:

$$PV_0 = \frac{\$18,149.48}{(1+0.04)^4} = \$15,514.25$$

The balance in the account throughout the entire eight-year period is shown in Figure 2.6 with the balance indicated both before and after the $5,000 withdrawals.

FIGURE 2.6   Balance in the Account that Requires a Deposit Today (Year 0) that Permits Withdrawals of $5,000 Each, Starting at the End of Year 5

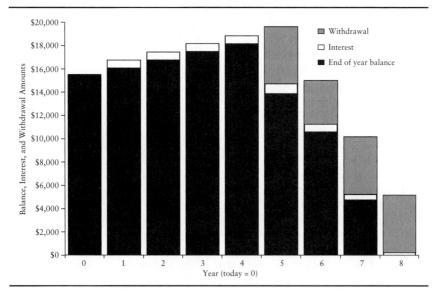

Let's look at a more complex deferred annuity. Consider making a series of deposits, beginning today, to provide for a steady cash flow beginning at some future time period. If interest is earned at a rate of 4% compounded per year, what amount must be deposited in a savings account each year for four years, starting today, so that $1,000 may be withdrawn each year for five years, beginning five years from today? As with any deferred annuity, we need to perform this calculation in steps:

Step 1: Calculate the present value of the $1,000 per year five-year ordinary annuity as of the end of the fourth year:

The present value of the annuity deferred to the end of the fourth period is

$$PV_4 = \$1,000 \sum_{t=1}^{5} \frac{1}{(1+0.04)^t} = \$1,000(4.4518)$$
$$= \$4,451.80$$

Therefore, there must be $4,451.80 in the account at the end of the fourth year to permit five $1,000 withdrawals at the end of each of the years 5, 6, 7, 8, and 9.

Step 2: Calculate the cash flow needed to arrive at the future value of that annuity due comprising four annual deposits earning 4% compounded interest, starting today.

The present value of the annuity at the end of the fourth year, $4,451.80, is the future value of the annuity due of four payments of an unknown amount. Using the formula for the future value of an annuity due,

$$\$4,451.80 = CF \sum_{t=1}^{4} (1+0.04)^{4-t+1} = CF(4.2465)(1.04)$$

and rearranging,

$$CF = \$4,451.80/4.4164 = \$1,008.02$$

Therefore, by depositing $1,008.02 today and the same amount on the same date each of the next three years, we will have a balance in the account of $4,451.80 at the end of the fourth period. With this period 4 balance, we will be able to withdraw $1,000 at the end of the following five periods.

LOAN AMORTIZATION

If an amount is loaned and then repaid in installments, we say that the loan is amortized. Therefore, loan amortization is the process of calculating the loan payments that amortize the loaned amount. We can determine the amount of the loan payments once we know the frequency of payments, the interest rate, and the number of payments.

Consider a loan of $100,000. If the loan is repaid in 24 annual installments (at the end of each year) and the interest rate is 5% per year, we calculate the amount of the payments by applying the relationship:

$$PV = \sum_{t=1}^{N} \frac{CF}{(1+i)^t}$$

$$\text{Amount loaned} = \sum_{t=1}^{N} \frac{\text{Loan payment}}{(1+i)^t}$$

$$\$100,000 = \sum_{t=1}^{24} \frac{\text{Loan payment}}{(1+0.05)^t}$$

We want to solve for the loan payment, that is, the amount of the annuity. Using a financial calculator or spreadsheet, the periodic loan payment is $7,247.09 ($PV$ = $100,000; N = 24; i = 5%). Therefore, the monthly payments are $7,247.09 each. In other words, if payments of $7,247.09 are made each year for 24 years (at the end of each year), the $100,000 loan will be repaid and the lender earns a return that is equivalent to a 5% interest on this loan.

We can calculate the amount of interest and principal repayment associated with each loan payment using a loan amortization schedule, as shown in Table 2.1.

The loan payments are determined such that after the last payment is made there is no loan balance outstanding. Thus, the loan is referred to as a *fully amortizing loan*. Even though the loan payment each year is the same, the proportion of interest and principal differs with each payment: the interest is 5% of the principal amount of the loan that remains at the beginning of the period, whereas the principal repaid with each payment is the difference between the payment and the interest. As the payments are made, the remainder is applied to repayment of the principal, which referred to as the scheduled principal repayment or the *amortization*. As the principal remaining on the loan declines, less interest is paid with each payment. We show the decline in the loan's principal graphically in Figure 2.7. The decline in the remaining principal is not a linear, but is curvilinear due to the compounding of interest.

TABLE 2.1 Loan Amortization on a $100,000 Loan for 24 Years and an Interest Rate of 5% per Year

Payment	Loan Payment	Beginning-of-the-Year Principal	Interest on Loan	Principal Paid Off = Payment – Interest	Remaining Principal
0					$100,000.00
1	$7,247.09	$100,000.00	$5,000.00	$2,247.09	97,752.91
2	7,247.09	97,752.91	4,887.65	2,359.44	95,393.47
3	7,247.09	95,393.47	4,769.67	2,477.42	92,916.05
4	7,247.09	92,916.05	4,645.80	2,601.29	90,314.76
5	7,247.09	90,314.76	4,515.74	2,731.35	87,583.41
6	7,247.09	87,583.41	4,379.17	2,867.92	84,715.49
7	7,247.09	84,715.49	4,235.77	3,011.32	81,704.17
8	7,247.09	81,704.17	4,085.21	3,161.88	78,542.29
9	7,247.09	78,542.29	3,927.11	3,319.98	75,222.32
10	7,247.09	75,222.32	3,761.12	3,485.97	71,736.34
11	7,247.09	71,736.34	3,586.82	3,660.27	68,076.07
12	7,247.09	68,076.07	3,403.80	3,843.29	64,232.78
13	7,247.09	64,232.78	3,211.64	4,035.45	60,197.33
14	7,247.09	60,197.33	3,009.87	4,237.22	55,960.11
15	7,247.09	55,960.11	2,798.01	4,449.08	51,511.03
16	7,247.09	51,511.03	2,575.55	4,671.54	46,839.49
17	7,247.09	46,839.49	2,341.97	4,905.12	41,934.37
18	7,247.09	41,934.37	2,096.72	5,150.37	36,784.00
19	7,247.09	36,784.00	1,839.20	5,407.89	31,376.11
20	7,247.09	31,376.11	1,568.81	5,678.28	25,697.83
21	7,247.09	25,697.83	1,284.89	5,962.20	19,735.63
22	7,247.09	19,735.63	986.78	6,260.31	13,475.32
23	7,247.09	13,475.32	673.77	6,573.32	6,901.99
24	7,247.09	6,901.99	345.10	6,901.99	0.00

FIGURE 2.7 Loan Amortization

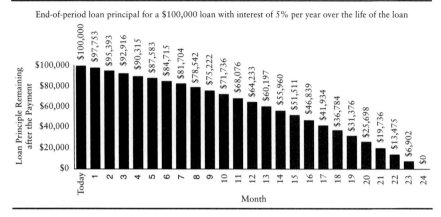

End-of-period loan principal for a $100,000 loan with interest of 5% per year over the life of the loan

Loan amortization works the same whether this is a mortgage loan to purchase a home, a term loan, or any other loan such as an automobile loan in which the interest paid is determined on the basis of the remaining amount of the loan. The calculation of the loan amortization can be modified to suit different principal repayments, such as additional lump-sum payments, known as balloon payments. For example, if there is a $10,000 balloon payment at the end of the loan in the loan of $100,000 repaid over 24 years, the calculation of the payment is modified as:

$$\text{Amount loaned} = \left[\sum_{t=1}^{N} \frac{\text{Loan payment}}{(1+i)^t} \right] + \frac{\text{Balloon payment}}{(1+i)^N}$$

$$\$100,000 = \left[\sum_{t=1}^{24} \frac{\text{Loan payment}}{(1+0.05)^t} \right] + \frac{\$10,000}{(1+i)^{24}}$$

The loan payment that solves this equation is $7,022.38 ($PV$ = $100,000; N = 24; i = 5%; FV = $10,000). The last payment (that is, at the end of the 24th year) is the regular payment of $7,022.38, plus the balloon payment, for a total of $17,022.38. As you can see in Figure 2.8, the loan amortization is slower when compared to the loan without the balloon payment.

The same mathematics work with term loans. Term loans are usually repaid in installments either monthly, quarterly, semiannually, or annually. Let's look at the typical repayment schedule for a term loan. Suppose that BigRock Corporation seeks a four-year term loan of $100 million. Let's assume for now that the term loan carries a fixed interest rate of 8% and that level payments are made monthly. If the annual interest rate is 8%, the rate per month is 8% ÷ 12 = 0.6667% per month. In a typical term loan, the payments are structured such that the loan is fully amortizing.

FIGURE 2.8   Loan Amortization with Balloon Payment

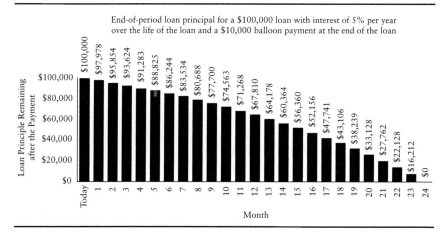

End-of-period loan principal for a $100,000 loan with interest of 5% per year over the life of the loan and a $10,000 balloon payment at the end of the loan

For this four-year, $100 million term loan with an 8% interest rate, the monthly payment is $2,441,292.23 (*PV* = $100,00,000; *N* = 48; *i* = 06667%). This amount is determined by solving for the annuity payment that equates the present value of the payments with the amount of the loan, considering an interest rate of 0.6667%. In Table 2.2 we show for each month the beginning monthly balance, the interest payment for the month, the amount of the monthly, and the ending loan balance. Notice that in our illustration, the ending loan balance is zero. That is, it is a fully amortizing loan.

In the loan amortization examples so far, we have assumed that the interest rate is fixed throughout the loan. However, in many loans the interest rate may change during the loan, as in the case of a floating-rate loan. The new loan rate at the reset date is determined by a formula. The formula is typically composed of two parts. The first is the reference rate. For example, in a monthly pay loan, the loan rate might be one-month London Interbank Offered Rate (LIBOR). The second part is a spread that is added to the reference rate. This spread is referred to as the quoted margin and depends on the credit of the borrower.

A floating rate loan requires a recalculation of the loan payment and payment schedule at each time the loan rate is reset. Suppose in the case of BigRock's term loan that the rate remains constant for the first three years, but is reset to 9% in the fourth year. This requires BigRock to pay off the principal remaining at the end of three years, the $28,064,562.84, in the remaining 12 payments. The revised schedule of payments and payoff for the fourth year require a payment of $2,454,287.47 (*PV* = $27,064,562.84; *N* = 12; *i* = 0.09 ÷ 12 = 0.75%), as shown in Table 2.3.

TABLE 2.2   Term Loan Schedule: Fixed Rate, Fully Amortized

Amount of loan	$100,000,000
Interest rate	8% per year
Number of years	4
Monthly payment	$2,441,292.33

Monthly Payment	Beginning-of-the-Year Principal	Interest on on Loan	Principal Paid Off = Payment – Interest	Remaining Principal
1	$100,000,000.00	$666,666.67	$1,774,625.57	$98,225,374.43
2	98,225,374.43	654,835.83	1,786,456.40	96,438,918.03
3	96,438,918.03	642,926.12	1,798,366.11	94,640,551.91
4	94,640,551.91	630,937.01	1,810,355.22	92,830,196.69
5	92,830,196.69	618,867.98	1,822,424.26	91,007,772.44
6	91,007,772.44	606,718.48	1,834,573.75	89,173,198.69
7	89,173,198.69	594,487.99	1,846,804.24	87,326,394.44
8	87,326,394.44	582,175.96	1,859,116.27	85,467,278.17
9	85,467,278.17	569,781.85	1,871,510.38	83,595,767.79
10	83,595,767.79	557,305.12	1,883,987.12	81,711,780.68
11	81,711,780.68	544,745.20	1,896,547.03	79,815,233.65
12	79,815,233.65	532,101.56	1,909,190.68	77,906,042.97
13	77,906,042.97	519,373.62	1,921,918.61	75,984,124.36
14	75,984,124.36	506,560.83	1,934,731.41	74,049,392.95
15	74,049,392.95	493,662.62	1,947,629.61	72,101,763.34
16	72,101,763.34	480,678.42	1,960,613.81	70,141,149.52
17	70,141,149.52	467,607.66	1,973,684.57	68,167,464.95
18	68,167,464.95	454,449.77	1,986,842.47	66,180,622.49
19	66,180,622.49	441,204.15	2,000,088.08	64,180,534.40
20	64,180,534.40	427,870.23	2,013,422.00	62,167,112.40
21	62,167,112.40	414,447.42	2,026,844.82	60,140,267.58
22	60,140,267.58	400,935.12	2,040,357.12	58,099,910.46
23	58,099,910.46	387,332.74	2,053,959.50	56,045,950.96
24	56,045,950.96	373,639.67	2,067,652.56	53,978,298.40
25	53,978,298.40	359,855.32	2,081,436.91	51,896,861.49
26	51,896,861.49	345,979.08	2,095,313.16	49,801,548.33
27	49,801,548.33	332,010.32	2,109,281.91	47,692,266.42
28	47,692,266.42	317,948.44	2,123,343.79	45,568,922.63
29	45,568,922.63	303,792.82	2,137,499.42	43,431,423.21
30	43,431,423.21	289,542.82	2,151,749.41	41,279,673.80

TABLE 2.2 (continued)

Monthly Payment	Beginning-of-the-Year Principal	Interest on on Loan	Principal Paid Off = Payment – Interest	Remaining Principal
31	$41,279,673.80	$275,197.83	$2,166,094.41	$39,113,579.39
32	39,113,579.39	260,757.20	2,180,535.04	36,933,044.35
33	36,933,044.35	246,220.30	2,195,071.94	34,737,972.42
34	34,737,972.42	231,586.48	2,209,705.75	32,528,266.66
35	32,528,266.66	216,855.11	2,224,437.12	30,303,829.54
36	30,303,829.54	202,025.53	2,239,266.70	28,064,562.84
37	28,064,562.84	187,097.09	2,254,195.15	25,810,367.69
38	25,810,367.69	172,069.12	2,269,223.12	23,541,144.57
39	23,541,144.57	156,940.96	2,284,351.27	21,256,793.30
40	21,256,793.30	141,711.96	2,299,580.28	18,957,213.02
41	18,957,213.02	126,381.42	2,314,910.81	16,642,302.21
42	16,642,302.21	110,948.68	2,330,343.55	14,311,958.66
43	14,311,958.66	95,413.06	2,345,879.18	11,966,079.48
44	11,966,079.48	79,773.86	2,361,518.37	9,604,561.11
45	9,604,561.11	64,030.41	2,377,261.83	7,227,299.28
46	7,227,299.28	48,182.00	2,393,110.24	4,834,189.04
47	4,834,189.04	32,227.93	2,409,064.31	2,425,124.74
48	2,425,124.74	16,167.50	2,425,124.74	0.00

TABLE 2.3 Term Loan Schedule: Reset Rate, Fully Amortized

Amount of loan	$100,000,000
Interest rate	8% per year for the first 3 years, 9% thereafter
Number of years	4
Monthly payment	$2,441,292.33 for the first 3 years, $2,454,287.47 for the fourth year

Monthly Payment	Beginning-of-the-Year Principal	Interest on on Loan	Principal Paid Off = Payment – Interest	Remaining Principal
37	$28,064,562.84	$210,484.22	$2,243,803.24	$25,820,759.59
38	25,820,759.59	193,655.70	2,260,631.77	23,560,127.82
39	23,560,127.82	176,700.96	2,277,586.51	21,282,541.32
40	21,282,541.32	159,619.06	2,294,668.41	18,987,872.91
41	18,987,872.91	142,409.05	2,311,878.42	16,675,994.49
42	16,675,994.49	125,069.96	2,329,217.51	14,346,776.99
43	14,346,776.99	107,600.83	2,346,686.64	12,000,090.35
44	12,000,090.35	90,000.68	2,364,286.79	9,635,803.56
45	9,635,803.56	72,268.53	2,382,018.94	7,253,784.62
46	7,253,784.62	54,403.38	2,399,884.08	4,853,900.54
47	4,853,900.54	36,404.25	2,417,883.21	2,436,017.33
48	2,436,017.33	18,270.13	2,436,017.34	0.00

THE CALCULATION OF INTEREST RATES AND YIELDS

The calculation of the present or future value of a lump-sum or set of cash flows requires information on the timing of cash flows and the compound or discount rate. However, there are many applications in which we are presented with values and cash flows, and wish to calculate the yield or implied interest rate associated with these values and cash flows. By calculating the yield or implied interest rate, we can then compare investment or financing opportunities. We first look at how interest rates are stated and how the effective interest rate can be calculated based on this stated rate, and then we look at how to calculate the yield, or rate of return, on a set of cash flows.

Annual Percentage Rate vs. Effective Annual Rate

A common problem in finance is comparing alternative financing or investment opportunities when the interest rates are specified in a way that makes it difficult to compare terms. The Truth in Savings Act of 1991 requires institutions to provide the annual percentage yield for savings accounts. As a result of this law, consumers can compare the yields on different savings arrangements. But this law does not apply beyond savings accounts. One investment may pay 10% interest compounded semiannually, whereas another investment may pay 9% interest compounded daily. One financing arrangement may require interest compounding quarterly, whereas another may require interest compounding monthly. To compare investments or financing with different frequencies of compounding, we must first translate the stated interest rates into a common basis. There are two ways to convert interest rates stated over different time intervals so that they have a common basis: the annual percentage rate and the effective annual interest rate.

One obvious way to represent rates stated in various time intervals on a common basis is to express them in the same unit of time—so we annualize them. The annualized rate is the product of the stated rate of interest per compound period and the number of compounding periods in a year. Let i be the rate of interest per period and n be the number of compounding periods in a year. The annualized rate, which is as we indicated earlier in this chapter also referred to as the nominal interest rate or the annual percentage rate (APR), is

$$APR = i \times n$$

Consider the following example. Suppose the Lucky Break Loan Company has simple loan terms: Repay the amount borrowed, plus 50%, in six months. Suppose you borrow $10,000 from Lucky. After six months, you must pay back the $10,000 plus $5,000. The APR on financing with Lucky is the interest rate per period (50% for six months) multiplied by the number of compound periods in a year (two six-month periods in a year). For the Lucky Break financing arrangement,

$$\text{APR} = 0.50 \times 2 = 1.00 \text{ or } 100\% \text{ per year}$$

But what if you cannot pay Lucky back after six months? Lucky will let you off this time, but you must pay back the following at the end of the next six months:

- The $10,000 borrowed.
- The $5,000 interest from the first six months.
- The 50% of interest on both the unpaid $10,000 and the unpaid $5,000 interest ($15,000 (0.50) = $7,500).

So, at the end of the year, knowing what is good for you, you pay off Lucky:

Amount of the original loan	$10,000
Interest from first six months	5,000
Interest on second six months	7,500
Total payment at end of the year	$22,500

Using the Lucky Break method of financing, you have to pay $12,500 interest to borrow $10,000 for one year's time. Because you have to pay $12,500 interest to borrow $10,000 over one year's time, you pay not 100% interest, but rather 125% interest per year ($12,500/$10,000 = 1.25 = 125%). What's going on here? It looks like the APR in the Lucky Break example ignores the compounding (interest on interest) that takes place after the first six months. And that's the way it is with all APRs. The APR ignores the effect of compounding. Therefore, this rate understates the true annual rate of interest if interest is compounded at any time prior to the end of the year. Nevertheless, APR is an acceptable method of disclosing interest on many lending arrangements, since it is easy to understand and simple to compute. However, because it ignores compounding, it is not the best way to convert interest rates to a common basis.

Another way of converting stated interest rates to a common basis is the effective rate of interest. The effective annual rate (EAR) is the true economic return for a given time period—it takes into account the compounding of interest—and is also referred to as the effective rate of interest.

Using our Lucky Break example, we see that we must pay $12,500 interest on the loan of $10,000 for one year. Effectively, we are paying

125% annual interest. Thus, 125% is the effective annual rate of interest. In this example, we can easily work through the calculation of interest and interest on interest. But for situations where interest is compounded more frequently, we need a direct way to calculate the effective annual rate. We can calculate it by resorting once again to our basic valuation equation:

$$FV = PV(1 + i)^n$$

Next, we consider that a return is the change in the value of an investment over a period and an annual return is the change in value over a year. Using our basic valuation equation, the relative change in value is the difference between the future value and the present value, divided by the present value:

$$\text{EAR} = \frac{FV - PV}{PV} = \frac{PV(1+i)^n}{PV}$$

Canceling PV from both the numerator and the denominator,

$$\text{EAR} = (1 + i)^n - 1 \tag{2.15}$$

Let's look how the EAR is affected by the compounding. Suppose that the Safe Savings and Loan promises to pay 6% interest on accounts, compounded annually. Since interest is paid once, at the end of the year, the effective annual return, EAR, is 6%. If the 6% interest is paid on a semiannual basis—3% every six months—the effective annual return is larger than 6% since interest is earned on the 3% interest earned at the end of the first six months. In this case, to calculate the EAR, the interest rate per compounding period—six months—is 0.03 (that is, 0.06/2) and the number of compounding periods in an annual period is 2:

$$\text{EAR} = (1 + 0.03)^2 - 1 = 1.0609 - 1 = 0.0609 \text{ or } 6.09\%$$

Extending this example to the case of quarterly compounding with a nominal interest rate of 6%, we first calculate the interest rate per period, i, and the number of compounding periods in a year, n:

$i = 0.06/4 = 0.015$ per quarter
$n = 4$ quarters in a year

The EAR is

$$\text{EAR} = (1 + 0.015)^4 - 1 = 1.0614 - 1 = 0.0614 \text{ or } 6.14\%$$

As we saw earlier in this chapter, the extreme frequency of compounding is continuous compounding. Continuous compounding is when interest is compounded at the smallest possible increment of time. In continuous compounding, the rate per period becomes extremely small:

$$i = \frac{APR}{\infty}$$

And the number of compounding periods in a year, n, is infinite. Therefore, the EAR is

$$EAR = e^{APR} - 1 \qquad (2.16)$$

where e is the natural logarithmic base.

For the stated 6% annual interest rate compounded continuously, the EAR is

$$EAR = e^{0.06} - 1 = 1.0618 - 1 = 0.0618 \text{ or } 6.18\%$$

The relation between the frequency of compounding for a given stated rate and the effective annual rate of interest for this example indicates that the greater the frequency of compounding, the greater the EAR.

Frequency of Compounding	Calculation	Effective Annual Rate
Annual	$(1 + 0.060)^1 - 1$	6.00%
Semiannual	$(1 + 0.030)^2 - 1$	6.09%
Quarterly	$(1 + 0.015)^4 - 1$	6.14%
Continuous	$e^{0.06} - 1$	6.18%

Figuring out the effective annual rate is useful when comparing interest rates for different investments. It doesn't make sense to compare the APRs for different investments having a different frequency of compounding within a year. But since many investments have returns stated in terms of APRs, we need to understand how to work with them.

To illustrate how to calculate effective annual rates, consider the rates offered by two banks, Bank A and Bank B. Bank A offers 9.2% compounded semiannually and Bank B other offers 9% compounded daily. We can compare these rates using the EARs. Which bank offers the highest interest rate? The effective annual rate for Bank A is $(1 + 0.046)^2 - 1 = 9.4\%$. The effective annual rate for Bank B is $(1 + 0.000247)^{365} - 1 = 9.42\%$. Therefore, Bank B offers the higher interest rate.

Yields on Investments

Suppose an investment opportunity requires an investor to put up $1 million and offers cash inflows of $500,000 after one year and $600,000 after two years. The return on this investment, or *yield*, is the interest rate that equates the present values of the $500,000 and $600,000 cash inflows to equal the present value of the $1 million cash outflow. This yield is also referred to as the *internal rate of return* (IRR) and is calculated as the rate that solves the following:

$$\$1,000,000 = \frac{\$500,000}{(1+\text{IRR})^1} + \frac{\$600,000}{(1+\text{IRR})^2}$$

Unfortunately, there is no direct mathematical solution (that is, closed-form solution) for the IRR, but rather we must use an iterative procedure. Fortunately, financial calculators and financial software ease our burden in this calculation. The IRR that solves this equation is 6.3941%:

$$\$1,000,000 = \frac{\$500,000}{(1.063941)^1} + \frac{\$600,000}{(1.063941)^2}$$

In other words, if you invest $1 million today and receive $500,000 in one year and $600,000 in two years, the return on your investment is 6.3941%.

Another way of looking at this same yield is to consider that an investment's IRR is the interest rate that makes the present value of all expected future cash flows—both the cash outflows for the investment and the subsequent inflows—equal to zero. We can represent the IRR as the rate that solves

$$\$0 = \sum_{t=1}^{N} \frac{CF_t}{(1+\text{IRR})^t}$$

Consider another example. Suppose an investment of $1 million produces no cash flow in the first year but cash flows of $200,000, $300,000, and $900,000 two, three, and four years from now, respectively. The IRR for this investment is the interest rate that solves

$$0 = \frac{-\$1,000,000}{(1+\text{IRR})^0} + \frac{0}{(1+\text{IRR})^1} + \frac{\$200,000}{(1+\text{IRR})^2} + \frac{\$300,000}{(1+\text{IRR})^3} + \frac{\$900,000}{(1+\text{IRR})^3}$$

Using a calculator or a computer, we get the precise answer of 10.172% per year.

We can use this approach to calculate the yield on any type of investment, as long as we know the cash flows—both positive and negative—and the timing of these flows. Consider the case of the yield to maturity on a bond. Most bonds pay interest semiannually—that is, every six months. Therefore, when calculating the yield on a bond, we must consider the timing of the cash flows to be such that the discount period is six months.

Consider a bond that has a current price of 90; that is, if the par value of the bond is $1,000, the bond's price is 90% of $1,000 or $900. And suppose that this bond has five years remaining to maturity and an 8% coupon rate. With five years remaining to maturity, the bond has 10 six-month periods remaining. With a coupon rate of 8%, this means that the cash flows for interest is $40 every six months. For a given bond, we therefore have the following information:

1. Present value = $900
2. Number of periods to maturity = 10
3. Cash flow every six months = $40
4. Additional cash flow at maturity = $1,000

The six-month yield, r_d, is the discount rate that solves the following:

$$\$900 = \left[\sum_{t=1}^{10} \frac{\$40}{(1+r_d)^t} \right] + \frac{\$1,000}{(1+r_d)^{10}}$$

Using a calculator or spreadsheet, the six-month yield is 5.315%. Bond yields are generally stated on the basis of an annualized yield, referred to as the *yield to maturity* (YTM) on a bond-equivalent basis. This YTM is analogous to the APR with semiannual compounding. Therefore, yield to maturity is 10.63%.

PRINCIPLES OF VALUATION

In later chapters, we apply the present value and yield concept to value financial assets such as stocks and bonds) and the valuation of capital budgeting projects being considered by a corporation. The fundamental principle of valuation is that the value of any asset is equal to the present value of its expected future cash flows. Thus, the valuation of an asset involves the following three steps:

Step 1. Estimate the expected future cash flows.

Step 2. Determine the appropriate interest rate or interest rates that should be used to discount the cash flows.

Step 3. Calculate the present value of the expected future cash flows found in Step 1 by the appropriate interest rate or interest rates determined in Step 2.

Estimating Cash Flows

Cash flow is simply the cash that is expected to be received in the future from owning an asset. An asset's cash flows represent the sum of each period's expected cash flow. The cash flows for most assets are not simple to estimate. Let's start with two simple ones and then move on to estimating the cash flow for more complex assets.

The cash flows for U.S. Treasury securities with a fixed interest rate are simple to project. While the probability of default of the U.S. government is not zero, it is close enough to that threshold so that default risk is ignored by the financial market. Consider a U.S. Treasury bond that has 25 years remaining to maturity and pays a coupon interest rate of 5%. Most bonds in the United State pay interest semiannually. Consequently, for this asset there are 50 cash flows consisting of 49 payments of coupon interest and one payment of coupon interest plus the principal. If the maturity value of this bond is $1 million, then the annual interest is $50,000 (5% × $1 million). The semiannual interest rate is $25,000. So, there will be 49 payments of $25,000 paid every six months. The last payment will be $1,025,000 which is the final coupon payment of $25,000 plus the principal repayment of $1 million. To summarize, this Treasury bonds cash flows are:

$25,000 semiannually for the next 24.5 years
$1,025,000 at the end of 25 years

Let's look at a corporate bond. The practice in computing the cash flows for such a bond is to assume that the issuer will not default and to project the cash flows in the same way as for a U.S. Treasury security. While the risk of default is ignored in projecting the cash flows, it is taken into consideration in the valuation process by discounting the cash flows at a higher interest rate than a comparable maturity U.S. Treasury security. So, for example, if a corporate bond with 25 years to maturity has a maturity value of $1 million and a coupon interest rate of 5%, its cash flows are the same as for the 25-year U.S. Treasury bond with a coupon rate of 5%.

Now let's look at what features of a bond would make estimating its cash flows problematic. These features include one or more of the following:

1. The issuer or the investor has the option to change the contractual due date of the repayment of the principal.
2. The coupon and/or principal payment is reset periodically based on a formula that depends on one or more market variables (e.g., interest rates, inflation rates, exchange rates, etc.).
3. The investor has the choice to convert or exchange the security into common stock or some other financial asset.

Referring back to this list, callable bonds, putable bonds, mortgage-backed securities, and asset-backed securities are examples of (1). Floating rate securities and Treasury Inflation Protected Securities (TIPS) are examples of (2). Convertible bonds and exchangeable bonds are examples of (3).

For securities that fall into the first category, a key factor determining whether the owner of the option (either the issuer of the security or the investor) will exercise the option to alter the security's cash flows is the level of interest rates in the future relative to the security's coupon rate. In order to estimate the cash flows for these types of securities, we must determine how the size and timing of their expected cash flows will change in the future. For example, when estimating the future cash flows of a callable bond, we must account for the fact that when interest rates change, the expected cash flows change. This introduces an additional layer of complexity to the valuation process because of the difficulty of estimating the cash flows.

Let's move from bonds to common stock. The cash flows for a share of common stock consist of the dividend payments and the projected stock price when the stock is eventually sold. As you can see, neither dividends nor the stock price when the stock is to be sold are known with certainty. This is what makes common stock valuation difficult.

For real estate, the cash flows are the projected net income, any tax benefits, and the projected sale price. While the tax benefits may be easy to determine assuming the tax law governing real estate investments does not change, the other components are subject to uncertainty. Hence, real estate investment are difficult to project.

Now we turn to investments made by corporations in plant and equipment, what are commonly referred to as capital budgeting projects. In Chapter 13, we will discuss how to estimate the cash flows for such investments. As will be seen, there are components of the cash flows that are difficult to estimate. Here is one simple example. Suppose a U.S. company is considering building a manufacturing plant in an emerging market economy. The cash flows for such a project will depend on sales, the costs of products in that country, and foreign exchange rate that will impact the U.S. dollar value of its cash flows.

Determining the Appropriate Interest Rate or Rates

Once we estimate the cash flows for an asset, the next step is to determine the appropriate interest rate for discounting each cash flow. The interest rate used to discount a particular asset's cash flows will depend on three basic factors: (1) the level of benchmark interest rates (i.e., U.S. Treasury rates); (2) the risks that the market perceives the investor in the asset is exposed to; and (3) the compensation the market expects to receive for these risks.

The minimum interest rate that an investor should require is the yield available in the marketplace on a default-free cash flow. For bonds with U.S. dollar-denominated cash flows, yields on U.S. Treasury securities serve as benchmarks for default-free interest rates. For now, we can think of the minimum interest rate that investors require as the yield on a comparable maturity Treasury security. The additional compensation or spread over the yield on the Treasury issue that investors require reflects the additional risks the investor faces by acquiring an asset that is not issued by the U.S. government. These risks include default risk, liquidity risk, exchange-rate risk, and the risks associated with any embedded options. These yield spreads will depend not only on the risks an individual issue is exposed to but also on the level of Treasury yields, the market's risk aversion, the business cycle, and so forth.

In financial theory, economic models have been developed to estimate the required interest rate investors should demand for the risk associated with an asset. These economic models are referred to as asset pricing models because given the interest rate that an investor should require, that interest rate can be used to value the asset's cash flows to determine it value. The most basic economic model is the capital asset pricing model which is the subject of Chapter 8. We will discuss other models in the same chapter.

For each cash flow estimated, the same interest rate can be used to calculate the present value. This is the traditional approach to valuation and it serves as a useful starting point in valuation. We discuss this traditional approach in the next section and use a single interest rate to determine present values. By doing this, however, we are implicitly assuming that the yield curve is flat. Since the yield curve is almost never flat and any asset can be thought of as a package of zero-coupon bonds, it is more appropriate to value each cash flow using an interest rate specific to when that cash flow is to be received.

Discounting the Expected Cash Flows

Once the expected (estimated) cash flows and the appropriate interest rate or interest rates that should be used to discount the cash flows are determined, the final step in the valuation process is to value the cash flows. The value of the cash flows is simply the present value of all the cash flows. The value of an asset is then the sum of the present value of all the expected cash flows. How the present value of the cash flows is computed was discussed earlier in this chapter.

In comparison to the other two steps in the valuation process, the computation of the present value of the projected cash flows is much easier. It is simply a mechanical process. Given the same projected cash flows for two assets and the same interest rates that should be used for discounting those cash flows, two analysts will come up with the same value. However, except in the simple cases discussed earlier, analysts will not necessarily project the cash flows for an asset, nor will they necessarily determine the same interest rate or interest rates. This is why there are differences in the view of investors of the valuation of assets.

SUMMARY

We can translate a present value into a value in the future through compounding. We can translate a future value into an equivalent value today through discounting. Financial mathematics consists of the mathematical tools we use to perform compounding and discounting.

The basic valuation equation, $FV = PV(1 + i)^N$, is used to translate present values into future values and to translate future values into present values. This basic relationship includes interest compounding—that is, interest earnings on interest already earned.

Using the basic valuation equation, we can translate any number of cash flows into a present or future value. When faced with a series of cash flows, we must value each cash flow individually, and then sum these individual values to arrive at the present value of the series. Our work can be cut a bit shorter if these cash flows are equal and occur at periodic intervals of time, referred to as an annuity.

We can use financial mathematics to value many different patterns of cash flows, including perpetuities, annuities due, and deferred annuities. Applying the tools to these different patterns of cash flows requires us to take care in specifying the timing of the various cash flows.

The interest on alternative investments is stated in different terms, so we must place these interest rates on a common basis so that we can determine the best alternative. Typically, we specify an interest rate on an annual basis, using either the annual percentage rate or the effective annual rate. The latter method is preferred since it takes into consideration the compounding of interest within a year. Effective rates on loans are calculated like annual percentage yields on savings accounts, by calculating the periodic rate and translating it into an effective annual rate. These effective rates are useful in comparing different borrowing or investing alternatives.

The fundamental principle of valuation is that the value of any asset is equal to the present value of its expected future cash flows. The three steps in the valuation of an asset are (1) estimate the expected future cash flows; (2) determine the appropriate interest rate or interest rates that should be used to discount the cash flows; and (3) calculate the present value of the expected future cash flows. The third step is purely mechanical. The first two steps are the complex steps in the valuation process.

CHAPTER 3

Basics of Financial Analysis

Financial analysis involves the selection, evaluation, and interpretation of financial data and other pertinent information to assist in evaluating the operating performance and financial condition of a company. The information that is available for analysis includes economic, market, and financial information. But some of the most important financial data are provided by the company in its annual and quarterly financial statements.

The operating performance of a company is a measure of how well a company has used its resources to produce a return on its investment. The financial condition of a company is a measure of its ability to satisfy its obligations, such as the payment of interest on its debt in a timely manner. An investor has many tools available in the analysis of financial information. These tools include:

- Financial ratio analysis
- Cash flow analysis
- Quantitative analysis

Cash flows provide a way of transforming net income based on an accrual system to a more comparable basis. Additionally, cash flows are essential ingredients in valuation because the value of a company today is the present value of its expected future cash flows. Therefore, understanding past and current cash flows may help in forecasting future cash flows and, hence, determine the value of the company. Moreover, understanding cash flow allows the assessment of the ability of a firm to maintain current dividends and its current capital expenditure policy without relying on external financing.

In this chapter, we describe and illustrate the basic tools of financial analysis: financial ratio analysis and cash flow analysis.

FINANCIAL RATIO ANALYSIS

In financial ratio analysis, we select the relevant information—primarily the financial statement data—and evaluate it. We show how to incorporate market data and economic data in the analysis of financial ratios. Finally, we show how to interpret financial ratio analysis, identifying the pitfalls that occur when it's not done properly.

Ratios and Their Classification

A financial ratio is a comparison between one bit of financial information and another. Consider the ratio of current assets to current liabilities, which we refer to as the *current ratio*. This ratio is a comparison between assets that can be readily turned into cash—current assets—and the obligations that are due in the near future—current liabilities. A current ratio of 2, or 2:1, means that we have twice as much in current assets as we need to satisfy obligations due in the near future.

Ratios can be classified according to the way they are constructed and the financial characteristic they are describing. For example, we will see that the current ratio is constructed as a coverage ratio (the ratio of current assets—available funds—to current liabilities—the obligation) that we use to describe a firm's liquidity (its ability to meet its immediate needs).

There are as many different financial ratios as there are possible combinations of items appearing on the income statement, balance sheet, and statement of cash flows. We can classify ratios according to the financial characteristic that they capture.

When we assess a firm's operating performance, a concern is whether the company is applying its assets in an efficient and profitable manner. When an investor assesses a firm's financial condition, a concern is whether the company is able to meet its financial obligations. The investor can use financial ratios to evaluate five aspects of operating performance and financial condition:

1. Return on investment
2. Liquidity
3. Profitability
4. Activity
5. Financial leverage

There are several ratios reflecting each of the five aspects of a firm's operating performance and financial condition. We apply these ratios to the Fictitious Corporation, whose balance sheets, income statements, and statement of cash flows for two years are shown in Tables 3.1, 3.2, and 3.3, respectively. We refer to the most recent fiscal year for which financial statements are available as the "current year." The "prior year" is the fiscal year prior to the current year.

The ratios we introduce here are by no means the only ones that can be formed using financial data, though they are some of the more commonly used. After becoming comfortable with the tools of financial analysis, an investor will be able to create ratios that serve a particular evaluation objective.

TABLE 3.1 Fictitious Corporation Balance Sheets for Years Ending December 31 (in thousands)

	Current Year	Prior Year
Assets		
Cash	$400	$200
Marketable securities	200	0
Accounts receivable	600	800
Inventories	1,800	1,000
Total current assets	$3,000	$2,000
Gross plant and equipment	$11,000	$10,000
Accumulated depreciation	(4,000)	(3,000)
Net plant and equipment	7,000	7,000
Intangible assets	1,000	1,000
Total assets	$11,000	$10,000
Liabilities and Shareholder Equity		
Accounts payable	$500	$400
Other current liabilities	500	200
Long-term debt	4,000	5,000
Total liabilities	$5,000	$5,600
Common stock, $1 par value;		
Authorized 2,000,000 shares		
Issued 1,500,000 and 1,200,000 shares	1,500	1,200
Additional paid-in capital	1,500	800
Retained earnings	3,000	2,400
Total shareholders' equity	6,000	4,400
Total liabilities and shareholder equity	$11,000	$10,000

TABLE 3.2 Fictitious Corporation Income Statements for Years Ending December 31 (in thousands)

	Current Year	Prior Year
Sales	$10,000	$9,000
Cost of goods sold	(6,500)	(6,000)
Gross profit	$3,500	$3,000
Lease expense	(1,000)	1,000
Administrative expense	(500)	(500)
Earnings before interest and taxes (EBIT)	$2,000	$2,000
Interest	(400)	(500)
Earnings before taxes	$1,600	$1,500
Taxes	(400)	(500)
Net income	$1,200	$1,000
Preferred dividends	(100)	(100)
Earnings available to common shareholders	$1,100	$900
Common dividends	(500)	(400)
Retained earnings	$600	$500

Return-on-Investment Ratios

Return-on-investment ratios compare measures of benefits, such as earnings or net income, with measures of investment. For example, if an investor wants to evaluate how well the firm uses its assets in its operations, he could calculate the return on assets—sometimes called the *basic earning power ratio*—as the ratio of earnings before interest and taxes (EBIT) (also known as operating earnings) to total assets:

$$\text{Basic earning power} = \frac{\text{Earnings before interest and taxes}}{\text{Total assets}}$$

For Fictitious Corporation, for the current year,

$$\text{Basic earning power} = \frac{\$2,000,000}{\$11,000,000} = 0.1818 \text{ or } 18.18\%$$

For every dollar invested in assets, Fictitious earned about 18 cents in the current year. This measure deals with earnings from operations; it does not consider how these operations are financed.

Another return-on-assets ratio uses net income—operating earnings less interest and taxes—instead of earnings before interest and taxes:

TABLE 3.3 Fictitious Company Statement of Cash Flows, Years Ended December 31 (in thousands)

	Current Year	Prior Year
Cash flow from (used for) operating activities		
Net income	$1,200	$1,000
Add or deduct adjustments to cash basis:		
Change in accounts receivables	$200	$(200)
Change in accounts payable	100	400
Change in marketable securities	(200)	200
Change in inventories	(800)	(600)
Change in other current liabilities	300	0
Depreciation	1,000	1,000
Cash flow from operations	$1,800	$1,800
Cash flow from (used for) investing activities		
Purchase of plant and equipment	$(1,000)	$0
Cash flow from (used for) investing activities	$(1,000)	$0
Cash flow from (used for) financing activities		
Sale of common stock	$1,000	$0
Repayment of long-term debt	(1,000)	(1,500)
Payment of preferred dividends	(100)	(100)
Payment of common dividends	(500)	(400)
Cash flow from (used for) financing activities	(600)	(1,900)
Increase (decrease) in cash flow	$200	$(100)
Cash at the beginning of the year	200	300
Cash at the end of the year	$400	$200

$$\text{Return on assets} = \frac{\text{Net income}}{\text{Total assets}}$$

(In actual application the same term, return on assets, is often used to describe both ratios. It is only in the actual context or through an examination of the numbers themselves that we know which return ratio is presented. We use two different terms to describe these two return-on-asset ratios in this chapter simply to avoid any confusion.)

For Fictitious in the current year:

$$\text{Return on assets} = \frac{\$1,200,000}{\$11,000,000} = 0.1091 \text{ or } 10.91\%$$

Thus, without taking into consideration how assets are financed, the return on assets for Fictitious is 18%. Taking into consideration how assets are financed, the return on assets is 11%. The difference is due to Fictitious financing part of its total assets with debt, incurring interest of $400,000 in the current year; hence, the return-on-assets ratio excludes taxes of $400,000 in the current year from earnings in the numerator.

If we look at Fictitious's liabilities and equities, we see that the assets are financed in part by liabilities ($1 million short term, $4 million long term) and in part by equity ($800,000 preferred stock, $5.2 million common stock). Investors may not be interested in the return the firm gets from its total investment (debt plus equity), but rather shareholders are interested in the return the firm can generate on their investment. The *return on equity* is the ratio of the net income shareholders receive to their equity in the stock:

$$\text{Return on equity} = \frac{\text{Net income}}{\text{Book value of shareholders' equity}}$$

For Fictitious Corporation, there is only one type of shareholder: common. For the current year,

$$\text{Return on equity} = \frac{\$1,200,000}{\$6,000,000} = 0.2000 \text{ or } 20.00\%$$

Recap: Return-on-Investment Ratios   The return-on-investment ratios for Fictitious Corporation for the current year are:

Basic earning power = 18.18%
Return on assets   = 10.91%
Return on equity   = 20.00%

These return-on-investment ratios indicate:

- Fictitious earns over 18% from operations, or about 11% overall, from its assets.
- Shareholders earn 20% from their investment (measured in book value terms).

These ratios do not provide information on:

- Whether this return is due to the profit margins (that is, due to costs and revenues) or to how efficiently Fictitious uses its assets.
- The return shareholders earn on their actual investment in the firm, that is, what shareholders earn relative to their actual investment, not the book value of their investment. For example, $100 may be invested in the stock, but its value according to the balance sheet may be greater than or, more likely, less than $100.

Du Pont System   The returns on investment ratios provides a "bottom line" on the performance of a company, but do not tell us anything about the "why" behind this performance. For an understanding of the "why," an investor must dig a bit deeper into the financial statements. A method that is useful in examining the source of performance is the Du Pont system. The *Du Pont system* is a method of breaking down return ratios into their components to determine which areas are responsible for a firm's performance. To see how it is used, let us take a closer look at the first definition of the return on assets:

$$\text{Basic earning power} = \frac{\text{Earnings before interest and taxes}}{\text{Total assets}}$$

Suppose the return on assets changes from 20% in one period to 10% the next period. We do not know whether this decreased return is due to a less efficient use of the firm's assets—that is, lower activity—or to less effective management of expenses (i.e., lower profit margins). A lower return on assets could be due to lower activity, lower margins, or both. Because an investor is interested in evaluating past operating performance to evaluate different aspects of the management of the firm and to predict future performance, knowing the source of these returns is valuable.

Let us take a closer look at the return on assets and break it down into its components: measures of activity and profit margin. We do this by relating both the numerator and the denominator to sales activity. Divide both the numerator and the denominator of the basic earning power by revenues:

$$\text{Basic earning power} = \frac{\text{Earnings before interest and taxes/Revenues}}{\text{Revenues total assets/Revenues}}$$

which is equivalent to

$$\text{Basic earning power}$$
$$= \left(\frac{\text{Earnings before interest and taxes}}{\text{Revenues}} \right) \left(\frac{\text{Revenues}}{\text{Revenues total assets}} \right)$$

This says that the earning power of the company is related to profitability (in this case, operating profit) and a measure of activity (total asset turnover).

Basic earning power = (Operating profit margin)(Total asset turnover)

When analyzing a change in the company's basic earning power, an investor could look at this breakdown to see the change in its components: operating profit margin and total asset turnover.

This method of analyzing return ratios in terms of profit margin and turnover ratios, referred to as the Du Pont System, is credited to the E.I. Du Pont Corporation, whose management developed a system of breaking down return ratios into their components.

Let's look at the return on assets of Fictitious for the two years. Its returns on assets were 20% in the prior year and 18.18% in the current year. We can decompose the firm's returns on assets for the two years to obtain:

Year	Basic Earning Power	Operating Profit Margin	Total Asset Turnover
Prior	20.00%	22.22%	0.9000 times
Current	18.18	20.00	0.9091 times

We see that operating profit margin declined over the two years, yet asset turnover improved slightly, from 0.9000 to 0.9091. Therefore, the return-on-assets decline is attributable to lower profit margins.

The return on assets can be broken down into its components in a similar manner:

$$\text{Return on assets} = \left(\frac{\text{Net income}}{\text{Revenues}} \right) \left(\frac{\text{Revenues}}{\text{Revenues total assets}} \right)$$

or

$$\text{Return on assets} = (\text{Net profit margin})(\text{Total asset turnover})$$

The basic earning power ratio relates to the return on assets. Recognizing that

$$\text{Net income} = \text{Earnings before tax}(1 - \text{Tax rate})$$

then

Net income = Earnings before interest and taxes

$$\times \left(\frac{\text{Earnings before taxes}}{\text{Earnings before interest and taxes}} \right) (1 - \text{Tax rate})$$

↑   ↑

Equity's share of earnings   Tax retention %

The ratio of earnings before taxes to earnings before interest and taxes reflects the interest burden of the company, where as the term (1 − tax rate) reflects the company's tax burden. Therefore,

$$\text{Return on assets} = \left(\frac{\text{Earnings before interest and taxes}}{\text{Revenues}} \right)$$

$$\times \left(\frac{\text{Revenues}}{\text{Revenues total assets}} \right)$$

$$\times \left(\frac{\text{Earnings before taxes}}{\text{Earnings before interest and taxes}} \right) (1 - \text{Tax rate})$$

or

$$\text{Return on assets} = (\text{Operating profit margin})(\text{Total asset turnover})$$
$$\times (\text{Equity's share of earnings})(\text{Tax retention \%})$$

The breakdown of a return-on-equity ratio requires a bit more decomposition because instead of total assets as the denominator, the denominator in the return is shareholders' equity. Because activity ratios reflect the use of all of the assets, not just the proportion financed by equity, we need to adjust the activity ratio by the proportion that assets are financed by equity (i.e., the ratio of the book value of shareholders' equity to total assets):

$$\text{Return on equity} = (\text{Return on assets}) \left(\frac{\text{Total assets}}{\text{Shareholders' equity}} \right)$$

$$\text{Return on equity} = \left(\frac{\text{Net income}}{\text{Revenues}} \right) \left(\frac{\text{Revenues}}{\text{Total assets}} \right) \left(\frac{\text{Total assets}}{\text{Shareholders' equity}} \right)$$

↑

Equity multiplier

The ratio of total assets to shareholders' equity is referred to as the equity multiplier. The equity multiplier, therefore, captures the effects of how a company finances its assets, referred to as its *financial leverage*. Multiplying the total asset turnover ratio by the equity multiplier allows us to break down the return-on-equity ratios into three components: profit margin, asset turnover, and financial leverage. For example, the return on equity can be broken down into three parts:

Return on equity = (Net profit margin)(Total asset turnover)(Equity multiplier)

Applying this breakdown to Fictitious for the two years:

Year	Return on Equity	Net Profit Margin	Total Asset Turnover	Total Debt to Assets	Equity Multiplier
Prior	22.73%	11.11%	0.9000 times	56.00%	2.2727
Current	20.00	12.00	0.9091	45.45%	1.8332

The return on equity decreased over the two years because of a lower operating profit margin and less use of financial leverage.

The investor can decompose the return on equity further by breaking out the equity's share of before-tax earnings (represented by the ratio of earnings before and after interest) and tax retention percentage. Consider the example in Figure 3.1(a), in which we provide a Du Pont breakdown of the return on equity for Microsoft Corporation for the fiscal year ending June 30, 2006. The return on equity of 31.486% can be broken down into three and then five components, as shown in this figure. We can also use this breakdown to compare the return on equity for the 2005 and 2006 fiscal years shown in Figure 3.1(b). As you can see, the return on equity improved from 2005 to 2006 and, using this breakdown, we can see that this was due primarily to the improvement in the asset turnover and the increased financial leverage.

This decomposition allows the investor to take a closer look at the factors that are controllable by a company's management (e.g., asset turnover) and those that are not controllable (e.g., tax retention). The breakdowns lead the investor to information on both the balance sheet and the income statement. And this is not the only breakdown of the return ratios—further decomposition is possible.

Liquidity

Liquidity reflects the ability of a firm to meet its short-term obligations using those assets that are most readily converted into cash. Assets that may be converted into cash in a short period of time are referred to as liquid assets; they are listed in financial statements as current assets. Current assets

FIGURE 3.1   The DuPont System Applied to Microsoft Corporation

(a) For the fiscal year ending June 30, 2006,

$$\text{Return on equity} = \frac{\text{Net income}}{\text{Total assets}} = \frac{\$12.599}{\$40.014} = 0.31486 \text{ or } 31.486\%$$

Breaking return on equity into three components,

$$\text{Return on equity} = \frac{\text{Net income}}{\text{Revenues}} \times \frac{\text{Revenues}}{\text{Total assets}} \times \frac{\text{Total assets}}{\text{Shareholders' equity}}$$

$$= \frac{\$12.599}{\$44.282} \times \frac{\$44.282}{\$69.597} \times \frac{\$69.597}{\$40.014} = 0.31486 \text{ or } 31.486\%$$

Breaking the return on equity into five components,

$$\text{Return on equity} = \left(\frac{\text{Earnings before interest and taxes}}{\text{Revenues}}\right) \times \left(\frac{\text{Earnings before taxes}}{\text{Earnings before interest and taxes}}\right) \times (1 - \text{Tax rate})$$

$$\times \left(\frac{\text{Revenues}}{\text{Total assets}}\right) \times \left(\frac{\text{Total assets}}{\text{Shareholders' equity}}\right)$$

$$\text{Return on equity} = \left(\frac{\$18.262}{\$44.282}\right) \times \left(\frac{\$18.262}{\$18.262}\right) \times (1 - 0.31010) \times \left(\frac{\$44.282}{\$69.597}\right) \times \left(\frac{\$69.597}{\$40.014}\right)$$

$$= 0.41240 \times 1.0 \times 0.68990 \times 0.63626 \times 1.73932$$

$$= 0.31486 \text{ or } 31.486\%$$

(b) Comparing the components between the June 30, 2006 fiscal year and the June 30, 2005 fiscal year,

$$\text{Return on equity} = \left(\frac{\text{Earnings before interest and taxes}}{\text{Revenues}}\right) \times \left(\frac{\text{Earnings before taxes}}{\text{Earnings before interest and taxes}}\right) \times (1 - \text{Tax rate})$$

$$\times \left(\frac{\text{Revenues}}{\text{Total assets}}\right) \times \left(\frac{\text{Total assets}}{\text{Shareholders' equity}}\right)$$

$$\frac{\text{Return on equity}}{\text{June 30, 2006}} = 0.41240 \times 1.0 \times 0.68990 \times 0.63626 \times 1.73932 = 31.486\%$$

$$\frac{\text{Return on equity}}{\text{June 30, 2006}} = 0.41791 \times 1.0 \times 0.73695 \times 0.56186 \times 1.47179 = 25.468\%$$

are often referred to as working capital, since they represent the resources needed for the day-to-day operations of the firm's long-term capital investments. Current assets are used to satisfy short-term obligations, or current liabilities. The amount by which current assets exceed current liabilities is referred to as the net working capital.

Operating Cycle   How much liquidity a firm needs depends on its operating cycle. The *operating cycle* is the duration from the time cash is invested in goods and services to the time that investment produces cash. For example, a firm that produces and sells goods has an operating cycle comprising four phases:

1. Purchase raw materials and produce goods, investing in inventory.
2. Sell goods, generating sales, which may or may not be for cash.
3. Extend credit, creating accounts receivable.
4. Collect accounts receivable, generating cash.

The four phases make up the cycle of cash use and generation. The operating cycle would be somewhat different for companies that produce services rather than goods, but the idea is the same—the operating cycle is the length of time it takes to generate cash through the investment of cash.

What does the operating cycle have to do with liquidity? The longer the operating cycle, the more current assets are needed (relative to current liabilities) since it takes longer to convert inventories and receivables into cash. In other words, the longer the operating cycle, the greater the amount of net working capital required.

To measure the length of an operating cycle we need to know:

- The time it takes to convert the investment in inventory into sales (that is, cash → inventory → sales → accounts receivable).
- The time it takes to collect sales on credit (that is, accounts receivable → cash).

We can estimate the operating cycle for Fictitious Corporation for the current year, using the balance sheet and income statement data. The number of days Fictitious ties up funds in inventory is determined by the total amount of money represented in inventory and the average day's cost of goods sold. The current investment in inventory—that is, the money "tied up" in inventory—is the ending balance of inventory on the balance sheet. The *average day's cost of goods sold* is the cost of goods sold on an average day in the year, which can be estimated by dividing the cost of goods sold (which is found on the income statement) by the number of days in the year. The average day's cost of goods sold for the current year is

$$\text{Average day's cost of goods sold} = \frac{\text{Cost of goods sold}}{365 \text{ days}}$$

$$= \frac{\$6,500,000}{365 \text{ days}} = \$17,808 \text{ per day}$$

In other words, Fictitious incurs, on average, a cost of producing goods sold of $17,808 per day.

Fictitious has $1.8 million of inventory on hand at the end of the year. How many days' worth of goods sold is this? One way to look at this is to imagine that Fictitious stopped buying more raw materials and just finished producing whatever was on hand in inventory, using available raw materials and work-in-process. How long would it take Fictitious to run out of inventory?

We compute the *days sales in inventory* (DSI), also known as the *number of days of inventory*, by calculating the ratio of the amount of inventory on hand (in dollars) to the average day's cost of goods sold (in dollars per day):

$$
\text{Days sales in inventory} = \frac{\text{Amount of inventory on hand}}{\text{Average day's cost of goods sold}}
$$

$$
= \frac{\$1,800,000}{\$17,808 \text{ day}} = 101 \text{ days}
$$

In other words, Fictitious has approximately 101 days of goods on hand at the end of the current year. If sales continued at the same price, it would take Fictitious 101 days to run out of inventory.

If the ending inventory is representative of the inventory throughout the year, then it takes about 101 days to convert the investment in inventory into sold goods. Why worry about whether the year-end inventory is representative of inventory at any day throughout the year? Well, if inventory at the end of the fiscal year-end is lower than on any other day of the year, we have understated the DSI. Indeed, in practice most companies try to choose fiscal year-ends that coincide with the slow period of their business. That means the ending balance of inventory would be lower than the typical daily inventory of the year. To get a better picture of the firm, we could, for example, look at quarterly financial statements and take averages of quarterly inventory balances. However, here for simplicity we make a note of the problem of representatives and deal with it later in the discussion of financial ratios.

It should be noted that as an attempt to make the inventory figure more representative, some suggest taking the average of the beginning and ending inventory amounts. This does nothing to remedy the representativeness problem because the beginning inventory is simply the ending inventory from the previous year and, like the ending value from the current year, is measured at the low point of the operating cycle. A preferred method, if data is available, is to calculate the average inventory for the four quarters of the fiscal year.

We can extend the same logic for calculating the number of days between a sale—when an account receivable is created—and the time it is collected in cash. If we assume that Fictitious sells all goods on credit, we can first calculate the average credit sales per day and then figure out how many days' worth of credit sales are represented by the ending balance of receivables.

The *average credit sales per day* are

$$\text{Credit sales per day} = \frac{\text{Credit sales}}{365 \text{ days}} = \frac{\$10,000,000}{365 \text{ days}} = \$27,397 \text{ per day}$$

Therefore, Fictitious generates $27,397 of credit sales per day. With an ending balance of accounts receivable of $600,000, the *days sales outstanding* (DSO), also known as the *number of days of credit*, in this ending balance is calculated by taking the ratio of the balance in the accounts receivable account to the credit sales per day:

$$\text{Number of days of credit} = \frac{\text{Accounts receivable}}{\text{Credit sales per day}}$$

$$= \frac{\$600,000}{\$27,297 \text{ per day}} = 22 \text{ days}$$

If the ending balance of receivables at the end of the year is representative of the receivables on any day throughout the year, then it takes, on average, approximately 22 days to collect the accounts receivable. In other words, it takes 22 days for a sale to become cash.

Using what we have determined for the inventory cycle and cash cycle, we see that for Fictitious

$$\text{Operating cycle} = \text{DSI} + \text{DSO} = 101 \text{ days} + 22 \text{ days} = 123 \text{ days}$$

We also need to look at the liabilities on the balance sheet to see how long it takes a firm to pay its short-term obligations. We can apply the same logic to accounts payable as we did to accounts receivable and inventories. How long does it take a firm, on average, to go from creating a payable (buying on credit) to paying for it in cash?

First, we need to determine the amount of an average day's purchases on credit. If we assume all the Fictitious purchases are made on credit, then the total purchases for the year would be the cost of goods sold less any amounts included in cost of goods sold that are not purchases. For example, depreciation is included in the cost of goods sold yet is not a purchase. Since we do not have a breakdown on the company's cost of goods sold showing how much was paid for in cash and how much was on credit, let us assume for simplicity that purchases are equal to cost of goods sold less depreciation. The average day's purchases then become

$$\text{Average day's purchases} = \frac{\text{Cost of goods sold} - \text{Depreciation}}{365 \text{ days}}$$

$$= \frac{\$6,500,000 - \$1,000,000}{365 \text{ days}} = \$15,068 \text{ per day}$$

The *days payables outstanding* (DPO), also known as the *number of days of purchases*, represented in the ending balance in accounts payable is calculated as the ratio of the balance in the accounts payable account to the average day's purchases:

$$\text{Days payables outstanding} = \frac{\text{Accounts payable}}{\text{Average day's purchases}}$$

For Fictitious in the current year,

$$\text{Days payables outstanding} = \frac{\$500,000}{\$15,065 \text{ per day}} = 33 \text{ days}$$

This means that on average Fictitious takes 33 days to pay out cash for a purchase.

The operating cycle tells us how long it takes to convert an investment in cash back into cash (by way of inventory and accounts receivable). The number of days of payables tells us how long it takes to pay on purchases made to create the inventory. If we put these two pieces of information together, we can see how long, on net, we tie up cash. The difference between the operating cycle and the number of days of purchases is the *cash conversion cycle* (CCC), also known as the *net operating cycle*:

Cash conversion cycle = Operating cycle – Number of days of payables

Or, substituting for the operating cycle,

$$\text{CCC} = \text{DSI} + \text{DSO} + \text{DPO}$$

The cash conversion cycle for Fictitious in the current year is

$$\text{CCC} = 101 + 22 - 33 = 90 \text{ days}$$

The CCC is how long it takes for the firm to get cash back from its investments in inventory and accounts receivable, considering that purchases may be made on credit. By not paying for purchases immediately (that is, using trade credit), the firm reduces its liquidity needs. Therefore, the longer the net operating cycle, the greater the required liquidity.

Measures of Liquidity The investor can describe a firm's ability to meet its current obligations in several ways. The *current ratio* indicates the firm's ability to meet or cover its current liabilities using its current assets:

$$\text{Current ratio} = \frac{\text{Current assets}}{\text{Current liabilities}}$$

For the Fictitious Corporation, the current ratio for the current year is the ratio of current assets, $3 million, to current liabilities, the sum of accounts payable and other current liabilities, or $1 million.

$$\text{Current ratio} = \frac{\$3,000,000}{\$1,000,000} = 3.0 \text{ times}$$

The current ratio of 3.0 indicates that Fictitious has three times as much as it needs to cover its current obligations during the year. However, the current ratio groups all current asset accounts together, assuming they are all as easily converted to cash. Even though, by definition, current assets can be transformed into cash within a year, not all current assets can be transformed into cash in a short period of time.

An alternative to the current ratio is the *quick ratio*, also called the *acid-test ratio*, which uses a slightly different set of current accounts to cover the same current liabilities as in the current ratio. In the quick ratio, the least liquid of the current asset accounts, inventory, is excluded:

$$\text{Quick ratio} = \frac{\text{Current assets} - \text{Inventory}}{\text{Current liabilities}}$$

We typically leave out inventories in the quick ratio because inventories are generally perceived as the least liquid of the current assets. By leaving out the least liquid asset, the quick ratio provides a more conservative view of liquidity.

For Fictitious in the current year,

$$\text{Quick ratio} = \frac{\$3,000,000 - 1,800,000}{\$1,000,000} = \frac{\$1,200,000}{\$1,000,000} = 1.2 \text{ times}$$

Still another way to measure the firm's ability to satisfy short-term obligations is the *net working capital-to-sales ratio*, which compares net working capital (current assets less current liabilities) with sales:

$$\text{Net working capital-to-sales ratio} = \frac{\text{Net working capital}}{\text{Sales}}$$

This ratio tells us the "cushion" available to meet short-term obligations relative to sales. Consider two firms with identical working capital of

$100,000, but one has sales of $500,000 and the other sales of $1,000,000. If they have identical operating cycles, this means that the firm with the greater sales has more funds flowing in and out of its current asset investments (inventories and receivables). The company with more funds flowing in and out needs a larger cushion to protect itself in case of a disruption in the cycle, such as a labor strike or unexpected delays in customer payments. The longer the operating cycle, the more of a cushion (net working capital) a firm needs for a given level of sales.

For Fictitious Corporation,

$$\text{Net working capital-to-sales ratio} = \frac{\$3,000,000 - 1,000,000}{\$10,000,000}$$
$$= 0.2000 \text{ or } 20\%$$

The ratio of 0.20 tells us that for every dollar of sales, Fictitious has 20 cents of net working capital to support it.

Recap: Liquidity Ratios Operating cycle and liquidity ratio information for Fictitious using data for the current year, in summary, is

Days sales in inventory	= 101 days
Days sales outstanding	= 22 days
Operating cycle	= 123 days
Days payables outstanding	= 33 days
Cash conversion cycle	= 90 days
Current ratio	= 3.0
Quick ratio	= 1.2
Net working capital–to-sales ratio	= 20%

Given the measures of time related to the current accounts—the operating cycle and the cash conversion cycle—and the three measures of liquidity—current ratio, quick ratio, and net working capital–to-sales ratio—we know the following about Fictitious Corporation's ability to meet its short-term obligations:

- Inventory is less liquid than accounts receivable (comparing days of inventory with days of credit).
- Current assets are greater than needed to satisfy current liabilities in a year (from the current ratio).
- The quick ratio tells us that Fictitious can meet its short-term obligations even without resorting to selling inventory.

■ The net working capital "cushion" is 20 cents for every dollar of sales (from the net working capital–to-sales ratio.)

What don't ratios tells us about liquidity? They don't provide us with answers to the following questions:

■ How liquid are the accounts receivable? How much of the accounts receivable will be collectible? Whereas we know it takes, on average, 22 days to collect, we do not know how much will never be collected.
■ What is the nature of the current liabilities? How much of current liabilities consists of items that recur (such as accounts payable and wages payable) each period and how much consists of occasional items (such as income taxes payable)?
■ Are there any unrecorded liabilities (such as operating leases) that are not included in current liabilities?

Profitability Ratios

Liquidity ratios indicate a firm's ability to meet its immediate obligations. Now we extend the analysis by adding *profitability ratios*, which help the investor gauge how well a firm is managing its expenses. *Profit margin ratios* compare components of income with sales. They give the investor an idea of which factors make up a firm's income and are usually expressed as a portion of each dollar of sales. For example, the profit margin ratios we discuss here differ only in the numerator. It is in the numerator that we can evaluate performance for different aspects of the business.

For example, suppose the investor wants to evaluate how well production facilities are managed. The investor would focus on gross profit (sales less cost of goods sold), a measure of income that is the direct result of production management. Comparing gross profit with sales produces the *gross profit margin*,

$$\text{Gross profit margin} = \frac{\text{Revenues} - \text{Cost of goods sold}}{\text{Revenues}}$$

This ratio tells us the portion of each dollar of sales that remains after deducting production expenses. For Fictitious Corporation for the current year,

$$\text{Gross profit margin} = \frac{\$10,000,000 - \$6,500,000}{\$10,000,000} = \frac{\$3,500,000}{\$10,000,000}$$
$$= 0.3500 \text{ or } 35\%$$

For each dollar of revenues, the firm's gross profit is 35 cents. Looking at sales and cost of goods sold, we can see that the gross profit margin is affected by:

- Changes in sales volume, which affect cost of goods sold and sales.
- Changes in sales price, which affect revenues.
- Changes in the cost of production, which affect cost of goods sold.

Any change in gross profit margin from one period to the next is caused by one or more of those three factors. Similarly, differences in gross margin ratios among firms are the result of differences in those factors.

To evaluate operating performance, we need to consider operating expenses in addition to the cost of goods sold. To do this, remove operating expenses (e.g., selling and general administrative expenses) from gross profit, leaving operating profit, also referred to as *earnings before interest and taxes* (EBIT). Therefore, the *operating profit margin* is

$$\begin{aligned} \frac{\text{Operating}}{\text{profit margin}} &= \frac{\text{Revenues} - \text{Cost of goods sold} - \text{Operating expenses}}{\text{Revenues}} \\ &= \frac{\text{Revenues earnings before interest and taxes}}{\text{Revenues}} \end{aligned}$$

For Fictitious in the current year,

$$\text{Operating profit margin} = \frac{\$2,000,000}{\$10,000,000} = 0.20 \text{ or } 20\%$$

Therefore, for each dollar of revenues, Fictitious has 20 cents of operating income. The operating profit margin is affected by the same factors as gross profit margin, plus operating expenses such as:

- Office rent and lease expenses.
- Miscellaneous income (for example, income from investments).
- Advertising expenditures.
- Bad debt expense.

Most of these expenses are related in some way to revenues, though they are not included directly in the cost of goods sold. Therefore, the difference between the gross profit margin and the operating profit margin is due to these indirect items that are included in computing the operating profit margin.

Both the gross profit margin and the operating profit margin reflect a company's operating performance. But they do not consider how these operations have been financed. To evaluate both operating and financing decisions, the investor must compare net income (that is, earnings after deducting interest and taxes) with revenues. The result is the *net profit margin*:

$$\text{Net profit margin} = \frac{\text{Net income}}{\text{Revenues}}$$

The net profit margin tells the investor the net income generated from each dollar of revenues; it considers financing costs that the operating profit margin does not consider. For Fictitious for the current year,

$$\text{Net profit margin} = \frac{\$1,200,000}{\$10,000,000} = 0.12 \text{ or } 12\%$$

For every dollar of revenues, Fictitious generates 12 cents in profits.

Recap: Profitability Ratios   The profitability ratios for Fictitious in the current year are:

Gross profit margin   = 35%
Operating profit margin = 20%
Net profit margin   = 12%

They indicate the following about the operating performance of Fictitious:

- Each dollar of revenues contributes 35 cents to gross profit and 20 cents to operating profit.
- Every dollar of revenues contributes 12 cents to owners' earnings.
- By comparing the 20-cent operating profit margin with the 12-cent net profit margin, we see that Fictitious has 8 cents of financing costs for every dollar of revenues.

What these ratios do not indicate about profitability is the sensitivity of gross, operating, and net profit margins to:

- Changes in the sales price.
- Changes in the volume of sales.

Looking at the profitability ratios for one firm for one period gives the investor very little information that can be used to make judgments regarding future profitability. Nor do these ratios provide the investor any information about why current profitability is what it is. We need more information to make these kinds of judgments, particularly regarding the future profitability of the firm. For that, turn to activity ratios, which are measures of how well assets are being used.

Activity Ratios

Activity ratios—for the most part, turnover ratios—can be used to evaluate the benefits produced by specific assets, such as inventory or accounts receivable, or to evaluate the benefits produced by the totality of the firm's assets.

Inventory Management   The *inventory turnover ratio* indicates how quickly a firm has used inventory to generate the goods and services that are sold. The inventory turnover is the ratio of the cost of goods sold to inventory:

$$\text{Inventory turnover ratio} = \frac{\text{Cost of goods sold}}{\text{Inventory}}$$

For Fictitious for the current year:

$$\text{Inventory turnover ratio} = \frac{\$6,500,000}{\$1,800,000} = 3.61 \text{ times}$$

This ratio indicates that Fictitious turns over its inventory 3.61 times per year. On average, cash is invested in inventory, goods and services are produced, and these goods and services are sold 3.6 times a year. Looking back to the number of days of inventory, we see that this turnover measure is consistent with the results of that calculation: There are 101 calendar days of inventory on hand at the end of the year; dividing 365 days by 101 days, or 365/101 days, we find that inventory cycles through (from cash to sales) 3.61 times a year.

Accounts Receivable Management   In much the same way inventory turnover can be evaluated, an investor can evaluate a firm's management of its accounts receivable and its credit policy. The *accounts receivable turnover* ratio is a measure of how effectively a firm is using credit extended to customers. The reason for extending credit is to increase sales. The downside to extending credit is the possibility of default—customers not paying when promised. The benefit obtained from extending credit is referred to as net credit sales—sales on credit less returns and refunds.

$$\text{Accounts receivable turnover} = \frac{\text{Net credit sales}}{\text{Accounts receivable}}$$

Looking at the Fictitious Corporation income statement, we see an entry for sales, but we do not know how much of the amount stated is on credit. In the case of evaluating a firm, an investor would have an estimate of the amount of credit sales. Let us assume that the entire sales amount represents net credit sales. For Fictitious for the current year:

$$\text{Accounts receivable turnover} = \frac{\$10,000,000}{\$600,000} = 16.67 \text{ times}$$

Therefore, almost 17 times in the year there is, on average, a cycle that begins with a sale on credit and finishes with the receipt of cash for that sale. In other words, there are 17 cycles of sales to credit to cash during the year.

The number of times accounts receivable cycle through the year is consistent with the days sales outstanding (22) that we calculated earlier—accounts receivable turn over 17 times during the year, and the average number of days of sales in the accounts receivable balance is 365 days/16.67 times = 22 days.

Overall Asset Management   The inventory and accounts receivable turnover ratios reflect the benefits obtained from the use of specific assets (inventory and accounts receivable). For a more general picture of the productivity of the firm, an investor can compare the sales during a period with the total assets that generated these revenues.

One way is with the *total asset turnover ratio*, which indicates how many times during the year the value of a firm's total assets is generated in revenues:

$$\text{Total assets turnover} = \frac{\text{Revenues}}{\text{Total assets}}$$

For Fictitious in the current year,

$$\text{Total assets turnover} = \frac{\$10,000,000}{\$11,000,000} = 0.91 \text{ times}$$

The turnover ratio of 0.91 indicated that in the current year, every dollar invested in total assets generates 91 cents of sales. Or, stated differently, the total assets of Fictitious turn over almost once during the year. Because total assets include both tangible and intangible assets, this turnover indicates how efficiently all assets were used.

An alternative is to focus only on fixed assets, the long-term, tangible assets of the firm. The *fixed asset turnover* is the ratio of revenues to fixed assets:

$$\text{Fixed asset turnover ratio} = \frac{\text{Revenues}}{\text{Fixed assets}}$$

For Fictitious in the current year:

$$\text{Fixed asset turnover ratio} = \frac{\$10,000,000}{\$7,000,000} = 1.43 \text{ times}$$

Therefore, for every dollar of fixed assets, Fictitious is able to generate $1.43 of revenues.

Recap: Activity Ratios The activity ratios for Fictitious Corporation are:

Inventory turnover ratio	=	3.61 times
Accounts receivable turnover ratio	=	16.67 times
Total asset turnover ratio	=	0.91 times
Fixed asset turnover ratio	=	1.43 times

From these ratios the investor can determine that:

- Inventory flows in and out almost four times a year (from the inventory turnover ratio).
- Accounts receivable are collected in cash, on average, 22 days after a sale (from the number of days of credit). In other words, accounts receivable flow in and out almost 17 times during the year (from the accounts receivable turnover ratio).

Here is what these ratios do not indicate about the firm's use of its assets:

- The sales not made because credit policies are too stringent.
- How much of credit sales is not collectible.
- Which assets contribute most to the turnover.

Financial Leverage Ratios

A firm can finance its assets with equity or with debt. Financing with debt legally obligates the firm to pay interest and to repay the principal as promised. Equity financing does not obligate the firm to pay anything because dividends are paid at the discretion of the board of directors. There is always some risk, which we refer to as *business risk*, inherent in any business enterprise. But how a firm chooses to finance its operations—the particular mix of debt and equity—may add financial risk on top of business risk. *Financial risk* is risk associated with a firm's ability to satisfy its debt obligations, and is often measured using the extent to which debt financing is used relative to equity.

Financial leverage ratios are used to assess how much financial risk the firm has taken on. There are two types of financial leverage ratios: component percentages and coverage ratios. Component percentages compare a firm's debt with either its total capital (debt plus equity) or its equity capital. Coverage ratios reflect a firm's ability to satisfy fixed financing obligations, such as interest, principal repayment, or lease payments.

Component Percentage Ratios   A ratio that indicates the proportion of assets financed with debt is the *debt-to-assets ratio*, which compares total liabilities (Short-term + Long-term debt) with total assets:

$$\text{Total debt-to-assets ratio} = \frac{\text{Debt}}{\text{Total assets}}$$

For Fictitious in the current year,

$$\text{Total debt-to-assets ratio} = \frac{\$5,000,000}{\$11,000,000} = 0.4546 \text{ or } 45.46\%$$

This ratio indicates that 45% of the firm's assets are financed with debt (both short term and long term).

Another way to look at the financial risk is in terms of the use of debt relative to the use of equity. The *debt-to-equity ratio* indicates how the firm finances its operations with debt relative to the book value of its shareholders' equity:

$$\text{Debt-to-equity ratio} = \frac{\text{Debt}}{\text{Book value of shareholders' equity}}$$

For Fictitious for the current year, using the book-value definition:

$$\text{Debt-to-equity ratio} = \frac{\$5,000,000}{\$6,000,000} = 0.8333 \text{ or } 83.33\%$$

For every one dollar of book value of shareholders' equity, Fictitious uses 83 cents of debt.

Both of these ratios can be stated in terms of total debt, as above, or in terms of long-term debt or even simply interest-bearing debt. And it is not always clear in which form—total, long-term debt, or interest-bearing—the ratio is calculated. Additionally, it is often the case that the current portion of long-term debt is excluded in the calculation of the long-term versions of these debt ratios.

One problem with using a financial ratio based on the book value of equity to analyze financial risk is that there is seldom a strong relationship between the book value and market value of a stock. The distortion in values on the balance sheet is obvious by looking at the book value of equity and comparing it with the market value of equity. The book value of equity consists of:

- The proceeds to the firm of all the stock issues since it was first incorporated, less any stock repurchased by the firm.
- The accumulative earnings of the firm, less any dividends, since it was first incorporated.

Let's look at an example of the book value versus the market value of equity. IBM was incorporated in 1911, so the book value of its equity represents the sum of all its stock issued and all its earnings, less any dividends paid since 1911. As of the end of 2006, IBM's book value of equity was approximately $28.5 billion, yet its market value was $142.8 billion.

Book value generally does not give a true picture of the investment of shareholders in the firm because:

- Earnings are recorded according to accounting principles, which may not reflect the true economics of transactions.
- Due to inflation, the earnings and proceeds from stock issued in the past do not reflect today's values.

Market value, on the other hand, is the value of equity as perceived by investors. It is what investors are willing to pay. So why bother with book value? For two reasons: First, it is easier to obtain the book value than the market value of a firm's securities, and second, many financial services report ratios using book value rather than market value.

However, any of the ratios presented in this chapter that use the book value of equity can be restated using the market value of equity. For example, instead of using the book value of equity in the debt-to-equity ratio, the market value of equity to measure the firm's financial leverage can be used.

Coverage Ratios The ratios that compare debt to equity or debt to assets indicate the amount of financial leverage, which enables an investor to assess the financial condition of a firm. Another way of looking at the financial condition and the amount of financial leverage used by the firm is to see how well it can handle the financial burdens associated with its debt or other fixed commitments.

One measure of a firm's ability to handle financial burdens is the *interest coverage ratio*, also referred to as the *times interest-covered ratio*. This ratio tells us how well the firm can cover or meet the interest payments associated with debt. The ratio compares the funds available to pay interest (that is, earnings before interest and taxes) with the interest expense:

$$\text{Interest coverage ratio} = \frac{\text{EBIT}}{\text{Interest expense}}$$

The greater the interest coverage ratio, the better able the firm is to pay its interest expense. For Fictitious for the current year,

$$\text{Interest coverage ratio} = \frac{\$2,000,000}{\$400,000} = 5 \text{ times}$$

An interest coverage ratio of 5 means that the firm's earnings before interest and taxes are five times greater than its interest payments.

The interest coverage ratio provides information about a firm's ability to cover the interest related to its debt financing. However, there are other costs that do not arise from debt but that nevertheless must be considered in the same way we consider the cost of debt in a firm's financial obligations. For example, lease payments are fixed costs incurred in financing operations. Like interest payments, they represent legal obligations.

What funds are available to pay debt and debt-like expenses? Start with EBIT and add back expenses that were deducted to arrive at EBIT. The ability of a firm to satisfy its fixed financial costs—its fixed charges—is referred to as the *fixed charge coverage ratio*. One definition of the fixed charge coverage considers only the lease payments:

$$\text{Fixed charge coverage ratio} = \frac{\text{EBIT} + \text{Lease expense}}{\text{Interest} + \text{Lease expense}}$$

For Fictitious for the current year,

$$\text{Fixed charge coverage ratio} = \frac{\$2,000,000 + \$1,000,000}{\$400,000 + \$1,000,000} = 2.14 \text{ times}$$

This ratio tells us that Fictitious's earnings can cover its fixed charges (interest and lease payments) more than two times over.

What fixed charges to consider is not entirely clear-cut. For example, if the firm is required to set aside funds to eventually or periodically retire debt—referred to as sinking funds—is the amount set aside a fixed charge? As another example, since preferred dividends represent a fixed financing charge, should they be included as a fixed charge? From the perspective of the common shareholder, the preferred dividends must be covered either to enable the payment of common dividends or to retain earnings for future growth. Because debt principal repayment and preferred stock dividends are paid on an after-tax basis—paid out of dollars remaining after taxes are paid—this fixed charge must be converted to before-tax dollars. The fixed charge coverage ratio can be expanded to accommodate the sinking funds and preferred stock dividends as fixed charges.

Up to now, we considered earnings before interest and taxes as funds available to meet fixed financial charges. EBIT includes noncash items such as depreciation and amortization. If an investor is trying to compare funds available to meet obligations, a better measure of available funds is cash flow from operations, as reported in the statement of cash flows. A ratio that considers cash flows from operations as funds available to cover interest payments is referred to as the *cash flow interest coverage ratio*.

$$\text{Cash flow interest coverage ratio}$$
$$= \frac{\text{Cash flow from operations} + \text{Interest} + \text{Taxes}}{\text{Interest}}$$

The amount of cash flow from operations that is in the statement of cash flows is net of interest and taxes. So we have to add back interest and taxes to cash flow from operations to arrive at the cash flow amount before interest and taxes in order to determine the cash flow available to cover interest payments.

For Fictitious for the current year,

$$\text{Cash flow interest coverage ratio} = \frac{\$1,800,000 + \$400,000 + \$400,000}{\$400,000}$$
$$= \frac{\$2,600,000}{\$400,000} = 6.5 \text{ times}$$

This coverage ratio indicates that, in terms of cash flows, Fictitious has 6.5 times more cash than is needed to pay its interest. This is a better picture of interest coverage than the five times reflected by EBIT. Why the difference? Because cash flow considers not just the accounting income, but noncash items as well. In the case of Fictitious, depreciation is a noncash charge that reduced EBIT but not cash flow from operations—it is added back to net income to arrive at cash flow from operations.

Recap: Financial Leverage Ratios Summarizing, the financial leverage ratios for Fictitious Corporation for the current year are:

Debt-to-assets ratio	=	45.45%
Debt-to-equity ratio	=	83.33%
Interest coverage ratio	=	5.00 times
Fixed charge coverage ratio	=	2.14 times
Cash flow interest coverage ratio	=	6.50 times

These ratios indicate that Fictitious uses its financial leverage as follows:

- Assets are 45% financed with debt, measured using book values.
- Long-term debt is approximately two-thirds of equity. When equity is measured in market value terms, long-term debt is approximately one-sixth of equity.

These ratios do not indicate:

- What other fixed, legal commitments the firm has that are not included on the balance sheet (for example, operating leases).
- What the intentions of management are regarding taking on more debt as the existing debt matures.

Common-Size Analysis

An investor can evaluate a company's operating performance and financial condition through ratios that relate various items of information contained in the financial statements. Another way to analyze a firm is to look at its financial data more comprehensively.

Common-size analysis is a method of analysis in which the components of a financial statement are compared with each other. The first step in common-size analysis is to break down a financial statement—either the balance sheet or the income statement—into its parts. The next step is to calculate the proportion that each item represents relative to some benchmark. This form of common-size analysis is sometimes referred to as vertical common-size analysis. Another form of common-size analysis is horizontal common-size analysis, which uses either an income statement or a balance sheet in a fiscal year and compares accounts to the corresponding items in another year. In common-size analysis of the balance sheet, the benchmark is total assets. For the income statement, the benchmark is sales.

Let us see how it works by doing some common-size financial analysis for the Fictitious Corporation. The company's balance sheet is restated in Table 3.4. This statement does not look precisely like the balance sheet we have seen before. Nevertheless, the data are the same but reorganized. Each item in the original balance sheet has been restated as a proportion of total assets for the purpose of common size analysis. Hence, we refer to this as the common-size balance sheet.

In this balance sheet, we see, for example, that in the current year cash is 3.6% of total assets, or $400,000/$11,000,000 = 0.036. The largest investment is in plant and equipment, which comprises 63.6% of total assets.

TABLE 3.4 Fictitious Corporation Common-Size Balance Sheets for Years Ending December 31

	Current Year		Prior Year	
Assets				
Cash	3.6%		2.0%	
Marketable securities	1.8%		0.0%	
Accounts receivable	5.5%		8.0%	
Inventory	16.4%		10.0%	
Current assets		27.3%		20.0%
Net plant and equipment		63.5%		70.0%
Intangible assets		9.2%		10.0%
Total assets		100.0%		100.0%
Liabilities and Shareholder Equity				
Accounts payable	4.6%		4.0%	
Other current liabilities	4.6%		1.0%	
Long-term debt	36.4%		50.0%	
Total liabilities		45.4%		56.0%
Shareholders' equity		54.6%		44.0%
Total liabilities and shareholder equity		100.0%		100.0%

On the liabilities side, that current liabilities are a small portion (9.1%) of liabilities and equity.

The common-size balance sheet indicates in very general terms how Fictitious has raised capital and where this capital has been invested. As with financial ratios, however, the picture is not complete until trends are examined and compared with those of other firms in the same industry.

In the income statement, as with the balance sheet, the items may be restated as a proportion of sales; this statement is referred to as the common-size income statement. The common-size income statements for Fictitious for the two years are shown in Table 3.5. For the current year, the major costs are associated with goods sold (65%); lease expense, other expenses, interest, taxes, and dividends make up smaller portions of sales. Looking at gross profit, EBIT, and net income, these proportions are the profit margins we calculated earlier. The common-size income statement provides information on the profitability of different aspects of the firm's business. Again, the picture is not yet complete. For a more complete picture, the investor must look at trends over time and make comparisons with other companies in the same industry.

TABLE 3.5 Fictitious Corporation Common-Size Income Statement for Years Ending December 31

	Current Year	Prior Year
Sales	100.0%	100.0%
Cost of goods sold	65.0%	66.7%
Gross profit	35.0%	33.3%
Lease and administrative expenses	15.0%	16.7%
Earnings before interest and taxes	20.0%	16.7%
Interest expense	4.0%	5.6%
Earnings before taxes	16.0%	16.7%
Taxes	4.0%	5.7%
Net income	12.0%	11.1%
Common dividends	6.0%	5.6%
Retained earnings	6.0%	5.5%

Using Financial Ratio Analysis

Financial analysis provides information concerning a firm's operating performance and financial condition. This information is useful for an investor in evaluating the performance of the company as a whole, as well as of divisions, products, and subsidiaries. An investor must also be aware that financial analysis is also used by investors and investors to gauge the financial performance of the company.

But financial ratio analysis cannot tell the whole story and must be interpreted and used with care. Financial ratios are useful but, as noted in the discussion of each ratio, there is information that the ratios do not reveal. For example, in calculating inventory turnover we need to assume that the inventory shown on the balance sheet is representative of inventory throughout the year. Another example is in the calculation of accounts receivable turnover. We assumed that all sales were on credit. If we are on the outside looking in—that is, evaluating a firm based on its financial statements only, such as the case of a financial investor or investor—and therefore do not have data on credit sales, assumptions must be made that may or may not be correct.

In addition, there are other areas of concern that an investor should be aware of in using financial ratios:

■ Limitations in the accounting data used to construct the ratios.

■ Selection of an appropriate benchmark firm or firms for comparison purposes.
■ Interpretation of the ratios.
■ Pitfalls in forecasting future operating performance and financial condition based on past trends.

CASH FLOW ANALYSIS

One of the key financial measures that an analyst should understand is the company's cash flow. This is because the cash flow aids the analyst in assessing the ability of the company to satisfy its contractual obligations and maintain current dividends and current capital expenditure policy without relying on external financing. Moreover, an analyst must understand why this measure is important for external parties, specifically stock analysts covering the company. The reason is that the basic valuation principle followed by stock analysts is that the value of a company today is the present value of its expected future cash flows. In this section, we discuss cash flow analysis.

Difficulties with Measuring Cash Flow

The primary difficulty with measuring a cash flow is that it is a flow: Cash flows into the company (i.e., cash inflows) and cash flows out of the company (i.e., cash outflows). At any point in time, there is a stock of cash on hand, but the stock of cash on hand varies among companies because of the size of the company, the cash demands of the business, and a company's management of working capital. So what is cash flow? Is it the total amount of cash flowing into the company during a period? Is it the total amount of cash flowing out of the company during a period? Is it the net of the cash inflows and outflows for a period? Well, there is no specific definition of cash flow—and that's probably why there is so much confusion regarding the measurement of cash flow. Ideally, a measure of the company's operating performance that is comparable among companies is needed—something other than net income.

A simple, yet crude method of calculating cash flow requires simply adding noncash expenses (e.g., depreciation and amortization) to the reported net income amount to arrive at cash flow. For example, the estimated cash flow for Procter & Gamble (P&G) for 2002, is

Estimated cash flow = Net income + Depreciation and amortization
= $4,352 million + 1,693 million
= $6,045 million

This amount is not really a cash flow, but simply earnings before depreciation and amortization. Is this a cash flow that stock analysts should use in valuing a company? Though not a cash flow, this estimated cash flow does allow a quick comparison of income across firms that may use different depreciation methods and depreciable lives. As an example of the use of this estimate of cash flow, *Guide to Using the Value Line Investment Survey*, published by Value Line, Inc., reports a cash flow per share amount, calculated as reported earnings plus depreciation, minus any preferred dividends, stated per share of common stock (p. 19).

The problem with this measure is that it ignores the many other sources and uses of cash during the period. Consider the sale of goods for credit. This transaction generates sales for the period. Sales and the accompanying cost of goods sold are reflected in the period's net income and the estimated cash flow amount. However, until the account receivable is collected, there is no cash from this transaction. If collection does not occur until the next period, there is a misalignment of the income and cash flow arising from this transaction. Therefore, the simple estimated cash flow ignores some cash flows that, for many companies, are significant.

Another estimate of cash flow that is simple to calculate is *earnings before interest, taxes, depreciation, and amortization* (EBITDA). However, this measure suffers from the same accrual-accounting bias as the previous measure, which may result in the omission of significant cash flows. Additionally, EBITDA does not consider interest and taxes, which may also be substantial cash outflows for some companies.[1]

These two rough estimates of cash flows are used in practice not only for their simplicity, but because they experienced widespread use prior to the disclosure of more detailed information in the statement of cash flows. Currently, the measures of cash flow are wide-ranging, including the simplistic cash flow measures, measures developed from the statement of cash flows, and measures that seek to capture the theoretical concept of *free cash flow.*

Cash Flows and the Statement of Cash Flows

Prior to the adoption of the statement of cash flows, the information regarding cash flows was quite limited. The first statement that addressed the issue of cash flows was the statement of financial position, which was required starting in 1971 (*APB Opinion No. 19*, "Reporting Changes in Financial Position"). This statement was quite limited, requiring an analysis of the sources and uses of funds in a variety of formats. In its earlier years of adoption, most companies provided this information using what is referred to as the *working capital concept*—a presentation of working capital provided and

---

[1] For a more detailed discussion of the EBITDA measure, see Eastman (1997).

applied during the period. Over time, many companies began presenting this information using the *cash concept*, which is a most detailed presentation of the cash flows provided by operations, investing, and financing activities.

Consistent with the cash concept format of the funds flow statement, the statement of cash flows is now a required financial statement. The requirement that companies provide a statement of cash flows applies to fiscal years after 1987 (*Statement of Financial Accounting Standards No. 95*, "Statement of Cash Flows"). This statement requires the company to classify cash flows into three categories, based on the activity: operating, investing, and financing. Cash flows are summarized by activity and within activity by type (e.g., asset dispositions are reported separately from asset acquisitions).

The reporting company may report the cash flows from operating activities on the statement of cash flows using either the *direct method*—reporting all cash inflows and outflows—or the *indirect method*—starting with net income and making adjustments for depreciation and other noncash expenses and for changes in working capital accounts. Though the direct method is recommended, it is also the most burdensome for the reporting company to prepare. Most companies report cash flows from operations using the indirect method. The indirect method has the advantage of providing the financial statement user with a reconciliation of the company's net income with the change in cash. The indirect method produces a cash flow from operations that is similar to the estimated cash flow measure discussed previously, yet it encompasses the changes in working capital accounts that the simple measure does not. For example, Procter & Gamble's cash flow from operating activities (taken from their 2002 statement of cash flows) is $7,742 million, which is over $1 billion more than the cash flow that we estimated earlier. (Procter & Gamble's fiscal year ended on June 30, 2002.)

The classification of cash flows into the three types of activities provides useful information that can be used by an analyst to see, for example, whether the company is generating sufficient cash flows from operations to sustain its current rate of growth. However, the classification of particular items is not necessarily as useful as it could be. Consider some of the classifications:

- Cash flows related to interest expense are classified in operations, though they are clearly financing cash flows.
- Income taxes are classified as operating cash flows, though taxes are affected by financing (e.g., deduction for interest expense paid on debt) and investment activities (e.g., the reduction of taxes from tax credits on investment activities).
- Interest income and dividends received are classified as operating cash flows, though these flows are a result of investment activities.

Whether these items have a significant effect on the analysis depends on the particular company's situation. Procter & Gamble, for example, has very little interest and dividend income, and its interest expense of $603 million is not large relative to its earnings before interest and taxes ($6,986 million). Table 3.6 shows that by adjusting P&G's cash flows for the interest expense only (and related taxes) changes the complexion of its cash flows slightly to reflect greater cash flow generation from operations and less cash flow reliance on financing activities.

The adjustment is for $603 million of interest and other financing costs, less its tax shield (the amount that the tax bill is reduced by the interest deduction) of $211 (estimated from the average tax rate of 35% of $603): adjustment = $603 (1 − 0.35) = $392.

For other companies, however, this adjustment may provide a less flattering view of cash flows. Consider Amazon.com's 2001 fiscal year results. Moving interest expense to financing, along with their respective estimated tax effects, results in a more accurate picture of the company's reliance on cash flow from financing as can be seen in Table 3.7.

Looking at the relation among the three cash flows in the statement provides a sense of the activities of the company. A young, fast-growing company may have negative cash flows from operations, yet positive cash flows from financing activities (i.e., operations may be financed in large part with external financing). As a company grows, it may rely to a lesser extent on external financing. The typical, mature company generates cash from operations and reinvests part or all of it back into the company. Therefore,

TABLE 3.6 Adjusted Cash Flow for P&G, 2002 (in millions)

In Millions	As Reported	As Adjusted
Cash flow from operations	$7,741	$8,134
Cash flow for investing activities	(6,835)	(6,835)
Cash flow from (for) financing activities	197	(195)

Source: Procter & Gamble 2002 Annual Report.

TABLE 3.7 Adjusted Cash Flow Amazon.com, 2001 (in millions)

In Millions	As Reported	As Adjusted
Cash flow from operations	$(120)	$(30)
Cash flow for investing activities	(253)	(253)
Cash flow from financing activities	(107)	17

Note: The adjustment is based on interest expense of $139 million, and a tax rate of 35%.
Source: Amazon.com 2001 10-K.

cash flow related to operations is positive (i.e., a source of cash) and cash flow related to investing activities is negative (i.e., a use of cash). As a company matures, it may seek less financing externally and may even use cash to reduce its reliance on external financing (e.g., repay debts). We can classify companies on the basis of the pattern of their sources of cash flows, as shown in Table 3.8. Though additional information is required to assess a company's financial performance and condition, examination of the sources of cash flows, especially over time, gives us a general idea of the company's operations. P&G's cash flow pattern is consistent with that of a mature company, whereas Amazon.com's cash flows are consistent with those of a fast-growing company that relies on outside funds for growth.

Fridson (1995) suggests reformatting the statement of cash flows as shown in Table 3.9. From the basic cash flow, the nondiscretionary cash needs are subtracted resulting in a cash flow referred to as *discretionary cash flow*. By restructuring the statement of cash flows in this way, it can be seen how much flexibility the company has when it must make business decisions that may adversely impact the long-run financial health of the enterprise.

For example, consider a company with a basic cash flow of $800 million and operating cash flow of $500 million. Suppose that this company pays dividends of $130 million and that its capital expenditure is $300 million. Then the discretionary cash flow for this company is $200 million found by subtracting the $300 million capital expenditure from the operating cash flow of $500 million. This means that even after maintaining a dividend payment of $130 million, its cash flow is positive. Notice that asset sales and other investing activity are not needed to generate cash to meet the dividend payments because in Table 3.9 these items are subtracted after accounting for the dividend payments. In fact, if this company planned to increase its capital expenditures, the format in Table 3.9 can be used to assess how much that expansion can be before affecting dividends or increasing financing needs.

TABLE 3.8   Patterns of Sources of Cash Flows

Cash Flow	Financing Growth Externally and Internally	Financing Growth Internally	Mature	Temporary Financial Downturn	Financial Distress	Downsizing
Operations	+	+	+	−	−	+
Investing activities	−	−	−	+	−	+
Financing activities	+	−	+ or −	+	−	−

TABLE 3.9   Suggested Reformatting of Cash Flow Statement to Analyze a Company's Flexibility

	Basic cash flow
Less:	Increase in adjusted working capital
	Operating cash flow
Less:	Capital expenditures
	Discretionary cash flow
Less:	Dividends
Less:	Asset sales and other investing activities
	Cash flow before financing
Less:	Net (increase) in long-term debt
Less:	Net (increase) in notes payable
Less:	Net purchase of company's common stock
Less:	Miscellaneous
	Cash flow

Notes:
1. The basic cash flow includes net earnings, depreciation, and deferred income taxes, less items in net income not providing cash.
2. The increase in adjusted working capital excludes cash and payables.
Source: This format was suggested by Fridson (1995).

Though we can classify a company based on the sources and uses of cash flows, more data is needed to put this information in perspective. What is the trend in the sources and uses of cash flows? What market, industry, or company-specific events affect the company's cash flows? How does the company being analyzed compare with other companies in the same industry in terms of the sources and uses of funds?

Let's take a closer look at the incremental information provided by cash flows. Consider Wal-Mart Stores, Inc., which had growing sales and net income from 1990 to 2005, as summarized in Figure 3.2. We see that net income grew each year, with the exception of 1995, and that sales grew each year.

We get additional information by looking at the cash flows and their sources, as graphed in Figure 3.3. We see that the growth in Wal-Mart was supported both by internally generated funds and, to a lesser extent, through external financing. Wal-Mart's pattern of cash flows suggests that Wal-Mart is a mature company that has become less reliant on external financing, funding most of its growth in recent years (with the exception of 1999) with internally generated funds.

FIGURE 3.2   Wal-Mart Stores, Inc., Revenues, Operating Profit, and Net Income, 1990–2005

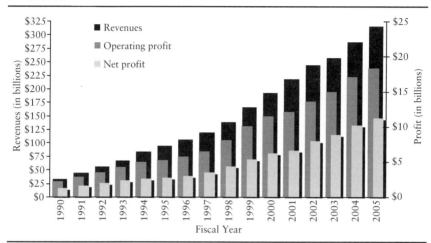

Source: Wal-Mart Stores, Inc., Annual Report, various years.

FIGURE 3.3   Wal-Mart Stores, Inc., Cash Flows, 1990–2005

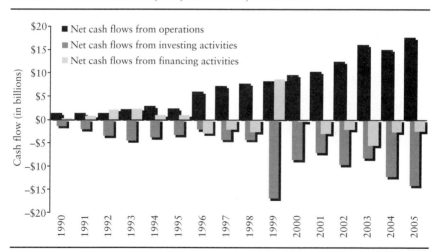

Source: Wal-Mart Stores, Inc., Annual Report, various years.

Free Cash Flow

Cash flows without any adjustment may be misleading because they do not reflect the cash outflows that are necessary for the future existence of a firm. An alternative measure, free cash flow, was developed by Jensen (1986) in his theoretical analysis of agency costs and corporate takeovers. In theory, *free cash flow* is the cash flow left over after the company funds all positive net present value projects. Positive net present value projects are those capital investment projects for which the present value of expected future cash flows exceeds the present value of project outlays, all discounted at the cost of capital. (The cost of capital is the cost to the company of funds from creditors and shareholders. The cost of capital is basically a hurdle: If a project returns more than its cost of capital, it is a profitable project.) In other words, free cash flow is the cash flow of the firm, less capital expenditures necessary to stay in business (i.e., replacing facilities as necessary) and grow at the expected rate (which requires increases in working capital).

The theory of free cash flow was developed by Jensen to explain behaviors of companies that could not be explained by existing economic theories. Jensen observed that companies that generate free cash flow should disgorge that cash rather than invest the funds in less profitable investments. There are many ways in which companies can disgorge this excess cash flow, including the payment of cash dividends, the repurchase of stock, and debt issuance in exchange for stock. The debt-for-stock exchange, for example, increases the company's leverage and future debt obligations, obligating the future use of excess cash flow. If a company does not disgorge this free cash flow, there is the possibility that another company—a company whose cash flows are less than its profitable investment opportunities or a company that is willing to purchase and lever-up the company—will attempt to acquire the free-cash-flow-laden company.

As a case in point, Jensen observed that the oil industry illustrates the case of wasting resources: The free cash flows generated in the 1980s were spent on low-return exploration and development and on poor diversification attempts through acquisitions. He argues that these companies would have been better off paying these excess cash flows to shareholders through share repurchases or exchanges with debt.

By itself, the fact that a company generates free cash flow is neither good nor bad. What the company does with this free cash flow is what is important. And this is where it is important to measure the free cash flow as that cash flow in excess of profitable investment opportunities. Consider the simple numerical exercise with the Winner Company and the Loser Company:

	Winner Company	Loser Company
Cash flow before capital expenditures	$1,000	$1,000
Capital expenditures, positive net present value projects	(750)	(250)
Capital expenditures, negative net present value projects	0	(500)
Cash flow	$250	$250
Free cash flow	$250	$750

These two companies have identical cash flows and the same total capital expenditures. However, the Winner Company spends only on profitable projects (in terms of positive net present value projects), whereas the Loser Company spends on both profitable projects and wasteful projects. The Winner Company has a lower free cash flow than the Loser Company, indicating that they are using the generated cash flows in a more profitable manner. The lesson is that the existence of a high level of free cash flow is not necessarily good—it may simply suggest that the company is either a very good takeover target or the company has the potential for investing in unprofitable investments.

Positive free cash flow may be good or bad news; likewise, negative free cash flow may be good or bad news:

	Good News	Bad News
Positive free cash flow	The company is generating substantial operating cash flows, beyond those necessary for profitable projects.	The company is generating more cash flows than it needs for profitable projects and may waste these cash flows on unprofitable projects.
Negative free cash flow	The company has more profitable projects than it has operating cash flows and must rely on external financing to fund these projects.	The company is unable to generate sufficient operating cash flows to satisfy its investment needs for future growth.

Therefore, once the free cash flow is calculated, other information (e.g., trends in profitability) must be considered to evaluate the operating performance and financial condition of the firm.

Calculating Free Cash Flow

There is some confusion when this theoretical concept is applied to actual companies. The primary difficulty is that the amount of capital expenditures necessary to maintain the business at its current rate of growth is generally not known; companies do not report this item and may not even be able to determine how much of a period's capital expenditures are attributed to maintenance and how much are attributed to expansion.

Consider Procter & Gamble's property, plant, and equipment for 2002, which comprise some, but not all, of P&G's capital investment:[2]

Additions to property, plant, and equipment	$1,679 million
Dispositions of property, plant, and equipment	(227)
Net change before depreciation	$1,452 million

How much of the $1,679 million is for maintaining P&G's current rate of growth and how much is for expansion? Though there is a positive net change of $1,452 million, does it mean that P&G is expanding? Not necessarily: The additions are at current costs, whereas the dispositions are at historical costs. The additions of $1,679 are less than P&G's depreciation and amortization expense for 2001 of $1,693 million, yet it is not disclosed in the financial reports how much of this latter amount reflects amortization. (P&G's depreciation and amortization are reported together as $1,693 million on the statement of cash flows.) The amount of necessary capital expenditures is therefore elusive.

Some estimate free cash flow by assuming that all capital expenditures are necessary for the maintenance of the current growth of the company. Though there is little justification in using all expenditures, this is a practical solution to an impractical calculation. This assumption allows us to estimate free cash flows using published financial statements.

Another issue in the calculation is defining what is truly "free" cash flow. Generally we think of "free" cash flow as that being left over after all necessary financing expenditures are paid; this means that free cash flow is after interest on debt is paid. Some calculate free cash flow before such financing expenditures, others calculate free cash flow after interest, and still others calculate free cash flow after both interest and dividends (assuming that dividends are a commitment, though not a legal commitment).

There is no one correct method of calculating free cash flow and different analysts may arrive at different estimates of free cash flow for a company. The problem is that it is impossible to measure free cash flow as dictated by the theory, so many methods have arisen to calculate this cash flow. A simple method is to start with the cash flow from operations and then deduct capital expenditures. For P&G in 2002:

---

[2] In addition to the traditional capital expenditures (i.e., changes in property, plant, and equipment), P&G also has cash flows related to investment securities and acquisitions. These investments are long-term and are hence part of P&G's investment activities cash outflow of $6,835 million.

Cash flow from operations $7,742
Deduct capital expenditures   (1,692)
Free cash flow $6,050

Though this approach is rather simple, the cash flow from the operations amount includes a deduction for interest and other financing expenses. Making an adjustment for the after-tax interest and financing expenses, as we did earlier for Procter & Gamble:

Cash flow from operations (as reported) $7,742
Adjustment   392
Cash flow from operations (as adjusted) $8,134
Deduct capital expenditures   (1,692)
Free cash flow $6,442

We can relate free cash flow directly to a company's income. Starting with net income, we can estimate free cash flow using four steps:

Step 1. Determine earnings before interest and taxes (EBIT).
Step 2. Calculate earnings before interest but after taxes.
Step 3. Adjust for noncash expenses (e.g., depreciation).
Step 4. Adjust for capital expenditures and changes in working capital.

Using these four steps, we can calculate the free cash flow for Procter & Gamble for 2002, as shown in Table 3.10.

Net Free Cash Flow

There are many variations in the calculation of cash flows that are used in analyses of companies' financial condition and operating performance. As an example of these variations, consider the alternative to free cash flow developed by Fitch, a company that rates corporate debt instruments. This cash flow measure, referred to as *net free cash flow* (NFCF), is free cash flow less interest and other financing costs and taxes. In this approach, free cash flow is defined as earnings before depreciation, interest, and taxes, less capital expenditures. Capital expenditures encompass all capital spending, whether for maintenance or expansion, and no changes in working capital are considered.

The basic difference between NFCF and free cash flow is that the financing expenses—interest and, in some cases, dividends—are deducted to arrive at NFCF. If preferred dividends are perceived as nondiscretionary—that is, investors come to expect the dividends—dividends may be included with the interest commitment to arrive at net free cash flow. Otherwise, dividends are

TABLE 3.10   Calculation of Procter & Gamble's Free Cash Flow for 2002, in Millions[a]

Step 1		
Net income	$4,352	
Add taxes	2,031	
Add interest	603	
Earnings before interest and taxes	$6,986	
Step 2		
Earnings before interest and taxes	$6,986	
Deduct taxes (@35%)	(2,445)	
Earnings before interest	$4,541	
Step 3		
Earnings before interest	$4,541	
Add depreciation and amortization	1,693	
Add increase in deferred taxes	389	
Earnings before noncash expenses	$6,623	
Step 4		
Earnings before noncash expenses		$6,623
Deduct capital expenditures		(1,679)
Add decrease in receivables	$96	
Add decrease in inventories	159	
Add cash flows from changes in accounts payable, accrued expenses, and other liabilities	684	
Deduct cash flow from changes in other operating assets and liabilities	(98)	
Cash flow from change in working capital accounts		841
Free cash flow		$5,785

[a] Procter & Gamble's fiscal year ended June 30, 2002. Charges in operating accounts are taken from Procter & Gamble's Statement of Cash Flows.

deducted from net free cash flow to produce cash flow. Another difference is that NFCF does not consider changes in working capital in the analysis.

Further, cash taxes are deducted to arrive at net free cash flow. Cash taxes are the income tax expense restated to reflect the actual cash flow related to this obligation, rather than the accrued expense for the period.

Cash taxes are the income tax expense (from the income statement) adjusted for the change in deferred income taxes (from the balance sheets). For Procter & Gamble in 2002:[3]

Income tax expense	$2,031
Deduct increase in deferred income tax	(389)
Cash taxes	$1,642

In the case of Procter & Gamble for 2002:

EBIT	$6,986
Add depreciation and amortization	1,693
Earnings before interest, taxes, depreciation, and amortization	$8,679
Deduct capital expenditures	(1,679)
Free cash flow	$7,000
Deduct interest	(603)
Deduct cash taxes	(1,642)
Net free cash flow	$4,755
Deduct cash common dividends	(2,095)
Net cash flow	$2,660

The free cash flow amount per this calculation differs from the $5,785 that we calculated earlier for two reasons: Changes in working capital and the deduction of taxes on operating earnings were not considered.

Net cash flow gives an idea of the unconstrained cash flow of the company. This cash flow measure may be useful from a creditor's perspective in terms of evaluating the company's ability to fund additional debt. From a shareholder's perspective, net cash flow (i.e., net free cash flow net of dividends) may be an appropriate measure because this represents the cash flow that is reinvested in the company.

USEFULNESS OF CASH FLOWS IN FINANCIAL ANALYSIS

The usefulness of cash flows for financial analysis depends on whether cash flows provide unique information or provide information in a manner that is more accessible or convenient for the analyst. The cash flow information provided in the statement of cash flows, for example, is not necessarily unique because most, if not all, of the information is available through

---

[3] Note that cash taxes require taking the tax expense and either increasing this to reflect any decrease in deferred taxes (that is, the payment this period of tax expense recorded in a prior period) or decreasing this amount to reflect any increase in deferred taxes (that is, the deferment of some of the tax expense).

analysis of the balance sheet and income statement. What the statement does provide is a classification scheme that presents information in a manner that is easier to use and, perhaps, more illustrative of the company's financial position.

An analysis of cash flows and the sources of cash flows can reveal the following information:

- *The sources of financing the company's capital spending.* Does the company generate internally (i.e., from operations) a portion or all of the funds needed for its investment activities? If a company cannot generate cash flow from operations, this may indicate problems up ahead. Reliance on external financing (e.g., equity or debt issuance) may indicate a company's inability to sustain itself over time.
- *The company's dependence on borrowing.* Does the company rely heavily on borrowing that may result in difficulty in satisfying future debt service?
- *The quality of earnings.* Large and growing differences between income and cash flows suggest a low quality of earnings.

Consider the financial results of Krispy Kreme Doughnuts, Inc., a wholesaler and retailer of donuts. Krispy Kreme grew from having fewer than 200 stores before its *initial public offering* (IPO) in 2000 to over 400 stores at the end of its 2005 fiscal year. Accompanying this growth in stores is the growth in operating and net income, as we show in Figure 3.4. The growth in income continued after the IPO as the number of stores increased, but the tide in income turned in the 2004 fiscal year and losses continued into the 2005 fiscal year as well.

Krispy Kreme's growth just after its IPO was financed by both operating activities and external financing, as we show in Figure 3.5. However, approximately half of the funds to support its rapid growth and to purchase some of its franchised stores in the 2000–2003 fiscal years came from long-term financing. This resulted in problems as the company's debt burden became almost three times its equity as revenue growth slowed by the 2005 fiscal year. Krispy Kreme demonstrated some ability to turn itself around in the 2006 fiscal year, partly by slowing its expansion through new stores.

Ratio Analysis

One use of cash flow information is in ratio analysis, primarily with the balance sheet and income statement information. Once such ratio is the cash flow–based ratio, the *cash flow interest coverage ratio*, which is a measure of financial risk. There are a number of other cash flow–based ratios that an

FIGURE 3.4   Krispy Kreme Doughnuts, Inc. Income, 1997–2006

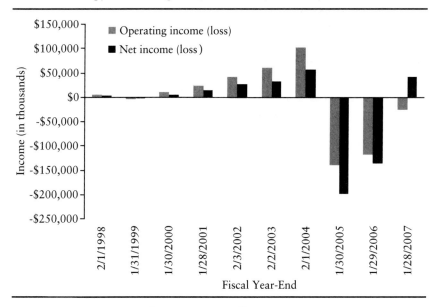

FIGURE 3.5   Krispy Kreme Doughnuts, Inc.'s Cash Flows, 1997–2006

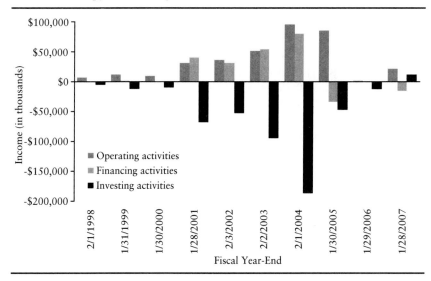

analyst may find useful in evaluating the operating performance and financial condition of a company.

A useful ratio to help further assess a company's cash flow is the *cash flow to capital expenditures ratio*, or *capital expenditures coverage ratio*:

$$\text{Cash flow to capital expenditures} = \frac{\text{Cash flow}}{\text{Capital expenditures}}$$

The cash flow measure in the numerator should be one that has not already removed capital expenditures; for example, including free cash flow in the numerator would be inappropriate.

This ratio provides information about the financial flexibility of the company and is particularly useful for capital-intensive firms and utilities (see Fridson, 1995, p. 173). The larger the ratio, the greater the financial flexibility. However, one must carefully examine the reasons why this ratio may be changing over time and why it might be out of line with comparable firms in the industry. For example, a declining ratio can be interpreted in two ways. First, the firm may eventually have difficulty adding to capacity via capital expenditures without the need to borrow funds. The second interpretation is that the firm may have gone through a period of major capital expansion and therefore it will take time for revenues to be generated that will increase the cash flow from operations to bring the ratio to some normal long-run level.

Another useful cash flow ratio is the *cash flow to debt ratio*:

$$\text{Cash flow to debt} = \frac{\text{Cash flow}}{\text{Debt}}$$

where debt can be represented as total debt, long-term debt, or a debt measure that captures a specific range of maturity (e.g., debt maturing in five years). This ratio gives a measure of a company's ability to meet maturing debt obligations. A more specific formulation of this ratio is Fitch's *CFAR* ratio, which compares a company's three-year average net free cash flow to its maturing debt over the next five years.[4] By comparing the company's average net free cash flow to the expected obligations in the near term (i.e., five years), this ratio provides information on the company's credit quality.

Using Cash Flow Information

The analysis of cash flows provides information that can be used along with other financial data to help assess the financial condition of a company. Consider the cash flow to debt ratio calculated using three different mea-

---

[4] See McConville (1996).

sures of cash flow—EBITDA, free cash flow, and cash flow from operations (from the statement of cash flows)—each compared with long-term debt, as shown in Figure 3.6 for Weirton Steel.

This example illustrates the need to understand the differences among the cash flow measures. The effect of capital expenditures in the 1988–1991 period can be seen by the difference between the free cash flow measure and the other two measures of cash flow; both EBITDA and cash flow from operations ignore capital expenditures, which were substantial outflows for this company in the earlier period.

Cash flow information may help identify companies that are more likely to encounter financial difficulties. Consider the study by Largay and Stickney (1980) that analyzed the financial statements of W. T. Grant during the 1966–1974 period preceding its bankruptcy in 1975 and ultimate liquidation. They noted that financial indicators such as profitability ratios, turnover ratios, and liquidity ratios showed some downward trends, but provided no definite clues to the company's impending bankruptcy. A study of cash flows from operations, however, revealed that company operations

FIGURE 3.6   Cash Flow to Debt Using Alternative Estimates of Cash Flow for Weirton Steel, 1988–1996

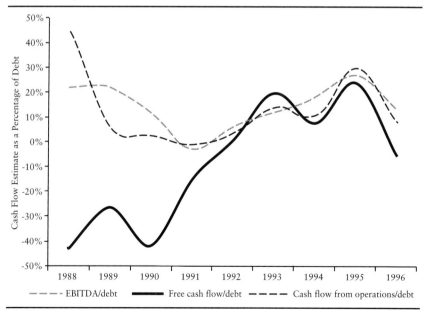

Source: Weirton Steel's 10-K reports, various years.

were causing an increasing drain on cash, rather than providing cash.[5] This necessitated an increased use of external financing, the required interest payments on which exacerbated the cash flow drain. Cash flow analysis clearly was a valuable tool in this case since W. T. Grant had been running a negative cash flow from operations for years. Yet none of the traditional ratios discussed above take into account the cash flow from operations. Use of the cash flow to capital expenditures ratio and the cash flow to debt ratio would have highlighted the company's difficulties.

Dugan and Samson (1996) examined the use of operating cash flow as an early warning signal of a company's potential financial problems. The subject of the study was Allied Products Corporation because for a decade this company exhibited a significant divergence between cash flow from operations and net income. For parts of the period, net income was positive while cash flow from operations was a large negative value. In contrast to W. T. Grant, which went into bankruptcy, the auditor's report in the 1991 Annual Report of Allied Products Corporation did issue a going-concern warning. Moreover, the stock traded in the range of $2 to $3 per share. There was then a turnaround of the company by 1995. In its 1995 annual report, net income increased dramatically from prior periods (to $34 million) and there was a positive cash flow from operations ($29 million). The stock traded in the $25 range by the Spring of 1996. As with the W. T. Grant study, Dugan and Samson found that the economic realities of a firm are better reflected in its cash flow from operations.

The importance of cash flow analysis in bankruptcy prediction is supported by the study by Foster and Ward (1997), who compared trends in the statement of cash flows components—cash flow from operations, cash flow for investment, and cash flow for financing—between healthy companies and companies that subsequently sought bankruptcy. They observe that healthy companies tend to have relatively stable relations among the cash flows for the three sources, correcting any given year's deviation from their norm within one year. They also observe that unhealthy companies exhibit declining cash flows from operations and financing and declining cash flows for investment one and two years prior to the bankruptcy. Further, unhealthy companies tend to expend more cash flows to financing sources than they bring in during the year prior to bankruptcy. These studies illustrate the importance of examining cash flow information in assessing the financial condition of a company.

---

[5] For the period investigated, a statement of changes of financial position (on a working capital basis) was required to be reported prior to 1988.

SUMMARY

The basic data for financial analysis is the financial statement data. We use this data to analyze relationships between different elements of a firm's financial statements. Through this analysis, we develop a picture of the operating performance and financial condition of a firm. Looking at the calculated financial ratios, in conjunction with industry and economic data, we can make judgments about past and future financial performance and condition.

We can classify ratios by the financial characteristic that we wish to measure—liquidity, profitability, activity, financial leverage, or return. Liquidity ratios tell us about a firm's ability to satisfy short-term obligations. These ratios are closely related to a firm's operating cycle, which tells us how long it takes a firm to turn its investment in current assets back into cash. Profitability ratios tell us how well a firm manages its assets, typically in terms of the proportion of revenues that are left over after expenses. Activity ratios tell us how efficiently a firm manages its assets, that is, how effectively a firm uses its assets to generate sales. Financial leverage ratios tell us (1) to what extent a firm uses debt to finance its operations and (2) its ability to satisfy debt and debt-like obligations. Return-on-investment ratios tell us how much of each dollar of an investment is generated in a period. The Du Pont system breaks down return ratios into their profit margin and activity ratios, allowing us to analyze changes in return on investments.

Common-size analysis expresses financial statement data relative to some benchmark item—usually total assets for the balance sheet and sales for the income statement. Representing financial data in this way allows an investor to spot trends in investments and profitability.

Interpretation of financial ratios requires an investor to put the trends and comparisons in perspective with the company's significant events. In addition to company-specific events, issues that can cause the analysis of financial ratios to become more challenging include the use of historical accounting values, changes in accounting principles, and accounts that are difficult to classify.

Comparison of financial ratios across time and with competitors is useful in gauging performance. In comparing ratios over time, an investor should consider changes in accounting and significant company events. In comparing ratios with a benchmark, an investor must take care in the selection of the companies that constitute the benchmark and the method of calculation.

The term *cash flow* has many meanings and the challenge is to determine the cash flow definition and calculation that is appropriate. The simplest calculation of cash flow is the sum of net income and noncash expenses.

This measure, however, does not consider other sources and uses of cash during the period.

The statement of cash flows provides a useful breakdown of the sources of cash flows: operating activities, investing activities, and financing activities. Though attention is generally focused on the cash flows from operations, what the company does with the cash flows (i.e., investing or paying off financing obligations) and what are the sources of invested funds (i.e., operations versus external financing) must be investigated. Minor adjustments can be made to the items classified in the statement of cash flows to improve the classification.

Examination of the different patterns of cash flows is necessary to get a general idea of the activities of the company. For example, a company whose only source of cash flow is from investing activities, suggesting the sale of property or equipment, may be experiencing financial distress.

Free cash flow is a company's cash flow that remains after making capital investments that maintain the company's current rate of growth. It is not possible to calculate free cash flow precisely, resulting in many different variations in calculations of this measure. A company that generates free cash flow is not necessarily performing well or poorly; the existence of free cash flow must be taken in context with other financial data and information on the company.

One of the variations in the calculation of a cash flow measure is net free cash flow, which is, essentially, free cash flow less any financing obligations. This is a measure of the funds available to service additional obligations to suppliers of capital.

REFERENCES

Bernstein, L.A. (1999). *Analysis of Financial Statements,* 5th ed., New York: Mc-Graw-Hill.

Dugan, M.T. and. Samson, W.D. (1996). Operating cash flow: Early indicators of financial difficulty and recovery. *Journal of Financial Statement Analysis* 1, no. 4 (Summer): 41–50.

Eastman, K. (1997). EBITDA: An overrated tool for cash flow analysis. *Commercial Lending Review* 12 (January-February): 64-69.

Fabozzi, F. J., Drake, P. P., and Polimeni, R. S. (2007). *The Complete CFO Handbook: From Accounting to Accountability.* Hoboken, NJ: John Wiley & Sons.

Fridson, M. (1995). *Financial Statement Analysis: A Practitioner's Guide.* New York: John Wiley & Sons.

Fridson, M., and Alvarez, F. (2002). *Financial Statement Analysis: A Practitioner's Guide,* 3rd ed. Hoboken, NJ: John Wiley & Sons.

Jensen, M. C. (1986). Agency costs of free cash flow, corporate finance, and take-overs. *American Economic Review* 76, no. 2: 323–329.

Largay, J. A. and Stickney, C. P. (1980). Cash flows, ratio analysis and the W. T. Grant company bankruptcy. *Financial Analysts Journal* (July/August): 51–54.

McConville, D. J. (1996). Cash flow ratios gains respect as useful tool for credit Rating. *Corporate Cashflow Magazine* (January): 18.

Peterson, P. P. and Fabozzi, F. J. (2006). *Analysis of Financial Statements*, 2nd ed. Hoboken, NJ: John Wiley & Sons.

Stumpp, P. M. (2001). Critical failings of EBITDA as a cash flow measure. In F. J. Fabozzi (ed.), *Bond Credit Analysis: Framework and Case Studies* (pp. 139–170). Hoboken, NJ: John Wiley & Sons.

Capital Markets and Capital Market Theory

The Financial System

It is through a country's financial system that entities with funds allocate those funds to those who have potentially more productive ways to deploy those funds, potentially leading to faster growth for a country's economy. A financial system makes possible a more efficient transfer of funds is by overcoming the information asymmetry problem between those with funds to invest and those needing funds. In general, *information asymmetry* means that one party to a transaction has more or superior information than the other party, resulting in an imbalance of power in a transaction.[1] In terms of a financial system, information asymmetry can lead to an inefficient allocation of financial resources. In Chapter 9, we look further at the problem of information asymmetry within the context of the principal-agent problem in financial management.

As explained in Chapter 1, the financial system has three components: (1) financial markets, (2) financial intermediaries, and (3) regulators of financial actitives. In this chapter, we look at each of these components and the motivation for their existence. In addition, as noted by Neave (2009), the financial system includes internally provided financing, which we cover in Chapter 9's discussion of dividend decision. We begin with a discussion of financial assets.

FINANCIAL ASSETS/FINANCIAL INSTRUMENTS

An *asset* is defined as any resource that is expected to provide future benefits and, hence, has economic value. Assets can be divided into two categories: tangible assets and intangible assets. The value of a *tangible asset* depends on its physical properties. Buildings, aircraft, land, and machinery are examples of tangible assets. An *intangible asset* represents a legal claim to some

---

[1] George Akerlof, Michael Spence, and Joseph Stiglitz shared the 2001 Nobel Memorial Prize in Economic Sciences for their work in the analysis of markets with asymmetric information.

future economic benefits. The value of an intangible asset bears no relation to the form, physical or otherwise, in which the claims are recorded. *Financial assets* are intangible assets where typically the future benefits come in the form of a claim to future cash. Another term used for a financial asset is a *financial instrument*. Certain types of financial instruments are referred to as *securities* and generally include stocks and bonds. Throughout this book, when we refer to an asset, we typically mean a financial asset.

For every financial instrument there is a minimum of two parties. The party that has agreed to make future cash payments is called the *issuer;* the party that owns the financial instrument and therefore the right to receive the payments made by the issuer is referred to as the *investor.*

Financial assets serve two principal economic functions. First, they allow the transference of funds from those entities who have surplus funds to invest to those who need funds to invest in tangible assets. Second, they permit the transference of funds in such a way as to redistribute the unavoidable risk associated with the cash flow generated by tangible assets among those seeking and those providing the funds. However, the claims held by the final wealth holders generally differ from the liabilities issued by those entities that are the final demanders of funds because of the activity of entities operating in financial systems, called *financial intermediaries*, who seek to transform the final liabilities into different financial assets preferred by the public. Financial intermediaries are discussed in more detail later.

Debt vs. Equity Intruments

A financial instrument can be classified by the type of claims that the investor has on the issuer. A financial instrument in which the issuer agrees to pay the investor interest plus repay the amount borrowed is a *debt instrument.* A debt instrument, also referred to as an *instrument of indebtedness*, can be in the form of a note, bond, or loan. The interest payments that must be made by the issuer are fixed contractually. For example, in the case of a debt instrument that is required to make payments in U.S. dollars, the amount can be a fixed dollar amount or it can vary depending upon some benchmark. That is, the dollar interest amount need not be a fixed dollar amount but may vary with some benchmark. The key point is that the investor in a debt instrument can realize no more than the contractual amount. For this reason, debt instruments are often referred to as *fixed income instruments.*

In contrast to a debt obligation, an *equity instrument* specifies that the issuer pay the investor an amount based on earnings, if any, after the obligations that the issuer is required to make to investors of the firm's debt instruments have been paid. Common stock and partnership shares are examples of equity instruments.

Some financial instruments fall into both categories in terms of their attributes. Preferred stock, a financial instrument that issued in the United States, is an example. This financial instrument has the attribute of a debt because typically the investor is only entitled to receive a fixed contractual amount. However, it is similar to an equity instrument because the payment is only made after payments to the investors in the firm's debt instruments are satisfied. Another "combination" instrument is a convertible bond, which allows the investor to convert debt into equity under certain circumstances. Because preferred stockholders typically are entitled to a fixed contractual amount, preferred stock is referred to as a *fixed income instrument*. Hence, fixed income instruments include debt instruments and preferred stock.

The classification of debt and equity is important for two legal reasons. First, in the case of a bankruptcy of the issuer, investors in debt instruments have a priority on the claim on the issuer's assets over equity investors. Second, in the United States, the tax treatment of the payments by the issuer differs depending on the type of class. Specifically, as we explain in later chapters, interest payments are tax deductible to the issuer while the distribution of earnings to equity investors (referred to as dividends) are not.

FINANCIAL MARKETS

A financial market is a market where financial instruments are exchanged. The more popular term used for the exchanging of financial instruments is that they are "traded." Financial markets provide the following three major economic functions:

- Price discovery
- Liquidity
- Reduced transaction costs

Price discovery means that the interactions of buyers and sellers in a financial market determine the price of the traded asset. Equivalently, they determine the required return that participants in a financial market demand in order to buy a financial instrument. Because the motivation for those seeking funds depends on the required return that investors demand, it is this function of financial markets that signals how the funds available from those who want to lend or invest funds will be allocated among those needing funds and raise those funds by issuing financial instruments.

Second, financial markets provide a forum for investors to sell a financial instrument and is said to offer investors "liquidity." This is an appealing feature when circumstances arise that either force or motivate an investor to sell a financial instrument. Without liquidity, an investor would be compelled to hold onto a financial instrument until either conditions arise that allow for the disposal of the financial instrument or the issuer is contractually obligated to pay it off. For a debt instrument, that is when it matures, whereas for an equity instrument that is until the company is either voluntarily or involuntarily liquidated. All financial markets provide some form of liquidity. However, the degree of liquidity is one of the factors that characterize different financial markets.

The third economic function of a financial market is that it reduces the cost of transacting when parties want to trade a financial instrument. In general, one can classify the costs associated with transacting into two types: search costs and information costs. *Search costs* in turn fall into categories: explicit costs and implicit costs. Explicit costs include expenses that may be needed to advertise one's intention to sell or purchase a financial instrument; implicit costs include the value of time spent in locating a counterparty to the transaction. The presence of some form of organized financial market reduces search costs. *Information costs* are costs associated with assessing a financial instrument's investment attributes. In a price efficient market, prices reflect the aggregate information collected by all market participants.

FINANCIAL INTERMEDIARIES

Despite the important role of financial markets, their role in allowing the efficient allocation for those who have funds to invest and those who need funds may not always work as described earlier. As a result, financial systems have found the need for a special type of financial entity called a *financial intermediary* when there are conditions that make it difficult for lenders or investors of funds to deal directly with borrowers of funds in financial markets. Financial intermediaries include depository institutions, insurance companies, regulated investment companies, investment banks, and insurance companies.

The role of financial intermediaries is to create more favorable transaction terms than could be realized by lenders/investors and borrowers dealing directly with each other in the financial market. This is accomplished by financial intermediaries in a two-step process: (1) obtaining funds from lenders or investors and (2) lending or investing the funds that they borrow to those who need funds. The funds that a financial intermediary acquires become, depending on the financial claim, either the liability of the financial intermediary or equity participants of the financial intermediary. The funds that a financial intermediary lends or invests become the asset of the financial intermediary.

Here are two examples using financial intermediaries that we will elaborate further upon below. In our first example, consider a commercial bank, a type of depository institution. Everyone knows that a bank accepts deposits from individuals, corporations, and governments. These depositors are the lenders to the commercial bank. The funds received by the commercial bank become the liability of the commercial bank. In turn, as explained later, a bank will lend these funds by either making loans or buying securities. The loans and securities become the assets of the commercial bank.

In our second example, consider a mutual fund (one type of regulated investment company that we will discuss later in this chapter). A mutual fund accepts funds from investors who in exchange receive mutual fund shares. In turn, the mutual funds invest those funds in a portfolio of financial instruments. The mutual fund shares represent an equity interest in the portfolio of financial instruments and the financial instruments are the assets of the mutual fund.

Basically, the process we just described has allowed a financial intermediary to transform financial assets that are less desirable for a large part of the investing public into other financial assets—their own liabilities—which are more widely preferred by the public. This asset transformation provides at least one of three economic functions:

- Maturity intermediation.
- Risk reduction via diversification.
- Cost reduction for contracting and information processing.

We'll describe each of these shortly.

There are other services that can be provided by financial intermediaries. They include:

- Facilitating the trading of financial assets for the financial intermediary's customers through brokering arrangements.
- Facilitating the trading of financial assets by using its own capital to take a position in a financial asset the financial intermediary's customer want to transact in.
- Assisting in the creation of financial assets for its customers and then either distributing those financial assets to other market participants.
- Providing investment advice to customers.
- Manage the financial assets of customers.
- Providing a payment mechanism.

Later in this chapter, when we discuss market participants, these other services of financial intermediaries will become clear. For example, we will see that the first and second functions services are brokerage and dealer or market maker services, respectively. The third service is the underwriting of securities.

We now discuss the three economic functions of financial intermediaries when they transform financial assets.

Maturity Intermediation

In our example of the commercial bank, two things should be noted. First, the maturity of the deposits made by lenders at the commercial bank are typically short term. As explained later, banks have deposits that are payable upon demand or have a specific maturity date, but most are less than three years. Second, the maturity of the loans made by a commercial bank may be considerably longer than three years. Think about what would happen if commercial banks did not exist in a financial system. In this scenario, borrowers would have to either (1) borrow for a shorter to term in order to match the length of time lenders are willing to loan funds; or (2) locate lenders that are willing to invest for the length of the loan sought.

Now put commercial banks back into the financial system. By issuing its own financial claims, the commercial bank in essence transforms a longer-term asset into a shorter-term one by giving the borrower a loan for the length of time sought and the depositor (lender) a financial asset for the desired investment horizon. This function of a financial intermediary is called *maturity intermediation.*

The implications of maturity intermediation for financial systems are twofold. The first implication is that lenders/investors have more choices with respect to the maturity for the financial instruments in which they invest and borrowers have more alternatives for the length of their debt obligations. The second implication is that because investors are reluctant to commit funds for a long period of time, they require long-term borrowers to pay a higher interest rate than on short-term borrowing. However, a financial intermediary is willing to make longer-term loans, and at a lower cost to the borrower than an individual investor would because the financial intermediary can rely on successive funding sources over a long time period (although at some risk). For example, a depository institution can reasonably expect to have successive deposits to be able to fund a longer-term investment. As a result, the cost of longer-term borrowing is likely to be reduced in an economy with financial intermediaries.

Risk Reduction via Diversification

Consider the second example above of a mutual fund. Suppose that the mutual fund invests the funds received from investors in the stock of a large number of companies. By doing so, the mutual fund diversifies and reduces its risk. Investors with a small sum to invest would find it difficult to achieve the same degree of diversification because of their lack of sufficient funds to buy shares of a large number of companies. Yet by investing in the mutual fund for the same dollar investment, investors can achieve this diversification, thereby reducing risk.

This economic function performed by financial intermediaries of transforming more risky assets into less risky ones is called *diversification*. Although individual investors with sufficient funds can achieve diversification on their own, they may not be able to accomplish it as cost effectively as financial intermediaries. Realizing cost-effective diversification in order to reduce risk by purchasing the financial assets of a financial intermediary is an important economic benefit for financial systems.

Reducing the Costs of Contracting and Information Processing

Investors purchasing financial assets must develop skills necessary to evaluate their risk and return attributes. After developing the necessary skills, investors can apply them in analyzing specific financial assets when contemplating their purchase or subsequent sale. Investors who want to make a loan to a consumer or business need to have the skill to write a legally enforceable contract with provisions to protect their interests. After the loan is made, investors would have to monitor the financial condition of the borrower and, if necessary, pursue legal action if any provisions of the loan agreement are violated. Although some investors might enjoy devoting leisure time to this task if they had the prerequisite skill set, most of investors find leisure time to be in short supply and want compensation for sacrificing it. The form of compensation could be a higher return obtained from an investment.

In addition to the opportunity cost of the time to process the information about the financial asset and its issuer, the cost of acquiring that information must also be considered. Such costs are referred to as *information processing costs*. The costs associated with writing loan agreements are referred to as *contracting costs*. Another aspect of contracting costs is the cost of enforcing the terms of the loan agreement.

With these points in mind, consider our two examples of financial intermediaries—the commercial bank and the mutual funds. The staffs of these two financial intermediaries include investment professionals trained to analyze financial assets and manage them. In the case of loan agreements, either standardized contracts can be prepared, or legal counsel can be part of the professional staff to write contracts involving more complex transactions. The investment professionals can monitor to activities of the borrower to assure compliance with the loan agreement's terms and where there is any violation take action to protect the interests of the financial intermediary.

It is clearly cost effective for financial intermediaries to maintain such staffs because investing funds is their normal business. There are economies of scale that financial intermediaries realize in contracting and processing information about financial assets because of the amount of funds that they manage. These reduced costs, compared to what individual investors would have to incur to provide funds to those who need them accrue to the benefit of (1) investors who purchase a financial claim of the financial intermediary; and (2) issuers of financial assets (a result of lower funding costs).

REGULATORS OF FINANCIAL ACTITIVIES

Most governments throughout the world regulate various aspects of financial activities because they recognize the vital role played by a country's financial system. As stated in a March 31, 2008 speech by Henry M. Paulson, Jr., Secretary of the U.S. Department of the Treasury:

> A strong financial system is vitally important—not for Wall Street, not for bankers, but for working Americans. When our markets work, people throughout our economy benefit—Americans seeking to buy a car or buy a home, families borrowing to pay for college, innovators borrowing on the strength of a good idea for a new product or technology, and businesses financing investments that create new jobs. And when our financial system is under stress, millions of working Americans bear the consequences. Government has a responsibility to make sure our financial system is regulated effectively. And in this area, we can do a better job. In sum, the ultimate beneficiaries from improved financial regulation are America's workers, families and businesses—both large and small.

The degree of regulation varies from country to country. Regulation takes one of four forms:

- Disclosure regulation
- Financial activity regulation
- Regulation of financial institutions
- Regulation of foreign participants

Disclosure regulation requires that an provide on a timely basis financial information and nonfinancial information that would be expected to affect the value of its security to actual and potential investors. Governments justify disclosure regulation by pointing out that the issuer has access to better information about the economic well being of the entity than those who ho own or are contemplating ownership of the securities. Economists refer to this uneven access or uneven possession of information as *asymmetric information*. In the United States, disclosure regulation is embedded in various securities acts passed since 1993 as are which delegates to the Securities and Exchange Commission (SEC) have the responsibility for gathering and publicizing relevant information and for punishing those issuers who supply fraudulent or misleading data. However, disclosure regulation does not attempt to prevent the issuance of risky assets. Rather, the SEC's sole motivation is to assure that issuers supply diligent and intelligent investors with the information needed for a fair evaluation of the securities.

Rules about traders of securities and trading on financial markets are what is referred to as *financial activity regulation*. Probably the best example of this type of regulation is rules prohibiting the trading of a security by those who, because of their privileged position in a corporation, know more about the issuer's economic prospects than the general investing public. Such individuals are referred to as *insiders* and include, yet are not limited to, corporate managers and members of the board of directors. Trading by insiders (referred to as *insider trading*) is another problem posed by asymmetric information. The SEC has is charged with the responsibility of monitoring the trades that corporate officers, directors, as well as major stockholders, execute in the securities of their firms. Another example of financial activity regulation is the rules imposed by the SEC regarding the structure and operations of exchanges where securities are traded. The justification for such rules is that it reduces the likelihood that members of exchanges may be able, under certain circumstances, to collude and defraud the general investing public. The SEC and another federal government entity, the Commodity Futures Trading Commission (CFTC), share responsibility for the federal regulation of trading in derivative instruments.

Later in this chapter we discuss financial institutions. The *regulation of financial institutions* is that form of governmental monitoring that restricts their activities. Such regulation is justified by governments because of the vital role played by financial institutions in a country's economy.

Government regulation of foreign participants involves the imposition of restrictions on the roles that foreign firms can play in a country's internal market and the ownership or control of financial institutions. Although many countries have this form of regulation, there has been a trend to lessen these restrictions.

Major federal legislation is listed in Table 4.1.

TABLE 4.1   Federal Regulation of Securities Markets in the United States Law
Description

Law	Description
Securities Act of 1933	Regulates new offerings of securities to the public. It requires the filing of a registration statement containing specific information about the issuing corporation and prohibits fraudulent and deceptive practices related to security offers.
Securities and Exchange Act of 1934	Establishes the Securities and Exchange Commission (SEC) to enforce securities regulations and extends regulation to the secondary markets.
Investment Company Act of 1940	Gives the SEC regulatory authority over publicly-held companies that are in the business of investing and trading in securities.
Investment Advisers Act of 1940	Requires registration of investment advisors and regulates their activities.
Federal Securities Act of 1964	Extends the regulatory authority of the SEC to include the over-the-counter securities markets.
Securities Investor Protection Act of 1970	Creates the Securities Investor Protection Corporation, which is charged with the liquidation of securities firms that are in financial trouble and which insures investors' accounts with brokerage firms.
Insider Trading Sanctions Act of 1984	Provides for treble damages to be assessed against violators of securities laws.
Insider Trading and Securities Fraud Enforcement Act of 1988	Provides preventative measures against insider trading and establishes enforcement procedures and penalties for the violation of securities laws.
Private Securities Litigation Reform Act of 1995	Limits shareholder lawsuits against companies, provides safe-harbor for forward-looking statement by companies, and provides for auditor disclosure of corporate fraud.
Securities Litigation Uniform Standards Act of 1998	Corrects the Private Securities Litigation Reform Act of 1995, reducing the ability of plaintiffs to bring securities fraud cases through state courts.
Sarbanes-Oxley Act of 2002	Wide-sweeping changes that provides reforms in corporate responsibility and financial disclosures, creates the Public Company Accounting Oversight Board, and increased penalties for accounting and corporate fraud.

Potential Changes in U.S. Regulatory Structure

In the United States, the regulatory structure is largely the result of financial crises that have occurred and abuse that legislators encountered, or thought they encountered, at one time. Most regulations were the result the stock market crash of 1929, the Great Depression in the 1930s, and the corporate scandals of the 1990s and early 2000s. Consequently, there remains some regulations that make little economic sense in the current financial market. Treasury Secretary Paulson, in a March 31, 2008 speech, notes that:

> Our current regulatory structure was not built to address the modern financial system with its diversity of market participants, innovation, complexity of financial instruments, convergence of financial intermediaries and trading platforms, global integration and interconnectedness among financial institutions, investors and markets. Moreover, our financial services companies are becoming larger, more complex and more difficult to manage. Much of our current regulatory system was developed after the Great Depression and it has developed through reaction—a pattern of creating regulators as a response to market innovations or to market stress.

As of this writing, the current U.S. regulatory system is based on an array of industry and market focused regulators. However, there have been proposals for a drastic overhaul of the U.S. regulatory system. The proposal by the U.S. Department of the Treasury in March 2008, popularly referred to as the "Blueprint for Regulatory Reform" would replace the prevailing complex array of regulators with a regulatory system based on functions. More specifically, there would be the following three regulators:

- Market stability regulator
- Prudential regulator
- Business conduct regulator

The *market stability regulator* would take on the traditional role of the Federal Reserve by giving it the responsibility and authority to ensure overall financial market stability. (We describe the Federal Reserve in the next chapter.) The Federal Reserve would be responsible for monitoring risks across the financial system. The *prudential regulator* would be responsible for the safety and soundness of firms with federal guarantees that we will describe in this book such as federal depository insurance and housing guarantees. The *business conduct regulator* would regulate business conduct across all types of financial firms. This regulator would take on most of the current responsibilities of the SEC and CFTC.

This change in regulatory structure is the long-term recommendation of the Blueprint for Regulatory Reform. This may not occur for 10 or 15 years, if at all. Using the history of U.S. reform as our guide, major changes do take that long to become legislation. For example, the major regulatory reform as of August 2007 was the Financial Services Modernization Act of 1999. Portions of that legislation were first recommended by a special commission of the Reagan administration in the early to mid-1980s.

CLASSIFICATION OF FINANCIAL MARKETS

Earlier we provided the general role of financial markets in a financial system. In this section, we will the many ways to classify financial markets.

Classification of a Country's Financial Markets

From the perspective of a given country, its financial market can be broken down into an internal market and an external market.

The *internal market*, which is also referred to as the *national market*, is made up of two parts: the domestic market and the foreign market. The *domestic market* is where issuers domiciled in the country issue securities and where those securities are subsequently traded. For example, from the perspective of the United States, securities issued by General Motors, a U.S. corporation, trade in the domestic market.

The *foreign market* is where securities of issuers not domiciled in the country are sold and traded. For example, from a U.S. perspective, the securities issued by Toyota Motor Corporation trade in the foreign market. The foreign market in the United States is called the "Yankee market." There are nicknames for the foreign market of other countries.[2] The regulatory authorities where the security is issued impose the rules governing the issuance of foreign securities. For example, non-U.S. corporations that seek to issue securities in the United States must comply with U.S. securities law. A non-Japanese corporation that wants to sell its securities in Japan must comply with Japanese securities law and regulations imposed by the Japanese Ministry of Finance.

The other sector of a country's financial market is the *external market*. This is the market where securities with the following two distinguishing features are trading: (1) at issuance they are offered simultaneously to investors in a number of countries; and (2) they are issued outside the jurisdiction

---

[2] For example, in Japan the foreign market is nicknamed the "Samurai market," in the United Kingdom the "Bulldog market," in the Netherlands the "Rembrandt market," and in Spain the "Matador market."

of any single country. The external market is also referred to as the *international market, offshore market*, and the *Euromarket* (despite the fact that this market is not limited to Europe).

Money Market

The money market is the sector of the financial market that includes financial instruments that have a maturity or redemption date that is one year or less at the time of issuance. Typically, money market instruments are debt instruments and include Treasury bills, commercial paper, negotiable certificates of deposit, repurchase agreements, and bankers acceptances. There is one form of equity, preferred stock, that can be viewed under certain conditions as a money market instrument.

Treasury bills (popularly referred to as *T-bills*) are short-term securities issued by the U.S. government; they have original maturities of either four weeks, three months, or six months. T-bills carry no stated interest rate. Instead, they are sold on a *discounted basis*. This means that the holder of a T-bill realizes a return by buying these securities for less than their maturity value and then receiving the maturity value at maturity.

Commercial paper is a promissory note—a written promise topay—issued by a large, creditworthy corporation or a municipality. This financial instrument has an original maturity that typically ranges from one day to 270 days. Most commercial paper is backed by bank lines of credit, which means that a bank is standing by ready to pay the obligation if the issuer is unable to. Commercial paper may be either interest bearing or sold on a discounted basis.

Certificates of deposit (CDs) are written promises by a bank to pay a depositor. Nowadays, they have original maturities from six months to three years. *Negotiable certificates of deposit* are CDs issued by large commercial banks that can be bought and sold among investors. Negotiable CDs typically have original maturities between one month and one year and are sold in denominations of $100,000 or more. Negotiable CDs are sold to investors at their face value and carry a fixed interest rate. On the maturity date, the investor is repaid the principal plus interest.

A *Eurodollar CD* is a negotiable CD for a U.S. dollar deposit at a bank located outside the United States or in U.S. International Banking Facilities. The interest rate on Eurodollar CDs is the London Interbank Offered Rate (LIBOR), which is the rate at which major international banks are willing to offer term Eurodollar deposits to each other.

Another form of short-term borrowing is the repurchase agreement. To understand a *repurchase agreement*, we will briefly describe why the instrument is created. There are participants in the financial system that use leverage in implementing trading strategies in the bond market. That is, the strategy will involve buying bonds with borrowed funds. Rather than borrowing from a bank, a market participant can use the bonds it has acquired as collateral for a loan. Specifically, the lender will loan a certain amount of funds to an entity in need of funds using the bonds as collateral. This common lending agreement is referred to as a *repurchase agreement* or *repo* because it specifies that the (1) the borrower sell the bonds to the lender in exchange for proceeds; and (2) a some specified future date, the borrower repurchases the bonds from the lender at a specified price. The specified price, called the *repurchase price*, is higher than the price at which the bonds are sold because it embodies the interest cost that the lender is charging the borrower. The interest rate in a repo is called the *repo rate*. Thus, a repo is nothing more than a collateralized loan. It is classified as a money market instrument because the term of a repo is typically less than one year.

Bankers' acceptances are short-term loans, usually to importers and exporters, made by banks to finance specific transactions. An acceptance is created when a draft (a promise to pay) is written by a bank's customer and the bank "accepts" it, promising to pay. The bank's acceptance of the draft is a promise to pay the face amount of the draft to whomever presents it for payment. The bank's customer then uses the draft to finance a transaction, giving this draft to her supplier in exchange for goods. Since acceptances arise from specific transactions, they are available in a wide variety of principal amounts. Typically, bankers' acceptances have maturities of less than 180 days. Bankers' acceptances are sold at a discount from their face value, and the face value is paid at maturity. Since acceptances are backed by both the issuing bank and the purchaser of goods, the likelihood of default is very small.

We mentioned that preferred stock under certain circumstances can be a money market instrument. Some preferred stock can be redeemed weekly by contract or via an option granted by the issuer that allows the preferred stockholder the right to force the issuer to redeem the preferred stock. In fact, there are mutual funds (a financial entity that we describe in the next chapter) that invest only in money market instruments. These mutual funds are referred to as *money market funds* and have restrictions as to what they can invest under U.S. securities law. Preferred stock would qualify if certain conditions are satisfied.

Capital Market

The *capital market* is the sector of the financial market where long-term financial instruments issued by corporations and governments trade. Here "long-term" refers to a financial instrument with an original maturity greater than one year and perpetual securities (those with no maturity). There are two types of capital market securities: those that represent shares of ownership interest, also called *equity*, issued by corporations, and those that represent indebtedness, issued by corporations and by the U.S., state, and local governments.

Earlier we described the distinction between equity and debt instruments. Equity includes common stock and preferred stock. Because common stock represents ownership of the corporation, and because the corporation has a perpetual life, common stock is a perpetual security; it has no maturity. In later chapters we describe common stock in more depth. *Preferred stock* also represents ownership interest in a corporation and can either have a redemption date or be perpetual.

A capital market debt obligation is a financial instrument whereby the borrower promises to repay the maturity value one year after issuance. These debt obligations can be broken into two categories: bank loans and debt securities. While at one time, bank loans were not considered capital market instruments, in recent years a market for the buying and selling of these debt obligations has developed. One form of bank loan that is bought and sold in the market is a *syndicated bank loan*. This is a loan in which a group (or syndicate) of banks provides funds to the borrower. The need for a group of banks arises because the amount sought by a borrower may be too large for any one bank to be exposed to the credit risk of that borrower.

Debt securities include (1) bonds, (2) notes, (3) medium-term notes, and (4) asset-backed securities. The distinction between a bond and a note has to do with the number of years until the obligation matures when the security is originally issued. Historically, a note is a debt security with a maturity at issuance of 10 years or less; a bond is a debt security with a maturity greater than10 years.[3]

The distinction between a note and a medium-term note has nothing to do with the maturity, but rather the way the security is issued. Throughout most of this book, we refer to a bond, a note, or a medium-term note as simply a *bond*. We will refer to the investors in any debt obligation as either the *debtholder, bondholder*, or *noteholder*. In Chapter 19, we describe the features and types of bonds.

---

[3] This distinction between notes and bonds is not precisely true, but is consistent with common usage of the terms *note* and *bond*. In fact, notes and bonds are distinguished by whether or not there is an indenture agreement, a legal contract specifying the terms of the borrowing and any restrictions, and identifying a trustee to watch out for the debtholders' interests. A bond has an indenture agreement, whereas a note does not.

Derivative Market

Financial markets are classified in terms of cash market and derivative markets. The *cash market*, also referred to as the *spot market*, is the market for the immediate purchase and sale of a financial instrument. In contrast, some financial instruments are contracts that specify that the contract holder has either the obligation or the choice to buy or sell another something at or by some future date. The "something" that is the subject of the contract is called the *underlying*. The underlying is a stock, a bond, a financial index, an interest rate, a currency, or a commodity. Because the price of such contracts derive their value from the value of the underlying, these contracts are called *derivative instruments* and the market where they are traded is called the *derivatives market.*

Derivatives instruments, or simply derivatives, include futures, forwards, options, swaps, caps, and floors. We postpone a discussion of these important financial instruments until Chapter 6 and their applications in corporate finance and portfolio management to later chapters.

The primary role of derivative instruments is to provide a transactionally efficient vehicle for protecting against various types of risk encountered by investors and issuers. In the absence of derivative instruments and the markets in which they trade, the global financial system throughout the world would not be as efficient or integrated as they are today. A May 1994 report published by the U.S. General Accounting Office (GAO) titled *Financial Derivatives: Actions Needed to Protect the Financial System* recognized the importance of derivatives for market participants. Page 6 of the report states:

> Derivatives serve an important function of the global financial marketplace, providing end-users with opportunities to better manage financial risks associated with their business transactions. The rapid growth and increasing complexity of derivatives reflect both the increased demand from end-users for better ways to manage their financial risks and the innovative capacity of the financial services industry to respond to market demands.

On February 10, 2000, in testimony before the U.S. Senate Committee on Agriculture, Nutrition, and Forestry, Alan Greenspan, then chairman of the Federal Reserve, stated that "Over-the-counter (OTC) derivatives have come to play an exceptionally important role in our financial system and in our economy. These instruments allow users to unbundle risks and allocate them to the investors most willing and able to assume them."

Admittedly, it is difficult to see at this early stage how derivatives are useful for controlling risk in an efficient way since too often the popular press focuses on how derivatives have misused by corporate treasurers or portfolio managers.

Primary Market

When a financial instrument is first issued, it is sold in the *primary market*. This is the market in which new issues are sold and new capital is raised. So it is the market whose sales directly benefit the issuer of the financial instrument. Issuance of securities must comply with the U.S. securities laws. The primary market can be classified as the public market and the private placement market.

Public Market Issurance   The public market offering of new issues typically involves the use of an investment bank. We'll discuss how investment banks are involved in this process, which is referred to as the *underwriting of securities*. Another method of offering new issues is through an auction process. Bonds by certain entities such as municipal governments and some regulated entities are issues in this way.

Private Placement Market   There are different regulatory requirements for securities that are issued to the general investing public and those that are privately placed. The two major securities law in the United States—the Securities Act of 1933 and the Securities Exchange Act of 1934—require that unless otherwise exempted, all securities offered to the general public must be registered with the SEC. One of the exemptions set forth in the 1933 Act is for "transactions by an issuer not involving any public offering." Although the 1933 Act does not provide specific guidelines as to what is a private offering or placement, Regulation D adopted by the SEC sets forth the specific guidelines that must be satisfied to qualify for exemption from registration. Regulations specifies that (1) in general, the securities cannot be offered through any form of general advertising or general solicitation that would prevail for public offerings; and (2) securities can only be sold to what the SEC refers to as "accredited" investors. The SEC defines "accredited" investors as those (1) with the capability to evaluate (or who can afford to employ an advisor to evaluate) the risk and return characteristics of the securities, and (2) with the resources to bear the economic risks.

Prior to 1990, a restriction imposed on buyers of privately placed securities is that they may not be resold for two years after acquisition. This lack of liquidity meant that buyers demanded a premium to compensate for this unappealing feature of a security for the first two years after acquisition. Rule 144A, which was approved by the SEC in 1990, eliminates the two-year holding period under certain circumstances. Specifically, Rule

144A permits large institutions—defined as one holding at least $100 million of the security—to trade the security purchased via in a private placement among themselves without having to register these securities with the SEC. As a result, the private placement market is now classified into two category: Rule 144A offerings and non-Rule 144A (commonly referred to as *traditional private placements*).

Secondary Market

A *secondary market* is one in which financial instruments are resold among investors. No new capital is raised and the issuer of the security does not benefit directly from the sale. Trading takes place among investors. Investors who buy and sell securities on the secondary markets may obtain the services of *stock brokers*, individuals who buy or sell securities for their clients.

Market Structure: Price Determination Mechanisms   Secondary markets are categorized based on the way in which they are traded, referred to as market structure. There are two overall market structures for trading financial instruments: order driven and quote driven. Market structure is means the mechanism by which buyers and sellers interact to determine price and quantity. In an *order-driven market structure*, buyers and seller orders submit their bids through their broker who relays these bids to a centralized location, where bids are matched and the transaction is executed An order-driven market is also referred to as an *auction market*. In a *quote-driven market structure*, intermediaries (market makers or dealers) quote the prices at which the public participants trade. Market makers provide a *bid quote* (to buy) and an *offer quote* (to sell) and realize revenues from the spread between these two quotes. Thus, market makers derive a profit from the spread and the turnover of their stocks. There are hybrid market structures that have elements of both a quote-driven and order-driven market structure.

Common stock is traded in both types of markets and we discuss this further in Chapter 19, where we discuss common stock portfolio management. Most trading in bonds is in a quote-driven market. Foreign exchange and currency is traded in a quote-driven market.

Exchange vs. Over-the-Counter Secondary Markets   Secondary markets are also classified in terms of organized exchanges and over-the-counter (OTC) markets. *Exchanges* are central trading locations where financial instruments are traded. The financial instruments must be those that are listed by the organized exchange. By listed, it is meant the financial instrument must satisfy requirements set forth by the exchange. In the case of common stock, the major organized exchange, which we describe in more detail in Chapter

18, is the New York Stock Exchange (NYSE). For the common stock of a corporation to be listed on the NYSE, for example, it must meet minimum requirements for pre-tax earnings, net tangible assets, market capitalization, and number and distribution of shares publicly held. In the United States, to qualify as an "exchange" approval must be obtained from the SEC.

In contrast, an OTC market is generally where unlisted financial instruments are traded. For common stock, there are listed and unlisted stocks. Although there are bonds that are listed, typically they are unlisted and therefore trade on an exchange. The same is true of loans. The foreign exchange market is an OTC market. Later we discuss derivatives markets. There are listed and unlisted derivative instruments.

Historically, exchanges were order-driven markets. As explained in Chapter 18, today some exchanges are hybrid of order-driven and quote-driven markets.

Market Efficiency

Investors do not like risk and they must be compensated for taking on risk—the larger the risk, the more the compensation. An important question about financial markets, which has implication for the different strategies that investors can pursue (as explained in Chapter 17), is: Can investors earn a return on financial assets beyond that necessary to compensate them for the risk? Economists refer to this excess compensation as an *abnormal return*. Whether this can be done in a particular financial market is an empirical question. If a strategy is identified that can generate abnormal returns, the attributes that lead one to implement such a strategy is referred to as a *market anomaly*.

This issue of how efficiently a financial market prices the assets traded in that market is referred to as *market efficiency*. An *efficient market* is defined as a financial market where asset prices rapidly reflect all available information. This means that all available information is already impounded in a asset's price, so investors should expect to earn a return necessary to compensate them for their opportunity cost, anticipated inflation, and risk. That would seem to preclude abnormal returns. But according to Fama (1970), there are the following three levels of efficiency:

- Weak form efficient
- Semistrong form efficient
- Strong form efficient

In the *weak form of market efficiency*, current asset prices reflect all past prices and price movements. In other words, all worthwhile information about previous prices of the stock has been used to determine today's price; the investor cannot use that same information to predict tomorrow's price and still earn abnormal profits.[4] Empirical evidence from the U.S. stock market suggests that in this market there is weak-form efficient. In other words, you cannot outperform ("beat") the market by using information on past stock prices.

In the *semistrong form of market efficiency*, the current asset prices reflect all publicly available information. The implication is that if investors employ investment strategies based on the use of publicly available information, they cannot earn abnormal profits. This does not mean that prices change instantaneously to reflect new information, but rather that information is impounded rapidly into asset prices. Empirical evidence supports the idea that U.S. stock market is for the most part semistrong form efficient. This, in turn, implies that careful analysis of companies that issue stocks cannot consistently produce abnormal returns.

In the *strong form of market efficiency*, asset prices reflect all public and private information. In other words, the market (which includes all investors) knows everything about all financial assets, including information that has not been released to the public. The strong form implies that you cannot make abnormal returns from trading on inside information (discussed later), where inside information is information that is not yet public.[5] In the U.S. stock market, this form of market efficiency is not supported by the empirical studies. In fact, we know from recent events that the opposite is true; gains are available from inside information. Thus, the U.S. stock market, the empirical evidence suggests, is essentially semistrong efficient but not in the strong form.

We have discussed the implications for investors of the different forms of market efficiency. The implications for market efficiency for issuers is that if the financial markets in which they issue securities are semistrong efficient, issuers should expect investors to pay a price for those shares that reflects their value. This also means that if new information about the issuer is revealed to the public (for example, concerning a new product), the price of the security should change to reflect that new information.

---

[4] This does not mean that trying it once may not prove fruitful. What it does mean is that, over the long run, you cannot earn abnormal returns from reading charts of past prices and predicting future prices from these charts. Do investors actually try this? Yes, as we see in Chapter 18 where we discuss strategies used in the stock market based on such activities.

[5] There is no exact definition of "inside information" in law. Laws pertaining to insider trading remain a gray area, subject to clarification mainly through judicial interpretation.

MARKET PARTICIPANTS

There is a large number of players in the financial system who buy and sell financial instruments. The Federal Reserve, in information about the financial markets that it publishes quarterly, classifies players into nine sectors. These sectors are:

- Households
- Governments
- Nonfinancial corporations
- Depository institutions
- Insurance companies
- Asset management firms
- Investment banks
- Nonprofit organizations
- Foreign investors

Households are self explanatory. In the following sections, we describe the other sectors.

Governments

The government sector includes:

- Federal government
- Government-owned corporations
- Government-sponsored enterprises
- State and local governments

The U.S. federal government raises funds by issuance of securities. The securities, referred to as Treasury securities, are issued by the U.S. Department of the Treasury via through an auction process.

The federal government has agencies that participate in the financial market by buying and selling securities. The federal government has chartered entities to provide funding for specific U.S. government projects. These entities are called *government-owned corporations*.[6] The best example is Tennessee Valley Authority (TVA), which was established by Congress in 1933 primarily to provide flood control, navigation, and agricultural and industrial development, and to promote the use of electric power in the Tennessee Valley region. Two other examples of government-owned corporations are the United States Postal Service and the National Railroad

---

[6] In other countries, the term state-owned corporation is used.

Passenger Corporation (more popularly know as Amtrak. In fact, of all the government-owned corporations, the TVA is the only one that is a frequent issuer of securities directly into the financial markets. Other government-owned corporations raise funds through the Federal Financing Bank (FFB). The FFB is authorized to purchase or sell obligations issued, sold, or guaranteed by other federal agencies.

Another type of government-chartered entity is one that is chartered to provide support for two sectors that are viewed as critically important to the U.S. economy: housing and agricultural sectors. These entities are called *government-sponsored enterprises* (GSEs). There are two types of GSEs. The first is a publicly owned shareholder corporation whose stock is publicly traded. There are three such GSEs: Fannie Mae, Freddie Mac, and the Federal Agricultural Mortgage Corporation. The first two are the most well known GSEs in September 2008 because of the key role that they play in the housing finance market. However, because of the financial difficulties faced by Fannie Mae and Freddie Mac, the U.S. government took control of these two GSEs by placing them into convervatorship. The other type of GSE is a funding entity of a federally chartered bank lending system and includes the Federal Home Loan Banks and the Federal Farm Credit Banks.

State and local governments are both issuer and investors in the financial markets. In addition, these entities establish authorities and commissions that issue securities in the financial market. Examples include the New York/New Jersey Port Authority. State and local governments invest when they have excess cash due to the mismatch between the timing of tax or other revenues and when those funds have to be spent. However, the major reason why they participate as investors is due to the funds available to invest from the pension funds that they sponsor for their employees. More specifically, many state and local governments provide a defined benefit program, a form pension where they guarantee benefits to the employees and their beneficiaries. The five largest state and local sponsors of defined pension funds (referred to as *public pension funds*) and their size (total assets) in billions as of September 30, 2007, according to *Pension & Investments* are the California Public Employees ($254.6), California State Teachers ($173.3), New York State Common ($164.3), Florida State Board ($142.5), and New York City Retirement ($127.9).

Nonfinancial Corporations

Corporations issue debt and equity instruments as well as invest in financial markets. The Federal Reserve classifies corporations that are not farms into two types: financial and nonfinancial. Financial corporations include depository institutions, insurance companies, and investment banks and they are included in separate sectors that will be discussed later. Nonfinancial corporations are all the rest.

Corporations participate as investors in the financial market by investing excess funds in the money market and, as with state and local governments, invest the funds of the defined benefit plans in which they sponsor. The largest corporate defined benefit pension funds in the United States are those of nonfinancial corporations. The five largest as of September 30, 2007 in terms of total asset (in billions) are General Motors ($133.8), AT&T ($117.5), General Electric ($88.2), IBM ($87.4), and Boeing ($81.1).

Some nonfinancial corporations have subsidiaries that are involved in the same activities as financial corporations. Their financial arms, refereed to as *captive finance companies*, participate in the financial market by lending funds. Examples include Ford Motor Credit (a subsidiary of Ford Motor) and General Electric Credit Corporation (a subsidiary of General Electric).

Depository Institutions

Depository institutions include commercial banks and thrifts. Thrifts include savings and loan associations, savings banks, and credit unions. As the name indicates, these entities accept deposits that represent their liabilities (debt) of the deposit-accepting institution. With the funds raised through deposits and nondeposit sources obtain by issuing debt obligations in the financial market, depository institutions make loans to various entities (businesses, consumers, and state and local governments).

Commercial banks are the largest type of depository institution and will be the focus here. As of the mid-2007, there were 7,350 commercial banks operating in the United States. Although less than 7% of commercial banks have total assets in excess of $1 billion, these banks hold more than 85% of total assets of commercial banks. The five largest banks in the United States as of year-end 2005 and their total assets in billions according to the Federal Reserve System, National Information Center are Bank of America Corp. ($1,082.2), J. P. Morgan Chase & Company ($1,014.0), Citigroup ($706.5), Wachovia Corp. ($472.1), and Wells Fargo & Company ($403.3).

Bank Services

The principal services provided by commercial banks can be broadly classified as follows: (1) individual banking, (2) institutional banking, and (3) global banking. Individual banking includes consumer lending, residential mortgage lending, consumer installment loans, credit card financing, automobile and boat financing, brokerage services, student loans, and individual-oriented financial investment services such as personal trust and investment services. Institutional banking includes loans to both nonfinancial and financial corporations government entities (state and local governments in the United States and foreign governments), commercial real estate financing, and leasing activities.

Global banking is where commercial banks compete head-to-head with another type of financial institution—investment banking firms that we discuss later and covers a broad range of activities involving corporate financing and capital market and foreign exchange products and services.[7] Corporate financing involves (1) procuring of funds for a bank's customers, which can go beyond traditional bank loans to involve the underwriting of securities and providing letters of credit and other types of guarantees; and (2) financial advice on such matters as strategies for obtaining funds, corporate restructuring, divestitures, and acquisitions. Capital market and foreign exchange products and services involve transactions where the bank may act as a dealer or broker in a service.

Bank Funding

Banks are highly leveraged financial institutions, meaning that most of their funds come from borrowing. One form of borrowing includes deposits. There are four types of deposit accounts issued by banks: demand deposits, savings deposits, time deposits, and money market demand accounts. Demand deposits, more popularly known as checking accounts can be withdrawn upon demand and offer minimal interest. Savings deposits pay interest (typically below market interest rates), do not have a specific maturity, and usually can be withdrawn upon demand. Time deposits, more popularly referred to as certificates of deposit or CDs, have a fixed maturity date and pay either a fixed or floating interest rate. A money market demand account pays interest based on short-term interest rates.

Nonborrowing deposit sources available to banks are (1) borrowing by the issuance of instruments in the money and bond markets; (2) borrowing reserves in the federal funds market; and (3) borrowing from the Federal Reserve through the discount window facility. The first source is self-explanatory. The last two require explanation.

---

[7] At one time, some of these activities were restricted by the Banking Act of 1933, which contained four sections (popularly referred to as the Glass-Steagall Act) barring commercial banks from certain investment banking activities. The restrictions were effectively repealed with the enactment of the Gramm-Leach-Bliley Act in November 1999, which expanded the permissible activities for banks and bank holding companies.

A bank cannot invest $1 for every $1 it raises via deposit because it must maintain a specified percentage of its deposits in a noninterest-bearing account at one of the 12 Federal Reserve Banks. These specified percentages are called *reserve ratios*, and the dollar amounts based on them that are required to be kept on deposit at a Federal Reserve Bank are called *required reserves*. The reserve ratios are established by the Federal Reserve Board (the "Fed") and is one of the monetary policy tools employed by the Fed. Reserve requirements in each period are to be satisfied by *actual reserves*, which are defined as the average amount of reserves held at the close of business at the Federal Reserve If actual reserves exceed required reserves, the difference is referred to as *excess reserves*. Because reserves are placed in noninterest-bearing accounts, an opportunity cost is associated with excess reserves. However, if there is shortfall, the Fed imposes penalties. Consequently, there is an incentive for banks to manage their reserves so as to satisfy reserve requirements as precisely as possible. There is a market where banks that are temporarily short of their required reserves can borrow reserves from banks with excess reserves. This market is called the *federal funds market,* and the interest rate charge to borrow funds in this market is called the *federal funds rate.*

Now let's look at how a bank can borrow at the Fed discount window. The Federal Reserve Bank is the banker's bank. This means that the Federal Reserve Bank is the bank of last resort. If a bank is temporarily short of funds, it can borrow from the Fed at its discount window. However, borrowing at the discount window requires that the bank seeking funds must put up collateral to do. That is, the Fed is willing to make a secured or collateralized loan. The Fed establishes (and periodically changes) the types of collateral that are eligible for borrowing a the discount window. The interest rate that the Fed charges to borrow funds at the discount window is called the *discount rate*. The Fed changes this rate periodically in order to implement monetary policy.

Bank Regulation

Because of their important role in financial markets, depository institutions are highly regulated and supervised by several federal and state government entities. At the federal level, supervision is undertaken by the Federal Reserve Board, the Office of the Comptroller of the Currency, and the Federal Deposit Insurance Corporation. Banks are insured by the Bank Insurance Fund (BIF), which is administered by the Federal Deposit Insurance Corporation (FDIC). Federal depository insurance began in the 1930s, and the insurance program is administered by the FDIC.

As already noted, the capital structure of banks is a highly leveraged one. That is, the ratio of equity capital to total assets is low, typically less than 8%. Consequently, there are concerns by regulators about potential insolvency resulting from the low level of capital provided by the owners. An additional concern is that the amount of equity capital is even less adequate because of potential liabilities that do not appear on the bank's balance sheet, so-called "off-balance sheet" obligations such as letters of credit and obligations on OTC derivatives. This is addressed by regulators via risk-based capital requirements.

The international organization that has established guidelines for risk-basked capital requirements is the Basel Committee on Banking Supervision ("Basel Committee"). This committee is made up of banking supervisory authorities from 13 countries. By "risk-based," it is meant that the capital requirements of a bank depend on the various risks to which it is exposed.

Insurance Companies

Insurance companies play an important role in an economy in that are risk bearers or the underwriters of risk for a wide range of insurable events. One form of insurance, financial guarantee insurance (more popularly referred to as bond insurance) has become an integral part of the financial markets. Moreover, beyond their risk bearer role, insurance companies are major participants in the financial market as investors.

To understand why, we will explain the basic economics of the insurance industry. As compensation for insurance companies selling protection against the occurrence of future events, the receive one or more payments over the life of the policy. The payment that they receive is called a *premium*. Between the time the premium is made by the policyholder to the insurance company and a claim on the insurance company is paid out (if such a claim is made), the insurance company can invest those proceeds in the financial market.

The insurance products sold by insurance companies are:

- *Life insurance.* Policies insure against death with the insurance company paying the beneficiary of the policy in the event of the death of the insured. Life policies can be for pure life insurance coverage (e.g, term life insurance) or can have an investment components (e.g., cash value life insurance).
- *Health insurance.* The risk insured is the cost of medical treatment for the insured.
- *Property and casualty insurance.* The risk insured against financial loss resulting from the damage, destruction, or loss to property of the

insured property attributable to an identifiable event that is sudden, unexpected, or unusual. The major types of such insurance are (1) a residential property house and its contents and (2) automobiles.

- *Liability insurance.* The risk insured against is litigation, the risk of lawsuits against the insured resulting from the actions by the insured or others.
- *Disability insurance.* This product insures against the inability of an employed person to earn an income in either the insured's own occupation or any occupation.
- *Long-term care insurance.* This product provides long-term coverage for custodial care for those no longer able to care for themselves.
- *Structured settlements.* These policies provide for fixed guaranteed periodic payments over a long period of time, typically resulting from a settlement on a disability or other type of policy.
- *Investment-oriented products.* The products offer have a major investment component. They include a *guaranteed investment contract* (GIC) and *annuities.* In the case of a GIC, a life insurance company agrees that upon the payment of a single premium it will, it will repay that premium plus a predetermined interest rate earned on that premium over the life of the policy. Basically, a GIC is insuring that the policyholder will receive a guaranteed interest rate rather than risk that interest rates decline over the life of the policy. In the case of an annuity, the policy holder pays a single premium for the policy and the life insurance company agrees to make periodic payments over time to the policyholder. While there are many forms of annuities, they all have two fundamental features: (1) whether the periodic payments begin immediately or are deferred to some future date and (2) whether the dollar amount is fixed (i.e., guaranteed dollar amount) or variable depending on the investment performance realized by the insurer.
- *Financial guarantee insurance.* The risk insured by this product is the credit risk that the issuer of an insured bond or other financial contract will fail to make timely payment of interest and principal. A bond or other financial obligation that has such a guarantee is said to have an insurance "wrap." A large percentage of bonds issued by municipal governments are insured bonds, as well as asset-backed securities.[8]

There are three types of companies that issue the insurance policies described above: (1) *life and health* (L&H) companies, (2) *property and casualty* (P&C) companies, and (3) *monoline* companies. The first two types of companies handle multiple products. As the name indicates, L&H companies issue life and health insurance, but they also insurance structured

---

[8] We discuss asset-backed securities in Chapter 12.

settlement and investment-oriented insurance products. The five largest L&H companies ranked by total assets as of mid-2006 are MetLife, Prudential Financial, Lincoln National Corporation, Principal Financial Group, and Nationwide Financial Services. The monoline companies, as the name indicates, provides only one produce: financial guarantees. Since late 2007, monoline companies have faced severe financial difficulties because of their role in insuring asset-backed securities backed by certain types of residential mortgage loans.

Asset Management Firms

Asset management firms manage the funds of individuals, businesses, and state and local governments and are compensated for this service by fees that they charge. The fee is tied to the amount that is managed for the client and, in some case, to the performance of the assets managed. Some asset management firms are subsidiaries of commercial banks, insurance companies, and investment banking firms.

The types of accounts, clients, and lines of business of asset management firms include:

- Regulated investment companies
- Exchange traded funds
- Separately managed accounts
- Hedge funds
- Pension funds

According to *Pension & Investments*, the two largest asset management firms in the world, based on the amount of *assets under management* (AUM) as of year-end 2006 were UBS AG (Switzerland) and Barclays Global Investors (United Kingdom). The five largest U.S. asset management firms were State Street Global Advisors, Fidelity Investments, Capital Group, Vanguard Group, and BlackRock.

Regulated Investment Companies

Regulated investment companies (RICs) are financial intermediaries that sell shares to the public and invest those proceeds in a diversified portfolio of securities. Asset management firms are retained to manage the portfolio of RICs. Various U.S. securities laws regulate these entities.

Each share sold represents a proportional interest in the portfolio of securities managed by the RIC on behalf of its shareholders. Additionally, the value of each share of the portfolio (not necessarily the price) is called the *net asset value* (NAV) and is computed as follows:

$$\text{NAV} = \frac{\text{Market value of portfolio} - \text{Liabilities}}{\text{Number of shares}}$$

For example, suppose that a RIC with 20 million shares outstanding has a portfolio with a market value of $430 million and liabilities of $30 million. The NAV is

$$\text{NAV} = \frac{\$430,000,000 - \$30,000,000}{20,000,000} = \$20$$

The NAV is determined only at the close of the trading day.

There are two types of RICs managed by asset management firms: open-end funds and closed-end funds.[9]

Open-end funds, commonly referred to simply as *mutual funds*, where the number of fund shares are not fixed. All new investments into the fund are purchased at the NAV and all redemptions (sale of the fund) or redeemed from the fund are purchased at the NAV. The total number of shares in the fund increases if more investments than withdrawals are made during the day, and vice versa. For example, assume that at the beginning of a day a mutual fund portfolio is valued at $300 million, with no liabilities, and 10 million shares outstanding. Thus, the NAV of the fund is $30. Assume that during the trading day investors deposit $5 million into the fund and withdraw $2 million, and the prices of all the securities in the portfolio remain constant. The $3 million net investment into fund means that 100,000 shares were issued ($3 million divided by $30). After the transaction, there are 10.1 million shares and the market value of the portfolio is $303 million. Hence, the NAV is $30, unchanged from the prior day.

If, instead, the portfolio's value and the number of shares change, the NAV will change. However, at the end of day, NAV will be the same regardless of the net shares added or redeemed. In the previous example, assume that at the end of the day the portfolio's value increases to $320 million. Because new investments and withdrawals are priced at the end-of-day NAV, which is now $32, the $5 million of new investments will be credited with 156,250 shares ($5 million/$32) and the $2 million redeemed will reduce the number of shares by 62,500 shares ($2 million/$32). Thus, at the end of the day the fund has 10,093,750 (10 million + 156,250 − 62,500). Since the portfolio has a total value of $323 million ($320 million plus the new investment of $3 million), the end-of-day NAV is $32 and not impacted by the transactions.

---

[9] There is a third type of RIC called a *unit trust*. This type of RIC is assembled, but not managed. Therefore, we do not discuss it here.

Unlike open-end funds, *closed-end funds* do not issue additional shares or redeem shares. That is, the number of fund shares is fixed at the number sold at the issuance. Instead, investors who want to sell their shares or investors who want to buy shares must do so in the secondary market where the shares are traded (either on an exchange or in the over-the-counter market). The price of the shares of a closed-end fund are determined by the supply and demand in the market in which these funds are traded. Hence, the fund share's price can trade below or above the NAV. Shares selling below NAV are said to be "trading at a discount," while shares trading above NAV are "trading at a premium." Investors who transact in closed-end fund shares must pay a brokerage commission at the time of purchase and at the time of sale.

Investors in RICs bear two types of costs: (1) a *shareholder fee*, usually called the *sales charge*, which is a "one-time" charge; and (2) an annual fund operating expense, usually called the *expense ratio*, which covers the fund's expenses. The largest expense component of the expense ratio is the *management fee* (also called the *investment advisory fees*), which is an annual fee paid to the asset management firm for its services.

RICs are available with different investment objectives and investing in different asset classes—stock funds, bond funds, and money market funds. The asset managers pursue the strategies that we describe in Chapters 18 and 19 where we cover stock and bond portfolio management. There are passively managed and actively managed funds. *Passive funds* (more commonly referred to as *indexed funds*) are designed to replicate a market index, such as the S&P 500 stock index in the case of common stock. In contrast, with *active funds* the fund advisor attempts to outperform an index and other funds by actively trading the fund portfolio.

Exchange Traded Funds

As an investment vehicle, open-end funds (i.e., mutual funds) are often criticized for two reasons. First, their shares are priced at, and can be transacted only at, the end-of-the-day or closing price. Specifically, transactions (i.e., purchases and sales) cannot be made at intraday prices, but only at closing prices. Second, while we did not discuss the tax treatment of open-end funds, we note that they are inefficient tax vehicles. This is because withdrawals by some fund shareholders may cause taxable realized capital gains for shareholders who maintain their positions.

As a result of these two drawbacks of mutual funds, in 1993 a new investment vehicle with many of the same features of mutual funds was introduced into the U.S. financial market—*exchange-traded funds* (ETFs). This investment vehicle is similar to mutual funds but trade like stocks on an exchange. Even though they are open-end funds, ETFs are, in a sense, similar to closed-end funds, which have small premiums or discounts from their NAV. In an ETF, the investment advisor assumes responsibility for maintaining the portfolio such that it replicates the index and the index's return accurately. Because supply and demand determine the secondary market price of these shares, the exchange price may deviate slightly from the value of the portfolio and, as a result, may provide some imprecision in pricing. Deviations remain small, however, because arbitrageurs can create or redeem large blocks of shares on any day at NAV, significantly limiting the deviations.

Another advantage of ETFs in addition to being to transact in ETFs at current prices throughout the day is the flexibility to place limit orders, stop orders, and orders to short sell and buy on margin, none of which can be done with open-end funds. These types of orders are discussed in Chapter 18. With respect to taxation, ETFs overcome the disadvantages of open-end funds but we will not discuss the advantages here.

There are ETFs which invest in a broad range of asset classes and new ones being introduced weekly.

Hedge Funds

The U.S. securities law does not provide a definition of the pools of investment funds run by asset managers that are referred to as *hedge funds*.[10] These entities as of this writing are not regulated. George Soros, chairman of Soros Fund Management, a firm that advises a privately owned group of hedge funds (the Quantum Group of Funds) defines a hedge fund as follows:

> Hedge funds engage in a variety of investment activities. They cater to sophisticated investors and are not subject to the regulations that apply to mutual funds geared toward the general public. Fund managers are compensated on the basis of performance rather than as a fixed percentage of assets. "Performance funds" would be a more accurate description. (Soros, 2000, p. 32)

The first page of a report by the President's Working Group on Financial Markets, *Hedge Funds, Leverage, and the Lessons of Long-Term Capital Management* published in April 1999, provides the following definition:

---

[10] The term *hedge fund* was first used by *Fortune* in 1966 to describe the private investment fund of Alfred Winslow Jones. In managing the portfolio, Jones sought to "hedge" the market risk of the fund by creating a portfolio that was long and short the stock market by an equal amount.

The term "hedge fund" is commonly used to describe a variety of different types of investment vehicles that share some common characteristics. Although it is not statutorily defined, the term encompasses any pooled investment vehicle that is privately organized, administered by professional money managers, and not widely available to the public.

The foregoing definitions, however, do not begin to describe the activities of hedge funds. The following definition of hedge funds offered by the United Kingdom's Financial Services Authority, the regulatory body of all providers of financial services in that country:[11]

The term can also be defined by considering the characteristics most commonly associated wih hedge funds. Usually, hedge funds:

- Are organised as private investment partnerships or offshore investment corporations.
- Use a wide variety of trading strategies involving position-taking in a range of markets.
- Employ an assortment of trading techniques and instruments, often including short-selling, derivatives and leverage.
- Pay performance fees to their managers.
- Have an investor base comprising wealthy individuals and institutions and a relatively high minimum investment limit (set at US$100,000 or higher for most funds).

The definitions listed here help us to understand several attributes of hedge funds. First and foremost, the word "hedge" in hedge funds is misleading because it is not a characteristic of hedge funds today. Second, hedge funds use a wide range of trading strategies and techniques in an attempt to not just generate abnormal returns but rather attempt to generate stellar returns regardless of how the market moves. The strategies used by a hedge fund can include one or more of the following:

- Leverage, which is the use of borrowed funds.
- Short selling, which is the sale of a financial instrument not owned in anticipation of a decline in that financial instrument's price.
- Derivatives to great leverage and control risk.
- Simultaneous buying and selling of related financial instruments to realize a profit from the temporary misalignment of their prices.

---

[11] Financial Services Authority (2002, p. 8).

Some of the strategies employed by hedge funds are described in later chapters and operate in all of the financial markets described in this book: cash market for stocks, bonds, and currencies and the derivatives markets.

Third, in evaluating hedge funds, investors are interested in the absolute return generated by the asset manager, not the relative return. *Absolute return* is simply the return realized rather than *relative return,* which is the difference between the realized return and the return on some benchmark or index, which is quite different from the criterion used when evaluating the performance of an asset manager as described in Chapter 17.

Fourth, the management fee structure for hedge funds is a combination of a fixed fee based on the market value of assets managed plus a share of the positive return. The latter is a performance-based compensation referred to as an *incentive fee.*

Separately Managed Accounts

Instead of investing directly in stocks or bonds, or by means of alternatives such as mutual funds, ETFs, or hedge funds, asset management firms offer individual and institutional investors the opportunity to invest in a *separately managed account* (also called an *individually managed account*). In such accounts, the investments selected by the asset manager are customized to the objectives of the investor. Although separately managed accounts offer the customers of an asset management an investment vehicle that overcomes all the limitations of RICs, they are more expensive than RICs in terms of the fees charged.

Pension Funds

A pension plan fund is established for the eventual payment of retirement benefits. A *plan sponsor* is the entity that establishes the pension plan. A plan sponsor can be:

- A private business entity on behalf of its employees, called a *corporate plan* or *private plan.*
- A federal, state, and local government on behalf of its employees, called a *public plan.*
- A union on behalf of its members, called a *Taft-Hartley plan.*
- An individual, called an *individually sponsored plan.*

Two basic and widely used types of pension plans are defined benefit plans and defined contribution plans. In addition, a hybrid type of plan, called a cash balance plan, combines features of both pension plan types.

In a *defined benefit* (DB) *plan*, the plan sponsor agrees to make specified dollar payments to qualifying employees beginning at retirement (and some payments to beneficiaries in case of death before retirement). Effectively, the DB plan pension obligations are a debt obligation of the plan sponsor and consequently the plan sponsore assumes the risk of having insufficient funds in the plan to satisfy the regular contractual payments that must be made to currently retired employees as well as those who will retire in the future.

A plan sponsor has several options available in deciding who should manage the plan's assets. The choices are:

- *Internal management.* The plan sponsor uses its own investment staff to manage the plan's assets.
- *External management.* The plan sponsor engages the services of one or more asset management firms to manage the plan's assets.
- *Combination of internal and external management.* Some of the plan's assets are managed internal by the plan sponsor and the balance are managed by one or more asset management firms.

Asset managers who manage the assets of defined benefit plans receive compensation in the form of a management fee.

There is federal legislation that regulates pension plans—the Employee Retirement Income Security Act of 1974 (ERISA). Responsibility for administering ERISA is delegated to the Department of Labor and the Internal Revenue Service. ERISA established fiduciary standards for pension fund trustees, managers, or advisors.

In a *defined contribution* (DC) *plan*, the plan sponsor is responsible only for making specified contributions into the plan on behalf of qualifying participants with the amount that it must contribute often being either a percentage of the employee's salary and/or a percentage of the employer's profits. The plan sponsor does not guarantee any specific amount at retirement. The amount that the employee receives at retirement is not guaranteed, but instead depends on the growth (therefore, performance) of the plan assets. The plan sponsor does offer the plan participants various options as to the investment vehicles in which they may invest. Defined contribution pension plans come in several legal forms: 401(k) plans, money purchase pension plans, and *employee stock ownership plans* (ESOPs).

A *hybrid pension plan* is a combination of a defined benefit and defined contribution plan with the most common type being a *cash balance plan.* This plan defines future pension benefits, not employer contributions. Retirement benefits are based on a fixed-amount annual employer contribution and a guaranteed minimum annual investment return. Each participant's account in a cash balance plan is credited with a dollar amount that resembles an employer contribution and is generally determined as a percentage of pay. Each participant's account is also credited with interest linked to some fixed or variable index such as the *consumer price index* (CPI). Typically, a cash balance plan provides benefits in the form of a lump sum distribution such as an annuity.

Investment Banks

As with commercial banks, investment banks are highly leveraged entities that play important roles in both the primary and secondary markets. The first role is assisting in the raising of funds by corporations, U.S. government agencies, state and local governments, and foreign entities (sovereigns and corporations). The second role is assisting investors who wish to invest funds by acting as brokers or dealers in secondary market transactions.

Investment banking fall into two categories: (1) firms affiliated with large financial services holding companies; and (2) firms that are independent of a large financial services holding company. The large investment firms are affiliated with large commercial bank holding companies. Examples of commercial bank holding companies, referred to as bank-affiliated investment banks, are Banc of America Securities (a subsidiary of Bank of America), JPMorgan Securities (a subsidiary of JPMorgan Chase), and Wachovia Securities (a subsidiary of (Wachovia). The second category of investment banks, referred to as independent investment banks, is a shrinking group. As of mid 2008, this group includes Goldman Sachs, Merrill Lynch, Morgan Stanley, Lehman Brothers, Greenhill & Company, and Houlihan Lokey Howard & Zukin.[12]

Another way of classifying investment banking firms is based on the types of activities (i.e., the lines of business) in which they participate: full-service investment banks and boutique investment banks. The former are active in a wide range of investment banking activities while the latter specialize in a limited number of those activities.

Investment banking activities include:

- Public offering of securities
- Private placement of securities
- Trading of securities
- Mergers, acquisitions, and financial restructuring advising
- Merchant banking
- Securities finance and prime brokerage services
- Asset management

---

[12] Prior to 2008. Bear Stearns fell into this group but was acquired via a government bailout plan by JPMorgan Chase.

We'll review each of these activities in this section.

Public Offerings of Securities

In assisting entities in the raising of funds in the public market, investment bankers perform one or more of the following three functions:

1. Advising the issuer on the terms and the timing of the offering.
2. Underwriting.
3. Distributing the issue to the public.

In its advisory role, the investment bankers may be required to design a security structure that is more appealing to investors than currently available financial instruments.

The underwriting function involves the way in which the investment bank agrees to place the newly issued security in the market on behalf of the issuer. The fee earned by the investment banking firm from underwriting is the difference between the price it paid and the price it reoffers the security to the public (called the *reoffering price*). This difference is referred to as the *gross spread*. There are two types of underwriting arrangements: firm commitment and best efforts. In a *firm commitment* arrangement, the investment bank purchases the newly issued security from the issuer at a fixed price and then sells the security to the public. The price at which it sells the securities to the public is called the *reoffering price*. In a best-efforts underwriting arrangement, the investment banking firm does not buy the newly issued security from the issuer. Instead, it agrees only to use its expertise to sell the security to the public and earns the gross spread on only what it can sell.

Typically in a firm commitment underwriting there will be several investment banks involved because of the capital commitment that must be made and the potential loss of the firm's capital if the newly issued security cannot be sold to the public at a higher price than the purchase price. This is done by forming a group of firms to underwrite the issue, referred to as an *underwriting syndicate* by the lead underwriter or underwriters. The gross spread is then divided among the lead underwriter(s) and the other firms in the underwriting syndicate

The distribution function is critical to both the issuer and the investment bank. To realize the gross spread, the entire securities issue must be sold to the public at the planned reoffering price and, depending on the size of the issue, may require a great deal of marketing effort. The members of the underwriting syndicate will sell the newly issued security to their investor client base. To increase the potential investor base, the lead underwriter(s) will often put together a *selling group*. This group includes the underwriting syndicate plus other firms not in the syndicate with the gross spread then divided among the lead underwriter(s), members of the underwriting syndicate, and members of the selling group.

Private Placement of Securities

As explained earlier in this chapter, rather than issue a new security in the public market, another method of issuance is via a private placement to a limited number of institutional investors such as insurance companies, investment companies, and pension funds. Private placement offerings are distinguished by type: non-Rule 144A offerings (traditional private placements) and Rule 144A offerings. Rule 144A offerings are underwritten by investment bankers.

Trading of Securities

An obvious activity of investment banks is providing transaction services for clients. Revenue is generated on transactions in which the investment bank acts as an agent or broker in the form of a commission. In such transactions, the investment bank is not taking a position in the transaction, meaning that it is not placing its own capital at risk. In other transactions, the investment bank may act as a market maker, placing its own capital at risk. Revenue from this activity is generated through (1) the difference between the price at which the investment bank sells the security and the price paid for the securities (called the bid-ask spread); and (2) appreciation of the price of the securities held in inventory. (Obviously, if the price of the securities decline, revenue will be reduced.) In Chapter 18 we describe the different types of institutional trades that institutional investors can execute through an investment bank.

In addition to executing trades in the secondary market for clients, as well as market making in the secondary market, investment banks do proprietary trading (referred to as *prop trading*). In this activity, the investment bank's traders position some of the firm's capital to bet on movements in the price of financial instruments, interest rates, or foreign exchange.

Mergers, Acquisitions, and Financial Restructuring Advising

Investment banks are active in mergers and acquisitions (M&A), leveraged buyouts (LBOs), restructuring and recapitalization of companies, and reorganization of bankrupt and troubled companies. They do so in one or more of the following ways: (1) identifying candidates for a merger or acquisition, M&A candidates; (2) advising the board of directors of acquiring companies or target companies regarding to price and nonprice terms for an exchange; (3) assisting firms that are the of an acquisition to fend off an unfriendly takeover attempt; (4) helping acquiring companies to obtain the needed funds to complete an acquisition; and (5) providing a "fairness opinion" to the board of directors regarding a proposed merger, acquisition, or sale of assets.

Another area where an investment banks advise is on a significant modification of a corporation's capital structure, operating structure, and/or corporate strategy with the objective of improving efficiency. Such modifications are referred to as *financial restructuring* of a firm. This may be the result of a firm seeking to avoid a bankruptcy, avoid a problem with creditors, or reorganize the firm as permitted by the U.S. bankruptcy code.

The activities described above generate fee income that can either be a fixed retainer or in the case of consummating a merger or acquisition, a fee based on the size of the transaction. Thus, for most of these activities, the investment bank's capital is not at risk. However, if the investment bank provides financing for an acquisition, it does place its capital at risk. This brings us to the activity of merchant banking.

Merchant Banking

The activity of merchant banking is one in which the investment bank commits its own capital as either a creditor or to take an equity stake. There are divisions or groups within an investment bank devoted to merchant banking. In the case of equity investing, this may be in the form of a series of private equity funds.

Securities Finance and Prime Brokerage Services

There are clients of investment banks that, as part of their investment strategy, may need to either (1) borrow funds in order to purchase a security or (2) borrow securities in order to sell a security short or to cover a short sale. The standard mechanism for borrowing funds in the securities market is via a repurchase agreement (referred to as a *repo*) rather through bank borrowing. A repo is a collateralized loan where the collateral is the security purchased. Investment banks earn interest on repo transactions. A customer can borrow a security in a transaction known as a *securities lending transaction*. In such transactions, the lender of the security earns a fee for lending the securities. The activity of borrowing funds or borrowing securities is referred to as *securities finance*.

Investment banks may provide a package of services to hedge fund and large institutional investors. This package of services, referred to as prime brokerage, includes securities finance that we just described as well as global custody, operational support, and risk management systems.

Asset Management

An investment bank may have one or more subsidiaries that manage assets for clients such as insurance companies, endowments, foundations, corporate and public pension funds, and high-net-worth individuals. These asset management divisions may also be mutual funds and hedge funds. Asset management generates fee income based on a percentage of the assets under management.

Nonprofit Organizations

Nonprofit organizations include *foundations* and *endowments*. These organizations are not motivated by profit or any monetary gain. Instead, the primary objective of such organizations is to financially support or actively engage in services that that benefit some specific public or private interest such as humanitarian aid, education, the arts, religion, and so on. The income realized by these entities from their investment portfolio is used for the operation of the foundation. The largest U.S. charitable foundation is the Bill & Melinda Gates Foundation with total assets as of 2008 of about $32 plus future commitments to add to that amount from Warren Buffett. The largest university endowment in the United States is Harvard University with assets of more than $34 billion in 2008, followed by Yale University with an assets in excess of $26 billion.

Foreign Investors

The sector referred to as *foreign investors* include individuals, nonfinancial business and financial entities that are not domiciled n the United States, as well as foreign central governments and supranationals. A foreign central bank is a monetary authority of the foreign country. There are two reasons why a foreign central bank participates in the U.S. financial market. The first reason is to stabilize their currency relative to the U.S. dollar. The second reason is to purchase a financial instrument with excess funds because it is perceived to be an attractive investment vehicle.

A supranational institution is an international entity that is created by two or more central governments through international treaties. Supranationals can be divided into two categories: multilateral development banks and others. The former are supranational financial institutions with the mandate to provide financial assistance with funds obtained from member countries to developing countries and to promote regional integration in specific geographical regions. The largest multilateral development banks are the European Investment Bank with more than $300 billion in total assets and the International Bank for Reconstruction and Development (popularly referred to as the World Bank) with more than $250 billion in total assets. The next two largest, the Inter-American Development Bank and Asian Development Bank, have less than a third of the assets of the two largest multilateral development banks.

SUMMARY

An asset is defined as any resource that has an economic value that is expected to provide future benefits. A financial asset or financial instrument is one form of intangible assets where typically the future benefits come in the form of a claim to future cash. The two principal economic functions of financial assets are: (1) they allow the exchange of funds from those entities who have surplus funds to invest to those who need funds to invest; and (2) they permit the transference of funds in such a way as to redistribute the unavoidable risk associated with the cash flow generated by tangible assets among those seeking and those providing the funds.

A financial instrument can be classified by the type of claims that the investor has on the issuer. A financial instrument in which the issuer agrees to pay the investor interest plus repay the amount borrowed is called a debt instrument and includes a note, bond or a loan. An equity instrument specifies that the issuer pay the investor an amount based on earnings, if any, after the obligations that the issuer is required to make to investors of the firm's debt instruments have been paid. Preferred stock has attributes of both a debt instrument and an equity instrument

A financial market is a market where financial instruments are exchanged and provide the three major economic functions: price discovery, liquidity, and reduced transaction costs. Financial systems have found the need for a special type of financial entity called a financial intermediary—depository institutions, insurance companies, regulated investment companies, investment banks, and insurance companies—when there are conditions that make it difficult for lenders/investors of funds to deal directly with borrowers of funds in financial markets. A financial intermediary accomplished this by transforming financial assets that are less desirable for a large part of the investing public into other financial assets—their own liabilities—which are more widely preferred by the public. This asset transformation provides the following three economic functions (1) maturity intermediation, (2) risk reduction via diversification, and (3) cost reduction for contracting and information processing.

Because of the importance of financial systems to an economy, governments regulate various aspects of financial markets and financial intermediaries. The different forms of regulation are disclosure regulation, financial activity regulation, regulation of financial institutions, and regulation of foreign participants. There have been proposals for a major overhaul of the U.S. regulatory system that would replace the prevailing complex array of regulators with a regulatory system based on functions that would include a market stability regulator, prudential regulator, and business conduct regulator.

There are different ways to classify financial markets. From the perspective of a given country, its financial market can be broken down into an internal market (domestic market and foreign market) and an international market. The money market is the sector of the financial market that includes financial instruments that have a maturity or redemption date that is one year or less at the time of issuance. The capital market is the sector of the financial market where long-term financial instruments issued by corporations and governments trade. Financial markets are classified in terms of cash market (or spot market) and derivative markets. Traded in the derivatives market are futures, forwards, options, swaps, caps, and floors. The primary role of derivative instruments is to provide a transactionally efficient means for protecting against various types of risk encountered by investors and issuers.

The primary market is where a financial instrument is first issued and hence the market whose sales directly benefit the issuer of the financial instrument. The issuance can be done via the public market or private placement market. In the public markets securities are either underwritten by investment bank or sold via an auction process. The private placement market includes Rule 144A offerings and non-Rule 144A (commonly referred to as traditional private placements).

It is in the secondary market where financial instruments are resold among investors. No new capital is raised and the issuer of the security does not benefit directly from the sale. Financial markets are classified based on the mechanism by which buyers and sellers interact to determine price and quantity: order driven and quote driven market structures. Secondary markets are also classified in terms of organized exchanges and over-the-counter markets.

Markets are classified according to the pricing efficiency, referred to as market efficiency. A financial market where asset prices rapidly reflect all available information is said to be an efficient market and such markets abnormal returns are precluded. There are the levels of market efficiency. Weak form of market efficiency means that current asset prices reflect all past prices and price movements. Semistrong form of market efficiency means that current asset prices reflect all publicly available information. Strong form of market efficiency means that current asset prices reflect all public and private information. The form of market efficiency has implications for investment management strategies.

There is a large number of players in the financial market who buy and sell financial instruments. The major players include households, governments, nonfinancial corporations, depository institutions, insurance companies, asset management firms, investment banks, nonprofit organizations, and foreign investors

The government sector includes the federal government, government-owned corporations, government-sponsored enterprises, and state and local governments. Corporations participate as investors in the financial market by investing excess funds in the money market and investing the funds of the defined benefit plans that they sponsor.

Depository institutions—commercial banks and thrifts (savings and loan associations, savings banks, and credit unions)—accept deposits and deploy those by making loans to businesses, consumers, and state and local governments. Commercial banks are the largest type of depository institution and the principal services that they provide can be broadly classified as: (1) individual banking, (2) institutional banking, and (3) global banking. In addition to deposits, commercial banks obtain funding by borrowing by the issuance of instruments in the money and bond markets, borrowing reserves in the federal funds market, and borrowing from the Federal Reserve through the discount window facility. Depository institutions are highly regulated. At the federal level, they are regulated by the Federal Reserve Board, the Office of the Comptroller of the Currency, and the Federal Deposit Insurance Corporation. The international organization that has established guidelines for risk-basked capital requirements is the Basel Committee on Banking Supervision.

Insurance companies are risk bearers. However, they are also major participants in the financial market as investors. Between the time the premium is made by the policyholder to the insurance company and a claim on the insurance company is paid out (if such a claim is made), the insurance company can invest those proceeds in the financial market. The insurance products sold by insurance companies are life insurance, health insurance, property and casualty insurance, liability insurance, disability insurance, long-term care insurance, structured settlements, investment-orient products (guaranteed investment contracts and annuities), and financial guarantee insurance. There are three types of companies that issue the insurance policies described above: (1) life and health (L&H) companies, (2) property and casualty (P&C) companies, and (3) monoline companies (which provide only financial guarantees).

Asset management firms are involved in the management of funds for individuals, businesses, state and local government entities, and endowments and foundations. The types of accounts, clients, and lines of business of asset management firms include regulated management companies, exchange traded funds, separately managed, hedge funds, and pension funds. *Regulated investment companies* (RICs) are financial intermediaries that sell shares to the public and invest those proceeds in a diversified portfolio of securities. There are two types of RICs managed by asset management firms: open-end funds (mutual funds) and closed-end funds. For open end funds, the number of fund shares are not fixed. All new investments into the fund are purchased at the NAV and all redemptions (sale of the fund) or redeemed from the fund are purchased at the NAV. Closed-end funds do not issue additional shares or redeem shares. That is, the number of fund shares is fixed at the number sold at the issuance. Instead, investors who want to sell their shares or investors who want to buy shares must do so in the secondary market where the shares are traded. RICs are available with different investment objectives and investing in different asset classes—stock funds, bond funds, and money market funds.

Exchange-traded funds overcome two drawbacks of open-end funds: (1) shares are priced at, and can be transacted only at, the end-of-the-day or closing price; and (2) they are inefficient tax vehicles. In an ETF, the investment advisor assumes responsibility for maintaining a portfolio such that it replicates the index and the index's return accurately. Because supply and demand determine the secondary market price of these shares, the exchange price may deviate slightly from the value of the portfolio and, as a result, may provide some imprecision in pricing. Deviations remain small, however, because arbitrageurs can create or redeem large blocks of shares on any day at NAV, significantly limiting the deviations.

While there is no standard definition for a hedge fund, they seek high absolute returns by employing a wide variety of trading strategies involving position-taking in a range of markets. They also employ an assortment of trading techniques and instruments that typically includes including short-selling, derivatives, and leverage. The fees that are charge include a management fee based on the amount of asset management and a performance fee (or incentive fee) based on profits.

Asset management firms manage funds for sponsors of pension plans. Sponsors of pension plans include private business entities on behalf of its employees (corporate plans or private plans), federal, state, and local governments on behalf of its employees (public plans), unions on behalf of its members (Taft-Hartley plans), and individuals on their own behalf (individually sponsored plan). The two basic and widely used types of pension plans are defined benefit plans and defined contribution plans. With a defined benefit plan, the plan sponsor agrees to make specified dollar payments to qualifying employees beginning at retirement (and some payments to beneficiaries in case of death before retirement). The funds can be managed internally, externally, or a combination of the two. The major federal legislation that regulates pension plans is the Employee Retirement Income Security Act of 1974 (ERISA). With a defined contribution plan, the plan sponsor is responsible only for making specified contributions into the plan on behalf of qualifying participants with the amount that it must contribute often being either a percentage of the employee's salary or a percentage of the employer's profits.

Investment banks assist entities in the raising funds in the primary market and assisting investors who wish to invest funds by acting as brokers or dealers in the secondary market. Investment banking are either affiliated with large financial services holding companies or independent of a large financial services holding company. Investment banking activities include the public offering of securities, private placement of securities, trading of securities, mergers, acquisitions, and financial restructuring advising, merchant banking, securities finance and prime brokerage services, and asset management.

Nonprofit organizations include foundations and endowments, whose primary objective is to financially support and actively engage in services that benefit some specific public or private interest such as humanitarian aid, education, the arts, religion, and so on. Foreign investors include individuals, nonfinancial business, and financial entities that are not domiciled n the United States, as well as foreign central governments and supranationals.

REFERENCES

Fama, E. F. (1970). Efficient capital markets: A review of theory and empirical work. *Journal of Finance* 25, no. 2: 383–417.

Financial Services Authority. (2002). *Hedge Funds and the FSA*, Discussion Paper 16.

Neave, E. (2009). *Modern Financial Markets and Institutions: Theory and Applications..* Hoboken, NJ: John Wiley & Sons.

Soros, G. (2000). *Open Society: Reforming Global Capitalism.* New York: Publish Affairs.

CHAPTER 5

Interest Rate Determination and the Structure of Interest Rates

Market participants make financing and investing decisions in a dynamic financial environment. They must understand the economy, the role of the government in the economy, and the financial markets and financial intermediaries that operate in the financial system. We have described the financial system in the previous chapter. Now we focus on a critical aspect of the financial environment that affects financial decisions: interest rates. We begin with two economic theories about the determinants of the level of interest rates and then discuss the role of the U.S. Federal Reserve System in influencing interest rates. Finally, because there is not one interest rate in an economy but a structure of interest rates ,we describe the factors that affect the structure of interest rates. We conclude the chapter with economic theories about the term structure of interest rates (i.e., relationship between interest rates and the maturity of debt instruments).

THEORIES ABOUT INTEREST RATE DETERMINATION

There are two economic theories of how the level of interest rates in an economy are determined:

- Loanable funds theory
- Liquidity preference theory

We describe both in this section.

Loanable Funds Theory

In an economy, households, business, and governments supply loanable funds (i.e., credit) in the capital market. The higher the level of interest rates, the more such entities are willing to supply loan funds; the lower the level of interest, the less they are willing to supply. These same entities demand loanable funds, demanding more when the level of interest rates is low and less when interest rates are higher. According to the *loanable funds theory*, formulated by the Swedish economist Knut Wicksell in the 1900s, the level of interest rates is determined by the supply and demand of loanable funds available in an economy's credit market (i.e., the sector of the capital markets for long-term debt instruments) More specifically, this theory suggests that investment and savings in the economy determine the level of long-term interest rates. Short-term interest rates, however, are determined by an economy's financial and monetary conditions.

Given the importance of loanable funds and that the major suppliers of loanable funds are commercial banks, the key role of this financial intermediary in the determination of interest rates should be clear. It is via monetary policy, as implemented by the Federal Reserve (informally, the Fed), that the supply of loanable funds from commercial banks can be altered and thereby change the level of interest rates. That is, the Federal Reserve, through the tools that it has available, can increase (decrease) the supply of credit available from commercial banks and thereby decrease (increase) the level of interest rates.

Liquidity Preference Theory

The loans funds theory of interest rates was widely accepted until an alternative theory was proposed by the English economist John Maynard Keynes (1936). This theory is called the *liquidity preference theory* because it explains how interest rates are determined based on the preferences of households to hold money balances rather than spending or investing those funds. Money balances can be held in the form of currency or checking accounts with the disadvantage that the maintenance of funds in this form earns no interest or a very low interest rate. A key element in the theory is the motivation for individuals to hold money balance despite the loss of interest income. Money is the most liquid of all financial assets and, of course, can easily be utilized to consume or to invest. The quantity of money held by individuals depends on their level of income and, consequently, for an economy the demand for money is directly related to an economy's income.

There is a trade-off between holding money balance for purposes of maintaining liquidity and investing or lending funds in less liquid debt instruments in order to earn a competitive market interest rate. The difference in the interest rate that can be earned by investing in interest-bearing debt instruments and money balances represents an opportunity cost for maintaining liquidity. The lower the opportunity cost, the greater the demand for money balances; the higher the opportunity cost, the lower the demand for money balance.

According to the liquidity preference theory, the level of interest rates is determined by the supply and demand for money balances. As explained next, the money supply is controlled by the policy tools available to the Fed as explained below. Recall that in the loan funds theory the level of interest rates is determined by supply and demand, but it is in the credit market.

THE FEDERAL RESERVE SYSTEM AND THE DETERMINATION OF INTEREST RATES

The United States has a central monetary authority known as the Federal Reserve System. The *Federal Reserve System*, which as we noted earlier is popularly referred to as the *Fed*, acts as the U.S. central bank, much like the Bank of England and the Bank of France are central banks in their respective countries. The role of a central bank is to carry out monetary policy that serves the best interests of the country's economic well-being.

Structure of the Federal Reserve System

The Federal Reserve System is comprised of 12 district banks, with the Federal Reserve Board of Governors (the "Board") overseeing the activities of the district banks. The members of the Board are appointed by the President of the United States and confirmed by the U.S. Senate, and each serves a term of 14 years, with terms staggered through time. The President also appoints the chairman of the board from among the members on the board. The chairman serves in this capacity for a term of four years. The board's role is to create rules and regulations that govern all depository institutions.

The Federal Reserve District Banks are not-for-profit institutions. Their responsibilities include:

- Handling the vast majority of check clearing in the United States
- Issuing money
- Acting as the bankers' bank

The Federal Reserve System consists of the Federal Reserve Banks and member commercial banks. All nationally chartered banks must join the system, but state-chartered banks may also join. A nationally chartered bank is a bank that receives its charter of incorporation (its right to do business) from the federal government, granted by the Comptroller of the Currency; a state-chartered bank receives its charter from the state. The

Comptroller of the Currency is a division of the U.S. Department of the Treasury and its role is to monitor banks' financial condition and compliance with regulations; states have similar agencies that monitor state-chartered banks. Because national banks represent the largest banking institutions in the United States, more than two-thirds of all bank assets are held by national banks.

The *Federal Open Market Committee* (FOMC) is a policy-making group within the Federal Reserve System. The committee is comprised of the seven members of the Federal Reserve Board, plus presidents or vice presidents of five Reserve banks. The FOMC is charged with making decisions regarding the Federal Reserve's open market operations, which consist of buying and selling of U.S. government securities. The open market operations of the Fed affect the cost and availability of credit in the economy.

Money Supply Defined

Market participants are interested in the supply and demand for money because it is the interaction of supply and demand that, according to the liquidity preference theory, affects the interest rates paid to borrow funds and the amount of interest earned on investing funds. The demand for money is determined by the availability of investment opportunities. The supply of money is determined, in large part, by the actions of a nation's central bank.

The decisions of the Fed affect the money supply of the United States. The money supply consists of cash and cash-like items. In fact, there are different definitions of the money supply, depending on the cash-like items you include. For example, the most basic definition of the money supply, denoted by *M1*, consists of:

- Cash (currency and bills) in circulation
- Demand deposits (non-interest earning deposits at banking institutions that can be withdrawn on demand)
- Other deposits that can be readily withdrawn using checks
- Travelers' checks

A broader definition of the money supply, denoted by *M2*, which consists of everything in M1, plus:

- Savings deposits
- Small denomination time deposits
- Money market mutual funds
- Money market deposit accounts

A still broader definition of money supply, denoted by *M3*, consists of everything in M2, plus:

- Large denomination time deposits
- Term repurchase agreements issued by commercial banks and thrift institutions, term Eurodollars held by U.S. residents
- Institution-owned balances in money market funds

A *savings deposit* is an amount held in an account with a financial institution for the purpose of accumulating money. A *time deposit* is a type of savings account at a financial institution. A *certificate of deposit* (CD) is an example of a time deposit. *Time* as used here describes the account because originally these accounts required that the saver notify the institution in advance (e.g., 90 days) of making a withdrawal. Though this practice of advance notification is no longer around, the term *time deposit* remains.

A *money market mutual fund* is a specific type of regulated investment company that invests only in short-term securities (i.e., money market instruments). A *money market deposit account* is an account at a depository institution that can be readily withdrawn. A *Eurodollar* is of U.S. dollars in foreign banks or in foreign branches of U.S. banks.

Goals of Monetary Policy

Monetary policy is the set of tools that a central bank can use to control the availability of loanable funds and the money supply. These tools can be used to achieve goals for the nation's economy. The 1977 amendment to the Federal Reserve Act sets forth the following two basic goals of monetary policy:[1]

1. Promote maximum sustainable output and employment.
2. Promote stable prices.

The Fed recognizes that in an economy, the amount of output and the employment rate are not affected by monetary policy in the long run, but rather are affected by other factors. Such factors include technological innovation and the rate of savings. Consequently, a monetary goal of achieving maximum sustainable output and employment means that the level of output and employment that the Fed seeks to affect should be consistent with these factors in the long run. However, there are business cycles where in the short-run, the Fed can influence either output or employment that is consistent with

---

[1] For a more detailed description of the goals of monetary policy, see Bernanke and Mishkin (1992).

long-run sustainable output and employment. Thus, a short-run objective of the Fed is to utilize monetary policy to stabilize an economy by bringing output and employment back in line with its long-term levels when deviations occur (i.e., when there are business cycles).

The concern, of course, is that action by Fed may push an economy beyond its long-run growth path for output and employment. As a result, this leads to pressure on an economy's resources (capacity), resulting in increasing higher inflation rates while failing in the long run to reduce the unemployment or increase output. That is, such an expansionary policy that could be pursued by the Fed leads to higher inflation, but no long-term benefit.

With respect to the goal of price stability, this means using monetary policy to achieve a low inflation environment. The reason is that in such an inflationary environment, households and businesses can make financial decisions without worrying about major price movements of goods and services in the future and, in comparison to output and employment, is one goal that the Fed can achieve in the long run.

Operating and Intermediate Target Variables

The Fed does not have direct control over the goals that are the final objectives of its policies. With monetary policy tools that we will describe later, the Fed cannot directly influence such complex economic variables as the prices of goods and services, the unemployment rate, the growth in output, and foreign exchange rates. Although the Fed can affect the rate of growth in the money supply using one of its policy tools—controlling reserves in the banking system—it cannot fully determine changes in the money supply. The growth in the money supply depends to a substantial extent on the preferences, actions, and expectations of numerous banks, borrowers, and consumers.

Consequently, the Fed seeks to achieve its goals through a form of chain reaction, which has the following chronology and structure. The Fed uses one or more of its policy tools to first influence what are referred to as *operating targets*. Operating targets are monetary and financial variables whose changes tend to bring about changes in what is called *intermediate targets*, which are variables that have a reasonably reliable linkage with the variables, such as output or employment, that constitute the Fed's goals. Intermediate targets may include interest rates or monetary aggregates. Thus, the Fed exerts whatever influence it has on the intermediate targets in an indirect way, by means of its control over the operating targets. For this reason, the Fed's power over the variables that make up its goals is quite indirect and dependent upon the linkages among the various targets and goals.

For monetary policy to be effective, the Fed must be able to identify the appropriate operating and intermediate target variables. The main characteristics of a suitable operating or intermediate target are:[2]

- Linkage
- Observability
- Responsiveness

By *linkage,* we mean that an operating target must have an expected connection with the intermediate target. In turn, the intermediate target must eventually impact the economy in a manner that is consistent with the Fed's goals.

The observability characteristic means that both operating targets and intermediate targets must be readily and regularly observable economic variables, in order for the Fed to be able to monitor its success in influencing their levels or rates of change.

The responsiveness characteristic means that in order to function as an operating target, a variable must respond quickly and in an expected way when the Fed's implements of one or more of its policy tools. Moreover, an appropriate intermediate target is one that reacts, in an anticipated way and a meaningfully short time, to changes in the operating target

Policy Tools for Implementing Monetary Policy

As just explained, the Fed cannot influence output and employment and control inflation directly, but rather through targets. Historically, the Fed's monetary policy has selected, as its operating target, either short-term interest rates or some measure of bank reserves. It would seem that the Fed might want to select both as operating targets. However, as explained by Poole (1970), the Fed must choose either a short-term rate or the level of some reserves and cannot choose to target both kinds of variables. Today, the Fed's operating target is short-term rates but there was a brief period, 1979–1982, where the Fed targeted reserves. Short-term rates appear to be the operating target selected by the central banks of most countries according to a study by the Bank for International Settlement (see Ho, 2008) rather than reserves.

The short-term rate that the Fed targets is the federal funds rate. Banks that have excess reserves charge other banks that need to borrow reserves when they have a shortfall. Since the lending of funds occurs at the end of the day and it is overnight lending, the federal funds rate is an overnight

---

[2] Friedman (1990) provides a formal treatment of the requirements for targets.

rate.[3] Yet, the federal funds rate is a market interest rate; consequently, the Fed cannot by decree change the federal funds rate. It can do so through its policy tools, which include:

- Open market operations.
- Changing the discount rate at the discount window.
- Changing the required reserve ratio.

Open market operations is the primary tool for implementing monetary policy and the other two are secondary tools. This policy tool involves the FOMC buying or selling government securities (Treasury and agency securities) to affect bank reserves, which in turn affects the federal funds available in the market. More specifically, the buying of securities by the Fed results in the Fed crediting the seller's account at a depository institution and thereby increasing reserve balances. An increase in reserve balances increases the supply of funds available in the federal fund markets and thereby reduces the federal funds rate. In contrast, the Fed's selling of securities reduces reserves, thereby decreasing the supply of funds available in the federal funds market. As a result, the sale of securities forces the federal funds upward.

A more transparent policy tool that can be used by the Fed is changing the interest rate at which it allows banks to borrow from it. Banks will do so as part of their reserve management strategy (i.e., satisfying required reserves). These loans are made by the district Federal Reserve Banks through a source referred to as the *discount window,* and the interest rate charged is called the *discount rate.* When a bank borrows at the discount window, the loan must be collateralized by eligible securities. In addition to setting the discount rate, the Fed specifies what qualifies as an eligible security that can be used as collateral. Notice that unlike the federal funds rate that is a rate on unsecured borrowing, the discount rate is a rate on collateralized borrowing.

The link to bank lending by changing the discount rate is as follows: Increasing the discount rate discourages borrowing by banks, which in turn discourages banks from lending funds. Lowering the discount rate has the opposite effect—encouraging bank lending.

As noted already, the policy tool that involves the changing of reserve requirements by changing the required ratio is typically not used. However, if the Fed elects to use it as a policy tool, the link is as follows. The money not held in reserve can be used to make loans and purchase securities. Changing reserve requirements affects monetary expansion; the lower

---

[3] Actually, there is not one federal funds rate. Since the lending of funds by one bank to another is done on an uncollateralized basis, the rate paid will vary with the credit worthiness of the borrowing bank. When we refer to the *federal funds rate* we mean the rate paid by the most creditworthy borrowers.

the reserve requirements, the more funds that can be put into the economy through loans and investments and, hence, the greater the supply of money in the economy. Raising the required reserve ratio reduces the effects of money expansion, and hence the money supply.

THE STRUCTURE OF INTEREST RATES

A casual examination of the financial pages of a journal would be enough to convene the idea that nobody talks about an "interest rate." There are interest rates reported for borrowing money and investing. These rates are not randomly determined; that is, there are factors that systematically how interest rates on different types of loans and debt instruments vary from each other. We refer to this as the *structure of interest rates* and we discuss the factors that affect this structure in this section.

The Base Interest Rate

The securities issued by the U.S. Department of the Treasury, popularly referred to as Treasury securities or simply Treasuries, are backed by the full faith and credit of the U.S. government. At the time of this writing, market participants throughout the world view U.S. Treasuries as being free of default risk, although there is the possibility that unwise economic policy by the U.S. government may alter that perception. While historically Treasury securities have served as the benchmark interest rates throughout the U.S. economy as well as in international capital markets, there are important benchmarks used by market participants that we will discuss later.

We have discussed earlier in this chapter the two theories about the determinants of the level of interest rate, which we will refer to as the base interest rate. A factor that is important in determining the level of rates is the expected rate of inflation. That is, the base interest rate can be expressed as:

Base interest rate = Real interest rate + Expected rate of inflation

The real interest rate is that that would exist in the economy in the absence of inflation.

The Risk Premium Between Non-Treasury and Treasury Securities with the Same Maturity

In Chapter 19, we will discuss the various sectors of the debt market and explain the myriad of debt instruments. Debt instruments not issued or backed by the full faith and credit of the U.S. government are available in the market at an interest rate or yield that is different from an otherwise comparable maturity Treasury security. We refer the difference between the interest rate offered on a non-Treasury security and a comparable maturity Treasury security as the *spread*. For example, if the yield on a five-year non-Treasury security is 5.4% and the yield on a 10-year Treasury security is 4%, the spread is said to be 1.4%. Rather than referring to the in percentage terms, such as 1.4%, market participants refer to the spread in terms of basis points. A basis point is equal to 0.01%. Consequently, 1% is equal to 100 basis points. In our example, the spread of 1.4% is equal to 140 basis points.

The spread exists because of the additional risk or risks to which an investor is exposed investing in a security that is not issued by the U.S. government. Consequently, the spread is referred to as a *risk premium*. Thus, we can express the interest rate offered on a non-Treasury security with the same maturity as a Treasury security as:

Interest rate = Base interest rate + Spread

or equivalently,

Interest rate = Base interest rate + Risk premium

While the spread or risk premium is typically positive, there are factors that can cause the risk premium to be negative as will be explained. The general factors that affect the risk premium between a non-Treasury security and a Treasury security with the same maturity are:

- The market's perception of the credit risk of the non-Treasury security.
- Any features provided for in the non-Treasury security that make them attractive or unattractive to investors.
- The tax treatment of the interest income from the non-Treasury security.
- The expected liquidity of the non-Treasury issue.

Risk Premium Due to Default Risk

Default risk refers to the risk that the issuer of a debt obligation may be unable to make timely payment of interest or the principal amount when it is due. Although market participants often use default risk and credit risk interchangeably, we will see in Chapter 19 that credit risk covers more than just default risk.

Most market participants gauge default risk in terms of credit rating assigned by the three major commercial rating companies: (1) Moody's Investors Service, (2) Standard & Poor's Corporation, and (3) Fitch Ratings. These companies, referred to as *rating agencies*, perform credit analyses of issuer's and issues and express their conclusions by a system of ratings. We postpone a detailed discussion of their letter grade rating systems until Chapter 19. For now, we just mention the essentials.

In all systems the term *high grade* means low credit risk or, conversely, high probability of future payments. Moody's designates the highest-grade bonds by the symbol Aaa; S&P and Fitch use the symbol AAA. The next highest grade is denoted by the symbol Aa (Moody's) or AA (S&P and Fitch); for the third grade all rating systems use A. The next three grades are Baa or BBB, Ba or BB, and B, respectively. There are also C grades. Moody's uses 1, 2, or 3 to provide a narrower credit quality breakdown within each class; S&P and Fitch use plus and minus signs for the same purpose. Bond issues that are assigned a rating in the top four categories are referred to as *investment-grade bonds*. Issues that carry a rating below the top four categories are referred to as *noninvestment-grade bonds*, or more popularly as *high-yield bonds* or *junk bonds*.

The spread or risk premium between Treasury securities and non-Treasury securities, which are identical in all respects except for credit rating, is referred to as a *credit spread*.

For example, on August 5, 2008, finance.yahoo.com reported (based on information supplied by ValuBond) that the five-year Treasury yield was 3.29% and the yield on five-year corporate bonds was as follows:

Credit Rating	Yield
AAA	5.01%
AA	5.50%
A	5.78%

Therefore, the credit spreads were:

Credit Rating	Credit Spread
AAA	5.01% – 3.29% = 1.72% = 172 basis points
AA	5.50% – 3.29% = 2.21% = 221 basis points
A	5.78% – 3.29% = 2.49% = 249 basis points

Note that the lower the credit rating, the higher the credit spread.

Inclusion of Attractive and Unattractive Provisions

We described the general characteristics of debt instruments in the previous chapter. The terms of the loan agreement may contain provisions that make the debt instrument more or less attractive compared to other debt instruments that do not have such provisions. When there is a provision that is attractive to an investor, the spread decreases relative to a Treasury security of the same maturity. The opposite occurs when there is an unattractive provision: The spread increases relative to comparable-maturity Treasury security.

The three most common features found in bond issues are (1) call provision, (2) put provision, and (3) conversion provision. A *call provision* grants the issuer the right to retire the bond issue prior to the scheduled maturity date. A bond issue that contains such a provision is said to be a *callable bond*. The inclusion of a call provision benefits the issuer by allowing it to replace that bond issue with a lower interest cost bond issue should interest rates in the market decline. Effectively, a call provision allows the issuer to alter the maturity of the bond issue. A call provision is an unattractive feature for the bondholder because the bondholder will not only be uncertain about maturity, but faces the risk that the issuer will exercise the call provision when interest rates have declined below the interest rate on the bond issue. As a result, the bondholder must reinvest the proceeds received when the bond issue is called into another bond issue paying a lower interest rate. This risk associated with a callable bond is called *reinvestment risk*. For this reason, investors require compensation for accepting reinvestment risk and they receive this compensation in the form of a higher spread or risk premium.

A bond issue with a *put provision* grants the bondholder the right to sell the issue back to the issuer at par value on designated dates. A bond that contains this provision is referred to as a *puttable bond*. Unlike a call provision, a put provision is an advantage to the bondholder. The reason is that, as explained in Chapter 19, if interest rates rise after the issuance of the bond, the price of the bond will decline. The put provision allows that bondholder to sell the bond back to the issuer, avoiding a market value loss on the bond and allowing the bondholder to reinvest the proceeds from the sale of the bond at a higher interest rate. Hence, a bond issue that contains a put provision will sell in the market at a lower spread than an otherwise comparable-maturity Treasury security.

A *conversion provision* grants the bondholder the right to exchange the bond issue for a specified number of shares of common stock. A bond with this provision is called a *convertible bond*. The conversion provision allows the bondholder the opportunity to benefit from a favorable movement in the price of the stock into which it can exchange bond. Hence, the conversion provision results in a lower spread relative to a comparable-maturity Treasury issue.

The three provisions we have described are effectively options. Unlike an option as described in Chapter 6, these provisions are referred to as *embedded options* because they are options embedded in a bond issue.

Taxability of Interest

The U.S. federal tax code specifies that interest income is taxable at the federal income tax level unless otherwise exempted. The federal tax code specifically exempts the interest income from qualified municipal bond issues from taxation at the federal level. Municipal bonds are securities issued by state and local governments and by their creations, such as "authorities" and special districts. The tax-exempt feature of municipal bonds is an attractive feature to an investor because it reduces taxes and, therefore, the spread is often such that the municipal bond issue sells in the market at a lower interest rate than a comparable-maturity bond issue.

For example, on August 5, 2008 finance.yahoo.com reported (based on information supplied by ValuBond) that the five-year Treasury yield was 3.29% and the yield on five-year municipal bonds was as follows:

Credit Rating	Yield
AAA	2.95%
AA	3.04%
A	3.27%

When comparing the yield on a municipal bond issue to that of the yield on a comparable-maturity Treasury issue, the market convention is not to compute the basis point difference (i.e., the spread) between the two bond issues. Instead, the market convention is to compute the ratio of the yield of municipal bond issue to yield of a comparable-maturity Treasury security. The resulting ratio is called the municipal yield ratio. On August 5, 2008, the municipal yield ratio for the three 5-year municipal bonds were:

Credit Rating	Municipal Yield Ratio
AAA	2.95%/3.29% = 0.90
AA	3.04%/3.29% = 0.92
A	3.27%/3.29% = 0.99

In selecting between a taxable bond (such as a corporate bond) and a municipal bond with the same maturity and credit rating, an investor can calculate the yield that must be offered on a taxable bond issue to give the same after-tax yield as a municipal bond issue. This yield measure is called the *equivalent taxable yield* and is determined as follows:

$$\text{Equivalent taxable yield} = \frac{\text{Tax-exempt yield}}{(1-\text{Marginal tax rate})}$$

For example, suppose an investor is considering the purchase of a AA rated five-year municipal bond on August 5, 2008 offering a yield of 3.04%. (the tax-exempt yield). Then

$$\text{Equivalent taxable yield} = \frac{0.0304}{(1-0.35)} = 4.68\%$$

That is, for an investor in the 35% marginal tax bracket, a taxable bond with a 4.68% yield would provide the equivalent of a 3.04% tax-exempt yield.

Expected Liquidity of a Bond Issue

When an investor wants to sell a particular bond issue, he or she is concerned whether the price that can be obtained from the sale will be close to the "true" value of the issue. For example, if recent trades in the market for a particular bond issue have been between 87.25 and 87.75 and market conditions have not changed, an investor would expect to sell the bond somewhere in the 87.25 to 87.75 range.

The concern that the investor has when contemplating the purchase of a particular bond issue is that he or she will have to sell it below its true value where the true value is indicated by recent transactions. This risk is referred to as *liquidity risk*. The greater the liquidity risk that investors perceive there is with a particular bond issue, the greater the spread or risk premium relative to a comparable-maturity Treasury security. The reason is that Treasury securities are the most liquid securities in the world.

TERM STRUCTURE OF INTEREST RATES

The price of a debt instrument will fluctuate over its life as yields in the market change. As explained and illustrated in Chapter 19, the price volatility of a bond is dependent on its maturity. More specifically, holding all other factors constant, the longer the maturity of a bond the greater the price volatility resulting from a change in market interest rates. The spread between any two maturity sectors of the market is called a *maturity spread*. Although this spread can be calculated for any sector of the market, it is most commonly calculated for the Treasury sector.

For example, this spread on August 6, 2008 Treasury issues for 2-year, 5-year, 10-year, and 30-year issues was follows:

Maturity	Yield
2-years	2.55%
5-years	3.29%
10-years	4.02%
30-years	4.64%

The maturity spreads were then:

5-year/2-year maturity spread:	3.29% − 2.55% = 74 basis points
10-year/2-year maturity spread:	4.02% − 2.55% = 147 basis points
10-year/5-year maturity spread:	4.02% − 3.29% = 73 basis points
30-year/2-year maturity spread:	4.64% − 2.55% = 209 basis points
30-year/5-year maturity spread:	4.64% − 3.29% = 135 basis points
30-year/10-year maturity spread:	4.64% − 4.02% = 62 basis points

The relationship between the yields on comparable securities but different maturities is called the *term structure of interest rates*. Again, the primary focus is the Treasury market. The graphic that depicts the relationship between the yield on Treasury securities with different maturities is known as the *yield curve* and, therefore, the maturity spread is also referred to as the *yield curve spread*. Figure 5.1 shows the shape of three hypothetical Treasury yield curves that have been observed from time to time in the United States.

Next we discuss the term structure of interest rates and the various economic theories to explain it.

Forward Rates and Spot Rates

The focus on the Treasury yield curve functions is due mainly because of its role as a benchmark for setting yields in many other sectors of the debt market. However, a Treasury yield curve based on observed yields on the Treasury market is an unsatisfactory measure of the relation between required yield and maturity. The key reason is that securities with the same maturity may

FIGURE 5.1   Three Observed Shapes for the Yield Curve

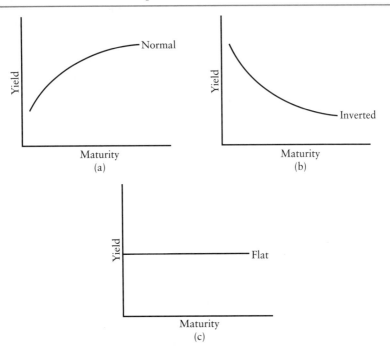

actually provide different yields. Hence, it is necessary to develop more accurate and reliable estimates of the Treasury yield curve. Specifically, the key is to estimate the theoretical interest rate that the U.S. Treasury would have to pay assuming that the security it issued is a zero-coupon security. Due its complexity, we will not explain how this is done. However, at this point all that is necessary to know is that there are procedures for estimating the theoretical interest rate or yield that the U.S. Treasury would have to pay for bonds with different maturities. These interest rates are called *Treasury spot rates*.

Valuable information for market participants can be obtained from the Treasury spot rates. These rates are called *forward rates*. First, we will see how these rates are obtained and then we will discuss theories about what determines forward rates. Finally, we will see how issuers can use the forward rates in making financing decisions.

Forward Rates

To see how a forward rate can be computed, consider the following two Treasury spot rates. Suppose that the spot rate for a zero-coupon Treasury security maturing in one year is 4% and a zero-coupon Treasury security maturing in two years is 5%. Let's look at this situation from the perspective of an investor who wants to invest funds for two years. The investor's choices are as follows:

Alternative 1. Investor buys a two-year zero-coupon Treasury security.

Alternative 2. Investor buys a one-year zero-coupon Treasury security and when it matures in one year the investor buys another one-year instrument.

With Alternative 1, the investor will earn the two-year spot rate and that rate is known with certainty. In contrast, with Alternative 2, the investor will earn the one-year spot rate, but the one-year spot one year from now is unknown. Therefore, for Alternative 2, the rate that will be earned over one year is not known with certainty.

Suppose that this investor expected that one year from now the one-year spot rate will be higher than it is today. The investor might then feel Alternative 2 would be the better investment. However, this is not necessarily true. To understand why it is necessary to know what a forward rate is, let's continue with our illustration.

The investor will be indifferent to the two alternatives if they produce the same total dollars over the two-year investment horizon. Given the two-year spot rate, there is some spot rate on a one-year zero-coupon Treasury security one year from now that will make the investor indifferent between the two alternatives. We will denote that rate by f.

The value of f can be readily determined given the two-year spot rate and the one-year spot rate. If an investor placed $100 in the two-year zero-coupon Treasury security (Alternative 1) earning 5%, the total dollars that will be generated at the end of two years is (i.e., the future value based on compounding as explained in Chapter 2) the following:

Total dollars at the end of two years for Alternative 1 = $100(1.05)^2 = 110.25

The proceeds from investing in the one-year Treasury security at 4% will generate the following total dollars at the end of one year:

Total dollars at the end of two years for Alternative 2 = $100(1.04) = 104

If one year from now this amount is reinvested in a zero-coupon Treasury security maturing in one year, which we denoted f, then

Total dollars at the end of two years for Alternative 2 = $104(1 + f)$

The investor will be indifferent between the two alternatives if the total dollars are the same. Setting the two equations for the total dollars at end of two years for the two alternatives equal we get

$$\$110.25 = \$104(1 + f)$$

Solving the preceding equation for f, we get

$$f = \frac{\$110.25}{\$104} - 1 = 0.06 = 6\%$$

Here is how we use this rate of 6%. If the one-year spot rate one year from now is less than 6%, then the total dollars at the end of two years would be higher by investing in the two-year zero-coupon Treasury security (Alternative 1). If the one-year spot rate one year from now is greater than 6%, then the total dollars at the end of two years would be higher by investing in a one-year zero-coupon Treasury security and reinvesting the proceeds one year from now at the one-year spot rate at that time (Alternative 2). Of course, if the one-year spot rate one year now is 6%, the two alternatives give the same total dollars at the end of two years.

Now that we have the forward rate f in which we are interested and we know how that rate can be used, let's return to the question that we posed at the outset. Suppose the investor expects that one year from now, the one-year spot rate will be 5.5%. That is, the investor expects the one-year spot rate one year from now will be higher than its current level. Should the investor select Alternative 2 because the one-year spot rate one year from now is expected to be higher? The answer is no. As we explained in the previous paragraph, if the spot rate is less than 6%, then Alternative 1 is the better alternative. Since this investor expects a rate of 5.5%, then he or she should select Alternative 1 despite the fact that he or she expects the one-year spot rate to be higher than it is today.

This is a somewhat surprising result for some investors. But the reason for this is that the market prices its expectations of future interest rates into the rates offered on investments with different maturities. This is why knowing the forward rates is critical. Some market participants believe that the forward rate is the market's consensus of future interest rates.

Similarly, borrowers need to understand what a forward rate is. For example, suppose a borrower must choose between a two-year loan and a series of two one-year loans. If the forward rate is less than the borrower's expectations of one-year rates one year from now, then the borrower will be better off with a two-year loan. If, instead, the borrower's expectations are that the one-year rate one year from now will be less than the forward rate, the borrower will be better off by choosing a series of two one-year loans.

In practice, a corporate treasurer needs to know both forward rates and what future spreads will be. Recall that a corporation pays the Treasury rate (i.e., the benchmark) plus a spread.

A natural question about forward rates is how well they do at predicting future interest rates. Studies have demonstrated that forward rates do not do a good job in predicting future interest rates. Then, why the big deal about understanding forward rates? The reason, as we demonstrated in our illustration of how to select between two alternative investments, is that the forward rates indicate how an investor's and borrower's expectations must differ from the market consensus in order to make the correct decision.

In our illustration, the one-year forward rate may not be realized. That is irrelevant. The fact is that the one-year forward rate indicated to the investor that if expectations about the one-year rate one month from now are less than 6%, the investor would be better off with Alternative 1.

For this reason, as well as others explained later, some market participants do not refer to forward rates as being market consensus rates. Instead, they refer to forward rates as *hedgeable rates*. For example, by investing in the two-year Treasury security, the investor was able to hedge the one-year rate one year from now. Similarly, a corporation issuing a two-year security is hedging the one-year rate one year from now.[4]

Determinants of the Shape of the Term Structure

At a given point in time, if we plot the term structure—the yield to maturity, or the spot rate, at successive maturities against maturity—we would observe one of the three shapes shown in Figure 5.1.

Panel A of Figure 5.1(a) shows a yield curve where the yield increases with maturity. This type of yield curve is referred to as an *upward-sloping yield curve* or a *positively sloped yield curve*. Two examples of an upward-sloping yield curve from two days are shown in tabular form below:

Day	3 mos.	6 mos.	1 yr.	2 yrs.	3 yrs.	5 yrs.	7 yrs.	10 yrs.	20 yrs.	30 yrs.
04/15/1992	3.70	3.84	4.14	5.22	5.77	6.66	7.02	7.37	NA	7.87
08/22/2007	3.12	4.08	4.10	4.15	4.19	4.34	4.46	4.63	5.01	4.96
04/18/2008	1.35	1.68	1.85	2.19	2.35	2.95	3.29	3.77	4.52	4.51

---

[4] Note, however, that it is only the benchmark interest rate that is being hedged. The spread that the corporation or the issuer will pay can change.

A distinction is made for upward sloping yield curves based on the steepness of the yield curve. The steepness of the yield curve is typically measured in terms of the maturity spread between the long-term and short-term yields. While there are many maturity candidates to proxy for long-term and short-term yields, many market participants use the maturity spread between the six-month and 30-year yield in our example.

The steepness of the two yield curves above is different. The maturity spread between the 30-year and six-month yield was 283 basis points (4.51% – 1.68%) on 4/18/2008 and 403 basis points (7.87% – 3.84%) on 4/14/1992. In practice, a Treasury positively sloped yield curve whose maturity spread as measured by the six-month and 30-year yields is referred to as a *normal yield curve* when the spread is 300 basis points or less. The yield curve on 4/18/2008 is therefore a normal yield curve. When the maturity spread is more than 300 basis points, the yield curve is said to be a *steep yield curve*. The yield curve on 4/15/1992 is a steep yield curve.

Figure 5.1(b) shows a *downward-sloping* or *inverted yield curve*, where yields in general decline as maturity increases. There have not been many instances in the recent history of the U.S. Treasury market where the yield curve exhibited this characteristic. Examples of downward sloping yield curves include the yield curves in mid-2000 and early 2007. For example:

Day	3 mos.	6 mos.	1 yr.	2 yrs.	3 yrs.	5 yrs.	7 yrs.	10 yrs.	20 yrs.	30 yrs.
02/21/2007	5.18	5.16	5.05	4.82	4.74	4.68	4.68	4.69	4.90	4.79
07/19/2000	6.33	6.15	6.46	6.4	6.31	6.35	6.16	6.29	5.92	6.33

The most notable is on August 14, 1981 Treasury yields at the time were at an historic high. The yield on the two-year was 16.91% and declined for each subsequent maturity until it reached 13.95% for the 30-year maturity.

Figure 5.1(c) depicts a *flat yield curve*. While the figure suggests that for a flat yield curve the yields are identical for each maturity, that is not what is observed in the maturity. Rather, the yields for all maturities are similar. The yield curves given below in tabular form are examples of a flat yield curve:

Day	3 mos.	6 mos.	1 yr.	2 yrs.	3 yrs.	5 yrs.	7 yrs.	10 yrs.	20 yrs.	30 yrs.
01/03/1990	7.89	7.94	7.85	7.94	7.96	7.92	8.04	7.99	N/A	8.04
05/23/2007	4.91	5.01	4.96	4.85	4.79	4.79	4.8	4.86	5.09	5.01

Notice the very small six-month–30-year maturity spread of less than 10 basis points.

A variant of the flat yield is one in which the yield on short-term and long-term Treasuries are similar but the yield on intermediate-term Treasuries are much lower than the six-month and 30-year yields. Such a yield curve is referred to as a *humped yield curve*. Examples of humped yield curves are the following:

Day	3 mos.	6 mos.	1 yr.	2 yrs.	3 yrs.	5 yrs.	7 yrs.	10 yrs.	20 yrs.	30 yrs.
11/24/2000	6.34	6.12	5.86	5.74	5.63	5.7	5.63	5.86	5.67	6.34
01/01/2007	5.87	5.58	5.11	4.87	4.82	4.76	4.97	4.92	5.46	5.35

Economic Theories of the Term Structure of Interest Rates

There are two major economic theories that have evolved to account for the observed shapes of the yield curve: the *expectations theory* and the *market segmentation theory*.

Expectations Theories

There are several forms of the expectations theory:

- Pure expectations theory
- Biased expectations theory

Both theories share an hypothesis about the behavior of short-term forward rates and also assume that the forward rates in current long-term bonds are closely related to the market's expectations about future short-term rates. The two theories differ, however, on whether or not other factors also affect forward rates, and how. The pure expectations theory postulates that no systematic factors other than expected future short-term rates affect forward rates; the biases expectations theory asserts that there are other factors.

Pure Expectations Theory According to the pure expectations theory, the forward rates exclusively represent the expected future rates. Thus, the entire term structure at a given time reflects the market's current expectations of the family of future short-term rates. Under this view, a rising term structure, as in Figure 5.1(a), must indicate that the market expects short-term rates to rise throughout the relevant future. Similarly, a flat term structure reflects an expectation that future short-term rates will be mostly constant, while a falling term structure must reflect an expectation that future short rates will decline steadily.

A major shortcoming of the pure expectations theory is that is ignores the risks inherent in investing in debt instruments. If forward rates were perfect predictors of future interest rates, then the future prices of bonds would be known with certainty. The return over any investment period would be certain and independent of the maturity of the debt instrument initially acquired and of the time at which the investor needed to liquidate the debt instrument. However, with uncertainty about future interest rates and hence about future prices of bonds, these debt instruments become risky investments in the sense that the return over some investment horizon is unknown.

Similarly, from a borrower's perspective, the cost of borrowing for any required period of financing would be certain and independent of the maturity of the debt instrument if the rate at which the borrower must refinance debt in the future is known. But with uncertainty about future interest rates, the cost of borrowing is uncertain if the borrower must refinance at some time over the periods in which the funds are initially needed.

Biased Expectations Theory Biased expectations theories take into account the shortcomings of the pure expectations theory. The two theories are:

- Liquidity theory
- Preferred habitat theory

According to the *liquidity theory*, the forward rates will not be an unbiased estimate of the market's expectations of future interest rates because they embody a premium to compensate for risk; this risk premium is referred to as a *liquidity premium*. Therefore, an upward-sloping yield curve may reflect expectations that future interest rates either (1) will rise, or (2) will be flat or even fall, but with a liquidity premium increasing fast enough with maturity so as to produce an upward-sloping yield curve.

The *preferred habitat theory* also adopts the view that the term structure reflects the expectation of the future path of interest rates as well as a risk premium. However, the preferred habitat theory rejects the assertion that the risk premium must rise uniformly with maturity. Proponents of the habitat theory say that the latter conclusion could be accepted if all investors intend to liquidate their investment at the first possible date, while all borrowers are eager to borrow long. However, this is an assumption that can be rejected for a number of reasons. The argument is that different financial institutions have different investment horizons and have a preference for the maturities in which they invest. The preference is based on the maturity of their liabilities. To induce a financial institution out of that maturity sector, a premium must be paid. Thus, the forward rates include a liquidity premium and compensation for investors to move out of their preferred maturity sector. Consequently, forward rates do not reflect the market's consensus of future interest rates.

Market Segmentation Theory

The *market segmentation theory* also recognizes that investors have preferred habitats dictated by saving and investment flows. This theory also proposes that the major reason for the shape of the yield curve lies in asset/liability management constraints (either regulatory or self-imposed) and/or creditors (borrowers) restricting their lending (financing) to specific maturity sectors. However, the market segmentation theory differs from the preferred habitat theory because the market segmentation theory assumes that neither investors nor borrowers are willing to shift from one maturity sector to another to take advantage of opportunities arising from differences between expectations and forward rates. Thus, for the segmentation theory, the shape of the yield curve is determined by supply of and demand for securities within each maturity sector.

Swap Rate Yield Curve

Another benchmark that is used by global investors is the swap rate. In Chapter 6 we describe interest rate swaps, a derivative instrument. In a generic interest rate swap, the parties exchange interest rate payments on specified dates: One party pays a fixed rate and the other party a floating rate over the life of the swap. In a typical swap the floating rate is based on a reference rate and the reference rate is typically LIBOR. The fixed interest rate that is paid by the fixed rate counterparty is called the swap rate. The relationship between the swap rate and maturity of a swap is called the *swap rate yield curve*, or more commonly referred to as the *swap curve*. Because the reference rate is typically LIBOR, the swap curve is also called the *LIBOR curve*.

The swap curve is used as a benchmark in many countries outside the United States. Unlike a country's government bond yield curve, however, the swap curve is not a default-free yield curve. Instead, it reflects the credit risk of the counterparty to an interest rate swap. Since the counterparty to an interest rate swap is typically a bank-related entity, the swap curve reflects the average credit risk of representative banks that provide interest rate swaps. More specifically, a swap curve is viewed as the *interbank yield curve*. It is also referred to as the *AA rated yield curve* because the banks that borrow money from each other at LIBOR have credit ratings of Aa/AA or above.

We see the effect of this credit risk when we compare the yield curve based on U.S. Treasuries with the swap rate curve. For example, consider the rates for August 22, 2008:

	1 yr.	2 yrs.	3 yrs.	4 yrs.	5 yrs.	7 yrs.	10 yrs.	30 yrs.
Yield curve, U.S. Treasuries	2.15	2.35	2.62	NA	3.07	3.39	3.82	4.44
Swap curve		3.05	3.38	3.73	3.95	4.10	4.36	4.58	4.92

The spread between these two curves ranges from 48 basis points for 30-year yield to 111 basis points for three-year yield.

There are reasons why investors prefer to use a country's swap curve if it available than a country's yield curve obtained from its government bonds. We will not describe these reasons here.[5]

SUMMARY

There are two economic theories that seek to explain the level of interest rates: the loanable funds theory and the liquidity preference theory. The loanable funds theory asserts that the level of interest rates in an economy is determined by the supply of and demand for loanable funds. According to the liquidity preference theory, the level of interest rates is determined by the supply of and demand for money balances.

The Federal Reserve System (the "Fed") is a network of banks that acts as the central banker for the United States. The money supply consists of cash and cash-like items. There are different definitions of what constitutes the money supply, depending on which cash-like items are included. Monetary policy, the set of tools that a central bank uses to control the availability of loanable funds and the money supply, has the following two goals in the United States: promote maximum sustainable output and employment and promote stable prices. Because the Fed policy does not have direct control over the goals that are the final objectives of its policies, in implementing monetary it uses one or more of its policy tools to first influence operating targets. Operating targets are monetary and financial variables whose changes tend to bring about changes in what are called intermediate targets, which are variables that have a reasonably reliable linkage with the variables, such as output or employment, that constitute the Fed's goals. The three tools of monetary policy are open market operations, changing the discount rate, and changing reserve requirements. Open market operations is the primary tool for implementing monetary policy and the other two are secondary tools.

Interest rates are determined by the base rate (rate on a Treasury security) plus a spread or risk premium. The factors that affect the risk premium for a non-Treasury security with the same maturity as a Treasury security

---

[5] These reasons are provided in Ron (2002).

are (1) the perceived creditworthiness of the issuer, (2) inclusion of provisions such as a call provision, put provision, or conversion provision, (3) taxability of interest, and (4) expected liquidity of an issue.

The term structure of interest rates shows the relationship between the yield on a bond and its maturity; the yield curve is the graph of the relationship between the yield on bonds of the same credit quality but different maturities. Valuable information for issuers and investors is provided in forward rates. Two major theories are offered to explain the observed shapes of the yield curve: the expectations theory and the market segmentation theory. There are two forms of the expectations theory: pure expectations theory and biased expectations theory. The two forms of the biased expectations theory are the liquidity theory and the preferred habit theory.

REFERENCES

Bernanke, B. and F. Mishkin (1992). Guideposts and signals in the conduct of monetary policy: Lessons from six industrialized countries, presented at the Seventh Annual Conference on Macroeconomics.

Friedman, B. M. (1990). Targets and instruments of monetary policy. Chapter 22 in Benjamin M. Friedman and Frank H. Hahn (eds.), *Handbook of Monetary Economics*. Amsterdam: North-Holland.

Ho, C. (2008). Implementing monetary policy in the 2000s: Operating procedures in Asia and beyond. BIS Working Paper 253, June.

Keynes, J. M. (1936). *The General Theory of Employment, Interest and Money*. London: Macmillan.

Poole, W. (1970). Optimal choice of monetary policy instrument in a simple stochastic macro model. *Quarterly Journal of Economics* 84, no. 2: 197–216.

Ron, U. (2002). A practical guide to swap curve construction. Chapter 6 in Frank J. Fabozzi (ed.), *Interest Rate, Term Structure, and Valuation Modeling*. New York: John Wiley & Sons.

Basics of Derivatives

Derivative instruments play an important role in financial markets as well as commodity markets by allowing market participants to control their exposure to different types of risk. In this chapter, we describe the various types of derivative contracts. The two basic derivative contracts are futures and forward contracts and options contracts. There are other types of derivative contracts that are economically equivalent to a package of these two basic contracts: swaps and caps and floors. We explain the investment characteristics of all of these contracts and the basic principle of pricing futures and forward contracts. In Chapters 20 and 21, we explain how derivative instruments are used in investment management and how the pricing of the derivatives may deviate from the pricing model explained in this chapter.

FUTURES AND FORWARD CONTRACTS

Basic Features of Futures Contracts

A *futures contract* is a legal agreement between a buyer and a seller in which:

1. The buyer agrees to take delivery of something at a specified price at the end of a designated period of time.
2. The seller agrees to make delivery of something at a specified price at the end of a designated period of time.

Of course, no one buys or sells anything when entering into a futures contract. Rather, those who enter into a contract agree to buy or sell a specific amount of a specific item at a specified future date. When we speak of the "buyer" or the "seller" of a contract, we are simply adopting the jargon of the futures market, which refers to parties of the contract in terms of the future obligation they are committing themselves to.

Let's look closely at the key elements of this contract. The price at which the parties agree to transact in the future is called the *futures price*. The designated date at which the parties must transact is called the *settlement date* or *delivery date*. The "something" that the parties agree to exchange is called *the underlying*.

To illustrate, suppose a futures contract is traded on an exchange where the underlying to be bought or sold is asset XYZ, and the settlement is three months from now. Assume further that Bob buys this futures contract, and Sally sells this futures contract, and the price at which they agree to transact in the future is $100. Then $100 is the futures price. At the settlement date, Sally will deliver asset XYZ to Bob. Bob will give Sally $100, the futures price. When an investor takes a position in the market by buying a futures contract (or agreeing to buy at the future date), the investor is said to be in a *long position* or to be *long futures*. If, instead, the investor's opening position is the sale of a futures contract (which means the contractual obligation to sell something in the future), the investor is said to be in a *short position* or *short futures*.

The buyer of a futures contract will realize a profit if the futures price increases; the seller of a futures contract will realize a profit if the futures price decreases. For example, suppose that one month after Bob and Sally take their positions in the futures contract, the futures price of asset XYZ increases to $120. Bob, the buyer of the futures contract, could then sell the futures contract and realize a profit of $20. Effectively, at the settlement date, he has agreed to buy asset XYZ for $100 and has agreed to sell asset XYZ for $120. Sally, the seller of the futures contract, will realize a loss of $20. If the futures price falls to $40 and Sally buys back the contract at $40, she realizes a profit of $60 because she agreed to sell asset XYZ for $100 and now can buy it for $40. Bob would realize a loss of $60. Thus, if the futures price decreases, the buyer of the futures contract realizes a loss while the seller of the futures contract realizes a profit, as we show in Figure 6.1.

Liquidating a Position

Most financial futures contracts have settlement dates in the months of March, June, September, or December. This means that at a predetermined time in the contract settlement month, the contract stops trading, and a price is determined by the exchange for settlement of the contract. For example, on January 4, 200X, suppose Bob buys and Sally sells a futures contract that settles on the third Friday of March of 200X. Then, on that date, Bob and Sally must perform—Bob agreeing to buy asset XYZ at $100, and Sally agreeing to sell asset XYZ at $100. The exchange will determine a settlement price for the futures contract for that specific date. For example, if the exchange determines a settlement price of $130, then Bob has agreed

FIGURE 6.1 Profit and Loss on a Futures Contract in XYZ with a Price of $100 and Settlement in Three Months

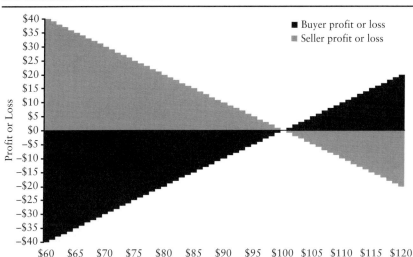

to buy asset XYZ for $100 but can settle the position for $130, thereby realizing a profit of $30. Sally would realize a loss of $30.

Instead of Bob or Sally entering into a futures contract on January 4, 200X, that settles in March, they could have selected a settlement in June, September, or December. The contract with the closest settlement date is called the *nearby futures contract*. The *next futures contract* is the one that settles just after the nearby contract. The contract farthest away in time from settlement is called the *most distant futures contract*.

A party to a futures contract has two choices regarding the liquidation of the position. First, the position can be liquidated prior to the settlement date. For this purpose, the party must take an offsetting position in the same contract. For the buyer of a futures contract, this means selling the same number of identical futures contracts; for the seller of a futures contract, this means buying the same number of identical futures contracts. An identical contract means the contract for the same underlying and the same settlement date. So, for example, if Bob buys one futures contract for asset XYZ with settlement in March 200X on January 4, 200X, and wants to liquidate a position on February 14, 200X, he can sell one futures contract for asset XYZ with settlement in March 200X. Similarly, if Sally sells one futures contract for asset XYZ with settlement in March 200X on January 4, 200X, and wants to liquidate a position on February 22, 200X, she can buy one futures contract for asset XYZ with settlement in March 200X. A futures contract on asset XYZ that settles in June 200X is not the same contract as a futures contract on asset XYZ that settles in March 200X.

The alternative is to wait until the settlement date. At that time, the party purchasing a futures contract accepts delivery of the underlying; the party that sells a futures contract liquidates the position by delivering the underlying at the agreed upon price. For some futures contracts that we shall describe later in later chapters, settlement is made in cash only. Such contracts are referred to as *cash settlement contracts*.

A useful statistic for measuring the liquidity of a contract is the number of contracts that have been entered into but not yet liquidated. This figure is called the contract's *open interest*. An open interest figure is reported by an exchange for every futures contracts traded on the exchange.

The Role of the Clearinghouse

Associated with every futures exchange is a clearinghouse, which performs several functions. One of these functions is to guarantee that the two parties to the transaction will perform. Because of the clearinghouse, the two parties need not worry about the financial strength and integrity of the other party taking the opposite side of the contract. After initial execution of an order, the relationship between the two parties ends. The clearinghouse interposes itself as the buyer for every sale and as the seller for every purchase. Thus, the two parties are then free to liquidate their positions without involving the other party in the original contract, and without worry that the other party may default.

Margin Requirements

When a position is first taken in a futures contract, the investor must deposit a minimum dollar amount per contract as specified by the exchange. This amount, called *initial margin,* is required as a deposit for the contract. The initial margin may be in the form of an interest-bearing security such as a Treasury bill. The initial margin is placed in an account, and the amount in this account is referred to as the *investor's equity.* As the price of the futures contract fluctuates each trading day, the value of the investor's equity in the position changes.

At the end of each trading day, the exchange determines the "settlement price" for the futures contract. The settlement price is different from the closing price, which is the price of the security in the final trade of the day (whenever that trade occurred during the day). By contrast, the settlement price is that value the exchange considers to be representative of trading at the end of the day. The exchange uses the settlement price to mark to market the investor's position, so that any gain or loss from the position is quickly reflected in the investor's equity account.

A *maintenance margin* is the minimum level (specified by the exchange) by which an investor's equity position may fall as a result of unfavorable price movements before the investor is required to deposit additional margin. The maintenance margin requirement is a dollar amount that is less than the initial margin requirement. It sets the floor that the investor's equity account can fall to before the investor is required to furnish additional margin. The additional margin deposited, called *variation margin,* is an amount necessary to bring the equity in the account back to its initial margin level. Unlike initial margin, variation margin must be in cash, not interest-bearing instruments. Any excess margin in the account may be withdrawn by the investor. If a party to a futures contract who is required to deposit a variation margin fails to do so within 24 hours, the futures position is liquidated by the clearinghouse.[1]

To illustrate the mark-to-market procedure, let's assume the following margin requirements for asset XYZ:

- Initial margin $7 per contract.
- Maintenance margin $4 per contract.

Suppose that Bob buys 500 contracts at a futures price of $100, and Sally sells the same number of contracts at the same futures price. The initial margin for both Bob and Sally is $3,500, which is determined by multiplying the initial margin of $7 by the number of contracts, 500. Bob and Sally must put up $3,500 in cash or Treasury bills or other acceptable collateral. At this time, $3,500 is the equity in the account.

The maintenance margin for the two positions is $2,000 (the maintenance margin per contract of $4 multiplied by 500 contracts). That means the equity in the account may not fall below $2,000. If it does, the party whose equity falls below the maintenance margin must put up additional margin, which is the variation margin.

Regarding the variation margin, note two things: First, the variation margin must be cash. Second, the amount of variation margin required is the amount to bring the equity up to the initial margin, not the maintenance margin.

---

[1] Although there are initial and maintenance margin requirements for buying securities on margin, the concept of margin differs for securities and futures. When securities are acquired on margin, the difference between the price of the security and the initial margin is borrowed from the broker. The security purchased serves as collateral for the loan, and the investor pays interest. For futures contracts, the initial margin, in effect, serves as "good-faith" money, an indication that the investor will satisfy the obligation of the contract. Normally, no money is borrowed by the investor.

Now, to illustrate the mark-to-market procedure, we will assume the following settlement prices at the end of four consecutive trading days after the transaction was entered into:

Trading Day	Settlement Price
1	$99
2	97
3	98
4	95

First consider Bob's position. At the end of trading day 1, Bob realizes a loss of $1 per contract, or $500 for the 500 contracts he bought. Bob's initial equity of $3,500 is reduced by $500 to $3,000. No action is taken by the clearinghouse, because Bob's equity is still above the maintenance margin of $2,000. At the end of the second day, Bob realizes a further loss as the price of the futures contract declines $2 to $97, resulting in an additional reduction in his equity position by $1,000. Bob's equity is then $2,000. Despite the loss, no action is taken by the clearinghouse, since the equity is not less than the $2,000 maintenance margin requirement. At the end of trading day 3, Bob realizes a profit from the previous trading day of $1 per contract, or $500. Bob's equity increases to $2,500. The drop in price from 98 to 95 at the end of trading day 4 results in a loss for the 500 contracts of $1,500 and a reduction of Bob's equity to $1,000. Since Bob's equity is now below the $2,000 maintenance margin, Bob is required to put up additional margin of $2,500 (variation margin) to bring the equity up to the initial margin of $3,500. If Bob cannot put up the variation margin, his position will be liquidated. That is, his contracts will be sold by the clearinghouse.

Now let's look at Sally's position. Since Sally sold the futures contract, she benefits if the price of the futures contract declines. As a result, her equity increases at the end of the first 2 trading days. In fact, at the end of trading day 1, she realizes a profit of $500, which increases her equity to $4,000. She is entitled to remove the $500 profit and utilize these funds elsewhere. Suppose she does, and, as a result, her equity remains at $3,500 at the end of trading day 1. At the end of trading day 2, she realizes an additional profit of $1,000 that she can withdraw. At the end of trading day 3, she realizes a loss of $500, because the price increased from $97 to $98. This results in a reduction of her equity to $3,000. Finally, on trading day 4, she realizes a profit of $1,500, making her equity $4,500. She can withdraw $1,000.

Leveraging Aspect of Futures

When taking a position in a futures contract, a party need not put up the entire amount of the investment. Instead, the exchange requires that only the initial margin be invested. To see the crucial consequences of this fact, suppose Bob has $100 and wants to invest in asset XYZ because he believes its price will appreciate. If asset XYZ is selling for $100, he can buy one unit of the asset in the cash market, the market where goods are delivered upon purchase. His payoff will then be based on the price action of one unit of asset XYZ.

Suppose that the exchange where the futures contract for asset XYZ is traded requires an initial margin of only 5%, which in this case would be $5. Then Bob can purchase 20 contracts with his $100 investment. (This example ignores the fact that Bob may need funds for variation margin.) His payoff will then depend on the price action of 20 units of asset XYZ. Thus, he can leverage the use of his funds. (The degree of leverage equals 1/margin rate. In this case, the degree of leverage equals 1/0.05, or 20.) While the degree of leverage available in the futures market varies from contract to contract, as the initial margin requirement varies, the leverage attainable is considerably greater than in the cash market.

At first, the leverage available in the futures market may suggest that the market benefits only those who want to speculate on price movements. This is not true. As we shall see, futures markets can be used to reduce price risk. Without the leverage possible in futures transactions, the cost of reducing price risk using futures would be too high for many market participants.

Basic Features of Forward Contracts

A forward contract, just like a futures contract, is an agreement for the future delivery of the underlying at a specified price at the end of a designated period of time. Futures contracts are standardized agreements as to the delivery date (or month) and quality of the deliverable, and are traded on organized exchanges. A forward contract differs in that it is usually nonstandardized (that is, the terms of each contract are negotiated individually between buyer and seller), there is no clearinghouse, and secondary markets are often non-existent or extremely thin. Unlike a futures contract, which is an exchange-traded product, a forward contract is an over-the-counter instrument.

Because there is no clearinghouse that guarantees the performance of a counterparty in a forward contract, the parties to a forward contract are exposed to *counterparty risk,* the risk that the other party to the transaction will fail to perform. Futures contracts are marked to market at the end of each trading day, while forward contracts usually are not. Consequently, futures contracts are subject to interim cash flows because additional margin may be required in the case of adverse price movements or because cash may be withdrawn in the case of favorable price movements. A forward contract may or may not be marked to market. Where the counterparties are two high-credit-quality entities, the two parties may agree not to mark positions to market. However, if one or both of the parties are concerned with the counterparty risk of the other, then positions may be marked to market. Thus, when a forward contract is marked to market, there are interim cash flows just as with a futures contract. When a forward contract is not marked to market, then there are no interim cash flows.

Other than these differences, what we said about futures contracts applies to forward contracts too.

Basics of Pricing of Futures and Forward Contracts

When using derivatives, a market participant should understand the basic principles of how they are valued. While there are many models that have been proposed for valuing financial instruments that trade in the cash (spot) market, the valuation of all derivative models are based on arbitrage arguments. Basically, this involves developing a strategy or a trade wherein a package consisting of a position in the underlying (that is, the underlying asset or instrument for the derivative contract) and borrowing or lending so as to generate the same cash flow profile as the derivative. The value of the package is then equal to the theoretical price of the derivative. If the market price of the derivative deviates from the theoretical price, then the actions of arbitrageurs will drive the market price of the derivative toward its theoretical price until the arbitrage opportunity is eliminated.

In developing a strategy to capture any mispricing, certain assumptions are made. When these assumptions are not satisfied in the real world, the theoretical price can only be approximated. Moreover, a close examination of the underlying assumptions necessary to derive the theoretical price indicates how a pricing formula must be modified to value specific contracts.

Here we describe how futures and forward are valued. The pricing of futures and forward contracts is similar. If the underlying asset for both contracts is the same, the difference in pricing is due to differences in features of the contract that must be dealt with by the pricing model.

We will illustrate the basic model for pricing futures contract. By "basic," we mean that we are extrapolating from the nuisances of the underlying for a specific contract. The issues associated with applying the basic pricing model to some of the more popular futures contracts are described in other chapters. Moreover, while the model described here is said to be a model for pricing futures, technically, it is a model for pricing forward contracts with no mark-to-market requirements.

Rather than deriving the formula algebraically, we demonstrate the basic pricing model using an example. We make the following six assumptions for a futures contract that has no initial and variation margin and for the underlying is asset U:

1. The price of asset U in the cash market is $100.
2. There is a known cash flow for asset U over the life of the futures contract.
3. The cash flow for asset U is $8 per year paid quarterly ($2 per quarter).
4. The next quarterly payment is exactly three months from now.
5. The futures contract requires delivery three months from now.
6. The current three-month interest rate at which funds can be lent or borrowed is 4% per year.

The objective is to determine what the futures price of this contract should be. To do so, suppose that the futures price in the market is $105. Let's see if that is the correct price. We can check this by implementing the following simple strategy:

- Sell the futures contract at $105.
- Purchase asset U in the cash market for $100.
- Borrow $100 for three months at 4% per year ($1 per quarter).

The purchase of asset U is accomplished with the borrowed funds. Hence, this strategy does not involve any initial cash outlay. At the end of three months, the following occurs

- $2 is received from holding asset U.
- Asset U is delivered to settle the futures contract.
- The loan is repaid.

This strategy results in the following outcome:

From settlement of the futures contract:

Proceeds from sale of asset U to settle the futures contract	=	$105
Payment received from investing in asset U for three months	=	2
Total proceeds	=	$107

From the loan:

Repayment of principal of loan	=	$100
Interest on loan (1% for three months)	=	1
Total outlay	=	$101
Profit from the strategy	=	$6

The profit of $6 from this strategy is guaranteed regardless of what the cash price of asset U is three months from now. This is because in the preceding analysis of the outcome of the strategy, the cash price of asset U three months from now never enters the analysis. Moreover, this profit is generated with no investment outlay; the funds needed to acquire asset U are borrowed when the strategy is executed. In financial terms, the profit in the strategy we have just illustrated arises froma riskless arbitrage between the price of asset U in the cash market and the price of asset U in the futures market.

In a well-functioning market, arbitrageurs who could realize this riskless profit for a zero investment would implement the strategy described above. By selling the futures and buying asset U in order to implement the strategy, this would force the futures price down so that at some price for the futures contract, the arbitrage profit is eliminated.

This strategy that resulted in the capturing of the arbitrage profit is referred to as a *cash-and-carry trade*. The reason for this name is that implementation of the strategy involves borrowing cash to purchase the underlying and "carrying" that underlying to the settlement date of the futures contract.

From the cash-and-carry trade we see that the futures price cannot be $105. Suppose instead that the futures price is $95 rather than $105. Let's try the following strategy to see if that price can be sustained in the market:

■ Buy the futures contract at $95.
■ Sell (short) asset U for $100.
■ Invest (lend) $100 for three months at 1% per year.

We assume once again that in this strategy that there is no initial margin and variation margin for the futures contract. In addition, we assume that there is no cost to selling the asset short and lending themoney. Given these assumptions, there is no initial cash outlay for the strategy just as with the cash-and-carry trade. Three months from now:

■ Asset U is purchased to settle the long position in the futures contract.
■ Asset U is accepted for delivery.
■ Asset U is used to cover the short position in the cash market.
■ Payment is made of $2 to the lender of asset U as compensation for the quarterly payment.

■ Payment is received from the borrower of the loan of $101 for principal and interest.

More specifically, the strategy produces the following at the end of three months:

From settlement of the futures contract:

Price paid for purchase of asset U to settle futures contract	=	$95
Proceeds to lender of asset U to borrow the asset	=	2
Total outlay	=	$97

From the loan:

Principal from loan	=	$100
Interest earned on loan ($1 for three months)	=	1
Total proceeds	=	$101
Profit from the strategy	=	$4

As with the cash-and-carry trade, the $4 profit from this strategy is a riskless arbitrage profit. This strategy requires no initial cash outlay, but will generate a profit whatever the price of asset U is in the cash market at the settlement date. In real-world markets, this opportunity would lead arbitrageurs to buy the futures contract and short asset U. The implementation of this strategy would be to raise the futures price until the arbitrage profit disappeared.

This strategy that is implemented to capture the arbitrage profit is known as a *reverse cash-and-carry trade*. That is, with this strategy, the underlying is sold short and the proceeds received from the short sale are invested.

We can see that the futures price cannot be $95 or $105. What is the theoretical futures price given the assumptions in our illustration? It can be shown that if the futures price is $99 there is no opportunity for an arbitrage profit. That is, neither the cash-and-carry trade nor the reverse cash-and-carry trade will generate an arbitrage profit.

In general, the formula for determining the theoretical price given the assumptions of the model is

$$\text{Theoretical futures price} = \text{Cash market price} + (\text{Cash market price}) \\ \times (\text{Financing cost} - \text{Cash yield}) \tag{6.1}$$

In the formula given by (6.1), "Financing cost" is the interest rate to borrow funds and "Cash yield" is the payment received from investing in the asset as a percentage of the cash price. In our illustration, the financing cost is 1% and the cash yield is 2%.

In our illustration, since the cash price of asset U is $100, the theoretical futures price is

$$\$100 + [\$100 \times (1\% - 2\%)] = \$99$$

The future price can be above or below the cash price depending on the difference between the financing cost and cash yield. The difference between these rates is called the *net financing cost*. A more commonly used term for the net financing cost is the *cost of carry*, or, simply, *carry*. *Positive carry* means that the cash yield exceeds the financing cost. (Note that while the difference between the financing cost and the cash yield is a negative value, carry is said to be positive.) *Negative carry* means that the financing cost exceeds the cash yield. Below is a summary of the effect of carry on the difference between the futures price and the cash market price:

Positive carry	Futures price will sell at a discount to cash price.
Negative carry	Futures price will sell at a premium to cash price.
Zero	Futures price will be equal to the cash price.

Note that at the settlement date of the futures contract, the futures price must equal the cash market price. The reason is that a futures contract with no time left until delivery is equivalent to a cash market transaction. Thus, as the delivery date approaches, the futures price will converge to the cash market price. This fact is evident from the formula for the theoretical futures price given by (6.1). The financing cost approaches zero as the delivery date approaches. Similarly, the yield that can be earned by holding the underlying approaches zero. Hence, the cost of carry approaches zero, and the futures price approaches the cash market price.

A Closer Look at the Theoretical Futures Price

In deriving theoretical futures price using the arbitrage argument, several assumptions had to be made. These assumptions as well as the differences in contract specifications will result in the futures price in the market deviating from the theoretical futures price as given by (6.1). It may be possible to incorporate these institutional and contract specification differences into the formula for the theoretical futures price. In general, however, because it is oftentimes too difficult to allow for these differences in building a model for the theoretical futures price, the end result is that one can develop bands or boundaries for the theoretical futures price. So long as the futures price in the market remains within the band, no arbitrage opportunity is possible.

Next, we will look at some of the institutional and contract specification differences that cause prices to deviate from the theoretical futures price as given by the basic pricing model.

Interim Cash Flows In the derivation of a basic pricing model, it is assumed that no interim cash flows arise because of changes in futures prices (that is, there is no variation margin). As noted earlier, in the absence of initial and variation margins, the theoretical price for the contract is technically the theoretical price for a forward contract that is not marked to market, rather than a futures contract.

In addition, the model assumes implicitly that any dividends or coupon interest payments are paid at the settlement date of the futures contract rather than at any time between initiation of the cash position and settlement of the futures contract. However, we know that interim cash flows for the underlying for financial futures contracts do have interim cash flows. We discuss this further for stock index futures contracts and bond futures contracts in Chapter 20.

Differences in Borrowing and Lending Rates In the formula for the theoretical futures price, it is assumed in the cash-and-carry trade and the reverse cash-and-carry trade that the borrowing rate and lending rate are equal. Typically, however, the borrowing rate is higher than the lending rate. The impact of this inequality is important and easy to quantify.

In the cash-and-carry trade, the theoretical futures price as given by (6.1) becomes

$$\begin{aligned}&\text{Theoretical futures price based on borrowing rate}\\&= \text{Cash market price} + (\text{Cash market price}) \qquad\qquad (6.2)\\&\quad \times (\text{Borrowing rate} - \text{Cash yield})\end{aligned}$$

For the reverse cash-and-carry trade, it becomes

$$\begin{aligned}&\text{Theoretical futures price based on lending rate}\\&= \text{Cash market price} + (\text{Cash market price}) \qquad\qquad (6.3)\\&\quad \times (\text{Lending rate} - \text{Cash yield})\end{aligned}$$

Equations (6.2) and (6.3) together provide a band between which the actual futures price can exist without allowing for an arbitrage profit. Equation (6.2) establishes the upper value for the band while equation (6.3) provides the lower value for the band. For example, assume that the borrowing rate is 6% per year, or 1.5% for three months, while the lending rate is 4% per year, or 1% for three months. Using equation (6.2), the upper value for the theoretical futures price is $99.5 and using equation (6.3) the lower value for the theoretical futures price is $99.

Transaction Costs   The two strategies to exploit any price discrepancies between the cash market and theoretical price for the futures contract requires the arbitrageur to incur transaction costs. In real-world financial markets, the costs of entering into and closing the cash position as well as round-trip transaction costs for the futures contract affect the futures price. As in the case of differential borrowing and lending rates, transaction costs widen the bands for the theoretical futures price.

Short Selling   The reverse cash-and-strategy trade requires the short selling of the underlying. It is assumed in this strategy that the proceeds from the short sale are received and reinvested. In practice, for individual investors, the proceeds are not received, and, in fact, the individual investor is required to deposit margin (securities margin and not futures margin) to short sell. For institutional investors, the underlying may be borrowed, but there is a cost to borrowing. This cost of borrowing can be incorporated into the model by reducing the cash yield on the underlying. For strategies applied to stock index futures, a short sale of the components stocks in the index means that all stocks in the index must be sold simultaneously. This may be difficult to do and therefore would widen the band for the theoretical future price.

Known Deliverable Asset and Settlement Date   In the two strategies to arbitrage discrepancies between the theoretical futures price and the cash market price, it is assumed that (1) only one asset is deliverable and (2) the settlement date occurs at a known, fixed point in the future as explained in Chapter 20.

Deliverable Is a Basket of Securities   Some futures contracts have as the underlying a basket of assets or an index. Stock index futures are the most obvious example and we will describe the problems with pricing in such instances in Chapter 20.

OPTIONS

We now turn to our second derivative contract, an option contract.

Basic Features of Options

An option is a contract in which the option seller grants the option buyer the right to enter into a transaction with the seller to either buy or sell an underlying asset at a specified price on or before a specified date. The specified price is called the strike price or exercise price and the specified date is called the *expiration date*. The option seller grants this right in exchange for a certain amount of money called the option premium or option price.

The option seller is also known as the option writer, while the option buyer is the option holder. The asset that is the subject of the option is called the *underlying*. The underlying can be an individual stock, a stock index, a bond, or even another derivative instrument such as a futures contract. The option writer can grant the option holder one of two rights. If the right is to purchase the underlying, the option is a *call option*. If the right is to sell the underlying, the option is a *put option*.

An option can also be categorized according to when it may be exercised by the buyer. This is referred to as the *exercise style*. A *European option* can only be exercised at the expiration date of the contract. An *American option*, in contrast, can be exercised any time on or before the expiration date. An option that can be exercised before the expiration date but only on specified dates is called a *Bermuda option* or an *Atlantic option*.

The terms of exchange are represented by the contract unit and are standardized for most contracts.

The option holder enters into the contract with an opening transaction. Subsequently, the option holder then has the choice to exercise or to sell the option. The sale of an existing option by the holder is a closing sale.

Let's use an illustration to demonstrate the fundamental option contract. Suppose that Jack buys a call option for $3 (the option price) with the following terms:

1. The underlying is one unit of asset ABC.
2. The exercise price is $100.
3. The expiration date is three months from now, and the option can be exercised anytime up to and including the expiration date (that is, it is an American option).

At any time up to and including the expiration date, Jack can decide to buy from the writer of this option one unit of asset ABC, for which he will pay a price of $100. If it is not beneficial for Jack to exercise the option, he will not; we'll explain shortly how he decides when it will be beneficial. Whether Jack exercises the option or not, the $3 he paid for it will be kept by the option writer. If Jack buys a put option rather than a call option, then he would be able to sell asset ABC to the option writer for a price of $100.

The maximum amount that an option buyer can lose is the option price. The maximum profit that the option writer can realize is the option price.

The option buyer has substantial upside return potential, while the option writer has substantial downside risk. We'll investigate the risk/reward relationship for option positions later in this chapter.

Options, like other financial instruments, may be traded either on an organized exchange or in the over-the-counter (OTC) market. The advantages of an exchange-traded option are as follows. First, the exercise price and expiration date of the contract are standardized. Second, as in the case of futures contracts, the direct link between buyer and seller is severed after the order is executed because of the interchangeability of exchange-traded options. The clearinghouse associated with the exchange where the option trades performs the same function in the options market that it does in the futures market. Finally, the transactions costs are lower for exchange-traded options than for OTC options.

The higher cost of an OTC option reflects the cost of customizing the option for the many situations where a corporation seeking to use an option to manage risk needs to have a tailor-made option because the standardized exchange-traded option does not satisfy its objectives. Some commercial and investment and banking firms act as principals as well as brokers in the OTC options market. OTC options are sometimes referred to as *dealer options*. While an OTC option is less liquid than an exchange-traded option, this is typically not of concern to the user of such an option.

Differences between Options and Futures Contracts

Notice that, unlike in a futures contract, one party to an option contract is not obligated to transact—specifically, the option buyer has the right but not the obligation to transact. The option writer does have the obligation to perform. In the case of a futures contract, both buyer and seller are obligated to perform. Of course, a futures buyer does not pay the seller to accept the obligation, while an option buyer pays the seller an option price.

Consequently, the risk/reward characteristics of the two contracts are also different. In the case of a futures contract, the buyer of the contract realizes a dollar-for-dollar gain when the price of the futures contract increases and suffers a dollar-for-dollar loss when the price of the futures contract drops. The opposite occurs for the seller of a futures contract. Because of this relationship, futures are referred to as having a "linear payoff."

Options do not provide this symmetric risk/reward relationship. The most that the buyer of an option can lose is the option price. While the buyer of an option retains all the potential benefits, the gain is always reduced by the amount of the option price. The maximum profit that the writer may realize is the option price; this is offset against substantial downside risk.

Because of this characteristic, options are referred to as having a *nonlinear payoff*.

The difference in the type of payoff between futures and options is extremely important because market participants can use futures to protect against symmetric risk and options to protect against asymmetric risk.

Risk and Return Characteristics of Options

Here we illustrate the risk and return characteristics of the four basic option positions—buying a call option, selling a call option, buying a put option, and selling a put option. The illustrations assume that each option position is held to the expiration date and not exercised early. Also, to simplify the illustrations, we ignore transactions costs.[2]

Buying Call Options

The purchase of a call option creates a position referred to as a *long call position*. To illustrate this position, assume that there is a call option on Asset X that expires in one month and has an exercise price of $60. The option price is $2. What is the profit or loss for the investor who purchases this call option and holds it to the expiration date?

The profit and loss from the strategy will depend on the price of Asset X at the expiration date. A number of outcomes are possible.

1. If the price of Asset X at the expiration date is less than $60 (the option price), then the investor will not exercise the option. It would be foolish to pay the option writer $60 when Asset X can be purchased in the market at a lower price. In this case, the option buyer loses the entire option price of $2. Notice, however, that this is the maximum loss that the option buyer will realize regardless of how low Asset X's price declines.
2. If Asset X's price is equal to $60 at the expiration date, there is again no economic value in exercising the option. As in the case where the price

---

[2] In addition, the illustrations do not address the cost of financing the purchase of the option price or the opportunity cost of investing the option price. Specifically, the buyer of an option must pay the seller the option price at the time the option is purchased. Thus, the buyer must finance the purchase price of the option or, assuming the purchase price does not have to be borrowed, the buyer loses the income that can be earned by investing the amount of the option price until the option is sold or exercised. In contrast, assuming that the seller does not have to use the option price as margin for the short position or can use an interest-earning asset as security, the seller has the opportunity to earn income from the proceeds of the option sale.

is less than $60, the buyer of the call option will lose the entire option price, $2.

3. If Asset X's price is more than $60 but less than $62 at the expiration date, the option buyer will exercise the option. By exercising, the option buyer can purchase Asset X for $60 (the exercise price) and sell it in the market for the higher price. Suppose, for example, that Asset X's price is $61 at the expiration date. The buyer of the call option will realize a $1 gain by exercising the option. Of course, the cost of purchasing the call option was $2, so $1 is lost on this position. By failing to exercise the option, the investor loses $2 instead of only $1.

4. If Asset X's price at the expiration date is equal to $62, the investor will exercise the option. In this case, the investor breaks even, realizing a gain of $2 that offsets the cost of the option, $2.

5. If Asset X's price at the expiration date is more than $62, the investor will exercise the option and realize a profit. For example, if the price is $70, exercising the option will generate a profit on Asset X of $10. Reducing this gain by the cost of the option, $2, the investor will realize a net profit from this position of $8.

Figure 6.2 shows in graph form the profit and loss for the buyer of the hypothetical call option. While the break-even point and the loss will depend on the option price and the exercise price, the profile shown in Exhibit 6.2 will hold for all buyers of call options. The shape indicates that the maximum loss is the option price and that there is substantial upside potential.

FIGURE 6.2   Profits and Losses of a Call Option to Buy the Stock at $60. The investor Pays $2 for this Call Option.

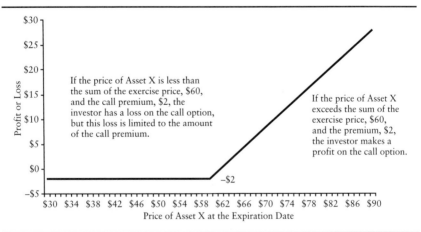

Writing (Selling) Call Options

The writer of a call option is said to be in a *short call position*. To illustrate the option seller's (i.e., writer's) position, we use the same call option we used to illustrate buying a call option. The profit and loss profile of the short call position (that is, the position of the call option writer) is the mirror image of the profit and loss profile of the long call position (the position of the call option buyer). That is, the profit of the short call position for any given price for Asset X at the expiration date is the same as the loss of the long call position. Consequently, the maximum profit that the short call position can produce is the option price. The maximum loss is not limited because it is the highest price reached by Asset X on or before the expiration date, less the option price; this price can be indefinitely high. Figure 6.3 shows the profit/loss profile for a short call position.

Buying Put Options

The buying of a put option creates a financial position referred to as a *long put position*. To illustrate this position, we assume a hypothetical put option on one unit of Asset X with one month to maturity and an exercise price of $100. Assume the put option is selling for $2 and the price of Asset X at the expiration date is $60. The profit or loss for this position at the expiration date depends on the market price of Asset X. The possible outcomes are:

FIGURE 6.3 Profits and Losses on the Writing of a Call Option that Allows the Call Option Buyer to Buy the Stock at $60. The Call Writer Receives $2 for this Option.

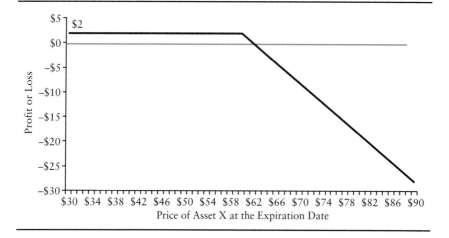

1. If Asset X's price is greater than $60, the buyer of the put option will not exercise it because exercising would mean selling Asset X to the writer for a price that is less than the market price. A loss of $2 (the option price) will result in this case from buying the put option. Once again, the option price represents the maximum loss to which the buyer of the put option is exposed.

2. If the price of Asset X at expiration is equal to $60, the put will not be exercised, leaving the put buyer with a loss equal to the option price of $2.

3. Any price for Asset X that is less than $60 but greater than $58 will result in a loss; exercising the put option, however, limits the loss to less than the option price of $2. For example, suppose that the price is $59 at the expiration date. By exercising the option, the option buyer will realize a loss of $1. This is because the buyer of the put option can sell Asset X, purchased in the market for $59, to the writer for $60, realizing a gain of $1. Deducting the $2 cost of the option results in a loss of $1.

4. At a $58 price for Asset X at the expiration date, the put buyer will break even. The investor will realize a gain of $2 by selling Asset X to the writer of the option for $60, offsetting the cost of the option ($2).

5. If Asset X's price is below $58 at the expiration date, the long put position (the put buyer) will realize a profit. For example, suppose the price falls at expiration to $46. The long put position will produce a profit of $12: a gain of $14 for exercising the put option less the $2 option price.

The profit and loss profile for the long put position is shown in graphical form in Figure 6.4. As with all long option positions, the loss is limited to the option price. The profit potential, however, is substantial: The theoretical maximum profit is generated if Asset X's price falls to zero. Contrast this profit potential with that of the buyer of a call option. The theoretical maximum profit for a call buyer cannot be determined beforehand because it depends on the highest price that can be reached by Asset X before or at the option expiration date.

Writing (Selling) Put Options

Writing a put option creates a position referred to as a *short put position*. The profit and loss profile for a short put option is the mirror image of the long put option. The maximum profit from this position is the option price. The theoretical maximum loss can be substantial should the price of the underlying fall; at the extreme, if the price were to fall all the way to zero,

FIGURE 6.4 Profits and Losses of a Put Option to Sell the Stock at $60. The Investor Pays $2 for this Put Option.

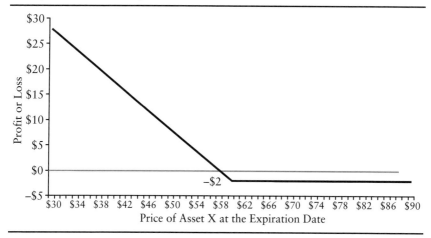

FIGURE 6.5 Profits and Losses on the Writing of a Put Option that Allows the Put Option Buyer to Sell the Stock at $60. The Put Writer Receives $2 for this Option.

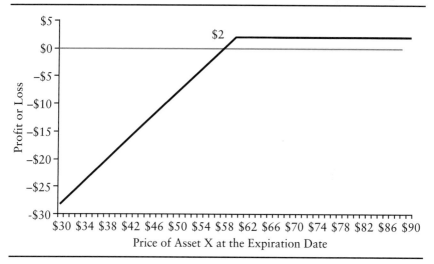

the loss would be as large as the exercise price less the option price. Figure 6.5 graphically depicts this profit and loss profile.

To summarize, buying calls or selling puts allows the investor to gain if the price of the underlying rises. Selling calls and buying puts allows the investor to gain if the price of the underlying falls.

Basic Components of the Option Price

The option price is a reflection of the option's *intrinsic value* and any additional amount over its intrinsic value. The premium over intrinsic value is often referred to as the *time premium*.

The Option Price

As with futures and forward contracts, the theoretical price of an option is also derived based on arbitrage arguments. However, as will be explained, the pricing of options is not as simple as the pricing of futures and forward contracts.

Basic Components of the Option Price

The theoretical price of an option is made up of two components: the intrinsic value and a premium over intrinsic value.

Intrinsic Value   The *intrinsic value* is the option's economic value if it is exercised immediately. If no positive economic value would result from exercising immediately, the intrinsic value is zero. An option's intrinsic value is easy to compute given the price of the underlying and the strike price.

For a call option, the intrinsic value is the difference between the current market price of the underlying and the strike price. If that difference is positive, then the intrinsic value equals that difference; if the difference is zero or negative, then the intrinsic value is equal to zero. For example, if the strike price for a call option is $100 and the current price of the underlying is $109, the intrinsic value is $9. That is, an option buyer exercising the option and simultaneously selling the underlying would realize $109 from the sale of the underlying, which would be covered by acquiring the underlying from the option writer for $100, thereby netting a $9 gain.

An option that has a positive intrinsic value is said to be *in-the-money*. When the strike price of a call option exceeds the underlying's market price, it has no intrinsic value and is said to be *out-of-the-money*. An option for which the strike price is equal to the underlying's market price is said to be *at-the-money*. Both at-the-money and out-of-the-money options have intrinsic values of zero because it is not profitable to exercise them. Our call option with a strike price of $100 would be (1) in the money when the market price of the underlying is more than $100; (2) out of the money when the market price of the underlying is less than $100, and (3) at the money when the market price of the underlying is equal to $100.

For a put option, the intrinsic value is equal to the amount by which the underlying's market price is below the strike price. For example, if the strike price of a put option is $100 and the market price of the underlying is $95, the intrinsic value is $5. That is, the buyer of the put option who simultaneously buys the underlying and exercises the put option will net $5 by exercising. The underlying will be sold to the writer for $100 and purchased in the market for $95. With a strike price of $100, the put option would be (1) in the money when the underlying's market price is less than $100; (2) out of the money when the underlying's market price exceeds $100; and (3) at the money when the underlying's market price is equal to $100.

Time Premium   The *time premium* of an option, also referred to as the *time value of the option*, is the amount by which the option's market price exceeds its intrinsic value. It is the expectation of the option buyer that at some time prior to the expiration date changes in the market price of the underlying will increase the value of the rights conveyed by the option. Because of this expectation, the option buyer is willing to pay a premium above the intrinsic value. For example, if the price of a call option with a strike price of $100 is $12 when the underlying's market price is $104, the time premium of this option is $8 ($12 minus its intrinsic value of $4). Had the underlying's market price been $95 instead of $104, then the time premium of this option would be the entire $12 because the option has no intrinsic value. All other things being equal, the time premium of an option will increase with the amount of time remaining to expiration.

An option buyer has two ways to realize the value of an option position. The first way is by exercising the option. The second way is to sell the option in the market. In the first example above, selling the call for $12 is preferable to exercising, because the exercise will realize only $4 (the intrinsic value), but the sale will realize $12. As this example shows, exercise causes the immediate loss of any time premium. It is important to note that there are circumstances under which an option may be exercised prior to the expiration date. These circumstances depend on whether the total proceeds at the expiration date would be greater by holding the option or exercising and reinvesting any received cash proceeds until the expiration date.

Put-Call Parity Relationship

For a European put and a European call option with the same underlying, strike price, and expiration date, there is a relationship between the price of a call option, the price of a put option, the price of the underlying, and the strike price. This relationship is known as the *put-call parity relationship*. The relationship is:

Put option price – Call option price = Present value of strike price + Present value of cash distribution – Price of underlying

Factors that Influence the Option Price

The factors that affect the price of an option include:

- Market price of the underlying.
- Strike price of the option.
- Time to expiration of the option.
- Expected volatility of the underlying over the life of the option.
- Short-term, risk-free interest rate over the life of the option.
- Anticipated cash payments on the underlying over the life of the option.

The impact of each of these factors may depend on whether (1) the option is a call or a put, and (2) the option is an American option or a European option. Table 6.1 summarizes how each of the six factors listed above affects the price of a put and call option. Here, we briefly explain why the factors have the particular effects.

Market Price of the Underlying Asset   The option price will change as the price of the underlying changes. For a call option, as the underlying's price increases (all other factors being constant), the option price increases. The opposite holds for a put option: As the price of the underlying increases, the price of a put option decreases.

Strike Price   The strike price is fixed for the life of the option. All other factors being equal, the lower the strike price, the higher the price for a call option. For put options, the higher the strike price, the higher the option price.

TABLE 6.1   Summary of Factors that Affect the Price of an Option

Factor	Effect of an Increase of Factor On	
	Call Price	Put Price
Market price of underlying	Increase	Decrease
Strike price	Decrease	Increase
Time to expiration of option	Increase	Increase
Expected volatility	Increase	Increase
Short-term, risk-free interest rate	Increase	Decrease
Anticipated cash payments	Decrease	Increase

Time to Expiration of the Option After the expiration date, an option has no value. All other factors being equal, the longer the time to expiration of the option, the higher the option price. This is because, as the time to expiration decreases, less time remains for the underlying's price to rise (for a call buyer) or fall (for a put buyer), and therefore the probability of a favorable price movement decreases. Consequently, as the time remaining until expiration decreases, the option price approaches its intrinsic value.

Expected Volatility of the Underlying over the Life of the Option All other factors being equal, the greater the expected volatility (as measured by the standard deviation or variance) of the underlying, the more the option buyer would be willing to pay for the option, and the more an option writer would demand for it. This occurs because the greater the expected volatility, the greater the probability that the movement of the underlying will change so as to benefit the option buyer at some time before expiration.

Short-Term, Risk-Free Interest Rate over the Life of the Option Buying the underlying requires an investment of funds. Buying an option on the same quantity of the underlying makes the difference between the underlying's price and the option price available for investment at an interest rate at least as high as the risk-free rate. Consequently, all other factors being constant, the higher the short-term, risk-free interest rate, the greater the cost of buying the underlying and carrying it to the expiration date of the call option. Hence, the higher the short-term, risk-free interest rate, the more attractive the call option will be relative to the direct purchase of the underlying. As a result, the higher the short-term, risk-free interest rate, the greater the price of a call option.

Anticipated Cash Payments on the Underlying over the Life of the Option Cash payments on the underlying tend to decrease the price of a call option because the cash payments make it more attractive to hold the underlying than to hold the option. For put options, cash payments on the underlying tend to increase the price.

Option Pricing Models

Earlier in this chapter, it was explained how the theoretical price of a futures contract and forward contract can be determined on the basis of arbitrage arguments. An option pricing model uses a set of assumptions and arbitrage arguments to derive a theoretical price for an option. Deriving a theoretical option price is much more complicated than deriving a theoretical futures or forward price because the option price depends on the expected volatility of the underlying over the life of the option.

Several models have been developed to determine the theoretical price of an option. The most popular one was developed by Fischer Black and Myron Scholes (1973) for valuing European call options on common stock. Because of the technical nature of this model, we describe it in the appendix to this chapter.

SWAPS

A *swap* is an agreement whereby two parties (called *counterparties*) agree to exchange periodic payments. The dollar amount of the payments exchanged is based on some predetermined dollar principal, which is called the *notional principal amount* or simply *notional amount*. The dollar amount each counterparty pays to the other is the agreed-upon periodic rate times the notional amount. The only dollars that are exchanged between the parties are the agreed-upon payments, not the notional amount.

A swap is an over-the-counter contract. Hence, the counterparties to a swap are exposed to counterparty risk.

Types of Swaps

The three types of swaps typically used by nonfinance corporations are interest rate swaps, currency swaps, commodity swaps, and credit default swaps. We illustrate these types of swaps in this section.

Interest Rate Swap

In an *interest rate swap*, the counterparties swap payments in the same currency based on an interest rate. For example, one of the counterparties can pay a fixed interest rate and the other party a floating interest rate. The floating interest rate is commonly referred to as the *reference rate*.

For example, suppose the counterparties to a swap agreement are Farm Equip Corporation (a manufacturing firm) and PNC Bank. The notional amount of this swap is $100 million and the term of the swap is five years. Every year for the next five years, Farm Equip Corporation agrees to pay PNC Bank 9% per year, while PNC Bank agrees to pay Farm Equip Corporation the one-year LIBOR as the reference rate. This means that every year, Farm Equip Corporation will pay $9 million (9% times $100 million) to PNC Bank. The amount PNC Bank will pay Farm Equip Corporation depends on LIBOR. For example, one-year LIBOR is 6%, PNC Bank will pay Farm Equip Corporation $6 million (6% times $100 million).

It is too early in this book to appreciate the motivation for the treasurer of Farm Equipment Corporation to use an interest rate swap. The motivation will be seen when we discuss financing techniques.

Currency Swaps

In a *currency swap*, two parties agree to swap payments based on different currencies. To illustrate a currency swap, suppose two counterparties are the High Quality Electronics Corporation (a U.S. manufacturing firm) and Citibank. The notional amount is $100 million and its Swiss franc (SF) equivalent at the time the contract was entered into is SF 127 million. The swap term is eight years. Every year for the next eight years the U.S. manufacturing firm agrees to pay Citibank Swiss francs equal to 5% of the Swiss franc notional amount, or SF 6.35 million. In turn, Citibank agrees to pay High Quality Electronics 7% of the U.S. notional principal amount of $100 million, or $7 million.

Again, the motivation for the management of High Quality Electronics Corporation for using a currency swap is difficult to appreciate because we have not covered how a firm finances itself. Currency swaps are used by corporations to raise funds outside of their home currency and then swap the payments into their home currency. This allows a corporation to eliminate currency risk (i.e., unfavorable exchange rate or currency movements) when borrowing outside of its domestic currency.

Commodity Swaps

In a commodity swap, the exchange of payments by the counterparties is based on the value of a particular physical commodity. Physical commodities include precious metals, base metals, energy stores (such as natural gas or crude oil), and food (including pork bellies, wheat, and cattle). Most commodity swaps involve oil.

For example, suppose that the two counterparties to this swap agreement are Comfort Airlines Company, a commercial airline, and Prebon Energy (an energy broker). The notional amount of the contract is 1 million barrels of crude oil each year and the contract is for three years. The swap price is $19 per barrel. Each year for the next three years, Comfort Airlines Company agrees to buy 1 million barrels of crude oil for $19 per barrel. So, each year Comfort Airlines Company pays $19 million to Prebon Energy ($19 per barrel times 1 million barrels) and receives 1 million barrels of crude oil.

The motivation for Comfort Airlines of using the commodity swap is that it allows the company to lock-in a price for 1 million barrels of crude oil at $19 per barrel regardless of how high crude oil's price increases over the next three years.

Credit Default Swaps

A *credit default swap* (CDS) is an OTC derivative that permits the buying and selling of credit protection against particular types of events that can adversely affect the credit quality of a bond such as the default of the borrower. Although it is referred to as a "swap," it does not follow the general characteristics of a swap described earlier. There are two parties: the *credit protection buyer* and *credit protection seller*. Over the life of the CDS, the protection buyer agrees to pay the protection seller a payment at specified dates to insure against the impairment of the debt of a *reference entity* due to a credit-related event. The reference entity is a specific issuer, say, Ford Motor Company. The specific credit-related events are identified in the contract that will trigger a payment by the credit protection seller to the credit protection buyer are referred to as *credit events*. If a credit event does occur, the credit protection buyer only makes a payment up to the credit event date and makes no further payment. At this time, the protection buyer is obligated to fulfill its obligation. The contract will call for the protection seller to compensate for the loss in the value of the debt obligation. The specific method for compensating the protection buyer is not important at this time for this brief description of this derivative contract.

Interpretation of a Swap

If we look carefully at a swap, we can see that it is not a new derivative instrument. Rather, it can be decomposed into a package of derivative instruments that we have already discussed. To see this, consider our first illustrative swap.

Every year for the next five years Farm Equip Corporation agrees to pay PNC Bank 9%, PNC Bank agrees to pay Farm Equip Corporation the reference rate, one-year LIBOR. Since the notional amount is $100 million, Farm Equip Corporation Manufacturing agrees to pay $9 million. Alternatively, we can rephrase this agreement as follows: Every year for the next five years, PNC Bank agrees to deliver something (one-year LIBOR) and to accept payment of $9 million. Looked at in this way, the counterparties are entering into multiple forward contracts: One party is agreeing to deliver something at some time in the future, and the other party is agreeing to accept delivery. The reason we say that there are multiple forward contracts is that the agreement calls for making the exchange each year for the next five years.

While a swap may be nothing more than a package of forward contracts, it is not a redundant contract for several reasons. First, in many markets where there are forward and futures contracts, the longest maturity does not extend out as far as that of a typical swap. Second, a swap is a more transactionally efficient instrument. By this we mean that in one transaction an entity can effectively establish a payoff equivalent to a package of forward contracts. The forward contracts would each have to be negotiated separately. Third, the liquidity of certain types of swaps has grown since the inception of swaps in 1981; some swaps now are more liquid than many forward contracts, particularly long-dated (i.e., long-term) forward contracts.

CAP AND FLOOR AGREEMENTS

There are agreements available in the financial market whereby one party, for a fee (referred to as a premium), agrees to compensate the other if a designated reference (such as a specified interest rate) is different from a predetermined level. The party that will receive payment if the designated reference differs from a predetermined level and pays a premium to enter into the agreement is called the buyer. The party that agrees to make the payment if the designated reference differs from a predetermined level is called the seller.

When the seller agrees to pay the buyer if the designated reference exceeds a predetermined level, the agreement is referred to as a *cap*. The agreement is referred to as a *floor* when the seller agrees to pay the buyer if a designated reference falls below a predetermined level.

In a typical cap or floor, the designated reference is either an interest rate or commodity price. The predetermined level is called the *exercise value*. As with a swap, a cap and a floor have a notional amount. Only the buyer of a cap or a floor is exposed to counterparty risk.

In general, the payment made by the seller of the cap to the buyer on a specific date is determined by the relationship between the designated reference and the exercise value. If the former is greater than the latter, then the seller pays the buyer an amount delivered as follows:

Notional amount × [Actual value of designated reference − Exercise value]

If the designated reference is less than or equal to the exercise value, then the seller pays the buyer nothing.

For a floor, the payment made by the seller to the buyer on a specific date is determined as follows. If the designated reference is less than the exercise value, then the seller pays the buyer an amount delivered as follows:

Notional amount × [Exercise value − Actual value of designated reference]

If the designated reference is greater than or equal to the exercise value, then the seller pays the buyer nothing.

The following example illustrates how a cap works. Suppose that the FPK Bookbinders Company enters into a five-year cap agreement with Fleet Bank with a notional amount of $50 million. The terms of the cap specify that if one-year LIBOR exceeds 8% on December 31 each year for the next five years, Fleet Bank (the seller of the cap) will pay FPK Bookbinders Company the difference between 8% (the exercise value) and LIBOR (the designated reference). The fee or premium FPK Bookbinders Company agrees to pay Fleet Bank each year is $200,000.

The payment made by Fleet Bank to FPK Bookbinders Company on December 31 for the next five years based on LIBOR on that date will be as follows. If one-year LIBOR is greater than 8%, then Fleet Bank pays $50 million × [Actual value of LIBOR − 8%]. If LIBOR is less than or equal to 8%, then Fleet Bank pays nothing.

So, for example, if LIBOR on December 31 of the first year of the cap is 10%, Fleet Bank pays FPK Bookbinders Company $1 million as shown here:

$$\$50 \text{ million} \times [10\% - 8\%] = \$1 \text{ million}$$

Interpretation of a Cap and Floor

In a cap or floor, the buyer pays a fee, which represents the maximum amount that the buyer can lose and the maximum amount that the seller of the agreement can gain. The only party that is required to perform is the seller. The buyer of a cap benefits if the designated reference rises above the exercise value because the seller must compensate the buyer. The exercise value can be a reference interest rate or an exchange rate, for example. The buyer of a floor benefits if the designated reference falls below the exercise value because the seller must compensate the buyer.

In essence, the payoff of these contracts is the same as that of an option. A call option buyer pays a fee and benefits if the value of the option's underlying (or equivalently, designated reference) is higher than the exercise price at the expiration date. A cap has a similar payoff. A put option buyer pays a fee and benefits if the value of the option's underlying (or equivalently, designated reference) is less than the exercise price at the expiration date. A floor has a similar payoff. An option seller is only entitled to the option price. The seller of a cap or floor is only entitled to the fee.

SUMMARY

The traditional purpose of derivative instruments is to provide an important opportunity to manage against the risk of adverse future price, exchange rate, or interest rate movements. The two basic derivative instruments are futures and forward contracts and options contracts.

Futures contracts are creations of exchanges, which require initial margin from parties. Each day, positions are marked to market. Additional (variation) margin is required if the equity in the position falls below the maintenance margin. The clearinghouse guarantees that the parties to the futures contract will satisfy their obligations. A forward contract differs in several important ways from a futures contract. In contrast to a futures contract, the parties to a forward contract are exposed to the risk that the other party to the contract will fail to perform. The positions of the parties are not necessarily marked to market, so there are no interim cash flows associated with a forward contract. Finally, unwinding a position in a forward contract may be difficult. A buyer (seller) of a futures contract realizes a profit if the futures price increases (decreases). The buyer (seller) of a futures contract realizes a loss if the futures price decreases (increases).

For futures and forward contracts, the theoretical price can be derived using arbitrage arguments. Specifically, a cash-and-carry trade can be implemented to capture the arbitrage profit for an overpriced futures or forward contract while a reverse cash-and-carry trade can be implemented to capture the arbitrage profit for an underpriced futures for forward contract. The basic model states that the theoretical futures price is equal to the cash market price plus the net financing cost. The net financing cost, also called the cost of carry, is the difference between the financing cost and the cash yield on the underlying.

An option grants the buyer of the option the right either to buy from (in the case of a call option) or to sell to (in the case of a put option) the seller (writer) of the option the underlying at a stated price called the exercise (strike) price by a stated date called the expiration date. The price that the option buyer pays to the writer of the option is called the option price or option premium. An American option allows the option buyer to exercise the option at any time up to and including the expiration date; a European option may be exercised only at the expiration date. The buyer of an option cannot realize a loss greater than the option price, and has all the upside potential. By contrast, the maximum gain that the writer (seller) of an option can realize is the option price; the writer is exposed to all the downside risk.

The two components of the price of an option are the intrinsic value and the time premium. The former is the economic value of the option if it is exercised immediately, while the latter is the amount by which the option price exceeds the intrinsic value. The option price is affected by six factors: (1) the market price of the underlying; (2) the strike price of the option; (3) the time remaining to the expiration of the option; (4) the expected volatility of the underlying as measured by the standard deviation; (5) the short-term, risk-free interest rate over the life of the option; and (6) the anticipated cash payments on the underlying. It is the uncertainty about the expected volatility of the underlying that makes valuing options more complicated than valuing futures and forward contracts. There are various models for determining the theoretical price of an option, the most well known being the Black-Scholes model.

In a swap, the counterparties agree to exchange periodic payments. The dollar amount of the payments exchanged is based on the notional principal amount. Swaps typically used by nonfinance companies are interest rate swaps, currency swaps, and commodity swaps. A swap has the risk/return profile of a package of forward contracts.

A cap is an agreement whereby the seller agrees to pay the buyer when a designated reference exceeds a predetermined level (the exercise value). A floor is an agreement whereby the seller agrees to pay the buyer when a designated reference is less than a predetermined level (the exercise value). The designated reference could be a specific interest rate or a commodity price. A cap is equivalent to a package of call options; a floor is equivalent to a package of put options.

APPENDIX: BLACK-SCHOLES OPTION PRICING MODEL

In the chapter, we explained the basic factors that affect the *value of an option*, also referred to as the *option price*. The option price is a reflection of the option's intrinsic value and any additional amount over its intrinsic value, called the time premium. In this appendix, we explain how the theoretical price of an option can be determined using a well-known financial model, the *Black-Scholes option pricing model*.[3] This model is viewed by many in the financial community as one of the path-breaking innovations in financial management and analysis. We do not provide the details with

---

[3] See Black and Scholes (1973).

respect to how the model was derived by its developers, Myron Scholes and Fischer Black. Rather, we will set forth the basics of the model.[4]

Theoretical Upper and Lower Values of an Option

By examining the features of an option and the value of its underlying asset, we can determine the highest and lowest values that an option may take on. These values are referred to as theoretical boundary conditions. The theoretical boundary conditions for the price of an option can be derived using simple economic arguments. For example, it can be shown that the minimum price for an American call option (i.e., an option that can be exercised at any time up to and including the expiration date) is its intrinsic value. That is,

Call option price ≥ maximum[0, Price of underlying – Strike price]

This expression says that the price of a call option will be greater than or equal to either the difference between the current price of the underlying asset and the strike price (intrinsic value) or zero, whichever is higher. Why zero? Because the option holder can simply choose not to exercise the option.

The boundary conditions can be "tightened" by using arbitrage arguments coupled with certain assumptions about the cash distribution of the underlying asset. For example, when the underlying is common stock, the cash distribution is the dividend payment.

The extreme case is an option pricing model that uses a set of assumptions to derive a single theoretical price for an option, rather than a range. As we shall see below, deriving a theoretical option price is complicated because the option price depends on the expected price volatility of the value of the underlying asset over the life of the option.

Black-Scholes Option Pricing Model

Several models have been developed to determine the theoretical value of an option. The most popular one was developed by Fischer Black and Myron Scholes in 1973 for valuing European call options on common stock. Recall that a European option is one that cannot be exercised prior to the expiration date.

Basically, the idea behind the arbitrage argument in deriving the option pricing model is that if the payoff from owning a call option can be replicated by (1) purchasing the stock underlying the call option; and (2) bor-

---

[4] Since the introduction of the Black-Scholes option pricing, there have been numerous modifications and extensions of the model. We will not review these in this appendix.

rowing funds, then the price of the option will be (at most) the cost of creating the payoff replicating strategy.

By imposing certain assumptions (to be discussed later) and using arbitrage arguments, the Black-Scholes option pricing model computes the fair (or theoretical) price of a European call option on a nondividend-paying stock with the following equation:

$$C = SN(d_1) - Xe^{-rt}N(d_2)$$

where

$$d_1 = \frac{\ln(S/K) + (r + 0.5s^2)t}{s\sqrt{t}}$$

$d_2 = d_1 - s\sqrt{t}$

ln = natural logarithm
C = call option price
S = price of the underlying asset
K = strike price
r = short-term risk-free rate
e = 2.718 (natural antilog of 1)
t = time remaining to the expiration date (measured as a fraction of a year)
s = standard deviation of the value of the underlying asset
N(.) = the cumulative probability density[5]

Notice that five of the factors that we indicated in the chapter that influence the price of an option are included in the formula. Anticipated cash dividends are not included because the model is for a nondividend-paying stock. In the Black-Scholes option pricing model, the direction of the influence of each of these factors is the same as stated in the chapter. Four of the factors—strike price, price of underlying asset, time to expiration, and risk-free rate—are easily observed. The standard deviation of the price of the underlying asset must be estimated.

The option price derived from the Black-Scholes option pricing model is "fair" in the sense that if any other price existed, it would be possible to earn riskless arbitrage profits by taking an offsetting position in the underlying asset. That is, if the price of the call option in the market is higher than

---

[5] The value for N(.) is obtained from a normal distribution function that is tabulated in most statistics textbooks or from spreadsheets that have this built-in function.

that derived from the Black-Scholes option pricing model, an investor could sell the call option and buy a certain quantity of the underlying asset. If the reverse is true, that is, the market price of the call option is less than the "fair" price derived from the model, the investor could buy the call option and sell short a certain amount of the underlying asset. This process of hedging by taking a position in the underlying asset allows the investor to lock in the riskless arbitrage profit.

To illustrate the Black-Scholes option pricing formula, assume the following values:

Strike price	= $45
Time remaining to expiration	= 183 days
Stock price	= $47
Expected price volatility	= standard deviation = 25%
Risk-free rate	= 10%

In terms of the values in the formula,

$S = \$47$
$K = \$45$
$t = 0.5$ (183 days/365, rounded)
$s = 0.25$
$r = 0.10$

Substituting these values into the Black-Scholes option pricing model, we get

$$d_1 = \frac{\ln(\$47 \,/\, \$45) + [0.10 + 0.5(0.25)^2]0.5}{0.25\sqrt{0.5}} = 0.6172$$

$$d_2 = 0.6172 - 0.25\sqrt{0.5} = 0.4404$$

From a normal distribution table,

$$N(0.6172) = 0.7315 \text{ and } N(0.4404) = 0.6702$$

Then

$$C = \$47(0.7315) - \$45(e^{-(0.10)(0.5)})(0.6702) = \$5.69$$

Let's look at what happens to the theoretical option price if the expected price volatility is 40% rather than 25%. Then

$$d_1 = \frac{\ln(\$47 \: / \: \$45) + [0.10 + 0.5(0.40)^2]0.5}{0.40\sqrt{0.5}} = 0.4719$$

$$d_2 = 0.4719 - 0.40\sqrt{0.5} = 0.1891$$

From a normal distribution table,

$$N(0.4719) = 0.6815 \text{ and } N(0.1891) = 0.5750$$

Then

$$C = \$47(0.6815) - \$45(e^{-(0.10)(0.5)})(0.5750) = \$7.42$$

Notice that the higher the assumed expected price volatility of the underlying asset, the higher the price of a call option.

In Figure 6.A1, we show the option value as calculated from the Black-Scholes option pricing model for different assumptions concerning (1) the standard deviation, (2) the risk-free rate, and (3) the time remaining to expiration. Notice that the option price varies directly with all three variables. That is, (1) the lower (higher) the volatility, the lower (higher) the option price; (2) the lower (higher) the risk-free rate, the lower (higher) the option price; and, (3) the shorter (longer) the time remaining to expiration, the lower (higher) the option price. All of this agrees with what we stated in this chapter about the effect of a change in one of the factors on the price of a call option.

Value of a Put Option

How do we determine the value of a put option? As explained in the chapter, there is a relationship among the price of the underlying asset, the call option price, and the put option price. This relationship, called the *put-call parity relationship*, is given below for European options:

Put option price = Call option price + Present value of strike price
− Price of the underlying asset

Or, using the notation we used previously,

$$P = C + Xe^{-rt} - S$$

If there are cash distributions on the underlying asset (e.g., dividends), these would be added to the right-hand side of this equation. The relationship is approximately true for American options.

FIGURE 6.A1   Comparison of Black-Scholes Call Option Prices Varying One Factor at a Time

Base case:

Strike price = $45   Current stock price = $47

Time remaining to expiration = 183 days   Risk-free rate = 10%

Expected price volatility = standard deviation = 25%

(a) Holding All Factors Constant Except Expected Price Volatility

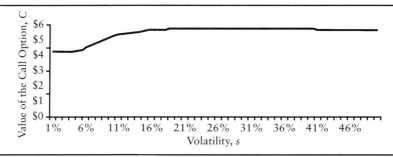

(b) Holding All Factors Constant Except for the Risk-Free Rate

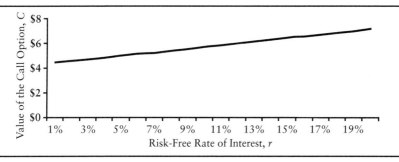

(c) Holding All Factors Constant Except for the Time Remaining to Expiration

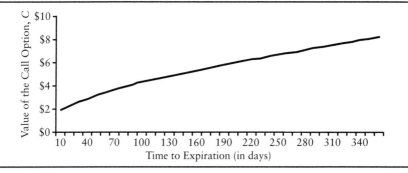

If this relationship does not hold, arbitrage opportunities exist. That is, portfolios consisting of long and short positions in the underlying asset and related options that provide an extra return with (practical) certainty will exist.

If we can calculate the fair value of a call option, the fair value of a put with the same strike price and expiration on the same stock can be calculated from the put-call parity relationship.

Black-Scholes Option Pricing Model Assumptions

The relation between the value of an option and the five factors in the Black-Scholes model are summarized in Table 6.A2. The Black-Scholes option pricing model is based on several restrictive assumptions. These assumptions were necessary to develop the hedge to realize riskless arbitrage profits if the market price of the call option deviates from the value obtained from the model.

The Option is European   The Black-Scholes option pricing model assumes that the call option is a European call option. Because the model is for a nondividend-paying stock, early exercise of an option will not be economical because by selling rather than exercising the call option, the option holder can recoup the option's time premium.[6]

Variance of the Price of the Underlying   The Black-Scholes model assumes that the variance of the price of the underlying asset is (1) constant over the life of the option and (2) known with certainty.

TABLE 6.A2   Relation Between Call and Put Option Features and the Value of an Option

Factor	Description	Relation to Call Option Value	Relation to Put Option Value
S	Value of the underlying asset, S	Direct relation	Inverse relation
X	Exercise price, X	Inverse relation	Direct relation
r	Time value of money, r	Direct relation	Inverse relation
s	Volatility of the value of the underlying asset, s	Direct relation	Direct relation
t	Time to maturity, t	Direct relation	Direct relation

---

[6] An option pricing model called the "lattice model" can easily handle American call options. For a description of this model, see Cox, Ross, and Rubinstein (1979).

Stochastic Process Generating Stock Prices   To derive an option pricing model, an assumption is needed about the way the price of the underlying asset may change over time. The Black-Scholes model is based on the assumption that the price of the underlying asset is generated by one kind of stochastic (random) process called a "diffusion process." In a diffusion process, the underlying asset's price can take on any positive value, but when it moves from one price to another, it must take on all values in between. That is, the stock price does not jump from one stock price to another, skipping over interim prices.

Risk-Free Rate   In deriving the Black-Scholes option pricing model, two assumptions are made about the risk-free rate. First, it is assumed that the interest rates for borrowing and lending are the same. Second, it is assumed that the interest rate was constant and known over the life of the option.

Dividends   The original Black-Scholes option pricing model is for a non-dividend-paying stock. In the case of a dividend-paying stock, it may be advantageous for the holder of the call option to exercise the option early. To understand why, suppose that a stock pays a dividend such that if the call option is exercised, dividends would be received prior to the option's expiration date. If the dividends plus the accrued interest earned from investing the dividends from the time they are received until the expiration date are greater than the option's time premium, then it would be optimal to exercise the option. In the case where dividends are not known with certainty, it will not be possible to develop a model using arbitrage arguments.[7]

Taxes and Transaction Costs   The Black-Scholes option pricing model ignores taxes and transaction costs. The model can be modified to account for taxes, but the problem is that there is not just one tax rate. Transaction costs include both commissions and the bid-ask spreads for the underlying asset and the option, as well as other costs associated with trading options.

REFERENCES

Black, F., and Scholes, M. (1973). Pricing of options and corporate liabilities. *Journal of Political Economy* 81, no. 3: 637–654.

Cox, J., Ross, S.A, and Rubinstein, M. (1979). Option pricing: A simplified approach. *Journal of Financial Economics* 7: 229–263.

[7] In the case of known dividends, a shortcut to adjust the Black-Scholes model is to reduce the stock price by the present value of the dividends. Fischer Black suggested an approximation technique to value a call option for a dividend-paying stock. A more accurate model for pricing call options in the case of known dividends has been developed by several researchers.

CHAPTER 7

Asset Valuation: Basic Bond and Stock Valuation Models

Valuation is the process of determining the fair value of a financial asset. The process is also referred to as "valuing" or "pricing" a financial asset. The fundamental principle of valuation is that the value of any financial asset is the present value of the expected cash flows. This principle applies regardless of the financial asset. Thus, the valuation of a financial asset involves the following three steps: (1) estimate the expected cash flows; (2) determine the appropriate interest rate or interest rates that should be used to discount the cash flows; and (3) calculate the present value of the expected cash flows using the interest rate or interest rates.

In this chapter, we apply the principles of valuation to value bonds and common stock. In the appendix, we explain how convertible bonds are valued.

It is important to remember that the user of any valuation model is exposed to *modeling risk*. This is the risk that the output of the model is incorrect because the assumptions on which it is based are incorrect. Consequently, it is imperative that the results of a valuation model be stress-tested for modeling risk by altering the assumptions.

VALUING BONDS

Valuation begins with the estimation of the cash flows. Cash flow is simply the cash that is expected to be received at some time from an investment. In the case of a bond, the cash flows consist of interest and principal repayment. It does not make any difference whether the cash flow is interest income or repayment of principal. The cash flows of a security are the collection of each period's cash flow. In the case of a simple bond that does not grant the issuer or the bondholder the option to alter the maturity date or exchange the bond for another type of financial instrument, the cash flows are easy to determine assuming that the issuer does not default. Such bonds that do not contain such option-type features are referred to as *option-free bonds*. The cash flows for an option-free bond is the periodic coupon payments and the principal payments at the bond's maturity date. Because most bonds issued in the United States pay interest, referred to as the coupon payment, every six month, the cash flows for an option-free bond are the semiannual coupon payment and the principal payment at the maturity date.

Bond valuation becomes more difficult when either the issuer or bondholder have an option to either alter the maturity of the bond or to convert the bond into another security. Bonds that have one or more such options are referred to generically as *bonds with embedded options*. These bonds include callable bond, putable bonds, and convertible bonds.[1] A *callable bond* is a bond issue that grants the issuer the right to retire (that is, call) the bond issue prior to the stated maturity date. A *putable bond* is a bond issue that grants the bondholder the right to have the issuer retire the bond issue prior to the stated maturity date. In the case of a *convertible bond*, the bondholder has the right to convert the bond issue into the issuer's common stock. Moreover, all convertible bonds are callable and some are putable.

Although our discussion in this chapter is on bonds such Treasury and corporate bonds, it is important to note that there are other sectors of the bond market that have even more complex structures that make valuation harder because of the difficulty of estimating the cash flows. For example, a major sector of the bond market is the market for securities backed by residential mortgage loans, called *mortgage-backed securities*. The cash flows for these securities are monthly and include the interest payment, the scheduled principal repayment,[2] and any amount in excess of the scheduled principal repayment. It is this last component of a mortgage-backed securities' cash flows—the payment in excess of the regularly scheduled principal payment—that make it difficult to project cash flows. This component of the cash flow is referred to as a *prepayment*. The right of the homeowners whose mortgage loan is included in the pool of loans backing the mortgage-backed security to prepay their loan at any time in whole or in part is an option. That option is effectively equivalent to the option in a callable bond because the borrower will find it attractive to make prepayments when mortgage rates in the market decline below the borrower's loan rate.

---

[1] Our description of bonds with embedded options considers only the most common types. There are bonds that allow the investor or the bondholder to select the currency in which the coupon and/or the principal may be repaid at the time of the payment. Effectively, this is an option on currency.

[2] Recall in Chapter 2 we explained the components of a loan repayment. The scheduled principal repayment is called the *amortization*.

In addition, there are securities that are backed by loans that are not residential mortgage loans. These securities are referred to as *asset-backed securities*. We discuss these securities when we describe asset securitization in Chapter 12. The structure of these securities is difficult due to defaults and potential prepayments, which cause uncertainty in the amount and timing of the cash flows. We will not discuss their valuation here.

A key factor determining whether the bond issuer in the case of a callable bond or the bondholder in the case of a putable bond would exercise an option to alter the maturity date is the prevailing level of interest rates relative to the bond's coupon rate. Specifically, for a callable bond, if the prevailing market rate that the issuer can realize by retiring the outstanding bond issue and issuing a new bond issue is sufficiently below the outstanding bond issue's coupon rate, so as to justify the costs associated with refunding the issue, the issuer is likely to call the issue. For a putable bond, if the interest rate on comparable bonds in the market rises such that the value of the putable bond falls below the value at which it must be repurchased by the issuer (i.e., the put price), then the investor will put the issue.

What this means is that to properly estimate the cash flows of a bond with an embedded option to alter the maturity date, it is necessary to incorporate into the analysis how interest rates can change in the future and how such changes affect the cash flows. This is done in bond valuation models by introducing a parameter that reflects the expected volatility of interest rates.

In the case of a convertible bond, the expected volatility of interest rates is important to consider because the bond issue is callable. However, even more important is the movement of the price of the issuer's common stock. So convertible bond valuation is even more complicated because of the difficulty of estimating the cash flows.

Determining the Appropriate Rate or Rates

Once the cash flows for a bond issue are estimated, the next step is to determine the appropriate interest rate. To do this, the investor must address the following three questions:

1. What is the minimum interest rate the investor should require?
2. How much more than the minimum interest rate should the investor require?
3. Should the investor require the same interest rate for each estimated cash flow or a unique interest rate for each estimated cash flow?

Minimum Interest Rate

The minimum interest rate that an investor should require is the yield available in the marketplace on a default-free cash flow. In the United States, this is the yield on a U.S. Treasury security. This is one of the reasons that the Treasury market is closely watched by market participants. The minimum interest rate that investors want is referred to as the *base interest rate*. There is not one base interest rate. There is a base interest rate for each maturity.

Premium Over the Base Interest Rate

The premium over the base interest rate on a Treasury security that investors will require reflects the additional risks the investor faces by acquiring a security that is not issued by the U.S. government. We discussed these risks in Chapter 5. This premium is called a *risk premium* or a *spread over Treasuries*. Thus we can express the interest rate offered on a non-Treasury security as

$$\text{Base interest rate} + \text{Risk premium}$$

or equivalently,

$$\text{Base interest rate} + \text{Spread}$$

The factors that affect the spread include (1) the issuer's perceived creditworthiness; (2) any embedded options; (3) the taxability of the interest received by investors; and (4) the expected liquidity of the security.

Perceived Creditworthiness of Issuer *Default risk* refers to the risk that the issuer of a bond may be unable to make timely principal or interest payments. As explained in Chapter 19, most market participants rely primarily on the nationally recognized statistical rating organizations (i.e., rating agencies) to assess the default risk of an issuer. The spread between Treasury securities and non-Treasury securities that are identical in all respects except for quality is referred to as a *quality spread* or *credit spread*.

Inclusion of Options As explained earlier, it is not uncommon for an issue to include a provision that gives the bondholder or the issuer an option to take some action against the other party. The presence of an embedded option has an effect on the spread of an issue relative to a Treasury security and the spread relative to otherwise comparable maturity issues that do not have an embedded option. In general, market participants will require a larger spread to a comparable-maturity Treasury security for an issue with an embedded option that is favorable to the issuer (e.g., a call option) than for an issue without such an option. In contrast, market participants will require a smaller spread to a comparable-maturity Treasury security for an issue with an embedded option that is favorable to the investor (e.g., put option or conversion option). In fact, for an issue with an option that is favorable to an investor, the coupon rate may be less than that on a comparable-maturity Treasury security.

Taxability of Interest Unless exempted under the federal income tax code, interest income is taxable at the federal level. In addition to federal income taxes, there may be state and local taxes on interest income. The federal tax code specifically exempts the interest income from qualified tax-exempt securities from taxation at the federal level. Most municipal securities are tax-exempt securities. Because of the tax-exempt feature of municipal bonds, the yield on a municipal bond is less than that on a Treasury security with the same maturity.

Expected Liquidity of an Issue Bonds trade with different degrees of liquidity. The greater the expected liquidity, the lower the yield that investors would require. Treasury securities are the most liquid securities in the world. The lower yield offered on Treasury securities relative to non-Treasury securities of the same maturity reflects the difference in liquidity.

Single or Multiple Interest Rates

For each cash flow estimated, the same interest rate can be used to calculate the present value. Alternatively, it can be argued that each cash flow is unique and, therefore, it may be more appropriate to value each cash flow using an interest rate specific to that cash flow. In the traditional approach to valuation discussed later, we will see that a single interest rate is used. In the arbitrage-free valuation approach, multiple interest rates are used.

Discounting the Estimated Cash Flows

Given the estimated cash flows and the appropriate interest rate or interest rates that should be used to discount the estimated cash flows, the final step in the valuation process is to value the cash flows.

To illustrate, consider an option-free bond that matures in four years, has a coupon rate of 10%, and has a maturity value of $100. For simplicity, let's assume for now that the bond pays interest annually, and the same discount rate of 8% should be used to calculate the present value of each cash flow. Then the cash flow for this bond is:

Year	Expected Cash Flow
1	$10
2	10
3	10
4	110

The present value of each cash flow is:

Year 1: Present value$_1$ $= \dfrac{\$10}{(1.08)^1} = \$9.2593$

Year 2: Present value$_2$ $= \dfrac{\$10}{(1.08)^2} = \$8.5734$

Year 3: Present value$_3$ $= \dfrac{\$10}{(1.08)^3} = \$7.9383$

Year 4: Present value$_4$ $= \dfrac{\$110}{(1.08)^4} = \$80.8533$

The value of this bond is then the sum of the present values of the four cash flows. That is, the present value is $106.6243 ($9.2593 + $8.5734 + $7.9383 + $80.8533).

Valuation Using Multiple Discount Rates

If instead of the same discount rate for each year, let's suppose that the appropriate discount rates are as follows: year 1, 6.8%; year 2, 7.2%; year 3, 7.6%; and year 4, 8%. Then the present value of each cash flow is:

Year 1: Present value$_1$ $= \dfrac{\$10}{(1.068)^1} = \$9.3633$

Year 2: Present value$_2$ $= \dfrac{\$10}{(1.072)^2} = \$8.7018$

Year 3: Present value$_3$ $= \dfrac{\$10}{(1.076)^3} = \$8.0272$

Year 4: Present value$_4$ $= \dfrac{\$110}{(1.08)^4} = \$80.8533$

The present value of this bond assuming the various discount rates is $106.9456.

Valuing Semiannual Cash Flows

In our illustrations, we assumed that the coupon payments are paid once per year. For most bonds, however, the payments are semiannual. This does not introduce any complexities into the calculation. The procedure is to simply adjust the coupon payments by dividing the annual coupon payment by 2 and adjust the discount rate by dividing the annual discount rate by 2. The time period t in the present value formula is treated in terms of six-month periods rather than years.

For example, consider once again the four-year 10% coupon bond with a maturity value of $100. The cash flow for the first 3.5 years is equal to $5 ($10/2). The last cash flow is $105. If an annual discount rate of 8% is used, the semiannual discount rate is 4%. The present value of each cash flow is then:

$$\text{Period 1: Present value}_1 = \frac{\$5}{(1.04)^1} = \$4.8077$$

$$\text{Period 2: Present value}_2 = \frac{\$5}{(1.04)^2} = \$4.6228$$

$$\text{Period 3: Present value}_3 = \frac{\$5}{(1.04)^3} = \$4.4449$$

$$\text{Period 4: Present value}_4 = \frac{\$5}{(1.04)^4} = \$4.2740$$

$$\text{Period 5: Present value}_5 = \frac{\$5}{(1.04)^5} = \$4.1096$$

$$\text{Period 6: Present value}_6 = \frac{\$5}{(1.04)^6} = \$3.9516$$

$$\text{Period 7: Present value}_7 = \frac{\$5}{(1.04)^7} = \$3.7996$$

$$\text{Period 8: Present value}_8 = \frac{\$105}{(1.04)^8} = \$76.7225$$

The bond's value is equal to $106.7327.

Valuing a Zero-Coupon Bond

For a zero-coupon bond, there is only one cash flow—the maturity value. The value of a zero-coupon bond that matures N years from now is

$$\frac{\text{Maturity value}}{(1 + i/2)^{2N}}$$

For example, a five-year zero-coupon bond with a maturity value of $100 discounted at an 8% interest rate is $67.5564

$$\frac{\$100}{(1.04)^{10}} = \$67.5564$$

Valuing a Bond between Coupon Payments

For coupon-paying bonds, a complication arises when we try to price a bond between coupon payments. The amount that the buyer pays the seller in such cases is the present value of the cash flow. But one of the cash flows, the very next cash flow, encompasses two components as shown below (assuming the buyer does not sell the bond prior to the next coupon payment date):

1. Interest earned by the seller.
2. Interest earned by the buyer.

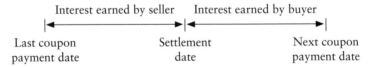

Interest earned by seller	Interest earned by buyer
Last coupon payment date	Settlement date	Next coupon payment date

The interest earned by the seller is the interest that has accrued since the last coupon payment was made and the settlement date. This interest is called *accrued interest*. The buyer must compensate the seller for the accrued interest. The buyer recovers the accrued interest when the next coupon payment is received.

When the price of a bond is computed using the present value calculations described earlier, it is computed with accrued interest embodied in the price. This price is referred to as the *full price*. (Some market participants refer to it as the *dirty price*.) It is the full price that the buyer pays the seller. From the full price, the accrued interest must be deducted to determine the *price* of the bond, sometimes referred to as the *clean price*.

We will not show here how the present value formula is modified to compute the full price when a bond is purchased between coupon periods. However, many financial calculators and spreadsheets have built-in programs to handle this complexity.

Traditional Approach to Valuation

The traditional approach to valuation has been to discount every cash flow of a bond by the same interest rate (or discount rate). For example, consider the three hypothetical 10-year Treasury securities shown in Table 7.1: a 12% coupon bond, an 8% coupon bond, and a zero-coupon bond. The cash flows for each bond are shown in the table. Since the cash flows of all three bonds are viewed as default free, the traditional practice is to use the same discount rate to calculate the present value of all three securities and use the same discount rate for the cash flow for each period. For the three hypothetical bonds, suppose that the yield on a 10-year Treasury trading at par value is 6.2169%. Then, the practice is to discount each cash flow using a discount rate of 6.2169%.

TABLE 7.1   Cash Flows for Three 10-Year Hypothetical Treasury Securities per $100 of Par Value (each period is six months)

	Coupon Rate		
Period	12%	8%	0%
1	$6	$4	$0
2	6	4	0
3	6	4	0
4	6	4	0
5	6	4	0
6	6	4	0
7	6	4	0
8	6	4	0
9	6	4	0
10	6	4	0
11	6	4	0
12	6	4	0
13	6	4	0
14	6	4	0
15	6	4	0
16	6	4	0
17	6	4	0
18	6	4	0
19	6	4	0
20	106	104	100

For a non-Treasury bond, a risk premium is added to the base interest rate (the Treasury rate). The risk premium is the same regardless of when a cash flow is to be received in the traditional approach. For a 10-year non-Treasury security, suppose that 90 basis points is the appropriate risk premium. Then all cash flows would be discounted at the base interest rate of 6.2169% plus 100 basis points, or 7.2169%. Using the traditional approach, the value of the 12%, 8%, and zero-coupon bonds would be $133.66, $105.51, and $49.21, respectively.

The Arbitrage-Free Valuation Approach

The fundamental flaw of the traditional approach is that it views each security as the same package of cash flows. For example, consider a 10-year U.S. Treasury bond with an 8% coupon rate. The cash flows per $100 of par value would be 19 payments of $4 every 6 months and $104 for 20 six-month periods from now. The traditional practice is to discount every cash flow using the same interest rate.

The proper way to view the 10-year 8% coupon bond is as a package of zero-coupon bonds. Each cash flow should be considered a zero-coupon bond whose maturity value is the amount of the cash flow and whose maturity date is the date that the cash flow is to be received. Thus, the 10-year 8% coupon bond should be viewed as 20 zero-coupon bonds. The reason this is the proper way to value a bond is that it does not allow a market participant to realize an arbitrage profit by taking apart or "stripping" a security and selling off the stripped securities at a higher aggregate value than it would cost to purchase the security in the market. This approach to valuation is referred to as the *arbitrage-free approach.*

By viewing any financial asset as a package of zero-coupon bonds, a consistent valuation framework can be developed. For example, under the traditional approach to bond valuation, a 10-year zero-coupon bond would be viewed as the same financial asset as a 10-year 8% coupon bond. Viewing a financial asset as a package of zero-coupon bonds means that these two bonds would be viewed as different packages of zero-coupon bonds and valued accordingly.

We depict the difference between the traditional valuation approach and the arbitrage-free approach in Table 7.2, in which we show how the three bonds described in Table 7.1 should be valued. With the traditional approach, the base interest rate for all three bonds is the yield on a 10-year U.S. Treasury security. With the arbitrage-free approach, the base interest rate for a cash flow is the theoretical rate that the U.S. Treasury would have to pay if it issued a zero-coupon bond with a maturity date equal to the maturity date of the estimated cash flow.

TABLE 7.2 Comparison of Traditional Approach and Arbitrage-Free Approach in Valuing a Treasury Security (each period is six months)

	Discount (base interest) Rate		Cash Flows For[a]		
Period	Traditional Approach	Arbitrage-Free Approach	12%	8%	0%
1	10-year Treasury rate	1-period Treasury spot rate	$6	$4	$0
2	10-year Treasury rate	2-period Treasury spot rate	6	4	0
3	10-year Treasury rate	3-period Treasury spot rate	6	4	0
4	10-year Treasury rate	4-period Treasury spot rate	6	4	0
5	10-year Treasury rate	5-period Treasury spot rate	6	4	0
6	10-year Treasury rate	6-period Treasury spot rate	6	4	0
7	10-year Treasury rate	7-period Treasury spot rate	6	4	0
8	10-year Treasury rate	8-period Treasury spot rate	6	4	0
9	10-year Treasury rate	9-period Treasury spot rate	6	4	0
10	10-year Treasury rate	10-period Treasury spot rate	6	4	0
11	10-year Treasury rate	11-period Treasury spot rate	6	4	0
12	10-year Treasury rate	12-period Treasury spot rate	6	4	0
13	10-year Treasury rate	13-period Treasury spot rate	6	4	0
14	10-year Treasury rate	14-period Treasury spot rate	6	4	0
15	10-year Treasury rate	15-period Treasury spot rate	6	4	0
16	10-year Treasury rate	16-period Treasury spot rate	6	4	0
17	10-year Treasury rate	17-period Treasury spot rate	6	4	0
18	10-year Treasury rate	18-period Treasury spot rate	6	4	0
19	10-year Treasury rate	19-period Treasury spot rate	6	4	0
20	10-year Treasury rate	20-period Treasury spot rate	106	104	100

[a] Per $100 of par value.

Therefore, to implement the arbitrage-free approach, it is necessary to determine the theoretical rate that the U.S. Treasury would have to pay to issue a zero-coupon Treasury bond for each maturity. Another name used for the zero-coupon Treasury rate is the *Treasury spot rate*. We will not discuss the process for computing the spot rate in this chapter. Spot rates are available from vendors of financial information such as Bloomberg and Reuters. The spot rate for a Treasury security of some maturity is the base interest rate that should be used to discount a default-free cash flow with the same maturity.

Valuation Using Treasury Spot Rates

For the purpose of the discussion to follow, we take the Treasury spot rate for each maturity as given. To illustrate how Treasury spot rates are used to

TABLE 7.3   Determination of the Theoretical Value of an 8% 10-Year Treasury

Period	Years	Cash Flow ($)	Spot Rate (%)	Present Value ($)
1	0.5	4	3.0000	3.9409
2	1.0	4	3.3000	3.8712
3	1.5	4	3.5053	3.7968
4	2.0	4	3.9164	3.7014
5	2.5	4	4.4376	3.5843
6	3.0	4	4.7520	3.4743
7	3.5	4	4.9622	3.3694
8	4.0	4	5.0650	3.2747
9	4.5	4	5.1701	3.1791
10	5.0	4	5.2772	3.0828
11	5.5	4	5.3864	2.9861
12	6.0	4	5.4976	2.8889
13	6.5	4	5.6108	2.7916
14	7.0	4	5.6643	2.7055
15	7.5	4	5.7193	2.6205
16	8.0	4	5.7755	2.5365
17	8.5	4	5.8331	2.4536
18	9.0	4	5.9584	2.3581
19	9.5	4	6.0863	2.2631
20	10.0	104	6.2169	56.3828
			Total	$115.2619

value a Treasury security, we use the hypothetical Treasury spot rates shown in the third column of Table 7.3 to value an 8% 10-year Treasury security. The present value of each period's cash flow is shown in the last column. The sum of the present values is the theoretical value for the Treasury security. For the 8% 10-year Treasury, it is $115.2619.

Credit Spreads and the Valuation of Non-Treasury Securities

The Treasury spot rates can be used to value any default-free security. The value of a non-Treasury security is found by discounting the cash flows by the Treasury spot rates (i.e., the base interest rates) plus a risk premium to reflect the additional risks we noted earlier that are associated with investing in a non-Treasury security.

In practice, the spot rate used to discount the cash flow of a non-Treasury security is the Treasury spot rate plus a constant credit spread. For example, suppose the six-month Treasury spot rate is 3% and the 10-year Treasury spot rate is 6%. Also, suppose that a suitable credit spread is 90 basis points. Then a 3.9% spot rate is used to discount a six-month cash flow of a non-Treasury bond and a 6.9% discount rate to discount a 10-year cash flow.

The drawback of this approach is that there is no reason to expect the credit spread to be the same regardless of when the cash flow is expected to be received. Instead, it might be expected that the credit spread increases with the maturity of the bond. That is, there is a *term structure for credit spreads*.

Dealer firms typically construct a term structure for credit spreads for a particular rating based on the input of traders. Generally, the credit spread increases with maturity. This is a typical shape for the term structure of credit spreads. In addition, the shape of the term structure is not the same for all credit ratings. The lower the credit rating, the steeper the term structure.

When the credit zero spreads for a given issuer are added to the Treasury spot rates, the resulting term structure is used to value bonds of issuers of the same credit quality. This term structure is referred to as the *benchmark spot rate curve* or *benchmark zero-coupon rate curve*.

For example, Table 7.4 reproduces the Treasury spot rate curve in Table 7.3. Also shown in the table is a hypothetical credit spread for a non-Treasury security. The resulting benchmark spot rate curve is in the next-to-the-last column. This spot rate curve is used to value the securities of this issuer. This is done in Table 7.4 for a hypothetical 8% 10-year issue for this issuer. The theoretical value is $109.3085. Notice that the theoretical value is less than that for an otherwise comparable Treasury security. The theoretical value for an 8% 10-year Treasury is $115.2619 (see Table 7.3). The theoretical value of the 12% and zero-coupon bonds using this same method are $139.0548 and $49.81585, respectively.

Valuing Bonds with Embedded Options

Thus far, the two approaches to valuation we have presented have dealt with the valuation of option-free bonds. Thus, a Treasury security and an option-free non-Treasury security can be valued using the procedures described previously. More general valuation models handle bonds with embedded options. Practitioners commonly use two models in such cases: the lattice model and the Monte Carlo simulation model. The lattice model is used to value callable bonds and putable bonds.[3] The Monte Carlo simula-

---

[3] This lattice model for valuing bonds with embedded options was developed in Kalotay, Williams, and Fabozzi (1993).

TABLE 7.4 Calculation of Theoretical Value of a Hypothetical 8% 10-Year Non-Treasury Security Using Credit Term Structure

Period	Years	Cash Flow ($)	Treasury Spot Rate (%)	Credit Spread (%)	Benchmark Spot (%)	Present Value ($)
1	0.5	4	3.0000	0.20	3.2000	3.9375
2	1.0	4	3.3000	0.20	3.5000	3.8647
3	1.5	4	3.5053	0.25	3.7553	3.7848
4	2.0	4	3.9164	0.30	4.2164	3.6829
5	2.5	4	4.4376	0.35	4.7876	3.5586
6	3.0	4	4.7520	0.35	5.1020	3.4455
7	3.5	4	4.9622	0.40	5.3622	3.3317
8	4.0	4	5.0650	0.45	5.5150	3.2270
9	4.5	4	5.1701	0.45	5.6201	3.1275
10	5.0	4	5.2772	0.50	5.7772	3.0206
11	5.5	4	5.3864	0.55	5.9364	2.9128
12	6.0	4	5.4976	0.60	6.0976	2.8043
13	6.5	4	5.6108	0.65	6.2608	2.6955
14	7.0	4	5.6643	0.70	6.3643	2.5971
15	7.5	4	5.7193	0.75	6.4693	2.4996
16	8.0	4	5.7755	0.80	6.5755	2.4033
17	8.5	4	5.8331	0.85	6.6831	2.3081
18	9.0	4	5.9584	0.90	6.8584	2.2018
19	9.5	4	6.0863	0.95	7.0363	2.0966
20	10.0	104	6.2169	1.00	7.2169	51.8085
					Total	$109.3085

tion model is used to value mortgage-backed securities and certain types of asset-backed securities.[4]

It is beyond the scope of this chapter to go into the details of these two models. What is critical to understand is that these valuation models use the principles of valuation described earlier in this chapter. Basically, these models look at possible paths that interest rates can take in the future and what the bond's value would be on a given interest rate path. A bond's value is then an average of these possible interest rate path values.

---

[4] See Fabozzi (1998).

There are four features common to the binomial and Monte Carlo valuation models. First, each model begins with the yield on Treasury securities and generates the Treasury spot rates. Second, each model makes an assumption about the expected volatility of short-term interest rates. This is a critical assumption in both models since it can significantly affect the bond's estimated value. Third, based on the volatility assumption, different paths that the short-term interest rate can take are generated. Fourth, the model is calibrated to the Treasury market. This means that if Treasury issue is valued using the model, the model will produce the observed market price.

VALUATION OF COMMON STOCK USING DIVIDEND DISCOUNT MODELS

There are various models that are used to value common stock. We do not describe all of the models. Rather our focus is on models that are referred to as *dividend discount models*. Dividends are cash payments made by a corporation to its owners. Most dividend discount models use current dividends, some measure of historical or projected dividend growth, and an estimate of the required rate of return. Popular models include the basic dividend discount model that assumes a constant dividend growth, and the multiple-phase models, which include the two-stage dividend growth and three-stage dividend growth models.

In this section, we discuss these dividend discount models and their limitations. We begin with a review of the various ways to measure dividends and then take a look at how dividends and stock prices are related.

Dividend Measures

Dividends are measured using three different measures:

- Dividends per share
- Dividend yield
- Dividend payout

The value of a share of stock today is the investors' assessment of today's worth of future cash flows for each share. Because future cash flows to shareholders are dividends, we need a measure of dividends for each share of stock to estimate future cash flows per share. The dividends per share is the dollar amount of dividends paid out during the period per share of common stock:

$$\text{Dividends per share} = \frac{\text{Dividends}}{\text{Number of shares outstanding}}$$

If a company has paid $600,000 in dividends during the period and there are 1.5 million shares of common stock outstanding, then

$$\text{Dividends per share} = \frac{\$600,000}{1,500,000 \text{ shares}} = \$0.40 \text{ per share}$$

The company paid out 40 cents in dividends per common share during this period.

The dividend yield, the ratio of dividends to price, is

$$\text{Dividend yield} = \frac{\text{Annual cash dividends per share}}{\text{Market price per share}}$$

The dividend yield is also referred to as the dividend-price ratio. Historically, the dividend yield for U.S. stocks has been a little less than 5% according to a study by Campbell and Shiller (1998). In an exhaustive study of the relation between dividend yield and stock prices, Campbell and Shiller find that:

- There is a weak relation between the dividend yield and subsequent 10-year dividend growth.
- The dividend yield does not forecast future dividend growth.
- The dividend yield predicts future price changes.

The weak relation between the dividend yield and future dividends may be attributed to the effects of the business cycle on dividend growth. The tendency for the dividend yield to revert to its historical mean has been observed by researchers.

Another way of describing dividends paid out during a period is to state the dividends as a portion of earnings for the period. This is referred to as the *dividend payout* ratio:

$$\text{Dividend payout ratio} = \frac{\text{Dividends}}{\text{Earnings available to common shareholders}}$$

If a company pays $360,000 in dividends and has earnings available to common shareholders of $1.2 million, the payout ratio is 30%:

$$\text{Dividend payout ratio} = \frac{\$360,000}{\$1,200,000} = 0.30 \text{ or } 30\%$$

This means that the company paid out 30% of its earnings to shareholders.

The proportion of earnings paid out in dividends varies by company and industry. For example, the companies in the steel industry typically pay out 25% of their earnings in dividends, whereas the electric utility companies pay out approximately 75% of their earnings in dividends.

If companies focus on dividends per share in establishing their dividends (e.g., a constant dividends per share), the dividend payout will fluctuate along with earnings. We generally observe that companies set the dividend policy such that dividends per share grow at a relatively constant rate, resulting in dividend payouts that fluctuate.

Dividends and Stock Prices

If an investor buys a common stock, he or she has bought shares that represent an ownership interest in the corporation. Shares of common stock are a perpetual security—that is, there is no maturity. The investor who owns shares of common stock has the right to receive a certain portion of any dividends—but dividends are not a sure thing. Whether or not a corporation pays dividends is up to its board of directors—the representatives of the common shareholders. Typically, we see some pattern in the dividends companies pay: Dividends are either constant or grow at a constant rate. But there is no guarantee that dividends will be paid in the future.

Preferred shareholders are in a similar situation as the common shareholders. They expect to receive cash dividends in the future, but the payment of these dividends is up to the board of directors. There are, however, three major differences between the dividends of preferred and common shares. First, the dividends on preferred stock usually are specified at a fixed rate or dollar amount, whereas the amount of dividends is not specified for common shares. Second, preferred shareholders are given preference: Their dividends must be paid before any dividends are paid on common stock. Third, if the preferred stock has a cumulative feature, dividends not paid in one period accumulate and are carried over to the next period. Therefore, the dividends on preferred stock are more certain than those on common shares.

It is reasonable to figure that what an investor pays for a share of stock should reflect what he or she expects to receive from it—a return on the investor's investment. What an investor receives are cash dividends in the future. How can we relate that return to what a share of common stock is worth? Well, the value of a share of stock should be equal to the present value of all the future cash flows an investor expects to receive from that share. To value stock, therefore, an investor must project future cash flows, which, in turn, means projecting future dividends. This approach to the valuation of common stock is referred to the discounted cash flow approach and the models used are what we referred to earlier as dividend discount models.

Basic Dividend Discount Models

As discussed, the basis for the *dividend discount model* (DDM) is simply the application of present value analysis, which asserts that the fair price of an asset is the present value of the expected cash flows. This model was first suggested by Williams (1938). In the case of common stock, the cash flows are the expected dividend payouts. The basic DDM model can be expressed mathematically as

$$P = \frac{D_1}{(1+r_1)^1} + \frac{D_2}{(1+r_2)^2} + \cdots \tag{7.1}$$

where

P = the fair value or theoretical value of the common stock

D_t = the expected dividend for period t

r_t = the appropriate discount or capitalization rate for period t

The dividends are expected to be received forever.

Practitioners rarely use the dividend discount model given by equation (7.1). Instead, one of the DDMs discussed next is typically used.

The Finite Life General Dividend Discount Model

The DDM given by equation (7.1) can be modified by assuming a finite life for the expected cash flows. In this case, the expected cash flows are the expected dividend payouts and the expected sale price of the stock at some future date. The expected sale price is also called the terminal price and is intended to capture the future value of all subsequent dividend payouts. This model is called the *finite life general DDM* and is expressed mathematically as

$$P = \frac{D_1}{(1+r_1)^1} + \frac{D_2}{(1+r_2)^2} + \cdots + \frac{D_N}{(1+r_N)^N} + \frac{P_N}{(1+r_N)^N} \tag{7.2}$$

where

P_N = the expected sale price (or terminal price) at the horizon period N

N = the number of periods in the horizon

and P, D_t, and r_t are the same as defined above.

Assuming a Constant Discount Rate

A special case of the finite life general DDM that is more commonly used in practice is one in which it is assumed that the discount rate is constant. That is, it is assumed each r_t is the same for all t. Denoting this constant discount rate by r, equation (7.2) becomes

$$P = \frac{D_1}{(1+r)^1} + \frac{D_2}{(1+r)^2} + \cdots + \frac{D_N}{(1+r)^N} + \frac{P_N}{(1+r)^N} \tag{7.3}$$

Equation (7.3) is called the constant discount rate version of the finite life general DDM. When practitioners use any of the DDM models presented in this section, typically the constant discount rate version form is used.

Let's illustrate the finite life general DDM assuming a constant discount rate assuming each period is a year. Suppose that the following data are determined for stock XYZ by a financial analyst:

$D_1 = \$2.00 \quad D_2 = \$2.20 \quad D_3 = \$2.30 \quad D_4 = \$2.55 \quad D_5 = \$2.65$
$P_5 = \$26 \quad\quad N = 5 \quad\quad\quad r = 0.10$

Based on these data, the fair price of stock XYZ is

$$P = \frac{\$2.00}{(1.10)^1} + \frac{\$2.20}{(1.10)^2} + \frac{\$2.30}{(1.10)^3} + \frac{\$2.55}{(1.10)^4} + \frac{\$2.65}{(1.10)^5} + \frac{\$26.00}{(1.10)^5} = \$24.895$$

Required Inputs

The finite life general DDM requires three forecasts as inputs to calculate the fair value of a stock:

1. Expected terminal price (P_N).
2. Dividends up to the assumed horizon $(D_1$ to $D_N)$.
3. Discount rates $(r_1$ to $r_N)$ or r (in the case of the constant discount rate version).

Thus, the relevant question is, How accurately can these inputs be forecasted?

The terminal price is the most difficult of the three forecasts. According to theory, P_N is the present value of all future dividends after N; that is, $D_{N+1}, D_{N+2}, \ldots, D_\infty$. Also, the future discount rate (r_t) must be forecasted. In practice, forecasts are made of either dividends (D_N) or earnings (E_N) first, and then the price P_N is estimated by assigning an "appropriate" requirement for yield, price-earnings ratio, or capitalization rate. Note that the present value of the expected terminal price $P_N/(1 + r)^N$ becomes very small if N is very large.

The forecasting of dividends is "somewhat" easier. Usually, past history is available, management can be queried, and cash flows can be projected for a given scenario. The discount rate r is the required rate of return. Forecasting r is more complex than forecasting dividends, although not nearly as difficult as forecasting the terminal price (which requires a forecast of future discount rates as well). As noted before, in practice for a given company, r is assumed to be constant for all periods and typically generated from the *capital asset pricing model* (CAPM). As explained in the next chapter, the CAPM provides the expected return for a company based on its systematic risk (beta).

Assessing Relative Value

Given the fair price derived from a dividend discount model, the assessment of the stock proceeds along the following lines. If the market price is below the fair price derived from the model, the stock is undervalued or cheap. The opposite holds for a stock whose market price is greater than the model-derived price. In this case, the stock is said to be overvalued or expensive. A stock trading equal to or close to its fair price is said to be fairly valued.

The DDM tells us the relative value but does not tell us when the price of the stock should be expected to move to its fair price. That is, the model says that based on the inputs generated by the analyst, the stock may be cheap, expensive, or fair. However, it does not tell us that if it is mispriced how long it will take before the market recognizes the mispricing and corrects it. As a result, an investor may hold on to a stock perceived to be cheap for an extended period of time and may underperform a benchmark during that period.

While a stock may be mispriced, an investor must also consider how mispriced it is in order to take the appropriate action (buy a cheap stock and sell or sell short an expensive stock). This will depend on by how much the stock is trading from its fair value and transaction costs. An investor should also consider that a stock may look as if it is mispriced (based on the estimates and the model), but this may be the result of estimates and the use of these estimates in the model that may introduce error in the valuation.

Constant Growth Dividend Discount Model

If future dividends are assumed to grow at a constant rate (g) and a single discount rate (r) is used, then the finite life general DDM assuming a constant growth rate given by equation (7.3) becomes

$$P = \frac{D_0(1+g)^1}{(1+r)^1} + \frac{D_0(1+g)^2}{(1+r)^2} + \frac{D_0(1+g)^3}{(1+r)^3} + \cdots + \frac{D_0(1+g)^N}{(1+r)^N} + \frac{P_N}{(1+r)^N} \qquad (7.4)$$

and it can be shown that if N is assumed to approach infinity, equation (7.4) is equal to

$$P = \frac{D_0(1+g)}{r-g} \qquad (7.5)$$

Equation (7.5) is called the *constant growth dividend discount model* (Gordon and Shapiro, 1956). An equivalent formulation for the constant growth DDM is

$$P = \frac{D_1}{r-g} \qquad (7.6)$$

where D_1 is equal to $D_0(1+g)$.

Consider a company that currently pays dividends of $3.00 per share. If the dividend is expected to grow at a rate of 3% per year and the discount rate is 12%, what is the value of a share of stock of this company? Using equation (7.5),

$$P = \frac{\$3.00(1+0.03)}{0.12-0.03} = \frac{\$3.09}{0.09} = \$34.33$$

If the growth rate for this company's dividends is 5%, instead of 3%, the current value is $45.00:

$$P = \frac{\$3.00(1+0.05)}{0.12-0.05} = \frac{\$3.15}{0.07} = \$45.00$$

Therefore, the greater the expected growth rate of dividends, the greater the value of a share of stock.

In this last example, if the discount rate is 14% instead of 12% and the growth rate of dividends is 3%, the value of a share of stock is

$$P = \frac{\$3.00(1+0.03)}{0.14-0.03} = \frac{\$3.09}{0.11} = \$28.09$$

Therefore, the greater the discount rate, the lower the current value of a share of stock.

Let's apply the model as given by equation (7.5) to estimate the price of three companies: Eli Lilly, Schering-Plough, and Wyeth Laboratories. The discount rate for each company was estimated using the capital asset pricing model assuming (1) a market risk premium of 5% and (2) a risk-free rate of 4.63%. The market risk premium is based on the historical spread between the return on the market (often proxied with the return on the S&P 500 Index) and the risk-free rate. Historically, this spread has been approximately 5%. The risk-free rate is often estimated by the yield on U.S. Treasury securities. At the end of 2006. 10-year Treasury securities were yielding approximately 4.625%. We use 4.63% as an estimate for the purposes of this illustration. The beta estimate for each company was obtained from the Value Line Investment Survey: 0.9 for Eli Lilly, 1.0 for Schering-Plough and Wyeth. The discount rate, r, for each company based on the CAPM that we describe in the next chapter is:

Eli-Lilly $r = 0.0463 + 0.9(0.05) = 9.125\%$
Schering-Plough $r = 0.0463 + 1.0(0.05) = 9.625\%$
Wyeth $r = 0.0463 + 1.0(0.05) = 9.625\%$

The dividend growth rate can be estimated by using the compounded rate of growth of historical dividends.

The compound growth rate, g, is found using the following formula:

$$g = \left(\frac{\text{Last dividend}}{\text{Starting dividend}} \right)^{1/\text{no. of years}} - 1$$

This formula is equivalent to calculating the geometric mean of 1 plus the percentage change over the number of years. Using time value of money math, the 2006 dividend is the future value, the starting dividend is the present value, the number of years is the number of periods; solving for the interest rate produces the growth rate.

Substituting the values for the starting and ending dividend amounts and the number of periods into the formula, we get:

Company	1991 Dividend	2006 Dividend	Estimated Annual Growth Rate
Eli-Lilly	$0.50	$1.60	8.063%
Schering-Plough	$0.16	$0.22	2.146%
Wyeth	$0.60	$1.01	3.533%

The value of D_0, the estimate for g, and the discount rate r for each company are summarized next:

Company	Current Dividend D_0	Estimated Annual Growth Rate g	Required Rate of Return r
Eli-Lilly	$1.60	8.063%	9.125%
Schering-Plough	$0.22	2.146%	9.625%
Wyeth	$1.01	3.533%	9.625%

Substituting these values into equation (7.5), we obtain

$$\text{Eli Lilly estimated price} = \frac{\$1.60(1+0.08063)}{0.09125-0.08063} = \frac{\$1.729}{0.0162} = \$162.79$$

$$\text{Schering-Plough estimated price} = \frac{\$0.022(1+0.02146)}{0.09625-0.02146} = \frac{\$0.225}{0.07479} = \$3.00$$

$$\text{Wyeth estimated price} = \frac{\$1.01(1+0.03533)}{0.09625-0.03533} = \frac{\$1.046}{0.06092} = \$17.16$$

Comparing the estimated price with the actual price, we see that this model does not do a good job of pricing these stocks:

Company	Estimated Price at the End of 2006	Actual Price at the End of 2006
Eli Lilly	$162.79	$49.87
Schering-Plough	$3.00	$23.44
Wyeth	$17.16	$50.52

Notice that the constant growth DDM is considerably off the mark for all three companies. The reasons include: (1) the dividend growth pattern for none of the three companies appears to suggest a constant growth rate; and (2) the growth rate of dividends in recent years has been much slower than earlier years (and, in fact, negative for Schering-Plough after 2003), causing growth rates estimated from the long time periods to overstate future growth. And this pattern is not unique to these companies.

Another problem that arises in using the constant growth rate model is that the growth rate of dividends may exceed the discount rate, r. Consider the following three companies and their dividend growth over the 16-year period from 1991 through 2006, with the estimated required rates of return:

Company	1991 Dividend	2006 Dividend	Estimated Growth Rate g	Estimated Required Rate of Return
Coca Cola	$0.24	$1.24	11.70%	7.625%
Hershey	$0.24	$1.03	10.198%	7.875%
Tootsie Roll	$0.04	$0.31	14.627%	8.625%

For these three companies, the growth rate of dividends over the prior 16 years is greater than the discount rate. If we substitute the D_0 (the 2006 dividends), the g, and the r into equation (7.5), the estimated price at the end of 2006 is negative, which doesn't make sense. Therefore, there are some cases in which it is inappropriate to use the constant rate DDM.

The potential for misvaluation using the constant rate DDM is highlighted by Fogler (1988) in his illustration using ABC prior to its being taken over by Capital Cities in 1985. He estimated the value of ABC stock to be $53.88, which was less than its market price at the time (of $64) and less than the $121 paid per share by Capital Cities.

Multiphase Dividend Discount Models

The assumption of constant growth is unrealistic and can even be misleading. Instead, most practitioners modify the constant growth DDM by assuming that companies will go through different growth phases. Within a given phase, dividends are assumed to growth at a constant rate. Molodovsky, May, and Chattiner (1965) were some of the pioneers in modifying the DDM to accommodate different growth rates.

Two-Stage Growth Model

The simplest form of a multiphase DDM is the two-stage growth model. A simple extension of equation (7.4) uses two different values of g. Referring to the first growth rate as g_1 and the second growth rate as g_2 and assuming that the first growth rate pertains to the next four years and the second growth rate refers to all years following, equation (7.4) can be modified as

$$P = \frac{D_0(1+g_1)^1}{(1+r)^1} + \frac{D_0(1+g_1)^2}{(1+r)^2} + \frac{D_0(1+g_1)^3}{(1+r)^3} + \frac{D_0(1+g_1)^4}{(1+r)^4}$$
$$+ \frac{D_0(1+g_2)^5}{(1+r)^5} + \frac{D_0(1+g_2)^6}{(1+r)^6} + \cdots$$

which simplifies to

$$P = \frac{D_0(1+g_1)^1}{(1+r)^1} + \frac{D_0(1+g_1)^2}{(1+r)^2} + \frac{D_0(1+g_1)^3}{(1+r)^3} + \frac{D_0(1+g_1)^4}{(1+r)^4} + P_4$$

Because dividends following the fourth year are presumed to grow at a constant rate g_2 forever, the value of a share at the end of the fourth year (that is, P_4) is determined by using equation (7.5), substituting $D_0(1+g_1)^4$ for D_0 (because period 4 is the base period for the value at end of the fourth year) and g_2 for the constant rate g:

$$P = \frac{D_0(1+g_1)^1}{(1+r)^1} + \frac{D_0(1+g_1)^2}{(1+r)^2} + \frac{D_0(1+g_1)^3}{(1+r)^3} + \frac{D_0(1+g_1)^4}{(1+r)^4}$$
$$+ \left[\frac{1}{(1+r)^4} \left(\frac{D_0(1+g_1)^4(1+g_2)}{r-g_2} \right) \right] \tag{7.7}$$

Suppose a company's dividends are expected to grow at a 4% for the next four years and then 8% thereafter. If the current dividend is $2.00 and the discount rate is 12%,

$$P = \frac{\$2.08}{(1+0.12)^1} + \frac{\$2.16}{(1+0.12)^2} + \frac{\$2.25}{(1+0.12)^3} + \frac{\$2.34}{(1+0.12)^4}$$
$$+ \left[\frac{1}{(1+0.12)^4} \left(\frac{\$2.53}{0.12-0.08} \right) \right] = \$46.87$$

If this company's dividends are expected to grow at the rate of 4% forever, the value of a share is $26.00; if this company's dividends are expected to grow at the rate of 8% forever, the value of a share is $52.00. But because the growth rate of dividends is expected to increase from 4% to 8% in four years, the value of a share is between those two values, or $46.87.

As can be seen from this example, the basic valuation model can be modified to accommodate different patterns of expected dividend growth.

Three-Stage Growth Model

The most popular multiphase model employed by practitioners appears to be the *three-stage DDM*.[5] This model assumes that all companies go through three phases, analogous to the concept of the product life cycle. In the growth phase, a company experiences rapid earnings growth as it produces new products and expands market share. In the transition phase the company's earnings begin to mature and decelerate to the rate of growth of

---

[5] The formula for this model can be found in Sorensen and Williamson (1985).

the economy as a whole. At this point, the company is in the maturity phase in which earnings continue to grow at the rate of the general economy.

Different companies are assumed to be at different phases in the three-phase model. An emerging growth company would have a longer growth phase than a more mature company. Some companies are considered to have higher initial growth rates and hence longer growth and transition phases. Other companies may be considered to have lower current growth rates and hence shorter growth and transition phases.

In the typical investment management organization, analysts supply the projected earnings, dividends, growth rates for earnings, and dividend and payout ratios using the fundamental security analysis described throughout this book. The basis for the three-stage model is that the current information on growth rates and the like are useful in determining the phase of the company and then the valuation model—whether one, two, or three—is applied to value the company's stock. Generally, the growth in the mature stage of a company's life cycle is assumed to be equal to the long-run growth rate for the economy. As a generalization, approximately 25% of the expected return from a company (projected by the DDM) comes from the growth phase, 25% from the transition phase, and 50% from the maturity phase. However, a company with high growth and low dividend payouts shifts the relative contribution toward the maturity phase, while a company with low growth and a high payout shifts the relative contribution toward the growth and transition phases.

SUMMARY

Valuation is the process of determining the fair value of a financial asset. The fundamental principle of valuation is that the value of any financial asset is the present value of the expected cash flows. The valuation process involves three steps: (1) estimating the expected cash flows; (2) determining the appropriate interest rate or interest rates that should be used to discount the cash flows; and (3) calculating the present value of the expected cash flows. For option-free bonds, the cash flows can easily be determined assuming that the issuer does not default. The difficulty in determining cash flows arises for bonds with embedded options.

The minimum interest rate or base rate that an investor should require is the yield available on Treasury securities since the cash flows of these securities are viewed as default-free cash flows. The risk premium over the interest rate on a Treasury security that investors will require reflects the additional risks the investor faces by acquiring a security that is not issued by the U.S. government. The interest rate offered on a non-Treasury security is the sum of the base interest rate plus the risk premium (or spread). The factors that affect the spread or risk premium include (1) the issuer's perceived creditworthiness; (2) provisions that grant either the issuer or the investor the option to do something; (3) the taxability of the interest; and (4) the expected liquidity of the security. In general, investors require a larger spread to a comparable Treasury security for an issue with an embedded option that is favorable to the issuer (e.g., a call option) than for an issue without such an option.

The traditional valuation methodology is to discount every cash flow of a bond by the same interest rate (or discount rate), thereby incorrectly viewing each bond as the same package of cash flows. The arbitrage-free approach values a bond as a package of cash flows, with each cash flow viewed as a zero-coupon bond and each cash flow discounted at its own unique discount rate.

Valuation models seek to estimate the fair or theoretical value of a bond and accommodate securities with embedded options. The two valuation models used to value bonds with embedded options are the lattice model and the Monte Carlo simulation model. The lattice model is used to value callable bonds and putable bonds. The Monte Carlo simulation model is used to value mortgage-backed securities. Basically, these two models look at possible paths that interest rates can take in the future and what the bond's value would be on a given interest rate path, with the bond's value being an average of the possible interest rate path values.

The discounted cash flow approach to valuing common stock requires projecting future dividends. Hence, the model used to value common stock is called a dividend discount model. Dividends are measured in a number of ways, including dividends per share, dividend yield, and dividend payout. The simplest dividend discount model is the constant growth model. More complex models include the multistage phase model. Stock valuation using a dividend discount model is highly dependent on the inputs used.

APPENDIX: VALUING CONVERTIBLE BONDS

A convertible bond is a bond that can be converted into common stock at the option of the bondholder. The conversion provision of a convertible bond grants the bondholder the right to convert the bond into a predetermined number of shares of common stock of the issuer. A convertible bond is, therefore, a bond with an embedded call option to buy the common stock of the issuer.[6]

---

[6] An *exchangeable security* grants the bondholder the right to exchange the bond for the common stock of a firm other than the issuer of the bond.

In illustrating the calculation of the various concepts described below, we will use a convertible bond issue Calgon Carbon Corporation (ticker symbol CCC) 5% $75 million convertible issue that matures in 2036. The notes were issued in August 2006 and cannot be converted unless the common stock is greater than or equal to 120% of the conversion price for a specified length of time. We look at this bond issue as of December 31, 2007. The value of the bonds on that date was $233.9 million.

The number of shares of common stock that the bondholder will receive from exercising the call option of a convertible security is called the *conversion ratio*. The conversion privilege may extend for all or only some portion of the bond's life, and the stated conversion ratio may fall over time.[7] For the CCC convertible issue, the conversion ratio is 196.0784 shares. This means that for each $1,000 of par value of this issue the bondholder exchanges for CCC common stocks, she will receive 196.0784 shares.

At the time of issuance of a convertible bond, the issuer effectively grants the bondholder the right to purchase the common stock at a price equal to

This price is referred to in the prospectus as the *stated conversion price*. The conversion price for the CCC convertible issue per $1,000 face value is

$$\text{Conversion price} = \frac{\$1,000}{196.0784} = \$5.10$$

The price of a share of CCC stock at the time of the note issue was $4.67. There are two approaches to valuation of convertible bonds: the traditional approach and the option-based approach. The latter approach uses the option pricing models as described in the appendix to Chapter 6 to value a convertible bond. The traditional approach makes no attempt to value the option that the bondholder has been granted.

Traditional Value of Convertible Bonds

The *conversion value*, or *parity value*, of a convertible bond or note is the value of the debt if it is converted immediately. That is,

Conversion value = Market price of common stock × Conversion ratio

The minimum price of a convertible security is the greater of its:

---

[7] It is always adjusted proportionately for stock splits and stock dividends.

1. Conversion value.
2. Value as a bond without the conversion option—that is, based on the convertible bond's cash flows if not converted.

This second value is called the bond's *straight value* or *investment value*. To estimate the straight value, we must determine the required yield on a nonconvertible bond with the same credit rating and similar investment characteristics. Given this estimated required yield, the straight value is then the present value of the bond's cash flows using this yield to discount the cash flows.

If the convertible bond does not sell for the greater of these two values, arbitrage profits could be realized. For example, suppose the conversion value is greater than the straight value, and the security trades at its straight value. An investor can buy the convertible bond at the straight value and convert it. By doing so, the investor realizes a gain equal to the difference between the conversion value and the straight value. Suppose, instead, the straight value is greater than the conversion value, and the security trades at its conversion value. By buying the convertible bond at the conversion value, the investor will realize a higher yield than a comparable straight bond.

At the time of the analysis (December 31, 2007), CCC's stock price was $15.89. For the CCC convertible issue, the conversion value per $1,000 of par value on December 31, 2007 was equal to

$$\text{Conversion value} = \$15.89 \times 196.0784 = \$3,115.69$$

Therefore, the conversion value per $100 of par value was $311.5686.

To simplify the analysis of the straight value of the bond, we discount the cash flows to maturity by the yield on the 10-year Treasury at the time of the analysis, 4.53%, plus a credit spread of 200 basis points that appeared to be appropriate at that time. The straight value, using a discount rate of 6.53% for theoretical purposes only, is 80.2046. Since the minimum value of the CCC convertible issue is the greater of the conversion value and the straight value, the minimum value is 80.2046.

The price an investor effectively pays for the common stock if the convertible security is purchased in the market and then converted into the common stock is called the *market conversion price* (also called the *conversion parity price*). It is found as follows:

$$\text{Market conversion price} = \frac{\text{Market price of convertible bond}}{\text{Conversion ratio}}$$

The market conversion price is a useful benchmark because, once the actual market price of the stock rises above the market conversion price, any further stock price increase is certain to increase the value of the convertible bond by at least the same percentage. Therefore, the market conversion price can be viewed as a break-even point.

An investor who purchases a convertible bond, rather than the underlying stock, pays a premium over the current market price of the stock. This premium per share is equal to the difference between the market conversion price and the current market price of the common stock. That is,

$$\text{Market conversion premium per share}$$
$$= \text{Market conversion price} - \text{Current market price}$$

The market conversion premium per share is usually expressed as a percentage of the current market price as follows:

$$\text{Market conversion premium ratio} = \frac{\text{Market conversion premium per share}}{\text{Market price of common stock}}$$

Why would someone be willing to pay a premium to buy the stock? Recall that the minimum price of a convertible bond is the greater of its conversion value or its straight value. Thus, as the common stock price declines, the price of the convertible bond will not fall below its straight value. The straight value therefore acts as a floor for the convertible bond's price.

Viewed in this context, the market conversion premium per share can be seen as the price of a call option. As explained in Chapter 6, the buyer of a call option limits the downside risk to the option price. In the case of a convertible bond, for a premium, the bondholder limits the downside risk to the straight value of the security. The difference between the buyer of a call option and the buyer of a convertible bond is that the former knows precisely the dollar amount of the downside risk, while the latter knows only that the most that can be lost is the difference between the convertible bond's price and the straight value. The straight value at some future date, however, is unknown; the value will change as interest rates in the economy change.

The calculation of the market conversion price, market conversion premium per share, and market conversion premium ratio for the CCC convertible issue based on market data as of the date of the analysis is shown next:[8]

---

[8] The market value of these $75 million face value notes, as reported in the company's 2007 annual report, was $233.9 million at the end of 2007. This translates into a $233.9 million/$75 million = $3.11867 value per $1 face value for these notes. The increase in the value of these notes is driven, in large part, by the increase in the value of the stock from $4.67 at the time the notes were issued to $15.89 at the end of 2007.

$$\text{Market conversion price} = \frac{\$3,118.67}{196.0784} = \$15.9052$$

$$\text{Market conversion premium per share} = \$15.9052 - \$15.89 = \$0.0152$$

$$\text{Market conversion premium ratio} = \frac{\$0.0152}{\$15.89} = 0.0957\%$$

The investment characteristics of a convertible note or bond depend on the common stock price. If the price is low, so that the straight value is considerably higher than the conversion value, the bond will trade much like a straight security. The convertible bond in such instances is referred to as a *fixed income equivalent* or a *busted convertible.*

When the price of the stock is such that the conversion value is considerably higher than the straight value, then the convertible bond will trade as if it were an equity instrument; in this case, it is said to be a *common stock equivalent.* In such cases, the market conversion premium per share will be small. As can be seen, the CCC convertible is trading like a common stock equivalent.

Between these two cases, fixed income equivalent and equity equivalent, the convertible security trades as a *hybrid security,* having the characteristics of both a bond and common stock.

An Option-Based Valuation Approach

The traditional valuation approach did not address the following questions:

1. What is a fair value for the conversion premium per share?
2. How do we handle convertible securities with call or put options?
3. How does a change in interest rates affect the stock price?

Consider first a noncallable/nonputable convertible bond. The investor who purchases this security would be entering into two separate transactions: (1) buying a noncallable/nonputable straight bond; and (2) buying a call option on the stock where the number of shares that can be purchased with the call option is equal to the conversion ratio.

The question is, what is the fair value for the call option? The fair value depends on the factors discussed in Chapter 6 that affect the price of a call option. One key factor is the expected price volatility of the stock: The more the expected price volatility, the greater the value of the call option. The theoretical value of a call option can be valued using the Black-Scholes option pricing model. As a first approximation to the value of a convertible security, the formula would be

Convertible bond's value = Straight value + Value of the call option on the stock

The value of the call option is added to the straight value because the investor has purchased a call option on the stock.

Now let's add in a common feature of a convertible bond: the issuer's right to call the bond. The issuer can force conversion by calling the security. For example, suppose the call price is 103 and the conversion value is 107. If the issuer calls the bond, the optimal strategy for the investor is to convert the bond and receive shares worth $107. The investor, however, loses any premium over the conversion value that is reflected in the market price. Therefore, the analysis of convertible bonds must take into account the value of the issuer's right to call. This depends, in turn, on (1) future interest rate volatility and (2) economic factors that determine whether it is optimal for the issuer to call the bond. The Black-Scholes option pricing model cannot handle this situation. To link interest rates and stock prices together (the third question we raise above), statistical analysis of historical movements of these two variables must be estimated and incorporated into the model.

Valuation models based on an option pricing approach have been suggested by several researchers.[9] Many dealers of convertible bonds have developed such models, which they make available to institutional clients. One example is the model developed by Merrill Lynch Equity Capital Markets that can handle a combination of call and put features found in convertible securities, as well as changing conversion ratios and provisional call features.[10] The key input to the theoretical valuation model is expected stock price volatility, expected interest rate volatility, the interest rate on the issuer's nonconvertible securities, the current common stock dividend, and the expected growth of common stock dividends. The inputs not known with certainty can be changed to test the sensitivity of the model.

Because the inputs into the valuation model are not known with certainty, it is important to test the sensitivity of the model.

REFERENCES

Bhattacharya, M. and Zhu, Y. (1997). Valuation and analysis of convertible securities. In F.J. Fabozzi (ed.), *The Handbook of Fixed Income Securities,* 5th Edition (pp. 791–817), Burr Ridge, IL: Irwin Professional Publishing.

Brennan, M. and Schwartz, E. (1977). Convertible bonds: Valuation and optimal strategies for call and conversion. *Journal of Finance* 32, no. 5: 1699–1715.

---

[9] See Brennan and Schwartz (1977, 1980), Ingersoll (1977), and Constantinides (1984).

[10] See Bhattacharya and Zhu (1997).

Brennan, M. and Schwartz, E. (1980). Analyzing convertible bonds. *Journal of Financial and Quantitative Analysis* 15, no. 4: 907–929.

Campbell, J. Y., and Shiller, R. J. (1998). Valuation ratios and the long-run stock market outlook. *Journal of Portfolio Management* 24, no. 2: 11–26.

Constantinides, G. (1984). Warrant exercise and bond conversion in competitive markets. *Journal of Financial Economics* 13, no. 3: 371–398.

Fabozzi, F. J. (1998). *Valuation of Fixed Income Securities and Derivatives,* 3rd ed. Hoboken, N.J., John Wiley & Sons.

Fogler, R. H. (1988). Security analysis, DDMs, and probability. In *Equity Markets and Valuation Methods* (pp. 51–52). Charlottesville, VA: The Institute of Chartered Financial Analysts.

Gordon, M., and Shapiro, E. (1956). Capital equipment analysis: The required rate of profit. *Management Science* 3, no. 1 (October): 102–110.

Ingersoll, J. (1977). A contingent-claims valuation of convertible securities. *Journal of Financial Economics* 10, no. 4: 289–322.

Kalotay, A. J., Williams, G.O., and Fabozzi, F.J. (1993). A model for the valuation of bonds and embedded options. *Financial Analysts Journal* 33 (May/June): 35–46.

Molodovsky, N., May, C., and Chattiner, S. (1965). Common stock valuation: Principles, tables, and applications. *Financial Analysts Journal* 21 (November/December): 111–117.

Sorensen, E., and Williamson, E. (1985). Some evidence on the value of dividend discount models. *Financial Analysts Journal* 41 (November/December): 60–69.

Williams, J. B. (1938). *The Theory of Investment Value.* Cambridge, MA: Harvard University Press.

CHAPTER 8

Asset Valuation:
The Theory of Asset Pricing

The pricing of assets is a topic that cuts across financial and asset management. In financial management, a firm wants to know the cost of capital and the return required before investing in a long-term investment project. In portfolio management, a key input in portfolio construction is the expected return for an asset. Asset pricing models describe the relationship between the risks of and the expected return. As we will see in later chapters, an estimate of the expected return that providers of capital require on investments is needed in order to value an asset. So, while we refer to asset pricing models in this chapter, we mean the expected return investors require given the risk associated with an investment.

The two most well-known equilibrium pricing models are the capital asset pricing model developed in the 1960s and the arbitrage pricing theory model developed in the mid-1970s. In this chapter, we describe these two models and we present their applications in later chapters.

CHARACTERISTICS OF AN ASSET PRICING MODEL

In well-functioning capital markets, an investor should be rewarded for accepting the various risks associated with investing in an asset. Risks are also referred to as "risk factors" or "factors." We can express an *asset pricing model* in general terms based on risk factors as follows:

$$E(R_i) = f(F_1, F_2, F_3, ..., F_N) \tag{8.1}$$

where

$E(R_i)$ = expected return for asset i
F_k = risk factor k
N = number of risk factors

Equation (8.1) says that the expected return is a function of N risk factors. The trick is to figure out what the risk factors are and to specify the precise relationship between expected return and the risk factors.

We can fine-tune the asset pricing model given by equation (8.1) by thinking about the minimum expected return we would want from investing in an asset. There are securities issued by the U.S. Department of the Treasury that offer a known return if held over some period of time. The expected return offered on such securities is called the risk-free return or the risk-free rate because there is believed to be no default risk. By investing in an asset other than such securities, investors will demand a premium over the risk-free rate. That is, the expected return that an investor will require is

$$E(R_i) = R_f + \text{Risk premium}$$

where R_f is the risk-free rate.

The "risk premium" or additional return expected over the risk-free rate depends on the risk factors associated with investing in the asset. Thus, we can rewrite the general form of the asset pricing model given by equation (8.1) as follows:

$$E(R_i) = R_f + f(F_1, F_2, F_3, ..., F_N) \tag{8.2}$$

Risk factors can be divided into two general categories. The first category is risk factors that cannot be diversified away. That is, no matter what the investor does, the investor cannot eliminate these risk factors. These risk factors are referred to as *systematic risk factors* or *nondiversifiable risk factors*. The second category is risk factors that can be eliminated via diversification. These risk factors are unique to the asset and are referred to as *unsystematic risk factors* or *diversifiable risk factors*.

CAPITAL ASSET PRICING MODEL

The first asset pricing model derived from economic theory was formulated by Sharpe (1964), Lintner (1965), Treynor (1961), and Mossin (1966) and is called the *capital asset pricing model* (CAPM). The CAPM has only one systematic risk factor—the risk of the overall movement of the market. This risk factor is referred to as *market risk*. So, in the CAPM, "market risk" and "systematic risk" are used interchangeably. Market risk means the risk associated with holding a portfolio consisting of all assets, that is, the market portfolio. As will be explained, in the market portfolio, an asset is held in proportion to its market value. So, for example, if the total market value of all assets is $X and the market value of asset j is $Y, then asset j will comprise $Y/$X of the market portfolio.

The CAPM is given by the following formula:

$$E(R_i) = R_f + \beta_i[E(R_M) - R_f] \qquad (8.3)$$

where

$E(R_M)$ = expected return on the "market portfolio"

β_i = measure of systematic risk of asset i relative to the "market portfolio"

We derive the CAPM later. For now, let's look at what this asset pricing model says.

The expected return for an asset i according to the CAPM is equal to the risk-free rate plus a risk premium. The risk premium is

$$\text{Risk premium in the CAPM} = \beta_i[E(R_M) - R_f]$$

First look at *beta* (β_i) in the risk premium component of the CAPM. Beta is a measure of the sensitivity of the return of asset i to the return of the market portfolio. A beta of 1 means that the asset or a portfolio has the same quantity of risk as the market portfolio. A beta greater than 1 means that the asset or portfolio has more market risk than the market portfolio, and a beta less than 1 means that the asset or portfolio has less market risk than the market portfolio. Later in this chapter we will see how beta is estimated.

The second component of the risk premium in the CAPM is the difference between the expected return on the market portfolio, $E(R_M)$, and the risk-free rate. It measures the potential reward for taking on the risk of the market above what can earned by investing in an asset that offers a risk-free rate.

Taken together, the risk premium is a product of the quantity of market risk (as measured by beta) and the potential compensation of taking on market risk (as measured by $[E(R_M) - R_f]$).

Let's use some values for beta to see if all of this makes sense. Suppose that a portfolio has a beta of zero. That is, the return for this portfolio has no market risk. Substituting zero for β in the CAPM, given by equation (8.3), we would find that the expected return is just the risk-free rate. This makes sense since a portfolio that has no market risk should have an expected return equal to the risk-free rate.

Consider a portfolio that has a beta of 1. This portfolio has the same market risk as the market portfolio. Substituting 1 for β in the CAPM given by equation (8.3) results in an expected return equal to that of the market portfolio. Again, this is what one should expect for the return of this portfolio since it has the same market risk exposure as the market portfolio.

If a portfolio has greater market risk than the market portfolio, beta will be greater than 1 and the expected return will be greater than that of the market portfolio. If a portfolio has less market risk than the market portfolio, beta will be less than 1 and the expected return will be less than that of the market portfolio.

Derivation of the CAPM

The CAPM is an equilibrium asset pricing model derived from a set of assumptions. Here, we demonstrate how the CAPM is derived.

Assumptions

The CAPM is an abstraction of the real world capital markets and, as such, is based on some assumptions. These assumptions simplify matters a great deal, and some of them may even seem unrealistic. However, these assumptions make the CAPM more tractable from a mathematical standpoint. The CAPM assumptions are as follows:

Assumption 1. Investors make investment decisions based on the expected return and variance of returns and subscribe to the Markowitz method of portfolio diversification.

Assumption 2. Investors are rational and risk averse.

Assumption 3. Investors all invest for the same period of time.

Assumption 4. Investors have the same expectations about the expected return and variance of all assets.

Assumption 5. There is a risk-free asset and investors can borrow and lend any amount at the risk-free rate.

Assumption 6. Capital markets are completely competitive and frictionless.

The first four assumptions deal with the way investors make decisions. The last two assumptions relate to characteristics of the capital market. These assumptions require further explanation. Many of these assumptions have been challenged resulting in modifications of the CAPM. There is branch of financial theory called *behavioral finance* that is highly critical of these assumptions, resulting in the formulation of a different CAPM theory that we describe later.

Let's look at Assumption 1. Prior to 1952, the notion of risk was not quantified in finance. In 1952, Harry Markowitz presented a normative theory of portfolio selection, now popularly referred to as the *theory of portfolio selection* or *modern portfolio theory*. A normative theory is one that describes a standard or norm of behavior that investors should pursue in constructing a portfolio, in contrast to a theory that is actually followed. The theory is based on the goal of constructing a portfolio that maximizes expected returns consistent with individually acceptable levels of risk. The measure of risk that Markowitz proposed to quantify investment risk is the variance of the return of an asset. The standard deviation of return is a statistical measure explained in all statistics books. The variance measures the dispersion of potential outcomes for a random variable. In the theory of portfolio selection, the random variable is the return of an asset (or a portfolio). The square root of the variance is the standard deviation.

We devote a good part of Chapter 17 to the theory of portfolio selection as formulated by Markowitz (1952). Here, we only describe the key elements of the theory so that the CAPM can be derived. Specifically, the theory of selection selection says:

1. Investors make decisions based on expected returns and the variance of returns. The expected return for an asset's return is typically estimated from historical mean of an asset's return over some time period. Consequently, the term "expected return" and "mean" are often used interchangeably. For this reason, the theory of portfolio selection is often referred to as *mean-variance portfolio analysis* or simple *mean-variance analysis*.

2. The focus of portfolio selection is not on the risk of individual securities but the risk of the portfolio. This theory shows that it is possible to combine risky assets and produce a portfolio whose expected return reflects its components, but with considerably lower risk. In other words, it is possible to construct a portfolio whose risk is smaller than the sum of all its individual parts.

Though practitioners realized that the risks of individual assets were related, prior to the theory of portfolio selection they were unable to formalize how combining them into a portfolio affected the risk at the portfolio level or how the addition of a new asset into a portfolio would change the portfolio's return/risk characteristics. This is because practitioners were unable to quantify the returns and risks of their investments. Further, in the context of the entire portfolio, they were also unable to formalize the interaction of the returns and risks across asset classes and individual assets. The failure to quantify these important measures and formalize these important relationships made the goal of constructing an optimal portfolio highly subjective and provided no insight into the return investors could expect and the risk they were undertaking. The key to the quantification was not only the expected return and variance, but the covariance or correlation between every pair of asset class or individual asset.

Obtaining the optimal portfolio given the expected return, variance, and all correlation pairs requires the use of an optimization tool from the field of operations research: mathematical programming. The output of the mean-variance analysis is a portfolio that maximizes the portfolio's expected return for a given level of risk (i.e., portfolio variance). Such a portfolio is called an *efficient portfolio* and in honor of Markowitz sometimes referred to as a *Markowitz efficient portfolio*. There is not just one efficient portfolio but a set of efficient portfolios: one for each level of risk. The set of all efficient portfolios is referred in the theory of portfolio selection as the *efficient frontier*. Again, this is made clearer in Chapter 16, where we provide the complete theory.

What is important to also understand at this time is the relationship between the theory of portfolio selection as formulated by Markowitz and asset pricing theory. Asset pricing theory formalizes the relationship that should exist between asset returns and risk if investors constructed and selected portfolios according to mean-variance analysis (our Assumption 1). In contrast to a normative theory, asset pricing theory is a positive theory—a theory that hypothesizes how investors behave rather than how investors should behave. Based on that hypothesized behavior of investors, a model that provides the expected return (a key input into constructing portfolios based on mean-variance analysis) is derived and is called an asset pricing model. Together the theory of portfolio selection and asset pricing theory provide a framework to specify and measure investment risk and to develop relationships between expected asset return and risk (and, therefore, between risk and required return of an investment). However, the theory of portfolio selection is a theory that is independent of any theories about asset pricing. The validity of theory of portfolio selection does not rest on the validity of asset pricing theory.

Assumption 2 indicates that in order to accept greater risk, investors must be compensated by the opportunity of realizing a higher return. We refer to the behavior of such investors as being *risk averse*.[1] What this means is that if an investor faces a choice between two portfolios with the same

---

[1] This is an oversimplified definition. Actually, a more rigorous definition of risk aversion is described by a mathematical specification of an investor's utility function. However, this complexity need not concern us here.

expected return, the investor will select the portfolio with the lower risk. Certainly, this is a reasonable assumption.

By Assumption 3, all investors are assumed to make investment decisions over some single-period investment horizon. The theory does not specify how long that period is (i.e., six months, one year, two years, and so on). In reality, the investment decision process is more complex than that, with many investors having more than one investment horizon. Nonetheless, the assumption of a one-period investment horizon is necessary to simplify the mathematics of the theory.

To obtain the efficient frontier (i.e., the set of efficient portfolios) which we will be used in developing the CAPM, it will be assumed that investors have the same expectations with respect to the inputs that are used to derive the efficient portfolios: asset returns, variances, and correlations/covariances. This is Assumption 4 and is referred to as the "homogeneous expectations assumption."

As we will see, the existence of a risk-free asset and unlimited borrowing and lending at the risk-free rate, Assumption 5, is important in deriving the CAPM. This is because efficient portfolios are created for portfolios consisting of risky assets. No consideration is given to how to create efficient portfolios when a risk-free asset is available. In the CAPM, it is assumed not only that there is a risk-free asset but that an investor can borrow funds at the same interest rate paid on a risk-free asset. This is a common assumption in many economic models developed in financed despite the fact it is well that that there is a different rate at which investors can borrow and lend funds.

Finally, Assumption 6 specifies that the capital market is perfectly competitive. In general, this means the number of buyers and sellers is sufficiently large, and all investors are small enough relative to the market so that no individual investor can influence an asset's price. Consequently, all investors are price takers, and the market price is determined where there is equality of supply and demand. In addition, according to this assumption, there are no transactions costs or impediments that interfere with the supply of and demand for an asset. Economists refer to these various costs and impediments as "frictions." The costs associated with frictions generally result in buyers paying more than in the absence of frictions and sellers receiving less.

In economic modeling, the model is modified by relaxing one or more of the assumptions. There are several extensions and modifications of the CAPM (see, for example, Black, 1972 and Merton, 1973), but we will not review them here. No matter the extension or modification, however, the basic implications are unchanged: investors are only rewarded for taking on systematic risk and the only systematic risk is market risk.

Capital Market Line

To derive the CAPM, we begin with the efficient frontier from the theory of portfolio selection, which is shown in Figure 8.1. Every point on the efficient frontier is derived as explained earlier and is the maximum portfolio return for a given level of risk. In the figure, risk is measured on the horizontal axis by the standard deviation of the portfolio's return, which is the square root of the variance.

In creating an efficient frontier, there is no consideration of a risk-free asset. In the absence of a risk-free rate, efficient portfolios can be constructed based on expected return and variance, with the optimal portfolio being the one portfolio that is tangent to the investor's indifference curve. The efficient frontier changes, however, once a risk-free asset is introduced and assuming that investors can borrow and lend at the risk-free rate (Assumption 6). This is illustrated in Figure 8.1.

Every combination of the risk-free asset and the efficient portfolio denoted by point M is shown on the line drawn from the vertical axis at the risk-free rate tangent to the efficient frontier. The point of tangency is denoted by M which represents portfolio M. All the portfolios on the line

FIGURE 8.1   The Capital Market Line

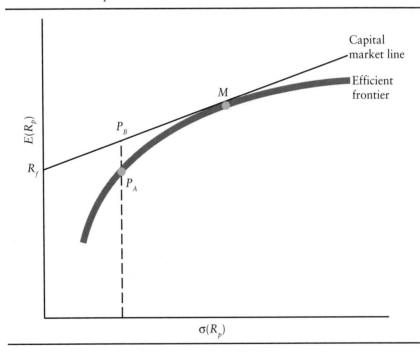

are feasible for the investor to construct. Portfolios to the left of portfolio M represent combinations of risky assets and the risk-free asset. Portfolios to the right of M include purchases of risky assets made with funds borrowed at the risk-free rate. Such a portfolio is called a *leveraged portfolio* because it involves the use of borrowed funds. The line from the risk-free rate that is tangent to portfolio M is called the *capital market line* (CML).

Let's compare a portfolio on the CML to a portfolio on the efficient frontier with the same risk. For example, compare portfolio P_A, which is on the efficient frontier, with portfolio P_B, which is on the CML and, therefore, is comprised of some combination of the risk-free asset and the efficient portfolio M. Notice that for the same risk, the expected return is greater for P_B than for P_A. By Assumption 2, a risk-averse investor will prefer P_B to P_A. That is, P_B will dominate P_A. In fact, this is true for all but one portfolio on the CML: portfolio M, which is on the efficient frontier.

With the introduction of the risk-free asset, we can now say that an investor will select a portfolio on the CML that represents a combination of borrowing or lending at the risk-free rate and the efficient portfolio M. The particular efficient portfolio on the CML that the investor selects depends on the investor's risk preference. This can be seen in Figure 8.2, which is the same as Figure 8.1, but has the investor's indifference curves included. The investor selects the portfolio on the CML that is tangent to the highest indifference curve, u_3 in the exhibit. Notice that without the risk-free asset, an investor could only get to u_2, which is the indifference curve that is tangent to the efficient frontier. Thus, the opportunity to borrow or lend at the risk-free rate results in a capital market where risk-averse investors will prefer to hold portfolios consisting of combinations of the risk-free asset and some portfolio M on the efficient frontier.

We can derive a formula for the CML algebraically. Based on the assumption of homogeneous expectations (Assumption 4), all investors can create an efficient portfolio consisting of w_f placed in the risk-free asset and w_M in the market portfolio, where w represents the corresponding percentage (weight) of the portfolio allocated to each asset. Therefore,

$$w_f + w_M = 1 \quad \text{or} \quad w_f = 1 - w_M$$

The expected return is equal to the weighted average of the expected return of the two assets. Therefore, the expected portfolio return, $E(R_p)$, is equal to

$$E(R_p) = w_f R_f + w_M E(R_M)$$

Since we know that $w_f = 1 - w_M$, we can rewrite $E(R_p)$ as follows:

FIGURE 8.2   Optimal Portfolio and the Capital Market Line

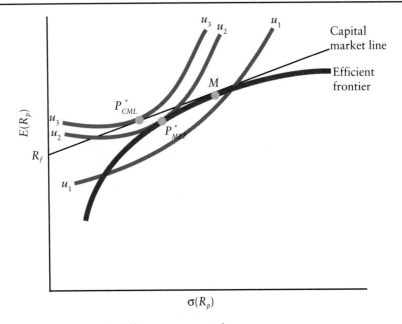

u_1, u_2, u_3 = indifference curves with $u_1 < u_2 < u_3$
M = market portfolio
R_f = risk-free rate
P^*_{CML} = optimal portfolio on capital market line
P^*_{MEF} = optimal portfolio on efficient frontier

$$E(R_p) = (1 - w_M)R_f + w_M E(R_M)$$

This can be simplified as follows:

$$E(R_p) = R_f + w_M[E(R_M) - R_f] \qquad (8.4)$$

The variance of the portfolio consisting of the risk-free asset and portfolio M can be found using the formula for the variance of a two-asset portfolio. It is

$$\text{var}(R_p) = w_f^2 \text{var}(R_f) + w_M^2 \text{var}(R_M) + 2w_f w_M \text{cov}(R_f, R_M)$$

The variance of the risk-free asset, $\text{var}(R_f)$, is equal to zero. This is because there is no possible variation in the return since the future return is known. The covariance between the risk-free asset and portfolio M, $\text{cov}(R_f,$

R_M), is zero. This is because the risk-free asset has no variability and therefore does not move at all with the return on portfolio M, a risky portfolio. Substituting these two values into the formula for the portfolio's variance, we get

$$\text{var}(R_p) = w_M^2 \, \text{var}(R_M)$$

In other words, the variance of the portfolio is represented by the weighted variance of portfolio M.

We can solve for the weight of portfolio M by substituting standard deviations for variances. Since the standard deviation (σ) is the square root of the variance, we can write

$$\sigma(R_p) = w_M \sigma(R_M)$$

and, therefore,

$$w_m = \frac{\sigma(R_p)}{\sigma(R_M)}$$

If we substitute the above result for w_M in equation (8.4) and rearrange terms we get the CML:

$$E(R_p) = R_f + \left[\frac{E(R_M) - R_f}{\sigma(R_M)} \right] \sigma(R_p) \qquad (8.5)$$

What Is Portfolio M?   Now that we know that portfolio M is pivotal to the CML, we need to know what portfolio M is. That is, how does an investor construct portfolio M? Fama (1970) demonstrated that portfolio M must consist of all assets available to investors, and each asset must be held in proportion to its market value relative to the total market value of all assets. That is, portfolio M is the market portfolio described earlier. So, rather than referring to the market portfolio, we can simply refer to the market.

Risk Premium in the CML   With homogeneous expectations, $\sigma(R_M)$ and $\sigma(R_p)$ are the market's consensus for the expected return distributions for portfolio M and portfolio p. The risk premium for the CML is

$$\left[\frac{E(R_M) - R_f}{\sigma(R_M)} \right] \sigma(R_p)$$

Let's examine the economic meaning of the risk premium.

The numerator of the first term is the expected return from investing in the market beyond the risk-free return. It is a measure of the reward for holding the risky market portfolio rather than the risk-free asset. The denominator is the market risk of the market portfolio. Thus, the first term measures the reward per unit of market risk. Since the CML represents the return offered to compensate for a perceived level of risk, each point on the CML is a balanced market condition, or equilibrium. The slope of the CML (that is, the first term) determines the additional return needed to compensate for a unit change in risk. That is why the slope of the CML is also referred to as the equilibrium market price of risk.

The CML says that the expected return on a portfolio is equal to the risk-free rate, plus a risk premium equal to the market price of risk (as measured by the reward per unit of market risk), multiplied by the quantity of risk for the portfolio (as measured by the standard deviation of the portfolio). That is,

$$E(R)_p = R_f + (\text{Market price of risk} \times \text{Quantity of risk})$$

Systematic and Unsystematic Risk

Now we know that a risk-averse investor who makes decisions based on expected return and variance should construct an efficient portfolio using a combination of the market portfolio and the risk-free rate. The combinations are identified by the CML. Based on this result, Sharpe (1964) derived an asset pricing model that shows how a risky asset should be priced. In the process of doing so, we can fine-tune our thinking about the risk associated with an asset. Specifically, we can show that the appropriate risk that investors should be compensated for accepting is not the variance of an asset's return but some other quantity. In order to do this, let's take a closer look at risk.

We can do this by looking at the variance of the portfolio. It can be demonstrated that the variance of the market portfolio containing N assets can be shown to be equal to

$$\text{var}(R_M) = w_{1M}\,\text{cov}(R_1, R_M) + w_{2M}\,\text{cov}(R_2, R_M) + \cdots + w_{NM}\,\text{cov}(R_N, R_M) \quad (8.6)$$

where w_{iM} is equal to the proportion invested in asset i in the market portfolio.

Notice that the portfolio variance does not depend on the variance of the assets comprising the market portfolio, but rather their covariance with the market portfolio. Sharpe defined the degree to which an asset covaries with the market portfolio as the asset's systematic risk. More specifically, he defined *systematic risk* as the portion of an asset's variability that can be attributed to a common factor. Systematic risk is the minimum level of risk that can be obtained for a portfolio by means of diversification across a large number of randomly chosen assets. As such, systematic risk is that which results from general market and economic conditions that cannot be diversified away.

Sharpe defined the portion of an asset's variability that can be diversified away as *nonsystematic risk*. It is also sometimes called *unsystematic risk*, *diversifiable risk*, *unique risk*, *residual risk*, and *company-specific risk*. This is the risk that is unique to an asset.

Consequently, total risk (as measured by the variance) can be partitioned into systematic risk as measured by the covariance of asset *i*'s return with the market portfolio's return and nonsystematic risk. The relevant risk for decision-making purposes is the systematic risk. We see how to measure the systematic risk later.

How diversification reduces nonsystematic risk for portfolios is illustrated in Figure 8.3. The vertical axis shows the variance of the portfolio return. The variance of the portfolio return represents the total risk for the

FIGURE 8.3   Systematic and Unsystematic Portfolio Risk

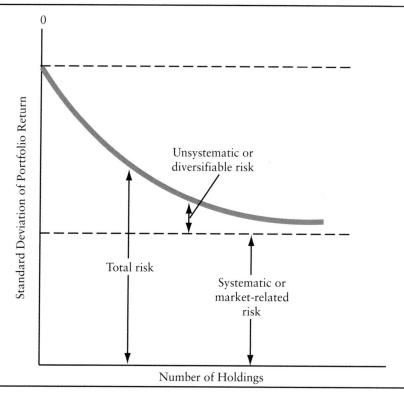

portfolio (systematic plus nonsystematic). The horizontal axis shows the number of holdings of different assets (e.g., the number of common stock held of different issuers). As can be seen, as the number of asset holdings increases, the level of nonsystematic risk is almost completely eliminated (that is, diversified away). Studies of different asset classes support this. For example, for common stock, several studies suggest that a portfolio size of about 20 randomly selected companies will completely eliminate nonsystematic risk leaving only systematic risk (see Wagner and Lau, 1971).

Security Market Line

The CML represents an equilibrium condition in which the expected return on a portfolio of assets is a linear function of the expected return of the market portfolio. Individual assets do not fall on the CML. Instead, Sharpe (1970) demonstrated that the following relationship holds for individual assets:

$$E(R_i) = R_f + \left[\frac{E(R_i) - R_f}{\text{var}(R_M)} \right] \text{cov}(R_i, R_M) \qquad (8.7)$$

Equation (8.7) is called the *security market line* (SML).

In equilibrium, the expected return of individual securities lies on the SML and not on the CML. This is true because of the high degree of nonsystematic risk that remains in individual assets that can be diversified out of portfolios. In equilibrium, only efficient portfolios lie on both the CML and the SML.

The SML also can be expressed as

$$E(R_i) = R_f + [E(R_i) - R_f] \left[\frac{\text{cov}(R_i, R_M)}{\text{var}(R_M)} \right]$$

How can the ratio in equation (8.8) be estimated for each asset? It can be estimated empirically using return data for the market portfolio and the return on the asset. The empirical analogue for equation (8.8) is

$$r_{it} - R_{ft} = \alpha_i + \beta_i [r_{Mt} - r_{ft}] + e_{it} \qquad (8.9)$$

where e_{it} is the error term. Equation (8.9) is called the *characteristic line*.

β_i, beta, in equation (8.9) is the estimate of the ratio in equation (8.8). That is,

$$\beta_i = \frac{\text{cov}(R_i, R_M)}{\text{var}(R_M)} \qquad (8.10)$$

Substituting β_i into the SML given by equation (8.8) gives the beta version of the SML:

$$E(R_i) = R_f + b_i[E(R_M) - R_f] \tag{8.11}$$

This is the CAPM form given by equation (8.3). This equation states that, given the assumptions of the CAPM, the expected return on an individual asset is a positive linear function of its index of systematic risk as measured by beta. The higher the beta, the higher the expected return.

An investor pursuing an active strategy will search for underpriced securities to purchase or retain and overpriced securities to sell or avoid (if held in the current portfolio, or sold short if permitted). If an investor believes that the CAPM is the correct asset pricing model, then the SML can be used to identify mispriced securities. A security is perceived to be underpriced (that is, undervalued) if the "expected" return projected by the investor is greater than the "required" return stipulated by the SML. A security is perceived to be overpriced (that is, overvalued), if the "expected" return projected by the investor is less than the "required" return stipulated by the SML. Said another way, if the expected return plots above (over) the SML, the security is "underpriced"; if it plots below the SML, it is "overpriced."

Tests of the CAPM

Now, that's the theory. The question is whether or not the theory is supported by empirical evidence. There has been probably more than 1,000 academic papers written on the subject. (Almost all studies use common stock to test the theory.) These papers cover not only the empirical evidence but the difficulties of testing the theory.

Let's start with the empirical evidence. There are two important results of the empirical tests of the CAPM that question its validity. First, it has been found that stocks with low betas have exhibited higher returns than the CAPM predicts and stocks with high betas have been found to have lower returns than the CAPM predicts. Second, market risk is not the only risk factor priced by the market. Several studies have discovered other factors that explain stock returns.

While on the empirical level there are serious questions raised about the CAPM, there is an important paper challenging the validity of these empirical studies. Roll (1977) demonstrates that the CAPM is not testable until the exact composition of the "true" market portfolio is known, and the only valid test of the CAPM is to observe whether the ex ante true market portfolio is mean-variance efficient. As a result of his findings, Roll states that he does not believe there ever will be an unambiguous test of the CAPM. He does not say that the CAPM is invalid. Rather, Roll says that there is likely to be no unambiguous way to test the CAPM and its implications due to the nonobservability of the true market portfolio and its characteristics.

ARBITRAGE PRICING THEORY MODEL

An alternative to the equilibrium asset pricing model just discussed, an asset pricing model based purely on arbitrage arguments was derived by Ross (1976). The model, called the *arbitrage pricing theory* (APT) *model*, postulates that an asset's expected return is influenced by a variety of risk factors, as opposed to just market risk as suggested by the CAPM. The APT model states that the return on a security is linearly related to H risk factors. However, the APT model does not specify what these risk factors are, but it is assumed that the relationship between asset returns and the risk factors is linear. Moreover, unsystematic risk can be eliminated so that an investor is only compensated for accepting the systematic risk factors.

Arbitrage Principle

Since the model relies on arbitrage arguments, we will digress at this point to define what is meant by arbitrage. In its simple form, arbitrage is the simultaneous buying and selling of an asset at two different prices in two different markets. The arbitrageur profits without risk by buying cheap in one market and simultaneously selling at the higher price in the other market. Investors don't hold their breath waiting for such situations to occur because they are rare. In fact, a single arbitrageur with unlimited ability to sell short could correct a mispricing condition by financing purchases in the underpriced market with proceeds of short sales in the overpriced market. (Short-selling means selling an asset that is not owned, in anticipation of a price decline.) This means that riskless arbitrage opportunities are short-lived.

Less obvious arbitrage opportunities exist in situations where a package of assets can produce a payoff (expected return) identical to an asset that is priced differently. This arbitrage relies on a fundamental principle of finance called the law of one price, which states that a given asset must have the same price regardless of the means by which one goes about creating that asset. The law of one price implies that if the payoff of an asset can be synthetically created by a package of assets, the price of the package and the price of the asset whose payoff it replicates must be equal.

When a situation is discovered whereby the price of the package of assets differs from that of an asset with the same payoff, rational investors will trade these assets in such a way so as to restore price equilibrium. This market mechanism is assumed by the APT model, and is founded on the fact that an arbitrage transaction does not expose the investor to any adverse movement in the market price of the assets in the transaction.

For example, let us consider how we can produce an arbitrage opportunity involving the three assets A, B, and C. These assets can be purchased today at the prices shown below, and can each produce only one of two payoffs (referred to as State 1 and State 2) a year from now:

Asset	Price	Payoff in State 1	Payoff in State 2
A	$70	$50	$100
B	60	30	120
C	80	38	112

While it is not obvious from the data presented above, an investor can construct a portfolio of assets A and B that will have the identical return as asset C in both State 1 and State 2. Let w_A and w_B be the proportion of assets A and B, respectively, in the portfolio. Then the payoff (that is, the terminal value of the portfolio) under the two states can be expressed mathematically as follows:

If State 1 occurs: $\$50w_A + \$30w_B$
If State 2 occurs: $\$100w_A + \$120w_B$

We create a portfolio consisting of A and B that will reproduce the payoff of C regardless of the state that occurs one year from now. Here is how: For either condition (State 1 and State 2), we set the expected payoff of the portfolio equal to the expected payoff for C as follows:

State 1: $\$50w_A + \$30w_B = \$38$
State 2: $\$100w_A + \$120w_B = \$112$

We also know that $w_A + w_B = 1$.

If we solved for the weights for w_A and w_B, which would simultaneously satisfy the previous equations, we would find that the portfolio should have 40% in asset A (that is, $w_A = 0.4$) and 60% in asset B (that is, $w_B = 0.6$). The cost of that portfolio will be equal to

$$(0.4)(\$70) + (0.6)(\$60) = \$64$$

Our portfolio (that is, package of assets) comprised of assets A and B has the same payoff in State 1 and State 2 as the payoff of asset C. The cost of asset C is $80 while the cost of the portfolio is only $64. This is an arbitrage opportunity that can be exploited by buying assets A and B in the proportions given above and shorting (selling) asset C.

For example, suppose that $1 million is invested to create the portfolio with assets A and B. The $1 million is obtained by selling short asset C. The proceeds from the short sale of asset C provide the funds to purchase assets A and B. Thus, there would be no cash outlay by the investor. The payoffs for States 1 and 2 are shown here:

Asset	Investment	Payoff in	
		State 1	State 2
A	$400,000	$285,715	$571,429
B	600,000	300,000	1,200,000
C	−1,000,000	−475,000	−1,400,000
Total	0	110,715	371,429

In either State 1 or 2, the investor profits without risk. The APT model assumes that such an opportunity would be quickly eliminated by the marketplace.

APT Model Formulation

The APT model postulates that an asset's expected return is influenced by a variety of risk factors, as opposed to just market risk of the CAPM. That is, the APT model asserts that the return on an asset is linearly related to H "factors." The APT does not specify what these factors are, but it is assumed that the relationship between asset returns and the factors is linear. Specifically, the APT model asserts that the rate of return on asset i is given by the following relationship:

$$R_i = E(R_i) + \beta_{i,1}F_1 + \beta_{i,2}F_2 + \cdots + \beta_{i,H}F_H + e_i$$

where

R_i = the rate of return on asset i

$E(R_i)$ = the expected return on asset i

F_h = the h-th factor that is common to the returns of all assets (h = 1, ..., H)

$\beta_{i,h}$ = the sensitivity of the i-th asset to the h-th factor

e_i = the unsystematic return for asset i

For an equilibrium to exist, the following conditions must be satisfied: Using no additional funds (wealth) and without increasing risk, it should not be possible, on average, to create a portfolio to increase return. In essence, this condition states that there is no "money machine" available in the market.

Ross (1976) derived the following relationship, which is what is referred to as the APT model:

$$E(R_i) = R_f + \beta_{i,F1}[E(R_{F1}) - R_F] + \beta_{i,F2}[E(R_{F2}) - R_F]$$
$$+ \cdots + \beta_{i,FH}[E(R_{FH}) - R_F] \qquad (8.12)$$

where $[E(R_{Fj}) - R_f]$ is the excess return of the jth systematic risk factor over the risk-free rate, and can be thought of as the price (or risk premium) for the jth systematic risk factor.

The APT model as given by equation (8.12) asserts that investors want to be compensated for all the risk factors that systematically affect the return of a security. The compensation is the sum of the products of each risk factor's systematic risk ($\beta_{i,FH}$), and the risk premium assigned to it by the financial market $[E(R_{Fh}) - R_f]$. As in the case of the CAPM, an investor is not compensated for accepting unsystematic risk.

It turns out that the CAPM is actually a special case of the APT model. If the only risk factor in the APT model as given by equation (8.12) is market risk, the APT model reduces to the CAPM. Now contrast the APT model given by equation (8.3). They look similar. Both say that investors are compensated for accepting all systematic risk and no nonsystematic risk. The CAPM states that systematic risk is market risk, while the APT model does not specify the systematic risk.

Supporters of the APT model argue that it has several major advantages over the CAPM or multifactor CAPM. First, it makes less restrictive assumptions about investor preferences toward risk and return. As explained earlier, the CAPM theory assumes investors trade off between risk and return solely on the basis of the expected returns and standard deviations of prospective investments. The APT model, in contrast, simply requires some rather unobtrusive bounds be placed on potential investor utility functions. Second, no assumptions are made about the distribution of asset returns. Finally, since the APT model does not rely on the identification of the true market portfolio, the theory is potentially testable.

Criticisms of the CAPM and the Behavioral Finance Approach

There have been attacks on the CAPM from those who believe that this cornerstone theory of finance is on shaky grounds. The three major attacks are

Attack 1. The use of the standard deviation or variance as a measure of risk does not capture what is observed what is observed in financial market regarding the probability distribution of asset returns.

Attack 2. The behavioral assumptions of the CAPM do not reflect the way investors make portfolio decisions in the real world.

Attack 3. There is evidence that there is more than one risk factor that affects asset returns.

Attack 1 is essentially a criticism of an assumption that the return distribution for asset returns follows a normal distribution. We will describe this below. Attack 2 is the criticism of financial economists who since the late 1970s have attacked economic theories based on observing how economic agents such as investors actually go about making decisions and how this is different from the assumptions made in many economic theories. Those who have attacked CAPM, as well as other theories in finance, have formulated alternative theories in the field of behavioral finance that we describe later in this chapter. Finally, an alternative economic theory of asset pricing, which we describe in the next section, is based on more than one risk factor.

Limitations of the Variance/Standard Deviation as a Risk Measure

Although we mentioned what the variance/standard deviation is, we did not say anything about the usefulness of this statistical concept in measuring risk. The usefulness of the variance as a risk measure depends upon the underlying return distribution. If the return distribution is normally distributed, then the variance is a useful measure. Figure 8.4 shows a normal distribution. The distribution is symmetric so outcomes (area under the normal distribution curve) are above and below the expected value are equally likely.

The normal distribution is one that receives not only a good deal of attention in finance. However, in most introductory statistics courses taken by business students and in empirical studies of the real-world financial markets, three things are suggested. First, real-world return distributions have fatter or heavier tails than the normal distribution. The "tails" of the return distribution are where the extreme outcomes occur. Figure 8.4 shows the tail of a normal distribution and another symmetric distribution that has fatter tails. If a probability distribution for the return of assets exhibits fat tails, extreme outcomes are more likely than would be predicted by the normal distribution. As a result, between periods when the market exhibits relatively modest changes in returns, there will be periods when there are changes that are much higher than the normal distribution predicts. Such extreme outcomes are referred to as crashes and booms.

FIGURE 8.4 Illustration of Kurtosis: Difference Between a Standard Normal Distribution and a Distribution with High Excess Kurtosis

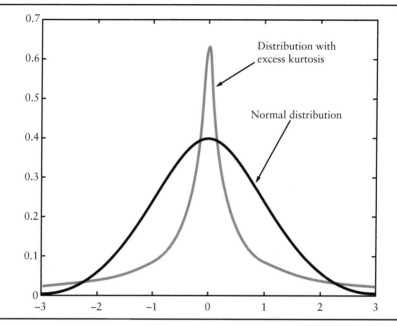

FIGURE 8.5 Distribution Skewed to the Right

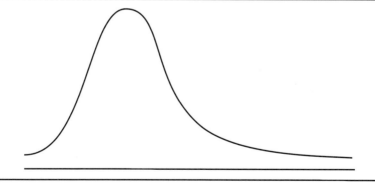

Second, a normal distribution assumes symmetry of asset returns. In many markets, return distributions have been found to be asymmetric. Figure 8.5 shows an asymmetric return distribution. The illustration shows a return distribution that is said to be "skewed to the right." As can be seen, the probability of very high outcomes are in the long tail of the distribution on the right. Hence, if an asset return distribution is one such as in Figure 8.5, asset returns have greater downside risk than suggested by a normal distribution.

The empirical evidence that refuted the assumption that return distributions are not normally distributed was first presented in the 1960s by Benoit Mandelbrot (Mandelbrot, 1963). He argued that return distributions follow a different probability distribution called a "stable Paretian distribution."[2] Although a discussion of a stable Paretian distribution is beyond the scope of this chapter, the important point here it has only been in recent years that more attention has been paid to this distribution in finance.[3]

The failure of asset return distributions to follow a normal distribution leads to the question of how risk should be measured. There is a growing literature in finance that has proposed alternative risk measures.

Criticisms of Behavioral Finance Theorists

In building economic models, economists must make assumptions about the behavior of economic agents in markets. More specifically, they make assumptions about how consumers make decisions about how much to spend and invest and how investors (or their agents such as portfolio managers) make decisions about selecting assets to include in their portfolio. The underlying economic theory that economists draw upon in formulating various theories of choice is utility theory.

Economists such as Adam Smith and John Maynard Keynes have argued that investor psychology affects security prices. Support for this view came in the late 1970 when two psychologists, Kahneman and Tversky (1979), demonstrated that the actions of economic agents in making investment decisions under uncertainty are inconsistent with the assumptions made by economists in formulating financial theories. Based on numerous experiments, Kahneman and Tversky attacked utility theory and presented their own their as to how investors made choices under uncertainty that they called "prospect theory."

Other attacks on the assumptions of traditional financial theory drawing from the field of psychology lead to the specialized field in finance known as *behavioral finance*.[4] Behavioral finance looks at how psychology affects investor decisions and the implications not only for the theory of portfolio selection which is a critical assumption made in deriving the CAPM, but other financial theories described later in this book such as option pricing theory.

---

[2] See also the work by Fama (1963).

[3] See Rachev, Mann, and Fabozzi (2005).

[4] For a further discussion of behavioral finance, see Statman (2008), Wilcox (2008), and Ricciardi (2008a, 2008b).

The foundations of behavioral finance draw from the research by Kahneman, Slovic, and Tversky (1982) and has the following three themes:[5]

Behavioral Finance Theme 1. When making investment decisions, investors make errors because they rely on rules of thumb.

Behavioral Finance Theme 2. Investors are influenced by form as well as substance in making investment decisions.

Behavioral Finance Theme 3. Prices in the financial market are affected by errors and decision frames.

Behavioral Finance Theme 1 involves the concept of *heuristics*. This term means a rule of thumb strategy or good guide to pursue so as to reduce the time required to make a decision. For example, in planning for retirement, a rule of thumb that has been suggested for having enough to retire is to invest 10% of annual pretax income. As for what to invest in to reach that retirement goal (that is, the allocation among asset classes), a rule of thumb that has been suggested is that the percentage that an investor should allocate to bonds should be determined by subtracting from 100 the investor's age. So, for example, a 45-year old individual should invest 55% of his or her retirement funds in bonds.

Although there are circumstances where heuristics can work fairly well, studies in the field of psychology suggest that heuristics can lead to systematic biases in decision making. This systematic bias is referred to by psychologists as *cognitive biases*. In the context of finance, these biases lead to errors in making investment decisions, what Shefrin (2002) refers to as *heuristic-driven biases*.

Now recall the first assumption made in deriving the CAPM. It is assumed that all investors estimate the mean and variance of every asset return and based on those estimates construct an optimal portfolio for each level of risk (i.e., the efficient frontier).

Behavioral Finance Theme 2 involves the concept of *framing*. This term means the way in which a situation or choice is presented to an investor. Behavioral finance theorists argue that the framing of investment choices can result in significantly different assessments by an investor as to the risk and return of each choice and therefore the ultimate decision made.[6] Shefrin and Statman (1985) provide an example of faulty framing coupled with a cognitive bias. Individual investors often fail to treat the value of their stock portfolio at market value. Instead, investors maintain a "mental account," where they continue to market the value of each stock in their portfolio at

---

[5] These themes are from Shefrin (2002).
[6] See Tversky and Kahneman (1961 and 1986).

the purchase price despite the change in the market value. The psychological reason for investor reluctance to acknowledge any losses on stocks in their portfolio that it keeps alive the prospect that those stocks that have realized losses will subsequently recover and produce a gain. When investors ultimately dispose of their stocks, they close the mental account and only at that time acknowledge the loss that had occurred on paper. Hence, investment decisions are affected by this mental accounting treatment rather than being based on the true economic impact that an investment decision would have on the investor.

Hence, the second theme of behavioral finance is many times referred to as "frame dependence" because theorists argue that investment decisions are affected by framing. Traditional finance theorists, in contrast, assume believe that "frame independence." This means, according to Shefrin (2001, p. 4), that investors "view all decisions through the transparent, objective lens of risk and return."

How errors caused by heuristics and framing dependence affect the pricing of assets is Behavioral Finance Theme 3. In Chapter 4, we discussed the efficiency of markets. Behavioral finance theorists argue that markets will be inefficient because asset prices will not reflect their fundamental value due to the way investors make decisions. For this reason, Shefrin (2001) labels this theme of behavioral finance as "inefficient markets."

We have tossed out quite a bit of theory so far in this chapter. In traditional finance, we have a cornerstone theory in finance—the CAPM as formulated by Sharpe and others—that rests on another critical theory—the theory of portfolio selection as formulated by Markowitz. In the other camp is the behavioral finance theory lead by the various theories and studies by Kahneman. These are not minor theories. They all lead to the awarding of the Nobel Prize in Economic Sciences for their contribution—Markowitz and Sharpe in 1990 "for their pioneering work in the theory of financial economics" and Kahneman in 2002 "for having integrated insights from psychological research into economic science, especially concerning human judgment and decision-making under uncertainty." That leaves us with two theories: traditional finance theory or behavioral finance theory. Which theory is correct?

In fairness, we have not provided the responses of the supporters of traditional finance theory to the criticisms of those who support behavioral finance theory. Nor have we presented the attacks on behavioral finance. Fortunately, Hirshleifer (2001) provided that analysis by describing the common objections to both theories. He refers to the traditional finance theory as the "fully rational approach" and behavioral finance theory as the "psychological approach." A criticism of both approaches is that they can go "theory fishing" to find theories in market data to support their respective position. Objections to the fully rational approach are (1) that the calculations required for the implementation of this approach are extremely difficult to do; and (2) that there is ample empirical evidence that fails to support rational behavior by investors. Objections to the psychological approach according to Hirshleifer are (1) that "alleged psychology biases are arbitrary" and (2) that the experiments performed by researchers that find alleged psychological biases are arbitrary.

SUMMARY

Asset pricing involves determining the expected return required by investors in order to invest in financial assets. The output of asset pricing models are used by financial managers in estimating a firm's cost of capital and by investors as the interest rate used in calculating the present value of an asset's cash flows in order to estimate the asset's fair value. The two most well-known equilibrium pricing models are the capital asset pricing model developed in the 1960s and the arbitrage pricing theory model developed in the mid 1970s.

In deriving the CAPM, assumptions are made. A key assumption is that investors make investment decisions in according with the theory of portfolio selection as formulated by Markowitz. The goal of portfolio selection is the construction of portfolios that maximize expected returns consistent with individually acceptable levels of risk. In the theory of portfolio selection risk is measured by the variance (or standard deviation) of historical returns and the expected return as the mean of historical returns. Hence, this theory is popularly referred to as mean-variance analysis. The CAPM goes on to formalize the relationship that should exist between asset returns and risk if investors behave in a hypothesized manner. Together, the theory of portfolio selection and CAPM Provide a framework to specify and measure investment risk and to develop relationships between expected asset return and risk (and hence between risk and required return on an investment).

The CAPM asserts that the only risk that is priced by rational investors is systematic risk, because that risk cannot be eliminated by diversification. Essentially, the CAPM says that the expected return of a security or a portfolio is equal to the rate on a risk-free security plus a risk premium. The risk premium in the CAPM is the product of the quantity of risk times the market price of risk.

The beta of a security or portfolio is an index of the systematic risk of the asset and is estimated statistically. Historical beta is calculated from a time series of observations on both the asset's return and the market portfolio's return. This assumed relationship is called the characteristic line and is not an equilibrium model for predicting expected return, but rather a description of historical data.

There have been numerous empirical tests of the CAPM, and, in general, these have failed to fully support the theory. Roll (1977) criticized these studies because of the difficulty of identifying the true market portfolio. Furthermore, Roll asserts that such tests are not likely to appear soon, if at all.

There have been two major criticisms of the theory of portfolio selection upon which the CAPM provides the foundation for. The first is a criticism to the notion that the return distribution for assets is symmetric and follows a normal distribution. If that is not the case, the variance/standard deviation may be a poor measure of risk. The second criticism comes from a branch of finance known as behavioral finance. This branch of finance, which draws from the field of psychology, asserts that investor behavior is far different from that postulated by those who formulate traditional finance theories.

The arbitrage pricing theory is developed purely from arbitrage arguments. It postulates that the expected return on a security or a portfolio is influenced by several factors. Proponents of the APT model cite its less restrictive assumptions as a feature that makes it more appealing than the CAPM. Moreover, testing the APT model does not require identification of the "true" market portfolio. It does, however, require empirical determination of the factors because they are not specified by the theory. Consequently, the APT model replaces the problem of identifying the market portfolio in the CAPM with the problem of choosing and measuring the underlying factors.

Despite the fact that the theories presented are controversial or may be difficult to implement in practice, there are several principles of investing that are not controversial and can be used in developing investment strategies. First, investing has two dimensions, risk and return. Therefore, focusing only on the actual return of an asset or portfolio without looking at the risk that had to be accepted to achieve that return is inappropriate. Second, it is also inappropriate to look at the risk of an individual asset when deciding whether it should be included in a portfolio. What is important is how the inclusion of an asset into a portfolio will affect the risk of the portfolio. Third, whether investors consider one risk or a thousand risks, risk can be divided into two general categories: systematic risks that cannot be eliminated by diversification, and unsystematic risk that can be diversified away. Finally, investors should be compensated only for accepting systematic risks. Thus, it is critical in formulating an investment strategy to identify the systematic risks.

REFERENCES

Black, F. (1972). Capital market equilibrium with restricted borrowing. *Journal of Business* 45, no. 3: 444–455.

Fama, E. F. (1963). Mandelbrot and the stable Paretian hypothesis. *Journal of Business*, 36 (October): 420–429.

Fama, E. F. (1970). Efficient capital markets: A review of theory and empirical work. *Journal of Finance* 25, 2: 383–417.

Hirshleifer, D. (2001). Investor psychology and asset pricing. *Journal of Finance*, 56: 1533–1597.

Kahneman, D. and Tversky, A. (1979). Prospect theory: An analysis of decision under risk. *Econometrica* 47 (March): 236–291

Kahneman, D. and Tversky, A. (1992). Advances in prospect theory: Cumulative representation of uncertainty. *Journal of Risk and Uncertainty* 5: 297–323.

Kahneman, D., Slovic, P. and Tversky, A. (1982) *Judgment under Uncertainty: Heuristics and Biases*. New York: Cambridge University Press.

Lintner, J. (1965). The valuation of risk assets and the selection of risky investments in stock portfolio and capital budgets. *Review of Economics and Statistics* 47, no. 1: 13–37.

Mandelbrot, B. B. (1963). The variation of certain speculative prices. *Journal of Business* 36: 394–419.

Markowitz, H. M. (1952). Portfolio selection. *Journal of Finance* 7, no. 1: 77–91.

Merton, R. C. (1973). An intertemporal capital asset pricing model. *Econometrica* 41 (September): 867–888.

Mossin, J. (1966). Equilibrium in a capital asset market. *Econometrica* 34 (October): 768–783.

Oberlechner, T. (2007). *The Psychology of Ethics in the Finance and Investment Industry*. Charlottesville, VA: Research Foundation of CFA Institute.

Ortobelli, S., Rachev, S. T., Stoyanov, S., Fabozzi, F. J., and Biglova, A. (2005). The proper use of risk measures in portfolio theory. *International Journal of Theoretical and Applied Finance*, 8 (December): 1–27.

Rachev, S. T., Menn, C., and Fabozzi, F. J. (2005). *Fat-Tailed and Skewed Asset Return Distributions: Implications for Risk Management, Portfolio Selection, and Option Pricing*. Hoboken, NJ: John Wiley & Sons.

Rachev, S. T., Ortobelli, S., Stoyanov, S., Fabozzi, F. J.,and Biglova, A. (2008). Desirable properties of an ideal risk measure in portfolio theory. *International Journal of Theoretical and Applied Finance*, 11 (February): 19–54.

Ricciardi, V. (2008a). The psychology of risk: The behavioral finance perspective. In F. J. Fabozzi (ed.), *The Handbook of Finance: Volume II* (pp. 85–112). Hoboken, NJ: John Wiley & Sons.

Ricciardi, V. (2008b). Risk: Traditional finance versus behavioral finance. In F. J. Fabozzi (ed.), *The Handbook of Finance: Volume III* (pp. 11–38). Hoboken, NJ: John Wiley & Sons.

Roll, R. (1977). A critique of the asset pricing theory's tests. *Journal of Financial Economics* 4 (March): 129–176.

Ross, R. A. (1976). The arbitrage theory of capital asset pricing. *Journal of Economic Theory* 13 (December): 343–362.

Sharpe, W. F. (1964). Capital asset prices. *Journal of Finance* 19, no. 3: 425–442.

Sharpe, W. F. (1970). *Portfolio Theory and Capital Markets*. New York: McGraw-Hill.

Shefrin, H. and Statman, M. (1985). The disposition to sell winners too early and ride losers too long: Theory and evidence. *Journal of Finance* 40: 777–790.

Shefrin, H. (2002). *Beyond Greed and Fear: Understanding Behavioral Finance and the Psychology of Investing*. New York: Oxford University Press.

Statman, M. (2008). What is behavioral finance. In F.J. Fabozzi (ed.), *The Handbook of Finance: Volume II* (pp. 79–84). Hoboken, NJ: John Wiley & Sons.

Treynor, J. L. (1961). Toward a theory of market value of risky assets. Unpublished paper, Arthur D. Little, Cambridge, MA.

Tversky, A. and Kahneman, D. (1961). The framing of decisions and the psychology of choice, *Science* 211: 453–458;

Tversky, A. and Kahneman, D. (1986). Rational choice and the framing of decisions. *Journal of Business* 59 (October, Part 2): S251–S278.

Wagner, W. H., and Lau, S. (1971). The effect of diversification on risks. *Financial Analysts Journal* 27, no. 3: 48–53.

Wilcox, J. W. (2008). Behavioral finance. In F. J. Fabozzi (ed.), *The Handbook of Finance: Volume II* (pp. 71–78). Hoboken, NJ: John Wiley & Sons.

Financial Management

Financial Management

Financial management encompasses many different types of decisions. We can classify these decisions into three groups: investment decisions, financing decisions, and decisions that involve both investing and financing. Investment decisions are concerned with the use of funds—the buying, holding, or selling of all types of assets: Should we buy a new die stamping machine? Should we introduce a new product line? Sell the old production facility? Buy an existing company? Build a warehouse? Keep our cash in the bank?

Financing decisions are concerned with the acquisition of funds to be used for investing and financing day-to-day operations. Should managers use the money raised through the firms' revenues? Should they seek money from outside of the business? A company's operations and investment can be financed from outside the business by incurring debts, such as though bank loans and the sale of bonds, or by selling ownership interests. Because each method of financing obligates the business in different ways, financing decisions are very important.

Many business decisions simultaneously involve both investing and financing. For example, a company may wish to acquire another firm—an investment decision. However, the success of the acquisition may depend on how it is financed: by borrowing cash to meet the purchase price, by selling additional shares of stock, or by exchanging existing shares of stock. If managers decide to borrow money, the borrowed funds must be repaid within a specified period of time. Creditors (those lending the money) generally do not share in the control of profits of the borrowing firm. If, on the other hand, managers decide to raise funds by selling ownership interests, these funds never have to be paid back. However, such a sale dilutes the control of (and profits accruing to) the current owners.

Whether a financial decision involves investing, financing, or both, it also will be concerned with two specific factors: expected return and risk. *Expected return* is the difference between potential benefits and potential costs. *Risk* is the degree of uncertainty associated with these expected returns.

In this chapter, we provide an overview of financial management: the forms of business enterprise, the objectives of financial management, and the relationship between financial managers and shareholders and other stakeholders.

FORMS OF BUSINESS ENTERPRISE

Financial management is not restricted to large corporations: It is necessary in all forms and sizes of businesses. The three major forms of business organization are the sole proprietorship, the partnership, and the corporation. These three forms differ in a number of factors, of which those most important to financial decision-making are:

- The way the firm is taxed.
- The degree of control owners may exert on decisions.
- The liability of the owners.
- The ease of transferring ownership interests.
- The ability to raise additional funds.
- The longevity of the business.

Sole Proprietorships

The simplest and most common form of business enterprise is the *sole proprietorship*, a business owned and controlled by one person—the proprietor. Because there are very few legal requirements to establish and run a sole proprietorship, this form of business is chosen by many individuals who are starting up a particular business enterprise. The sole proprietor carries on a business for his or her own benefit, without participation of other persons except employees. The proprietor receives all income from the business and alone decides whether to reinvest the profits in the business or use them for personal expenses.

A proprietor is liable for all the debts of the business; in fact, it is the proprietor who incurs the debts of the business. If there are insufficient business assets to pay a business debt, the proprietor must pay the debt out of his or her personal assets. If more funds are needed to operate or expand the business than are generated by business operations, the owner either contributes his or her personal assets to the business or borrows. For most sole proprietorships, banks are the primary source of borrowed funds. However, there are limits to how much banks will lend a sole proprietorship, most of which are relatively small.

For tax purposes, the sole proprietor reports income from the business on his or her personal income tax return. Business income is treated as the proprietor's personal income.

The assets of a sole proprietorship may also be sold to some other firm, at which time the sole proprietorship ceases to exist. Or the life of a sole proprietorship ends with the life of the proprietor, although the assets of the business may pass to the proprietor's heirs.

Partnerships

A *partnership* is an agreement between two or more persons to operate a business. A partnership is similar to a sole proprietorship except instead of one proprietor, there is more than one. The fact that there is more than one proprietor introduces some issues: Who has a say in the day-to-day operations of the business? Who is liable (that is, financially responsible) for the debts of the business? How is the income distributed among the owners? How is the income taxed? Some of these issues are resolved with the partnership agreement; others are resolved by laws. The partnership agreement describes how profits and losses are to be shared among the partners, and it details their responsibilities in the management of the business.

Most partnerships are *general partnerships*, consisting only of general partners who participate fully in the management of the business, share in its profits and losses, and are responsible for its liabilities. Each general partner is personally and individually liable for the debts of the business, even if those debts were contracted by other partners.

A *limited partnership* consists of at least one general partner and one *limited partner*. Limited partners invest in the business, but do not participate in its management. A limited partner's share in the profits and losses of the business is limited by the partnership agreement. In addition, a limited partner is not liable for the debts incurred by the business beyond his or her initial investment.

A partnership is not taxed as a separate entity. Instead, each partner reports his or her share of the business profit or loss on his or her personal income tax return. Each partner's share is taxed as if it were from a sole proprietorship.

The life of a partnership may be limited by the partnership agreement. For example, the partners may agree that the partnership is to exist only for a specified number of years or only for the duration of a specific business transaction. The partnership must be terminated when any one of the partners dies, no matter what is specified in the partnership agreement. Partnership interests cannot be passed to heirs; at the death of any partner, the partnership is dissolved and perhaps renegotiated.

One of the drawbacks of partnerships is that a partner's interest in the business cannot be sold without the consent of the other partners. So a partner who needs to sell his or her interest because of, say, personal financial needs may not be able to do so. Still another problem involves ending a partnership and settling up, mainly because it is difficult to determine the value of the partnership and of each partner's share.

Another drawback is the partnership's limited access to new funds. Short of selling part of their own ownership interest, the partners can raise money only by borrowing from banks—and here too there is a limit to what a bank will lend a (usually small) partnership.

In certain businesses—including accounting, law, architecture, and physician's services—firms are commonly organized as partnerships. The use of this business form may be attributed primarily to state laws, regulations of the industry, and certifying organizations meant to keep practitioners in those fields from limiting their liability. Many states have allowed some types of business, such as accounting firms, that were previously restricted to the partnership form to become limited liability companies (a form of business discussed later).

Corporations

A *corporation* is a legal entity created under state laws through the process of incorporation. The corporation is an organization capable of entering into contracts and carrying out business under its own name, separate from it owners. To become a corporation, state laws generally require that a firm must do the following: (1) file articles of incorporation, (2) adopt a set of bylaws, and (3) form a board of directors.

The *articles of incorporation* specify the legal name of the corporation, its place of business, and the nature of its business. This certificate gives "life" to a corporation in the sense that it represents a contract between the corporation and its owners. This contract authorizes the corporation to issue units of ownership, called *shares*, and specifies the rights of the owners, the *shareholders*.

The bylaws are the rules of governance for the corporation. The bylaws define the rights and obligations of officers, members of the board of directors, and shareholders. In most large corporations, it is not possible for each owner to participate in monitoring the management of the business. Therefore, the owners of a corporation elect a board of directors to represent them in the major business decisions and to monitor the activities of the corporation's management. The board of directors, in turn, appoints and oversees the officers of the corporation. Directors who are also employees of the corporation are called *insider directors*; those who have no other position within the corporation are *outside directors* or *independent directors*. Generally it is believed that the greater the proportion of outside directors, the greater the board's independence from the management of the company. The proportion of outside directors on corporate boards varies significantly.

The state recognizes the existence of the corporation in the corporate charter. Corporate laws in many states follow a uniform set of laws referred to as the *Model Business Corporations Act*. (A *Model act* is a statute created and proposed by the National Conference of Commissioners of Uniform State Laws. A Model act is available for adoption—with or without modification—by state legislatures.) Once created, the corporation can enter into contracts, adopt a legal name, sue or be sued, and continue in existence forever. Though owners may die, the corporation continues to live. The liability of owners is limited to the amounts they have invested in the corporation through the shares of ownership they purchased.

Unlike the sole proprietorship and partnership, the corporation is a taxable entity. It files its own income tax return and pays taxes on its income. That income is determined according to special provisions of the federal and state tax codes and is subject to corporate tax rates different from personal income tax rates.

If the board of directors decides to distribute cash to the owners, that money is paid out of income left over after the corporate income tax has been paid. The amount of that cash payment, or dividend, must also be included in the taxable income of the owners (the shareholders). Therefore, a portion of the corporation's income (the portion paid out to owners) is subject to double taxation: once as corporate income and once as the individual owner's income.

The dividend declared by the directors of a corporation is distributed to owners in proportion to the numbers of shares of ownership they hold. If Owner A has twice as many shares as Owner B, he or she will receive twice as much money.

The ownership of a corporation, also referred to as stock or equity, is represented as shares of stock. A corporation that has just a few owners who exert complete control over the decisions of the corporation is referred to as a *close corporation* or a *closely-held corporation*. A corporation whose ownership shares are sold outside of a closed group of owners is referred to as a *public corporation* or a *publicly-held corporation*. Mars Inc., producer of M&M candies and other confectionery products, is a closely-held corporation; Hershey Foods, also a producer of candy products among other things, is a publicly-held corporation.

The shares of public corporations are freely traded in securities markets, such as the New York Stock Exchange. Hence, the ownership of a publicly-held corporation is more easily transferred than the ownership of a proprietorship, a partnership, or a closely-held corporation.

Companies whose stock is traded in public markets are required to file an initial registration statement with the Securities and Exchange Commission, a federal agency created to oversee the enforcement of U.S. securities laws. The statement provides financial statements, articles of incorporation, and descriptive information regarding the nature of the business, the debt and stock of the corporation, the officers and directors, any individuals who own more than 10% of the stock, among other items.

Other Forms of Business

In addition to the proprietorship, partnership, and corporate forms of business, an enterprise may be conducted using other forms of business, such as the master limited partnership, the professional corporation, the limited liability company, and the joint venture.

A *master limited partnership* is a partnership with limited partner ownership interests that are traded on an organized exchange. For example, more than two dozen master limited partnerships are listed on the New York Stock Exchange, including the Cedar Fair, Global Partners, and Sunoco Logistics Partners partnerships. Ownership interests, which represent a specified ownership percentage, are traded in much the same way as the shares of stock of a corporation. One difference, however, is that a corporation can raise new capital by issuing new ownership interests, whereas a master limited partnership cannot. It is not possible to sell more than a 100% interest in the partnership, yet it is possible to sell additional shares of stock in a corporation. Another difference is that the income of a master limited partnership is taxed only once, as partners' individual income.

Another variant of the corporate form of business is the professional corporation. A *professional corporation* is an organization that is formed under state law and treated as a corporation for federal tax law purposes, yet that has unlimited liability for its owners—the owners are personally liable for the debts of the corporation. Businesses that are likely to form such corporations are those that provide services and require state licensing, such as physicians', architects', and attorneys' practices since it is generally felt that it is in the public interest to hold such professionals responsible for the liabilities of the business.

More recently, companies are using a hybrid form of business, the *limited liability company* (LLC), which combines the best features of a partnership and a corporation. In 1988, the Internal Revenue Service (IRS) ruled that the LLC be treated as a partnership for tax purposes, while its owners are not liable for its debts. Since this ruling, every state has passed legislation permitting limited liability companies.

Though state laws vary slightly, in general, the owners of the LLC have limited liability. The IRS considers the LLC to be taxed as a partnership if the company has no more than two of the following characteristics: (1) limited liability, (2) centralized management, (3) free transferability of ownership interests, and (4) continuity of life. If the company has more than two of these, it will be treated as a corporation for tax purposes, subjecting the income to taxation at both the company level and the owners'.

A *joint venture*, which may be structured as either a partnership or as a corporation, is a business undertaken by a group of persons or entities (such as a partnership or corporation) for a specific business activity and, therefore, does not constitute a continuing relationship among the parties. For tax and other legal purposes, a joint venture partnership is treated as a partnership and a joint venture corporation is treated as a corporation.

U.S. corporations have entered into joint ventures with foreign corporations, enhancing participation and competition in the global marketplace. Joint ventures are becoming increasingly popular as a way of doing business. Participants—whether individuals, partnerships, or corporations—get together to exploit a specific business opportunity. Afterward, the venture can be dissolved. Recent alliances among communication and entertainment firms have sparked thought about what the future form of doing business will be. Some believe that what lies ahead is a virtual enterprise—a temporary alliance without all the bureaucracy of the typical corporation—that can move quickly and decisively to take advantage of profitable business opportunities.

Prevalence

The advantages and disadvantages of the three major forms of business from the point of view of financial decision-making are summarized in Table 9.1. Firms tend to evolve from proprietorship to partnership to corporation as they grow and as their needs for financing increase. Sole proprietorship is the choice for starting a business, whereas the corporation is the choice to accommodate growth. The great majority of business firms in the United States are sole proprietorships, but most business income is generated by corporations.

THE OBJECTIVE OF FINANCIAL MANAGEMENT

So far we have seen that financial managers are primarily concerned with investment decisions and financing decisions within business organizations.

TABLE 9.1 Characteristics of the Three Basic Forms of Business

Sole Proprietorship

Advantages	*Disadvantages*
1. The proprietor is the sole business decision-maker.	1. The proprietor is liable for all debts of the business (unlimited liability).
2. The proprietor receives all income from business.	2. The proprietorship has a limited life.
3. Income from the business is taxed once, at the individual taxpayer level.	3. There is limited access to additional funds.

General Partnership

Advantages	*Disadvantages*
1. Partners receive income according to terms in partnership agreement.	1. Each partner is liable for all the debts of the partnership.
2. Income from business is taxed once as the partners' personal income.	2. The partnership's life is determined by agreement or the life of the partners.
3. Decision-making rests with the general partners only.	3. There is limited access to additional funds.

Corporation

Advantages	*Disadvantages*
1. The firm has perpetual life.	1. Income paid to owners is subjected to double taxation.
2. Owners are not liable for the debts of the firm; the most that owners can lose is their initial investment.	2. Ownership and management are separated in larger organizations.
3. The firm can raise funds by selling additional ownership interest.	
4. 4. Income is distributed in proportion to ownership interest.	

The great majority of these decisions are made within the corporate business structure, which better accommodates growth and is responsible for 89% of U.S. business income. One such issue concerns the objective of financial decision-making. What goal (or goals) do managers have in mind when they choose between financial alternatives—say, between distributing current income among shareholders and investing it to increase future income? There is actually one financial objective: the maximization of the economic well-being, or wealth, of the owners. Whenever a decision is to be made, management should choose the alternative that most increases the wealth of the owners of the business.

The Measure of Owner's Economic Well-Being

The price of a share of stock at any time, or its *market value*, represents the price that buyers in a free market are willing to pay for it. The *market value of shareholders' equity* is the value of all owners' interest in the corporation. It is calculated as the product of the market value of one share of stock and the number of shares of stock outstanding:

Market value of shareholders' equity
= Market value of a share of stock × Number of shares of stock outstanding

The number of shares of stock outstanding is the total number of shares that are owned by shareholders. For example, at the end of December 2007, there were 1.88 billion Walt Disney Company shares outstanding. The price of Disney stock at the end of 2007 was $32.28 per share. Therefore, the market value of Disney equity at the end of 2007 was over $60 billion.

Investors buy shares of stock in anticipation of future dividends and increases in the market value of the stock. How much are they willing to pay today for this future—and hence uncertain—stream of dividends? They are willing to pay exactly what they believe it is worth today, an amount that is called the *present value*, an important financial concept. The present value of a share of stock reflects the following factors:

- The uncertainty associated with receiving future payments.
- The timing of these future payments.
- Compensation for tying up funds in this investment.

The market price of a share is a measure of owners' economic well-being. Does this mean that if the share price goes up, management is doing a good job? Not necessarily. Share prices often can be influenced by factors beyond the control of management. These factors include expectations regarding the economy, returns available on alternative investments (such as bonds), and even how investors view the firm and the idea of investing.

These factors influence the price of shares through their effects on expectations regarding future cash flows and investors' evaluation of those cash flows. Nonetheless, managers can still maximize the value of owners' equity, given current economic conditions and expectations. They do so by carefully considering the expected benefits, risk, and timing of the returns on proposed investments.

Economic Profit vs. Accounting Profit: Share Price vs. Earnings Per Share

When you studied economics, you saw that the objective of the firm is to maximize profit. In finance, however, the objective is to maximize owners' wealth. Is this a contradiction? No. We have simply used different terminology to express the same goal. The difference arises from the distinction between accounting profit and economic profit.

Economic profit is the difference between revenues and costs, where costs include both the actual business costs (the explicit costs) and the implicit costs. The implicit costs are the payments that are necessary to secure the needed resources, the *cost of capital*. With any business enterprise, someone supplies funds, or capital, that the business then invests. The supplier of these funds may be the business owner, an entrepreneur, or banks, bondholders, and shareholders. The cost of capital depends on both the time value of money—what could have been earned on a risk-free investment—and the uncertainty associated with the investment. The greater the uncertainty associated with an investment, the greater the cost of capital.

Consider the case of the typical corporation. Shareholders invest in the shares of a corporation with the expectation that they will receive future dividends. But shareholders could have invested their funds in any other investment, as well. So what keeps them interested in keeping their money in the particular corporation? Getting a return on their investment that is better than they could get elsewhere, considering the amount of uncertainty of receiving the future dividends. If the corporation cannot generate economic profits, the shareholders will move their funds elsewhere.

Accounting profit, however, is the difference between revenues and costs, recorded according to accounting principles, where costs are primarily the actual costs of doing business. The implicit costs—opportunity cost and normal profit—which reflect the uncertainty and timing of future cash flows, are not taken into consideration in accounting profit. Moreover accounting procedures, and, therefore, the computation of accounting profit, can vary from firm to firm. For both these reasons, accounting profit is not a reasonable gauge of shareholders' return on their investment, and the maximization of accounting profit is not equivalent to the maximization of shareholder wealth. When economic profit is zero, as an example, investors are getting a return that just compensates them for bearing the risk of the investment. When accounting profit is zero, investors would be much better off investing elsewhere and just as well off by keeping their money under their mattresses.

Many U.S. corporations, including Coca-Cola, Briggs & Stratton, and Boise Cascade, are embracing a relatively new method of evaluating and rewarding management performance that is based on the idea of compensating management for economic profit, rather than for accounting profit. The most prominent of recently developed techniques to evaluate a firm's performance are economic value-added and market value-added.

Economic value-added (EVA®) is another name for the firm's economic profit. Key elements of estimating economic profit are:

1. Calculating the firm's operating profit from financial statement data, making adjustments to accounting profit to better reflect a firm's operating results for a period.
2. Calculating the cost of capital.
3. Comparing operating profit with the cost of capital.

The difference between the operating profit and the cost of capital is the estimate of the firm's economic profit, or economic value-added. One of the first to advocate using economic profit in compensating management is Stewart (1991).

A related measure, *market value added* (MVA), focuses on the market value of capital, as compared to the cost of capital. The key elements of market value added are:

1. Calculating the market value of capital.
2. Calculating the amount of capital invested (i.e., debt and equity).
3. Comparing the market value of capital with the capital invested.

The difference between the market value of capital and the amount of capital invested is the market value added. In theory, the market value added is the present value of all expected future economic profits.

Share Prices and Efficient Markets

We have seen that the price of a share of stock today is the present value of the dividends and share price the investor expects to receive in the future. What if these expectations change?

Suppose you buy a share of stock of IBM. The price you are willing to pay is the present value of future cash flows that you expect from dividends paid on one share of IBM stock and from the eventual sale of that share. This price reflects the amount, the timing, and the uncertainty of these future cash flows. Now what happens if some news—good or bad—is announced that changes the expected IBM dividends? If the market in which these shares are traded is efficient, the price will fall very quickly to reflect that news.

In an efficient market, the price of assets—in this case shares of stock—reflects all publicly available information. As information is received by investors, share prices change rapidly to reflect the new information. How rapidly? In U.S. stock markets, which are efficient markets, information affecting a firm is reflected in share prices of its stock within minutes.

What are the implications for financing decisions? In efficient markets, the current price of a firm's shares reflects all publicly available information. Hence, there is no good time or bad time to issue a security. When a firm issues stock, it will receive what that stock is worth—no more and no less. Also, the price of the shares will change as information about the firm's activities is revealed. If the firm announces a new product, investors use whatever information they have to figure out how this new product will change the firm's future cash flows and, therefore, the value of the firm and share price, accordingly. Moreover, in time, the price will be such that investors' economic profit approaches zero.

Financial Management and the Maximization of Owners' Wealth

Financial managers are charged with the responsibility of making decisions that maximize owners' wealth. For a corporation, that responsibility translates into maximizing the value of shareholders' equity. If the market for stocks is efficient, the value of a share of stock in a corporation should reflect investors' expectations regarding the future prospects of the corporation. The value of a stock will change as investors' expectations about the future change. For financial managers' decisions to add value, the present value of the benefits resulting from decisions must outweigh the associated costs, where costs include the costs of capital.

If there is a separation of the ownership and management of a firm—that is, the owners are not also the managers of the firm—there are additional issues to confront. What if a decision is in the best interests of the firm, but not in the best interest of the manager? How can owners ensure that managers are watching out for the owners' interests? How can owners motivate managers to make decisions that are best for the owners? We address these issues and more in the next section.

THE AGENCY RELATIONSHIP

If you are the sole owner of a business, you make the decisions that affect your own well-being. But what if you are a financial manager of a business and you are not the sole owner? In this case, you are making decisions for owners other than yourself; you, the financial manager, are an agent. An *agent* is a person who acts for—and exerts powers of—another person or group of persons. The person (or group of persons) the agent represents is referred to as the *principal*. The relationship between the agent and his or her principal is an agency relationship. There is an agency relationship between the managers and the shareholders of corporations.

Problems with the Agency Relationship

In an agency relationship, the agent is charged with the responsibility of acting for the principal. Is it possible the agent may not act in the best interest of the principal, but instead act in his or her own self-interest? Yes—because the agent has his or her own objective of maximizing personal wealth.

In a large corporation, for example, the managers may enjoy many fringe benefits, such as golf club memberships, access to private jets, and company cars. These benefits (also called *perquisites* or *perks*) may be useful in conducting business and may help attract or retain management personnel, but there is room for abuse. What if the managers start spending more time at the golf course than at their desks? What if they use the company jets for personal travel? What if they buy company cars for their teenagers to drive? The abuse of perquisites imposes costs on the firm—and ultimately on the owners of the firm. There is also a possibility that managers who feel secure in their positions may not bother to expend their best efforts toward the business. This is referred to as *shirking*, and it too imposes a cost to the firm.

Finally, there is the possibility that managers will act in their own self-interest, rather than in the interest of the shareholders when those interests clash. For example, management may fight the acquisition of their firm by some other firm, even if the acquisition would benefit shareholders. Why? In most takeovers, the management personnel of the acquired firm generally lose their jobs. Envision that some company is making an offer to acquire the firm that you manage. Are you happy that the acquiring firm is offering the shareholders of your firm more for their stock than its current market value? If you are looking out for their best interests, you should be. Are you happy about the likely prospect of losing your job? Most likely not.

Many managers faced this dilemma in the merger mania of the 1980s. So what did they do? Among the many tactics, they did the following:

- Some fought acquisition of their firms—which they labeled *hostile takeovers*—by proposing changes in the corporate charter or even lobbying for changes in state laws to discourage takeovers.
- Some adopted lucrative executive compensation packages—called *golden parachutes*—that were to go into effect if they lost their jobs.

Such defensiveness by corporate managers in the case of takeovers, whether it is warranted or not, emphasizes the potential for conflict between the interests of the owners and the interests of management.

Costs of the Agency Relationship

There are costs involved with any effort to minimize the potential for conflict between the principal's interest and the agent's interest. Such costs are called *agency costs*, and they are of three types: monitoring costs, bonding costs, and residual loss.

Monitoring costs are costs incurred by the principal to monitor or limit the actions of the agent. In a corporation, shareholders may require managers to periodically report on their activities via audited accounting statements, which are sent to shareholders. The accountants' fees and the management time lost in preparing such statements are monitoring costs. Another example is the implicit cost incurred when shareholders limit the decision-making power of managers. By doing so, the owners may miss profitable investment opportunities; the foregone profit is a monitoring cost.

The board of directors of corporation has a *fiduciary duty* to shareholders; that is the legal responsibility to make decisions (or to see that decisions are made) that are in the best interests of shareholders. Part of that responsibility is to ensure that managerial decisions are also in the best interests of the shareholders. Therefore, at least part of the cost of having directors is a monitoring cost.

Bonding costs are incurred by agents to assure principals that they will act in the principal's best interest. The name comes from the agent's promise or bond to take certain actions. A manager may enter into a contract that requires him or her to stay on with the firm even though another company acquires it; an implicit cost is then incurred by the manager, who foregoes other employment opportunities.

Even when monitoring and bonding devices are used, there may be some divergence between the interests of principals and those of agents. The resulting cost, called the *residual loss*, is the implicit cost that results because the principal's and the agent's interests cannot be perfectly aligned even when monitoring and bonding costs are incurred.

Motivating Managers: Executive Compensation

One way to encourage management to act in shareholders' best interests, and so minimize agency problems and costs, is through executive compensation—how top management is paid. There are several different ways to compensate executives, including:

- *Salary.* The direct payment of cash of a fixed amount per period.
- *Bonus.* A cash reward based on some performance measure, say, earnings of a division or the company.
- *Stock appreciation right.* A cash payment based on the amount by which the value of a specified number of shares has increased over a specified period of time (supposedly due to the efforts of management).
- *Performance shares.* Shares of stock given the employees, in an amount based on some measure of operating performance, such as earnings per share.
- *Stock option.* The right to buy a specified number of shares of stock in the company at a stated price—referred to as an exercise price at some time in the future. The exercise price may be above, at, or below the current market price of the stock.
- *Restricted stock grant.* The grant of shares of stock to the employee at low or no cost, conditional on the shares not being sold for a specified time.

The salary portion of the compensation—the minimum cash payment an executive receives—must be enough to attract talented executives. But a bonus should be based on some measure of performance that is in the best interests of shareholders—not just on the past year's accounting earnings. For example, a bonus could be based on gains in market share. Recently, several companies have adopted programs that base compensation, at least in part, on value added by managers as measured by economic profits.

The basic idea behind stock options and restricted stock grants is to make managers owners, since the incentive to consume excessive perks and to shirk are reduced if managers are also owners. As owners, managers not only share the costs of perks and shirks, but they also benefit financially when their decisions maximize the wealth of owners. Hence, the key to motivation through stock is not really the *value* of the stock, but rather *ownership* of the stock. For this reason, stock appreciation rights and performance shares, which do not involve an investment on the part of recipients, are not effective motivators.

Stock options do work to motivate performance if they require owning the shares over a long time period; are exercisable at a price significantly *above* the current market price of the shares, thus encouraging managers to get the share price up, and require managers to tie up their own wealth in the shares. Unfortunately, the design and implementation of executive stock option programs have not always been designed in ways to sufficiently motivate executives.

Currently, there is a great deal of concern in some corporations because executive compensation is not linked to performance. In recent years, many

U.S. companies have downsized, restructured, and laid off many employees and allowed the wages of employees who survive the cuts to stagnate. At the same time, corporations have increased the pay of top executives through both salary and lucrative stock options. If these changes lead to better value for shareholders, shouldn't the top executives be rewarded?

There are two issues here. First, such a situation results in anger and disenchantment among both surviving employees and former employees. Second, the downsizing, restructuring, and lay-offs may not result in immediate (or even, eventual) increased profitability.

Another problem is that the reports disclosing these compensation packages to shareholders (the proxy statements) have often been confusing. The changes in securities laws in response to the Sarbanes-Oxley Act of 2002 and other related changes in rules and regulations require more transparency in the reporting of compensation of top executives.

Owners have one more tool with which to motivate management—the threat of firing. As long as owners can fire managers, managers will be encouraged to act in the owners' interest. However, if the owners are divided or apathetic—as they often are in large corporations—or if they fail to monitor management's performance and the reaction of directors to that performance, the threat may not be credible. The removal of a few poor managers can, however, make this threat palpable.

Shareholder Wealth Maximization and Accounting "Irregularities"

Recently, there have been a number of scandals and allegations regarding the financial information that is being reported to shareholders and the market. Financial results reported in the income statements and balance sheets of some companies indicated much better performance than the true performance or much better financial condition than actual. Examples include Xerox, which was forced to restate earnings for several years because it had inflated pre-tax profits by $1.4 billion, Enron, which was accused of inflating earnings and hiding substantial debt, and Worldcom, which failed to properly account for $3.8 billion of expenses. Along with these financial reporting issues, the independence of the auditors and the role of financial analysts have been brought to the forefront. For example, the public accounting firm of Arthur Andersen was found guilty of obstruction of justice in 2002 for their role in the shredding of documents relating to Enron. As an example of the problems associated with financial analysts, the securities firm of Merrill Lynch paid a $100 million fine for their role in hyping stocks to help win investment-banking business.

It is unclear at this time the extent to which these scandals and problems were the result of simply bad decisions or due to corruption. The eagerness of managers to present favorable results to shareholders and the market appears to be a factor in several instances. And personal enrichment at the expense of shareholders seems to explain some cases. Whatever the motivation, *chief executive officers* (CEOs), *chief financial officers* (CFOs), and board members are being held directly accountable for financial disclosures. The Sarbanes-Oxley Act, passed in 2002, addresses these and other issues pertaining to disclosures and governance in public corporations. This Act addresses audits by independent public accountants, financial reporting and disclosures, conflicts of interest, and corporate governance at public companies. Each of the provisions of this Act can be traced to one or more scandals that occurred in the few years leading up to the passage of the Act.

The accounting scandals created an awareness of the importance of corporate governance, the importance of the independence of the public accounting auditing function, the role of financial analysts, and the responsibilities of CEOs and CFOs. However, the recent events related to subprime mortgage lending and investing suggests that more reform may be necessary to insure transparency of financial information and a better linkage between pay and performance.

Shareholder Wealth Maximization and Social Responsibility

When financial managers assess a potential investment in a new product, they examine the risks and the potential benefits and costs. If the risk-adjusted benefits do not outweigh the costs, they will not invest. Similarly, managers assess current investments for the same purpose; if benefits do not continue to outweigh costs, they will not continue to invest in the product but will shift their investment elsewhere. This is consistent with the goal of shareholder wealth maximization and with the allocative efficiency of the market economy.

Discontinuing investment in an unprofitable business may mean closing down plants, laying off workers, and, perhaps destroying an entire town that depends on the business for income. So decisions to invest or disinvest may affect great numbers of people.

All but the smallest business firms are linked in some way to groups of persons who are dependent to a degree on the business. These groups may include suppliers, customers, the community itself, and nearby businesses, as well as employees and shareholders. The various groups of persons that depend on a firm are referred to as its *stakeholders*; they all have some *stake* in the outcome of the firm. For example, if the Boeing Company lays off workers or increases production, the effects are felt by Seattle and the surrounding communities.

Can a firm maximize the wealth of shareholders and stakeholders at the same time? Probably. If a firm invests in the production of goods and services that meet the demand of consumers in such a way that benefits exceed costs, the firm will be allocating the resources of the community efficiently, employing assets in their most productive use. If later the firm must disinvest—perhaps close a plant—it has a responsibility to assist employees and other stakeholders who are affected. Failure to do so could tarnish its reputation, erode its ability to attract new stakeholder groups to new investments, and ultimately act to the detriment of shareholders.

The effects of a firm's actions on others are referred to as *externalities*. Pollution is an externality that keeps increasing in importance. Suppose the manufacture of a product creates air pollution. If the polluting firm acts to reduce this pollution, it incurs a cost that either increases the price of its product or decreases profit and the market value of its stock. If competitors do not likewise incur costs to reduce their pollution, the firm is at a disadvantage and may be driven out of business through competitive pressure.

The firm may try to use its efforts at pollution control to enhance its reputation in the hope that this will lead to a sales increase large enough to make up for the cost of reducing pollution. This is called a *market solution*: The market places a value on the pollution control and rewards the firm (or an industry) for it. If society really believes that pollution is bad and that pollution control is good, the interests of owners and society can be aligned.

It is more likely, however, that pollution control costs will be viewed as reducing owners' wealth. Then firms must be forced to reduce pollution through laws or government regulations. But such laws and regulations also come with a cost—the cost of enforcement. Again, if the benefits of mandatory pollution control outweigh the cost of government action, society is better off. In such a case, if the government requires all firms to reduce pollution, then pollution control costs simply become one of the conditions under which owner wealth-maximizing decisions are to be made.

DIVIDEND AND DIVIDEND POLICIES

Many corporations pay cash dividends to their shareholders and, despite the tax consequences of these dividends and the fact that these funds could otherwise be plowed back into the corporation for investment purposes, these dividends are often viewed as a signal of the corporation's future prosperity. Corporations may also "pay" stock dividends or split the stock, dividing the equity pie into smaller pieces, the announcement of which is often viewed as positive news by investors. Funds can be paid out to shareholders other than in the form of a cash dividend; corporation may repurchase their shares from shareholders through open market purchases, tender offers, or targeted block repurchases.

Dividends

A dividend is the cash, stock, or any type of property a corporation distributes to its shareholders. The board of directors may declare a dividend at any time, but dividends are not a legal obligation of the corporation—it is the board's choice. Unlike interest on debt securities, if a corporation does not pay a dividend, there is no violation of a contract and no legal recourse for shareholders.

Most dividends are in the form of cash. Cash dividends are payments made directly to shareholders in proportion to the shares they own. Cash dividends are paid on all outstanding shares of stock. A few companies pay special or extra dividends occasionally—identifying these dividends apart from their regular dividends.

We usually describe the cash dividends that a company pays in terms of *dividends per share* and is calculated as follows:

$$\text{Dividends per share} = \frac{\text{Common stock dividends}}{\text{Number of common shares outstanding}}$$

Another way of describing cash dividends is in terms of the percentage of earnings paid out in dividends, referred to as the *dividend payout*. The dividend payout can be expressed in terms of dividends and shares outstanding:

$$\text{Dividend payout} = \frac{\text{Common stock dividends}}{\text{Earnings available to common shareholders}}$$

If we divide both the numerator and the denominator by the number of common shares outstanding, we can rewrite the dividend payout as:

$$\text{Dividend payout} = \frac{\text{Dividends per share}}{\text{Earnings per share}}$$

Dividend Reinvestment Plans

Many U.S. corporations allow shareholders to reinvest automatically their dividends in the shares of the corporation paying them. A *dividend reinvestment plan* (DRP) is a program that allows shareholders to reinvest their dividends, buying additional shares of stock of the company instead of receiving the cash dividend. A DRP offers benefits to both shareholders and the corporation. Shareholders buy shares without transactions costs—brokers' commissions—and at a discount from the current market price. The corporation is able to retain cash without the cost of a new stock issue. Alas, the dividends are taxed as income before they are reinvested, even though the shareholders never see the dividend. The result is similar to a dividend cut, but with a tax consequence for the shareholders: The cash flow that would have been paid to shareholders is plowed back into the corporation. Many corporations are finding high rates of participation in DRPs. If so many shareholders want to reinvest their dividends—even after considering the tax consequences—why is the corporation paying dividends? This suggests that there is some rationale, such as signaling (discussed later in this chapter), which compels corporations to pay dividends.

Stock Distributions

In addition to cash dividends, a corporation may provide shareholders with dividends in the form of additional shares of stock or, rarely, some types of property owned by the corporation When dividends are not in cash, they are usually additional shares of stock. Additional shares of stock can be distributed to shareholders in two ways: paying a stock dividend and splitting the stock.

A *stock dividend* is the distribution of additional shares of stock to shareholders. Stock dividends are generally stated as a percentage of existing share holdings. If a corporation pays a stock dividend, it is not transferring anything of value to the shareholders. The assets of the corporation remain the same and each shareholder's proportionate share of ownership remains the same. All the corporation is doing is cutting its equity pie into more slices and at the same time cutting each shareholder's portion of that equity into more slices. So why pay a stock dividend?

There are a couple of reasons for paying dividends in the form of stock dividends. One is to provide information to the market. A company may want to communicate good news to the shareholders without paying cash. For example, if the corporation has an attractive investment opportunity and needs funds for it, paying a cash dividend doesn't make any sense—so the corporation pays a stock dividend instead. But is this an effective way of communicating good news to the shareholders? It costs very little to pay a stock dividend—just minor expenses for recordkeeping, printing, and distribution. But if it costs very little, do investors really believe in devices where management is not putting "its money where its mouth is"?

Another reason given for paying a stock dividend is to reduce the price of the stock. If the price of a stock is high relative to most other stocks, there may be higher costs related to investors' transactions of the stock, as in a higher broker's commission. By paying a stock dividend—which slices the equity pie into more pieces—the price of the stock should decline. Let's see how this works. Suppose an investor owns 1,000 shares, each worth $50 per share, for a total investment of $50,000. If the corporation pays the investor a 5% stock dividend, the investor then owns 1,050 shares after the dividend. Is there any reason for your holdings to change in value? Nothing economic has gone on here—the company has the same assets, the same liabilities, and the same equity—total equity is just cut up into smaller pieces. There is no reason for the value of the portion of the equity this investor owns to change. But the price *per share* should decline: from $50 per share to $47.62 per share. The argument for reducing the share price only works if the market brings down the price substantially, from an unattractive trading range to a more attractive trading range in terms of reducing brokerage commissions and enabling small investors to purchase even lots of 100 shares.

A stock split is something like a stock dividend. A *stock split* splits the number of existing shares into more shares. For example, in a 2:1 split—referred to as "two for one"—each shareholder gets two shares for every one owned. If an investor owns 1,000 shares and the stock is split 2:1, the investor then owns 2,000 shares after the split. Has the portion of the investor's ownership in the company changed? No, the investor now simply owns twice as many shares—and so does every other shareholder. If the investor owned 1% of the corporation's stock before the split, the investor still owns 1% after the split.

So why split? Like a stock dividend, the split reduces the trading price of shares. If an investor owns 1,000 shares of the stock trading for $50 per share prior to a 2:1 split, the shares should trade for $25 per share after the split.

Aside from a minor difference in accounting, stock splits and stock dividends are essentially the same. The stock dividend requires a shift within the stockholders' equity accounts, from retained earnings to paid-in capital, for the amount of the distribution; the stock split requires only a memorandum entry.

A 2:1 split has the same effect on a stock's price as a 100% stock dividend, a 1.5 to 1 split has the same effect on a stock's price as a 50% stock dividend, and so on. The basis of the accounting rules is related to the reasons behind the distribution of additional shares. If firms want to bring down their share price, they tend to declare a stock split; if firms want to communicate news, they often declare a stock dividend.

How can investors tell what the motivation is behind stock dividends and stock splits? They cannot, but they can get a general idea of how investors interpret these actions by looking at what happens to the corporation's share price when a corporation announces its decision to pay a stock dividend or split its stock, or reverse split. If the share price tends to go up when the announcement is made, the decision is probably good news; if the price tends to go down, the stock dividend is probably bad news. This is supported by evidence that indicates corporation's earnings tend to increase following stock splits and dividends.[1]

The share price of companies announcing stock distributions and stock splits generally increase at the time of the announcement. The stock price typically increases by 1% to 2% when the split or stock dividend is announced. When the stock dividend is distributed or the split is effected (on the "ex" date), the share's price typically declines according to the amount of the distribution. Suppose a firm announces a 2:1 split. Its share price may increase by 1% to 2% when this is announced, but when the shares are split, the share price will go down to approximately half of its presplit value.[2] The most likely explanation is that this distribution is interpreted as good news—that management believes that the future prospects of the company are favorable or that the share price is more attractive to investors.

Dividend Policy

A dividend policy is a corporation's decision about the payment of cash dividends to shareholders. There are several basic ways of describing a corporation's dividend policy:

- No dividends.
- Constant growth in dividends per share.
- Constant payout ratio.
- Low regular dividends with periodic extra dividends.

The corporations that typically do not pay dividends are those that are generally viewed as younger, faster growing companies. For example, Microsoft Corporation was founded in 1975 and went public in 1986, but it did not pay a cash dividend until January 2003.

A common pattern of cash dividends tends to be the constant growth of dividends per share. Another pattern is the constant payout ratio. Many other companies in the food processing industry, such as Kellogg and Tootsie Roll Industries, pay dividends that are a relatively constant percentage of earnings. Some companies display both a constant dividend payout and a constant growth in dividends. This type of dividend pattern is characteristic of large, mature companies that have predictable earnings growth—the divi-

---

[1] See, for example, McNichols and Dravid (1990).
[2] See, for example, Grinblatt, Masulis, and Titman (1984).

dends growth tends to mimic the earnings growth, resulting in a constant payout.

U.S. corporations that pay dividends tend to pay either constant or increasing dividends per share. Dividends tend to be lower in industries that have many profitable opportunities to invest their earnings. But as a company matures and finds fewer and fewer profitable investment opportunities, a greater portion of its earnings are paid out in dividends.

Many corporations are reluctant to cut dividends because the corporation's share price usually falls when a dividend reduction is announced. For example, the U.S. auto manufacturers cut dividends during the recession in the early 1990s. As earnings per share declined the auto makers did not cut dividends until earnings per share were negative—and in the case of General Motors, not until it had experienced two consecutive loss years. But as earnings recovered in the mid-1990s, dividends were increased. (General Motors increased dividends until cutting them once again in 2006 as it incurred substantial losses.) Corporations tend to only raise their regular quarterly dividend when they are sure they can keep it up in the future. By giving a special or extra dividend, the corporation is able to provide more cash to the shareholders without committing itself to paying an increased dividend each period into the future.

There is no general agreement whether dividends should or should not be paid. Here are several views:

- *The Dividend Irrelevance Theory.* The payment of dividends does not affect the value of the firm since the investment decision is independent of the financing decision.
- *The "Bird in the Hand" Theory.* Investors prefer a certain dividend stream to an uncertain price appreciation.
- *The Tax-Preference Explanation.* Due to the way in which dividends are taxed, investors should prefer the retention of funds to the payment of dividends.
- *The Signaling Explanation.* Dividends provide a way for the management to inform investors about the firm's future prospects.
- *The Agency Explanation.* The payment of dividends forces the firm to seek more external financing, which subjects the firm to the scrutiny of investors.

The Dividend Irrelevance Theory

The dividend irrelevance argument was developed by Merton Miller and Franco Modigliani (1961). Basically, the argument is that if there is a *perfect market*—no taxes, no transactions costs, no costs related to issuing new securities, and no costs of sending or receiving information—the value of the corporation is unaffected by payment of dividends.

How can this be? Suppose investment decisions are fixed—that is, the company will invest in certain projects *regardless* how they are financed. The value of the corporation is the present value of all future cash flows of the company—which depend on the investment decisions that management makes, *not* on how these investments are financed. If the investment decision is fixed, whether a corporation pays a dividend or not does not affect the value of the corporation.

A corporation raises additional funds either through earnings or by selling securities—sufficient to meet its investment decisions and its dividend decision. The dividend decision therefore affects only the financing decision—how much capital the company has to raise to fulfill its investment decisions.

The Miller and Modigliani argument implies that the dividend decision is a residual decision. If the company has no profitable investments to undertake, the firm can pay out funds that would have gone to investments to shareholders. And whether or not the company pays dividends is of no consequence to the value of the company. In other words, dividends are irrelevant.

But companies don't exist in a perfect world with a perfect market. Are the imperfections (taxes, transactions costs, etc.) enough to alter the conclusions of Miller and Modigliani? It isn't clear.

The "Bird in the Hand" Theory

A popular view is that dividends represent a *sure thing* relative to share price appreciation. The return to shareholders is comprised of two parts: the return from dividends—the *dividend yield*—and the return from the change in the share price—the *capital yield*. Corporations generate earnings and can either pay them out in cash dividends or reinvest earnings in profitable investments, increasing the value of the stock and, hence, share price. Once a dividend is paid, it is a certain cash flow. Shareholders can cash their quarterly dividend checks and reinvest the funds. But an increase in share price is not a sure thing. It only becomes a sure thing when the share's price increases over the price the shareholder paid and he or she sells the shares.

We can observe that prices of dividend-paying stocks are less volatile than nondividend-paying stocks. But are dividend-paying stocks less risky because they pay dividends? Or are less risky firms more likely to pay dividends? Most of the evidence supports the latter. Companies that have greater risk—business risk, financial risk, or both—tend to pay little or no dividends. In other words, companies whose cash flows are more variable tend to avoid large dividend commitments that they could not satisfy during periods of poorer financial performance.

The Tax-Preference Explanation

If dividend income is taxed at the same rates as capital gain income, investors may prefer capital gains because of the time value of money: capital gains are only taxed when realized—that is, when the investor sells the stock—whereas dividend income is taxed when received. If, on the other hand, dividend income is taxed at rates higher than that applied to capital gain income, investors should prefer stock price appreciation to dividend income because of both the time value of money and the lower rates.

Historically, capital gain income has been taxed in the U.S. at rates lower than that applied to dividend income for individual investors. However, the current situation for individuals is that dividend income and capital gain income are taxed at the same rates.[3] Even with the same rates applied to income, capital gain income is still preferred because the tax on any stock appreciation is deferred until the stock is sold.

But the tax impact is different for different types of shareholders. A corporation receiving a dividend from another corporation may take a *dividends received deduction*—a deduction of a large portion of the dividend income. (The dividends received deduction ranges from 70% to 100%, depending on the ownership relation between the two corporations.) Therefore, corporations pay taxes on a small portion of their dividend income. Still other shareholders may not even be taxed on dividend income. For example, a pension fund beneficiary does not pay taxes on the dividend income it gets from its investments (these earnings are eventually taxed when the pension is paid out to the employee after retirement).

Even if dividend income were taxed at rates higher than that of capital gains, investors could take investment actions that affect this difference. First, investors that have high marginal tax rates may gravitate towards stocks that pay little or no dividends. This means the shareholders of dividend paying stocks have lower marginal tax rates. This is referred to as a *tax clientele*—investors who choose stocks on the basis of the taxes they have to pay. Second, investors with high marginal tax rates can use legitimate investment strategies—such as borrowing to buy stock and using the deduction from the interest payments on the loan to offset the dividend income in order to reduce the tax impact of dividends. Several strategies that can be used to reduce the taxes on dividend income are discussed by Miller and Scholes (1979). However, Peterson, Peterson, and Ang (1985) document

---

[3] The Jobs & Growth Tax Relief Reconciliation Act of 2003 lowered the tax rate individuals pay on dividends to 15% or 5%, depending on the individual's other income, at the same time lowering the tax rate on capital gains to the same 15% or 5% rates. Though these tax rate cuts were intended to expire in 2008, they were extended by the Tax Relief and Health Care Act of 2006.

that investors do not appear to take advantage of these strategies and end up paying substantial taxes on dividend income.

The Signaling Explanation

Companies that pay dividends seem to maintain a relatively stable dividend, either in terms of a constant or growing dividend payout or in terms of a constant or growing dividend per share. And when companies change their dividend—either increasing or reducing ("cutting") the dividend—the price of the company's shares seems to be affected: When a dividend is increased, the price of the company's shares typically goes up; when a dividend is cut, the price usually goes down. This reaction is attributed to investors' perception of the meaning of the dividend change: Increases are good news, decreases are bad news.

The board of directors is likely to have some information that investors do not have, a change in dividend may be a way for the board to signal this private information. Because most boards of directors are aware that when dividends are lowered, the price of a share usually falls, most investors do not expect boards to increase a dividend unless they thought the company could maintain it into the future. Realizing this, investors may view a dividend increase as the board's increased confidence in the future operating performance of the firm.

The Agency Explanation

The relation between the owners and the managers of a firm is an agency relationship: The owners are the principals and the managers are the agents. Management is charged with acting in the best interests of the owners. Nevertheless, there are possibilities for conflicts between the interests of the two. If the firm pays a dividend, the firm may be forced to raise new capital outside of the firm—that is, issue new securities instead of using internally generated capital—subjecting them to the scrutiny of equity research analysts and other investors. This extra scrutiny helps reduce the possibility that managers will not work in the best interests of the shareholders. But issuing new securities is not costless. There are costs of issuing new securities—flotation costs. In "agency theory speak," these costs are part of *monitoring costs*—incurred to help monitor the managers' behavior and insure behavior is consistent with shareholder wealth maximization.

The payment of dividends also reduces the amount of free cash flow under control of management. Free cash flow is the cash in excess of the cash needed to finance profitable investment opportunities. A profitable investment opportunity is any investment that provides the company with a return greater than what shareholders could get elsewhere on their money—that is, a return greater than the shareholders' opportunity cost.

Because free cash flow is the cash flow left over after all profitable projects are undertaken, the only projects left are the unprofitable ones. Should free cash be reinvested in the unprofitable investments or paid out to shareholders? Of course if boards make decisions consistent with shareholder wealth maximization, any free cash flow should be paid out to shareholders since—by the definition of a profitable investment opportunity—the shareholders could get a better return investing the funds they receive.

If the company pays a dividend, funds are paid out to shareholders. If the company needs additional funds, it could be raised by issuing new securities; in this event, shareholders wishing to reinvest the funds received as dividends in the firm could buy these new securities. One view of the role of dividends is that the payment of dividends therefore reduces the cash flow in the hands of management, reducing the possibility that managers will invest funds in unprofitable investment opportunities.

Summing Up: To Pay Dividends or Not

We can figure out reasons why a company should or should not pay dividends, but not why they actually do or do not—this is the "dividend puzzle" coined by Fisher Black (1976). But we do know from looking at dividends and the market's reaction to them that:

- If a company increases its dividends or pays a dividend for the first time, this is viewed as good news—its share price increases.
- If a company decreases its dividend or omits it completely, this is viewed as bad news—its share price declines.

That is why corporations must be aware of the relation between dividends and the value of the common stock in establishing or changing dividend policy.

Stock Repurchases

Corporations have repurchased their common stock from their shareholders. A corporation repurchasing its own shares is effectively paying a cash dividend, with one important difference: taxes. Cash dividends are ordinary taxable income to the shareholder. A firm's repurchase of shares, on the other hand, results in a capital gain or loss for the shareholder, depending on the price paid when they were originally purchased. If the shares are repurchased at a higher price, the difference may be taxed as capital gains, which may be taxed at rates lower than ordinary income.

The company may repurchase its own stock by any of three methods: (1) a tender offer, (2) open market purchases, and (3) a targeted block repurchase.

A *tender offer* is an offer made to all shareholders, with a specified deadline and a specified number of shares the corporation is willing to buy back. The tender offer may be a fixed price offer, where the corporation specifies the price it is willing to pay and solicits purchases of shares of stock at that price. A tender offer may also be conducted as a *Dutch auction* in which the corporation specifies a minimum and a maximum price, soliciting bids from shareholders for any price within this range at which they are willing to sell their shares. After the corporation receives these bids, they pay all tendering shareholders the maximum price sufficient to buy back the number of shares they want. A Dutch auction reduces the chance that the firm pays a price higher than needed to acquire the shares. Dutch auctions are gaining in popularity relative to fixed-price offers. For example, Wendy's International announced in October 2006 that it would buy back shares in a Dutch auction tender offer. In this offer, the company specified the range of prices it is willing to pay—in this case $33.00 to $36.00 per share—and the number of shares. The company then allowed the auction mechanism to work to determine the price. As a result of this auction, Wendy's bought back 22.4 million shares at $35.75 per share in November of 2006, representing 19% of the company's outstanding common stock. There were 27.9 million shares tendered, but only 22.4 million shares at or below the purchase price.

A corporation may also buy back shares directly in the open market. This involves buying the shares through a broker. A corporation that wants to buy shares may have to spread its purchases over time so as not to drive the share's price up temporarily by buying large numbers of shares.

The third method of repurchasing stock is to buy it from a specific shareholder. This involves direct negotiation between the corporation and the shareholder. This method is referred to as a *targeted block repurchase*, since there is a specific shareholder (the "target") and there are a large number of shares (a "block") to be purchased at one time. Targeted block repurchases, also referred to as "greenmail," were used in the 1980s to fight corporate takeovers.

Corporations repurchase their stock for a number of reasons. First, a repurchase is a way to distribute cash to shareholders at a lower cost to both the firm and the shareholders than dividends. If capital gains are taxed at rates lower than ordinary income, which until recently has been the case with U.S. tax law, repurchasing is a lower cost way of distributing cash. However, since shareholders have different tax rates—especially when comparing corporate shareholders with individual shareholders—the benefit is mixed. The reason is that some shareholders' income is tax-free (e.g., pension funds), some shareholders are only taxed on a portion of dividends (e.g., corporations receiving dividends from other corporations), and some shareholders are taxed on the full amount of dividends (e.g., individual tax-payers).

Another reason to repurchase stock is to increase earnings per share. A company that repurchases its shares increases its earnings per share simply because there are fewer shares outstanding after the repurchase. But there are two problems with this motive. First, cash is paid to the shareholders, so less cash is available for the corporation to reinvest in profitable projects. Second, because there are fewer shares, the earnings pie is sliced in fewer pieces, resulting in higher earnings per share. The individual "slices" are bigger, but the pie itself remains the same size.

Looking at how share prices respond to gimmicks that manipulate earnings, there is evidence that a company cannot fool the market by playing an earnings per share game. The market can see through the earnings per share to what is really happening and that the firm will have less cash to invest.

Still another reason for stock repurchase is that it could tilt the debt-equity ratio so as to increase the value of the company. By buying back stock—thereby reducing equity—the company's assets are financed to a greater degree by debt. Does this seem wrong? It's not. To see this, suppose a corporation has a balance sheet consisting of assets of $100 million, liabilities of $50 million, and $50 million of equity. That is, the corporation has financed 50% of its assets with debt, and 50% with equity. If this corporation uses $20 million of its assets to buy back stock worth $20 million, its balance sheet will have assets of $80 million financed by $50 of liabilities and $30 million of equity. It now finances 62.5% of its assets with debt and 37.5% with equity.

If financing the firm with more debt is good—that is, the benefits from deducting interest on debt outweigh the cost of increasing the risk of bankruptcy—repurchasing stock may increase the value of the firm. But there is the flip-side to this argument: Financing the firm with more debt may be bad if the risk of financial distress—difficulty paying legal obligations—outweighs the benefits from tax deductibility of interest.

So, repurchasing shares from this perspective would have to be judged on a case-by-case basis to determine if it's beneficial or detrimental.

One more reason for a stock repurchase is that it reduces total dividend payments—without seeming to. If the corporation cuts down on the number of shares outstanding, the corporation can still pay the same amount of dividends *per share*, but the *total* dividend payments are reduced. If the shares are correctly valued in the market (there is no reason to believe otherwise), the payment for the repurchased shares equals the reduction in the value of the firm—and the remaining shares are worth the same as they were before.

Some argue that a repurchase is a signal about future prospects. That is, by buying back the shares, the management is communicating to investors that the company is generating sufficient cash to be able to buy back shares. But does this make sense? Not really. If the company has profitable investment opportunities, the cash could be used to finance these investments, instead of paying it out to the shareholders.

A stock repurchase may also reduce agency costs by reducing the amount of cash the management has on hand. Similar to the argument suggested for dividend payments, repurchasing shares reduces the amount of free cash flow and, therefore, reduces the possibility that management will invest it unprofitably. Many companies use stock buybacks to mitigate the dilution resulting from executive stock options, as well as to shore up their stock price. According to a press releases by Standard & Poor's (2005, 2006), companies in the S&P 500, for example, repurchased a record dollar amount of shares in 2005 and 2006, as much as they spent on capital expenditures.[4] The effect of these buybacks has been to increase earnings per share for the S&P 500 by 20% in 2006.

Repurchasing shares tends to shrink the firm: Cash is paid out and the value of the firm is smaller. Can repurchasing shares be consistent with wealth maximization? Yes. If the best use of funds is to pay them out to shareholders, repurchasing shares maximizes shareholders' wealth. If the firm has no profitable investment opportunities, it is better for a firm to shrink by paying funds to the shareholders than to shrink by investing in lousy investments.

So how does the market react to a company's intention to repurchase shares? A number of studies have looked at how the market reacts to such announcements. In general, the share price goes up when a firm announces it is going to repurchase its own shares. It is difficult to identify the reason the market reacts favorably to such announcements since so many other things are happening at the same time. By piecing bits of evidence together, however, we see that it is likely that investors view the announcement of a repurchase as good news—a signal of good things to come.

SPECIAL CONSIDERATIONS IN INTERNATIONAL FINANCIAL MANAGEMENT

Financial management decisions of most firms are not confined to domestic borders. Many financing and investment decisions involve economies and firms outside a firm's own domestic borders either directly, through international transactions, or indirectly, through the effects of international issues

---

[4] See also Taub (2006).

on the domestic economy. *International financial management* is the management of a firm's assets and liabilities considering the global economy in which the firm operates. In this section, we discuss special factors that must be considered in international corporate financial management.

Multinational Firms

A multinational company is a firm that does business in two or more countries. Most large U.S. corporations are multinational firms, deriving a large part of their income from operations beyond the U.S. borders.

Companies expand beyond their domestic borders for many reasons, including:

- *To gain access to new markets.* Growth in the domestic market may slow, but there may be opportunities to grow in other countries. For example, as the domestic discount retail market became saturated in the mid-1990s, Wal-Mart opened stores in Mexico.
- *To gain access to resources.* Companies that rely on natural resources, such as oil companies, establish access to these resources by establishing subsidiaries in other countries. This assures these companies of their basic materials to maintain uninterrupted operations.
- *To reduce political and regulatory hurdles.* Shifting operations to other countries may be necessary to overcome the many hurdles established by nations to protect their domestic businesses. For example, in the 1970s, Japanese auto firms established manufacturing and assembly plants in the United States to avoid import quotas imposed by the United States.
- *To diversify.* Over any given period of time, the level of business activity may be different in different countries. This results in opportunities to reduce the overall fluctuations in a firm's business revenues and costs by doing business abroad. For example, in the 1980s, the Japanese economy was flourishing, while the U.S. economy was in a recession; in contrast, during the early 1990s, the Japanese economy did poorly, while the U.S. economy was prospering.
- *To gain access to technology.* As technology is developed in other countries, a firm may expand operations in other countries, say, through joint ventures, to assure access to patents and other developments that ensure its competitiveness both domestically and internationally.

The many changes in the world political economy have enhanced opportunities. These changes include changes in domestic laws and regulations, such as increased import quotas and the reduction in regulations on banking activities, and changes outside the United States, such as North American

Free Trade Agreement (NAFTA) and the European Free Trade Association (EFTA).

Foreign Currency

Doing business outside of one's own country requires dealing with the currencies of other countries. Financial managers must be aware of the issues relating to dealing with multiple currencies. In particular, the financial manager must be aware of exchange rate and the related currency risk.

Exchange Rates

The *exchange rate* is the number of units of a given currency that can be purchased for one unit of another country's currency; the exchange rate tells us about the relative value of any two currencies.

Countries have different policies concerning their currency exchange rate. In the *floating exchange rate system*, the currency's foreign exchange rate is allowed to fluctuate freely by supply and demand for the currency. Another type of policy is the *fixed exchange rate system*, where the government intervenes to offset changes in exchange rates caused by changes in the currency's supply and demand. The third type of policy is a *managed floating exchange rate system*, which falls somewhere between the fixed and floating systems. In the managed floating rate system, the currency's exchange rates are allowed to fluctuate in response to changes in supply and demand, but the government may intervene to stabilize the exchange rate in the short-run, avoiding short-term wild fluctuations in the exchange rate.

The value of a country's currency depends on many factors, including the imports and exports of goods and services. As the demand and supply of countries' currencies rises and falls, the exchange rates, which reflect the currencies' relative values, change if rates are allowed to "float." Another factor that affects the relative value of currencies is the movement of investment capital from one country to another. If interest rates are higher in one country, investors may buy the currency of that country in order to buy the interest-bearing securities in that country. This shifting of investment capital increases the demand for the currency of the country with the higher interest rate.

When a currency loses value relative to other currencies, we say that the currency has "depreciated" if the change is due to changes in supply and demand, or has been "devalued" if the change is due to government intervention. If the currency gains value relative other currencies, we say that the currency has "appreciated" or been "revalued."

Currency Risk

The uncertainty of exchange rates affects a financial manager's decisions. Consider a U.S. firm making an investment that produces cash flows in British pounds, £. Suppose you invest £10,000 today and expect to get £12,000 one year from today. Further suppose that £1 = $1.48 today, so the firm is investing $1.48 times 10,000 = $14,800. If the British pound does not change in value relative to the U.S. dollar, the firm would have a return of 20%:

$$\text{Return} = \frac{£12,000 - £10,000}{£10,000} \text{ or } \frac{\$17,760 - \$14,800}{\$14,800} = 20\%$$

But what if one year from now £1 = $1.30 instead? The firm's return would be less than 20% because the value of the pound has dropped in relation to the U.S. dollar. The firm is making an investment of £10,000, or $14,800, and getting not $17,760, but rather $1.30 times £12,000 = $15,600 in one year. If the pound loses value from $1.48 to $1.30, the firm's return on your investment is

$$\text{Return} = \frac{\$15,600 - \$14,800}{\$14,800} = \frac{\$800}{\$14,800} = 5.41\%$$

Currency risk, also called *exchange-rate risk*, is the risk that the relative values of the domestic and foreign currencies will adversely change in the future, changing the value of the future cash flows. Financial managers must consider currency risk in investment decisions that involve other currencies and make sure that the returns on these investments are sufficient compensation for the risk of changing values of currencies.

The buying and selling of foreign currency takes place in the foreign exchange market, which is an over-the-counter market consisting of banks and brokers in major world financial centers. Trading in foreign currencies may be done in the spot market, which is the buying and selling of currencies for immediate delivery, or in the *forward market*, which is the buying and selling of contracts for future delivery of currencies. If a U.S. firm needs euros in 90 days, it can buy today a contact for delivery of euros in 90 days.

Forward contracts can be used to reduce uncertainty regarding foreign exchange rates. By buying a contract for euros for 90 days from now, the firm is locking in the exchange rate of U.S. dollars for euros. This use of forward contracts in this manner is referred to as *hedging*. By hedging, the financial manager can reduce a firm's exposure to currency risk.

Purchasing Power Parity

If there are no barriers or costs to trade across borders (including costs to move the good or service), the price of a given product will be the same regardless of where it is sold. This is referred to as the *law of one price*. Applied to a situation in which there are different currencies on either side of the borders, this means that after adjusting for the difference in currencies, the price of a good or service is the same across borders. In the case of different currencies, the law of one price is known as *purchasing power parity* (PPP).

If purchasing power parity holds, we can evaluate the exchange rate of two currencies by looking at the price of a good or service in the two different countries. In a light-hearted look at purchasing power parity, the financial magazine, the *Economist*, periodically publishes the price of the McDonald's Big Mac in different countries. The *Economist* uses the price of the Big Mac in different countries, along with information on current exchange rates, to predict future exchange rates. For example, in April 2002, the Big Mac price in China was 10.50 yuan, which was equivalent to $1.27 using the exchange rate in existence then of 8.28 yuan/USD [*Economist*, April 25, 2002]. Comparing this Big Mac price with that of the Big Mac in the U.S. at the time, $2.49, this suggests—if you believe that this is a good indicator of relative valuation—that the yuan in undervalued by 49% relative to the U.S. dollar.[5]

Any mispricing in terms of current exchange rates is interpreted as a sign of future changes in currency valuations. In most situations, there are barriers (e.g., import or export quotas) and costs (e.g., tariffs) associated with moving goods across borders. Therefore, purchasing power parity does not likely hold precisely. There is a variation of purchasing power parity that states that changes in the relative inflation rates between two countries is reflected in the change in the exchange rate between the two currencies.

Tax Considerations

Taxes paid by corporate entities can be classified into two types: income taxes and indirect taxes. The former includes taxes paid to the central government based on corporate income and possibly any local income taxes. Indirect taxes include real estate value-added and sales taxes, as well as miscellaneous taxes on business transactions. In this section, we provide an overview of the key corporate income tax issues that affect investing decisions and financing decisions in foreign countries.

---

[5] The yuan has increased in value relative to the U.S. dollar since 2002. In September 2008, for example, the value of a yuan per USD was 6.8210.

Establishing a Business Entity

The United States has several forms of taxable entities: individuals, partnerships, and corporations. The choice of the structure is determined by a myriad of factors, including the minimization of taxes (income taxes and other business taxes), the desire for limited liability, and the ease with which ownership can be transferred. The same factors also influence the structure a firm elects when establishing a subsidiary in a foreign country. The form of business entity chosen by major commercial entities in the United States is the corporation.

As examples of the business entities that are available outside the United States, let's look at Germany and France. Germany has six forms of commercial enterprises: (1) the corporation (*Aktiengellschaft*—abbreviated AG); (2) limited liability company (*Gesellschaft mit beschrankter Haftung*—GmbH); (3) general commercial partnership (*offene Handelgellschaft*—oHG); (4) limited partnership (*Kommanditgesellschaft*—KG); (5) limited partnership with share capital (*Kommanditgesellschaft auf Aktien*—KGaA); and (6) branch of a domestic or foreign company (*Zweignierderlassung*). Corporate income taxes are assessed on AGs, GmbHs, and nonresident companies that establish German branches. The other forms are not taxed at the entity level but at the individual level; that is, the income is allocated to the individual partners who are then taxed at their appropriate tax rate. The preferred form used by foreigners is either the GmbH or a branch.

The principal forms of French commercial enterprises are (1) the corporation (*societe annonyme*—abbreviated SA); (2) limited liability company (*societe a responsabilite limitee*—SARL); (3) general partnership (*societe en nom collectif*—SCS); (4) partnership limited by shares (*societe en commandite par actions*—SCPA); (5) joint ventures; and (6) branch (*succursale*). The commercial entities liable for corporate income taxes are SAs, SARLs, SCPAs, and nonresident companies with branches. The other entities may elect to be taxed as corporate entities or as individuals. Foreign entities predominately use SAs and SARLs.

Corporate Income Tax Rates

The basic corporate income tax imposed by central governments is a fixed percentage or an increasing percentage of the statutorily determined corporate income. The rate varies significantly from country to country. Countries typically tax resident corporations on worldwide income regardless of whether the income is repatriated. Nonresident corporations, that is, corporations whose corporate seat and place of management are outside the country, are typically subject only to corporate taxes derived from within the country.

To list the basic tax rates by country would be misleading for several reasons. First, the calculation of corporate income varies based on the types of revenues that may or may not be included as taxable and permissible deductions. Second, there may be a refund for corporate income distributed to shareholders that lowers the effective tax rate or an additional corporate tax paid on distributed income that raises the effective tax rate. Third, there may be a different tax rate based on the characteristics of the commercial entity, such as its size. Fourth, the effective tax rate may be different for undistributed income and income distributed to shareholders. Finally, the tax rate can vary for resident and nonresident business entities.

Several countries impose no tax or minimal tax rates. These countries are referred to as *tax havens*. The Cayman Islands and Bermuda are examples. Tax havens are used by some entities to avoid or reduce taxes. The use of tax havens by U.S. entities was significantly reduced by the Tax Reform Act of 1986.

A country's tax authorities withhold taxes on income derived in their country by nonresident corporations. The withholding tax rate may vary, depending on the type of income: dividends, interest, or royalties. Major trading countries often negotiate tax treaties to reduce the double taxation of corporate income.

A corporation's effective tax rate on its worldwide income therefore depends on tax treaties between its home country and all the foreign countries where it has established a nonresident corporation. Moreover, the rate also depends on whether a corporation is permitted a credit by the tax authorities in its home country against taxes paid in foreign countries. Many countries permit this credit, called a *foreign tax credit*. The limitation is usually that the tax credit paid to a foreign country may not exceed the amount that would have been paid in the home country.

Determining Taxable Income

Varying definitions of taxable revenue and deductible expenses cause the determination of corporate profits to vary from country to country. By far, the largest variance can be attributed to the differences in the treatment of items that are deductible for tax purposes. Different methods of treating of noncash expenses such as depreciation and inventory valuation can affect the calculation of taxable income.

Two other considerations affect the determination of taxable income. Both of these matters relate to the deductibility of items that foreign tax authorities view as legitimate expenses but are incurred to minimize taxes in the foreign country. The first is the deductibility of interest expense when that expense may be viewed as excessive. The second is the inflation of expenses associated with the sale or purchase of goods and services by a nonresident company with an associated company (that is, a parent company or another subsidiary of the parent) outside the foreign country. These two factors are interest expense and transfer prices used in intercompany transactions.

Interest Expense   In most countries, the interest expense associated with borrowed funds is tax deductible. (However, some countries allow the dividend-paying company to receive a tax credit for distributed profits.) Dividends, in contrast, are treated as distributed profits and are not tax deductible. This difference is particularly important when a parent company provides financing to a foreign subsidiary. Interest paid by a subsidiary to its parent is deductible for the subsidiary but taxable for the parent. Dividends, in contrast, are taxable for both the subsidiary and the parent.

An increasing number of firms have employed financing arrangements to take advantage of the tax advantage associated with debt. It can be done in two ways. First, a financing agreement can be called "debt," even though it is effectively a form of equity. For example, an instrument may be called a debt obligation but, unlike legitimate debt, it allows the "borrower" to miss periodic payments if sufficient cash flow is unavailable. Or the priority of the "creditors" can be subordinated to all other creditors and to preferred stockholders. Both of these provisions indicate that the instrument may be more appropriately classified as a form of equity rather than debt. Second, several companies have employed capital structures that predominately consist of debt. Such companies are commonly referred to as *thin capitalization.*

In some countries, tax authorities have challenged whether, in fact, some of the debt should be appropriately recharacterized as equity for tax purposes, thereby eliminating the deductibility of interest for the reclassified portion. The recharacterization of debt to equity may be due to the terms of the individual agreement or security regardless of the ratio of debt to equity. When a company's debt-to-equity ratio is high, tax authorities may seek to recharacterize a portion of the debt to equity for tax purposes.

Tax authorities or finance ministries use other methods to attempt to curtail what they perceive to be an abuse of borrowing to benefit from interest deductibility. One way is to place an explicit restriction on the amount of interest that may be deductible. To restrict resident companies controlled by foreign entities from being thinly capitalized, some countries, requiring approval of the investments by foreign entities, do not grant that approval unless they deem the capitalization adequate. When approval is necessary, minimum equity or maximum debt levels may be imposed. Or countries can use restrictions on the transfer of funds abroad to mitigate the problem of thin capitalization.

Intercompany Transactions and Transfer Prices   As just explained, to minimize taxes in foreign countries with high tax rates, a firm may use excessive debt in controlled entities. To further reduce taxes, the interest rate on the "loan" may be above market rates. An excessive interest rate charged to subsidiaries in high tax countries is but one expense that a company with foreign operations can consider to reduce worldwide taxes.

It is common for a company's subsidiaries in different countries to buy and sell goods from each other. The price for the goods in such intercompany transactions is called a *transfer price*. Establishing transfer prices to promote goal congruence within a multinational company is a complicated topic. In practice, goal congruence seems to be of secondary importance to the minimization of worldwide taxes—income taxes and import duty taxes—in the establishment of transfer prices.

The following illustration demonstrates how the establishment of a transfer price affects income taxes. Suppose that a parent company resides in the United States where it faces a marginal tax rate of 35% and has only one subsidiary located in a foreign country where the marginal tax rate is 42%. The parent company manufactures a product for $20 a unit and sells 100,000 units to the subsidiary each year. The subsidiary, in turn, further processes each unit at a cost of $10 per unit and sells the finished product for $80 per unit. The parent company's sale represents its revenue, and the subsidiary's purchase represents part of its production cost. It is assumed that fixed costs for the parent and the subsidiary are $1,000,000 and $500,000, respectively.

Table 9.2(a) shows the taxes and the net income of the parent, the subsidiary, and the company as a whole if the transfer price is set at $40 per unit. Panel b of the table shows the same analysis if the parent company sets a transfer price of $60 per unit. Notice that by increasing the transfer price from $40 to $60, worldwide income increases by $140,000, the same amount by which worldwide taxes decline.

SUMMARY

The decision-making of financial managers can be broken down into two broad classes: investment decisions and financing decisions. Investment decisions are those decisions that involve the use of the firm's funds. Financing decisions are those decisions that involve the acquisition of the firm's funds. Financial managers assess the potential risks and rewards associated with investment and financing decisions through the application of financial analysis. The information necessary for financial decisions and analysis includes the accounting information that describes the company and its indus-

TABLE 9.2 Illustration of Effect of Transfer Price on Worldwide Net Income

Assumptions: Units sold by parent = 100,000

U.S. parent tax rate = 35%

Subsidiary tax rate = 42%

	Price and Costs in U.S. Dollars	
	Parent	Subsidiary
Selling price	Transfer price	$80
Unit variable manufacturing cost	$20	Transfer price + $10
Fixed manufacturing costs	$1,000,000	$500,000

(a) Transfer price = $40

	U.S. Parent Company Alone	Subsidiary
Revenue	$4,000,000	$8,000,000
Variable manufacturing costs	2,000,000	5,000,000
Fixed manufacturing costs	1,000,000	500,000
Taxable income	$1,000,000	$2,500,000
Income taxes	350,000	1,050,000
Net income after taxes	$650,000	$1,450,000

Worldwide income taxes = $1,400,000
Worldwide net income after taxes = $2,100,000

(b) Transfer price = $60

	U.S. Parent Company Alone	Subsidiary
Revenue	$6,000,000	$8,000,000
Variable manufacturing costs	2,000,000	7,000,000
Fixed manufacturing costs	1,000,000	500,000
Taxable income	$3,000,000	$500,000
Income taxes	1,050,000	210,000
Net income after taxes	$1,950,000	$290,000

Worldwide income taxes = $1,260,000
Worldwide net income after taxes = $2,240,000

try as well as economic information relating to the company, the industry, and the economy in general.

A business enterprise may be formed as a sole proprietorship, a partnership, corporation, or a hybrid of one or more of these forms. The hybrid forms include the master limited partnership, the professional corporation, the limited liability company, and the joint venture. The choice of the form of business is influenced by concerns about the life of the enterprise, the liability of its owners, the taxation of income, and access to funds. In turn, the form of business influences financial decision-making through its effect on taxes, governance, and the liability of owners. Corporations are entities created by law that limit the liability of owners and subject income to an additional layer of taxation. The corporation's owners—the shareholders—are represented by the board of directors, which oversees the management of the firm.

The objective of financial decision-making in a business is the maximization of the wealth of owners. For a corporation, this is equivalent to the maximization of the market value of the stock. If markets for securities are price efficient, share prices will reflect all available information. When information is revealed to investors, it is rapidly figured into share prices.

Since managers' self-interest may not be consistent with owners' best interests, owners must devise ways to align mangers' and owners' interests. One means of doing this is through executive compensation. By designing managers' compensation packages to encourage long-term investment in the stock of a corporation, the interests of managers and shareholders can be aligned.

Recent financial problems and scandals have created an awareness of the responsibility of CEOs, CFOs, and board members to shareholders and the market. Shareholder wealth maximization is consistent with the best interests of stakeholders and society if market forces reward firms for taking actions that are in society's interest or if the government steps in to force actions that are in society's interest.

Part of shareholders' return is in the form of cash payments called dividends. Whether a corporation should pay dividends is debatable, given that even with similar tax rates on dividend income and capital gain income, capital gains are preferred because of the time value of money. Some believe that dividends serve a purpose: either providing information about the firm's future prospects or forcing the corporation to sell more securities to raise the money to pay the dividends.

Besides cash dividends, firms may distribute additional shares of stock to shareholders through a stock dividend or a stock split. While distributing additional shares does not change the value of the stock, the announcement of the distribution may provide information about management's expectations of the firm's future prospects.

Corporations can repurchase shares in the open market, use a tender offer, or buy shares in a targeted block repurchase. Corporations can repurchase shares either to change their capital structure, reduce dividend payments, signal future prospects, or to reduce free cash flow.

International financial management is the management of a firm's assets and liabilities in the global economy. Issues such as foreign currency exchange, taxes, and unique risks, such as political and currency risk, make the financial management of a firm more challenging.

Companies do business outside of their own country's borders to gain access to new markets, to enhance production efficiency, to gain access to resources, to reduce hurdles to expand in other nations, to diversify, and to gain access to certain technology. Financial managers of companies doing business abroad must be aware of foreign currency exchange and its associated risk. Changes in foreign currency exchange rates can affect a company's profitability.

Making decisions in foreign countries, however, requires an understanding of domestic tax regulations as well as foreign tax regulations. Taxes paid by corporate enterprises are income taxes (taxes paid to the central government based on corporate income and possibly any local income taxes) and indirect taxes (real estate value-added and sales taxes, as well as miscellaneous taxes on business transactions).

REFERENCES

Baker, H., Farrelly, G., and Edelman, R. (1985). A survey of management views on dividend policy. *Financial Management* 14, no. 3: 78–84.

Baker, H., and Powell, G. (1999). How corporate managers view dividend policy. *Quarterly Journal of Business and Economics* 38, no. 2: 17–35.

Barclay, M., Holderness, C., and Sheehan, D. (2006). Dividends and corporate shareholders. Working Paper, University of Rochester.

Barclay, M., Smith, C., and Watts, R. (1995). The determinants of corporate leverage and dividend policies. *Journal of Applied Corporate Finance* 7, no. 4: 4–19.

Bar-Yosef, S. and Huffman, L. (1986). The information content of dividends: A signaling approach. *Journal of Financial and Quantitative Analysis* 21 (March): 47–58.

Benartzi, S., Michaely, R., and Thaler, R. (1997). Do changes in dividends signal the future or the past? *Journal of Finance* 52, no. 3: 1007–1034.

Black, F. (1976). The dividend puzzle. *Journal of Portfolio Management* 2, no. 2 (Winter): 5–8.

Black, F. and Scholes, M. (1974). The effects of dividend yield and dividend policy on common stock prices and returns. *Journal of Financial Economics* 1, no. 1: 1–22.

Brav, A., Graham, J., Harvey, C. and Michaely, R. (2005). Payout policy in the 21st century. *Journal of Financial Economics* 77, no. 3: 483–527

Chaplinsky, S. and Seyhun, H.N. (1990). Dividends and taxes: Evidence on tax-reduction strategies. *Journal of Business* 63, no. 2: 239–260.

Divecha, A. and Morse, D. (1983). Market responses to dividend increases and changes in payout ratios. *Journal of Financial and Quantitative Analysis* 18, no. 2: 163–173

Grinblatt, M., Masulis, R., and Titman, S. (1984). The valuation effects of stock splits and stock dividends. *Journal of Financial Economics* 13, no. 4: 461–490.

Jensen, M. C. (1998). *Foundations of Organizatonal Strategy*. Cambridge, MA: Harvard University Press.

Jensen, M. C. (2000). *A Theory of the Firm. Governance, Residual Claims, and Organizational Form*. Cambridge, MA: Harvard University Press.

Jensen, M. C. and Meckling, W. H. (1976). Theory of the firm: Managerial behavior, agency costs and ownership structure. *Journal of Financial Economics* 3, no. 4: 305–360.

Lakonishok, J. and Lev, B. (1987). Stock splits and stock dividends: Why, who, and when. *Journal of Finance* 42, no. 4: 913–932.

Lang, L. and Litzenberger, R. (1989). Dividend announcements: Cash flow signaling vs. free cash flow hypothesis. *Journal of Financial Economics* 24, no. 1: 181–191.

Lublin, J. (1996). AT&T board faces protest over CEO pay. *Wall Street Journal* (April 16): A3 and A6.

McNichols, M. and Dravid, A. (1990). Stock dividends, stock splits, and signaling. *Journal of Finance* 45, no. 3: 857–879.

Miller, M. and Modigliani, F. (1961). Dividend policy, growth and the valuation of shares. *Journal of Business* 34, no. 4: 411–433.

Miller, M. and Scholes, M. (1979). Dividend and taxes. *Journal of Financial Economics* 6, no. 4: 333–364.

Miller, M., and Scholes, M. (1982). Dividend and taxes: Some empirical evidence. *Journal of Political Economy* 90, no. 6: 1118–1141.

Peterson, P., Peterson, D., and Ang, J. (1985). Direct evidence on the marginal rate of taxation on dividend income. *Journal of Financial Economics* 4, no. 2 (June): 267–282.

Sarbanes-Oxley Act of 2002, Public Law 107-204.

Standard and Poor's (2005). S&P 500 companies using excess cash to reduce share count. Press Release, September 9.

Standard and Poor's (2006). S&P 500 3rd Quarter buybacks at $110 billion. Press Release, November 27.

Schooley, D. and Barney, L. (1994). Using dividend policy and managerial ownership to reduce agency costs. *Journal of Financial Research* 17, no. 3: 363–373.

Stewart, G. B. (1991). *The Quest for Value*. New York: HarperCollins.

Taub, S. (2006). Stock buybacks at "unprecedented level." *CFO.com*, September 18.

CHAPTER 10

Financial Strategy and Financial Planning

A company's strategy plan is a method of achieving the goal of maximizing shareholder wealth. This strategic plan requires both long-term and short-term financial planning that brings together forecasts of the company's sales with financing and investment decision-making. Budgets, such as the cash budget and the production budget, are used to manage the information used in this planning, whereas performance measures, such as the balanced scorecard and economic value added, are used to evaluate progress toward the strategic goals.

A business that is able to deploy its assets to the best possible use creates value and advances the efficient allocation of resources for society as a whole. Owners, employees, customers, and anyone else who has a stake in the business enterprise are all better off when its management makes decisions that puts its assets to their best use. But just as there may be alternative routes to a destination, there may be alternative ways to allocate resources. A *strategy* is a plan of action of how to reach an objective. And just as some routes may get you where you are going faster, some strategies may be better than others.

Suppose a company has decided it has an advantage over its competitors in marketing and distributing its products in the global market. The company's strategy may be to expand into the European market, followed by an expansion into the Asian market. Once the company has its strategy, it needs a plan, in particular the *strategic plan*, which is the set of actions the company intends to use to follow its strategy.

The investment opportunities that enable the company to follow its strategy comprise the company's *investment strategy*. The company may pursue its strategy of expanding into European and Asian markets by either establishing itself or acquiring businesses already in these markets. This is where capital budgeting analysis comes in: Management evaluates the possible investment opportunities to see which ones, if any, provide a return greater than necessary for the investment's risk. And let's not forget the investment in working capital, the resources the company needs to support its day-to-day operations.

Suppose as a result of evaluating whether to establish or acquire businesses, our company decides it is better—in terms of maximizing the value of the company—to acquire selected European businesses. The next step is to figure out how it is going to pay for these acquisitions. Management must make sure that the company has sufficient funds to meet its operating needs, as well as its investment needs. This is where the company's financing strategy enters the picture. Where should the needed funds come from? What is the precise timing of the needs for funds? To answer these questions, working capital management (in particular, short-term financing) and the capital structure decision (the mix of long-term sources of financing) enter the picture.

When the chief financial officer under the supervision of the board of directors looks at the company's investment decisions and considers how to finance them, this is budgeting. *Budgeting* is mapping out the sources and uses of funds for future periods. Budgeting requires both economic analysis (including forecasting) and accounting. Economic analysis includes both marketing and production analysis to develop forecasts of future sales and costs. Accounting techniques are used as a measurement device: But instead of using accounting to summarize what has happened (its common use), in budgeting, companies use accounting to represent what the management expects to happen in the future. The process is summarized in Figure 10.1.

Once these plans are put into effect, the management must compare what happens with what was planned. This is referred to as post auditing, which companies use to:

- Evaluate the performance of management.
- Analyze any deviations of actual results from planned results.
- Evaluate the planning process to determine just how good it is.

The purpose of this chapter is to explain strategic planning and how financial planning and budgeting are used in this process. A discussion of capital budgeting, working capital management, and financing strategies are not covered in this chapter, but in other chapters in this book.

STRATEGY AND VALUE

The strategic plan is the path that the company intends to follow to achieve its objective, which is to put its assets to their best use, adding value. In this

FIGURE 10.1   Strategy and Budgeting

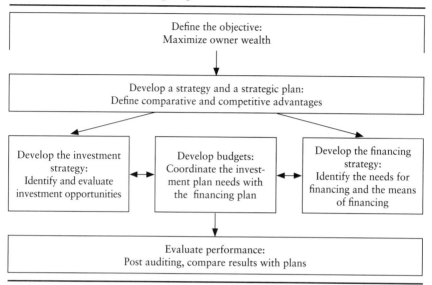

strategic plan is a method to make investments that will add value to the company. The way to add value is to invest in projects that have positive net present values. But where do these positive net present values come from? They come from the company's comparative advantage or its competitive advantages.

Comparative and Competitive Advantages

A *comparative advantage* is the advantage one company has over others in terms of the cost of producing or distributing goods or services. For example, Wal-Mart Stores, Inc. had for years a comparative advantage over its competitors (such as Kmart) through its vast network of warehouses and its distribution system. Wal-Mart invested in a system of regional warehouses and its own trucking system. Combined with bulk purchases and a unique customer approach (such as its "greeters"), Wal-Mart's comparative advantages in its warehousing and distribution systems helped it grow to be a major (and very profitable) retailer in a very short span of time. However, as with most comparative advantages, it took a few years for competitors to catch up and for Wal-Mart's advantages to disappear.

A *competitive advantage* is the advantage one company has over another because of the structure of the markets, input and output markets, in which they both operate. For example, one company may have a competitive advantage due to barriers to other companies entering the same market. This happens in the case of governmental regulations that limit the number of companies in a market, as with banks, or in the case of government-granted monopolies. A company itself may create barriers to entry (although with the help of the government) that include patents and trademarks. NutraSweet Company, a unit of Monsanto Company, had the exclusive patent on the artificial sweetener, aspartame, which it marketed under the brand name NutraSweet. However, this patent expired December 14, 1992. The loss of the monopoly on the artificial sweetener reduced the price of aspartame from $70 per pound to $20 to $35 per pound, since other companies could produce and sell aspartame products starting December 15, 1992.[1] (It should be noted that Monsanto sold its sweetener division in 2000.) NutraSweet had a competitive advantage as long as it had the patent. But as soon as the patent expired, this competitive advantage was lost and competitors were lining up to enter the market. Estimates of the value of patents vary by country and industry, but studies have shown that up to one quarter of the return from research and development is attributed to patents.[2]

Only by having some type of advantage can a company invest in something and get more back in return. So first, a management has to figure out where the company has a comparative or competitive advantage before the company's strategy can be determined.

Strategy and Adding Value

Often companies conceptualize a strategy in terms of the consumers of the company's goods and services. For example, management may have a strategy to become the world's leading producer of microcomputer chips by producing the best quality chip or by producing chips at the lowest cost, developing a cost (and price) advantage over its competitors. So management's focus is on product quality and cost. Is this strategy in conflict with maximizing owners' wealth? No.

To add value, management must focus on the returns and risks of future cash flows to stockholders. And management looks at a project's net present value when making decisions regarding whether to invest in it. A strategy of gaining a competitive or comparative advantage is consistent with maximizing shareholder wealth. This is because projects with positive net present value arise when the company has a competitive or comparative advantage over other companies.

Suppose a new piece of equipment is expected to generate a return greater than what is expected for the project's risk (its cost of capital). But

[1] See Therrien, Oster, and Hawkins (1992, p. 42).
[2] See, for example, Schankerman (1998).

how can a company create value simply by investing in a piece of equipment? How can it maintain a competitive advantage? If investing in this equipment can create value, wouldn't the company's competitors also want this equipment? Of course—if they could use it to create value, they would surely be interested in it.

Now suppose that the company's competitors face no barriers to buying the equipment and exploiting its benefits. What will happen? The company and its competitors will compete for the equipment, bidding up its price. When does it all end? When the net present value of the equipment is zero.

Suppose instead that the company has a patent on the new piece of equipment and can thus keep its competitors from exploiting the equipment's benefits. Then there would be no competition for the equipment and the company would be able to exploit it to add value.

Consider an example where trying to gain a comparative advantage went wrong. Schlitz Brewing Company attempted to reduce its costs to gain an advantage over its competitors: It reduced its labor costs and shortened the brewing cycle. Reducing costs allowed it to reduce its prices below competitors' prices. But product quality suffered—so much that Schlitz lost market share, instead of gaining it.

Schlitz Brewing, for example, attempted to gain a comparative advantage, but was not true to a larger strategy to satisfy its customers—who apparently wanted quality beer more than they wanted cheap beer. And the loss of market share was reflected in Schlitz's declining stock price.[3]

Value can be created only when the company has a competitive or comparative advantage. If a company analyzes a project and determines that it has a positive net present value, the first question should be: Where did it come from?

FINANCIAL PLANNING AND BUDGETING

A strategy is the direction a company takes to meet its objective. A strategic plan is how a company intends to go in that direction. For management, a strategic investment plan includes policies to seek out possible investment opportunities: Do we spend more on research and development? Do we look globally? Do we attempt to increase market share?

A strategic plan also includes resource allocation. If a firm intends to expand, where does it get the capital to do so? If a firm requires more capital, the timing, amount, and type of capital (whether equity or debt) comprise elements of a firm's financial strategic plan. These things must be planned to implement the strategy.

---

[3] The case of Schlitz Brewing is detailed in Day and Fahey (1990).

IMPORTANCE OF FINANCIAL PLANNING

Financial planning allocates a firm's resources to achieve its investment objectives. Financial planning is important for several reasons.

First, financial planning helps managers assess the impact of a particular strategy on their firm's financial position, its cash flows, its reported earnings, and its need for external financing.

Second, by formulating financial plans, management is in a better position to react to any changes in market conditions, such as slower than expected sales, or unexpected problems, such as a reduction in the supply of raw materials. By constructing a financial plan, management becomes more familiar with the sensitivity of the firm's cash flows and its financing needs to changes in sales or some other factor.

Third, creating a financial plan helps management understand the trade-offs inherent in its investment and financing plans. For example, by developing a financial plan, management is better able to understand the trade-off that exists between having sufficient inventory to satisfy customer demands and the need to finance the investment in inventory.

Financial planning consists of the company's investment and financing plans. Once we know the firm's investment plan, management needs to figure out when funds are needed and where they will come from. This is accomplished by developing a *budget*, which is basically the company's investment and financing plans expressed in dollar terms. A budget can represent details such as what to do with cash in excess of needs on a daily basis, or it can reflect broad statements of a firm's business strategy over the next decade. Figure 10.2 illustrates the budgeting process.

Budgeting for the short term (less than a year) is usually referred to as *operational budgeting*; budgeting for the long term (typically three to five years ahead) is referred to as *long-run planning* or *long-term planning*. But since long-term planning depends on what is done in the short term, the operational budgeting and long-term planning are closely related.

BUDGETING PROCESS

The budgeting process involves putting together the financing and investment strategy in terms that allow those responsible for the financing of the company to determine what investments can be made and how these investments should be financed. In other words, budgeting pulls together decisions regarding capital budgeting, capital structure, and working capital.

Consider Sears. Its store renovation plan is part of its overall strategy of regaining its share of the retail market by offering customers better

FIGURE 10.2   The Budgeting Process of a Company

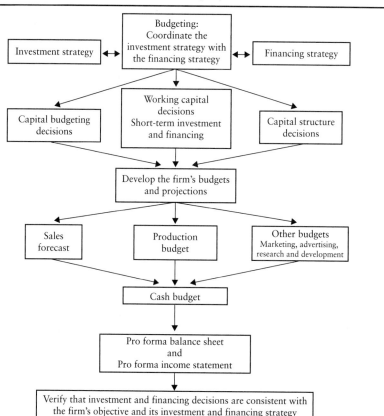

quality and service. Fixing up its stores is seen as an investment strategy. Sears evaluates its renovation plan using capital budgeting techniques (e.g., net present value). But the renovation program requires financing—this is where the capital structure decision comes in. If it needs more funds, where do they come from? Debt? Equity? Both? And let's not forget the working capital decisions. As Sears renovates its stores, will this change its need for cash on hand? Will the renovation affect inventory needs? If Sears expects to increase sales through this program, how will this affect its investment in accounts receivable? And what about short-term financing? Will Sears need more or less short-term financing when it renovates?

While Sears is undergoing a renovation program, it needs to estimate what funds it needs, in both the short run and the long run. This is where cash budget and pro forma financial statements are useful. The starting point is generally a sales forecast, which is related closely to the purchasing, production, and other forecasts of the firm. What are Sears's expected sales in the short term? In the long term? Also, the amount that Sears expects to sell affects its purchases, sales personnel, and advertising forecasts. Putting together forecasts requires cooperation among Sears's marketing, purchasing, and finance staff.

Once Sears has its sales and related forecasts, the next step is a cash budget, detailing the cash inflows and outflows each period. Once the cash budget is established, pro forma balance sheet and income statements can be constructed. Following this, Sears must verify that its budget is consistent with its objective and its strategies.

Budgeting generally begins four to six months prior to the end of the current fiscal period. Most companies have a set of procedures that must be followed in compiling the budget. The budget process is usually managed by either the CFO, a vice president of planning, the director of the budget, the vice president of finance, or the controller. Each division or department provides its own budgets that are then merged into a company's centralized budget by the manager of the budget.

A budget looks forward and backward. It identifies resources that the company will generate or need in the near and long term, and it serves as a measure of the current and past performance of departments, divisions, or individual managers. But management has to be careful when measuring deviations between budgeted and actual results to separately identify deviations that were controllable from deviations that were uncontrollable. For example, suppose management develops a budget expecting $10 million sales from a new product. If actual sales turn out to be $6 million, do we interpret this result as poor performance on the part of management? Maybe, maybe not: If the lower-than-expected sales are due to an unexpected downturn in the economy, probably not; but yes, if they are due to what turns out to be obviously poor management forecasts of consumer demand.

SALES FORECASTING

Sales forecasts are an important part of financial planning. Inaccurate forecasts can result in shortages of inventory, inadequate short-term financing arrangements, and so on.

If a firm's sales forecast misses its mark, either understating or overstating sales, there are many potential problems. Consider Coleco Industries, which missed its mark. This company introduced a toy product in 1983, its Cabbage Patch doll, which enjoyed runaway popularity. In fact, this doll was so popular that Coleco could not keep up with demand. It was in such demand and inventory so depleted that fights broke out in toy stores, some parents bribed store personnel to get scarce dolls just before Christmas, and fake dolls were being smuggled into the country.

Coleco missed its mark, significantly underestimating the demand for these dolls. While having a popular toy may seem like a dream for a toy manufacturer, this doll turned into a nightmare. With no Cabbage Patch dolls on the toy shelves, other toy manufacturers introduced dolls with similar (but not identical) features, capturing some of Coleco's market. Also, many consumers—the parents—became irate at Coleco's creating the demand for the toy through advertising, but not having sufficient dolls to satisfy the demand.

Coleco Industries tried but failed to introduce a toy as successful as the Cabbage Patch doll. It filed for bankruptcy in 1988, with most of its assets (including its Cabbage Patch doll line) sold to Hasbro Inc., a rival toy company. Hasbro was then acquired by Mattel, Inc.

To predict cash flows management forecasts sales, which are uncertain because they are affected by future economic, industry, and market conditions. Nevertheless, management can usually assign meaningful degrees of uncertainty to its forecasts. Sales can be forecasted by regression analysis, market surveys, or opinions of management. We discuss each in this section.

Forecasting with Regression Analysis

Regression analysis is a statistical method that enables us to fit a straight line that on average represents the best possible graphical relationship between sales and time. This best fit is called the *regression line*. One way regression analysis can be used is to simply extrapolate future sales based on the trend in past sales. Another way of using regression analysis is to look at the relation between two measures, say, sales and capital expenditures.

While regression analysis gives us what may seem to be a precise measure of the relationship among variables, there are a number of warnings that management must heed in using it:

- Using historical data to predict the future assumes that the past relationships will continue into the future, which is not always true.
- The period over which the regression is estimated may not be representative of the future. For example, data from a recessionary period of time will not tell much about a period that is predicted to be an economic boom.
- The reliability of the estimate is important: If there is a high degree of error in the estimate, the regression estimates may not be useful.
- The time period over which the regression is estimated may be too short to provide a basis for projecting long-term trends.

■ The forecast of one variable may require forecasts of other variables. For example, the management may be convinced that sales are affected by *gross domestic product* (GDP) and use regression to analyze this relationship. But to use regression to forecast sales, management must first forecast GDP. In this case, management's forecast of sales is only as good as the forecast of GDP.

Market Surveys

Market surveys of customers can provide estimates of future revenues. In the case of IBM, for example, management would need to focus on the computer industry and, specifically, on the personal computer, minicomputer, and mainframe computer markets. For each of these markets, management would have to assess IBM's market share and also the expected sales for each market. Management should expect to learn from these market surveys:

■ Product development and introductions by IBM and its competitors.
■ The general economic climate and the projected expenditures on computers.

In general, management can use the company's own market survey department to survey its customers. Or it can employ outside market survey specialists.

Management Forecasts

In addition to market surveys, the firm's managers may be able to provide forecasts of future sales. The experience of a firm's management and their familiarity with the firm's products, customers, and competitors make them reliable forecasters of future sales.

The firm's own managers should have the expertise to predict the market for the goods and services and to evaluate the costs of producing and marketing them. But there are potential problems in using management forecasts. Consider the case of a manager who forecasts rosy outcomes for a new product. These forecasts may persuade the firm to allocate more resources—such as a larger capital budget and additional personnel—to that manager. If these forecasts come true, the firm will be glad these additional resources were allocated. But if these forecasts turned out to be too rosy, the firm has unnecessarily allocated these resources.

Forecasting is an important element in planning for both the short-term and the long-term. But forecasts are made by people. Forecasters tend to be optimistic, which usually results in rosier-than-deserved forecasts of future sales. In addition, people tend to focus on what worked in the past, so past successes carry more weight in developing forecasts than an analysis of the future.

One way to avoid this is to make managers responsible for their forecasts, rewarding accurate forecasts and penalizing managers for being way off the mark.

SEASONAL CONSIDERATIONS

A company's operating activities typically vary throughout the year, depending on seasonal demand and supply factors. Seasonality influences a company's short-term investment and financing activities.

Let us look at a few U.S. corporations' quarterly revenues to get an idea of different seasonal patterns of activity:

- Coca-Cola, a beverage producer.
- Amazon.com, an online retailer.
- Walt Disney, a film and amusement firm.
- Nike, a shoe manufacturer.
- Delta Airlines, a national airline.

The quarterly revenues for each of these firms is plotted in Figure 10.3 from the first quarter 2003 through the third quarter 2006. The seasonal patterns are quite different:

- Coca-Cola tends to have increased sales in the summer months, driven, most likely, by their larger segment, soft drinks.
- Amazon.com has a high degree of seasonality, with sales dependent on the December holiday season, with sales highest in the fourth quarter.
- Walt Disney Company has sales that tend to increase around the fourth quarter of each year, influenced by their two major product lines, film production, and amusement parks.
- Nike has seasonal sales, with sales increasing around the "back-to-school" time of year.
- Delta Airlines' sales increase somewhat during the summer months, due to summer vacation travel, but this seasonality is not as pronounced as that of, say, Nike or Disney.

Looking closer at what seasonality has to do with cash flows, let's focus on the likely cash flow pattern for Amazon.com. Sales are greatest in the fourth quarter of the year due to holiday shopping. As a retail operation

FIGURE 10.3   Revenues of Selected U.S. Companies, Quarterly, First Quarter 2003 through Third Quarter 2006

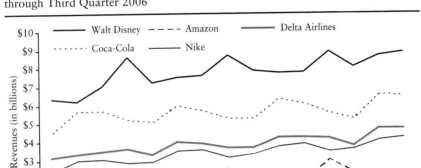

Source: Company annual reports and 10-Q filings, various years.

that does not extend credit, its cash inflows will be highest in the fourth quarter also.

But what about cash outflows? To have the merchandise to sell in the fourth quarter, Amazon.com must increase its inventory prior to or during the fourth quarter. Depending on its credit arrangements with its suppliers, cash will be flowing out of the firm before or during the fourth quarter. This means that for some period of time Amazon.com will have more cash going out than coming in, and then more cash coming in than going out.

BUDGETING

In budgeting, we bring together analyses of cash flows, projected income statements, and projected balance sheets. The cash flow analyses are most important, though the financial management staff needs to generate the income statement and balance sheet as well.

Most firms extend or receive credit, so cash flows and net income do not coincide. Typically, the finance staff must determine cash flows from accounting information on revenues and expenses. Combining sales projections with estimates of collections of accounts receivable results in an estimate of cash receipts.

How are sales estimates translated into cash receipts? First, how long it takes to collect accounts needs to be estimated. Management can estimate the typical time it takes to collect on accounts using the financial ratio,

$$\text{Number of days of credit} = \frac{\text{Accounts receivable}}{\text{Credit sales per day}}$$

This ratio indicates how long it takes, on average, to collect on accounts receivable.

An alternative and more precise method is to look at the *aging of receivables*—how long each account has been outstanding—and use this information to track collections. However, this requires a detailed estimate of the age of all accounts and their typical collection period.

Whether an overall average or an aging approach is used, several factors in the cash collections estimate need to be considered:

- An estimate of bad debts—accounts that will not be collected at all.
- An analysis of the trend in the number of days it takes customers to pay on account.
- An estimate of the seasonal nature of collections of accounts; often customers' ability to pay is influenced by the operating cycle of their own firm.

As with revenues and cash receipts, there is a relation between expenses and cash disbursements. Firms typically do not pay cash for all goods and services; purchases are generally bought on account (creating accounts payable) and wages and salaries are paid periodically (weekly, bimonthly, or monthly). Therefore, a lagged relationship exists between expenses and cash payments.

An idea of the time it takes to pay for purchases on account with the number of days of purchases can be obtained from the following ratio:

$$\text{Number of days of purchases} = \frac{\text{Accounts payable}}{\text{Average day's purchases}}$$

The time it takes to pay for wages and salaries can be estimated by looking at the firm's personnel policies. Putting these two pieces together, the estimate of how long it takes to pay for the goods and services can be acquired.

Cash Budget

A *cash budget* is a detailed statement of the cash inflows and outflows expected in future periods. This budget helps management identify financing and investment needs. A cash budget can also be used to compare actual cash flows against planned cash flows so that management can evaluate both management's performance and management's forecasting ability.

Cash flows come into the company from:

- Operations, such as receipts from sales and collections on accounts receivable.
- The results of financing decisions, such as borrowings, sales of shares of common stock, and sales of preferred stock.
- The results of investment decisions, such as sales of assets and income from marketable securities.

Cash flows leave the company from:

- Operations, such as payments on accounts payable, purchases of goods, and the payment of taxes.
- Financing obligations, such as the payment of dividends and interest, and the repurchase of shares of stock or the redemption of bonds.
- Investments, such as the purchase of plant and equipment.

As we noted before, the cash budget is driven by the sales forecast. Consider the following sales forecasts for the Imagined Company for January through June:

Month	Forecasted Sales	Month	Forecasted Sales
January	$1,000	April	$2,000
February	2,000	May	1,000
March	3,000	June	1,000

Using the forecasted sales, along with a host of assumptions about credit sales, collections on accounts receivable, payments for purchases, and financing, we can construct a cash budget, which tells us about the cash inflows and the cash outflows.

Let's look at Imagined's cash budget for January of Year 1. Sales are expected to be $1,000. Now let's translate sales into cash flows, focusing first on the cash flows from operations.

Let's assume that an analysis of accounts receivable over the prior year, Year 0, reveals that:

- 10% of a month's sales are paid in the month of the sale.
- 60% of a month's sales are paid in the month following the sale.

■ 30% of a month's sales are paid in the second month following the sale.

This means that only 10% of the $1,000 sales, or $100, is collected in January of Year 1. But this also means that in January Imagined collects 60% of Year 0's December sales and 30% of Year 0's November sales. If sales in December and November of Year 0 were $1,000 and $2,000, respectively, this means that January collections are:

Collections on January Year 1 sales	$100	← 10% of $1,000
Collections on December Year 0 sales	600	← 60% of $1,000
Collections on November Year 0 sales	600	← 30% of $2,000
Total cash inflow from collections	$1,300	

Now let's look at the cash flows related to Imagined's payment for its goods. We first have to make an assumption about how much Imagined buys and when it pays for its goods and services. First, assume that Imagined has a cost of goods (other than labor) of 50%. This means that for every $1 it sells, it has a cost of 50%. Next, assume that Imagined purchases goods two months in advance of when the firm sells them (this means the number of days of inventory is around 60 days). Finally, let's assume that Imagined pays 20% of its accounts payable in the month it purchases the goods and 80% of its accounts payable in the month after it purchases the goods.

Putting this all together, we forecast that in January, Imagined will purchase 50% of March's forecasted sales, or 50% of $3,000 = $1,500. Imagined will pay 20% of these purchases in January, or 20% of $1,500 = $300. In addition, Imagined will be paying 80% of the purchases made in December of Year 0. And December of Year 0's purchases are 50% of *February* of Year 1's projected sales. So in January of Year 1, Imagined will pay 50% of 80% of $2,000, which is 50% of $1,600 or $800.

We assume that Imagined has additional cash outflows for wages (5% of current month's sales) and selling and administrative expenses (also 10% of current month's sales). Imagined's cash outflows related to operations in January consist of:

Payments of current month's purchases	$300	← 20% of $1,500
Payments for previous month's purchases	800	← 80% of $1,600
Wages	50	← 5% of $1,000
Selling and administrative expenses	100	← 10% of $1,000
Operating cash outflows	$1,250	

The cash flows pertaining to Imagined Company's operations are shown in the top portion of Table 10.1. In January, there is a net cash inflow from operations of $50. Extending what we did for January's cash flows to the next five months as well, we get a projection of cash inflows and outflows from operations. As you can see, there are net outflows from operations in February and March, and net inflows in other months.

But cash flows from operations do not tell us the complete picture. Management also considers Imagined's nonoperating cash flows. Does the company intend to buy or retire any plant and equipment? Does it intend to retire any debt? Does it need to pay interest on any debt? And so on. These projections are inserted in the lower portion of Table 10.1.

But there is one catch here: Cash inflows must equal cash outflows. So management has to decide where Imagined is going to get its cash if its inflows are less than its outflows. And we have to decide where it is going to invest its cash if its outflows are less than its inflows.

Let's assume that Imagined plans to borrow from one of its banks where it has a line of credit when it needs short-term financing and it will pay off its bank loans or invest in marketable securities (if it has no outstanding bank loans) if it has more cash than needed. In our example, let's group cash and marketable securities into one item, referred to as "cash."

The bank loan–marketable securities decision is a residual decision: Management makes policy decisions about such things as when the company pays out accounts, but it uses the bank loan or marketable securities investment as a "plug" figure to help balance the cash inflows and outflows. This plug is very important—it tells management what financing arrangement needs to be in place (such as a line of credit) or that management needs to make decisions regarding short-term investments.

Comparing inflows with outflows from operations, we see that if Imagined requires a minimum cash balance of $1,000, it needs to use bank financing in January, February, May, and June. Management can also see that if Imagined does not need to maintain a cash balance above $2,000, it can pay off some of its bank loans in April.

Table 10.1 provides a forecast of cash inflows and outflows for several months into the future. But these are forecasts and lots of things can happen between now and then. The actual cash flows can easily differ from the forecasted cash flows. Furthermore, a host of assumptions and decisions have been made by the management along the way, some that the board may be able to influence, such as dividend payments, and some that management has no control over, such as how long customers take to pay. Economic conditions, market conditions, and other factors will affect actual cash flows.

Two tools that can help management assess the uncertainty of cash flows are sensitivity analysis and simulation analysis. *Sensitivity analysis* involves

TABLE 10.1 Imagined Company Monthly Cash Budget, January through June of Year 1

	January	February	March	April	May	June
Sales	$1,000	$2,000	$3,000	$2,000	$1,000	$1,000
Operating Cash Flows						
Cash Inflows						
Collections on accounts receivables:						
Collections on current month's sales	$100	$200	$300	$200	$100	$100
Collections from previous month's sales	600	600	1,200	1,800	1,200	600
Collections from two months' previous sales	600	300	300	600	900	600
Operating cash inflows	$1,300	$1,100	$1,800	$2,600	$2,200	$1,300
Cash Outflows						
Payments of purchases on account:						
Payments for current month's purchases	$300	$200	$100	$100	$100	$100
Payments for previous month's purchases	800	1,200	800	400	400	400
Wages	50	100	150	100	50	50
Selling and administrative expenses	100	200	300	200	100	100
Operating cash outflows	$1,250	$1,700	$1,350	$800	$650	$650
Operating net cash flow	$50	($600)	$450	$1,800	$1,550	$650
Nonoperating Cash Flows						
Cash Inflows						
Retirements of plant and equipment	$0	$0	$0	$500	$0	$0
Issuance of long-term debt	0	3,000	0	0	0	0
Issuance of common stock	0	0	0	0	0	0
Nonoperating cash inflows	$0	$3,000	$0	$500	$0	$0

343

TABLE 10.1 (continued)

	January	February	March	April	May	June
Cash Outflows						
Acquisitions of plant and equipment	$1,000	$3,000	$0	$0	$3,500	$0
Payment of cash dividends	0	0	100	0	0	100
Retirement of long-term debt	0	0	0	0	0	1,000
Retirement of common stock	0	0	0	0	0	0
Interest on long-term debt	10	10	10	10	10	10
Taxes	69	165	271	168	53	53
Nonoperating cash outflows	$1,079	$3,175	$381	$178	$3,563	$1,163
Nonoperating cash flows	−$1,079	−$175	−$381	$322	−$3,563	−$1,163
Analysis of cash and marketable securities						
Balance, beginning of month	$1,500.00	$1,000.00	$1,000.00	$1,069.25	$2,000.00	$1,000.00
Net cash flows for the month	(1,029.00)	(775.33)	69.25	2,122.34	(2,012.55)	(513.05)
Balance without any change in bank loans	$471.00	$224.67	$1,069.25	$3,191.59	($12.55)	$486.95
Bank loans to maintain minimum balance	529.00	775.33	0.00	0.00	1,012.55	513.05
Available to pay off bank loans	0.00	0.00	0.00	1,191.59	0.00	0.00
Balance, end of month	$1,000.00	$1,000.00	$1,069.25	$2,000.00	$1,000.00	$1,000.00

Assumptions:

(1) Cash sales are 10% of current month's sales.
(2) Collections on accounts receivable are 60% of previous month's sales and 30% of the previous two month's sales.
(3) Purchases are 50% of two-months-ahead sales.
(4) Payments on accounts are 20% of current month's purchases, plus 80% of previous month's purchases.
(5) Wages are 5% of current month's sales.
(6) Selling and administrative expenses are 10% of current month's sales.
(7) July and August sales are forecasted to be $1,000 each month.

changing one of the variables in the analysis and looking at its affect on the cash flows. This gives management an idea of what cash flows may be under certain circumstances. Management can pose different scenarios: What if customers take 60 days to pay instead of 30? What if sales are actually $1,000 in February instead of $2,000?

But sensitivity analysis can become unmanageable if management starts changing two or more things at a time. A manageable approach to doing this is with computer simulation. *Simulation analysis* allows management to develop a probability distribution of possible outcomes, given a probability distribution for each variable that may change.

Suppose management can develop a probability distribution—that is, a list of possible outcomes and their related likelihood of occurring—for sales.[4] And suppose management can develop a probability distribution for costs of the raw materials that are needed in producing the product. Using simulation, a probability distribution of cash flows can be produced, providing information on the uncertainty of the firm's future cash flows, as shown in Figure 10.4. Once management produces the probability distribution of future cash flows, management has an idea of the possible cash flows and can plan accordingly. The cash budget produced using the possible cash flows is a *flexible budget*. With this information, management can then determine the more appropriate short-term financing and short-term investments to consider.

FIGURE 10.4   Simulation and Cash Flow Uncertainty

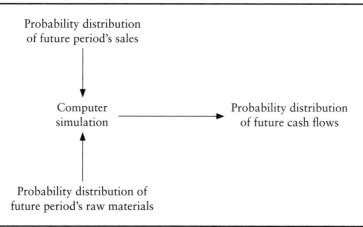

---

[4] A probability distribution is the set of possible outcomes and their likelihood of occurrence.

PRO FORMA FINANCIAL STATEMENTS

A *pro forma balance sheet* is a projected balance sheet for a future period—a month, quarter, or year—that summarizes assets, liabilities, and equity. A *pro forma income statement* is the projected income statement for a future period—a month, quarter, or year—that summarizes revenues and expenses. Together both projections help management identify the company's investment and financing needs.

The analysis of accounts and percent-of-sales methods are two ways of projecting financial statements.

Analysis of Accounts

The *analysis of accounts method* starts with the cash budget. Before putting together the pro forma income statement and balance sheet, management needs to see how the various asset, liability, and equity accounts change from month to month, based on the information provided in the cash budget. The analysis of accounts is shown in Table 10.2, where each account is analyzed starting with the beginning balance and making any necessary adjustments to arrive at the ending balance.

Management can see how the cash budget interacts with the pro forma income statement and balance sheet by looking at the change in accounts receivable. Consider what happens in January of Year 1:

The Analysis of Accounts Receivable . . .		. . . Affects Financial Planning through the . . .
Balance at the beginning of the month	$2,000 →	pro forma balance sheet (accounts receivable)
Plus credit sales during January	+900 →	pro forma income statement (sales) and pro forma balance sheet (accounts receivable)
Less collections on accounts during January	−1,200 →	cash budget (cash flow from operations)
Balance at the end of the month	$1,700 →	pro forma balance sheet (accounts receivable)

As can be seen, the balances in these accounts are all interrelated with the cash budget.

In doing a cash budget, management has begun to make projections based on the following information:

■ Changes in the cash account are determined by the difference between cash inflows and outflows.

TABLE 10.2 Imagined Company Analysis of Monthly Changes in Accounts, January through June of Year 1

	January	February	March	April	May	June
Accounts receivable						
Month's beginning balance	$2,000	$1,700	$2,600	$3,800	$3,200	$2,000
Plus credit sales during the month	900	1,800	2,700	1,800	900	900
Less collections on accounts	1,200	900	1,500	2,400	2,100	1,200
Month's ending balance	$1,700	$2,600	$3,800	$3,200	$2,000	$1,700
Inventory						
Month's beginning balance	$2,500	$3,500	$3,500	$2,500	$2,000	$2,000
Plus purchases	1,500	1,000	500	500	500	500
Plus wages and other production expenses	50	100	150	100	50	50
Less goods sold	550	1,100	1,650	1,100	550	550
Month's ending balance	$3,500	$3,500	$2,500	$2,000	$2,000	$2,000
Accounts payable						
Month's beginning balance	$2,000	$2,400	$2,000	$1,600	$1,600	$1,600
Plus purchases on account	1,200	800	400	400	400	400
Less payments on account	800	1,200	800	400	400	400
Month's ending balance	$2,400	$2,000	$1,600	$1,600	$1,600	$1,600
Bank loans						
Month's beginning balance	$1,000	$1,529	$2,304	$2,304	$1,113	$2,125
Plus borrowings	529	775	0	0	1,013	513
Less repayment of loans	0	0	0	1,192	0	0
Month's ending balance	$1,529	$2,304	$2,304	$1,113	$2,125	$2,638

TABLE 10.2 (continued)

	January	February	March	April	May	June
Plant and equipment						
Month's beginning balance	$10,000	$10,890	$13,751	$13,614	$12,982	$16,318
Plus acquisitions	1,000	3,000	$0	0	3,500	0
Less retirements	0	0	0	500	0	0
Less depreciation[a]	110	139	137	131	165	163
Month's ending balance	$10,890	$13,751	$13,614	$12,982	$16,318	$16,154
Long-term debt						
Month's beginning balance	$5,000	$5,000	$8,000	$8,000	$8,000	$8,000
Plus issuances of long-term debt	0	3,000	0	0	0	0
Less retirements of long-term debt	0	0	0	0	0	1,000
Month's ending balance	$5,000	$8,000	$8,000	$8,000	$8,000	$7,000
Common equity						
Month's beginning balance	$8,000	$8,161	$8,547	$9,079	$9,470	$9,592
Plus earnings retained during the month	161	386	532	391	123	24
Plus issuances of common stock	0	0	0	0	0	0
Less retirements of common stock	0	0	0	0	0	0
Month's ending balance	$8,161	$8,547	$9,079	$9,470	$9,592	$9,616

[a] 1% of gross plant and equipment.

- Changes in accounts receivables are determined by sales and collections projections.
- Changes in inventory are determined by purchase and sales projections.
- Changes in plant and equipment are determined by capital budgeting.
- Changes in long-term debt are determined by financing projections.
- Changes in common equity are determined by both the financing projections and the projected retained earnings.
- Changes in retained earnings are determined by the projected income.

If all these pieces are put together, management has a pro forma balance sheet for Imagined Company, as shown in Table 10.3. Looking at the cash budget in Table 10.1, the analysis of accounts in Table 10.2, and the balance sheet in Table 10.3, management can follow through to see the interactions among the various assets, liabilities, equity accounts, and cash flows as was done for accounts receivable.

The pro forma income statement for Imagined Company is shown in the lower part of Table 10.3. Though management's interest is ultimately in cash flows, the income statement provides useful summary information on the expected performance of the firm in months to come. As can be seen in Table 10.3, net income tends to increase in March, which accompanies the increased revenues in that month.

Management is interested in the pro forma balance sheet and income statement not just as a product of the cash flow analysis. Suppose the bank financing is secured financing, limited to 80% of accounts receivable. If this is the case, the company may be limited as to how much can be borrowed from the bank in any particular month. Management is also interested in the balance sheet since some of the short-term or long-term debt may have covenants that prescribe the firm to maintain specific relations among its accounts, for example, a current ratio of 2:1. In addition, management may be concerned about the company's perceived riskiness. If management must borrow heavily at certain times within a year, does this affect the riskiness of the outstanding debt obligations, thereby increasing the cost of financing?

These considerations point out the importance of reviewing the projected balance sheet. In fact, these considerations may point out the need for management to explicitly build constraints into the budget to ensure certain financial ratios are maintained each month. These constraints add complexity to an already complex system of relationships, the detail of which is beyond the scope of this text.

TABLE 10.3 Imagined Company Monthly Pro Forma Balance Sheet and Income Statement, January through June of Year 1

Pro Forma Balance Sheet

	January	February	March	April	May	June
Assets						
Cash and marketable securities	$1,000	$1,000	$1,069	$2,000	$1,000	$1,000
Accounts receivable	1,700	2,600	3,800	3,200	2,000	1,700
Inventories	3,500	3,500	2,500	2,000	2,000	2,000
Plant and equipment	10,890	13,751	13,614	12,982	16,318	16,154
Total Assets	$17,090	$20,851	$20,983	$20,182	$21,318	$20,854
Liabilities and equity						
Accounts payable	$2,400	$2,000	$1,600	$1,600	$1,600	$1,600
Bank loans	1,529	2,304	2,304	1,113	2,125	2,638
Long-term debt	5,000	8,000	8,000	8,000	8,000	7,000
Common equity	8,161	8,547	9,079	9,470	9,592	9,616
Total Liabilities and Equity	$17,090	$20,851	$20,983	$20,182	$21,318	$20,854

TABLE 10.3 (continued)
Pro Forma Income Statement

	January	February	March	April	May	June
Sales	$1,000	$2,000	$3,000	$2,000	$1,000	$1,000
Less cost of goods sold	550	1,100	1,650	1,100	550	550
Less depreciation	110	139	138	131	165	163
Gross profit	$340	$761	$1,212	$769	$285	$287
Less selling and administrative expenses	100	200	300	200	100	100
Earnings before interest and taxes	$240	$561	$912	$569	$185	$187
Less interest	10	10	10	10	10	10
Earnings before taxes	$230	$551	$902	$559	$175	$177
Less taxes	69	165	271	168	53	53
Net income	$161	$386	$632	$391	$123	$124
Less cash dividends	0	0	100	0	0	100
Retained earnings	$161	$386	$532	$391	$123	$24

Percent-of-Sales Method

The *percent-of-sales method* uses historical relationships between sales and each of the other income statement accounts and between sales and each of the balance sheet accounts. There are two steps to this method.

First, previous periods' income statement and balance sheet accounts are restated in terms of a percentage of sales for the year. Let's look at the Imagined Corporation's balance sheet and income statement for Year 1 shown in the leftmost column of Table 10.4. Because we are projecting monthly sales, each item in both statements is restated as a percent of December Year 1 sales, as shown in the second column of this table.

Second, based on the forecasted sales for the future years and the percentages each account represents, projections for January through June are calculated. For example, cost of goods sold is 55% of sales. Because January sales are predicted to be $1,000, cost of goods sold is predicted to be 55% of $1,000, or $550. Because sales for February is predicted to be $2,000, cost of goods sold for February are predicted to be $1,100. It is likewise for balance sheet accounts. Cash and marketable securities are 75% of monthly sales, so the company expects $750 in this account in January. Each of the balance sheet and income statement accounts is forecasted January through June, as shown in Table 10.4.

This method of creating pro forma statements is simple. But it may make inappropriate assumptions, such as that: (1) all costs vary with sales, even though most firms have fixed costs; or (2) assets and liabilities change along with sales, even though firms tend to make capital investments that generate cash flows far into the future, not necessarily in the year they are put in place.

And there is another drawback: The percent-of-sales method focuses on accounts in the financial statements, not cash flows. Because of this, it cannot help identify when a company needs cash and when it has excess cash to invest.

But the percent-of-sales method is used frequently because of its simplicity. And since we are dealing with forecasts, which are themselves estimates (and not actual fact), the simpler approach is sometimes more attractive.

LONG-TERM FINANCIAL PLANNING

Long-term planning is similar to what we have just completed for the operational budget for January through June of Year 1, but for a longer span of time into the future and with less detail.

TABLE 10.4 Pro Forma Financial Statements for January through June of Year 1, Using the Percent-of-Sales Method
Pro Forma Balance Sheet

	As of the End of Year 0	Percentage of December Year 0 Sales	Forecasted Accounts for Year 1					
			January	February	March	April	May	June
Cash and marketable securities	$1,500	75%	$750	$1,500	$2,250	$1,500	$750	$750
Accounts receivable	2,000	100%	1,000	2,000	3,000	2,000	1,000	$1,000
Inventories	2,500	125%	1,250	2,500	3,750	2,500	1,250	$1,250
Plant and equipment	10,000	500%	5,000	10,000	15,000	10,000	5,000	$5,000
Total Assets	$16,000	800%	$8,000	$16,000	$24,000	$16,000	$8,000	$8,000
			$0	$0	$0	$0	$0	$0
Accounts payable	$2,000	100%	$1,000	$2,000	$3,000	$2,000	$1,000	$1,000
Bank loans	1,000	50%	500	1,000	1,500	1,000	$500	$500
Long-term debt	5,000	250%	2,500	5,000	7,500	5,000	2,500	2,500
Common stock and paid-in capital	2,000	100%	1,000	2,000	3,000	2,000	1,000	1,000
Retained earnings	6,000	300%	3,000	6,000	9,000	6,000	3,000	3,000
Total Liabilities and Equity	$16,000	800%	$8,000	$16,000	$24,000	$16,000	$8,000	$8,000

TABLE 10.4 (continued)
Pro Forma Income Statement

	December Year 0	Percentage of December Year 0 Sales	Forecasted Accounts for Year 1					
			January	February	March	April	May	June
Sales	$2,000	100%	$1,000	$2,000	$3,000	$2,000	$1,000	$1,000
Less cost of goods sold	1,100	55%	550	1,100	1,650	1,100	550	550
Less depreciation	200	10%	100	200	300	200	100	100
Gross profit	$700	35%	350	700	1,050	700	350	350
Less selling and administrative expenses	10	1%	5	10	15	10	5	5
Earnings before interest and taxes	$690	35%	$345	$690	$1,035	$690	$345	$345
Less interest	20	1%	10	20	30	20	10	10
Earnings before taxes	$670	34%	$335	$670	$1,005	$670	$335	$335
Less taxes	12	1%	6	12	18	12	6	6
Net income	$658	33%	$329	$658	$987	$658	$329	$329
Previous December's sales	$1,000							
Previous November's sales	$2,000							

Projections for Year 1 through Year 6 are shown in Table 10.5, where the cash budget is shown in panel A and the pro forma financial statements are shown in panel B. Notice that management is not as concerned about the details, say, concerning the source of cash flows from operations, but rather the bottom line. However, these statements must be compiled as was done with the operational budget: Based on projections and assumptions that are built into our cash budget, management integrates the investment decisions with the financing decisions.

By looking at the long-term plan, management gets an idea of how the firm intends to meet its objective of maximizing shareholder wealth. For example, in the operational budget management would be concerned about meeting monthly cash demands and we assume Imagined Company borrows from banks to meet any cash shortages. But with the long-term plan, management can address the issue of what capital structure (the mix of debt and equity) the firm wants in the long-run. In the case of Imagined Company, in our illustration it is assumed that:

- Any bank loans are reduced to $1,000 at the end of each year.
- When long-term capital is needed, the CFO raises one-half using debt, one-half issuing new equity.
- When the firm is able to reduce its reliance on external funds, it will reduce its long-term debt.

Long-term plans should be evaluated periodically as well as operational budgets. Since the two are closely tied (what is done in the short-term influences what happens in the long-term), it is convenient to update both types of budgets simultaneously.

FINANCIAL MODELING

A *financial model* is the set of relationships that are behind the calculations performed in putting together the cash budget and the pro forma statements. In financial modeling, management generally focuses on the essential features of the budget and statements, and tries not to get bogged down in the details. In our Imagined Company example, we looked at the relation between cash and marketable securities, but we avoided getting into detail of where the cash is held or which securities to buy or sell.

In the case of Imagined Company, the following relations between cash inflows and sales are modeled:

Cash inflows = 10%(This month's sales) + 60%(Preceding month's sales)

+ 30%(Second preceding month's sales)

TABLE 10.5 Imagined Company Long-Term Planning, Year 1 through Year 6

(a) Cash Budget

Projected Sales	$20,000	$22,000	$25,000	$26,000	$27,000	$28,000
	Year 1	Year 2	Year 3	Year 4	Year 5	Year 6
Operating Cash Flows						
Cash Inflows						
Cash sales	$2,000	$2,200	$2,500	$2,600	$2,700	$2,800
Collections on account:	19,000	19,820	21,250	22,040	24,100	26,270
Operating cash inflows	$21,000	$22,020	$23,750	$24,640	$26,800	$29,070
Cash Outflows						
Payments of purchases on account:	$10,067	$10,917	$12,375	$12,958	$13,458	$13,958
Wages	1,000	1,100	1,250	1,300	1,350	1,400
Selling and administrative expenses	2,000	2,200	2,500	2,600	2,700	2,800
Operating cash outflows	$13,067	$14,217	$16,125	$16,858	$17,508	$18,158
Operating net cash flows	$7,933	$7,803	$7,625	$7,782	$9,292	$10,912
Nonoperating Cash Flows						
Cash inflows						
Retirement of plant and equipment	$500	$0	$0	$0	$1,000	$2,000
Nonoperating cash inflows	$500	$0	$0	$0	$1,000	$2,000

TABLE 10.5 (continued)

Projected Sales	$20,000	$22,000	$25,000	$26,000	$27,000	$28,000
	Year 1	Year 2	Year 3	Year 4	Year 5	Year 6
Nonoperating Cash Flows						
Cash outflows						
Maturing long-term debt	$1,000	$1,000	$1,000	$1,000	$1,000	$1,000
Acquisitions of plant and equipment	10,000	7,500	7,500	5,000	1,000	5,000
Payment of cash dividends	400	400	400	400	400	400
Interest on long-term debt	0,300	0,350	0,400	0,350	0,300	0,250
Taxes	1,308	1,317	1,454	1,520	1,773	1,901
Nonoperating cash outflows	$13,008	$10,567	$10,754	$8,270	$4,473	$8,551
Nonoperating net cash flows	−$12,508	−$10,567	−$10,754	−$8,270	−$3,473	−$6,551
Analysis of cash						
Cash balance, beginning of year	$1,500	$1,500	$1,500	$1,500	$1,500	$4,000
Net cash flows during year	−4,575	−2,764	−3,129	−488	5,819	4,360
Cash balance without any financing	−$3,075	−$1,264	−$1,629	$1,012	$7,319	$8,360
Long-term debt issuance	2,287	1,382	1,564	244	0	0
Common stock issuance	2,287	1,382	1,564	244	0	0
Available to pay off long-term debt	0	0	0	0	3,319	4,360
Cash balance, end of year	$1,500	$1,500	$1,500	$1,500	$4,000	$4,000

TABLE 10.5 (continued)
Imagined Company Long-Term Planning, Analysis of Accounts

	Year 1	Year 2	Year 3	Year 4	Year 5	Year 6
Accounts receivable						
Year's beginning balance	$2,000	$1,000	$980	$2,230	$3,590	$3,790
Plus credit sales during the year	$18,000	19,800	22,500	23,400	24,300	25,200
Less collections on accounts	$19,000	19,820	21,250	22,040	24,100	26,270
Year's ending balance	$1,000	$980	$2,230	$3,590	$3,790	$2,720
Inventory						
Year's beginning balance	$2,500	$2,500	$2,500	$2,500	$2,500	$2,500
Plus purchases	10,000	11,000	12,500	13,000	13,500	14,000
Plus wages and other production expenses	1,000	1,100	1,250	1,300	1,350	1,400
Less goods sold	11,000	12,100	13,750	14,300	14,850	15,400
Year's ending balance	$2,500	$2,500	$2,500	$2,500	$2,500	$2,500
Accounts payable						
Year's beginning balance	$2,000	$1,933	$2,017	$2,142	$2,183	$2,225
Plus purchases on account	10,000	11,000	12,500	13,000	13,500	14,000
Less payments on account	10,067	10,917	12,375	12,958	13,458	13,958
Year's ending balance	$1,933	$2,017	$2,142	$2,183	$2,225	$2,267

TABLE 10.5 (continued)

	Year 1	Year 2	Year 3	Year 4	Year 5	Year 6
Bank loans						
Year's beginning and ending balance	$1,000	$1,000	$1,000	$1,000	$1,000	$1,000
Plant and equipment						
Year's beginning balance	$10,000	$17,160	$21,701	$25,697	$27,013	$23,772
Plus acquisitions	9,500	7,500	7,500	5,000		3,000
Less depreciation	2,340	2,959	3,504	3,684	3,242	3,213
Year's ending balance	$17,160	$21,701	$25,697	$27,013	$23,772	$23,559
Long-term debt						
Year's beginning balance	$5,000	$6,287	$6,669	$7,234	$6,478	$2,159
Plus long-term debt issued	2,287	1,382	1,564	244		
Less long-term debt retired or matured	1,000	1,000	1,000	1,000	4,319	5,360
Year's ending balance	$6,287	$6,669	$7,234	$6,478	$2,159	-$3,202
Common equity						
Year's beginning balance	$8,000	$12,939	$16,995	$21,551	$24,942	$28,678
Plus issuance of new shares of stock	2,287	1,382	1,564	244	0	0
Plus earnings retained during the year	2,652	2,674	2,992	3,146	3,736	4,036
Year's ending balance	$12,939	$16,995	$21,551	$24,942	$28,678	$32,714

TABLE 10.5 (continued)

(b) Imagined Company Pro Forma Financial Statements, Year 1 through Year 6

Pro Forma Balance Sheet

	Year 1	Year 2	Year 3	Year 4	Year 5	Year 6
Assets						
Cash and marketable securities	$1,500	$1,500	$1,500	$1,500	$4,000	$4,000
Accounts receivable	1,000	980	2,230	3,590	3,790	2,720
Inventories	2,500	2,500	2,500	2,500	2,500	2,500
Plant and equipment	17,160	21,701	25,697	27,013	23,772	23,559
Total Assets	$22,160	$26,681	$31,927	$34,603	$34,062	$32,779
Liabilities and Equity						
Accounts payable	$1,933	$2,017	$2,142	$2,183	$2,225	$2,269
Bank loans	1,000	1,000	1,000	1,000	1,000	1,000
Long-term debt	6,287	6,669	7,234	6,478	2,159	(3,202)
Stockholders' equity	12,939	16,995	21,551	24,942	28,678	32,714
Total Liabilities and Equity	$22,160	$26,681	$31,927	$34,603	$34,062	$32,779

TABLE 10.5 (continued)
Pro Forma Income Statement

	Year 1	Year 2	Year 3	Year 4	Year 5	Year 6
Sales	$20,000	$22,000	$25,000	$26,000	$27,000	$28,000
Less cost of goods sold	11,000	12,100	13,750	14,300	14,850	15,400
Less depreciation	2,340	2,959	3,504	3,684	3,242	3,213
Gross profit	$6,660	$6,941	$7,746	$8,016	$8,908	$9,387
Less selling and administrative expenses	2,000	2,200	2,500	2,600	2,700	2,800
Earnings before interest and taxes	$4,660	$4,741	$5,246	$5,416	$6,208	$6,587
Less interest	300	350	400	350	300	250
Earnings before taxes	$4,360	$4,391	$4,846	$5,066	$5,908	$6,337
Less taxes	1,308	1,317	1,454	1,520	1,773	1,901
Net income	$3,052	$3,074	$3,392	$3,546	$4,136	$4,436
Less cash dividends	400	400	400	400	400	400
Retained earnings	$2,652	$2,674	$2,992	$3,146	$3,736	$4,036

Cash outflows are similar, but instead of collecting on sales and receivables, we are paying expenses and paying on our accounts payable:

$$\text{Cash outflows} = \underbrace{20\%(\text{This month's purchases}) + 80\%(\text{Last month's purchases})}_{\text{Payments on purchases}}$$

$$+ \underbrace{5\%(\text{This month's sales})}_{\text{Wages}} + \underbrace{10\%(\text{This month's sales})}_{\text{Other expenses}}$$

Purchases are determined by projected sales, so we can rewrite this as

$$\text{Cash outflows} = 20\%(\text{Sales forecasted two months out})$$
$$+ 80\%(\text{Next month's sales}) + 15\%(\text{This month's sales})$$

The cash inflows and outflows from operations are therefore dependent on the forecast of sales in future periods. By changing forecasted sales, the cash inflows and outflows change as well.

Management could continue modeling the relations expressed in the cash budget and pro forma financial statements until all the relationships are represented. Once this is done, management has created a financial model of the firm. By playing what if with the model—changing one item and observing what happens to the rest—management can see the consequences of different actions.

Building the financial model forces management to think through the relationships and consequences of investment and financing decisions. Much of the computation in financial modeling can be accomplished using computers and spreadsheet programs.

The task of modeling financial relationships is made easier by computer programs. These programs reduce the modeling effort because they enable the user to program a financial model using understandable phrases instead of programming code.

PERFORMANCE EVALUATION

Planning and forecasting are important, but without some type of performance evaluation, the execution of a strategy and the accuracy of forecasting cannot be addressed. There are many performance evaluation measures and systems available. We will address two of these, economic value added and the balanced scorecard, to provide examples of how these may assist in assessing performance.

Economic Value Added

Arising from the need for better methods of evaluating performance, several consulting companies advocate performance evaluation methods that are applied to evaluate a company's performance as a whole and to evaluate specific managers' performances. These methods are, in some cases, supplanting traditional methods of measuring performance, such as the return on assets discussed in other chapters of this book. As a class, these measures are often referred to as value-based metrics or economic value added measures. There is a cacophony of acronyms to accompany these measures, including *economic value added* (EVA®), *market value added* (MVA), *cash flow return on investment* (CFROI), *shareholder value added* (SVA), *cash value added* (CVA), and *refined economic value added* (REVA).[5]

A company's management creates value when decisions provide benefits that exceed the costs. These benefits may be received in the near or distant future. The costs include both the direct cost of the investment as well as the less obvious cost, the cost of capital. The cost of capital is the explicit and implicit costs associated with using investors' funds. The attention to the cost of capital sets the value-based metrics apart from traditional measures of performance such as the return on investment.

The most prominent of the techniques to evaluate a company's performance are the value-added measures of *economic profit* and *market value-added* (MVA). Another prominent valuation approach is the discounted cash flow approach, advocated by McKinsey and Co. This approach involves forecasting future periods' free cash flows, forecasting a company's continuing value at the end of the forecast period, and discounting the future free cash flows and the continuing value at the company's weighted average cost of capital. Because this approach involves valuation based on forecasts, it is not a suitable device for evaluating performance, though it is useful in setting performance targets.[6]

These measures have links to our fundamental valuation techniques. Value-added measures are based on the same valuation principles as the *net present value* (NPV) capital budgeting technique.[7] Keep in mind that value is not created out of thin air, but rather from a company's strategy that exploits its comparative or competitive advantage.

Whereas the NPV for a specific investment project is the estimate of change in the value of equity if the company invests in the project, an economic value added is an estimate of the change in the value of the company. Further, whereas NPV is forward looking, assisting management in making

---

[5] For a further discussion of these measures, see Fabozzi and Grant (2000).
[6] See Copeland, Koller, and Murrin (1994).
[7] For an explanation of this technique, see Chapter 13.

decisions dealing with the use of capital in the future, measuring a period's performance, value-added measures focus on the decisions that have been made during a period and the cost of capital that supported those investment decisions to help management gauge how well the company has performed.

There are a number of value-added measures available. The most commonly used measures are economic profit and market value added.

Economic Profit/Economic Value Added

Economic value added, also referred to as *economic profit*, is the difference between operating profits and the cost of capital, where the cost of capital is expressed in dollar terms. The application to an entire company involves, essentially, calculating the NPV of all investment projects, both those involving existing assets (that is, past investment decisions) and those projected.

Although the application of economic value added is relatively new in the measurement of performance, the concept of economic profit is not new—it was first noted by Alfred Marshall in the nineteenth century.[8] What this recent emphasis on economic profit has done is focus attention away from accounting profit and toward economic profit.

Key elements of estimating economic value added are:

- The calculation of the company's operating profit from financial statement data, making adjustments to accounting profit to better reflect a company's results for a period.
- The calculation of the company's cost of capital.
- The comparison of operating profit with the cost of capital.

The difference between the operating profit and the cost of capital is the estimate of the company's economic profit, or economic value added.

The cost of capital is the rate of return required by the suppliers of capital to the company. For a business that finances its operations or investments using both debt and equity, the cost of capital includes not only the explicit interest on the debt, but also the implicit minimum return that owners require. This minimum return to owners is necessary so that owners keep their investment capital in the company.

Even advocates of economic profit do not prescribe a particular formula for calculating economic profit. Economic profit has ambiguous elements, most notably the adjustments to operating income and the cost of capital. Conceivably, two consultants could calculate economic profit, yet draw different conclusions regarding companies' relative performance.

---

[8] See Marshall (1890, p. 142).

Market Value Added

A measure closely related to economic profit is *market valued added*. Market value added is the difference between the company's market value and its capital. Essentially, market value added is a measure of what the company's management has been able to do with a given level of resources (the invested capital): Market value added is the difference between the market value of the firm (that is, debt and equity), less the capital invested. Like economic profit, market value added is in terms of dollars and the goal of the company is to increase added value.

The key elements of market value added are:

- The calculation of the market value of capital.
- The calculation of the capital invested.
- The comparison of the market value of capital with the capital invested.

The difference between the market value of capital and the amount of capital invested is the market value added. The primary distinction between economic value added and market value added is that the latter incorporates market data in the calculation.

Balanced Scorecard

The traditional measures of a company's performance are generally historical, financial measures. With the popularity of economic value added and market value measures, many companies began to adopt forward-looking financial measures. Taking a step further, many companies are adopting the concept of a balanced scorecard. A *balanced scorecard* is a management tool used to:

- Help put a company's strategic plan into action.
- Use measurement devices to evaluate performance relative to the strategic plan.
- Provide feedback mechanisms to allow for continuous improvement toward the strategic goals.

Kaplan and Norton (1991, 2001) developed the concept of a balanced scorecard to address the need of companies to balance the needs of customers, financial needs, internal management needs, and the needs for innovation and learning within the enterprise. They contend that single metrics do not adequately address the strategic objectives of a company; rather, multiple measures—both lagging and leading indicators—should be used to meet a company's strategic goals. These measures, referred to as *key performance indicators*, include short-term and long-term measures, financial and nonfinancial measures, and historical and leading measures. The balanced scorecard, therefore, goes beyond the traditional financial measures of the rate of return and profitability to capture other dimensions of a company's performance and use this information to help attain the company's strategic goals.

The Process

The balanced scorecard is really a process of determining the company's strategy, identifying measures to evaluate whether the company is meeting its short-term and long-term goals, setting targets, and then providing feedback from these measures. This process is illustrated in Figure 10.5. The actual balanced scorecard does not prescribe the measures to use, but rather specifies the dimensions of the company that should be considered in the system.

The Measures

The developers of the balanced scorecard argue that measures and metrics used to evaluate different business units and the company should represent different dimensions of performance, including financial performance, customer relations, internal business processes, and organizational learning and

FIGURE 10.5 The Balanced Scorecard Process

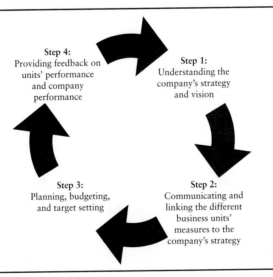

Step 4:
Providing feedback on units' performance and company performance

Step 1:
Understanding the company's strategy and vision

Step 3:
Planning, budgeting, and target setting

Step 2:
Communicating and linking the different business units' measures to the company's strategy

FIGURE 10.6 Relation between Strategy and Dimensions of Performance

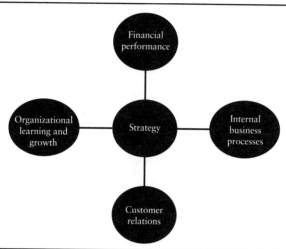

growth. These dimensions are shown in Figure 10.6. However, no specific measures are prescribed; rather, the choice of measures should be tailored to the company's individual situation. The basic idea, however, is to select the *key performance indicators* (KPIs) that capture the four dimensions.

Within each of these dimensions, there may be any number of different measures. These measures are generally tailored to the specific business and should be consistent with the company's or unit's goals. We provide a number of possible metrics within each of these dimensions in Table 10.6.

TABLE 10.6 Possible Performance Indicators in the Four Suggested Dimensions

Financial Performance	Customer Relations
Return on investment	Customer profitability
Net profit margin	Repeat customers
Economic value added	Customer surveys
Market value added	Number of customer complaints
Growth rate of revenues	On-time delivery
	Service response times

Internal Business Processes	Organizational Learning and Growth
Dealer quality	Employee motivation
Process cost	Employee empowerment
Number of units requiring reworking	Information systems capabilities
Length of operating cycle	Employee capabilities
Volume of goods shipped	Number of employee suggestions
Optimal asset utilization	Hours spent on training employees

How Do Companies Use the Balanced Scorecard?

The idea of using metrics to gauge a company or unit's performance is not new. What the balanced scorecard concept does is remind companies to evaluate themselves and their path to their strategic goals by including the different dimensions of performance, therefore providing a more comprehensive look at the company.

This comprehensive look, however, does not come with a ready-equipped list of key measures or drivers. Nor does the balanced scorecard come with a system of examining these measures, which may quickly turn into a case of too much information. Based on research by The Hackett Group, as described in Kersner (2004), on average a company's management may be faced with examining 83 financial and 49 internal business-process metrics. Limiting the number of measures to key drivers is preferred, but this is not necessarily the way in which this concept has been applied in practice.

Aside from the wealth of metrics available and used, the development of a balanced scorecard requires balancing. Yet, in practice, there are generally a greater proportion of financial measures relative to the other dimensions. This is likely due to the traditional use of financial measures in gauging performance, along with the ease of obtaining or calculating these measures. However, most of the financial measures used by companies are historical measures that do not provide the richness that the scorecard system requires to address the company's strategy.

The purpose behind the balanced scorecard approach is to help companies measure and manage their performance with respect to the company's strategic goals. As with many methods that seek to change the way companies manage themselves, the success of the method depends on its support throughout the company and its implementation. Whereas some companies' managers believe that the scorecard helps the company work toward its strategic goals, others do not feel that approach is helpful.[9] The evidence regarding whether companies using the balanced scorecard outperform firms that do not use such an approach is mixed. David and Albright (1994) find that balanced scorecard firms outperformed firms that did not use the balanced scorecard. Contrary evidence is found in Ittner, Larcker, and Randall (2003).

Scorecard for the Balanced Scorecard

According to its advocates, a balanced scorecard does the following for a company:

---

[9] See, for example, the survey information provided by Nomura Research Institute as reported in Morisawa and Kurosaki (2003).

- The balanced scorecard encourages looking beyond historical financial measures to look at measures that permeate throughout the company and its operations.
- The balanced scorecard approach requires the flow of information both down-line—providing goals, measures, and schedules to different parts of the organization—and up-line—providing information and measures upward in the organization to allow evaluation of progress toward strategic initiatives.
- The balanced scorecard provides a framework for feedback for continuous improvement.
- The balanced scorecard encourages a company's management to keep the strategic goals in mind in both the choice of measures and use of any feedback from those measures.

Here is what the balanced scorecard cannot do for a company:

- The balanced scorecard does not detail what measures or how many a company should use, only the broad classification of such measures.
- The balanced scorecard does not establish the precise feedback mechanism, only that a company should develop such a mechanism to allow for continuous improvement.

STRATEGY AND VALUE CREATION

The company's chief financial officer is in a good position to link the corporate strategy with value creation. Most surveys indicate that CFOs feel that their focus is shifting from historical assessment of performance to forward-looking tasks such as the development of strategy and decision-making. For example, a March 2006 report prepared by CFO Research Services in collaboration with Deloitte Consulting[10] found that CFOs not only participate in the development of a company's strategy, but in many cases the CFO is also charged with executing the strategy and measuring the company's progress toward the strategic goals. The CFO role has expanded from the traditional functions—controller, financial reporting, compliance and support—to include serving the company's strategy through financial decision-making. This expansion has broadened the role

---

[10] "Different Paths to One Truth: Finance Brings Value Discipline to Strategy Execution."

from a service function to an activist function. According to an April 2005 report[11] prepared by CFO Research Services and Booz Allen Hamilton:

> Activism—again, defined as finance in a role beyond controllership and decision support—occurs more often among survey respondents who say their finance teams have become more closely engaged with the board of directors in the last two years.

This survey, however, indicates that those companies with closer relations with the board of directors are also firms that have greater pressure from analysts, high turnover in top management, and a need to change the company's operating model—in other words, those companies under the microscope of the business community.

It is interesting that surveys suggest an inconsistency in the CFO's role in a company's strategy and value creation.[12] The majority of CFOs feel that strategy is their top priority, yet they also feel that this is not the perception of the CFO's role among other functions within the company:

> ... found that 60% of the CFOs surveyed cite their role in the development/formulation of corporate strategy as a priority. Yet only 25% say the rest of the organization views finance as a value added function to be consulted on all important decisions.

A 2005 survey, by Financial Executives International Canada, "The Role of the CFO Today and Beyond", found that CFOs are directly accountable for financial analysis (93%), financial risk management (92.3%), forecasting and projections (87.3%), business and financial systems and reporting (82.4%), and financing and capital structure changes (79.6%). In terms of functions in which CFOs are closely involved, the top three functions are involvement in the operational risk management (70.4%), writing some or all of the strategic plan (69%), and strategic and business planning (59.9%). The results of this survey illustrate the breadth of the CFOs responsibility.

Sources of Value Creation

A company's strategy is a path to create value. But value cannot be created out of thin air. Value creation—that is, generating economic profit—requires identifying comparative and competitive advantages and developing a strategy that exploits these advantages.

---

[11] CFO Research Services and Booz Allen Hamilton, "The Activist CFO—Alignment with Strategy, Not Just with the Business," p. 15.

[12] See Frigo (2003, p. 9).

FIGURE 10.7 Porter's Five Forces

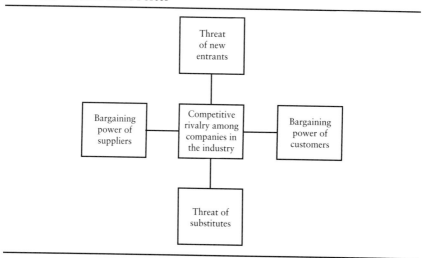

One way to look at these advantages is to use the framework introduced by Michael Porter (1998). He analyzed competitive structure of industries and identified five competitive forces that capture an industry's competitive rivalry, as illustrated in Figure 10.7:

- Bargaining power of suppliers.
- Threat of new entrants.
- Threat of substitute products.
- Bargaining power of buyers.
- Degree of rivalry.

More specifics about these forces follow:

- The bargaining power of suppliers is a force related to the providers of inputs—both goods and services. Suppliers' bargaining power is greater when the market in which they operate is dominated by a few large companies, there are no substitutes for the input, the cost of switching inputs is high, the buyers are fragmented with little buying power, and the suppliers may integrate forward to capture higher prices and margins.
- The bargaining power of customers is high when they purchase large quantities of goods or services, the buyers are concentrated, the suppliers have high fixed costs, and there are ready substitutes or the buyer could produce the good or service itself.

■ The threat of new entrants is high when there are few barriers to entry. A barrier to entry is an impediment such as economies of scale, high initial start-up costs, cost advantages due to experience of existing participants, loyalty among customers, protections such as patents, licenses, or copyrights, or regulatory or government action that limits entrants into the industry.

■ The threat of substitutes is high when there is little brand loyalty among customers, there are no close customer relations, there are low costs to switching goods or services, and there are substitutes that are lower priced.

■ The competitive rivalry among existing members of the industry is affected by the number and relative size of the companies in the industry, the strategies of the companies, the differentiation among products, and the growth of the sales in the industry.

Porter's forces are, basically, an elaboration of the theories of economics that tell us how a company creates economic profit. Though Porter's forces may seem oversimplistic in a dynamic economy, they provide a starting point for analysis of a company's ability to add value. Porter argues that an individual company may create a competitive advantage through relative cost, differentiation, and relative prices. Management, in evaluating a company's current and future performance, can use these forces and strategies to identify the company's sources of economic profit.

Management should never ignore the basic economics that lie behind value creation. If a company has a unique advantage, this can lead to value creation. If the advantage is one that can be replicated easily by others, this advantage—and hence any value creation related to it—may erode quickly. The herding behavior of companies, seeking to mimic the strategies of the better-performing companies, may result in the erosion of value from that strategy. This herding behavior therefore requires that strategic planning be dynamic and that feedback from performance evaluation is important in this planning process. Therefore, strategic planning should be a continual process that requires setting strategic objectives, developing the strategy, periodically measuring progress toward those goals, and then reevaluating the strategic objectives and strategy.

SUMMARY

The goal of management is to maximize shareholder wealth. As with any goal, it requires a strategy. As part of its strategy, the firm needs to plan the sources and uses of funds. The investment strategy is the plan of what investment opportunities are needed to meet the firm's goals. The financing strategy is the plan of where the firm is going to get the funds to make these investments.

Financial planning is where decisions, actions, and goals are brought together with forecasts about the firm's sales. In financial planning we need to know what sales will be to determine what cash flows will be. We can forecast sales using regression analysis, market surveys, or management forecasts. The cash budget is used to coordinate the investment decisions—which often require cash outlays—with the financing decisions—where the cash is coming from. Pro forma financial statements can be generated using the percent of sales method or analyzing accounts based on the cash budget. Whereas the percent of sales method is simpler, the analysis of accounts gives the financial manager a better idea of the cash flows of the firm and their relation to the financial statements.

Long-term financial planning is less detailed than the operational budgets, but not less important. Long-term planning helps keep financial managers focused on the objective of the firm and the strategy to achieve it. Financial modeling is a useful tool in looking at the array of relationships that exist in financial planning. It enables managers to examine the consequences of their decisions. In assessing progress toward strategic goals, management can use measures such as economic value added and the balanced scorecard. Understanding value creation and its relation to the strategic plan requires an understanding of the sources of value creation.

REFERENCES

Copeland, T., Koller, T., and Murrin, J. (1994). *Valuation: Measuring and Managing the Value of Companies* 2nd ed., New York: John Wiley & Sons.

Davis, S. and Albright, T. (1994). An investigation of the effect of balanced scorecard implementation on financial performance. *Management Accounting Research* 15, no. 2: 135–153.

Day, G. S. and Fahey, L. (1990). Putting strategy into shareholder value analysis. *Harvard Business Review* 68, no. 2: 156–162.

Fabozzi, F. J. and Grant, J. L. (eds.) (2000). *Value Based Metrics: Foundations and Practice*. Hoboken, NJ: John Wiley & Sons.

Frigo, M. L. (2003). Strategy, value creation, and the CFO. *Strategic Finance* 84, no. 7 (January): 9.

Ittner, C. D., Larcker, D. F., and Randall, T. (2003). Performance implications of strategic performance measurement in financial services firms. *Accounting, Organizations and Society* 28, nos. 7–8: 715–741.

Kaplan, R. S. and Norton, D. P. (1996). *The Balanced Scorecard*, Boston: Harvard Business School Press.

Kaplan, R. S. and Norton, D. P. (2001). *The Strategy-Focused Organization.* Boston: Harvard Business School Press.

Kersner, J. (2004). Swamped. *CFO.* (November): 62–68.

Marshall, A. (1980). *Principles of Economics,* vol. 1, New York: Macmillan.

Morisawa, T. and Kurosaki, H. (2003). Using the balanced scorecard in reforming corporate management systems. NRI Papers no. 71.

Porter, M. (1998). *Competitive Strategy: Techniques for Analyzing Industries and Competitors.* New York: Simon & Schuster.

Schankerman, M. (1998). How valuable is patent protection? Estimates by technology field. *Rand Journal of Economics* 29, no. 1: 77–107.

Stewart, G. B. (1991). *The Quest for Value.* New York: Harper Collins.

Therrien, L., Oster, P., and Hawkins, C. (1992). How sweet it isn't at nutra-sweet. *Business Week* (December 14): 42.

CHAPTER 11

The Corporate Financing Decision

A business invests in new plant and equipment to generate additional revenues and income—the basis for its growth. One way to pay for investments is to generate capital from the company's operations. Earnings generated by the company belong to the owners and can either be paid to them—in the form of cash dividends—or plowed back into the company.

The owners' investment in the company is referred to as *owners' equity* or, simply, *equity*. If earnings are plowed back into the company, the owners expect it to be invested in projects that will enhance the value of the company and, hence, enhance the value of their equity. But earnings may not be sufficient to support all profitable investment opportunities. In that case management is faced with a decision: Forego profitable investment opportunities or raise additional capital. New capital can be raised by either borrowing or selling additional ownership interests or both.

The decision about how the company should be financed, whether with debt or equity, is referred to as the capital structure decision. In this chapter, we discuss the capital structure decision. There are different theories about how the firm should be financed and we review these theories in this chapter. In the appendix to this chapter, we present a theory about the capital structure proposed by Franco Modigliani and Merton Miller.

DEBT VS. EQUITY

The capital structure of a company is some mix of the three sources of capital: debt, internally generated equity, and new equity. But what is the right mixture? The best capital structure depends on several factors. If a company finances its activities with debt, the creditors expect the interest and principal—fixed, legal commitments—to be paid back as promised. Failure to pay may result in legal actions by the creditors. If the company finances its activities with equity, the owners expect a return in terms of cash dividends, an appreciation of the value of the equity interest, or, as is most likely, some combination of both.

Suppose a company borrows $100 million and promises to repay the $100 million plus $5 million in one year. Consider what may happen when the $100 is invested:

- If the $100 million is invested in a project that produces $120 million, the company pays the lender the $105 million the company owes and keeps the $15 million profit.
- If the project produces $105 million, the company pays the lender $105 million and keeps nothing.
- If the project produces $100 million, the company pays the lender $105 million, with $5 million coming out of company funds.

So if the company reinvests the funds and gets a return more than the $5 million (the cost of the funds), the company keeps all the profits. But if the project returns $5 million or less, the lender still gets her or his $5 million. This is the basic idea behind *financial leverage*—the use of financing that has fixed, but limited payments.

If the company has abundant earnings, the owners reap all that remains of the earnings after the creditors have been paid. If earnings are low, the creditors still must be paid what they are due, leaving the owners nothing out of the earnings. Failure to pay interest or principal as promised may result in financial distress. *Financial distress* is the condition where a company makes decisions under pressure to satisfy its legal obligations to its creditors. These decisions may not be in the best interests of the owners of the company.

With equity financing there is no obligation. Though the company may choose to distribute funds to the owners in the form of cash dividends, there is no legal requirement to do so. Furthermore, interest paid on debt is deductible for tax purposes, whereas dividend payments are not tax deductible.

One measure of the extent debt is used to finance a company is the *debt ratio,* the ratio of debt to equity:

$$\text{Debt ratio} = \frac{\text{Debt}}{\text{Equity}}$$

This is relative measure of debt to equity. The greater the debt ratio, the greater the use of debt for financing operations, relative to equity financing. Another measure is the *debt-to-assets ratio,* which is the extent to which the assets of the company are financed with debt:

$$\text{Debt-to-assets ratio} = \frac{\text{Debt}}{\text{Total assets}}$$

This is the proportion of debt in a company's capital structure, measured using the book, or carrying value of the debt and assets.

It is often useful to focus on the long-term capital of a company when evaluating the capital structure of a company, looking at the interest-bearing debt of the company in comparison with the company's equity or with its capital. The *capital* of a company is the sum of its interest-bearing debt and its equity. The debt ratio can be restated as the ratio of the interest-bearing debt of the company to the equity:

$$\text{Debt-equity ratio} = \frac{\text{Interest-bearing debt}}{\text{Equity}}$$

and the debt-to-assets can be restated as the proportion of interest-bearing debt of the company's capital:

$$\text{Debt-to-capital ratio} = \frac{\text{Interest-bearing debt}}{\text{Total capital}}$$

By focusing on the long-term capital, the working capital decisions of a company that affect current liabilities such as accounts payable, are removed from this analysis.

The equity component of all of these ratios is often stated in book, or carrying value terms. However, when taking a markets perspective of the company's capital structure, it is often useful to compare debt capital with the market value of equity. In this latter formulation, for example, the total capital of the company is the sum of the market value of interest-bearing debt and the market value of equity.

If market values of debt and equity are the most useful for decision-making, should management ignore book values? No, because book values are relevant in decision-making also. For example, bond covenants are often specified in terms of book values or ratios of book values. As another example, dividends are distinguished from the return of capital based on the availability of the book value of retained earnings. Therefore, though the focus is primarily on the market values of capital, management must also keep an eye on the book value of debt and equity as well.

There is a tendency for companies in some sectors and industries to use more debt than others. We can make some generalizations about differences in capital structures across sectors:

- Companies that are more reliant upon research and development for new products and technology—for example, pharmaceutical companies—tend to have lower debt-to-asset ratios than companies without such research and development needs.

- Companies that require a relatively heavy investment in fixed assets tend to have lower debt-to-asset ratios.

Considering these generalizations and other observations related to differing capital structures, why do some industries tend to have companies with higher debt ratios than other industries? By examining the role of financial leveraging, financial distress, and taxes, we can explain some of the variation in debt ratios among industries. And by analyzing these factors, we can explain how the company's value may be affected by its capital structure.

THE CONCEPT OF LEVERAGE

The capital structure decision involves managing the risks associated with the company's business and financing decisions. The concept of *leverage*—in both operations and financing decisions—plays a role in the company's risk because leverage exaggerates outcomes, good or bad.

Leverage and Operating Risk

The concept of leverage and the degree of leverage can be used to describe the operating risk of a company, which is a component of a company's business risk. *Business risk* is the uncertainty associated with the earnings from operations.

Business risk is inherent in the type of business and can be envisioned as being comprised of sales risk and operating risk. *Sales risk* is the risk associated with sales as a result of economic and market forces that affect the volume and prices of goods or services sold. *Operating risk* is the risk associated with the cost structure of the company's assets. A cost structure is comprised of both fixed operating costs and variable operating costs. The greater the fixed costs relative to variable costs, the greater the leverage and, hence, operating risk. If sales were to decline, the greater the fixed costs in the operating cost structure the more exaggerated the effect on operating earnings.

In the context of the operating risk of a company, the degree of leverage is referred to as the *degree of operating leverage*, or DOL. In this case, the fixed costs operate as a fulcrum in this leverage are specifically the fixed operating costs.

We can demonstrate the concept of leverage by taking a look at operating leverage. Consider the simple example of a company that has both fixed and variable expenses. Suppose it has one product, with a sales price of $100 per unit and variable costs of $40 per unit. This means that the company has a $60 profit per unit before considering any fixed expenses.

This $60 is the product's *contribution margin*—the amount that is available to cover any fixed expenses. Suppose the company's fixed expenses are $20 million. If the company produces and sells 250,000 units, it has a loss of $5 million; whereas if it produces and sells 1 million units, it has a profit of $40 million. The company would have to produce and sell 1/3 million units before covering its fixed expenses; producing and selling more than 1/3 million produces a profit and producing less than 1/3 million generates a loss. This 1/3 million is the *break-even point*: the number of units produced and sold such that the product of the units sold and unit price just covers both the variable and fixed expenses.

The relation between the fixed costs, F, and the contribution margin can be specified in terms of the break-even quantity, Q_{BE}, the price per unit, P, the variable cost per unit, V, and the fixed costs:

$$Q_{BE} = \frac{F}{(P - V)}$$

Looking at the profit from a wider range of units produced and sold, as shown in Figure 11.1, the profit is upward sloping, with a slope of $60: producing one additional unit produces a change in profit of $60, which is the contribution margin. In contrast, consider a similar scenario, but with a variable cost per unit of $20 and fixed costs of $40. In this case, the break-even number of units produced and sold is 500,000. However, this latter case has a greater use of fixed costs. This produces a profit-units relation as also shown in Figure 11.1, with a slope of $80. In the latter case, there is more leverage: a greater relative use of fixed costs increases the losses and increases the profits.

Another way of quantifying the relation between the contribution margin and the fixed costs is using the *degree of operating leverage* (DOL) measure:

$$DOL = \frac{Q(P - V)}{Q(P - V) - F}$$

where Q is the number of units produced and sold, P is the sales price per unit, V is the variable cost per unit produced and sold, and F is the total fixed operating cost.

The DOL provides a measure of the sensitivity of the profit at a given level of production. In the previous example, with variable costs of $40 per unit and fixed costs of $20 million, the degree of leverage at 1 million units produced and sold is

$$DOL = \frac{1(\$100 - 40)}{1(\$100 - 40) - \$20} = \frac{\$60}{\$40} = 1.5$$

FIGURE 11.1   Leverage and Fixed Costs

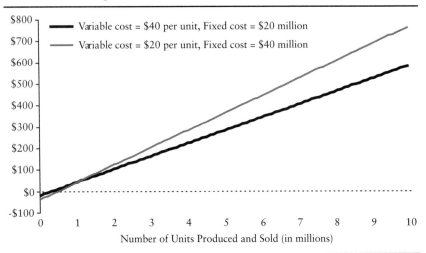

At 2 million units, the degree of leverage is

$$\text{DOL} = \frac{2(\$100 - 40)}{2(\$100 - 40) - \$20} = \frac{\$120}{\$100} = 1.2$$

In other words, the DOL leverage depends on the level of production. The degree of leverage is undefined at the break-even point—1/3 million units in this case—because the profit in the denominator is zero. The DOL beyond the break-even point declines: as the company moves farther away from the break-even point, the effect of leverage—and hence risk—lessens, as shown in Figure 11.2.

As you can see, the DOL differs between the two scenarios, with the cost structure with a greater reliance of fixed costs having greater operating leverage. The DOL is a measure of the operating risk. Business risk, therefore, is the combined effect of both sales risk and operating risk, both of which affect the risk associated with operating earnings.

Leverage and Financial Risk

The effect of the mixture of fixed and variable costs on operating earnings is akin to the effect of debt financing on earnings to owners. With respect to a firm's capital structure it is referred to as financial leverage, which we describe shortly. The greater the fixed financing costs in the capital structure, the greater the leveraging effect on earnings to owners for a given change in

FIGURE 11.2 The Degree of Leverage for Increasing Number of Units Produced and Sold beyond the Break-Even Point

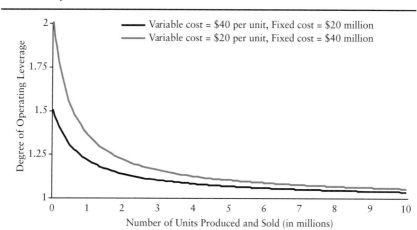

operating earnings. The degree of leverage attributed to the capital structure of a company is referred to as the *degree of financial leverage* (DFL).

Both operating leverage and financial leverage have a bearing on a company's financial risk. This is because of the compounding effect of operating leverage upon financial leverage, to affect the total leverage of the company. In fact, there is a multiplicative effect of the two leverages, such that the degree of total leverage of a company, DTL, is the product of its degree of operating leverage and its degree of financial leverage:

$$DTL = DOL \times DFL$$

Therefore, the greater the business risk of the company, the greater the risk associated with a company's earnings to owners. The import of this is that management must consider both the degree of operating leverage and the degree of financial leverage in managing the risk of the company.

CAPITAL STRUCTURE AND FINANCIAL LEVERAGE

Debt and equity financing create different types of obligations for the company. Debt financing obligates the company to pay creditors interest and principal—usually a fixed amount—when promised. If the company earns more than necessary to meet its debt payments, it can either distribute the surplus to the owners or reinvest. Equity financing does not obligate the company to distribute earnings. The company may pay dividends or repurchase stock from the owners, but there is *no* obligation to do so.

The fixed and limited nature of the debt obligation affects the risk of the earnings to the owners. Consider Capital Corporation that has $20 million of assets, all financed with equity. There are 1 million shares of Capital Corporation stock outstanding, valued at $20 per share. The company's current balance sheet is simple:

Capital Corporation Balance Sheet (in millions)

Assets	$20	Debt	$0
		Equity	20

Suppose Capital Corporation has investment opportunities requiring $10 million of new capital. Further suppose Capital Corporation can raise the new capital either of three ways:

Alternative 1. Issue $10 million equity (500 thousand shares of stock at $20 per share).

Alternative 2. Issue $5 million of equity (250 thousand shares of stock at $20 per share) and borrow $5 million with an annual interest of 10%.

Alternative 3. Borrow $10 million with an annual interest of 10%.

Under each alternative, the capital structure as summarized in Table 11.1.

It may be unrealistic to assume that the interest rate on the debt in Alternative 3 will be the same as the interest rate for Alternative 2 because in Alternative 3 there is more credit risk. For purposes of illustrating the point of leverage, however, let's keep the interest rate the same.

TABLE 11.1   Alternative Capital Structures for Capital Corporation: Balance Sheet (in millions)

Alternative 1:			
Assets	$30	Debt	$0
		Equity [1.5 million shares]	30
Alternative 2:			
Assets	$30	Debt	$5
		Equity [1.25 million shares]	25
Alternative 3:			
Assets	$30	Debt	$10
		Equity [1 million shares]	20

Stated differently, the debt ratio and the debt-to-asset ratio of Capital Corporation under each alternative are the following:

Alternative	Debt-Equity Ratio	Debt-to-Capital Ratio
1	0.0%	0.0%
2	20.0%	16.7%
3	50.0%	33.3%

How can these ratios be interpreted? The debt ratio of 20% for Alternative 2 indicates that the company finances its assets using $1 of debt for every $5 of equity. The debt-to-assets ratio means that 16.7% of the assets are financed using debt or, in other words, almost 17 cents of every $1 of assets is financed with debt.

Suppose Capital Corporation has $4.5 million of operating earnings. This means it has a $4.5/$30 = 15% *return on assets* (ROA). And suppose there are no taxes. To illustrate the concept of financial leverage, consider the effect of this leverage on the earnings per share of a company. The *earnings per share* (EPS) under the different alternatives are given in Table 11.2. The three parts of this table show the EPS based on different assumptions for the ROA: 15%, 10%, and 5%. Notice that if the company is earning a return that is the same as the cost of debt, 10%, the earnings per share are not affected by the choice of financing. If the return on assets is 15%, Alternative 3 has the highest earnings per share, but if the return on assets is 5%, Alternative 3 has the lowest earnings per share.

This example illustrates the role of debt financing on the risk associated with earnings: the greater the use of debt vis-à-vis equity, the greater the risk associated with earnings to owners. Or, using the leverage terminology, the greater the degree of financial leverage, the greater the financial risk. Additionally, by comparing the outcomes for the different operating earnings scenarios—$4.5, $3.0, and $1.5 million—the effect of adding financial risk in addition to the operating risk magnifies the risk to the owners.

Comparing the results of each of the alternative financing methods provides information on the effects of using debt financing. As more debt is used in the capital structure, the greater the "swing" in EPS. The EPS under each financing alternative and each ROA assumption shown in Table 11.3.

When debt financing is used instead of equity (Alternative 3), the owners don't share the earnings—all they must do is pay their creditors the interest on debt. But when equity financing is used instead of debt (Alternative 1), the owners must share the increased earnings with the additional owners, diluting their return on equity and earnings per share.

TABLE 11.2   Earnings Per Share for Three Alternative Capital Structures and Different Return on Assets Assumed

(a) 15% return on assets assumed

	Alternative 1: $10 million Equity	Alternative 2: $5 million Equity and $5 million Debt	Alternative 3: $10 million of Debt
Operating earnings in millions	$4.5	$4.5	$4.5
Less interest expense in millions	0.0	0.5	1.0
Net income in millions	$4.5	$4.0	$3.5
Number of shares in millions	÷1.5	÷ 1.25	÷ 1.0
Earnings per share	$3.00	$3.20	$3.50

(b) 10% return on assets assumed

	Alternative 1: $10 million Equity	Alternative 2: $5 million Equity and $5 million Debt	Alternative 3: $10 million of Debt
Operating earnings in millions	$3.0	$3.0	$3.0
Less interest expense in millions	0.0	0.5	1.0
Net income in millions	$3.0	$2.5	$2.0
Number of shares in millions	÷1.5	÷ 1.25	÷ 1.0
Earnings per share	$2.00	$2.00	$2.00

(c) 5% return on assets assumed

	Alternative 1: $10 million Equity	Alternative 2: $5 million Equity and $5 million Debt	Alternative 3: $10 million of Debt
Operating earnings in millions	$1.5	$1.5	$1.5
Less interest expense in millions	0.0	0.5	1.0
Net income in millions	$1.5	$1.0	$0.50
Number of shares in millions	÷1.5	÷ 1.25	÷ 1.0
Earnings per share	$1.00	$0.80	$0.50

FINANCIAL LEVERAGE AND RISK

The use of financial leverage (that is, the use of debt in financing a company) increases the range of possible outcomes for owners of the company. As we saw previously, the use of debt financing relative to equity financing increases both the upside and downside potential earnings for owners. In

TABLE 11.3 EPS for Three Financing Alternatives and Return on Asset Assumptions

Financing Alternative	Earnings per Share Assuming		
	ROA = 5%	ROA = 10%	ROA = 15%
1. $10 million equity	$1.00	$2.00	$3.00
2. $5 million equity, $5 million debt	$0.80	$2.00	$3.20
3. $10 million debt	$0.50	$2.00	$3.50

other words, financial leverage increases the risk to owners. Now that we understand the basics of leverage, let's quantify its effect on the risk of earnings to owners.

Another way to view the choice of financing is to calculate the degree of financial leverage, DFL:

$$DFL = \frac{\text{Earnings before interest and taxes}}{\text{Earnings before interest and taxes} - \text{Interest}}$$

Calculating the DFL for the three alternatives at a 10% ROA, or $3 million in operating earnings, we see that Alternative 3 as the highest degree of financial leverage:

Alternative	Degree of Financial Leverage at $3 million in Operating Earnings
1	1.0
2	1.2
3	1.5

The degree of financial leverage is interpreted in a manner similar to that of DOL: A DFL of 1.25 indicates that if operating earnings increase by 1%, net profit, and hence earnings per share will increase by 1.2%. In the case of Alternative 2, with a DFL of 1.2, when operating earnings change from $3 million to $4.5 million (that is, a 50% increase), earnings to owners go from $2 per share to $3.2 per share, an increase of 50% × 1.2 or 60%.

The Leverage Effect

Equity owners can reap most of the rewards through financial leverage when their company does well. But they may suffer a downside when the company does poorly. What happens if earnings are so low that it cannot cover interest payments? Interest must be paid no matter how low the earnings. How can money be obtained with which to pay interest when earnings are insufficient? It can be obtained in three ways:

- By reducing the assets in some way, such as using working capital needed for operations or selling buildings or equipment.
- By taking on more debt obligations.
- By issuing more shares of stock.

Whichever the company chooses, the burden ultimately falls upon the owners.

This leveraging effect is illustrated in Figure 11.3 for Capital Corporation. Note that we have broadened the number of possible return on asset outcomes ranging from 0% to 30%. Alternative 3 provides for the most upside potential for the equity holders, it also provides for the most downside potential as well. Hence, Alternative 1—all equity— offers the more conservative method of financing operations.

The three alternatives have identical earnings per share when there is a 10% return on assets. Capital Corporation's 10% return on assets is referred to as the *EPS indifference point*: the return where the earnings per share are

FIGURE 11.3   Capital Corporation's Earnings per Share for Different Operating Earnings for Each of the Three Financing Alternatives

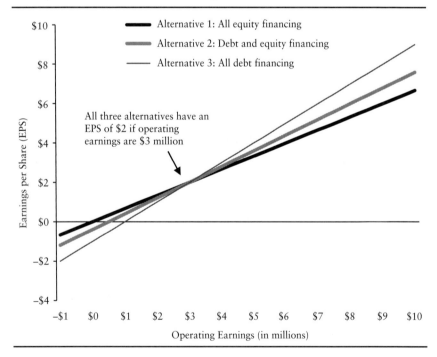

the same under the financing alternatives. Above a 10% return on assets (that is, above operating earnings of $3,000), Alternative 3 offers the most to owners. But Alternative 3 also has the most downside potential, producing the worst earnings to owners below this 10% return on assets.

Leverage and Financial Flexibility

The use of debt also reduces a company's financial flexibility. A company with debt capacity that is unused, sometimes referred to as *financial slack*, is more prepared to take advantage of investment opportunities in the future. This ability to exploit these future, strategic options is valuable and, hence taking on debt increases the risk that the company may not be sufficiently nimble to act on valuable opportunities.

There is evidence that suggests that companies that have more cash flow volatility tend to build up more financial slack and, hence, their investments are not as sensitive to their ability to generate cash flows internally. (See Booth and Cleary (2006).) Rather, the financial slack allows them to exploit investment opportunities without relying on recent internally generated cash flows.

In the context of the effect of leverage on risk, this means that companies that tend to have highly volatile operating earnings may want to maintain some level of financial flexibility by not taking on significant leverage in the form of debt financing.

Governance Value of Debt Financing

A company's use of debt financing may provide additional monitoring of a company's management and decisions, reducing agency costs. As explained later in this chapter, agency costs are the costs that arise from the separation of the management and the ownership of a company, which is particularly acute in large corporations. These costs are the costs necessary to resolve the agency problem that may exist between management and ownership of the company and may include the cost of monitoring company management. These costs include the costs associated with the board of directors and providing financial information to shareholders and other investors.

An agency problem that may arise in a company is how effectively a company uses its cash flows. The free cash flow of a company is, basically, its cash flow less any capital expenditures and dividends. One theory that has been widely regarded is that by using debt financing, the company reduces its free cash flows and, hence company must reenter the debt market to raise new capital. (See Jensen (1986).) It is argued that this benefits the company in two ways. First, there are fewer resources under control of management and less chance of wasting these resources in unprofitable investments. Second, the continual dependence of the debt market for capital imposes a monitoring, or governance discipline on the company that would not have been there otherwise.

CAPITAL STRUCTURE AND TAXES

We've seen how the use of debt financing increases the risk to owners; the greater the use of debt financing (vis-à-vis equity financing), the greater the risk. Another factor to consider is the role of taxes. In the U.S., income taxes play an important role in a company's capital structure decision because the payments to creditors and owners are taxed differently. In general, interest payments on debt obligations are deductible for tax purposes, whereas dividends paid to shareholders are not deductible. This bias affects a company's capital structure decision.

Interest Deductibility and Capital Structure

The deductibility of interest represents a form of a government subsidy of financing activities. By allowing interest to be deducted from taxable income, the government is sharing the company's cost of debt. To see how this subsidy works, compare two companies: Company U (unlevered) and Company L (levered). Suppose both have the same $5 million taxable income before interest and taxes and contributed capital of $35 million. Company U is financed entirely with equity, whereas Company L is financed with $10 million debt that requires an annual payment of 10% interest. If the tax rate for both companies is 30%, the tax payable and net income to owners are calculated as follows:

	Company U (no debt)	Company L ($10 million debt)
Taxable income before taxes and interest in millions	$5.0	$5.0
Less interest expense in millions	0.0	1.0
Taxable income before taxes in millions	$5.0	$4.0
Less taxes at 30% of taxable income in millions	1.5	1.2
Net income to owners	$3.5	$2.8

By financing its activities with debt, paying interest of $1 million, Company L reduces its tax bill by $0.3 million. Company L's creditors receive $1 million of income, the government receives $1.2 million of income, and the owners receive $2.8 million. The $0.3 represents money Company L does not pay because it is allowed to deduct the $1 million interest. This reduction in the tax bill is a type of subsidy.

If Company LL (Lots of Leverage) has the same operating earnings and tax rate as Companies U and L, but uses $20 million of debt at the 10% interest rate, the interest expense is $2 million and net income to owners are as $2.1 million.

Comparing Company LL relative to Company L, we see that the interest expense is more, taxes are less, and net income to owners less:

	Company L ($10 million debt)	Company LL ($20 million debt)
Taxable income before taxes and interest in millions	$5.0	$5.0
Less interest expense in millions	1.0	2.0
Taxable income before taxes in millions	$4.0	$3.0
Less taxes at 30% of taxable income in millions	1.2	0.9
Net income to owners	$2.8	$2.1

If Company L were to increase its debt financing from $10 to $20 million, like Company LL's, the total net income to the suppliers of capital—the creditors and owners—is increased $0.3 million, from $3.8 to $4.1 million, determined as follows:

	Company U (no debt)	Company L ($10 million debt)	Company LL ($20 million debt)
Income to creditors in millions	$0.0	$1.0	$2.0
Income to owners in millions	3.5	2.8	2.1
Total income to suppliers of capital	$3.5	$3.8	$4.1

Consider this distribution of income between creditors and owners. The total income to the suppliers of capital increases from the use of debt. For example, the difference in the total income to suppliers of capital of Company U compared to Company LL is $0.6 million. This difference is due to a tax subsidy by the government: by deducting $2 million in interest expense, Company LL benefits by reducing taxable income by $2 million and reducing taxes by $2 million × 30% = $0.6 million.

If we assume that there are no direct or indirect costs to financial distress, the cost of capital for the company should be the same, no matter the method of financing. With a 10% cost of capital, the value to the suppliers of capital is split, as shown in Table 11.4.

Who benefits from this tax deductibility? The owners. The owners of Company U have a return on equity of $3.5 million/$35 million = 10%. Compare this to the owners of Company L, for which owners have a return on equity of $2.8 million/$25 million = 11.2%, and to the owners of Company LL, who have a return on equity of $2.1 million/$15 million = 14%. The owners of the levered firms benefit from the tax deductibility of interest in terms of the return on their investment.

Interest Tax Shield

An interesting element introduced into the capital structure decision is the reduction of taxes due to the payment of interest on debt. We refer to the benefit from interest deductibility as the *interest tax shield*, because the in-

TABLE 11.4 Value to Suppliers of Capital of Companies U, L, and LL

	Company (no debt)	Company ($10 million debt)	Company ($20 million debt)
	(in millions)		
Value, dividing the income stream by the 10% discount rate:			
Value to creditors	$0	$10	$20
Value to owners	<u>35</u>	<u>28</u>	<u>21</u>
Value of the company	$35	$38	$41
Capital contributed by:			
By creditors	$0	$10	$20
By owners	<u>35</u>	<u>25</u>	<u>15</u>
Total contributed capital	$35	$35	$35
The difference between value and contributed capital:			
Added value from debt	$0	$3	$6

terest expense *shields* income from taxation. The tax shield from interest deductibility is

$$\text{Tax shield} = \text{Tax rate} \times \text{Interest expense}$$

If Company L has \$10 million of 10% debt and is subject to a tax of 30% on net income, the tax shield is

$$\text{Tax shield} = 0.30\ [\$10\ (0.10)] = 0.30(\$1) = \$0.3 \text{ million}$$

A \$1 million interest expense means that \$1 million of income is not taxed at 30%.

Recognizing that the interest expense is the interest rate on the debt, r_d, multiplied by the face value of debt, D, the tax shield for a company with a tax rate of τ is

$$\text{Tax shield} = \text{Tax rate} \times \text{Interest rate} \times \text{Face value of debt}$$

$$\text{Tax shield} = \tau\ r_d\ D$$

How does this tax shield affect the value of the company? The tax shield reduces the net income of the company that goes to pay taxes. We should specify that the tax rate is the *marginal tax rate*—the tax rate on the next dollar of income.

And since management is concerned with how interest protects income from taxation, the focus should be on how it shields taxable income beyond the income that is shielded by all other tax deductible expenses.

Unused Tax Shields

The value of a tax shield depends on whether the company can use an interest expense deduction. In general, if a company has deductions that *exceed* income, the result is a *net operating loss*. The company does not have to pay taxes in the year of the loss and may "carry" this loss to another tax year.

This loss may be applied against previous years' taxable income (with some limits). The previous years' taxes are recalculated and a refund of taxes previously paid is requested. If there is insufficient previous years' taxable income to apply the loss against, any unused loss is carried over into future years (with some limits), reducing future years' taxable income.

Therefore, when interest expense is larger than income before interest, the tax shield is realized immediately—*if* there is sufficient prior years' taxable income. If prior years' taxable income is *insufficient* (that is, less than the operating loss created by the interest deduction), the tax shield is less valuable because the financial benefit is not received until some later tax year (if at all). In this case, we discount the tax shield to reflect both the uncertainty of benefiting from the shield and the time value of money.

To see how an interest tax shield may become less valuable, let's suppose The Unfortunate Company has the following financial results:

	The Unfortunate Company		
	Year 1	Year 2	Year 3
Taxable income before interest	$7,000	$8,000	$6,000
Interest expense	5,000	5,000	5,000
Taxable income	$2,000	$3,000	$1,000
Tax rate	0.40	0.40	0.40
Tax paid	$800	$1,200	$400

Suppose further that the Unfortunate Company has the following result for Year 4:

	Year 4
Taxable income before interest	$1,000
Less: Interest expense	8,000
Net operating loss	–$7,000

And suppose the tax code permits a carryback of two years and a carryover of 20 years. The Unfortunate Company can take the net operating loss of $7,000 and apply it against the taxable income of previous two years, beginning with Year 1:

	Year 1	Year 2	Year 3
Taxable income before interest	$7,000	$8,000	$6,000
Interest expense	5,000	5,000	5,000
Taxable income—original	$2,000	$3,000	$1,000
Application of Year 4 loss		–3,000	–1,000
Taxable income—recalculated		$0	$0
Taxes paid	$1,200	$400	
Tax due—recalculated	0	0	
Refund of taxes paid	$1,200	$400	

By carrying back the part of the loss, the Unfortunate Company has applied $4,000 of its Year 4 loss against the previous years' taxable income: $3,000(Year 2) + $1,000(Year 3) and receives a tax refund of $1,200 + 400 = $1,600. There remains an unused loss of $7,000 – $4,000 = $3,000. This loss can be applied toward future tax years' taxable income, reducing taxes in future years. But since we don't get the benefit from the $3,000 unused loss—the $3,000 reduction in taxes—until sometime in the future, the benefit is worth less than if we could use it today.

The Unfortunate Company, with an interest deduction of $8,000, benefits from $5,000 of the deduction; $1,000 against current income and $4,000 against previous income. Therefore, the tax shield from the $8,000 is not $3,200 (40% of $8,000), but rather $2,000 (40% of $5,000), plus the present value of the taxes saved in future years. The present value of the taxes saved in future years depends on:

- The uncertainty that Unfortunate Company will generate taxable income.
- The time value of money.

The Unfortunate Company's tax shield from the $8,000 interest expense is less than what it could have been because the company could not use all of it now.

The bottom line of the analysis of unused tax shields is that the benefit from the interest deductibility of debt depends on whether or not the company can use the interest deductions.

CAPITAL STRUCTURE AND FINANCIAL DISTRESS

A company that has difficulty making payments to its creditors is in financial distress. Not all companies in financial distress ultimately enter into the legal status of bankruptcy. However, extreme financial distress may very well lead to bankruptcy. While bankruptcy is often a result of financial difficulties arising from problems in paying creditors, some bankruptcy filings are made prior to distress when a large claim is made on assets (for example, class action liability suit).

Costs of Financial Distress

The costs related to financial distress without legal bankruptcy can take different forms. For example, to meet creditors' demands, a company takes on projects expected to provide a quick payback. In doing so, the financial manager may choose a project that decreases owners' wealth or may forgo a profitable project.

Another cost of financial distress is the cost associated with lost sales. If a company is having financial difficulty, potential customers may shy away from its products because they may perceive the company unable to provide maintenance, replacement parts, and warranties. Lost sales due to customer concerns represent a cost of financial distress—an opportunity cost, something of value (sales) that the company would have had if it were not in financial difficulty.

Still another example of a cost of financial distress is the cost associated with suppliers. If there is concern over the company's ability to meet its obligations to creditors, suppliers may be unwilling to extend trade credit or may extend trade credit only at unfavorable terms. Also, suppliers may be unwilling to enter into long-term contracts to supply goods or materials. This increases the uncertainty that the company will be able to obtain these items in the future and raises the costs of renegotiating contracts.

The Role of Limited Liability

Limited liability limits owners' liability for obligations to the amount of their original investment in the shares of stock. Limited liability for owners of some forms of business creates a valuable right and an interesting incentive for shareholders. This valuable right is the right to default on obligations to creditors—that is, the right not to pay creditors. Because the most shareholders can lose is their investment, there is an incentive for the company to take on very risky projects: If the projects turn out well, the company pays creditors only what it owes and keeps the remainder and if the projects turn out poorly, it pays creditors what it owes—*if* there is anything left.

The fact that owners with limited liability can lose only their initial investment—the amount they paid for their shares—creates an incentive for owners to take on riskier projects than if they had unlimited liability: They have little to lose and much to gain. Owners of a company with limited liability have an incentive to take on risky projects since they can only lose their investment in the company. But they can benefit substantially if the payoff on the investment is high.

For companies whose owners have limited liability, the more the assets are financed with debt, the greater the incentive to take on risky projects, leaving creditors "holding the bag" if the projects turn out to be unprofitable. This is a problem: A conflict of interest between shareholders' interests and creditors' interests. The investment decisions are made by management (who represent the shareholders) and, because of limited liability, there is an incentive for management to select riskier projects that may harm creditors who have entrusted their funds (by lending them) to the company.

The right to default is a call option: The owners have the option to buy back the entire company by paying off the creditors at the face value of their debt. As with other types of options, the option is more valuable, the riskier the cash flows. However, creditors are aware of this and demand a higher return on debt (and hence a higher cost to the company). Jensen and Meckling (1976) analyze the agency problems associated with limited liability. They argue that creditors are aware of the incentives the company has to take on riskier project. Creditors will demand a higher return and may also require protective provisions in the loan contract. The result is that shareholders ultimately bear a higher cost of debt.

Bankruptcy and Bankruptcy Costs

When a company is having difficulty paying its debts, there is a possibility that creditors will foreclose (that is, demand payment) on loans, causing the company to sell assets that could impair or cease the company's operations. But if some creditors force payment, this may disadvantage other creditors. So what has developed is an orderly way of dealing with the process of the company paying its creditors—the process is called *bankruptcy*.

Bankruptcy in the United States is governed by the Bankruptcy Code, which is found under U.S. Code Title 11. A company may be reorganized under Chapter 11 of this Code, resulting in a restructuring of its claims, or liquidated under Chapter 7.

Chapter 11 bankruptcy provides the troubled company with protection from its creditors while it tries to overcome its financial difficulties. A company that files bankruptcy under Chapter 11 continues as a going concern during the process of sorting out which of its creditors get paid and how much. On the other hand, a company that files under bankruptcy Chapter 7, under the management of a trustee, terminates its operations, sells its assets, and distributes the proceeds to creditors and owners.

We can classify *bankruptcy costs* into direct and indirect costs. Direct costs include the legal, administrative, and accounting costs associated with the filing for bankruptcy and the administration of bankruptcy. The indirect costs of bankruptcy are more difficult to evaluate. Operating a company while in bankruptcy is difficult, since there are often delays in making decisions, creditors may not agree on the operations of the company, and the objectives of creditors may be at variance with the objective of efficient operation of the company.

Another indirect cost of bankruptcy is the loss in value of certain assets. If the company has assets that are intangible or for which there are valuable growth opportunities or options, it is less likely to borrow because the loss of value in the case of financial distress is greater than, say, a company with marketable assets.[1] Because many intangible assets derive their value from the continuing operations of the company, the disruption of operations during bankruptcy may change the value of the company. The extent to which the value of a business enterprise depends on intangibles varies among industries and among companies; so the potential loss in value from financial distress varies as well. For example, a drug company may experience a greater disruption in its business activities, than say, a steel manufacturer, since much of the value of the drug company may be derived from the research and development that leads to new products.

Financial Distress and Capital Structure

The relationship between financial distress and capital structure is simple: As more debt financing is used, fixed legal obligations increase (interest and principal payments), and the ability of the company to satisfy these increasing fixed payments decreases. Therefore, as more debt financing is used, the probability of financial distress and then bankruptcy increases.

For a given decrease in operating earnings, a company that uses debt to a greater extent in its capital structure (that is, a company that uses more financial leverage), has a greater risk of not being able to satisfy the debt obligations and increases the risk of earnings to owners.

Another factor to consider in assessing the probability of financial distress is the business risk of the company. As discussed earlier, the business risk interacts with the financial risk to affect the risk of the company.

Management's concern in assessing the effect of financial distress on the value of the company is the present value of the expected costs of financial distress. And the present value depends on the probability of financial distress: The greater the probability of financial distress, the greater the expected costs of financial distress.

The present value of the costs of financial distress increase with the increasing relative use of debt financing because the probability of financial distress increases with increases in financial leverage. In other words, as the debt ratio increases, the present value of the costs of financial distress increases, lessening some of the value gained from the use of tax deductibility of interest expense.

Summarizing the factors that influence the present value of the cost of financial distress:

---

[1] This is based on the reasoning in Myers and Majluf (1984).

1. The probability of financial distress increases with increases in business risk.
2. The probability of financial distress increases with increases in financial risk.
3. Limited liability increases the incentives for owners to take on greater business risk.
4. The costs of bankruptcy increase the more the value of the company depends on intangible assets.

Management does not know the precise manner in which the probability of distress increases as the debt-to-equity ratio increases. Yet, it is reasonable to think that:

- The probability of distress increases as a greater proportion of the company's assets are financed with debt.
- The benefit from the tax deductibility of interest increases as the debt-to-equity ratio increases.
- The present value of the cost of financial distress increases as the debt-to-equity ratio increases.

THE COST OF CAPITAL

The capital structure of a company is intertwined with the company's cost of capital. The *cost of capital* is the return that must be provided for the use of an investor's funds. If the funds are borrowed, the cost is related to the interest that must be paid on the loan. If the funds are equity, the cost is the return that investors expect, both from the stock's price appreciation and dividends. The cost of capital is a *marginal* concept. That is, the cost of capital is the cost associated with raising one more dollar of capital.

There are two reasons for determining a corporation's cost of capital. First, the cost of capital is often used as a starting point (a benchmark) for determining the cost of capital for a specific project. Often in capital budgeting decisions, the firm's cost of capital is adjusted upward or downward depending on whether the project's risk is more than or less than the firm's typical project.

Second, many of a firm's projects have risk similar to the risk of the firm as a whole. So the cost of capital of the firm is a reasonable approximation for the cost of capital of one of its projects that are under consideration for investment.

A firm's cost of capital is the cost of its long-term sources of funds: debt, preferred stock, and common stock. And the cost of each source reflects the risk of the assets the firm invests in. A firm that invests in assets having little risk will be able to bear lower costs of capital than a firm that invests in assets having a high risk. Moreover, the cost of each source of funds reflects the hierarchy of the risk associated with its seniority over the other sources. For a given firm, the cost of funds raised through debt is less than the cost of funds from preferred stock which, in turn, is less than the cost of funds from common stock. This is because creditors have seniority over preferred shareholders, who have seniority over common shareholders. If there are difficulties in meeting obligations, the creditors receive their promised interest and principal before the preferred shareholders who, in turn, receive their promised dividends before the common shareholders.

For a given firm, debt is less risky than preferred stock, which is less risky than common stock. Therefore, preferred shareholders require a greater return than the creditors and common shareholders require a greater return than preferred shareholders. Figuring out the cost of capital requires us to determine the cost of each source of capital the firm expects to use, along with the relative amounts of each source of capital the firm expects to raise. Putting together all these pieces, the firm can then estimate the marginal cost of raising additional capital.

The estimation of the firm's cost of capital consists of three steps. In the first step the proportion of each source of capital to be used in the calculations is determined. This should be based on the target capital structure selected by the firm, not book values as per the balance sheet. The second step is then the calculation of the cost of each financing source. The cost of debt and preferred stock is fairly simple to obtain, but the cost of equity is by far much more difficult to estimate. There are several models available for estimating the cost of equity. What is critical to understand is that these different models can generate significantly different estimates for the cost of common stock and, as a result, the estimated cost of capital will be highly sensitive to the model selected. The proportions of each source must be determined before calculating the cost of each source since the proportions may affect the costs of the sources of capital. The last step is to weight the cost of each source of funding by the proportion of that source in the target capital structure.

For example, suppose the firm's target capital structure is as follows: 40% debt, 10% preferred stock, and 50% common stock. Assume further that management estimates that the cost for raising an additional dollar of debt, preferred stock, and common equity is 5%, 6%, and 12%, respectively. If the company's marginal tax rate is 40%, the after-tax cost of debt is 5% × (1 − 0.4) = 3%. Returning to the illustration, the weighted average cost of capital is 7.8%:

$$(40\% \times 3\%) + (10\% \times 6\%) + (50\% \times 12\%) = 7.8\%$$

This means that for every \$1 the firm plans to obtain from financing, the cost is 7.8%.

As a company adjusts its capital structure, its cost of capital changes. Up to a point, using more debt relative to equity will lower the cost of capital because the after-tax cost of debt is less than the cost of equity. There is some point, however, when the likelihood and, hence, cost of financial distress increases and may in fact outweigh the benefit from taxes. After this point—wherever this may be—the cost of both debt and equity increases because both are much riskier.

Therefore, the trade-off theory of capital structure dictates that as the company uses more debt relative to equity, the value of the company is enhanced from the benefit of the interest tax shields. But the theory also states that there is some point at which the likelihood of financial distress increases such that there are ever-increasing likelihood of bankruptcy. Therefore:

■ The value of the company declines as more and more debt is used, relative to equity.
■ The cost of capital increases because the costs of the different sources of capital increase.

Though the trade-off theory simplifies the world too much, it gives the management an idea of the trade-offs involved. Introduce the value of financial flexibility and the governance value of debt, and management has the key inputs to consider in the capital structure decision.

THE AGENCY RELATIONSHIP AND CAPITAL STRUCTURE

In Chapter 9 where we discussed the agency-principal relationship. A company that takes on debt may be making an effective use of free cash flows, hence, reducing agency costs associated with the available free cash flow. Taking on additional debt also increases monitoring because creditors and rating agencies will be monitoring the ability of the company to pays its obligations. Therefore, taking on additional debt may enhance the value of the company by reducing agency costs, offsetting some of the effect on the value of the company of increasing financial risk.

Another agency issue that arises with regard to the use of debt is the use of debt as a takeover defense. A *takeover defense* is any mechanism that discourages or prevents a hostile takeover. By taking on additional debt, a company can make itself unattractive to potential suitors. Some companies borrow to repurchase their common shares specifically as an antitakeover device, increasing financial leverage dramatically. Whether this is beneficial to the company depends on a number of factors, especially the motivation. Most research into the effects of takeover defenses concludes that the use of takeover defenses may reduce the value of the company, especially if motivated by self-interest on the part of the target company's management.[2] Jandik and Makhija (2005) conclude in their study of unsuccessful takeovers that if the increase in debt results in better monitoring, such as that afforded by bank borrowing, the company benefits from the increase in debt; on the other hand, if the increase in debt results in management entrenchment, the effect on the value of the company is negative. In other words, the use of takeover defenses that are motivated by self-interest may impose a cost to owners.

OPTIMAL CAPITAL STRUCTURE: THEORY AND PRACTICE

Management can try to evaluate whether there is a capital structure that maximizes the value of the company. This capital structure, if it exists, is referred to as the *optimal capital structure*. However, even if the company's optimal capital structure cannot be determined precisely, management should understand that there is an economic benefit from the tax deductibility of taxes, but eventually this benefit may be reduced by the costs of financial distress.

So what good is this analysis of the trade-off between the value of the interest tax shields and the costs of distress if we cannot apply it to a specific company? While we cannot specify a company's optimal capital structure, we do know the factors that affect the optimum. The analysis demonstrates that there is a benefit from taxes and the discipline of debt but, eventually, these benefits reduce financial flexibility and may increase the likelihood of financial distress.

Benefits of debt financing	Costs of debt financing
■ Interest tax shield	■ Financial flexibility
■ Governance value	■ Financial distress and bankruptcy

Capital Structures among Different Industries

The analysis of the capital structure trade-off suggests several financial characteristics of companies that affect the choice of capital structure:

---

[2] See for example Sinha (1991) and Field and Karpoff (2002).

- The greater the marginal tax rate, the greater the benefit from the interest deductibility and, therefore, the more likely a company is to use debt in its capital structure.
- The greater the business risk of a company, the greater the present value of financial distress and, therefore, the less likely the company is to use debt in its capital structure.
- The greater extent that the value of the company depends on intangible assets, the less likely it is to use debt in its capital structure.

It is reasonable to expect these financial characteristics to differ among industries, but be similar within an industry. The marginal tax rate should be consistent within an industry since:

- The marginal tax rates are the same for all profitable companies.
- The tax law provides specific tax deductions and credits (for example, depreciation allowances and research and development credits) that creates some differences across industries, but generally applies to all companies within an industry because the asset structure and the nature of investment is consistent within an industry.
- The companies in an industry are subject to the same economic and market forces that may cause tax shields to be unusable. Therefore, it is reasonable to assume that capital structures should be similar within industry groups.

Capital Structures within Industries

The capital structures among companies within industries differ for several possible reasons. First, within an industry there may not be a homogeneous group of companies. For example, Kellogg Co., Brach's Candy, and Sara Lee Corporation are all considered members of the food product industry, but they have quite different types of business risk. The problem of industry groupings is exacerbated by conglomeration, with many industries now include companies with dissimilar product lines.

Adding to the difficulty in comparing companies is the Financial Standards Accounting Board (FASB) requirement that companies consolidate the accounting data of majority-owned subsidiaries. For example, the capital structure of the automobile manufacturers looks quite different with the financing subsidiaries included in the calculation of their debt ratios.

Trade-Off Theory and Observed Capital Structures

The trade-off theories can explain some of the capital structure variations that we observe. Companies whose value depends to a greater extent on intangibles, such as in the semiconductor and drug industries, tend to have lower debt ratios. Companies in volatile product markets, such as the electronics and telecommunications industries, tend to have lower debt ratios.

However, the trade-off theories cannot explain all observed capital structure behavior. We observe profitable companies in the drug manufacturing industry that have no long-term debt. Though these companies do have a large investment in intangibles, they choose not to take on *any* debt at all, even though taking on some debt could enhance the value of their companies.

We also see companies that have high business risk and high debt ratios. Companies in the air transportation industry experience a volatile product market, with a high degree of operating leverage. Companies in this industry must invest heavily in jets, airport gates, and reservations systems, and have a history of difficulty with labor. However, these companies also have high debt ratios, with upwards to 80% of their assets financed with debt. One possible explanation for airlines taking on a great deal of financial leverage on top of their already high operating leverage is that their assets, such as jets and gates, can be sold quickly, offsetting the effects of their greater volatility in operating earnings. Whereas the high business risk increases the probability of financial distress, the liquidity of their assets reduces the probability of distress. But hindsight tells us more about the airline industry. The overcapacity of the industry just prior to the recession of 1989–1991 meant that there was not much of a market for used jets and planes. Hence, there was little liquidity in the airline assets at this time and, therefore, the airlines suffered significantly during this economic recession: Of the 14 companies in existence just prior to 1989, four companies entered bankruptcy (Continental, Pan Am, Midway, and America West), and two were liquidated (Eastern Airlines and Braniff).

Other Possible Explanations

Looking at the financing behavior of companies in conjunction with their dividend and investment opportunities, we can make several observations:

- Companies prefer using internally generated capital (retained earnings) to externally raised funds (issuing equity or debt).
- Companies try to avoid sudden changes in dividends.
- When internally generated funds are greater than needed for investment opportunities, companies pay off debt or invest in marketable securities.
- When internally generated funds are less than needed for investment opportunities, companies use existing cash balances or sell off marketable securities.

■ If companies need to raise capital externally, they issue the safest security first; for example, debt is issued before preferred stock, which is issued before common equity.

The trade-off among taxes and the costs of financial distress lead to the belief that there is some optimal capital structure, such that the value of the company is maximized. Yet it is difficult to reconcile this with some observations in practice. Why?

One possible explanation is that the trade-off analysis is incomplete. We didn't consider the relative costs of raising funds from debt and equity. Because there are no out-of-pocket costs to raising internally generated funds (retained earnings), it may be preferred to debt and to externally raised funds. Because the cost of issuing debt is less than the cost of raising a similar amount from issuing common stock (typically flotation costs of 2.2% versus 7.1%), debt may be preferred to issuing stock.

Another explanation for the differences between what we observe and what we believe should exist is that companies may wish to build up financial slack, in the form of cash, marketable securities, or unused debt capacity, to avoid the high cost of issuing new equity.

Still another explanation is that management may be concerned about the signal given to investors when equity is issued. It has been observed that the announcement of a new common stock issue is viewed as a negative signal, since the announcement is accompanied by a drop in the value of the equity of the company. It is also observed that the announcement of the issuance of debt does not affect the market value of equity. Therefore, management must consider the effect that the new security announcement may have on the value of equity and therefore may shy away from issuing new equity.

The concern over the relative costs of debt and equity and the concern over the interpretation by investors of the announcement of equity financing leads to a preferred ordering, or *pecking order,* of sources of capital: first internal equity, then debt, then preferred stock, then external equity (new common stock). A result of this preferred ordering is that companies prefer to build up funds, in the form of cash and marketable securities, so as not to be forced to issue equity at times when internal equity (that is, retained earnings) is inadequate to meet new profitable investment opportunities.[3]

A CAPITAL STRUCTURE PRESCRIPTION

The analysis of the trade-off and pecking order explanations of capital structure suggests that there is no satisfactory explanation. What management

---

[3] For a more complete discussion of the pecking order explanation, especially the role of asymmetric information, see Myers (1985).

can take from an examination of these possible explanations is that there are several factors to consider in making the capital structure decision:

■ *Taxes.* The tax deductibility of interest makes debt financing attractive. However, the benefit from debt financing is reduced if the company cannot use the tax shields.
■ *Risk.* Because financial distress is costly, even without legal bankruptcy, the likelihood of financial distress depends on the business risk of the company, in addition to any risk from financial leverage.
■ *Type of asset.* The cost of financial distress is likely to be more for companies whose value depends on intangible assets and growth opportunities.
■ *Financial slack.* The availability of funds to take advantage of profitable investment opportunities is valuable. Therefore, having a store of cash, marketable securities, and unused debt capacity is valuable.

Management's task is to assess the business risk of the company, predicting the usability of tax deductions in the future, evaluating how asset values are affected in the event of distress, and estimating the relative issuance costs of the alternative sources of capital. In the context of all these considerations, management can observe other companies in similar situations, using their decisions and consequences as a guide.

SUMMARY

The capital structure decision involves managing the risks associated with the company's business and financing decisions. The concept of leverage, operating and financial, plays a role in the company's risk because leverage exaggerates both favorable and unfavorable outcomes. Financial leverage is the use of fixed cost sources of funds. The effect of using financial leverage is to increase both the expected returns and the risk to owners.

Taxes provide an incentive to take on debt because interest paid on debt is a deductible expense for tax purposes, shielding income from taxation. But the possibility of incurring direct and indirect costs of financial distress discourages taking on high levels of debt. Taxes and financial distress costs result in a trade-off. For low debt ratios, the benefit of taxes more than overcomes the present value of the costs of financial distress, resulting in increases in the value of the company for increasing debt ratios. But beyond some debt ratio, the benefit of taxes is overcome by the costs of financial distress; the value of the company decreases as debt is increased beyond this point. An explanation for the capital structures that we observe is that companies prefer to raise capital internally, but will raise capital externally according to a pecking order from safe to riskier securities.

In an agency relationship, the agent has the responsibility of acting for the principal. An explanation for the capital structures that we observe is that firms prefer to raise capital internally, but will raise capital externally according to a pecking order from safe to riskier securities.

Management may not be able to figure out the best capital structure for a company. However, a good checklist of factors to consider in the capital structure decision: taxes, business risk, asset type, issuance costs, and investor interpretations of security issuance announcements.

APPENDIX: CAPITAL STRUCTURE: LESSONS FROM MODIGLIANI AND MILLER

Franco Modigliani and Merton Miller provide a theory of capital structure that is a framework for the discussion of the factors most important in a company's capital structure decision: taxes, financial distress, and risk. Though this theory does not give a prescription for capital structure decisions, it does offer a method of examining the role of these important factors that provide the financial manager with the basic decision-making tools in analyzing the capital structure decision. Within their theory, Modigliani and Miller demonstrate that without taxes and costs of financial distress, the capital structure decision is irrelevant to the value of the company.

The capital structure decision becomes value-relevant when taxes are introduced into the situation, such that an interest-tax shield from the tax deductibility of interest on debt obligations encourages the use of debt because this shield becomes a source of value. Financial distress becomes relevant because costs associated distress mitigate the benefits of debt in the capital structure, offsetting or partially offsetting the benefit from interest deductibility. The value of a company—meaning the value of all its assets—is equal to the sum of its liabilities and its equity (the ownership interest). Does the way we finance the company's assets affect the value of the company and hence the value of its owners' equity? Yes. How does it affect the value of the company? As explained in this chapter, it depends.

M&M Irrelevance Proposition

Franco Modigliani and Merton Miller developed the basic framework for the analysis of capital structure and how taxes affect the value of the company (Modigliani and Miller, 1957). The essence of this framework is that what matters in the value of the company is the company's operating cash flows and the uncertainty associated with these cash flows.

Modigliani and Miller (M&M) reasoned that if the following conditions hold, the value of the company is not affected by its capital structure:

> *Condition 1.* Individuals and corporations can borrow and lend at the same terms (referred to as *equal access*).
>
> *Condition 2.* There is no tax advantage associated with debt financing vis-à-vis to equity financing.
>
> *Condition 3.* Debt and equity trade in a market where assets that are substitutes for one another, they trade at the same price.

Under the first condition, individuals can borrow and lend on the same terms as the business entities. Therefore, if individuals are seeking a given level of risk they can either: (1) borrow or lend on their own, or (2) invest in a business that borrows or lends. In other words, if an individual investor wants to increase the risk of the investment, the investor could choose to invest in a company that uses debt to finance its assets. Or the individual could invest in a company with no financial leverage and take out a personal loan—increasing the investor's own financial leverage.

The second condition isolates the effect of financial leverage. If deducting interest from earnings is allowed in the analysis, it would be difficult to figure out what effect financial leverage itself has on the value of the company. M&M relax this later, but at this point assume no tax advantage exists between debt or equity securities—either for the company or the investor. The third condition ensures that assets are priced according to their risk and return characteristics. This condition establishes what is referred to as a *perfect market*: If assets are traded in a perfect market, the value of assets with the same risk and return characteristics trade for the same price.

Under these conditions, the value of a company is the same, no matter how it chooses to finance itself. The *total* cash flow to owners and creditors is the same and the value of the company is the present value of the company's operating cash flows *ad infinitum*. If cash flows are expected to be the same each year, the value of the company is the present value of this perpetual stream of cash flows:

$$\text{Value of the company} = \frac{\text{Cash flow per period}}{\text{Capitalization rate}}$$

The discount rate is referred to as the *capitalization rate*, which is the rate that translates future earnings into a current value. The capitalization rate reflects the uncertainty associated with the expected earnings in the future. The more uncertain the future earnings, the less a dollar of future income is worth today and, therefore, the greater the capitalization rate. But the uncertainty regarding the cash flows generated by the assets is not affected by how the assets are financed. How the assets are financed affects the amount of cash flows each party—creditors and owners—receives.

Modigliani and Miller show that the discount rate for the cash flows to equity owners is higher when the company uses debt. Specifically, they show that the discount rate of the cash flows to owners is equal to the discount rate of a company with no financial leverage plus the compensation for bearing risk appropriate to the amount of debt in the capital structure.

The compensation for bearing risk, as reasoned by Modigliani and Miller, should be the risk premium weighted by the relative use of debt in the capital structure. The *risk premium* referred to in this case is the difference between the discount rate for the net income to owners and the discount rate on earnings to creditors (the interest). The latter earnings stream assumed to be risk-free: Interest is paid to creditors no matter how well or how poorly the company is doing; hence, it is considered risk-free to creditors.

Let r_s represent the capitalization rate for the company's operating cash flows, r_e represent the discount rate for a risky cash flows to owners, r_d represent the discount rate for risk-free debt cash flows, and D and E, respectively, be the value of debt and equity in the a company's capital structure. The cost of capital for the company as a whole is the weighted average of the costs of debt and equity:

$$r_s = \frac{D}{D+E} r_d + \frac{E}{D+E} r_e$$

As demonstrated by M&M, the discount rate that is applied to the cash flows to owners is the rate applied to the all-equity company, plus a premium for risk:

$$r_e = r_s + \left[(r_s - r_d)\left(\frac{D}{E}\right) \right]$$

(Note that the above equation for r_e is developed by algebraically rearranging the weighted cost of capital formula to solve for r_e.) Therefore, the greater the use of debt, the greater is D/E and, hence the greater the risk premium.

Consider a company with expected annual cash flows of $8 million per year, ad infinitum. Suppose that the appropriate discount rate for an all-equity company, r_s, is 8%. The value of the company is $8/0.08 = $100 million.

If this company has 20% debt in its capital structure with a cost of 5%:

	Cash Flow (in millions)	Cost of Capital	Value (in millions)
Debt	$1.00	5.00%	$20.00
Equity	7.00	8.75%	80.00
Company	$8.00	8.00%	$100.00

If this company has 40% debt in its capital structure with a cost of 5%:

	Cash Flow (in millions)	Cost of Capital	Value (in millions)
Debt	$2	5%	$40
Equity	6	10%	60
Company	$8	8%	$100

In other words, when there are no taxes and no costs to financial distress, no matter how the cash flows are sliced, the value of the "pie" is $100 million. As shown in Figure 11.4, the relation between the value of the company and the proportion of debt in the capital structure is quite uninteresting.

If there are no taxes and no costs to financial distress, the choice of capital structure is irrelevant. The reasoning is simple:

- The transactions involving the capital structure do not change total cash flows.
- It is the cash flows that are relevant to valuation. The value of the company is determined by its operating assets.

FIGURE 11.4   Capital Structure Irrelevance When There Are No Tax Deductibility of Interest and No Costs of Financial Distress

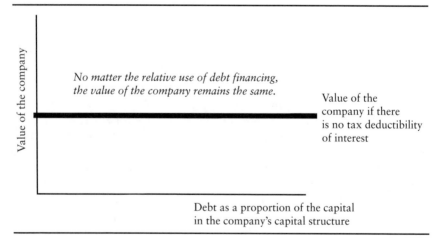

■ How the financial "pie" is divided among creditors and owners does not affect the total value.

Consider the view of investors. Investors do not pay more for the ownership of the company that borrows if they could have borrowed as well. And because the value of the company is the present value of cash flows, if there are no taxes, debt and equity choices should not affect the value of the company.

M&M show that in the simplified world without taxes or costs of distress, the value of the company depends on the cash flows of the company, *not* on how the company's cash flows are divided between creditors and owners. An implication of the Modigliani and Miller analysis is that the use of debt financing increases the risk of the future cash flows to owners and, therefore, increases the discount rate investors use to value these future earnings. Modigliani and Miller reason that the effect that the increased expected cash flows has on the value of equity is just offset by the increased discount rate applied to these riskier earnings, keeping the cost of capital the same no matter the capital structure.

M&M with Tax Deductibility of Interest Paid on Debt

M&M's second proposition is that when interest on debt are deducted in determining taxable income, but dividends are not, the value of the company is enhanced because of this tax deductibility of interest. When Modigliani and Miller introduce the tax deductibility of interest into the framework, the use of debt has a distinct advantage over financing with stock. The deductibility of interest represents a form of a government subsidy of financing activities; the government is sharing the company's cost of debt. We refer to the benefit from interest deductibility as the *interest tax shield* because the interest expense *shields* income from taxation. The tax shield from interest deductibility is the amount by which taxes are reduced by the deduction for interest.

How does this tax shield affect the value of the company? The tax shield is valuable because it reduces the net income of the company that goes to the government in the form of taxes. In any given year, this is the product of the tax rate and the interest expense. If this tax shield is anticipated each year, *ad infinitum*, the value of this tax shield is calculated as the present value of a perpetuity. If is the interest rate on debt, r_d, and the amount of debt is D, the interest on debt $r_d D$. The tax shield is the amount of income shielded from taxation by the interest deduction, which is $\tau r_d D$. Capitalizing this at r_d, the value of the tax shield is $\tau r_d D / r_d = \tau D$; in other words, the present value of this tax shield is τD.

Suppose that the company has cash flows of $8 million per year in perpetuity and the discount rate for this company if all equity financed is 8%.

The value of the company is $100 based on these cash flows. And suppose the company is financed with $20 million of debt and $80 million of equity. If the interest rate on debt is 5%, then there is $1 million per year in interest. If the marginal tax rate is 40%, the tax benefit is $1 million × 40% = $0.4 million. In perpetuity, this interest cash flow stream has a value today of $0.4 million/0.05 = $8 million. The $8 million is the value enhancement from the tax shield from debt. (As a practical matter, if a company is not profitable, the tax shield is less valuable because the full value of the tax deductibility of interest cannot be realized immediately.)

If we represent the value of the unlevered company as V_U and the value of the levered company as V_L, the value of this levered company considering the benefit from taxes is

$$V_L = V_U + \tau D$$

and the cost of capital for the company is adjusted for the deductibility of interest on debt, which lowers the company's cost of debt.

Let r_e represent the cost of equity financing, and let D and E represent the values of debt and equity, respectively. The cost of debt to the company is less than r_d because of the deductibility of interest on debt; specifically, the after-tax cost of debt is $r_d(1 - t)$. The weighted average cost of capital, r_s—that is, the cost of capital for the company considering the costs of both debt and equity in proportion to usage in the capital structure—is

$$r_s = \left(\frac{D}{D+E} r_d(1-t) \right) + \frac{E}{D+E} r_e$$

Of the "pie," the creditors' slice is $20 million, whereas the owners' slice is $88 million. (In this example with 20% of debt, the value of debt is $20, the value of equity without considering the value of the tax shield is $7 million/0.0875 = $80 million, and the value of the tax shield, which accrues to the owners, is $0.4 million/0.05 = $8 million.)

	Cash Flow (in millions)	Cost of Capital	Value (in millions)
Debt	$1.00	5.00%	$20.00
Equity			
From residual operating cash flows	7.00	8.75%	80.00
From tax shield	0.40	5.00%	8.00
Company	$8.40	7.77%	$108.00

In other words, the "pie" has grown and the owners are the beneficiaries of addition to the size of the pie from the tax deductibility of interest.

If there are no costs associated with financial distress:

- The value of the company increases with ever-increasing use of debt financing because of the value enhancement from the use of the interest tax shield, as we show in Figure 11.5(a).
- The cost of capital for the company decreases with ever-increasing use of debt financing because the after-tax cost of debt affects the cost of capital for the company as a whole such that the increase use of the debt reduces the cost of capital, as we show in Figure 11.5(b).

Is there a limit? As long as there are no costs to financial distress, the only limit is the existence of at least a small percentage of equity in the capital structure.

Capital Structure Theory and Costs to Financial Distress

If the debt burden is too much, the company may experience financial distress, resulting in an increasing cost of capital: At some point, the value of the company declines and the cost of capital increases with increasing use of debt financing. Financial distress results in both direct and indirect costs

FIGURE 11.5 Capital Structure Irrelevance when There Is Tax Deductibility of Interest, But No Costs of Financial Distress
(a) Value of the company

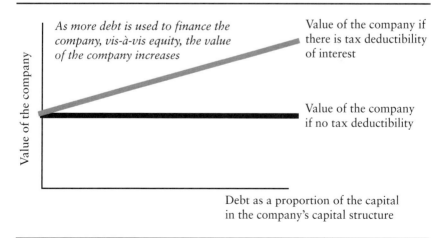

FIGURE 11.5   (continued)
(b) Cost of capital

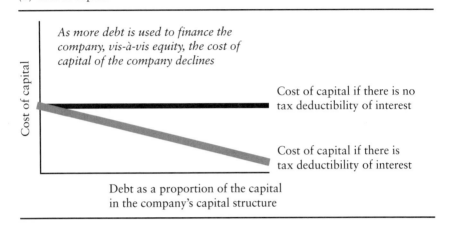

including legal costs, opportunity costs for projects, the effect on the relationship with customers and suppliers.

At some capital structure, these costs begin to offset the benefit of the interest deductibility of debt. The *optimal capital structure* is the point at which the value of the company is maximized. Up until the optimal capital structure, the benefits from the tax deductibility of interest outweigh the cost of financial distress. When the amount of financial leverage exceeds the optimal capital structure, the benefits from the tax deductibility of interest are outweighed by the cost of financial distress. This is shown in Figure 11.6. Because of the relation between the value of the company and the cost of capital, the capital structure that maximizes the value of the company is the same capital structure that minimizes the cost of capital.

The problem is that we cannot determine before hand what the optimal capital structure is for a given company. The theory is not prescriptive in terms of identifying this precise point. What we can observe is when a company takes on too much debt and distress occurs. The optimal capital structure depends, in large part, on the business risk of the company: the greater the business risk of the company, the sooner this optimal capital structure is reached.

So what good is the theory of capital structure if financial managers cannot determine the optimal capital structure? The M&M theory, along with subsequent, related theories and evidence, provides a framework for decision-making:

1. There is a benefit to taking on debt—to a point.

FIGURE 11.6   Capital Structure Irrelevance When There Is Tax Deductibility of Interest and Costs of Financial Distress
(a) Value of the company

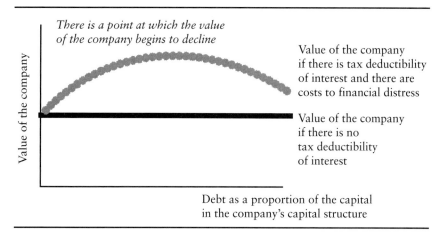

(b) Cost of capital

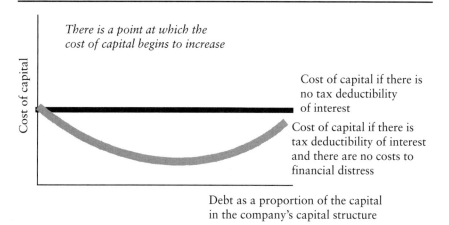

2. The cost of capital of a company decreases with ever-increasing use of debt financing—to a point.
3. The optimal capital structure depends on the risk associated with the company's operating cash flows.

The Traditional Trade-Off Model and Current Capital Structure Theory and Practice

The M&M theory offers a trade-off model of capital structure: some balance exists between the present value of the interest tax shields and the present value of the costs of financial distress. We simply cannot determine, based on this theory, where this point is for a given company.

Since M&M introduced their theory of capital structure in a series of articles, there have been many other considerations offered by researchers, including:

- Agency costs (Jensen and Meckling, 1976) that may obfuscate the maximization of shareholders' wealth.
- Asymmetric information and signaling (Myers, 1984; Myers and Majluf, 1984) that result in a pecking order of financing choices.
- Nonfinancial stakeholder issues (Grinblatt and Titman, 2002) that may affect the costs of financial distress.

These additional considerations complicate the analysis, but do not replace the fundamental concept that there is a trade-off between the benefits of debt and the costs of having too much debt.

The empirical evidence regarding the drivers of capital structure suggests that the trade-off and the pecking-order theories explain some of the capital structures that we observe, these theories do not explain all. Consider the survey results by Graham and Harvey (2001):

- The role of the interest tax deductibility in the choice of capital structure appears to be more important in regulated and dividend-paying companies.
- The costs of financial distress *per se* are not as important as the credit rating of debt; hence, the effect of an increasing debt burden on the credit quality of the company's debt is a consideration.
- The volatility of earnings is important in the capital structure decision, suggesting that the cost of financial distress affect the decision.

Summary

The theory that Modigliani and Miller developed has stood the test of time because it offers the basic logic behind capital structure decisions: companies are interested in maximizing the value of the company and therefore factor in the benefits from interest deductibility and the costs of financial distress. Though their model is not prescriptive, it identifies the primary factors in the decision and offers the reasoning of how these factors affect the value of a company.

REFERENCES

Booth, L. and Cleary, S. (2006). Cash flow volatility, financial slack, and investment decisions. Working Paper, University of Toronto (January).

Field, L .C. and Karpoff, J. M. (2002). Takeover defenses of IPO frms. *Journal of Finance* 57, no. 5:1857–1889.

Garvy, G. T. and Hanka, G. (1999). Capital Structure and corporate control: The effect of antitakeover statutes on firm leverage. *Journal of Finance* 54, no. 2: 519–546.

Graham, J. R. and Harvey, C. R. (2001). The theory and practice of corporate finance: evidence from the field. *Journal of Financial Economics* 60: 287–243.

Grinblatt, M., and Titman, S. (2002). *Financial Markets and Corporate Strategy*, Boston: Irwin/McGraw-Hill.

Jandik, T. and Makhija, A. (2005). Debt, debt structure and corporate performance after unsuccessful takeovers: Evidence from targets that remain independent. *Journal of Corporate Finance* 11: 882–914.

Jensen, M. C. (1986). Agency cost of free cash flow, corporate finance, and takeovers. *American Economic Review* 76, no. 2: 323–329.

Jensen, M. C. and Meckling, W. (1976). Theory of the firm: Managerial behavior, agency costs, and ownership structure. *Journal of Financial Economics* 4: 305–360.

Modigliani, F. and Miller, M. (1958). "The cost of capital, corporation finance, and the theory of investment. *American Economic Review* 48, no. 3: 261–297.

Modigliani, F. and Miller, M. (1963). Corporate income taxes and the cost of capital: A correction. *American Economic Review* 53, no. 3: 433–443.

Myers, S. C. (1977). Determinants of corporate borrowing. *Journal of Financial Economics* 5: 147–176.

Myers, S. C. (1985). The capital structure puzzle. *Midland Corporate Finance Journal* 3, no. 3: 65–76.

Myers, S. C. and Majluf, N. S. (1984). Corporate financing and investment decisions when firms have information investors do not have. *Journal of Financial Economics* (June): 187–221.

Sinha, S. (1991). Share repurchases as a takeover defense. *Journal of Financial and Quantitative Analysis* 26, no. 2: 233–244.

CHAPTER 12

Financial Engineering, Asset Securitization, and Project Financing

A specialty area in finance is the area of financial engineering. In fact, there are graduate degrees in this subject and even departments of business or engineering schools that carry this title. Yet, there is no standard definition of financial engineering. For example, Professor Neil Pearson provides the following two definitions of financial engineering for his courses in financial engineering and risk management at the University of Illinois:[1]

(Definition 1) Financial engineering is the application of the mathematical tools commonly used in physics and engineering to financial problems, especially the pricing and hedging of derivative instruments.

(Definition 2) Financial engineering is the use of financial instruments such as forwards, futures, swaps, options, and related products to restructure or rearrange cash flows in order to achieve particular financial goals, particularly the management of financial risk. If we define financial engineering this way, it is almost synonymous with financial risk management.

The International Association of Financial Engineers (IAFE) defines financial engineering as follows:[2]

- Financial engineering is the application of mathematical methods to the solution of problems in finance.
- It is also known as financial mathematics, mathematical finance, and computational finance.

---

[1] Department of Finance, University of Illinois, "Areas of Specialization" (2008), www.business.uiuc.edu/Finance/areas.aspx?code=E.

[2] International Association of Financial Engineers, "Resources: What is Financial Engineering" (2007), www.iafe.org/resources_what.html.

■ Financial engineering draws on tools from applied mathematics, computer science, statistics, and economic theory.

In this chapter we see how financial engineering is used in corporate finance. That is, we will look at how financial engineering is used in corporate finance deal structuring. For this purpose we will use the definition provided by Finnerty (2008, p. 91):

> Financial engineering involves the design of innovative securities, which provide superior, previously unavailable risk/return combinations. This process often includes coupling new derivative products with traditional securities to manage risks more cost effectively. The key to developing better risk-management vehicles is to design financial instruments that either provide new and more desirable risk-return combinations or furnish the desired future cash-flow profile at lower cost than existing instruments.

This specialty area in corporate financial engineering is commonly referred to as *structured finance*. Though there are many structured finance products and processes, they share some basic characteristics:

■ Complex products or processes that involve a pool of underlying assets.
■ Liabilities whose cash flows are either linked to a pool of assets or referenced to a specified index, most likely divided into classes referred to as tranches.
■ Embedded derivatives.
■ A special-purpose entity that links the pool of assets, the liabilities, and the derivatives that provides a legal entity apart from the originator of the structured finance product.

The key is that the structured finance product or process serves to rearrange the cash flows of the underlying assets into different securities that may have different cash flow and risk characteristics.

In this chapter, we explain how financial engineering is used to structure transactions. We begin with how a financial manager can use derivatives to create structured notes. Then we explain one of the most popular uses of financial engineering: asset securitization. Finally, we look another financial engineering application, project financing.

CREATION OF STRUCTURED NOTES

For a plain-vanilla bond structure, (1) the coupon interest rate is either fixed over the life of the security or floating at a fixed spread to a reference rate; and (2) the principal is a fixed amount that is due on a specified date. There are bonds that have slight variations that are common in the marketplace. A callable bond may have a redemption date that is prior to the scheduled maturity date. The option to call the bond prior to the maturity date resides with the issuer; the benefit of calling the issue depends on the market interest rate at which the callable bond issue can be refinanced. Similarly, a putable bond has a maturity date that can be shortened, but in this case the option resides with the bondholder; if the market rate on comparable bonds exceeds the coupon rate, the bondholder will exercise. A convertible bond typically has at least two embedded options. The first is the bondholder's right to convert the bond into common stock. The second is the issuer's right to call the bond. Some convertible bonds are also putable.

Callable, putable, and convertible bonds are considered traditional securities, as are other similar structures such as extendible and retractable bonds.[3] There are bonds with embedded options that have much more complicated provisions for one or more of the following: interest rate payable, redemption amount, and timing of principal repayment. The interest or redemption amount can be tied to the performance or the level of one or more interest rates or noninterest rate benchmarks. As a result, the potential performance (return and risk) of such securities will be substantially different from those offered by plain-vanilla bond structures. These securities are popularly referred to as *structured notes*.

In a survey article on structured notes, Telpner (2004, p. 6) defines structured notes as "fixed-income securities—sometimes referred to as hybrid securities that present the appearance of fixed-income securities—that combine derivative elements and do not necessarily reflect the risk of the issuer." Here the key element is that the issuer is not necessarily taking on the opposite risk of the investors.

In their book on the structured notes market, Peng and Dattatreya (1995, p. 2) write, "Structured notes are fixed income debentures linked to derivatives." They go on to say:

> A key feature of structured notes is that they are created by an underlying swap transaction. The issuer rarely retains any of the risks embedded in the structured note and is almost hedged out of

[3] An extendible bond grants the issuer the right to extend the redemption date beyond the stated maturity date. A retractable bond grants the bondholder the right to redeem on a date prior to the original maturity date.

the risks of the note by performing a swap transaction with a swap counterparty. This feature permits issuers to produce notes of almost any specification, as long as they are satisfied that the hedging swap will perform for the life of the structured note. To the investor, this swap transaction is totally transparent since the only credit risk to which the investor is exposed is that of the issuer.

In this definition, the focus is not on the issuer selling a debt instrument with derivative-type payoffs to investors, but the issuer protecting itself against the risks associated with the potential payoffs it must make to investors by hedging those risks. That is, the upside potential available to investors in a structured note does not reflect risk to the issuer. While Peng and Dattatreya say that this can be done with a swap transaction, any other derivative can be employed to hedge the risk faced by an issuer.[4]

A structured note can be issued in the public market, or as a private placement or a 144A security.[5] It can take the form of either commercial paper, a medium-term note, or a corporate bond. The issuer must be of high credit quality so that credit risk is minimal in order to accomplish the objectives that motivated the creation of the structured note. Issuers include highly rated corporations, banks, and U.S. government agencies. Because credit risk increases over time, the type of issuer and the form of the security are tied to the planned holding period of the investor.

Motivation for Investors

The motivation for the purchase of structured notes by investors includes (1) the potential for enhancing yield; (2) participating indirectly in the bond market; (3) obtaining exposure to alternative asset classes; (4) acquiring exposure to a particular market but not a particular aspect of it;[6] and (5) controlling risks.

The potential for yield enhancement was the motivation behind the popularity of structured notes in the sustained low-interest-rate environment in

---

[4] A *swap* is a transaction that results in the exchange of a stream of cash flows among parties. For example, a swap may involve two parties: one that has a fixed payment cash flow stream and another that has a floating (that is, variable) cash flow stream. These parties can agree to exchange these cash flow streams in a swap agreement. The basics of swaps are described in Chapter 6.

[5] A 144A security is one that satisfies the requirements of Rule 144A of the Securities Act of 1933, which exempts securities sold to qualified institutional buyers from the registration requirements of the Act.

[6] For example, a U.S. investor may want exposure to Japanese equities, but not yen assets, so the investor can buy U.S.-dollar-denominated bonds that have a payoff linked to the Japanese stock market index.

the late 1980s. After the high interest rates (double digits) that prevailed in the early 1980s, institutional investors faced interest rates that were not sufficient to satisfy the liabilities for the financial products they created during the high-interest-rate environment. Local governments had come to rely on interest income from higher interest rates in order to fund operations and avoid raising property and personal taxes. Structured notes offered the potential to provide a higher return than that prevailing in the market for plain-vanilla debt obligations if certain market scenarios occurred.

The ability of issuers to hedge risk using derivatives allows them to create securities for investors who wish to participate in the bond market indirectly. For example, a structured note could be created that allowed exposure to a change in the yield curve, the change in the spread between two reference interest rates, or the direction of interest rates (e.g., a leveraged payoff if interest rates declined).

Structured notes that have payoffs based on the performance of asset classes other than bonds allow investors to participate in other markets in which they may be prohibited from investing by regulatory or client constraint. For example, suppose that an investor who must restrict portfolio holdings to investment-grade bonds wishes to participate in the equity market. The investor would not be permitted to invest in equities. However, by investing in an investment-grade bond whose payoff is based on the performance of the equity market, the investor has obtained exposure to the equity market. For this reason, some market participants refer to structured notes as "rule busters."

Finally, a structured note can be used to hedge exposure that an investor may not be able to hedge more efficiently using derivative products. For example, suppose that an investor is concerned with exposure in its current portfolio to changes in credit spreads. While there are currently credit derivatives that would allow the investor to hedge this exposure, suppose that the investor is not permitted to utilize them. An investor can have an issuer create a structured note that has a payoff based on a particular credit spread. The issuer can protect itself by taking a position in the credit derivatives market.

What is the benefit of all this customization for the issuer? By creating a customized product for an investor, the issuer seeks a lower funding cost than if it had issued a bond with a plain-vanilla structure.

How do borrowers or their agents find investors who are willing to buy structured notes? In a typical plain-vanilla bond offering, the sales force of the underwriting firm solicits interest in the issue from its customer base. That is, the sales forces will make an inquiry to investors about their needs and preferences. In the structured note market, the process is often quite different. Because of the small size of an offering and the flexibility to customize the offering in the swap market, investors can approach an issuer through its agent about designing a security for their needs. This process of customers inquiring of issuers or their agents to design a security is called a *reverse inquiry*.

Creating Structured Notes

Peng and Dattatreya describe the three main steps in creating a structured note:[7]

1. Conceptual stage.
2. Identification process.
3. Structuring or construction stage.

In customizing a structured note for a client, the investment banker must understand the client's motivation. This is the conceptual stage of the process. We described earlier why investors look to the structured note market for customization. The investor provides the motivation through reverse inquiry.

In the identification process, the investment banker identifies the underlying components that will be packaged to create the structured note based on the requirements identified in the conceptual stage. This process begins with specifying five customization factors: nationality, rate profile, risk-return, maturity, and credit. The nationality factor specifies the country where the client would like to have some investment exposure. In the case of structured notes where the underlying is an interest rate, the rate factor determines the directional play (e.g., rising or falling interest rates, flattening or steepening yield curve) that is to be embedded in the structure. The amount of risk to be embedded in the structured note is the risk-return customization factor. Both the maturity and credit customization factors determine the instrument that will be used and the type of issuer.

In the structuring or construction stage, the investment banker gathers the pertinent market data and issuer-specific information. This information includes the target funding cost for the issuer (after underwriting fees) and the desired coupon and principal structure based on information from the conceptual and identification stages. In determining the cost of the structure, recognition must be given to the hedging cost that will be incurred when using the derivative instrument or instruments. Other specifications depend on the complexity of the structure. For example, a structure may require that the correlation of the factors driving the price of the underlying instruments in the structure be estimated.

---

[7] See Chapter 8 in Peng and Dattatreya (1995).

Two Examples of Structured Notes

A wide range of structured notes have been created in the market. Here we will discuss only two types: interest-rate structured notes (more specifically, an inverse floater) and an equity-linked structured note. The derivative instrument used in the creation of these two structured notes, swaps, were described in Chapter 6.

Interest-Rate Linked Structured Notes

The general coupon formula for a floating rate security (floater) is

$$\text{Coupon rate} = \text{Reference rate} + \text{Quoted margin}$$

The reference rate is the specified benchmark for the security's rate, such as LIBOR or the rate on a three-month U. S. Treasury Bill. The quoted margin is the contracted additional amount that is paid over and above the reference rate. Typically, the coupon formula on floaters is such that the coupon rate increases when the reference rate increases, and decreases when the reference rate decreases. There are structured notes whose coupon rate moves in the opposite direction from the change in the reference rate. Such issues are called *inverse floaters* or *reverse floaters*.

The coupon reset formula for an inverse floater is

$$\text{Coupon rate} = K - [L \times (\text{Reference rate})]$$

L is the leverage factor, whereas K is a specified fixed rate. When L is greater than 1, the security is referred to as a *leveraged inverse floater*. For example, suppose L is 1. Then the coupon reset formula is

$$\text{Coupon rate} = K - (\text{Reference rate})$$

Suppose the reference rate is one-month LIBOR, K is 12%, and L is equal to 1. The coupon formula is

$$\text{Coupon rate} = 12\% - (1\text{-month LIBOR})$$

If in some month the one-month LIBOR at the coupon reset date is 5%, the coupon rate for the period is 7%. If in the next month the month LIBOR declines to 4.5%, the coupon rate increases to 7.5%.

Notice that if the month's LIBOR exceeds 12%, then the coupon reset formula produces a negative coupon rate. To prevent this, there is a floor imposed on the coupon rate. Typically, the floor is zero. There is also a cap on the inverse floater. This occurs if the one-month LIBOR is zero. In that unlikely event, the maximum coupon rate is 12% for our hypothetical inverse floater. Therefore, the cap is the value of K in the coupon reset formula for an inverse floater.

An inverse floater can be created when an investment banking firm underwrites a fixed rate bond and simultaneously enters into an interest rate swap with the issuer, where the maturity of the swap is generally less than the maturity of the structured note that will be issued. The investor owns an inverse floater for the swap's tenor (that is, the term of the swap agreement), which then converts to a fixed rate bond (the underlying collateral) when the swap contract expires. An inverse floater created using a swap is called an *indexed inverse floater*.

To see how this can be accomplished, assume the following. The CFO wants to issue $200 million on a fixed rate basis for 20 years. An investment banker suggests two simultaneous transactions:

Transaction 1. Issue a $200 million, 20-year bond in which the coupon rate is determined by the following rules for a specific reference rate:

For years 1 through 5:   Coupon rate = 14% – Reference rate
For years 6 through 10:   Coupon rate = 5%

Transaction 2. Enter into a five-year interest rate swap with the investment bank with a notional principal amount of $200 million in which semiannual payments are exchanged as follows using the same reference rate:

Issuer pays the reference rate
Issuer receives 6%

Note that for the first five years, the investor owns an inverse floater because if the reference rate increases the coupon rate decreases, whereas if the reference rate decreases the coupon rate increases. However, even though the security issued pays an inverse floating rate, the combination of the two transactions results in fixed rate financing for the issuer:

Rate issuer receives
From the investment bank for its swap payment: 6%

Rate issuer pays
To security holders as interest: 14% – Reference rate
To the investment bank for its swap obligation: Reference rate

Net payments
(14% – Reference rate) + Reference rate – 6% = 8%

So what is the bottom line? The issuer has issued a floating rate security, but effectively pays a fixed rate of 8%. Why would a company enter into these transactions instead of simply issuing a fixed rate security? Because the company may find it easier to find a buyer for the floating rate security, and can shift the risk of changes in the reference rate to another party—in this case the investment bank.

Equity-Linked Structured Notes

An equity swap is an agreement between two parties to exchange a set of future cash flows. An equity swap can be used to design a bond issue with a coupon rate tied to the performance of an equity index. Such a bond issue is referred to as an *equity-linked structured note*. Such notes may be designed many different ways, but the basic idea is to blend the features of a low or zero-coupon bond with potential for the investor to participate in the upward movement of an equity index.

To illustrate how this is done, suppose the Universal Information Technology Company (UIT) seeks to raise $100 million for the next five years on a fixed rate basis. UIT's investment banker indicates that if bonds with a maturity of five years were issued, the interest rate on the issue would have to be 8.4%. At the same time, there are institutional investors who are seeking to purchase bonds but are interested in making a play on (i.e., betting on) the future performance of the stock market. These investors are willing to purchase a bond whose annual interest rate is based on the actual performance of the S&P 500 stock market index.

The banker recommends to UIT's CFO that it consider issuing a five-year bond whose annual interest rate is based on the actual performance of the S&P 500. The risk with issuing such a bond is that UIT's annual interest cost is uncertain because it depends on the performance of the S&P 500. However, suppose that the following two transactions are arranged:

1. On January 1, UIT agrees to issue, using the banker as the underwriter, a $100 million five-year bond whose annual interest rate is the actual performance of the S&P 500 that year minus 300 basis points. The minimum interest rate, however, is set at zero. The annual interest payments are made on December 31.
2. UIT enters into a five-year, $100 million notional amount equity swap with the banker in which each year for the next five years UIT agrees to pay 7.9% to the banker, and the banker agrees to pay the actual per-

FIGURE 12.1 Bond Structure: Conventional vs. S&P Linked Note
(a) Conventional Bond Issue

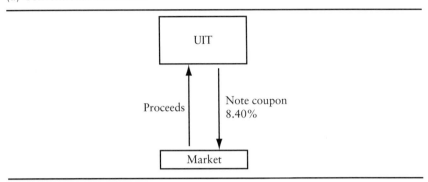

(b) S&P Linked Note

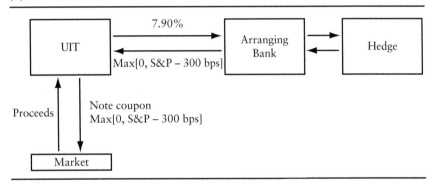

formance of the S&P 500 that year minus 300 basis points. The terms of the swap call for the payments to be made on December 31 of each year. Thus, the swap payments coincide with the payments that must be made on the bond issue. Also as part of the swap agreement, if the S&P 500 minus 300 basis points (bps) results in a negative value, the banker pays nothing to UIT.[8]

Figure 12.1 diagrams the payment flows for this swap. Consider what has been accomplished with these two transactions from the perspective of UIT. Specifically, focus on the payments that must be made by UIT on the bond issue and the swap and the payments that it will receive from the swap. These are summarized as follows:

---

[8] The trading desk of the investment banking firm can hedge this risk with a basis swap that pays a fixed or floating cash flow in return for receiving the return on the S&P.

Interest payments on bond issue:	S&P 500 return − 300 bps
Swap payment from the banker:	S&P 500 return − 300 bps
Swap payment to the banker:	7.9%
Net interest cost:	7.9%

Thus, the net interest cost is a fixed rate despite the bond issue paying an interest rate tied to the S&P 500. This was accomplished with the equity swap.

There are several questions that should be addressed. First, what was the advantage to UIT to entering into this transaction? Recall that if UIT issued a bond, the banker estimated that UIT would have to pay 8.4% annually. Thus, UIT has saved 50 basis points (8.4% minus 7.9%) per year. Second, why would investors purchase this bond issue? In real-world markets, there are restrictions imposed on institutional investors as to the types of investment or by other portfolio guidelines. For example, an institutional investor may be prohibited by a client or by other portfolio guidelines from purchasing common stock. However, it may be permitted to purchase a bond of an issuer, such as UIT, despite the fact that the interest rate is tied to the performance of common stocks. Third, is the banker exposed to the risk of the performance of the S&P 500? In the swap market, there are ways for the banker to protect itself.

ASSET SECURITIZATION

As an alternative to raising funds via borrowing, a popular financing vehicle is asset securitization. With traditional secured bonds, it is necessary for the issuer to generate sufficient earnings to repay the debt obligation. So, for example, if a manufacturer of farm equipment issues a bond in which the bondholders have a first mortgage lien on one of its plants, the ability of the manufacturer to generate cash flow from all of its operations is required to pay off the bondholders. In contrast, in an asset securitization transaction, the burden of the source of repayment shifts from the cash flow of the issuer to the cash flow of a pool of financial assets or a third party that guarantees the payments if the pool of financial assets does not generate sufficient cash flow. For example, if the manufacturer of farm equipment has receivables from installment sales contracts to customers (i.e., a financial asset for the farm equipment company) and uses these receivables in a structured financing as described below, payment to the buyers of the bonds backed by these receivables depends only on the ability to collect the receivables. That is, it does not depend on the ability of the manufacturer of the farm equipment to generate cash flow from operations.

In this section we describe asset securitization. It should be noted that since the summer of 2007, there were major problems in the mortgage-backed securities market, one type of asset class that has been securitized. However, while those problems have slowed down the issuance of the securitization of other asset classes, asset securitization remains an important mechanism for raising firms by nonfinancial firms.

Illustration of an Asset Securitization Transaction

Let's use an illustration to describe an asset securitization transaction. In our illustration, we will use a hypothetical firm, Farm Equipment Corporation. This company is assumed to manufacture farm equipment. Some of its sales are for cash, but the bulk of its sales are from installment sales contracts. Effectively, an installment sale contract is a loan to the buyer of the farm equipment who agrees to repay Farm Equipment Corporation over a specified period of time. For simplicity, we will assume that the loans are typically for four years. The collateral for the loan is the farm equipment purchased by the borrower. The loan specifies an interest rate that the buyer pays.

The credit department of Farm Equipment Corporation makes the decision as to whether to extend credit to a customer. That is, the credit department will receive a credit application from a customer and, based on criteria established by the firm, will decide on whether to extend a loan and the amount. The criteria for extending credit or a loan are referred to as *underwriting standards*. Because Farm Equipment Corporation is extending the loan, it is referred to as the *originator* of the loan.

Moreover, Farm Equipment Corporation may have a department that is responsible for servicing the loan. *Servicing* involves collecting payments from borrowers, notifying borrowers who may be delinquent, and, when necessary, recovering and disposing of the collateral (i.e., farm equipment in our illustration) if the borrower does not make loan repayments by a specified time. While the servicer of the loans need not be the originator of the loans, in our illustration we are assuming that Farm Equipment Corporation is the servicer.

Now let's get to how these loans can be used in a securitization transaction. We will assume that Farm Equipment Corporation has more than $200 million of installment sales contracts. This amount is shown on the corporation's balance sheet as an asset. We will further assume that Farm Equipment Corporation wants to raise $200 million. Rather than issuing corporate bonds for $200 million (for the reasons explained later), the treasurer decides to raise the funds via a securitization.

To do so, the Farm Equipment Corporation will set up a legal entity referred to as a *special-purpose entity* (SPE), also referred to as a *special-*

purpose vehicle (SPV). At this point, we will not explain the purpose of this legal entity, but it will be made clearer later that the SPE is critical in a securitization transaction. In our illustration, the SPE that is set up is called FE Asset Trust (FEAT). Farm Equipment Corporation will then sell to FEAT $200 million of the loans. Farm Equipment Corporation will receive from FEAT $200 million in cash, the amount it wanted to raise. But where does FEAT get $200 million? It obtains those funds by selling securities that are backed by the $200 million of loans. The securities are called *asset-backed securities*. The asset-backed securities issued in a transaction securitization are also referred to as bond classes or *tranches*. The structure is diagrammed in Figure 12.2.

A simple transaction can involve the sale of just one bond class with a par value of $200 million. We will call this Bond Class A. Suppose that 200,000 certificates are issued for Bond Class A with a par value of $1,000 per certificate. Then, each certificate holder would be entitled to 1/200,000 of the payment from the collateral. Each payment made by the borrowers (i.e., the buyers of the farm equipment) consists of principal repayment and interest.

A securitization transaction is typically more complicated. For example, there can be rules for distribution of principal and interest other than on a pro rata basis to different bond classes. It may be difficult to understand why such a structure should be created. What is important to understand is that there are institutional investors who have needs for bonds with different maturities and price volatility characteristics. A securitization transaction can be designed to create bond classes with investment characteristics that are more attractive to institutional investors to satisfy those needs.

FIGURE 12.2 Illustration of Asset Securitization Process

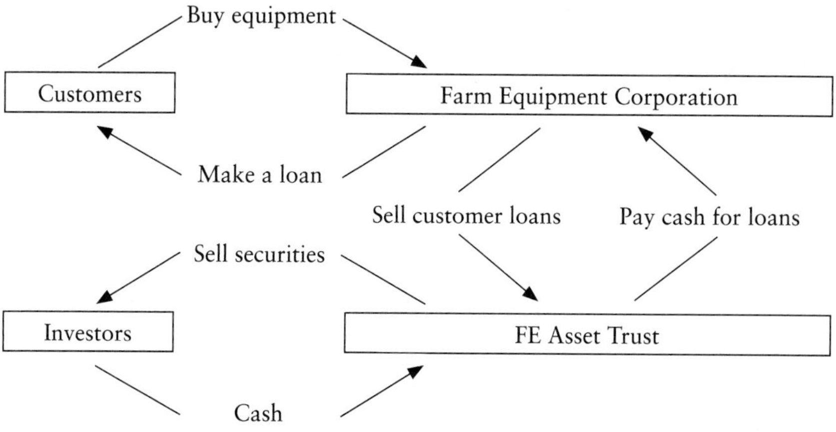

An example of a more complicated transaction is one in which two bond classes are created, Bond Class A1 and Bond Class A2. The par value for Bond Class A1 is $90 million and for Bond Class A2 is $110 million. The priority rule can simply specify that Bond Class A1 receives all the principal that is paid by the borrowers (i.e., the buyers of the farm equipment) until all of Bond Class A1 has paid off its $90 million and then Bond Class A2 begins to receive principal. Bond Class A1 is then a shorter-term bond than Bond Class A2.

As will be explained later, there are typically structures where there is more than one bond class, but the two bond classes differ as to how they will share any losses resulting from defaults of the borrowers in the underlying collateral pool. In such a structure, the bond classes are classified as *senior bond classes* and *subordinate bond classes* and the structure is referred to as a *senior-subordinate structure*. Losses are realized by the subordinate bond classes before there are any losses realized by the senior bond classes. For example, suppose that FEAT issued $180 million par value of Bond Class A, the senior bond class, and $20 million par value of Bond Class B, the subordinate bond class. As long as there are no defaults by the borrower greater than $20 million, then Bond Class A will be repaid fully its $180 million.

Reasons for Using a Securitization Transaction

There are three principal reasons why a corporation may elect to issue an asset-backed security rather than a corporate bond.[9] They are:

1. The potential for reducing funding costs.
2. To diversify funding sources.
3. To accelerate earnings for financial reporting purposes.

Potential for Reducing Funding Costs

To understand the potential for reducing funding costs by issuing an asset-backed security rather than a corporate bond, suppose that in our illustration Farm Equipment Corporation has a triple-B credit rating. If it wants to raise funds equal to $200 million and it issues a corporate bond, its funding cost would be whatever the benchmark Treasury yield is plus a yield spread for triple-B issuers. Suppose, instead, that Farm Equipment Corporation uses $200 million of its installment sales contracts (i.e., the loans it has made to customers) as collateral for a bond issue. What will be its funding cost? It probably will be the same as if it issued a corporate bond. The reason is that

[9] For banks, a key motivation for securitizing assets such as loans is for relief from risk-based capital requirements.

if Farm Equipment Corporation defaults on any of its outstanding debt, the creditors will go after all of the corporate assets, including the loans to its customers.

However, suppose that Farm Equipment Corporation can create another legal entity and sell the loans to that entity. That entity is the special-purpose vehicle that we described earlier in our hypothetical transaction. In our illustration, it is Farm Equipment Asset Trust (FEAT). If the sale of the loans by Farm Equipment Corporation to FEAT is done properly—that is, the sale of the loans is at the fair market value—FEAT then *legally* owns the receivables, not Farm Equipment Corporation. This means that if Farm Equipment Corporation is forced into bankruptcy, its creditors *cannot* try to recover the loans (sold to FEAT) because they are legally owned by FEAT. What is the implication of structuring a transaction in this way?

When FEAT sells bonds backed by the loans (i.e., the asset-backed securities), those interested in buying the bonds will evaluate the credit risk associated with collecting the payments due on the loans independent of the credit rating of Farm Equipment Corporation. What credit rating will be received for the bonds issued by FEAT? Whatever FEAT wants the credit rating to be! It may seem strange that the issuer (the SPE, FEAT) can get any credit rating it wants, but that is the case. The reason is that FEAT will show the characteristics of the collateral for the asset-backed securities (i.e., the loans to Farm Equip's customers) to a credit rating agency. In turn, the rating agency will evaluate the credit quality of the collateral and inform the issuer what must be done to obtain a desired credit rating.

More specifically, the issuer will be asked to "credit enhance" the structure. There are various forms of credit enhancement that we will review later. Basically, the rating agencies will look at the potential losses from the collateral and make a determination of how much credit enhancement is needed for the bond classes issued to achieve the targeted rating sought by the issuer. The higher the credit rating sought by the issuer, the more credit enhancement a rating agency will require for given collateral. Thus, Farm Equipment Corporation, which we assumed is triple-B rated, can obtain funding using the loans to its customers as collateral to obtain a better credit rating for the bonds issued than its own credit rating. In fact, with enough credit enhancement, it can issue a bond of the highest credit rating, triple A.

The key to a corporation issuing bonds with a higher credit rating than the corporation's own credit rating is the SPE. Its role is critical because it is the SPE (FEAT in our illustration) that legally separates the assets used as collateral from the corporation that is seeking financing (Farm Equipment Corporation in our illustration).

Why wouldn't a corporation always seek the highest credit rating (triple A) for the bonds backed by the collateral in a securitization transaction? The answer is that credit enhancement does not come without a cost. As described later, there are various credit enhancement mechanisms and they increase the costs associated with borrowing via the issuance of asset-backed securities. So, the corporation must assess the trade-off when it is seeking a higher rating between the additional cost of credit enhancing the bonds versus the reduction in funding cost by issuing a bond with a higher credit rating.

It is important to realize that if a bankruptcy of the corporation seeking funds occurs (Farm Equipment Corporation in our illustration), a bankruptcy judge may decide that the assets of the SPE are assets that the creditors of the corporation seeking financing may go after. This is an unresolved legal issue in the United States. Legal experts have argued that this is unlikely. In the prospectus of an asset-backed security, there will be a legal opinion addressing this issue. This is the reason why special-purpose vehicles in the United States are referred to as *bankruptcy-remote* entities.

Diversifying Funding Sources

An issuer seeking to raise funds via securitization must establish itself as an issuer in the asset-backed securities market. Once that is done, it can look at both the corporate bond market and the asset-backed securities market to determine the better funding source. That is, it will compare the all-in-cost of funds in the corporate bond market and the asset-backed securities market and select the one with the lower cost.

Credit Enhancement

The way credit enhancement works is some third party is either paid a fee (or an insurance premium) or earns extra yield on a security in the structure to assume credit risk. There are two forms of credit enhancement—external and internal. *External credit enhancement* involves third-party guarantees such as insurance or a letter of credit. *Internal credit enhancement* includes overcollateralization, senior-subordinated structure, and reserves. Deals will often have more than one form of credit enhancement. The rating agencies specify the amount of credit enhancement to obtain a specific credit rating. The issuer decides on what mechanisms to use.

It is critical for the issuer to examine each form of credit enhancement prior to issuance to determine the enhancement mechanism or combination of credit enhancement mechanisms that is most cost effective. Over time, due to changing market conditions, the least expensive form of credit enhancement today may not be the least expensive in a subsequent securitization transaction.

As explained earlier, the reason why an issuer does not simply seek a triple-A rating for all the securities in the structure is that there is a cost to doing so. The issuer must examine the cost of credit enhancing a structure to obtain a triple-A rating versus the reduction in the yield (i.e., the increase in price) at which it can offer the securities due to a triple-A rating. In general, in deciding to improve the credit rating on some securities in a structure, the issuer will evaluate the trade-off associated with the cost of enhancement versus the reduction in yield required to sell the security.

Next we describe the various forms of credit enhancement mechanisms.

Third-Party Guarantees

Perhaps the easiest form of credit enhancement to understand is insurance or a letter of credit. In this form of credit enhancement, an insurance provider agrees, for a fee, to guarantee the performance of a certain amount of the collateral against defaults. If, for example, a loan in the collateral pool goes into default and the underlying collateral is repossessed and then sold at a loss resulting in a partial payoff of the outstanding loan balance, the bondholders would be in a position not to recover the principal outstanding for that loan. To provide protection to the bondholders, an insurance provider will pay the difference between the loan payoff amount and the amount due to the bondholders, thereby absorbing the loss.

The rating agencies decide on the creditworthiness of the insurance provider to determine the credit rating of the bonds. Perhaps the biggest perceived disadvantage to this form of credit enhancement is so-called event risk. Triple-A rated bondholders, for example, can enjoy triple-A status only as long as the enhancement provider retains its triple-A credit rating status. If the credit enhancement provider is downgraded (i.e., its credit rating is lowered by a rating agency), as we have seen in 2007 and 2008 in the case of mortgage-backed securities, the bonds guaranteed by the enhancement provider are typically downgraded as well.

Overcollateralization

One form of internal credit enhancement is *overcollateralization*. In this form of credit protection, credit enhancement is provided by issuing bonds with a par value that is less than the par value of the loans or receivables in the collateral pool. For example, if there are $200 million of loans in a collateral pool and the issuer wanted to use overcollateralization for credit enhancement to achieve, say, a triple-A credit rating for the bonds to be issued, the issuer would obtain from the rating agencies an indication as to how many bonds it could issue versus the $200 million par value of loans in the collateral pool to obtain the target credit rating. Depending on the characteristics of the loans and their perceived creditworthiness, the rating agencies might allow $190 million of par value of bonds to be issued.

This means that cash flows for $200 million par value of loans are available to bondholders but only $million par value of bonds need to be paid interest and principal. The cash flows from the extra $10 million of loans can either flow into a "reserve account," where the flows are reserved until such a time as they are needed to cover losses or the funds are used to retire bonds early. If a $3 million loss is realized by the collateral pool, there will still be enough cash flow from the other loans to ensure that the triple-A rated bonds receive their payments. After all the bonds have been retired, the remaining funds in the reserve account and any remaining collateral are distributed to the originator (assuming the originator has not sold its interest in the collateral).

The cost of such an arrangement is implicit in the price paid for $200 million par value of collateral versus the proceeds of issuing only $190 million par value of bonds.

Senior-Subordinate Structure

Another form of internal credit enhancement is the senior-subordinate structure mentioned earlier. This involves the subordination of some bond classes for the benefit of attaining a high investment-grade rating for other bond classes in the structure. Based on an analysis of the collateral, a rating agency will decide how many triple-A bonds can be issued, how many double-A bonds, and so forth down to nonrated bonds. A structure can have simply two bond classes, a senior bond class and a subordinate bond class. Or it can have several subordinate bond classes in addition to the senior bond class.

For example, suppose that a senior-subordinate structure for $200 million of collateral for the Farm Equipment Corporation is as follows:

Bond Class	Rating	Percent of Structure	Par Value
A	AAA	65%	$130 million
B	AA	20	40 million
C	BBB	10	20 million
D	Not rated	5	10 million

Bond class A is the senior bond class. The subordinate bond classes are B, C, and D.

The rule for recognizing losses is as follows. As a loss on the collateral is realized, that loss is first applied to bond class D. When bond class D has no balance, the next dollar of loss is applied to bond class C, and then bond class B. After all the subordinate bond classes are wiped out due to losses, the losses are realized by the senior bond class.

The cost of this form of credit enhancement is based on the proceeds for selling the bonds, which is, in turn, determined by the demand for the bonds. The yields that must be offered on the bond classes are affected by the yields demanded by investors. The lower the credit rating of the bond class (i.e., the more likely the bond class is to realize a loss), the more yield is demanded and the lower will be the proceeds received from the sale of the bonds for that bond class. The proceeds for the sale of all the bonds have to be compared to the cost of the collateral pool.

One of the perceived advantages of internal credit enhancements such as the overcollateralization and the senior-subordinate structure is the lack of event risk that accompanies external credit enhancement (i.e., a third-party guarantee). The assets in the collateral pool provide all credit support and investors are at risk only with regard to the performance of those assets.

Reserve Funds

Reserve funds come in two forms, cash reserve funds and excess spread. Cash reserve funds are straight deposits of cash generated from issuance proceeds. In this case, part of the underwriting profits from the deal are deposited into a fund and used to offset any losses. Excess spread accounts involve the allocation of excess spread into a separate reserve account after paying out the coupon to bondholders, the servicing fee, and all other expenses on a monthly basis.

Securitization and Funding Costs

We stated that one of the motivations for securitization is the potential reduction in funding costs. Here we will discuss this issue further. As explained in the appendix to Chapter 11, Modigliani and Miller (1958) addressed an important economic issue about firm valuation: Does the breaking up of the financial claims of a firm alter the firm's value? They concluded that in a world with no taxes and no market frictions, the capital structure of a firm is irrelevant. That is, the splitting of the claims between creditors and equity owners will not change the firm's value. Later, Modigliani and Miller (1961) corrected their position to take into account the economic benefits of the interest tax shield provided by debt financing. In the presence of taxes, the firm's optimal capital structure is one in which it is 100% debt financed.

Over the 50 years following the original Modigliani and Miller paper, several theories have been put proposed to explain why we observe less than

100% debt financing by firms. The leading explanation is that firms do not engage in 100% debt financing because of the costs of financial distress. A company that has difficulty making payments to its creditors is in financial distress. Not all companies in financial distress ultimately enter into the legal status of bankruptcy. However, extreme financial distress may very well lead to bankruptcy.[10] The relationship between financial distress and capital structure is straightforward: As more debt financing is employed, fixed legal obligations increase (interest and principal payments), and the ability of the firm to satisfy these increasing fixed payments decreases. Consequently, the probability of financial distress and then bankruptcy increases as more debt financing is employed. So, as the debt ratio increases, the present value of the costs of financial distress increase, reducing some of the value gained from the use of tax deductibility of interest expense.

The same type of question is being asked of asset securitization: Does asset securitization increase a firm's value? Effectively, asset securitization breaks up a company into a set of various financial assets or cash flow streams. Some of those various subsets of financial assets are isolated from the general creditors of the originator and benefit solely the investors in the asset-backed securities issued. In a world without asset securitization each investor has a risk in the unclassified, composite company as a whole. There are, of course, secured lenders whose claims are backed by specific collateral, but such collateral value is also liable to be eaten up by the generic business risks of the entity. Does the decomposition of the company's cash flow and granting specific debt holders a position of priority over other debt holders serve an economic purpose? If there is any advantage for this special category of debt holders with priority on the claims of designated financial assets, is it at the cost of the other investors in the firm, and, therefore, the aggregation of the risk-return profile of these different types of investors just the sum of a firm's value without securitization?

Structural Arbitrage Argument

Asset securitization rests on the essential principle that there is an arbitrage in breaking up a set of cash flows into another set of cash flows with different risk and return characteristics—risk-reward tranching—and, as a result, the sum of the parts is different from the whole. Participants in financial markets include investors with different needs to satisfy their investment objectives and hence different risk-reward appetites. Consequently, the carving up of different exposures to credit risk and interest rate risk through

---

[10] While bankruptcy is often a result of financial difficulties arising from problems in paying creditors, some bankruptcy filings are made prior to distress, when a large claim is made on assets (for example, class action liability suit).

structuring in a securitization makes economic sense. Essentially, the capital structure of the firm is itself evidence of the efficiency of the structural arbitrage—if there was no efficiency in creating corporate claims with different priorities, we would have a generic common claim on the assets of the corporation. If the pecking order of priorities in the capital structure itself has an economic value, securitization simply carries that idea further.

Arbitrage activity is the most apparent example of the alchemy of securitization. An arbitrage vehicle acquires financial assets and funds the acquisition by issuing asset-backed securities, thereby making an arbitrage profit in the process. While there is no reason for the weighted average cost of the funding to be lower than the weighted average return from the assets acquired, the market proves that there is an arbitrage involved in stratifying the risks in the asset portfolio.

The principle of structural arbitrage is one of the principles in securitization. While this has been disputed by theorists, it has been observed quite clearly in the market. Schwarz (2002, 2004) argues that securitization does reduce funding costs and therefore is not a zero-sum game. His arguments are based on the economic rationale for secured lending: Because secured lending by definition puts the secured lender at priority to the unsecured one, costs are lowered. Schwarz also argues that securitization allows a firm to enter the capital market directly and certainly capital market funding is more efficient than funding by financial intermediaries. While financial intermediaries play an important function in terms of credit creation and capital allocation, funding should come from where it eventually comes—households.

Increased Financial Leverage Argument

There was an increased focus on securitization following the bankruptcy of Enron in 2001 due to the role played by special purpose vehicles that it used. Moody's published its view in *Moody's Perspective 1987–2002: Securitization and its Effect on the Credit Strength of Companies*. In this paper, Moody's posed the question as to whether securitization provides access to low-cost funding and provided the following response:

> Not really. Many in the market believe that securitization offers "cheap funding" because the pricing on the debt issued in a securitization transaction is typically lower than pricing on the company's unsecured borrowings. However, the securitization debt is generally backed by high-quality assets, cash held in reserve funds, and may be overcollateralized. This means that the relatively lower pricing comes at the expense of providing credit enhancement to support the securitization debt.

While it may be true that credit enhancement using overcollateralization or some other mechanism is an inherent cost for the securitization transaction, what is important to understand is the nature of credit enhancement. In typical corporate funding, because equity investors are a firm's first-loss capital, equity is the credit enhancement for the lenders to a firm. The extent of such credit enhancement in typical corporate funds, that is the appropriate leverage ratios for the firm, is in general extraneously specified either by lending practices or in the case of regulated entities such as banks, regulatory requirements. This may force a firm to require much higher credit enhancements in the form of equity than warranted. In contrast, in a securitization, the required credit enhancement is linked directly to the expected losses in the portfolio and, therefore, the risks of the portfolio of financial assets.

If it is accepted as true that equity is a costlier funding source than debt funding, the higher leverage requirements attributable to traditional lending to firms in an industry or by regulatory capital requirements imposing higher weighted average funding costs on the firm. Greater financial leverage is permitted by employing securitization and, therefore, a lower funding cost or correspondingly higher returns on equity are attainable. This is achieved not from more efficient operations but from higher leverage.

A rating arbitrage argument has been offered as to why one would expect securitization to result in lower weighted average costs. *Rating arbitrage* occurs because securitization allows the corporate ratings of the originator to remain unaffected and the transaction to be rated solely on the strength of its assets and the credit enhancement mechanisms in the structure. The auto industry provides an excellent example. When the U.S. automakers General Motors and Ford were downgraded, they did not reduce their securitization volume. In fact, the evidence as cited earlier indicates the opposite. Volumes not only increased, but the asset-backed securities received a triple-A rating. Moreover, the existing asset-backed securities outstanding prior to May 2005 were in fact upgraded to the triple-A level, essentially because of an increase in credit support levels.

PROJECT FINANCING

Among its many applications, structured finance may be used by corporations to fund major projects so that the lenders look to the cash flow from the project being financed rather than corporation or corporations seeking funding. This financing technique is called *project financing* (or *project finance*) and uses the special purpose vehicle to accomplish its financing objectives. Both project financing and asset securitization use SPVs, yet project financing involves cash flows from operating assets, whereas asset securitization involves cash flows from financial assets, such as loans or as receivables.

As Finnerty (2007, p. 1) notes:

> Although project financings have certain common features, financing on a project basis necessarily involves tailoring the financing package to the circumstances of a particular project. Expert financial engineering is often as critical to the success of a large project as are the traditional forms of engineering.

Industries engaged in the production, processing, transportation, or use of energy have been particularly attracted to project financing techniques because of the needs of such companies for new capital sources. Enterprises located in countries privatizing state-owned companies have made extensive use of project financing. However, the same principles used to finance a major pipeline, copper mine, or a power plant can be used to finance a cannery, a hotel, a ship, or a processing plant.

In this section, we look at the basic features of project financing.

What Is Project Financing?

Although *project financing* has been used to describe all types of financing of projects, both with and without recourse, the term has evolved in recent years to have a more precise definition:

> A financing of a particular economic unit in which a lender is satisfied to look initially to the cash flows and earnings of that economic unit as the source of funds from which a loan will be repaid and to the assets of the economic unit as collateral for the loan.[11]

A key word in the definition is "initially." While a lender may be willing to look initially to the cash flows of a project as the source of funds for repayment of the loan, the lender must also feel comfortable that the loan will in fact be paid on a worst-case basis. This may involve undertakings or direct or indirect guarantees by third parties who are motivated in some way to provide such guarantees.

Project financing has great appeal when it does not have a substantial impact on the balance sheet or the creditworthiness of the sponsoring entity or entities. Boards of directors are receptive to proceeding with projects that can be very highly leveraged or financed entirely or substantially on their own merits.

---

[11] Nevitt and Fabozzi (2001, p. 1).

The initiating party in a project is its *promoter* or *sponsor*. A project may have one or several sponsors, all of whom are equity investors in the project. The motivation of construction companies acting as sponsors is to profit in some way from the construction or operation of the project. The motivation of operating companies for sponsoring a project may be simply to make a profit from selling the product produced by the project. In many instances the motivation for the project is to provide processing or distribution of a basic product of the sponsor or to ensure a source of supply vital to the sponsor's business.

The ultimate goal in project financing is to arrange a borrowing for a project that will benefit the sponsor but at the same time have absolutely no recourse to the sponsor and, therefore, no effect on its credit standing or balance sheet. One way this can be accomplished is by using the credit of a third party to support the transaction. Such a third party then becomes a sponsor. However, a project is rarely financed independently on its own merits without credit support from sponsors who are interested as third parties and who will benefit in some way from the project.

There is considerable room for disagreement between lenders and borrowers as to what constitutes a feasible project financing. Borrowers prefer their projects to be financed independently, off their balance sheets, with appropriate disclosures in financial reports indicating the exposure of the borrower to a project financing. Lenders, on the other hand, are not in the venture capital business and they are not equity risk takers. Lenders want to feel secure that they are going to be repaid either by the project, the sponsor, or an interested third party. Therein lies the challenge of most project financings.

The key to a successful project financing is structuring the financing of a project with as little recourse as possible to the sponsor, while at the same time providing sufficient credit support through guarantees or undertakings of a sponsor or third party so that lenders will be satisfied with the credit risk.

For lenders and investors, the essence of project finance is the analysis of project risks, including construction risk, operating risk, market risk (applying to both inputs and outputs of a project), regulatory risk, insurance risk, and currency risk. These risks often are allocated contractually to parties best able to manage them through construction guarantees, power purchase agreements and other types of output contracts, fuel and raw material supply agreements, transportation contracts, indemnifications, insurance policies, and other contractual agreements. But with many projects today in virtually all sectors, sponsors, lenders, and bank investors are exposed to significant market risk. Though recourse to the sponsors is usually limited, sponsors often provide credit support to the project through guarantees or other contractual undertakings. For example, an industrial sponsor of a cogeneration project may contract to buy steam from a project and another sponsor may contract to sell power to it. Also, the sponsors' economic interests in the success of a project are strong elements in the project's creditworthiness.

Reasons for Jointly Owned or Sponsored Projects

There has been an increasing trend towards jointly owned or controlled projects. Although most corporations prefer sole ownership and control of a major project, particularly projects involving vital supplies and distribution channels, there are factors that encourage the formation of jointly owned or controlled projects that consist of partners with mutual goals, talents, and resources. These factors include:[12]

- The undertaking is beyond a single corporation's financial and/or managerial resources.
- The partners have complementary skills or economic goals.
- The economics of a large project lower the cost of the product or service substantially over the possible cost of a smaller project if the partners proceeded individually.
- The risks of the projects are shared.
- One or more of the partners can use the tax benefits (i.e., depreciation and any tax credit).
- Greater debt leverage can be obtained.

The joint sponsors will select the legal form of the SPV (corporation, partner, limited partnership, limited liability company, contractual joint venture, or trust) that will be satisfy their tax and legal objectives.

Credit Exposures in a Project Financing

To place a project financing into perspective, it is helpful to review the different credit exposures that occur at different times in the course of a typical project financing.

Risk Phases

Project financing risks can be divided into three time frames in which the elements of credit exposure assume different characteristics:

- Engineering and construction phase.

---

[12] Nevitt and Fabozzi (2001, p. 265).

- Start-up phase.
- Operations according to planned specifications.

Different guarantees and undertakings of different partners may be used in each time frame to provide the credit support necessary for structuring a project financing.

Engineering and Construction Phase

Projects generally begin with a long period of planning and engineering. Equipment is ordered, construction contracts are negotiated, and actual construction begins. After commencement of construction, the amount at risk begins to increase sharply as funds are advanced to purchase material, labor, and equipment. Interest charges on loans to finance construction also begin to accumulate.

Start-Up Phase

Project lenders do not regard a project as completed on conclusion of the construction of the facility. They are concerned that the plant or facility will work at the costs and to the specifications that were planned when arranging the financing. Failure to produce the product or service in the amounts and at the costs originally planned means that the projections and the feasibility study are incorrect and that there may be insufficient cash to service debt and pay expenses.

Project lenders regard a project as acceptable only after the plant or facility has been in operation for a sufficient period of time to ensure that it will in fact produce the product or service at the price, in the amounts, and to the standards assumed in the financial plan that formed the basis for the financing. This startup risk period may run from a few months to several years.

Operations According to Specification

Once the parties are satisfied that the plant is running to specification, the final operating phase begins. During this phase, the project begins to function as a regular operating company. If correct financial planning was done, revenues from the sale of the product produced or service performed should be sufficient to service debt—interest and principal—pay operating costs, and provide a return to sponsors and investors.

Different Lenders for Different Risk Periods

Some projects are financed from beginning to end with a single lender or single group of lenders. However, most large projects employ different lenders or groups of lenders during different risk phases. This is because of the different risks involved as the project facility progresses through construction to operation, and the different ability of lenders to cope with and accept such risks.

Some lenders like to lend for longer terms and some prefer short-term lending. Some lenders specialize in construction lending and are equipped to monitor engineering and construction of a project, some are not. Some lenders will accept and rely on guarantees of different sponsors during the construction, start-up, or operation phases, and some will not. Some lenders will accept the credit risk of a turnkey operating project, but are not interested in the high-risk lending during construction and start-up.

Interest rates will also vary during the different risk phases of project financing and with different credit support from sponsors during those time periods.

Short-term construction lenders are very concerned about the availability of long-term "take-out" financing by other lenders upon completion of the construction or start-up phase. Construction lenders live in fear of providing their own unplanned take out financing. Consequently, from the standpoint of the construction lender, take out financing should be in place at the outset of construction financing.

Key Elements of a Successful Project Financing

There are several elements that both sponsors and lenders to a project financing should review in order to increase the likelihood that a project financing will be successful. The key ones follow:[13]

- A satisfactory feasibility study and financial plan has been prepared with realistic assumptions regarding future inflation rates and interest rates.
- The cost of product or raw materials to be used by the project is assured.
- A supply of energy at reasonable cost has been assured.
- A market exists for the product, commodity, or service to be produced.
- Transportation is available at a reasonable cost to move the product to the market.
- Adequate communications are available.
- Building materials are available at the costs contemplated.

---

[13] Nevitt and Fabozzi (2001, p. 7).

- The contractor is experienced and reliable.
- The operator is experienced and reliable.
- Management personnel are experienced and reliable.
- Untested technology is not involved.
- The contractual agreement among joint venture partners, if any, is satisfactory.
- The key sponsors have made an adequate equity contribution.
- Satisfactory appraisals of resources and assets have been obtained.
- Adequate insurance coverage has been arranged.
- The risk of cost overruns have been addressed.
- The risk of delay has been considered.
- The project will have an adequate return for the equity investor.
- Environmental risks are manageable.

When the project involves a sovereign entity, the following critical elements are important to consider to ensure the success of a project:

- A stable and friendly political environment exists; licences and permits are available; contracts can be enforced; and legal remedies exist.
- There is no risk of expropriation.
- Country risk is satisfactory.
- Sovereign risk is satisfactory.
- Currency is available and foreign exchange risks have been addressed.
- Protection has been arranged from criminal activities such as kidnaping and extortion.
- A satisfactory commercial legal system protects property and contractual rights.

Credit Impact Objective

While the sponsor or sponsors of a project financing ideally would prefer that the project financing be a nonrecourse borrowing that does not in any way affect its credit standing or balance sheet, many project financings are aimed at achieving some other particular credit impact objective, such as any one or several of the following:[14]

- To avoid being shown as debt on the face of the balance sheet so as not to affect financial ratios.
- To avoid being shown in a particular footnote to the balance sheet.
- To avoid being within the scope of restrictive covenants in an indenture or loan agreement that precludes direct debt financing or leases for the project.

[14] Nevitt and Fabozzi (2001, p. 4).

- To avoid being considered as a cash obligation that would dilute interest coverage ratios and affect the sponsor's credit standing with the rating services.
- To limit direct liability to a certain period of time such as during construction and/or the start-up period, so as to avoid a liability for the remaining life of the project.
- To keep the project off the balance sheet during construction or until the project generates revenues.

Any one or a combination of these objectives may be sufficient reason for a borrower to seek the structure of a project financing.

Liability for project debt for a limited time period may be acceptable in situations in which liability for such debt is unacceptable for the life of the project. Where a sponsor cannot initially arrange long-term nonrecourse debt for a project that will not impact its balance sheet, the project may still be feasible if the sponsor is willing to assume the credit risk during the construction and start-up phase, provided lenders are willing to shift the credit risk to the project after the project facility is completed and operating. Under such an arrangement, most of the objectives of an off-balance-sheet project financing and limited credit impact can be achieved after the initial risk period of construction and start-up. In some instances, the lenders may be willing to rely on revenue produced by unconditional take-or-pay contracts from users of the product or services to be provided by the project to repay debt.[15] In other instances, the condition of the market for the product or service may be such that sufficient revenues are assured after completion of construction and start-up so as to convince lenders to rely on such revenues for repayment of their debts.

Other Benefits of a Project Financing

There are often other side benefits resulting from segregating a financing as a project financing that may have a bearing on the motives of the company seeking such a structure. These benefits include:[16]

---

[15] A *take-or-pay contract* is a long-term contract to make periodic payments over the life of the contract in certain minimum amounts as payments for a service or a product. The payments are in an amount sufficient to service the debt needed to finance the project and to pay the project's operating expenses. The obligation to make minimum payments is unconditional and must be paid whether or not the service or product is actually furnished or delivered. In contrast, a *take-and-pay contract* is a contact in which payment is contingent upon delivery and the obligation to pay is not unconditional.

[16] Nevitt and Fabozzi (2001, p. 5).

- Credit sources may be available to the project that would not be available to the sponsor.
- Guarantees may be available to the project that would not be available to the sponsor.
- A project financing may enjoy better credit terms and interest costs in situations in which a sponsor's credit is weak.
- Higher leverage of debt to equity may be achieved.
- Legal requirements applicable to certain investing institutions may be met by the project but not by the sponsor.
- Regulatory problems affecting the sponsor may be avoided.
- For regulatory purposes, costs may be clearly segregated as a result of a project financing.
- Construction financing costs may not be reflected in the sponsor's financial statements until such time as the project begins producing revenue.

In some instances, any one of the reasons stated above may be the primary motivation for structuring a new operation as a project financing.

Disincentives to Project Financing

Project financings are complex. The documentation tends to be complicated, and the cost of borrowing funds may be higher than with conventional financing. If the undertakings of a number of parties are necessary to structure the project financing, or if a joint venture is involved, the negotiation of the original financing agreements and operating agreements will require patience, forbearing, and understanding. Decision-making in partnerships and joint ventures is never easy, since the friendliest of partners may have diverse interests, problems, and objectives. However, the rewards and advantages of a project financing will often justify the special problems that may arise in structuring and operating the project.

SUMMARY

While there are many interpretations as to the meaning of financial engineering, the use by financial managers, referred to as corporate financial engineers, involves designing innovative securities that offer a risk-return profile that is superior to risk-return profiles currently available in the marketplace. As a result, this reduces the issuer's funding costs. In the creation of such securities, derivatives are typically used in combination with typical securities.

Structured notes are bonds with embedded options that have much more complicated provisions for interest rate payable, redemption amount, and timing of principal repayment that have the risk and return substantially different from those offered by plain-vanilla bond structures. Typically derivative instruments are used in creating structured notes so that the issuer can hedge the risk associated with the issue.

Investor motivation for purchasing structured notes includes the potential for enhancing yield, acquiring a view on the bond market, obtaining exposure to alternative asset classes, acquiring exposure to a particular market but not a particular aspect of it, and controlling risks. Corporations are willing to issue structured notes in order to reduce their all-in-cost of funds. The main steps in creating a structured note are the conceptual stage, the identification process, and the structuring or construction stage.

Asset securitization is the process of creating securities backed by a pool of financial assets. It provides an alternative to the issuance of a corporate bond. The securities issued in a securitization transaction are backed by loans, accounts receivable, or notes receivable and are referred to as asset-backed securities. It is the collateral combined with any third-party guarantees that will determine the ability of an issuer to pay the obligation to the holders of the asset-backed securities. To obtain a desired credit rating sought by a corporation by using a securitization financing, both the cash flow of a financial asset and a third-party credit support may be needed.

The four principal reasons why a corporation may elect to issue asset-backed securities rather than a corporate bond are (1) potential for lower funding cost; (2) diversification of funding sources; (3) acceleration of earnings for financial reporting purposes; and (4) potential for reducing capital requirements for regulated entities.

The key to a corporation issuing asset-backed securities with a higher credit rating than the corporation's own credit rating via a securitization is the special-purpose vehicle. Its role is critical because it is the special-purpose vehicle that legally separates the assets used as collateral from the corporation that is seeking financing.

There are two forms of credit enhancement that can be used in a structured finance transaction. External credit enhancement involves third-party guarantees such as insurance or a letter of credit. Internal credit enhancement includes overcollateralization, senior-subordinated structures, and reserves.

Project financing involves the financing of a particular economic unit whereby the lenders to the project are initially satisfied to rely on the cash flows and earnings of that economic unit as the source of funds for paying off their loans and to the assets of the economic unit as collateral for the loan. While both project financing and asset securitization utilize SPVs to accomplish their financing objectives, project financings involve cash flows from operating assets, whereas most asset securitizations involve cash flows from financial assets, such as loans or as receivables.

REFERENCES

Fabozzi, F. J., Davis, H., and Choudhry, M. (2007). *Introduction to Structured Finance*. Hoboken, NJ: John Wiley & Sons.

Finnerty, J. D. (1988). Financial engineering in corporate finance: An overview. *Financial Management* 17, no. 4: 14–33.

Finnerty, J. D. (2007). *Project Financing: Asset-Based Financial Engineering*. Hoboken, NJ: John Wiley & Sons.

Finnerty, J. D. (2008). Securities innovation. In F. J. Fabozzi (ed.), *The Handbook of Finance*, vol. I (pp. 61–92). Hoboken, NJ: John Wiley & Sons.

Finnerty, J. D., and Emery, D. R. (2002). Corporate securities innovation: An update. *Journal of Applied Finance* 12, no. 1 (Spring/Summer): 21–47.

Modigliani, F. and Miller, M. (1958). The cost of capital, corporation finance, and the theory of investment. *American Economic Review* 48, no. 3 (1958): 261–297.

Modigliani, F. and Miller, M. (1963). Corporate income taxes and the cost of capital: A correction. *American Economic Review* 53, no. 3: 433–443.

Nevitt, P. K. and Fabozzi, F. J. (2001). *Project Financing*, 7th ed. London: Euromoney.

Peng, S. Y. and Dattatreya, R. (1995). *The Structured Note Market*. Chicago: Probus Publishing.

Schwarcz, S. L. (2003). Enron and the use and abuse of special purpose entities in corporate structures. *University of Cincinnati Law Review* 40: 1309.

Schwarcz, S. L. (2004). Securitization post-Enron. *Cardozo Law Review* (Symposium Issue on Threats to Asset-Based Finance) 25 (May): 1539–1575.

Telpner, J. S. (2004). A survey of structured notes. *Journal of Structured and Project Finance* 9, no. 4 (Winter): 6–19.

CHAPTER 13

Capital Budgeting: Process and Cash Flow Estimation

Companies continually invest funds in assets, and these assets produce income and cash flows that the company may then either reinvest in more assets or pay to the owners. These assets represent the company's capital. *Capital* is the company's total assets, including both tangible and intangible assets. These assets include physical assets (such as land, buildings, equipment, and machinery), as well as assets that represent property rights, such as accounts receivable, securities, patents, and copyrights. When we refer to *capital investment*, we are referring to the company's investment in its assets, where the term "capital" also has come to mean the funds used to finance the company's assets and, in some contexts, refers to the sum of equity and interest-bearing debt.

Capital budgeting decisions involve the long-term commitment of a company's scarce resources in capital investments. These decisions play a prominent role in determining whether a company will be successful. The commitment of funds to a particular capital project can be enormous and may be irreversible. Whereas some capital budgeting decisions are routine decisions that do not change the course or risk of a company, there are strategic capital budgeting decisions that will either have an impact on the company's future market position in its current product lines or permit it to expand into a new product line in the future

The company's capital investment decision may be comprised of a number of distinct decisions, each referred to as a *project*. A capital project is a set of assets that are contingent on one another and are considered together. For example, suppose a company is considering the production of a new product. This capital project requires the company to acquire land, build facilities, and purchase production equipment. And this project may also require the company to increase its investment in its working capital—inventory, cash, or accounts receivable. *Working capital* is the collection of assets needed for day-to-day operations that support a company's long-term investments.

There are several techniques that are used in practice to evaluate capital budgeting proposals. These include the payback and discounted payback techniques, net present value technique, profitability index technique, internal rate of return technique, and modified internal rate of return technique. While used in practice, some of these techniques are limited in their ability to help managers identify proposed capital projects that are profitable and are not necessarily consistent with maximization of shareholder wealth. Moreover, where capital rationing exists, some techniques give conflicting rankings of the relative attractiveness of capital projects.

Evaluating whether a company should invest in a capital project requires an analysis of whether the project adds value to the company. Essential in the analysis of the attractiveness of a capital project is an assessment of the project's risk. The analysis of the risk of a project is challenging because most capital projects are unique and a project's contribution to the company's risk is difficult to quantify. There are several tools available to help incorporate a project's risk into the decision.

This chapter and the next cover the capital budgeting decision. In this chapter, we cover two topics. First, we explain the capital budgeting budgeting process and the classification of investment project. Second, we show to estimate the expected change to a company's future cash flow as a result of an capital investment decision. As will become apparent, estimating cash flow is an imprecise art at best. In the next chapter, we look at the techniques used to evaluate capital budgeting projects.

INVESTMENT DECISIONS AND OWNERS' WEALTH MAXIMIZATION

Managers must evaluate a number of factors in making investment decisions. Not only does the financial manager need to estimate how much the company's future cash flows will change if it invests in a project, but the manager must also evaluate the uncertainty associated with these future cash flows.

The value of the company today is the present value of all its future cash flows. But we need to understand better where these future cash flows come from. They come from assets that are already in place, which are the assets accumulated as a result of all past investment decisions, and future investment opportunities.

The value of a company is therefore the present value of the company's future cash flows, where these future cash flows include the cash flows from all assets in place and the cash flows from future investment opportunities. These future cash flows are discounted at a rate that represents investors' assessments of the uncertainty that these cash flows will flow in the amounts and when expected. As you can see, we need to evaluate the risk of these future cash flows in order to understand the risk of any investment opportunity on the value of the company.

Cash flow risk comes from two basic sources:

- *Sales risk*. The degree of uncertainty related to the number of units that will be sold and the price of the good or service.
- *Operating risk*. The degree of uncertainty concerning operating cash flows that arises from the particular mix of fixed and variable operating costs.

Sales risk is related to the economy and the market in which the company's goods and services are sold. Operating risk, for the most part, is determined by the product or service that the company provides and is related to the sensitivity of operating cash flows to changes in sales. We refer to the combination of these two risks as *business risk*.

A project's business risk is reflected in the discount rate, which is the rate of return required to compensate the suppliers of capital (bondholders and owners) for the amount of risk they bear. From the perspective of investors, the discount rate is the *required rate of return* (RRR). From the company's perspective, the discount rate is the *cost of capital*—what it costs the company to raise a dollar of new capital.

For example, suppose a company invests in a new project, Project X. How does the investment affect the company's value?

- If Project X generates cash flows that just compensate the suppliers of capital for the risk they bear on this project (that is, it earns the cost of capital), the value of the company does not change.
- If Project X generates cash flows greater than needed to compensate them for the risk they take on, it earns more than the cost of capital, increasing the value of the company.
- If Project X generates cash flows *less* than needed, it earns less than the cost of capital, decreasing the value of the company.

How do we know whether the cash flows are more than or less than needed to compensate for the risk that they will indeed need? If we discount all the cash flows at the cost of capital, we can assess how this project affects the present value of the company. If the expected change in the value of the company from an investment is:

- Positive, the project returns more than the cost of capital.
- Negative, the project returns less than the cost of capital.

- Zero, the project returns the cost of capital.

Capital budgeting is the process of identifying and selecting investments in long-lived assets; that is, selecting assets expected to produce benefits over more than one year.

CAPITAL BUDGETING PROCESS

Because a company must continually evaluate possible investments, capital budgeting is an ongoing process. However, before a company begins thinking about capital budgeting, it must first determine its corporate strategy—its broad set of objectives for future investment. For example, the Walt Disney Company has stated that its objective is to "be one of the world's leading producers and providers of entertainment and information, using its portfolio of brands to differentiate its content, services and consumer products."

How does a company achieve its corporate strategy? By making investments in long-lived assets that maximize owners' wealth. Selecting these projects is what capital budgeting is all about.

Stages in the Capital Budgeting Process

Though every company has its own set of procedures and processes for capital budgeting, we can generalize the process as consisting of five stages.

Stage 1. Investment screening and selection.
Stage 2. Capital budgeting proposal.
Stage 3. Budgeting approval and authorization.
Stage 4. Project tracking.
Stage 5. Post-completion audit.

We discuss each stage in this section.

Stage 1. Investment Screening and Selection

Projects consistent with the corporate strategy are identified by production, marketing, and research and development management of the company. Once identified, projects are evaluated and screened by estimating how they affect the future cash flows of the company and, hence, the value of the company.

Because companies often face a large number of investment opportunities, many companies institute some form of initial screening, identifying those projects that merit more intense research and analysis. The initial screening may take the form of using a simple criterion, such as project payback, to each project.

Stage 2. Capital Budget Proposal

A capital budget is proposed for the projects surviving the screening and selection process. The budget lists the recommended projects and the dollar amount of investment needed for each. This proposal may start as an estimate of expected revenues and costs, but as the project analysis is refined, data from marketing, purchasing, engineering, accounting, and finance functions are put together.

Stage 3. Budgeting Approval and Authorization

Projects included in the capital budget are authorized, allowing further fact gathering and analysis, and approved, allowing expenditures for the projects. In some companies, the projects are authorized and approved at the same time. In others, a project must first be authorized, requiring more research before it can be formally approved. Formal authorization and approval procedures are typically used on larger expenditures; smaller expenditures are at the discretion of management.

No matter the specific procedure that a company adopts, the approval and authorization of capital projects must be consistent with the company's strategic plan. The feedback from the capital budgeting process to the strategic plan—in terms of the availability and feasibility of projects consistent with the strategic plan—is important.[1]

In many organizations, managers of the different divisions compete for budgeting approval and authorization. This internal competition, when combined with profit-sharing, provides for an efficient allocation of the company's scarce resources.[2] Hence, by having divisions, products, or other forms of segmentation complete, the company insures an efficient allocation of capital funds through the budget approval process.

Stage 4. Project Tracking

After a project is approved, work on it begins. The manager reports periodically on its expenditures, as well as on any revenues associated with it. This is referred to as *project tracking*, the communication link between the decision makers and the operating management of the company. For example,

---

[1] Dayananda, et al. (2002).
[2] Marino and Zabojnik (2004).

tracking can identify cost over-runs and uncover the need for more marketing research.

Stage 5. Postcompletion Audit

No matter the number of stages in a company's capital budgeting process, most companies include some form of *postcompletion audit* that involves a comparison of the actual cash from operations of the project with the estimated cash flow used to justify the project.[3] There are two reasons why the postcompletion audit is beneficial. First, many companies find that the knowledge that a postcompletion audit will be undertaken causes project proposers to be more careful before endorsing a project. Second, it will aid senior management identify proposers who are consistently optimistic or pessimistic with respect to cash flow estimates. Senior management is then be in a better position to evaluate the bias that may be expected when a particular individual or group proposes a project.

Thorough postcompletion audits are typically performed on selected projects, usually the largest projects in a given year's budget for the company or for each division. For control purposes, this function should not be performed by the group that proposed the project. Instead, a centralized group such as the internal audit department should be responsible for making the review and rendering a report to senior management.

A focus of the postcompletion audit is on the amount and timing of the project cash flows. In a study of forecasting errors in capital budgeting projects, Soares, Coutinho, and Martins (2007) found that the source of forecast errors were predominantly errors in forecasting sales, rather then operating costs.

CLASSIFYING INVESTMENT PROJECTS

There are different ways managers classify capital investment projects. One way of classifying projects is by project life, whether short-term or long-term. We do this because in the case of long-term projects, the time value of money plays an important role in long-term projects. Another ways of classifying projects is by their risk. The riskier the project's future cash flows, the greater the role of the cost of capital in decision-making. Still another way of classifying projects is by their dependence on other projects. The relationship between a project's cash flows and the cash flows of some other project of the company must be incorporated explicitly into the analysis since we want to analyze how a project affects the total cash flows of the company.

---

[3] See Pierce and Tsay (1992) and Neale (1995).

Classification According to Their Economic Life

An investment generally provides benefits over a limited period of time, referred to as its economic life. The *economic life* or *useful life* of an asset is determined by:

- Physical deterioration.
- Obsolescence.
- The degree of competition in the market for a product.

The economic life is an estimate of the length of time that the asset will provide benefits to the company. After its useful life, the revenues generated by the asset tend to decline rapidly and its expenses tend to increase.

Typically, an investment requires an immediate expenditure and provides benefits in the form of cash flows received in the future. If benefits are received only within the current period—within one year of making the investment—we refer to the investment as a *short-term investment*. If these benefits are received beyond the current period, we refer to the investment as a *long-term investment* and refer to the expenditure as a *capital expenditure*. An investment project may comprise one or more capital expenditures. For example, a new product may require investment in production equipment, a building, and transportation equipment.

Short-term investment decisions involve, primarily, investments in current assets: cash, marketable securities, accounts receivable, and inventory. The objective of investing in short-term assets is the same as long-term assets: maximizing owners' wealth. Nevertheless, we consider them separately for two practical reasons:

1. Decisions about long-term assets are based on projections of cash flows far into the future and require us to consider the time value of money.
2. Long-term assets do not figure into the daily operating needs of the company.

Decisions regarding short-term investments, or current assets, are concerned with day-to-day operations. A company needs some level of current assets to act as a cushion in case of unusually poor operating periods, when cash flows from operations are less than expected.

Classification According to Their Risk

Suppose you are faced with two investments, A and B, each promising a $10 million cash inflow 10 years from today. If A is riskier than B, what are they worth to you today? If you are risk averse, you would consider A less valuable than B because the chance of getting the $10 million in 10 years is less for A than for B. Therefore, valuing a project requires considering the risk associated with its future cash flows.

The investment's risk and return can be classified according to the nature of the project represented by the investment:

- *Replacement projects.* Investments in the replacement of existing equipment or facilities.
- *Expansion projects.* Investments in projects that broaden existing product lines and existing markets.
- *New products and markets.* Projects that involve introducing a new product or entering into a new market.
- *Mandated projects.* Projects required by government laws or agency rules.

Replacement projects include the maintenance of existing assets to continue the current level of operating activity. Projects that reduce costs, such as replacing old equipment or improving the efficiency, are also considered replacement projects. Evaluating replacement projects requires us to compare the value of the company with the replacement asset to the value of the company without that same replacement asset. What we are really doing in this comparison is looking at *opportunity costs*: what cash flows would have been if the company had stayed with the old asset.

There is little risk in the cash flows from replacement projects. The company is simply replacing equipment or buildings already operating and producing cash flows. And the company typically has experience in managing similar new equipment.

Expansion projects, which are intended to enlarge a company's established product or market, also involve little risk. However, investment projects that pertain to introducing new products or entering into new markets are riskier because the company has little or no management experience in the new product or market.

A company is forced or coerced into its mandated projects. These are government-mandated projects typically found in "heavy" industries, such as utilities, transportation, and chemicals, all industries requiring a large portion of their assets in production activities. Government agencies, such as the Occupational Health and Safety Agency (OSHA) or the Environmental Protection Agency (EPA), may impose requirements that companies install specific equipment or alter their activities (such as how they dispose of waste).

We can further classify mandated projects into two types: contingent and retroactive. Suppose, as a steel manufacturer, we are required by law to include pollution control devices on all smoke stacks. If we are considering a new plant, this mandated equipment is really part of our new plant investment decision—the investment in pollution control equipment is contingent on our building the new plant. On the other hand, if a company is required by law to place pollution control devices on existing smoke stacks, the law is retroactive. A company does not have a choice. The company must invest in the equipment whether it increases the value of the company or not. In this case, the company has three choices: (1) select from among possible equipment that satisfies the mandate; (2) weigh the decision whether to halt production in the offending plant; (3) if available, consider the purchase of pollution emissions allowances.[4]

Classification According to Their Dependence on Other Projects

In addition to considering the future cash flows generated by a project, a company must consider how the project affects the assets already in place—the results of previous project decisions—as well as other projects that may be undertaken. Projects can be classified according to the degree of dependence with other projects: independent projects, mutually exclusive projects, contingent projects, and complementary projects.

An *independent project* is one whose cash flows are not related to the cash flows of any other project. Therefore, accepting or rejecting an independent project does not affect the acceptance or rejection of other projects. Projects are *mutually exclusive* if the acceptance of one precludes the acceptance of other projects. For example, suppose a manufacturer is considering whether to replace its production facilities with more modern equipment. The company may solicit bids among the different manufacturers of this equipment. The decision consists of comparing two choices, either keeping its existing production facilities or replacing the facilities with the modern equipment of one manufacturer. Because the company cannot use more than one production facility, it must evaluate each bid and choose the most attractive one. The alternative production facilities are mutually exclusive projects: the company can accept only one bid.

Contingent projects are dependent on the acceptance of another project. Suppose a greeting card company develops a new character, Pippy, and is considering starting a line of Pippy cards. If Pippy catches on, the company will consider producing a line of Pippy t-shirts—but *only* if the Pippy character becomes popular. The t-shirt project is a contingent project.

Another form of dependence is found in *complementary projects*, where the investment in one enhances the cash flows of one or more other projects. Consider a manufacturer of personal computer equipment and software. If

[4] See Insley (2003).

it develops new software that enhances the abilities of a computer mouse, the introduction of this new software may enhance its mouse sales as well.

ESTIMATING CASH FLOWS OF CAPITAL BUDGETING PROJECTS

Incremental Cash Flows

A company invests only to make its owners "better off," meaning increasing the value of their ownership interest. A company will have cash flows in the future from its past investment decisions. When it invests in new assets, it expects the future cash flows to be greater than without this new investment. Otherwise it doesn't make sense to make this investment. The difference between the cash flows of the company with the investment project and the cash flows of the company without the investment project—both over the same period of time—is referred to as the *project's incremental cash flows*.

We have to look at how it will change the future cash flows of the company to evaluate an investment. How much does the value of the company changes as a result of the investment? The change in a company's value as a result of a new investment is the difference between its benefits and its costs:

Project's change in the value of the company
= Project's benefits − Project's costs

A more useful way of evaluating the change in the value of the company is to breakdown the project's cash flows into two components:

1. The present value of the cash flows from the project's operating activities (revenues and operating expenses), referred to as the *project's operating cash flows* (OCF).
2. The present value of the *investment cash flows*, which are the expenditures needed to acquire the project's assets and any cash flows from disposing the project's assets.

This can be expressed as

$$\begin{array}{c}\text{Change in the value}\\ \text{of the company}\end{array} = \begin{array}{c}\text{Present value of the change}\\ \text{in operating cash flows}\\ \text{provided by the project}\end{array} + \begin{array}{c}\text{Present value of}\\ \text{investment}\\ \text{cash flows}\end{array}$$

The present value of a project's operating cash flows is typically positive (indicating predominantly cash inflows) and the present value of the investment cash flows is typically negative (indicating predominantly cash outflows).

Investment Cash Flows

Investment cash flows take into account asset acquisition costs and disposal costs.

Asset Acquisition

The analysis of an investment must consider all the cash flows associated with acquiring and disposing of assets. In any project, there are a number of different types of investment cash flows to consider, including the cost of acquisition (e.g., cost of the asset, set-up expenditures, including shipping and installation, and any tax credit). The tax credit may be an investment tax credit or a special credit, such as a credit for a pollution control device-depending on the prevailing tax law.

Suppose the company buys equipment that costs $100 million and it costs $1 million to install it. If the company is eligible for a 7% tax credit on this equipment (that is, 7% of the total cost of buying and installing the equipment) the change in the company's cash flow from acquiring the asset is $93.93 million:

Cash outflow from acquiring assets, in millions
= $100 + $1 − 0.07 ($101)
= $93.93 million

What about expenditures made in the past for assets or research that would be used in the project we're evaluating? Suppose the company spent $1 million over the past three years developing a new type of toothpaste. Should the company consider this $1 million spent on research and development when deciding whether to produce this new project we are considering? No, these expenses have already been made and do not affect how the new product changes the future cash flows of the company. This $1 million is a *sunk cost* and it is not considered in the analysis of the new project. Whether or not the company goes ahead with this new product, this $1 million has been spent. A sunk cost is any cost that has already been incurred that does not affect future cash flows of the company.

Consider another example. Suppose the company owns a building that is currently empty. If the company suddenly has an opportunity to use it for the production of a new product. Is the cost of the building relevant to the new product decision? The cost of the building itself is a sunk cost because it was an expenditure made as part of some previous investment decision. The cost of the building does not affect the decision to go ahead with the new product.

Suppose the company was using the building in some way producing cash (say, renting it or selling it) and the new project is going to take over the entire building. The cash flows given up represent opportunity costs that must be included in the analysis of the new project. In the case of a company that could rent the building, these forgone cash flows are not asset acquisition cash flows, but rather must be considered part of the project's future operating cash flows.

Further, if the company incur costs in renovating the building to manufacture the new product, the renovation costs are relevant and should be included in our asset acquisition cash flows.

Asset Disposition

At the end of the useful life of an asset, the company may be able to sell the asset or may have to pay another party to haul it away or close it down. If the company is making a decision that involves replacing an existing asset, the cash flow from disposing of the old asset must be considered because it is a cash flow relevant to the acquisition of the new asset.

If the company disposes of an asset, whether at the end of its useful life or when it is replaced, two types of cash flows must be considered: what the company expects to receive or expects to pay in disposing of the asset and any tax consequences resulting from the disposal. The proceeds are what the company expects to sell the asset for if sold. If the company must pay for the disposal of the asset, this cost is a cash outflow.

$$\begin{array}{c} \text{Cash flow from} \\ \text{disposing assets} \end{array} = \begin{array}{c} \text{Proceeds or payment} \\ \text{from disposing assets} \end{array} - \begin{array}{c} \text{Taxes from} \\ \text{disposing assets} \end{array}$$

Consider the investment in a gas station. The current owner wants to sell the station to another gas station proprietor. But if a buyer cannot be found and the station is abandoned, the current owner may be required to remove the underground gasoline storage tanks to prevent environmental damage. Thus, a cost is incurred at the end of the asset's life.

The tax consequences are a bit more complicated. Taxes depend on (1) the expected sales price; (2) the carrying value of the asset for tax purposes (called the *tax basis*) at the time of disposition; and (3) the tax rate at the time of disposal.

If a company sells the asset for more than its tax basis, but less than its original cost, the difference between the sales price and the tax basis is a gain, taxable at ordinary tax rates. If a company sells the asset for more than its original cost, then the gain is broken into two parts: the capital gain (the difference between the sales price and the original cost) and recapture of depreciation (the difference between the original cost and the tax basis).

The *capital gain* is the benefit from the appreciation in the value of the asset and may be taxed at special rates, depending on the tax law at the time of sale. The *recapture of depreciation* represents the amount by which the company has overdepreciated the asset during its life. This means that more depreciation has been deducted from income (hence reducing taxes) than necessary to reflect the actual depreciation of the asset. The recapture portion is taxed at the ordinary tax rates, because this excess depreciation taken all these years has reduced taxable income.

If a company sells an asset for less than its tax basis, the result is a *capital loss*. In this case, the asset's value has decreased by more than the amount taken for depreciation for tax purposes. A capital loss is given special tax treatment:

- If there are capital gains in the same tax year as the capital loss, the gains and losses are combined, so that the capital loss reduces the taxes paid on capital gains.
- If there are not sufficient capital gains to offset against the capital loss, the remaining capital loss is used to reduce ordinary taxable income.

The benefit from a loss on the sale of an asset is the amount by which taxes are reduced. The reduction in taxable income is referred to as a *tax shield* because the loss shields some income from taxation. For example, if a company has a loss of $1,000 on the sale of an asset and has a tax rate of 40%, this means that its taxable income is $1,000 less and its tax liability is $400 less than it would have been without the sale of the asset.

Suppose a company is evaluating an asset that costs $10,000 that it expects to sell in five years. Suppose further that the tax basis of the asset for tax purposes will be $3,000 after five years and that the company's tax rate is 40%. What are the expected cash flows from disposing this asset?

If the company expects to sell the asset for $8,000 in five years, $10,000 − $3,000 = $7,000 of the asset's cost will be depreciated; yet the asset lost only $10,000 − $8,000 = $2,000 in value. Therefore, the company has over-depreciated the asset by $5,000. Because this overdepreciation represents deductions to be taken on the company's tax returns over the five years that don't reflect the actual depreciation in value (the asset does not lose $7,000 in value, only $2,000), this $5,000 is taxed at ordinary tax rates. If the company's tax rate is 40%, the tax will be 40% × $5,000 = $2,000.

The cash flow from disposition is the sum of the direct cash flow (someone pays us for the asset or the company pays someone to dispose of it) and the tax consequences. In this example, the cash flow is the $8,000 we expect someone to pay the company for the asset, less the $2,000 in taxes we expect the company to pay, or $6,000 cash inflow Suppose instead that the company expects to sell this asset in five years for $12,000. Again, the asset is overdepreciated by $7,000. In fact, the asset is not expected to depreciate, but rather appreciate over the five years. The $7,000 in depreciation is recaptured after five years and taxed at ordinary rates: 40% of $7,000, or $2,800. The $2,000 capital gain is the appreciation in the value of the asset and may be taxed at special rates. If the tax rate on capital gain income is assumed to be 30%, the company would expect to pay 30% of $2,000, or $600 in taxes on this gain. Selling the asset in five years for $12,000 therefore results in an expected cash inflow of $12,000 − $2,800 − $600 = $8,600.

Suppose the company expects to sell the asset in five years for $1,000. If the company can reduce its ordinary taxable income by the amount of the capital loss, $3,000 − $1,000 = $2,000, its tax liability will be 40% of $2,000, or $800 because of this loss. As mentioned earlier, this reduction in the taxes is a tax shield since the loss "shields" $2,000 of income from taxes. Combining the $800 tax reduction with the cash flow from selling the asset, the $1,000, gives the company a cash inflow of $1,800.

The calculation of the cash flow from disposition for the alternative sales prices of $8,000, $12,000, and $1,000 are discussed next.

Expected Cash Flows from the Disposition of an Asset

Suppose a company is evaluating an asset that costs $10,000 that it expects to sell in five years. Suppose further that the tax basis of the asset will be $3,000 after five years and that the company's tax rate is 40%. What are the expected cash flows from disposing this asset?

Case 1. Sell the Asset for More than its Tax Basis, but Less than its Original Cost

If the company expects to sell the asset for $8,000 in five years, $10,000 − $3,000 = $7,000 of the asset's cost will be depreciated, yet the asset lost only $10,000 − $8,000 = $2,000 in value. Therefore, the company has overdepreciated the asset by $5,000. Since this overdepreciation represents deductions to be taken on the company's tax returns over the five years that don't reflect the actual depreciation in value (the asset doesn't lose $7,000 in value, only $2,000), this $5,000 is taxed at ordinary tax rates. If the company's tax rate is 40%, the tax = 40% × $5,000 = $2,000.

The cash flow from disposition is the sum of the direct cash flow (someone pays the company for the asset or the company pays another party to dispose of it) and the tax consequences. In this example, the cash flow is the $8,000 the company expects someone to pay for the asset, less the $2,000 in taxes the company expects to pay, or $6,000 cash inflow.

Tax on Disposition	
Sales price	$8,000
Less: Tax basis	3,000
Gain	$5,000
Ordinary tax rate	0.40
Tax on recapture	$2,000
Cash Flows	
Proceeds from disposition	$8,000
Less: tax on gain	2,000
Cash flow	$6,000

Case 2. Sell the Asset for More than the Original Cost

Suppose instead that the company expects to sell this asset in five years for $12,000. Again, the asset is overdepreciated by $7,000. In fact, the asset is not expected to depreciate, but rather appreciate over the five years. The $7,000 in depreciation is recaptured after five years and taxed at ordinary rates: 40% of $7,000, or $2,800. The $2,000 capital gain is the appreciation in the value of the asset and may be taxed at special rates. Assuming the tax rate on capital gain income is 30%, the company expects to pay 30% of $2,000, or $600 in taxes on this gain. Selling the asset in five years for $12,000 therefore results in an expected cash inflow of $12,000 – 2,800 – 600 = $8,600.

Tax on Disposition	
Sales price	$12,000
Less: Original cost	10,000
Capital gain	$2,000
Capital gains tax rate	0.30
Tax on capital gain	$600
Original cost	$10,000
Less: Tax basis	3,000
Gain (recapture)	$7,000
Ordinary tax rate	0.40
Tax on recapture	$2,800

Cash Flows	
Cash flow from sale	$12,000
Less: Tax on capital gain	600
Less: Tax on recapture	2,800
Cash flow	$8,600

Case 3. Sell the Asset for Less than its Tax Basis

Suppose the company expects to sell the asset in five years for $1,000. If the company can reduce its ordinary taxable income by the amount of the capital loss, $3,000 − 1,000 = $2,000, its tax liability be 40% of $2,000, or $800 because of this loss. The loss "shields" $2,000 of income from taxes. Combining the $800 tax reduction with the cash flow from selling the asset, the $1,000, gives the company a cash inflow of $1,800.

Tax Shield on Disposition	
Tax basis	$3,000
Sales price	1,000
Loss on sale	$2,000
Ordinary tax rate	0.40
Tax shield on loss	$800
Cash Flows	
Proceeds from disposition	$1,000
Plus tax shield on loss	800
Cash flow	$1,800

Disposition of New Investment   Consider the investment in a gas station. The current owner may want to leave the business (retire, whatever), selling the station to another gas station proprietor. But if a buyer cannot be found because of lack of gas buyers in the area, the current owner may be required to remove the underground gasoline storage tanks to prevent environmental damage. Thus, a cost is incurred at the end of the asset's life.

The tax consequences are a bit more complicated. Taxes depend on the expected sales price and the tax basis at the time of disposition. If a company sells the asset for more than its tax basis but less than its original cost, the difference between the sales price and the tax basis is a gain, taxable at ordinary tax rates.

If a company sells the asset for more that its original cost, then the gain is broken into two parts: (1) a capital gain, which is the difference between the sales price and the original cost; and (2) recapture depreciation, which is the difference between the original cost and the tax basis. The capital gain is the benefit from the appreciation in the value of the asset and may be taxed at special rates, depending on the tax law at the time of sale. The recapture portion is taxed at the ordinary tax rates since this excess depreciation taken all these years has reduced taxable income.

If a company sells an asset for less than its tax basis, the result is a capital loss. In this case, the asset's value has decreased by more than the amount taken for depreciation for tax purposes. A capital loss is given special tax treatment as discussed earlier. The benefit from a loss on the sale of an asset is the amount by which taxes are reduced (i.e., the tax shield). If the company has a loss of $1,000 on the sale of an asset and has a tax rate of 40%, this means that its taxable income is $1,000 less and its taxes are $400 less than they would have been without the sale of the asset.

The relevant book value of an asset in the case of determining the tax gain or loss—and hence the related cash flow—is the tax basis of the asset. The tax basis is the difference between the original cost of the asset and any accumulated depreciation, where this accumulated depreciation is the prescribed depreciation according to the tax code.

Consider an asset purchased at the beginning of 20X1 for $1 million. If this is a three-year MACRS asset, its depreciation, accumulated depreciation, and tax basis each year is the following (MACRS depreciation rates are the rates prescribed by the U.S. Internal Revenue Code for depreciation for tax purposes):

Year	MACRS Rate (%)	Depreciation	Accumulated Depreciation	Tax Basis at End of Year
20X1	33.33	$333,300	$333,300	$666,700
20X2	44.45	444,500	777,800	222,200
20X3	14.81	148,100	925,900	74,100
20X4	7.41	74,100	1,000,000	0

Whether there is a gain or a loss on the sale of this asset depends on whether the sales prices is above the tax basis (hence, a gain), or below the tax basis (hence, a loss). If the sales price is above the original cost of $1 million, the total gain is broken into two parts—that which is above the original cost (Sales price − Original cost), which is taxed at capital gains rates, and that which is below (Original cost − Tax basis), which is taxed at ordinary rates.

What is the gain or loss if the asset described above is sold:

At the end of 20X2, for $250,000? Gain = $250,000 − $222,200 = $27,800	This gain is taxed at ordinary rates because the sales price of $250,000 is less than original cost of $1 million.

(Continued)

(Continued)

At the end of 20X3, sold for $50,000? Loss = $50,000 − $74,100 = −$24,100	This is a capital loss because it is sold at less than the tax basis at the time of the sale.
At the end of 20X4 for $1,100,000? Gain = $1,1000,000 − $666,700 = $433,300	The gain is taxed in two parts: ■ $100,000 taxed as a capital gain. ■ $333,300 taxed at ordinary rates.

Disposition of Existing Asset(s)   Let's also not forget about disposing of any existing assets. Suppose the company bought equipment 10 years ago and at that time expected to be able to sell it 15 years later for $10,000. If the company decides today to replace this equipment, it must consider what it is giving up by not disposing of an asset as planned.

■ If the company does not replace the equipment today, it would continue to depreciate it for five more years and then sell it for $10,000.
■ If the company replaces the equipment today, it would not have five more years' depreciation on the replaced equipment and it would not have $10,000 in five years (but perhaps some other amount today).

This $10,000 in five years, less any taxes, is a forgone cash flow that we must consider in the investment cash flows. Also, the depreciation the company would have had on the replaced asset must be considered in analyzing the replacement asset's operating cash flows. So, any time that a company is making a decision pertaining to replacing an asset, the forgone depreciation must be accounted for.

Operating Cash Flows

In the simplest form of investment, there will be a cash outflow when the asset is acquired and there may be either a cash inflow or an outflow at the end of its economic life. In most cases these are not the only cash flows —the investment may result in changes in revenues, expenditures, taxes, and working capital. These are operating cash flows since they result directly from the operating activities—the day-to-day activities of the company.

What we are after here are estimates of operating cash flows. We cannot know for certain what these cash flows will be in the future, but we must attempt to estimate them. What is the basis for these estimates? We base them on marketing research, engineering analyses, operations, analysis of our competitors—and our managerial experience.

Change in Revenues

Suppose we are a food processor considering a new investment in a line of frozen dinner products. If we introduce a new ready-to-eat dinner product that is not frozen, our marketing research will indicate how much we should expect to sell. But where do these new product sales come from? Some may come from consumers who do not already buy frozen dinner products. But some of the not-frozen dinner product sales may come from consumers who choose to buy the not-frozen dinners product instead of frozen dinners. It would be nice if these consumers are giving up buying our competitors' frozen dinners. Yet some of them may be giving up buying our frozen dinners. So, when we introduce a new product, we are really interested in how it changes the revenues of the entire company (that is, the incremental revenues), rather than the sales of the new product alone.

We also need to consider any foregone revenues—opportunity costs—related to our investment. Suppose our company owns a building currently being rented to another company. If we are considering terminating that rental agreement so we can use the building for a new project, we need to consider the foregone rent—what we would have earned from the building. Therefore, the revenues from the new project are really only the additional revenues—the revenues from the new project minus the revenue that we could have earned from renting the building.

Thus, when a company undertakes a new project, the financial managers want to know how it changes the company's total revenues, not merely the new product's revenues.

Change in Expenses

When a company takes on a new project, all the costs associated with it will change the company's expenses. If the investment involves changing the sales of an existing product, we need to estimate the change in unit sales. Once we have an estimate in how sales may change, we can develop an estimate of the additional costs of producing the additional number of units by consulting with production management. And, we will want an estimate of how the product's inventory may change when production and sales of the product change.

If the investment involves changes in the costs of production, we compare the costs without this investment with the costs with this investment. For example, if the investment is the replacement of an assembly line machine with a more efficient machine, we need to estimate the change in the company's overall production costs such as electricity, labor, materials, and management costs.

A new investment may change not only production costs but also operating costs, such as rental payments and administration costs. Changes in operating costs as a result of a new investment must be considered as part of the changes in the company's expenses. Increasing cash expenses are cash outflows, and decreasing cash expense are cash inflows.

Change in Taxes

Taxes figure into the operating cash flows in two ways. First, if revenues and expenses change, taxable income and, therefore, taxes change. That means we need to estimate the change in taxable income resulting from the changes in revenues and expenses resulting from a new project to determine the effect of taxes on the company. Second, the deduction for depreciation reduces taxes. Depreciation itself is not a cash flow. But depreciation reduces the taxes that must be paid, shielding income from taxation. The tax shield from depreciation is like a cash inflow.

Suppose a company is considering a new product that is expected to generate additional sales of $200,000 and increase expenses by $150,000. If the company's tax rate is 40%, considering only the change in sales and expenses, taxes go up by $50,000 × 40% or $20,000. This means that the company is expected to pay $20,000 more in taxes because of the increase in revenues and expenses.

Let's change this around and consider that the product will generate $200,000 in revenues and $250,000 in expenses. Considering only the change in revenues and expenses, if the tax rate is 40%, taxes go down by $50,000 × 40%, or $20,000. This means that we reduce our taxes by $20,000, which is like having a cash inflow of $20,000 from taxes. Now, consider depreciation. When a company buys an asset that produces income, the tax laws allow it to depreciate the asset, reducing taxable income by a specified percentage of the asset's cost each year. By reducing taxable income, the company is reducing its taxes. The reduction in taxes is like a cash inflow since it reduces the company's cash outflow to the government.

Suppose a company has taxable income of $50,000 before depreciation and a flat tax rate of 40%. If the company is allowed to deduct depreciation of $10,000, how has this changed the taxes it pays?

	Without Depreciation	**With Depreciation**
Taxable income	$50,000	$40,000
Tax rate	0.40	0.40
Taxes	$20,000	$16,000

Depreciation reduces the company's tax-related cash outflow by $20,000 – $16,000 = $4,000 or, equivalently, by $10,000 × 40% = $4,000. A reduction is an outflow (taxes in this case) is an inflow. The effect depreciation has on taxes is the depreciation tax shield.

Consider another depreciation example, this time involving replacing an existing asset with another, which affects both depreciation and the cash flow associated with the depreciation tax shield. Suppose the machine being replaced was bought at the beginning of 20X1 for $75,000. This asset has been depreciated as a five-year asset using MACRS. If the machine is replaced at the beginning of 20X4 with a new machine that costs $50,000 and is also a five-year asset, how does the change in depreciation affect the cash flows if the company's tax rate is 30%? We can calculate the effect two ways:

1. Calculate the change in depreciation and calculate the tax shield related to the change in depreciation. The change in depreciation is $10,000 – $8,640 = $1,360. (The machine purchased in 20X1 is now in its fourth year in 20X4, with depreciation of 11.52% × $75,000 = $8,640.) The change in the depreciation tax shield is 30% of $1,360, or $408.
2. Compare the depreciation and related tax shield from the old and the new machines. For example, the depreciation tax shield on the old machine for 20X4 would have been $8,640 × 30% = $2,592, whereas the depreciation tax shield on the new machine is $10,000 × 30% = $3,000. Therefore, the change in the cash flow from depreciation is $3,000 – $2,592 = $408.

Analysis of a capital investment decision requires a focus on incremental cash flows. Therefore, the difference in the depreciation and the tax shield from depreciation must be considered in the operating cash flows rather than simply the depreciation and depreciation tax shield associated with the new asset. For this replacement decision, the differences in the depreciation and depreciation tax shields are as follows:

Year	Depreciation on the Asset Being Replaced	Depreciation on the New Asset	Difference in Depreciation	Difference in the Depreciation Tax Shield
20X4	$8,640	$10,000	$1,360	$408.0
20X5	8,640	16,000	7,360	2,208.0
20X6	4,320	9,600	5,280	1,584.0
20X7	0	5,760	5,760	1,728.0
20X8	0	5,760	5,760	1,728.0
20X9	0	2,880	2,880	864.0

Change in Working Capital

Working capital consists of short-term assets, also referred to as current assets, which support the day-to-day operating activity of the business. Net working capital is the difference between current assets and current liabilities. Net working capital is what would be left over if the company had to pay off its current obligations using its current assets. The adjustment we make for changes in net working capital is attributable to two sources:

1. A change in current asset accounts for transactions or precautionary needs.
2. The use of the accrual method of accounting.

An investment may increase the company's level of operations, resulting in an increase in the net working capital needed (also considered transactions needs). If the investment is to produce a new product, the company may have to invest more in inventory (raw materials, work-in-process, and finished goods). If to increase sales means extending more credit, then the company's accounts receivable will increase. If the investment requires maintaining a higher cash balance to handle the increased level of transactions, the company will need more cash. If the investment makes the company's production facilities more efficient, it may be able to reduce the level of inventory.

Because of an increase in the level of transactions, the company may want to keep more cash and inventory on hand for precautionary purposes. That is because as the level of operations increase, the effect of any fluctuations in demand for goods and services may increase, requiring the company to keep additional cash and inventory "just in case." The company may increase working capital as a precaution because if there is greater variability of cash and inventory, a greater safety cushion will be needed. On the other hand, if a project enables the company to be more efficient or lowers costs, it may lower its investment in cash, marketable securities, or inventory, releasing funds for investment elsewhere in the company.

We also use the change in working capital to adjust accounting income (revenues less expenses) to a cash basis because cash flow is ultimately what we are valuing, not accounting numbers. But since we generally have only the accounting numbers to work from, we use this information, making adjustments to arrive at cash.

To see how this works, let's look at the cash flow from sales. Not every dollar of sales is collected in the year of sale. Customers may pay some time after the sale. Using information from the accounts receivable department about how payments are collected, we can determine the change in the cash flows from revenues. Suppose we expect sales in the first year to increase by $20,000 per month and it typically takes customers 30 days to pay. The change in cash flows from sales in the first year is $20,000 × 11 = $220,000—not $20,000 × 12 = $240,000. The way we adjust for this difference between what is sold and what is collected in cash is to keep track of the change in working capital, which is the change in accounts receivable in this case. An increase in working capital is used to adjust revenues downward to calculate cash flow:

Change in revenues	$240,000
Less the increase in accounts receivable	20,000
Change in cash inflow from sales	$220,000

On the other side of the balance sheet, if the company is increasing its purchases of raw materials and incurring more production costs, such as labor, the company may increase its level of short-term liabilities, such as accounts payable and salary and wages payable.

Suppose expenses for materials and supplies are forecasted at $10,000 per month for the first year and it takes the company 30 days to pay. Expenses for the first year are $10,000 × 12 = $120,000, yet cash outflow for these expenses is only $10,000 × 11 = $110,000 since the company does not pay the last month's expenses until the following year. Accounts payable increases by $10,000, representing one month's of expenses. The increase in net working capital (increase in accounts payable → increases current liabilities → increases net working capital) reduces the cost of goods sold to give us the cash outflow from expenses:

Cost of goods sold	$120,000
Less the increase in accounts payable	10,000
Change in cash flow from expenses	$110,000

A new project may result in either an increase in net working capital, a decrease in net working capital, or no change in net working capital.

Further, working capital may change at the beginning of the project and at any point during the life of the project. For example, as a new product is introduced, sales may be terrific in the first few years, requiring an increase in cash, accounts receivable, and inventory to support these increased sales. But all of this requires an increase in working capital—a cash outflow.

But later sales may fall off as competitors enter the market. As sales and production fall off, the need for the increased cash, accounts receivable, and inventory falls off also. As cash, accounts receivable, and inventory are reduced, there is a cash inflow in the form of the reduction in the funds that become available for other uses within the company.

A change in net working capital can be thought of specifically as part of the initial investment—the amount necessary to get the project going. Or it can be considered generally as part of operating activity—the day-to-day business of the company. So where do we classify the cash flow associated with net working capital? With the asset acquisition and disposition represented in the new project or with the operating cash flows?

Note that in many applications, we can arbitrarily classify the change in working capital as either investment cash flows or operating cash flows. And the classification doesn't really matter since it's the bottom line, the net cash flows, that matter. How we classify the change in working capital does not affect a project's attractiveness. However, we will take care in our examples to classify the change in working capital according to whether it is related to operating or investment cash flows so you can see how to make the appropriate adjustments.

Putting it All Together

Here's what we need to put together to calculate the change in the company's operating cash flows related to a new investment we are considering:

- Changes in revenues and expenses.
- Cash flow from changes in taxes from changes in revenues and expenses.
- Cash flow from changes in cash flows from depreciation tax shields.
- Changes in net working capital.

There are many ways of compiling the component cash flow changes to arrive at the change in operating cash flow. We will start by first calculating taxable income, making adjustments for changes in taxes, noncash expenses, and net working capital to arrive at operating cash flow.

Suppose a company is evaluating a project that is expected to increase sales by $200,000 and expenses by $150,000. Accounts receivable are expected to increase by $20,000 and accounts payable are expected to increase by $5,000, but no changes in cash or inventory are expected. Further, suppose the project's assets will have a $10,000 depreciation expense for tax purposes. If the tax rate is 40%, what is the operating cash flow from this project?

Change in sales	$200,000
Less change in expenses	150,000
Less change in depreciation	10,000
Change in taxable income	$40,000

Less taxes	16,000
Change in income after taxes	$24,000
Add depreciation	10,000
Less increase in working capital	15,000
Change in operating cash flow	$19,000

So that we can mathematically represent how to calculate the change in operating cash flows for a project, let's use the delta symbol (Δ) to indicate change in:

ΔOCF	=	change in operating cash flow
ΔR	=	change in revenues
ΔE	=	change in expenses
ΔD	=	change in depreciation
t	=	tax rate
ΔNWC	=	change in working capital

The change in the operating cash flow is

$$\Delta OCF = (\Delta R - \Delta E - \Delta D)(1 - t) + \Delta D - \Delta NWC$$

We can also write this as

$$\Delta OCF = (\Delta R - \Delta E)(1 - t) + \Delta Dt - \Delta NWC$$

Applying these equations to the previous example,

$$\Delta OCF = (\Delta R - \Delta E - \Delta D)(1 - t) + \Delta D - \Delta NWC$$
$$= (\$200,000 - \$150,000 - \$10,000)(1 - 0.40) + \$10,000 - \$15,000$$
$$= \$19,000$$

or, using the rearrangement of the equation,

$$\Delta OCF = (\Delta R - \Delta E)(1 - t) + \Delta Dt - \Delta NWC$$
$$= (\$200,000 - \$150,000)(1 - 0.40) + \$10,000(0.40) - \$15,000$$
$$= \$19,000$$

Looking at one more example for the calculation of operating cash flows, consider evaluating equipment that is expected to reduce expenses by $100,000 during the first year. And, since the new equipment is more efficient than the existing equipment, the existing equipment will be sold and replaced by this new equipment. Suppose that the depreciation on the equipment to be replaced would be $20,000 for the coming year, but that the depreciation on the new equipment would be $30,000. Therefore, depreciation increases by $10,000 if the new equipment is bought. If the marginal tax rate is 30%, the depreciation tax shield increases from $6,000 to $9,000 for the coming year.

Net Cash Flows

By now we should know that an investment's cash flows consist of: (1) cash flows related to acquiring and disposing the assets represented in the investment; and (2) how it affects cash flows related to operations. To evaluate any investment project, we must consider both to determine whether or not the company is better off with or without it.

The sum of the cash flows from asset acquisition and disposition and from operations is referred to as *net cash flows* (NCF). And this sum is calculated for each period. In each period, we add the cash flow from asset acquisition and disposition and the cash flow from operations. For a given period,

$$\text{Net cash flow} = \frac{\text{Investment}}{\text{cash flow}} + \frac{\text{Change in operating}}{\text{cash flow (i.e., } \Delta\text{OCF)}}$$

The analysis of the cash flows of investment projects can become quite complex. But by working through any problem systematically, line-by-line, you will be able to sort out the information and focus on those items that determine cash flows.

To illustrate, suppose that the Acme Company is evaluating replacing its production equipment that produces anvils. The worksheet for calculating the cash flows for this illustration is shown in Table 13.1. The current equipment was purchased 10 years ago at a cost of $1.5 million. Acme depreciated its current equipment using MACRS, considering the equipment to be a five-year MACRS asset. If Acme sells the current equipment, it estimates that $100,000 can be realized from the sale. The new equipment would cost $2.5 million and would be depreciated as a five-year MACRS asset. The new equipment would not affect sales, but would result in a costs savings of $400,000 each year of the asset's 10-year useful life. At the end of its 10-year life, Acme estimates that it can sell the equipment for $30,000. Also, because the new equipment would be more efficient, Acme would have less work-in-process anvils, reducing inventory needs initially by $20,000. Acme's marginal tax rate is 40%. Assume that the equipment purchase (and sale of the old equipment) occurs at the end of the Year 0 and that the first year of operating this equipment is Year 1 and the last year of operating the equipment is Year 10.

TABLE 13.1 Worksheet for Computing the New Cash Flow for Acme Company

	Year 0	Year 1	Year 2	Year 3	Year 4	Year 5	Year 6	Year 7	Year 8	Year 9	Year 10
Initial payment	-$2,500,000										
Sale of new	$100,000										$30,000
Tax on sale of new	-$40,000										-$12,000
Change in working capital, ΔNWC	$20,000										-$20,000
Investment cash flows	-$2,420,000										-$2,000
Change in revenues, ΔR		$0	$0	$0	$0	$0	$0	$0	$0	$0	$0
Change in expenses, ΔE		-$400,000	-$400,000	-$400,000	-$400,000	-$400,000	-$400,000	-$400,000	-$400,000	-$400,000	-$400,000
Change in depreciation, ΔD		$500,000	$800,000	$480,000	$288,000	$288,000	$144,000	$0	$0	$0	$0
Change in taxable income, (ΔR − ΔE − ΔD)		-$100,000	-$400,000	-$80,000	$112,000	$112,000	$256,000	$400,000	$400,000	$400,000	$400,000
Change in taxes, t(ΔR − ΔE − ΔD)		-$40,000	-$160,000	-$32,000	$44,800	$44,800	$102,400	$160,000	$160,000	$160,000	$160,000
Change in after-tax income, (1 − t)(ΔR − ΔE − ΔD)		-$60,000	-$240,000	-$48,000	$67,200	$67,200	$153,600	$240,000	$240,000	$240,000	$240,000
Change in depreciation, ΔD		$500,000	$800,000	$480,000	$288,000	$288,000	$144,000	$0	$0	$0	$0
Change in operating cash flows		$440,000	$560,000	$432,000	$355,200	$355,200	$297,600	$240,000	$240,000	$240,000	$240,000
Net cash flow	-$2,420,000	$440,000	$560,000	$432,000	$355,200	$355,200	$297,600	$240,000	$240,000	$240,000	$238,000

The information for this illustration is:

- Tax basis of current equipment = $0
- Sale of current equipment = $100,000
- Tax on sale of current equipment = $40,000
- Initial outlay for new= –$2,500,000
- ΔE = $400,000
- ΔNWC = –$20,000 (initially)
- ΔNWC = $20,000 (at end of project)

Depreciation:

Year 1: 0.2000 ($2,500,000) = $500,000
Year 2: 0.3200 ($2,500,000) = $800,000
Year 3: 0.1920 ($2,500,000) = $480,000
Year 4: 0.1152 ($2,500,000) = $288,000
Year 5: 0.1152 ($2,500,000) = $288,000

Simplifications

To actually analyze a project's cash flows, we need to make several simplifications:

- We assume that cash flows into or out of the company at certain points in time, typically at the end of the year, although we realize a project's cash flows into and out of the company at irregular intervals.
- We assume that the assets are purchased and put to work immediately.
- By combining inflows and outflows in each period, we are assuming that all inflows and outflows in a given period have the same risk.

Because there are so many flows to consider, we focus on flows within a period (say a year), assuming they all occur at the end of the period. We assume this to reduce the number of things we have to keep track of. Whether or not this assumption matters depends: (1) the difference between the actual time of cash flow and when we assume it flows at the end of the period (that is, a flow on January 2 is 364 days from December 31, but a flow on December 30 is only one day from December 31); and (2) the opportunity cost of funds. Also, assuming that cash flows occur at specific points in time simplifies the financial mathematics we use in valuing these cash flows.

Keeping track of the different cash flows of an investment project can be taxing. Developing a checklist of things to consider can help you wade through the analysis of a project's cash flows.

SUMMARY

One of the most important functions in financial management is the evaluation of capital expenditures. Decisions involving capital expenditures are known as capital budgeting decisions. Unlike working capital decisions, capital budgeting decisions commit funds for a time period longer than one year and may have an impact of a company's strategic position within its industry. The capital budgeting process encompasses the initial investment screening and selection through the postcompletion audit of the project. Classifying capital projects along different dimensions (that is, economic life, risk, and *dependence on other projects)* is necessary because of these characteristics of the project affect the analysis of the projects.

Determining whether an investment's benefits outweigh its costs requires that management first estimate the future cash flows associated with the investment. The evaluation of a project requires estimating not only the initial outlay, but the expected cash flows at the end of the project's useful life. The estimation of operating cash flows requires estimation of revenues, expenses, taxes, any tax shield (or benefit) from taxes, as well as any anticipated changes in working capital needs.

The goal in estimating cash flows is to arrive at the company's incremental cash flow for each period. This incremental cash flow includes both any investing and any operating cash flows related to the project. When a company undertakes a new project, management wants to know how it changes the company's total revenues, not merely the new product's revenues.

The task of estimating the cash flows appears, at first, to be quite daunting, but this is an exercise that all companies must go through for every capital project. The amount of material that must be sorted through to determine the relevant information for this estimation is often substantial and it is the responsibility of the staff responsible for capital budgeting of the company to sort through this material, determine the relevant information, and organize it in such a way to enable the estimation of the cash flows in every period of the project's life.

REFERENCES

Dayananda, D., Irons, R., Harrison, S., and Herbohn, J. (2002). *Capital Budgeting: Financial Appraisal of Investment Projects.* New York: Cambridge University Press.

Insley, M. C. (2003). On the option to invest in pollution control under a regime of tradable emissions allowances. *Canadian Journal of Economics* 36, no. 4: 860–883.

Marino, A. M., and Zabojnik, J. (1994). Internal competition for corporate resources and incentives in teams. *RAND Journal of Economics* 35, no. 4: 710–727.

Neale, C.W. (1995). Post-completion audits: Avoiding the pitfalls. *Managerial Auditing Journal* 10, no. 1: 17–24.

Peterson, P. and Fabozzi, F. J. (2002). *Capital Budgeting: Theory and Practice.* Hoboken, NJ: John Wiley & Sons.

Pierce, B. J. and Tsay. J. J. (1992). A study of the post-completion audit practices of large American corporations: Experience from 1978 and 1988. *Journal of Management Accounting Research* 4 (Fall): 131–155.

Soares, J., Coutinho, M. C., and Martins, C. V. (2007). Forecasting errors in capital budgeting: A multi-company post-audit study. *Engineering Economist* 52, no. 1: 21–39.

CHAPTER 14

Capital Budgeting Techniques

The value of a company today is the present value of all its future cash flows, where these future cash flows come from assets that are already in place and from future investment opportunities. These future cash flows are discounted at a rate that represents investors' assessments of the uncertainty that they will flow in the amounts and when expected. Management makes decisions by evaluating which capital projects, if any, are expected to enhance the value of the company. This process is referred to as capital budgeting.

The capital budgeting decisions for a project requires analysis of: (1) the project's future cash flows; (2) the degree of uncertainty associated with the project's future cash flows; and (3) the value of the project's future cash flows considering their uncertainty. The estimation of cash flows involves estimating with a project's incremental cash flows, comprising changes in operating cash flows (change in revenues, expenses, and taxes), and changes in investment cash flows (the firm's incremental cash flows from the acquisition and disposition of the project's assets).

The degree of uncertainty, or risk, is reflected in a project's cost of capital. The cost of capital is what the company must pay for the funds to finance its investments. The cost of capital may be an explicit cost (for example, the interest paid on debt) or an implicit cost (for example, the expected price appreciation of its shares of common stock).

In this chapter, we focus on evaluating the future cash flows. Given estimates of incremental cash flows for a project and given a cost of capital that reflects the project's risk, we look at alternative techniques that are used to select projects. We also explain the basics of how to incorporate risk when evaluating projects.

EVALUATION TECHNIQUES

Look at the incremental cash flows for Project X and Project Y shown in Table 14.1. Can you tell by looking at the cash flows for Investment A whether

TABLE 14.1 Estimated Cash Flows for Investments X and Y

	End of Period Cash Flows	
Year	Project X	Project Y
0	–$1,000,000	–$1,000,000
1	0	325,000
2	200,000	325,000
3	300,000	325,000
4	900,000	325,000

or not it enhances wealth? Or, can you tell by just looking at Investments A and B which one is better? Perhaps with some projects you may think you can pick out which one is better simply by gut feeling or eyeballing the cash flows. But why do it that way when there are precise methods to evaluate investments by their cash flows?

The first step is to determine the cash flows from each investment and then assess the uncertainty of all the cash flows in order to evaluate investment projects and select the investments that maximize wealth.

In this chapter, there are six techniques discussed that are commonly used by companies to evaluate investments in long-term assets:

1. Net present value
2. Profitability index
3. Internal rate of return
4. Modified internal rate of return
5. Payback period
6. Discounted payback period

The focus of the analysis of these techniques is on how well each technique discriminates among the different projects, steering the decision-maker toward the projects that maximize the value of the company.

An evaluation technique should:

- Consider all the future incremental cash flows from the project.
- Consider the time value of money.
- Consider the uncertainty associated with future cash flows.
- Have an objective criterion by which to select a project.

Projects selected using a technique that satisfies all four criteria will, under most general conditions, maximize owners' wealth. In addition to judging whether each technique satisfies these criteria, this chapter also looks at which ones can be used in special situations, such as when a dollar limit is placed on the capital budget.

The Cost of Capital, the Required Rate of Return, and the Discount Rate

In several of the capital budgeting evaluation techniques, the uncertain future cash flows of a project are discounted to the present at some interest rate that reflects the degree of uncertainty associated with this future cash flow. These *discounted cash flow techniques* are the net present value method, the profitability index, and the modified internal rate of return. In each of these, the more uncertain the future cash flow, the less the cash flow is worth today—this means that a higher discount rate is used to translate it into a value today. In the case of the internal rate of return, the uncertainty is reflected in the hurdle rate that must be exceeded by the project's return: the greater the uncertainty of future cash flows, the higher is this hurdle rate.

This rate—whether a discount rate or a hurdle rate—reflects the opportunity cost of funds. This opportunity cost of funds reflects the *cost of capital* to be paid the suppliers of capital (the creditors and owners).

The cost of capital comprises the *required rate of return* (RRR) (that is, the return suppliers of capital demand on their investment) and the cost of raising new capital if the firm cannot generate the needed capital internally (that is, from retaining earnings). The cost of capital and the required rate of return are the same concept, but from different perspectives. Therefore, we will use the terms interchangeably in our study of capital budgeting.

This rate is the project's cost of capital—the return required by the suppliers of capital (creditors and owners) to compensate them for time value of money and the risk associated with the investment. The more uncertain the future cash flows, the greater the cost of capital.

NET PRESENT VALUE

If an investment requires the payment of $1 million today and promises to return $1.5 million two years from today and if the opportunity cost for projects of similar risk is 12%, is this a good investment? To determine whether this is a good investment the initial investment of $1 million is compared with the $1.5 million cash flow expected in two years. Because the discount rate of 10% reflects the degree of uncertainty associated with the $1.5 million expected in two years, today it is worth:

$$\text{Present value of \$1.5 million to be received in 2 years} = \frac{\$1.2 \text{ million}}{(1+0.10)^2}$$

$$= \$1.2397 \text{ million}$$

By investing $1 million today, the company is getting in return, a promise of a cash flow in the future that is worth $1.2397 million today. The company is expected to increase its value by $1.2397 – $1 million = $0.2397 million if it makes this investment. In other words, the expected value added with this investment is $0.2397 million.

Another way of stating this is that the present value of the $1.5 million cash inflow is $1.2397 million, which is more than the $1 million today's cash outflow to make the investment. Subtracting today's cash outflow to make an investment from the present value of the cash inflow from the investment provides the increase or decrease in the company's value, which is referred to as the investment's *net present value*.

The net present value is the present value of all expected cash flows.

Net present value = Present value of all expected cash flows

The word "net" in this term indicates that all cash flows—both positive and negative—are considered. Often the changes in operating cash flows are inflows and the investment cash flows are outflows. Therefore, we tend to refer to the net present value as the difference between the present value of the cash inflows and the present value of the cash outflows.

Calculating the Net Present Value

We can represent the *net present value* (NPV) using summation notation, where t indicates any particular period, CF_t represents the cash flow at the end of period t, r represents the cost of capital, and N the number of periods comprising the economic life of the investment:

NPV = Present value of cash inflows – Present value of cash outflows

$$= \sum_{t=1}^{N} \frac{CF_t}{(1+r)^t}$$

Cash inflows are positive values of CF_t and cash outflows are negative values of CF_t. For any given period t, the cash flows (positive and negative) are collected and net together.

Take another look at Projects X. Using a 10% cost of capital, the present values of the cash flows are:

| | Project X | |
Year	Cash Flow	Discounted Cash Flow
0	–$1,000,000	–$1,000,000.00
1	0	0.00
2	200,000	165,289.26
3	300,000	225,394.44
4	900,000	614,712.11
		NPV = +$5,395.81

This NPV indicates that with investing in Project X, there is an expected increase in the value of the company by $5,395.81. Calculated in a similar manner, the NPV of Project Y is $30,206.27.

A positive NPV means that the investment increases the value of the company—the return is more than sufficient to compensate for the required return of the investment. A negative NPV means that the investment decreases the value of the company—the return is less than the cost of capital. A zero NPV means that the return just equals the return required by the owners to compensate them for the degree of uncertainty over the investment's future cash flows and the time value of money. Given what we now know:

If ...	this means that ...	and the company ...
NPV > $0	the investment is expected to increase shareholder wealth	should accept the project.
NPV < $0	the investment is expected to decrease shareholder wealth	should reject the project.
NPV = $0	the investment is expected not to change shareholder wealth	should be indifferent between accepting or rejecting the project.

Project X is expected to increase the value of the company by $5,395.81, whereas Project Y is expected to add $30,206.27 in value. If these are independent investments, both should be taken on because both increase the value of the company. If X and Y are mutually exclusive, such that the only choice is either X or Y, then Y is preferred since it has the greater NPV. Projects are said to be mutually exclusive if accepting one precludes the acceptance of the other.

The Investment Profile

A financial manager may want to see how sensitive the decision to accept a project is to changes in the estimate of the project's cost of capital. The *investment profile* (also known as the *net present value profile*) is a depiction of the NPVs for different discount rates, which allows an examination of the sensitivity in how a project's NPV changes as the discount rate changes. The investment profile is a graphical depiction of the relation between the NPV of a project and the discount rate: The profile shows the NPV of a project for each discount rate, within some range.

The NPV profile for Projects X is shown in Figure 14.1 for discount rates from 0% to 20%. As shown in the figure, the NPV of Project X is positive for discount rates from 0% to 10.172%, and negative for discount rates higher than 10.172%. As explained later in this chapter, the 10.172% is the internal rate of return; that is, the discount rate at which the net present value is equal to zero. Therefore, Project X increases owners' wealth if the project's cost of capital is less than 10.172% and decreases owners' wealth if the cost of capital is greater than 10.172%.

Imposing the NPV profile of Project Y onto the NPV profile of Project X, as shown in the graph in Figure 14.2, the projects may be compared. If Projects X and Y are mutually exclusive projects—that is, the company may invest in only one or neither project—this graph clearly shows that the project selected depends on the discount rate. For higher discount rates, Project X's NPV is less than that of Project Y. This is because most of Project X's present value is attributed to the large cash flows four and five years into the future. The present value of the more distant cash flows is more sensitive to changes in the discount rate than is the present value of cash flows nearer the present.

FIGURE 14.1   The Investment Profile of Project X

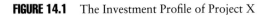

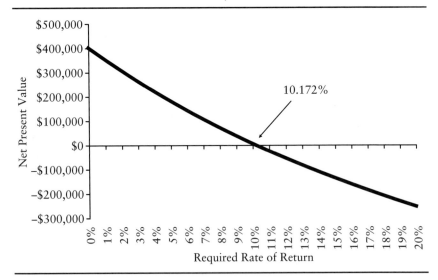

FIGURE 14.2   Investment Profiles of Investments X and Y

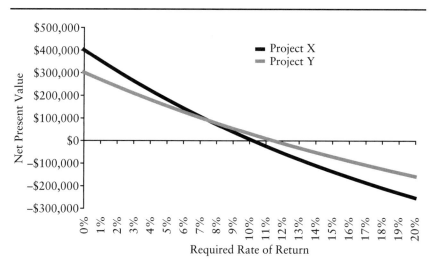

If the discount rate is less than 7.495%, Project X adds more values than Project Y. If the discount rate is more than 7.495% but less than 11.338%, Project Y increases wealth more than Project X. If the discount rate is greater than 11.338%, we should invest in neither project because both would decrease wealth.

The 7.495% is the *cross-over discount rate*, which is the discount rate that produces identical NPV's for the two projects. If the discount rate is 7.495%, the NPV of both investments is $88,660. (The precise cross-over rate is 7.49475%, at which the NPV for both projects is $88,659.)

PROFITABILITY INDEX

The *profitability index* uses some of the same information we used for the net present value, but it is stated in terms of an index. Whereas the NPV is

NPV = Present value of cash inflows − Present value of cash outflows

$$= \sum_{t=1}^{N} \frac{CF_t}{(1+r)^t}$$

The profitability index, *PI*, is

$$PI = \frac{\text{Present value of cash inflows}}{\text{Present value of cash outflows}} = \frac{\sum\limits_{t=1}^{N} \dfrac{CIF_t}{(1+r)^t}}{\sum\limits_{t=1}^{N} \dfrac{COF_t}{(1+r)^t}}$$

where CIF and COF are cash inflows and cash outflows, respectively. For Project X, the CIF is:

	Project X	
Year	Cash Flow	Discouted Cash Flow
1	$0	$0.00
2	200,000	165,289.26
3	300,000	225,394.44
4	900,000	614,712.11

$$\sum_{t=1}^{N} \frac{CIF_t}{(1+r)^t} = +\$1,005,395.81$$

Therefore, the profitability index is

$$PI_X = \frac{\$1,005,395.81}{\$1,000,000} = 1.0054$$

The index value is greater than one, which means that the investment produces more in terms of benefits than costs. An advantage of using the profitability index is that it translates the dollar amount of NPV into an indexed value, providing a measure of the benefit per dollar investment. This is helpful in ranking projects in cases in which the capital budget is limited.

The decision rule for the profitability index depends on the PI relative to 1.0, which means

If ...	this means that ...	and you ...
$PI > 1.0$	the investment is expected to increase shareholder wealth	should accept the project.
$PI < 1.0$	the investment is expected to decrease shareholder wealth	should reject the project.
$PI = 1.0$	the investment is expected not to change shareholder wealth	should be indifferent between accepting or rejecting the project.

INTERNAL RATE OF RETURN

Suppose an investment opportunity requires an initial investment of $1 million and has expected cash inflows of $0.6 million after one year and another $0.6 million after two years. This opportunity is shown in Figure 14.3 using a time line.

The return on this investment (denoted by *internal rate of return* or IRR, in the next equation) is the discount rate that causes the present values of the $0.6 million cash inflows to equal the present value of the $1 million cash outflow, calculated as

$$\$1 = \frac{\$0.6}{(1+\text{IRR})^1} + \frac{\$0.6}{(1+\text{IRR})^2}$$

Another way to look at this is to consider the investment's cash flows discounted at the IRR of 10%. The NPV of this project if the discount rate is 13.0662% (the IRR in this example), is zero:

$$0 = \frac{\$0.6}{(1+0.13662)^1} + \frac{\$0.6}{(1+0.13662)^2} - \$1$$

An investment's internal rate of return is the discount rate that makes the present value of all expected future cash flows equal to zero. We can represent the IRR as the rate that solves

$$\$0 = \sum_{t=1}^{N} \frac{CF_t}{(1+\text{IRR})^t}$$

Going back to Project X, the IRR for this project is the discount rate that solves

$$0 = \frac{\$0}{(1+\text{IRR})^1} + \frac{\$200,000}{(1+\text{IRR})^2} + \frac{\$300,000}{(1+\text{IRR})^3} + \frac{\$900,000}{(1+\text{IRR})^4} - \$1,000,000$$

Using a calculator or a computer, we get the answer of 10.172% per year.

FIGURE 14.3 Timeline of Investment Opportunity

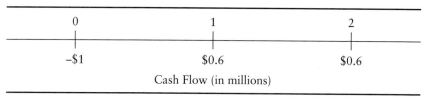

0	1	2
−$1	$0.6	$0.6

Cash Flow (in millions)

Looking back at the investment profiles of Projects X and Y, each profile crosses the horizontal axis (where NPV = 0) at the discount rate that corresponds to the investment's IRR. This is no coincidence: by definition, the IRR is the discount rate that causes the project's NPV to equal zero.

The IRR is a yield—what is earned, on average, per year. How do you use it to decide which investment, if any, to choose? Let's revisit Projects X and Y and the IRRs we just calculated for each. If, for similar risk investments, owners earn 10% per year, then both Projects X and Y are attractive. They both yield more than the rate owners require for the level of risk of these two investments:

Project	IRR	Cost of Capital
X	10.172%	10%
Y	11.388%	10%

The decision rule for the IRR is to invest in a project if it provides a return greater than the cost of capital. The cost of capital, in the context of the IRR, is a *hurdle rate*—the minimum acceptable rate of return. For independent projects and situations in which there is no capital rationing, the following holds true:

If ...	this means that ...	and you ...
IRR > cost of capital	the investment is expected to increase shareholder wealth	should accept the project.
IRR < cost of capital	the investment is expected to decrease shareholder wealth	should reject the project.
IRR = cost of capital	the investment is expected not to change shareholder wealth	should be indifferent between accepting or rejecting the project.

The IRR and Mutually Exclusive Projects

What if the financial manager is forced to choose between Projects X and Y because the projects are mutually exclusive? Project Y has a higher IRR than Project X—so at first glance we might want to accept Project Y. What about the NPV of Projects X and Y? What does the NPV tell us to do? If we use the higher IRR, it tells us to go with Project Y. If we use the higher NPV and the cost of capital is 10%, we go with Project X. Which is correct? Choosing the project with the higher NPV is consistent with maximizing owners' wealth. Why? Because if the cost of capital is 10%, we would calculate different NPVs and come to a different conclusion, as shown using the investment profiles in Figure 14.2.

When evaluating mutually exclusive projects, the project with the highest IRR may not be the one with the best NPV. (It may or may not—and that is the problem. It is possible to make a value-maximizing decision by using the IRR method, but it is also possible to make a decision that is not value-maximizing by using IRR.) The IRR may give a different decision than NPV when evaluating mutually exclusive projects because of the assumption about what rate can be earned when reinvesting the cash flows. While we have not discussed this assumption, it is a property of any yield calculation and the IRR is a yield calculation. To realize the computed yield, it is assumed that the cash flows are reinvested at the computed IRR. Thus we have:

- NPV assumes cash flows reinvested at the cost of capital.
- IRR assumes cash flows reinvested at the internal rate of return.

This reinvestment assumption may cause different decisions in choosing among mutually exclusive projects when:

- The timing of the cash flows is different among the projects.
- There are scale differences (that is, very different cash flow amounts).
- The projects have different useful lives.

With respect to the role of the timing of cash flows in choosing between two projects: Project Y's cash flows are received sooner than Project X's. Part of the return on either is from the reinvestment of its cash inflows. And in the case of Y, there is more return from the reinvestment of cash inflows. The question is what is done by the company with the cash inflows from a project when they are received. We generally assume that when the company receives cash inflows, they are reinvested in other assets.

With respect to the reinvestment rate assumption in choosing between these projects: Suppose we can reasonably expect to earn only the cost of capital on our investments. Then for projects with an IRR above the cost of capital we would be overstating the return on the investment using the IRR.

With respect to the NPV method: if the best we can do is reinvest cash flows at the cost of capital, the NPV assumes reinvestment at the more reasonable rate (the cost of capital). If the reinvestment rate is assumed to be the project's cost of capital, evaluating projects on the basis of the NPV and select the one that maximizes owners' wealth.

The IRR and Capital Rationing

Capital rationing means that there is a limit on the capital budget. Suppose Projects X and Y are *independent projects*. Projects are independent if the acceptance of one does not prevent the acceptance of the other. And suppose the capital budget is limited to $1 million. In our example, the financial manager would therefore forced to choose between Projects X or Y. Choosing the project with the highest IRR, Project Y should be chosen. But Project Y is expected to increase wealth less than Project X at the projects' 10% cost of capital. Therefore, ranking investments on the basis of their IRRs may not maximize wealth.

This dilemma is similar to that in the case of mutually exclusive projects using the projects' investment profiles. The discount rate at which Project X's NPV is zero is where Project X's IRR is 10.172%, where the project's investment profile crosses the horizontal axis. Likewise, the discount rate at which Project Y's NPV is zero is where Project Y's IRR is 11.388%. The discount rate at which Project X's and Y's investment profiles cross is the cross-over rate, 7.495%. For discount rates less than 7.495%, Project X has the higher NPV. For discount rates greater than 7.495%, Project Y has the higher NPV. If Project Y is chosen because it has a higher IRR and if Project Y's cost of capital is less than 7.495%, the company has not chosen the project that produces the greatest value.

The source of the problem in the case of capital rationing is that the IRR is a percentage, not a dollar amount. Because of this, we cannot determine how to distribute the capital budget to maximize wealth because the investment or group of investments producing the highest yield does not mean they are the ones that produce the greatest wealth.

Multiple Internal Rates of Return

The typical project usually involves only one large negative cash flow initially, followed by a series of future positive flows. But that's not always the case. Suppose you are involved in a project that uses environmentally sensitive chemicals. It may cost a great deal to dispose of them. And that will mean a negative cash flow at the end of the project.

Suppose we are considering a project that has cash flows as follows:

Year	End of Year Cash Flow
0	−$1,000
1	+1,000
2	+500
3	−2,100

What is this project's IRR? One possible solution is IRR = 7.77%, yet another possible solution is IRR = 33.24%. That is, both IRRs will make the present value of the cash flows equal to zero.

FIGURE 14.4 The Case of Multiple IRRs

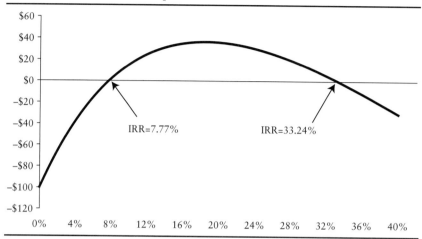

The NPV of these cash flows are shown in Figure 14.4 for discount rates from 0% to 40%. Remember that the IRR is the discount rate that causes the NPV to be zero. In terms of Figure 14.4, this means that the IRR is the discount rate where the NPV is zero, the point at which the present value changes sign—from positive to negative or from negative to positive. In the case of this project, the present value changes from negative to positive at 7.77% and from positive to negative at 33.24%.

Is it reasonable to expect that a project's cash flows will experience only one sign change during its useful life? It depends on the type of project. For example, projects requiring environmental mitigation or significant retooling may to have negative cash flows during or at the end of the project's useful life.

MODIFIED INTERNAL RATE OF RETURN

The *modified internal rate of return* (MIRR) is a yield on an investment considering a specific rate on the reinvestment of funds. The NPV method assumes that cash inflows from a project are reinvested at the project's cost of capital, whereas the IRR method assumes that cash inflows are reinvested at the project's IRR. These assumptions are built into the mathematics of the methods, but they may not represent the actual opportunities of the company. The modified IRR method is an alternative that considers a specific reinvestment rate for cash inflows from a project.

To better understand this reinvestment rate assumption, consider Project X. The IRR is 10.17188%. If each of the cash inflows from Project

X is reinvested at 10.17188%, the sum of these future cash flows will be $1,472,272.53 at the end of Year 4:

Number of Periods Earning a Return	Future Value of Cash Flow Reinvested at 10.17188%
3	$0.00
2	242,756.88
1	330,515.65
0	<u>900,000.00</u>
	$1,473,272.53

The $1,473,272.53 is referred to as the project's *terminal value*. (For example, Year 2's cash flow of $200,000 is reinvested at 10.17188% for two years (that is, for Year 3 and Year 4), or $200,000 (1 + 0.1017188)^2 = $242,756.88.) The terminal value is how much the company has from an investment if all proceeds are reinvested at the assumed reinvestment rate. In our illustration, we assumed the reinvestment rate is the IRR. So what is the return on this project? Using the terminal value as the future value and the investment as the present value:

$$FV = \$1,473,272.53$$
$$PV = \$1,000,000.00$$
$$N = 4 \text{ years}$$
$$r = \sqrt[4]{\frac{\$1,473,273}{\$1,000,000}} - 1 = 10.17188\%$$

In other words, by investing $1,000,000 at the end of Year 0 and receiving $1,473,272.53 produces an average annual return of 10.1718%, which is the project's IRR.

Calculating the Modified Internal Rate of Return

The MIRR is the return on the project assuming reinvestment of the cash flows at a specified rate. Consider Project X if the reinvestment rate is 5%:

Number of Periods Earning a Return	Future Value of Cash Flow Reinvested at 5%
3	$0
2	220,500
1	315,000
0	<u>900,000</u>
	$1,435,500

The MIRR is 9.4588% when:

Terminal value = $1,435,500
Present value = $1,000,000
N = 4 years

$$\text{MIRR} = \sqrt[4]{\frac{\$1,435,500}{\$1,000,000}} - 1 = 9.4588\%$$

If, instead, the reinvestment rate is 6%:

Number of Periods Earning a Return	Future Value of Cash Flow Reinvested at 6%
3	$0
2	224,720
1	318,000
0	900,000
	$1,442,720

The MIRR is 9.5962% when:

Terminal value = $1,442,720
Present value = $1,000,000
N = 4 years

$$\text{MIRR} = \sqrt[4]{\frac{\$1,442,720}{\$1,000,000}} - 1 = 9.5962\%$$

The opportunity of the company to reinvest the cash inflows at a higher rate (5% versus 6%) increases the attractiveness of the project, from an MIRR of 9.4588% to 9.5962%.

The MIRR is therefore a function of both the reinvestment rate and the pattern of cash flows, with higher reinvestment rates leading to greater MIRRs. Shown in Figure 14.5 are the MIRRs of both Project X and Project Y plotted for different reinvestment rates. Project Y's MIRR is more sensitive to the reinvestment rate because more of its cash flows are received sooner relative to Project X's cash flows.

Representing this technique in a formula,

FIGURE 14.5   MIRRs for Project X and Project Y

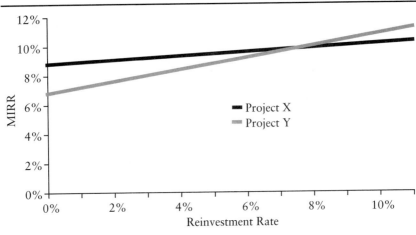

$$MIRR = \sqrt[N]{\dfrac{\displaystyle\sum_{t=1}^{N} CIF_t(1+i)^{N-t}}{\displaystyle\sum_{t=1}^{N} \dfrac{COF_t}{(1+i)^t}}}$$

where the CIF_t are the cash inflows and the COF_t are the cash outflows. In the previous example, the present value of the cash outflows is equal to the $1,000,000 initial cash outlay, whereas the future value of the cash inflows is $1,435,500.

The decision rule for the modified internal rate of return is to invest in a project if it provides a return greater than the cost of capital. The cost of capital, in the context of the MIRR, is a hurdle rate—the minimum acceptable rate of return. For independent projects and situations in which there is no capital rationing, the following holds true:

If ...	this means that ...	and you ...
MIRR > cost of capital	the investment is expected to return more than required	should accept the project.
MIRR < cost of capital	the investment is expected to return less than required	should reject the project.
MIRR = cost of capital	the investment is expected to return what is required	are indifferent between accepting or rejecting the project.

PAYBACK PERIOD

The *payback period* for a project is the time it takes for the cash inflows to add up to the initial cash outflow. In other words, how long it takes to recover the initial cash outflow. The payback period is also referred to as the *payoff period* or the *capital recovery period*. If $10 million is invested today and the investment is expected to generate $5 million one year from today and $5 million two years from today, the payback period is two years—it takes two years to recoup the $10 million investment.

Suppose a company is considering Projects X and Y, each requiring an investment of $1 million today (consider today to be the last day of the Year 0) and promising cash flows at the end of each of the following years through Year 4. How long does it take to recover the $1,000,000 investment? The payback period for Project X is four years:

Year	Project X	Accumulated Cash Flows
0	–$1,000,000	
1	$0	–$1,000,000
2	200,000	–800,000
3	300,000	–500,000
4	900,000	+400,000

By the end of Year 3, the entire $1 million is not paid back, but by Year 4 the accumulated cash flow hits (and exceeds) $1 million. Therefore, the payback period for Project X is four years. The payback period for Project Y is also four years. It is not until the end of Year 4 that the $1 million initial investment (and more) is recovered.

Is Project X or Y more attractive? According to the payback period method, a shorter payback period is better than a longer payback period. Yet there is no clear-cut rule for what length of time is best. Assuming that all cash flows occur at the end of the year, Project X provides the same payback as Project Y. Therefore, the two projects cannot be distinguished from one another. In addition to having no well-defined decision criteria, payback period analysis favors investments with "front-loaded" cash flows: an investment looks better in terms of the payback period the sooner its cash flows are received no matter what its later cash flows look like.

Payback period analysis is a type of "break-even" measure. It tends to provide a measure of the economic life of the investment in terms of its payback period. The more likely the life exceeds the payback period, the more attractive the investment. The economic life beyond the payback period is referred to as the *postpayback duration*. If postpayback duration is zero, the investment is worthless, no matter how short the payback. This is because the sum of the future cash flows is no greater than the initial investment outlay. And since these future cash flows are really worth less today than in the future, a zero postpayback duration means that the present value of the future cash flows is less than the project's initial investment.

The payback method should only be used as a coarse initial screen of investment projects. But it can be a useful indicator of some things. Because a dollar of cash flow in the early years is worth more than a dollar of cash flow in later years, the payback period method provides a simple, yet crude measure of the liquidity of the investment.

The payback period also offers some indication on the risk of the investment. In industries where equipment becomes obsolete rapidly or where there are very competitive conditions, investments with earlier payback are more valuable. That's because cash flows farther into the future are more uncertain and therefore have lower present value. In the personal computer industry, for example, the fierce competition and rapidly changing technology requires investment in projects that have a payback of less than one year since there is no expectation of project benefits beyond one year.

Because the payback method does not indicate the particular payback period that maximizes wealth, it cannot be used as the primary screening device for investment in long-lived assets.

DISCOUNTED PAYBACK PERIOD

The *discounted payback period* is the time needed to pay back the original investment in terms of discounted future cash flows. In this technique, each cash flow is discounted back to the beginning of the investment at a rate that reflects both the time value of money and the uncertainty of the future cash flows.

Returning to Projects X and Y, suppose that each has a cost of capital of 10%. The first step in determining the discounted payback period is to discount each year's cash flow to the beginning of the investment (the end of the Year 0) at the cost of capital. Here is an example:

	Project X		Project Y	
Year	Cash Flows	Accumulated Discounted Cash Flows	Cash Flows	Accumulated Discounted Cash Flows
0	−$1,000,000.00	−$1,000,000.00	−$1,000,000.00	−$1,000,000.00
1	0.00	−1,000,000.00	295,454.55	−704,545.45
2	165,289.26	−834,710.74	268,595.04	−435,950.41
3	225,394.44	−609,316.30	244,177.31	−191,773.10
4	614,712.11	5,395.81	221,979.37	30,206.27

How long does it take for each investment's discounted cash flows to pay back its $1 million investment? The discounted payback period for both Projects X and Y is four years.

It appears that the shorter the payback period, the better, whether using discounted or nondiscounted cash flows. But how short is better? This is not clear. All that is known is that an investment "breaks-even" in terms of discounted cash flows at the discounted payback period—the point in time when the accumulated discounted cash flows equal the amount of the investment.

Using the length of the payback as a basis for selecting investments, Projects X and Y cannot be distinguished. But by using the discounted payback period, valuable cash flows for both investments—those beyond what is necessary for recovering the initial cash outflow—are ignored. Therefore, the discounted payback period method is not recommended for evaluating capital projects.

ISSUES IN CAPITAL BUDGETING

Not all discounted cash flows methods are appropriate in all circumstances. As explained in this section, when faced with mutually exclusive projects, scale differences, different project lives, or capital rationing, care must be exercised in these circumstances.

Scale Differences

Scale differences between projects—that is, differences in the amount of the initial investment—can lead to conflicting investment decisions among the discounted cash flow techniques. Consider two projects, Project Bigger and Project Smaller, that each have a cost of capital of 5% per year with the following cash flows:

	Cash Flows	
End of Year	Project Bigger	Project Smaller
0	-$5,000	-$2,500
1	1,250	650
2	1,250	650
3	1,250	650
4	1,250	650

Applying the discounted cash flow techniques to each project we get:

Technique	Project Bigger	Project Smaller
NPV	$411.85	$314.16
IRR	7.93%	9.43%
MIRR	6.68%	7.52%
PI	1.08	1.13

If there is no limit to the capital budget—that is, there is no capital rationing—then both projects are acceptable, value-increasing projects as indicated by all four techniques. However, if the projects are mutually exclusive projects or there is a limit to the capital budget, then the four methods provide differing accept-reject decisions.

If Project Bigger and Project Smaller are mutually exclusive projects, which project should a company prefer? If the company goes strictly by the PI, IRR, or MIRR criteria, it would choose Project Smaller. But is this the better project? Project Bigger provides more value—$411.85 versus $314.16. The techniques that ignore the scale of the investment—PI, IRR, and MIRR—may lead to an incorrect decision.

If the company is subject to capital rationing—say a limit of $5,000—and the two projects are independent projects, which project should the company choose? The company can only choose one—spend $2,500 or $5,000, but not $7,500. Applying the PI, IRR, or MIRR criteria, the company would choose Project Smaller. But is this the better project? Again, the techniques that ignore the scale of the investment—PI, IRR, and MIRR—leading to an incorrect decision.

Unequal Lives

If projects have unequal lives, the comparison, strictly on the basis of these techniques, may lead to an incorrect decision, whether choosing among mutually exclusive projects or subject to capital rationing. Consider the projects whose cash flows are provided in Figure 14.6. Project AA has a life of five years, Project BB a life of 10 years, and Project CC a life of 15 years. Projects AA and CC have a cost of capital of 4% and Project BB has a cost of capital of 5%.

Applying the four discounted cash flow techniques without considering their different lives suggests that Project CC provides the most value added; and Project CC produces the higher IRR benefit per $1 invested:

Technique	AA	BB	CC
NPV	$157.47	$235.48	$334.21
IRR	9.43%	9.61%	8.44%
MIRR	7.09%	7.24%	6.02%
PI	1.16	1.24	1.33

However, comparing these projects without any adjustment for the different lives ignores the fact that at the completion of the shorter projects, there is reinvestment necessary that is not reflected in the straightforward application of the techniques. In other words, this is an "apples to oranges" comparison if an adjustment is not made. One alternative is to find the common denominator life for the projects. In the case of these projects, this would be 30 years. This requires then looking at Project AA as reinvested in the same project five more times, resulting in a "life" for analysis of 30 years.

The common denominator approach may be cumbersome when there are many projects. An alternative is to use the *equivalent annual annuity* method. This method requires two steps:

FIGURE 14.6 Projects with Different Economics Lives

	Projects' End-of-Year Cash Flows		
Year	AA	BB	CC
0	−$1,000	−$1,000	−$1,000
1	260	160	120
2	260	160	120
3	260	160	120
4	260	160	120
5	260	160	120
6		160	120
7		160	120
8		160	120
9		160	120
10		160	120
11			120
12			120
13			120
14			120
15			120

Step 1. Calculate the annual annuity that is equivalent to the NPV of the project, considering the discount rate and the original life of the project. In the case of Project AA, the annuity amount is $35.37.

Step 2. Calculate the present value of this annuity if received *ad infinitum*. In the case of Project AA, this is $35.37/0.04 = $884.32.

The second step is only necessary if the comparison involves projects with different costs of capital. If the costs of capital are the same for the projects, the ranking of the projects in Step 1 is identical to that of Step 2. For the three projects we get the following:

	Project		
	AA	**BB**	**CC**
Equivalent annual annuity	$35.37	$30.50	$30.06
Value in perpetuity	$884.32	$609.91	$751.47

After adjusting for the different lives, the conclusion is that Project AA provides the most value added of the three projects.

COMPARING TECHNIQUES

When dealing with mutually exclusive projects, the NPV method leads us to invest in projects that maximize wealth, that is, capital budgeting decisions consistent with owners' wealth maximization. When dealing with a limit on the capital budget, the NPV and PI methods lead to the set of projects that maximize wealth.

The advantages and disadvantages of each of the techniques for evaluating investments are summarized in Table 14.2. As indicated in this table, the discounted cash flow techniques—NPV, IRR, PI, and MIRR—are preferred to the non-discounted cash flow techniques because these techniques consider (1) all cash flows, (2) the time value of money, and (3) the risk of future cash flows. The discounted cash flow techniques are also useful because we can apply objective decision criteria—criteria can be used to estimate whether the projects are adding value.

However, not all discounted cash flow techniques are right for every situation. There are questions that must be asked when evaluating an investment and the answers will determine which technique is the one to use for that investment:

- Are the projects mutually exclusive or independent?
- Are the projects subject to capital rationing?

TABLE 14.2   Advantages and Disadvantages to the Use of the Techniques

Net Present Value

Advantages	Disadvantages
1. Tells whether the investment will increase the company's value.	1. Requires an estimate of the cost of capital in order to calculate the net present value.
2. Considers all the cash flows.	
3. Considers the time value of money.	2. Expressed in terms of dollars, not as a percentage.
4. Considers the future cash flows' risk through the cost of capital.	

Profitability Index

Advantages	Disadvantages
1. Tells whether an investment increases the company's value.	1. Requires an estimate of the cost of capital in order to calculate the profitability index.
2. Considers all cash flows of the project.	
3. Considers the time value of money.	2. May not give the correct decision when used to compare mutually exclusive projects.
4. Considers the future cash flows' risk through the cost of capital.	
5. Useful in ranking and selecting projects when capital is rationed.	

Internal Rate of Return

Advantages	Disadvantages
1. Tells whether an investment increases the company's value.	1. Requires an estimate of the cost of capital in order to make a decision.
2. Considers all cash flows of the project.	2. May not give the value-maximizing decision when used to compare mutually exclusive projects.
3. Considers the time value of money.	
4. Considers the future cash flows' risk through the cost of capital in the decision rule.	3. May not give the value-maximizing decision when used to choose projects when there is capital rationing.
	4. Cannot be used in situations in which the sign of the cash flows of a project change more than once during the project's life.

Modified Internal Rate of Return

Advantages	Disadvantages
1. Tells whether an investment increases the company's value.	1. Requires an estimate of the cost of capital in order to make a decision.
2. Considers all cash flows of the project.	2. May not give the value-maximizing decision when used to compare mutually exclusive projects.
3. Considers the time value of money.	
4. Considers the future cash flows' risk through the cost of capital in the decision rule.	3. May not give the value-maximizing decision when used to choose projects when there is capital rationing.

TABLE 14.2 (continued)

Payback Period	
Advantages	Disadvantages
1. Simple to compute.	1. No concrete decision criteria to indicate
2. Provides some information on the risk of	whether an investment increases the
the investment.	company's value.
3. Provides a crude measure of liquidity.	2. Ignores cash flows beyond the payback
	period.
	3. Ignores the time value of money.
	4. Ignores the future cash flows' risk.

Discounted Payback Period	
Advantages	Disadvantages
1. Considers the time value of money.	1. No concrete decision criteria that indi-
2. Considers the project's cash flows' risk	cate whether the investment increases the
through the cost of capital.	company's value.
	2. Requires an estimate of the cost of capi-
	tal in order to calculate the payback.
	3. Ignores cash flows beyond the discounted
	payback period.

- Do the projects have the same risk?
- Do the projects have the same scale of investment?

The advantages and disadvantages of each method are listed in Table 14.2. Here are some simple rules:

1. If projects are independent and not subject to capital rationing, we can evaluate them and determine those projects that maximize wealth based on any of the discounted cash flow techniques.
2. If the projects are mutually exclusive, have the same investment outlay, and have the same risk, we must use only the NPV or the MIRR techniques to determine the projects that maximize wealth.
3. If projects are mutually exclusive and are of different risks or are of different scales, NPV is preferred over MIRR.

If the capital budget is limited, either the NPV or the PI can be used. The decision-maker must be careful, however, not to select projects simply on the basis of their NPV or PI (that is, ranking on NPV and selecting the highest NPV projects), but rather how NPV of the total capital budget can be maximized. In other words, which set of capital projects will maximize owners' wealth?

CAPITAL BUDGETING TECHNIQUES IN PRACTICE

Among the evaluation techniques in this chapter, the one we can be sure about is the NPV method. This method will steer a financial manager toward the project that maximizes wealth in the most general circumstances. But what evaluation technique is really used in practice?

What is known about what goes on in practice is from anecdotal evidence and surveys.[1] Observations from these indicate:

- Techniques that use discounted cash flows are preferred over technique that fail to take into consideration the time value of money.
- There is an increased use of the net present value method.
- Most decision-makers use more than one technique to evaluate the same projects, with a discounted cash flow techniques used as a primary method and payback period used as a secondary method.
- The most commonly used technique is the net present value method, though the internal rate of return method is still widely used.

Up until recently, studies suggested that the IRR method was the most popular method, which was troublesome because it may lead to decisions about projects that are not in the best interest of owners in certain circumstances.

Is the use of payback period also troublesome? Not necessarily. The payback period is generally used as a screening device for larger companies, eliminating those projects that cannot even break even. However, surveys suggest that smaller companies do rely on the payback method.[2] Further, the payback period can be viewed as a measure of a yield. If the future cash flows are the same amount each period and if these future cash flows can be assumed to be received each period forever—essentially, a perpetuity—then 1/payback period is a rough guide to a yield on the investment. Use of the simpler techniques, such as payback period, does not mean that a company has unsophisticated capital budgeting.

Remember that evaluating the cash flows is only one aspect of the process:

- Cash flows must first be estimated.
- Cash flows are evaluated using NPV, PI, IRR, MIRR or a payback method.
- Project risk must be assessed to determine the cost of capital.

---

[1] See Ryan and Ryan (2002) and Graham and Harvey (2002).
[2] For example, Graham and Harvey (2002) found that the payback period method ranked fourth in terms of percentage of the CFOs who used this technique.

The choice of the method used to evaluate the projects is just one of the many important decisions in the capital budgeting process.

CAPITAL BUDGETING AND THE JUSTIFICATION OF NEW TECHNOLOGY

Although the "mechanics" of calculating the measures in this chapter given (1) the initial cash flows; (2) the cash flow from operations; and (3) the required return (or hurdle rate) are not complicated, remember that the most complex activity of the capital budgeting procedure is estimating cash flows.

Some observers of capital budgeting practices have cited examples of how capital budgeting techniques have not been properly utilized.[3] That is, despite the evidence that more firms are using NPV, that does not mean that the right decisions about investment opportunities are being made. The examples cited have focused on the failure of capital budgeting techniques to evaluate the acquisition of new technological equipment and information management projects.

When new technological equipment, such as a newly created computer-aided production process, is considered for acquisition, the cash flows must be estimated. Does management do a good job of estimating the potential benefits from such technologies? Informed observers believe that this may not be the case despite the widespread use of capital budgeting techniques.

Underestimating the potential benefits when projecting cash flows results in a bias in favor of rejecting a new technology. But there are more problems. The estimated cash flows must be discounted. It is not uncommon for firms to select a very high required return to evaluate new technologies. While there is nothing wrong with assigning a high discount rate to a project involving new technologies, but this discount rate should reflect the project's risk, considering the benefits that the project may provide in terms of diversification. Unfortunately, for some firms the analysis underlying the setting of a high required rate ranges from little to none; or, put another way, for some firms the high required rate is arbitrarily determined.

Why does a high required return (or, equivalently discount rate or hurdle rate) bias the acceptance of new technologies? Recall our old friend, the time value of money. We know that the further into the future the positive cash flows, the lower will be all of the discounted flow measures we described in this chapter. We also know that the higher the discount rate the lower the NPV and profitability index. (In the case of the IRR, it will have to exceed the high hurdle rate.) Now consider a typical new technology that is being considered by a firm. It may take one or more years to get the new technol-

---

[3] See, for example, Hayes and Garvin (1982).

ogy up and running. Consequently, positive cash flow may not be seen for several years. A high discount rate coupled with positive cash flows not coming in for several years will bias the decision in the direction of rejecting a new technology. For example, suppose a discount rate of 22% is required on a project and that a positive cash flow is not realized for at least four years. Then the present value of a positive cash flow of $1 four years from now at 22% is $0.45; for a positive cash flow of $1 10 years from now, the present value is $0.14. On the other hand, if the correct discount rate is, say, 13%, then the present value of a $1 positive cash flow would be $0.61 if it received four years from now and $0.29 if it is received 10 years from now. You can see the dramatic impact of an unwarranted high discount rate. Add to this the underestimation of the positive cash flows by not properly capturing all the benefits from the introduction of a new technology, and you can see why U.S. firms may have been reluctant to acquire new technologies using "state-of-the-art" capital budgeting techniques. Is it any wonder that respondents to a study conducted by the Automation Forum found that the financial justification of automated equipment was the number one impediment to its introduction into U.S. firms two decades ago.[4]

In addition to the possible understatement of future cash flows, or the overstatement of the discount rate, associated with investment projects employing new technology, there is the potential problem of ignoring the real options that are present in these types of projects. A *real option* is an option associated with an investment project that has value arising from the option the company possesses, such as to defer investment in the project, abandon the project, or expand the project. It may be the case that the new technology that provides a comparative or competitive advantage is unique, patented technology. If this is the case, the company may have a real option to defer investment, which enhances the value of the project beyond the value attributed simply to discounted cash flows. According to survey evidence reported by Graham and Harvey (2002), less than 30% of CFOs incorporate the value of these real options in the capital budgeting decision.

All of this is not to say that the capital budgeting techniques described in this chapter should not be used to analyze whether to acquire new technologies. Quite the contrary. We believe that if properly employed—that is, good cash flow estimation capturing all the benefits and cost that can be realized from introducing a new technology, and the proper estimation of an appropriate discount rate—these techniques can help identify opportunities available from new technologies.

In fact, because of the failure to recognize the wide ranging impact of the acquisition of new technologies, the Garnter Group in the 1980s proposed the concept of *total cost ownership* (TCO). This measure, sometimes also

---

[4] See Dorian (1987).

referred to as the *total cost of operation*, is used to evaluate the direct and indirect impact related to the acquisition of new capital investment, taking into account all economic costs beyond the purchase cost and all the potential benefits. These economic costs include in addition to the acquisition costs changes in operating costs, conversion costs, and the cost of training personnel on the new equipment. On the benefit side, avoiding the potential loss of reputation from say security breaches or improved risk mangement system are recognized as well as any productivity or performance improvements. Basically, if all costs and benefits are properly accounted for in the capital budgeting framework set forth in this chapter and the previous one, the same conclusions about acquiring new technologies as obtained from TCO analysis will be reached. It has been the failure of those employing traditional capital budgeting to take into account the less obvious costs/benefits of ownership in acquiring new equipment, particularly new technologies, that TCO highlights, making it a popular tool employed by decision-makers. Still, despite the best efforts of management, it may be difficult to quantify the value of new technology and, therefore, difficult to use traditional capital budgeting techniques or TCO.

INCORPORATING RISK INTO CAPITAL BUDGETING ANALYSIS

Capital budgeting decisions require analyzing a proposed project's future cash flows, the uncertainty with its future cash flows, and the value of the future cash flows. When looking at the available investment opportunities, management must determine the project or set of projects that is expected to add the most value to the company. This requires evaluating how each project's benefits compare with its costs. The projects that are expected to increase owners' wealth the most are the best ones. In weighing a project's benefits and its costs, the costs include both the cash flow necessary to make the investment (the investment outlay) and the opportunity costs of not using the cash tied up in this investment.

The benefits are the future cash flows generated by the investment. But nothing in the future is certain, so there is risk associated with the future cash flows. Therefore, for an evaluation of any investment to be meaningful, management must represent how much risk there is that its cash flows will differ from what is expected in terms of both the amount and the timing of the cash flows.

Risk is the degree of uncertainty and is typically incorporated in one of two ways: (1) discount future cash flows using a higher discount rate, the greater the cash flow's risk; or (2) require a higher return on a project, the greater the cash flow's risk. Of course, risk is incorporated into the decision-making regarding projects that maximize owners' wealth. In this chapter, the sources of cash flow uncertainty and how to incorporate risk in the capital budgeting decision are examined.

Project Risk

When management estimates what it costs to invest in a given project and what benefits are expected from the project in the future, it is with uncertainty. The uncertainty arises from different sources, depending on the type of investment being considered, as well as the circumstances and the industry in which the company is operating. Uncertainty may arise from many sources, including:

- *Economic conditions.* Will consumers be spending or saving? Will the economy be in a recession? Will the government stimulate spending? What will be the rate of inflation?
- *Market conditions.* Is the market competitive? How long does it take competitors to enter into the market? Are there any barriers, such as patents or trademarks, that will keep competitors away? Is there sufficient supply of raw materials and labor? How much will raw materials and labor cost in the future?
- *Interest rates.* What will be the cost of raising capital in future years?
- *Taxes.* What will tax rates be? Will Congress alter the tax system?
- *International conditions.* Will the exchange rate between different countries' currencies where the company transacts change? Are the governments of the countries in which the company does business stable?

These sources of uncertainty influence future cash flows and their risk. To evaluate and select among projects that will maximize owners' wealth, management must assess the uncertainty associated with a project's cash flows.

Management worries about risk because the suppliers of capital—the creditors and owners—demand compensation for taking on risk. They can either provide their funds to the company to make investments or they could invest their funds elsewhere. Therefore, there is an opportunity cost to consider: what the suppliers of capital could earn elsewhere for the same level of risk. This return required by the suppliers of capital is the *required rate of return*, which comprises the compensation to suppliers of capital for their opportunity cost of not having the funds available (the time value of money) and compensation for risk. From the perspective of the company, this required rate of return is the cost to raise capital and hence is referred to as the cost of capital:

$$\text{Cost of capital} = \text{Compensation for the time value of money}$$
$$+ \text{Compensation for risk}$$

Discounting the expected future cash inflows and outflows of a project to the present produces what is often referred to as the project's net present value. The project is expected to add value to the company if the net present value is positive. In other words, if the net present value is positive, we expect the value of owners' wealth to increase. If, on the other hand, the net present value is negative, we do not expect the project to add value, but rather we expect it to reduce the value of owners' interest in the company.

In making investment decisions, financial managers must estimate the cost of capital. This estimation requires estimating the time value of money—the price of time—and the premium for risk. The time value of money is, basically, the return on a risk-free asset. The challenge for the financial manager is the estimate of the risk premium. For a given project, what is the appropriate risk premium? This requires first specifying the risk of the project. Considering that a company typically invests in many assets and is, essentially, a portfolio of asset, the issue arises: Is the risk of a project relevant for investment decision-making the total risk of the project or the risk of the project considering how the project affects the risk of the company?

Measuring Project Risk

If management has some idea of the uncertainty associated with a project's future cash flows—its possible outcomes—and the probabilities associated with these outcomes, then there is some measure of the risk of the project. But this is the project's risk in isolation from the company's other projects. This is the risk of the project ignoring the effects of diversification and is referred to as the project's *total risk* or *stand-alone risk.*

Because most companies have other assets, the stand-alone risk of the project under consideration may not be the relevant risk for analyzing the project. A company is a portfolio of assets and the returns of these different assets do not necessarily move together; that is, they are not perfectly positively correlated with one another. Management is therefore not concerned about the stand-alone risk of a project, but rather how the addition of the project to the company's portfolio of assets changes the risk of the company's portfolio.

Taking this a step further, consider that the shares of many companies may be owned by investors who themselves hold diversified portfolios. These investors are concerned about how the company's investments affect the risk of their own personal portfolios. When owners demand compensation for risk, they are requiring compensation for market risk, the risk they cannot diversify away. Recognizing this, a company considering taking on a new project should be concerned with how it changes the market risk of a company. Therefore, if the company's owners hold diversified investments—which is a safe assumption to make for all large corporations—it is the project's market risk that is relevant to the company's decision-making.

Even though management generally believes that it is the project's market risk that is important to analyze, stand-alone risk should not be ignored. If we are making decisions for a small, closely held company, whose owners do not hold well-diversified portfolios, the stand-alone risk gives us a good idea of the project's risk. And many small businesses fit into this category.

Even if it is a large corporation making an investment decision, and that corporation has many products and whose owners are well-diversified, the analysis of stand-alone risk may be useful. Stand-alone risk is often closely related to market risk: In many cases, projects with higher stand-alone risk may also have higher market risk. And a project's stand-alone risk is easier to measure than market risk. A project's stand-alone risk may be gauged by evaluating the project's future cash flows using statistical measures, sensitivity analysis, and simulation analysis.

Measuring a Project's Market Risk

If an investor is looking at an investment in a share of stock, it is possible to look at that stock's returns and the returns of the entire market over the same period of time as a way of measuring its market risk. While this is not a perfect measurement, it at least provides an estimate of the sensitivity of that particular stock's returns as compared to the returns of the market as a whole. But what about the market risk of a new product? There is no way to look at how that new product has affected the company's stock return.

Though it is not possible to look at a project's returns and see how they relate to the returns on the market as a whole, management can do the next best thing: Estimate the market risk of the stock of another company whose only line of business is the same as the project's risk. If we could find such a company, we could look at its stock's market risk and use that as a first step in estimating the project's market risk.

In finance, the Greek letter beta, β, is typically used to denote a measure of market risk. β is a measure of the sensitivity of an asset's returns to change in the returns of the market. β is an elasticity measure: If the return on the market increases by 1%, the return on an asset with a β of 2.0 is expected to increase by about 2%; if the return on the market decreases by 1%, the return on an asset with a β of 1.5 is expected to decrease by about 1.5%, and so on. The *asset beta*, therefore, is a measure of the asset's market risk. To distinguish the beta of an asset from the beta we used for a company's stock, the asset's beta is denoted by β_{asset} and the beta of a company's stock by β_{equity}.

Market Risk and Financial Leverage

If a company has no debt, the market risk of its common stock is the same as the market risk of its assets. That is, the beta of its equity, β_{equity}, is the same as its asset's beta, β_{asset}. However, it is rarely the case that a company has no debt in its capital structure, so we must consider the effect of financial leverage on a company's equity beta.

Financial leverage is the use of debt obligations that require fixed contractual payments to finance a company's assets. The greater the use of debt obligations, the more financial leverage and the more risk associated with cash flows to owners. The effect of using debt is to increase the risk of the company's equity. If the company has debt obligations, the market risk of its common stock is greater than its assets' risk (that is, β_{equity} is greater than β_{asset}) due to financial leverage.

Consider an asset's beta, β_{asset}. This beta depends on the asset's risk, not on how the company chose to finance it. Management can choose to finance it with equity only, in which case β_{equity} is greater than βasset. But what if, instead, management chooses to finance it partly with a mixture of debt and equity? When this is done, the creditors and the owners share the risk of the asset, so the asset's risk is split between them, but not equally because of the nature of the claims. Creditors have seniority and receive a fixed amount (interest and principal), so there is less risk to the creditors compared to the owners associated with a dollar of debt financing than with a dollar of equity financing of the same asset. So the market risk borne by the creditors is different from the market risk borne by owners.

Representing the market risk of creditors as β_{debt} and the market risk of owners as β_{equity}, the asset's market risk is the weighted average of the company's debt beta, β_{debt}, and equity beta, β_{equity} because the asset's risk is shared between creditors and owners. If the proportion of the company's capital from creditors is ω_{debt} and the proportion of the company's capital from owners is β_{equity}, then

$$\beta_{asset} = \beta_{debt}(\text{Proportion of assets financed with debt})$$
$$+ \beta_{equity}(\text{Proportion of assets financed with equity})$$

or

$$\beta_{asset} = \beta_{debt}\omega_{debt} + \beta_{equity}\omega_{equity}$$

But interest on debt is deducted to arrive at taxable income, so the claim that creditors have on the company's assets does not cost the company the full amount, but rather the after-tax claim, so the burden of debt financing is actually less due to interest deductibility. Further, the beta of debt is generally assumed to be zero (that is, there is no market risk associated with debt). With D representing the market value of debt, E representing the market value of equity, and τ the marginal tax rate, the relation between the asset beta and the equity beta is

$$\beta_{asset} = \beta_{debt} \frac{(1-\tau)D}{[(1-\tau)D]+E} + \beta_{equity} \frac{E}{[(1-\tau)D]+E}$$

Assuming $\beta_{debt} = 0$, and rearranging,

$$\beta_{asset} = \beta_{equity} \left[\frac{1}{\left(1+(1-\tau)\dfrac{D}{E}\right)} \right]$$

This means that an asset's beta is related to the company's equity beta, with adjustments for financial leverage. If a company does not use debt, $\beta_{equity} = \beta_{asset}$, and if the company does use debt, $\beta_{equity} > \beta_{asset}$.

Therefore, a β_{equity} may be translated into a β_{asset} by removing the influence of the company's financial risk from β_{equity}. To accomplish this, the following must be known:

- The company's marginal tax rate.
- The amount of the company's debt financing in market value terms.
- The amount of the company's equity financing in market value terms.

The process of translating an equity beta into an asset beta is referred to as "unlevering" because the effects of financial leverage are removed from the equity beta, β_{equity}, to arrive at a beta for the company's assets, β_{asset}. Therefore, this beta is an estimate of the market risk of a company's assets.

Using a Pure-Play There are many instances in which a company invests in assets with differing risks and management is faced with estimating the cost of capital of a project. Using the company's asset beta would be inappropriate because the asset beta reflects the market risk of all of the company's assets and this may not be the same risk as for the project being evaluated. One approach to handle this dilemma is to estimate the cost of capital of a company that has a single line of business that is similar to the project under consideration.

A company with a single line of business is referred to as a *pure-play*. Selecting the company or companies that have a single line of business, where this line of business is similar to the project's, helps in estimating the market risk of a project.

One method of estimating the pure-play's equity beta is regressing the returns on the pure-play's stock and the returns on the market. Once the pure-play's equity beta is calculated, management "unlevers" it by adjusting it for the financial leverage of the pure-play company.

Suppose a pure-play company has the following financial data:

β_{equity} = 1.1
Tax rate = 0.34
Debt = $3,914 million
Equity = $4,468 million

Its asset beta, β_{asset}, is 0.6970:

$$\beta_{asset} = 1.1 \left[\frac{1}{\left[\left(1 + (1 - 0.34)\dfrac{\$3,914}{\$4,468} \right) \right]} \right] = 0.6970$$

Because many U.S. corporations whose stock's returns are readily available have more than one line of business, finding an appropriate pure-play company may be difficult. Care must be taken to identify those that have lines of business similar to the project's. If an appropriate pure-play can be identified, this method can be used in estimating a project's cost of capital. (Estimating a pure-play asset beta is useful in many other applications, including valuing divisions or segments of a business and valuing small businesses.)

Adjusted Present Value

The use of the project's cost of capital to discount the cash flows of that project to the present is one method of incorporating the effect of financial leverage into the evaluation of a project. Another method is the *adjusted present value* (APV) method, which involves separating the value of the project and the value of the project's leverage.[5] The basic expression of APV is

---

[5] The adjusted present value method is based on the work of Myers (1974).

Adjusted present value = Value of project if all-equity financed

$$+ \underbrace{\left(\begin{array}{cc} \text{Value of the tax} & \text{PV of expected costs} \\ \text{benefits from debt} & \text{of financial distress} \end{array} \right)}_{\text{PV of the project's financial leverage}}$$

The value of the project if all-equity financed is the present value of the project's cash flows, discounted at a rate that reflects the asset's market risk. (Using the capital asset pricing model to determine the cost of capital for the all-equity financed project, the cost of capital is equal to the risk-free rate of interest plus the product of the market premium and the asset's beta. The product of the market premium and the asset's beta is the compensation for bearing risk.)

The value of the tax benefits from debt is the present value of the tax-shield from interest deductibility. For a given period, the tax shield is the product of the interest in that period and the marginal tax rate. The present value of the expected costs of financial distress is the present value of the probability-weighted costs of bankruptcy:

PV of expected costs of financial distress

= Probability of financial distress × PV of the costs of financial distress

Suppose management is evaluating a project that has a required initial outlay of $10 million and expected cash inflows of $3 million for each of the next five years. And suppose that the marginal tax rate is 35% and that the company's capital structure has a debt-equity ratio of 25%, a before-tax cost of debt of 5%, and a cost of equity of 9%. The cost of equity is calculated by using the following estimates: the company's stock beta of 1.5, an expected risk-free rate of interest of 3%, and a market risk premium of 4%.

A debt-equity ratio of 25% means that the company's capital structure consists of 20% debt and 80% equity. (The proportion of debt in the capital structure is calculated by dividing the debt-equity ratio by one plus the debt-equity ratio.) Using the weighted average cost of capital and the net present value method, the project's cost of capital is

Project's cost of capital = [(0.20)(0.05)(1 − 0.4)] + [(0.80)(0.09)] = 7.8%

The NPV of the project is therefore $2.01415 million.

The APV of the project requires first calculating the value of the project if all-equity financed. The unlevered beta for the project—that is, the beta if the company was all-equity financed—is 1.304:

$$\beta_{asset} = 1.5 \left[\frac{1}{1 + [(1 - 0.40)0.25]} \right] = 1.0304$$

Therefore, the cost of equity is

$$r_e = 0.03 + [1.0304\ (0.04)] = 0.08217 \text{ or } 8.217\%$$

The value of the all-equity-financed project is calculated by discounting the project's cash flows at 8.217% and subtracting the cost of the project. The result is a value of the equity-financed project of $1.9098 million.

The value of the tax shields requires first calculating the tax shield each period and discounting these at the before-tax cost of debt. If debt is 20% of the project's cost and the debt is constant through the life of the project at 20% of $10 million, or $2 million, the interest expense each year is 5% of $2 million, or $0.1 million. The tax shield each period is therefore 40% of $0.1 million, or $0.04 million. Discounting these tax shields at 5% produces a present value of the tax benefit from debt of $0.1732 million.

Putting these two value pieces together produces:

$$APV = \$1.9098 \text{ million} + \$0.1732 \text{ million} = \$2.0830 \text{ million}$$

The NPV using the weighted average cost of capital (WACC) is $2.0415 million, which is less than the APV that we calculated of $2.0830 million. Because we assumed a constant capital structure over the life of the project, the WACC and APV will differ in this example only because we incorporated financial leverage into the WACC for the NPV, but have not incorporated it in the APV as yet. If we back into the effect of financial distress, which is the only missing component in the APV, the PV of the costs of distress is $2.0830 million − $2.0415 million = $0.415 million. A challenge in using APV is that it is difficult to come up with the estimate of the likelihood and cost of financial distress. (In some applications, the cost of financial distress is ignored if the company's capital structure is not believed to be sufficiently levered such that the costs of distress would be material.)

The difference between APV and NPV methods can be seen once it is assumed that the capital structure will change over the life of the project. If the NPV is calculated in the standard manner, using a WACC that does not change over the life of the project, this most likely will understate or overstate the value of the project if the capital structure changes. The only way to have equivalence between APV and the NPV in the case of a changing capital structure is to recalculate the WACC in the NPV method when the capital structure changes, which would be cumbersome. If, for example, the capital structure is expected to change each period, the WACC used for discounting the project cash flows must therefore change each period.

Extending this example to consider a changing capital structure, assume that the debt of $2 million is paid off over the life of the project, with $0.4 million of debt paid off each year. In this case, the interest expense, and hence tax shield, declines each year and the capital structure becomes less levered over the life of the project. We compare the NPV and the APV for the constant and declining capital structure scenarios in Table 14.3. In Table 14.3(a), the capital structure is constant and the difference between the NPV and the APV is the present value of financial distress, as discussed previously. In Table 14.3(b) of this table, the APV is less than in Table 14.3(a) because the present value of the tax shields is less. In this case, the difference between the NPV and the APV is not only the cost of financial distress, but also the effect of the changing capital structure (which changes the weights in the WACC and hence the NPV), which affects the value of the tax shields. (Without a great deal more complexity, it is not possible to detail the effects on the capital structure and how the WACC must change to maintain equivalence to the APV and NPV. This is because not only do the weights in the WACC change, but also as the capital structure changes, the costs of debt and equity both change as well.)

The APV is easier to use relative to the NPV in the case of the changing capital structure because adjusting for the effects of the changing capital structure is less complex. This is summarized in Table 14.4.

TABLE 14.3 NPV and APV

(a) Constant capital structure

In Millions	Year					
	0	1	2	3	4	5
Project cash flow	$(10.000)	$3.000	$3.000	$3.000	$3.000	$3.000
Debt principal		$2.000	$2.000	$2.000	$2.000	$2.000
Interest on debt		$0.100	$0.100	$0.100	$0.100	$0.100
Interest tax shield		$0.040	$0.040	$0.040	$0.040	$0.040

NPV if constant WACC = $2.0415 million

APV components:

    Value of all equity financed project = $1.9098 million

    Value of interest tax shields = 0.1732 million

  APV without costs of financial distress = $2.0830 million

TABLE 14.3 (continued)
(b) Declining capital structure
Assuming that debt is paid off evenly throughout the life of the project and that the before-tax cost of debt declines uniformly from 5% to 4.6%.

In Millions	Year					
	0	1	2	3	4	5
Project cash flow	$(10.000)	$3.000	$3.000	$3.000	$3.000	$3.000
Debt principal		$2.000	$1.600	$1.200	$0.800	$0.400
Interest on debt		$0.100	$0.080	$0.060	$0.040	$0.020
Interest tax shield		$0.040	$0.032	$0.024	$0.016	$0.008
Before-tax cost of debt		5.0%	4.9%	4.8%	4.7%	4.6%

NPV if constant WACC	=	$2.0415 million
APV components:		
Value of all equity financed project	=	$1.9098 million
Value of interest tax shields	=	0.1077 million
APV without costs of financial distress	=	$2.0185 million

TABLE 14.4 Capital Structure Change and APV vs. NPV

Capital Structure Change	APV Is Affected Because	NPV Is Affected Because
Debt-equity declines over the life of the project.	▪ The before-tax cost of debt may decline.[a]	▪ The before-tax cost of debt may decline. ▪ The cost of equity may decline. ▪ The weight assigned to debt decreases and the weight assigned to equity increases.
Debt-equity increases over the life of the project.	▪ The before-tax cost of debt may increase.	▪ The before-tax cost of debt may increase. ▪ The cost of equity may increase. ▪ The weight assigned to debt increases and the weight assigned to equity decreases.

[a] Hence, the present value of the tax shields is affected. Whether the present value of the tax shields increases or decreases depends on the rate of the decrease in the tax shields versus the decline in the cost of debt.

The NPV, however, has the distinct advantage over the APV of being simpler to use when the capital structure is assumed constant throughout the life of the project. In the case of the NPV, estimates of the costs and probability of financial distress are not necessary; rather the influence of the likelihood and cost of financial distress is already impounded in the costs of debt and the costs of equity and, hence, the WACC.

The challenge in using APV is that management must specify the costs of financial distress and the probability, which are difficult to quantify. If the value effects of financial distress are ignored, the APV is overstated and, hence, the value added of the project is overstated.

Incorporating Risk in the Capital Budgeting Decision

Using the discounted cash flow capital budgeting techniques, the project's cost of capital used to evaluate a project should reflect the project's risk.

Risk-Adjusted Rate

The cost of capital is the cost of funds from the providers of capital, creditors and owners. This cost is the return required by these suppliers of capital. The greater the risk of a project, the greater the return required and, hence, the greater the cost of capital.

One view of the project's cost of capital is that it is the sum of what suppliers of capital demand for providing funds, which is comprised of two parts:

1. The return if the project were risk-free, which provides compensation for the time value of money.
2. The compensation for risk.

The compensation for the time value of money includes compensation for any anticipated inflation. The risk-free rate of interest, such as the yield on a long-term U.S. Treasury bond, is typically used to represent the time value of money. The compensation for risk is the extra return required because the project's future cash flows are uncertain. Because the relevant risk is the project's market risk, investors should require a greater return, the greater the project's market risk.

Project's Cost of Capital Based on the CAPM Method   A commonly used method of estimating a project's cost of capital is to use the return formula from the capital asset pricing model. This requires first specifying the premium for bearing the average amount of risk for the market as a whole and then, using a measure of market risk, fine tuning this to reflect the market risk of the project. The market risk premium for the market as a whole is the difference between the average expected market return, r_m, and the expected risk-free rate of interest, r_f. If a company buys an asset whose market risk was the same as that of the market as a whole, the company expects a return of $r_m - r_f$ to compensate investors for market risk.

Adjusting the market risk premium for the market risk of the particular project requires multiplying the market risk premium by that project's asset beta, β_{asset}:

$$\text{Compensation for market risk} = \beta_{asset}(r_m - r_f)$$

This is the extra return necessary to compensate for the project's market risk. The asset beta fine-tunes the risk premium for the market as a whole to reflect the market risk of the particular project. If we then add the risk-free interest rate, we arrive at the cost of capital:

$$\text{Cost of capital} = r_f + \beta_{asset}(r_m - r_f)$$

Suppose the expected risk-free rate of interest is 4% and the expected return on the market as a whole is 10%. If the β_{asset} is 2, this means that if there is a 1% change in the market risk premium, a 2% change in the return on the project is expected. In this case, the cost of capital is 16%:

$$\text{Cost of capital} = 0.04 + 2(0.10 - 0.04) = 0.16 \text{ or } 16\%$$

If instead the β_{asset} is 0.75, the cost of capital is 8.5%:

$$\text{Cost of capital} = 0.04 + 0.75(0.06) = 0.085 \text{ or } 8.5\%$$

Because the cost of capital is the result of a calculation using several inputs, it is important to test the sensitivity of the cost of capital to these inputs.

Adjusting the Company's Cost of Capital It is often the case that management is not able to estimate the project's market risk, nor even the expected risk-free rate. Another way to estimate the cost of capital for a project without estimating the risk premium directly is to use the company's WACC as a starting point. The WACC is the company's marginal cost of raising one more dollar of capital—the cost of raising one more dollar in the context of all the company's projects considered altogether, not just the project being evaluated. The WACC of the company can then be adjusted to suit the perceived risk of the project:

- If a new project being considered is riskier than the average project of the company, the cost of capital of the new project is greater than the average cost of capital.
- If the new project is less risky, its cost of capital is less than the average cost of capital.
- If the new project is as risky as the average project of the company, the new project's cost of capital is equal to the average cost of capital.

However, altering the company's cost of capital to reflect a project's cost of capital requires judgment. How much do we adjust it? If the project is riskier than the typical project, do we add 2%? 4%? 10%? There is no prescription here. It depends on the judgment and experience of the decision maker. But this is where the measures of a project's stand-alone risk can be used to help form that judgment.

Real Options

A significant challenge in capital budgeting is dealing with risk. The traditional methods of evaluating projects are being challenged by an alternative approach that applies option-pricing theory to real assets, referred to as *real options valuation* (ROV). The interest in ROV arises from the fact that the traditional methods do not consider directly the options available in many investment projects. Though the importance of options in investment opportunities has long been recognized, it is only recently that a great deal of attention has been paid to incorporating options in a meaningful way. (For example, Myers (1977) recognized the importance of considering investment opportunities as growth options.)

Consider the typical options inherent in an investment opportunity:

- Almost every project has an option to abandon, though there may be constraints (e.g., legally binding contracts) that affect when this option can be exercised.
- Many projects have the option to expand.
- Many projects have an option to defer investment, putting off the major investment outlays to some future date.

So how does management consider these options within the context of the traditional methods? One approach is to use sensitivity analysis or simulation analysis. And while these analyses allow a look at the possible outcomes of a decision, they do not provide guidance regarding which course of action—of the many—to take. Another approach is the use of a decision tree analysis, associating probabilities to each of the possible outcomes for an event and mapping out the possible outcomes and the value of the investment opportunity associated with these different outcomes. And while this approach is workable when there are few options associated with a project, option pricing provides a method of analysis that is more comprehensive.

The basic idea of ROV is to consider that the value of a project extends beyond its value as measured by the net present value; in other words, the value of a project is supplemented by the value of the options. Because the options are considered strategic decisions, the revised or supplemented net present value is often referred to as the *strategic NPV*. Consider an investment opportunity that has one option associated with it. The strategic NPV is the sum of the traditional NPV (the static NPV) and the value of the option:

$$\text{Strategic NPV} = \text{Static NPV} + \text{Value of the option}$$

Certainty Equivalents

An alternative to adjusting the discount rate to reflect risk is to adjust the cash flow to reflect risk. We do this by converting each cash flow and its risk into its certainty equivalent. A *certainty equivalent* is the certain cash flow that is considered to be equivalent to the risky cash flow. For example, if the risky cash flow two years into the future is $1.5 million, the certainty equivalent is the dollar amount of a certain cash flow (that is, a sure thing) that the firm considers to be worth the same. This certainty equivalent could be $1 million, $0.8 million, $1.4 million, or any other amount—which depends on both the degree of risk of the $1.5 million risky cash flow and the judgment of the decision-maker.

The certainty equivalent approach of incorporating risk into the net present value analysis is useful for several reasons:

- It separates the time value of money and risk. Risk is accounted for in the adjusted cash flows, while the time value of money is accounted for in the discount rate.
- It allows each year's cash flows to be adjusted separately for risk. This is accomplished by converting each year's cash flows into a certainty equivalent for that year. The certainty equivalent factor may be different for each year.
- The decision-maker can incorporate preferences for risk. This is done in determining the certainty equivalent cash flows.

However, there are some disadvantages to using the certainty equivalent approach that stymie its application in practice:

- *The net present value of the certainty equivalent is not easily interpreted.* We no longer have the clearer interpretation of the net present value as the increment in shareholder wealth.
- *There is no reliable way of determining the certainty equivalent value for each year's cash flow.*

Assessment of Project Risk in Practice

Most U.S. companies consider risk in some manner in evaluating investment projects. But considering risk is usually a subjective analysis as opposed to the more objective results obtainable with simulation or sensitivity analysis.

Surveys indicate that companies that use discounted cash flow techniques, such as net present value and internal rate of return methods, tend to use a risk-adjusted cost of capital, but generally use the company's weighted average cost of capital as a benchmark.[6] But a significant portion of companies use a single cost of capital for all projects, which can be problematic. Suppose a company uses the same cost of capital for all its projects. If all of them have the same risk and the cost of capital being used is appropriate for this level of risk, there is no problem. But what if a company uses the same cost of capital but the projects each have different levels of risk?

The company's cost of capital reflects the company's average risk project. What happens when this cost of capital is applied in discounted cash flow techniques, such as the net present value or the internal rate of return, to all projects? This will result in the company:

- Rejecting profitable projects (which would have increased owners' wealth) that have risk below the risk of the average risk project because the company has discounted the project's future cash flows too much.
- Accepting unprofitable projects whose risk is above the risk of the average project, because the company did not discount the project's future cash flows enough.

The effect of the use of the single cost of capital is demonstrated using the following illustration. Consider the following three projects, each requiring an investment of $1 million:

---

[6] See, for example, the survey by Graham and Harvey (2002).

	Projects		
	AAA	BBB	CCC
Project's cost of capital	12%	10%	8%
NPV at project's cost of capital	−$30,000	+$90,000	$30,000
NPV at company's cost of capital	+$10,000	+$90,000	−$20,000
Decision			
Based on project's cost of capital	Reject	Accept	Accept
Based on company's cost of capital	Accept	Accept	Reject

Assuming that each project is independent and there is no limit to the capital budget, projects BBB and CCC should be accepted. Therefore, the value added based on using projects' cost of capital is $90,000. If the company's cost of capital is used, then AAA is accepted when it should not have been (reducing the value of the company by $30,000) and project CCC is rejected, when it could have been adding value of $30,000. In this example, we see that the use of the single discount rate results in a forgone opportunity (from the rejection of the lower risk project) and a value-destroying decision (the acceptance of a negative net present value project).

Companies that use a risk-adjusted discount rate usually do so by classifying projects into risk classes by the type of project. For example, a company with a cost of capital of 10% may use a 14% cost of capital for new products and a much lower rate of 8% for replacement projects. Given a set of costs of capital, management need only figure out what class a project belongs to and then apply the rate assigned to that class.

Companies may also make adjustments in the cost of capital for factors other than the type of project. For example, companies investing in projects in foreign countries will sometimes make an adjustment for the additional risk of the foreign project, such as exchange rate risk, inflation risk, and political risk.

There are tools available to assist the decision-maker in measuring and evaluating project risk. But much of what is actually done in practice is subjective. Judgment, with a large dose of experience, is used more often than scientific means of incorporating risk. Is this bad? Well, the scientific approaches to measurement and evaluation of risk depend, in part, on subjective assessments of risk, the probability distributions of future cash flows, and judgments about market risk. So it is possible that bypassing the more technical analyses in favor of completely subjective assessment of risk may result in cost-of-capital estimates that better reflect the project's risk. But then again, it may not. The proof may be in the pudding, but it is difficult to assess the "proof" because it can never be determined how well a company may have done had it used more technical techniques.

SUMMARY

In this chapter, we discussed and illustrated the six most commonly used techniques for evaluating capital budgeting proposals (the net present value, profitability index, internal rate of return, modified internal rate of return, payback period, and discounted payback period), as well as how to deal with risk in capital budgeting analysis. Each technique offers some advantages and disadvantages. The discounted flow techniques are superior to the payback period and the discounted payback period. Care must be taken in selecting a technique to be used when evaluating mutually exclusive projects or projects subject to capital rationing, The net present value method is consistent with owners' wealth maximization whether mutually exclusive projects are being evaluated or there is capital rationing.

Not all discounted cash flows methods are appropriate in all circumstances. When faced with mutually exclusive projects, scale differences, different project lives, or capital rationing, care must be exercised in using the most appropriate method for these special cases. When there are scale differences, use the net present value. When evaluating projects that have different economics lives, the different lives before selecting projects must be taken into account.

While capital budgeting techniques are used to evaluate the acquisition of new technologies, there are biases introduced. Specifically, both the potential wide-ranging cash flow consequences are not always recognized and unwarranted high required returns are set.

Evaluating capital projects requires assessing the risk associated with the future cash flows. This risk may be measured in terms of the stand-alone risk or the market risk, though in most cases the focus is on the project's market risk. Risk is typically incorporated into decision-making by using a cost of capital that reflects the project's risk. The adjusted present value method is an alternative method for evaluating a capital project that incorporates the effect of financial leverage. The method involves separating the value of the project's financial leverage from the value of the project.

The relevant risk for the evaluation of a project is the project's market risk, which is also referred to as the asset beta. This risk may be estimated by looking at the market risk of companies in a single line of business similar to that of the project, a pure-play. An alternative to finding a pure-play is to classify projects according to the type of project (e.g., expansion) and assign costs of capital to each project type according to subjective judgment of risk.

Most companies adjust for risk in their assessment of the attractiveness of projects. However, this adjustment is typically accomplished by evaluating risk subjectively and ad-hoc adjustments to the company's cost of capital to arrive at a cost of capital for a particular project.

Estimating the options associated with an investment opportunity may reveal value in a project that is not reflected using traditional capital budgeting techniques. There are options associated with every investment opportunity, including the option to defer the investment and the option to abandon the investment.

An alternative approach to dealing with risk in a capital project is through the use of certainty equivalents, which are risk-free values that correspond to the risky cash flows.

REFERENCES

Graham, J. and Harvey, C. R. (2002). How do CFOs Make capital budgeting and capital structure decisions? *Journal of Applied Corporate Finance* 15, no. 1: 8–23.

Hayes, R. H. and Garvin, D. (1982). Managing as if tomorrow mattered. *Harvard Business Review* 60, no. 3 (May–June): 70–79.

Myers, S. C. (1974). Interactions in corporate financing and investment decisions: Implications for capital budgeting. *Journal of Finance* 29, no. 1: 1–25.

Myers, S. C. (1977). Determinants of corporate borrowing. *Journal of Financial Economics* 5, no. 2: 147–176.

CHAPTER 15

Managing Current Assets

Current assets are assets that could reasonably be converted into cash within one operating cycle or one year, whichever takes longer. An operating cycle begins when the firm invests cash in the raw materials used to produce its goods or services and ends with the collection of cash for the sale of those same goods or services. For example, if a company manufactures and sells candy products, its operating cycle begins when it purchases the raw materials for the products (e.g., sugar) and ends when it cycle of most businesses is less than one year, we tend to think of current assets as those assets that can be converted into cash in one year. *Current assets* consist of cash, marketable securities, accounts receivable, and inventories.

Cash comprises both currency and assets that are immediately transformable into cash. Marketable securities are securities that can be readily sold when cash is needed. Every company needs to have a certain amount of cash to fulfill immediate needs, and any cash in excess of immediate needs is usually invested temporarily in marketable securities. Investments in marketable securities are simply viewed as a short-term place to store funds.

Accounts receivable are amounts due from customers who have purchased the firm's goods or services but haven't yet paid for them. To encourage sales, many firms allow their customers to "buy now and pay later," perhaps at the end of the month or within 30 days of the sale. Accounts receivable therefore represents money that the firm expects to collect soon. Inventories represent the total value of the firm's raw materials, work-in-process, and finished (but as yet unsold) goods. A manufacturer of toy trucks would likely have plastic and steel on hand as raw materials, work-in-process consisting of truck parts and partly completed trucks, and finished goods consisting of trucks packaged and ready for shipping.

The working capital decision requires an evaluation of the benefits and costs associated with each component. In this chapter, we will look at the management of cash, marketable securities, receivables, and inventory and explain how to evaluate the benefits and costs associated with the investment in these assets.

MANAGEMENT OF CASH AND MARKETABLE SECURITIES

Managers base decisions about investing in long-term projects on judgments about future cash flows, the uncertainty of those cash flows, and the opportunity costs of the funds to be invested. Decisions pertaining to short-term assets are made in similar ways, but over much shorter time horizons. Thus considerations of risk takes a smaller role in our discussions in the next few chapters, while the operating cycle becomes more important.

A company's operating cycle is the time it takes to turn the investment of cash (e.g., buying raw materials) back into cash (e.g., collecting on accounts receivables). As our opening example shows, the operating cycle in part determines how long it takes for a firm to generate cash from its short-term assets and, therefore, the risk and cost of its investment in current assets, or working capital. *Working capital* is the capital that managers can immediately put to work to generate the benefits of capital investment. Working capital is also known as *current capital* or *circulating capital*.

Firms invest in current assets for the same reasons that they invest in long-term, capital assets: to maximize owners' wealth. But, because managers evaluate current assets over a shorter time frame (less than a year), they focus more on their cash flows and less on the time value of money.

How much should a firm invest in current assets? That depends on several factors:

- The type of business and product.
- The length of the operating cycle.
- Customs, traditions, and industry practices.
- The degree of uncertainty of the business.

The type of business, whether retail, manufacturing, or service, affects how a firm invests. In some industries, large investments in machinery and equipment are necessary. In other industries, such as retail firms, less is invested in plant and equipment and other long-term assets, and more is invested in current assets such as inventory.

The firm's operating cycle—the time it takes the firm to turn its investment in inventory into cash—affects how much the firm ties up in current assets. The operating cycle comprises the time it takes to: manufacturer the goods, sell them and collect on their sale. The net operating cycle considers the benefit from purchasing goods on credit; the net operating cycle is the operating cycle less the number of days of purchases. The longer the net operating cycle, the larger the investment in current assets.

CASH MANAGEMENT

Cash flows *out of* a firm as it pays for the goods and services it purchases from others. Cash flows into the firm as customers pay for the goods and services they purchase. When we refer to *cash*, we mean the amount of cash and cash-like assets—currency, coin, and bank balances. When we refer to *cash management*, we mean management of cash inflows and outflows, as well as the stock of cash on hand.

Monitoring Cash Needs

A company can monitor its cash needs through cash forecasting. *Cash forecasting* is analyzing how much and when cash is needed, and how much and when to generate it. Cash forecasting requires pulling together and consolidating the short-term projections that relate to cash inflows and outflows. These cash flows may be a part of the capital budget, production plans, sales forecasts, or collection on accounts.

To understand the cash needs and generation, managers have to understand how long it takes to generate cash once an investment in inventory is made. We're referring to the operating cycle—the time it takes to make cash out of cash.

If we consider cash disbursements, we get a better picture of the net cash—the *net operating cycle*—the time it takes to make cash from cash plus the time we delay payment on our purchases:

Net operating cycle = Operating cycle – Number of days of purchases

Estimating net operating cycle gives a manager information on how long it takes to generate cash from current assets. The longer the net operating cycle, the more cash needed on hand.

To understand cash flows, the manager also has to have a fairly good idea of the uncertainty of the firm's cash needs and cash generation. Cash flows are uncertain because sales are uncertain, and so is the uncertainty regarding when the firm will collect payment on what it sells, as well as uncertainty about production costs and capital outlays. Forecasting cash flows requires the coordination of marketing, purchasing, production, and financial management.

Reasons for Holding Cash Balances

Firms hold some of their assets in the form of cash for several reasons. They need cash to meet the transactions in their day-to-day operations. Referred to as the *transactions balance*, the amount of cash needed for this purpose differs from firm to firm, depending on the particular flow of cash into and out of the firm. The amount depends on:

1. The size of the transactions made by the firm.
2. The firm's operating cycle, which depends on the firm's production process, purchasing policies, and collection policies.

There is always some degree of uncertainty about future cash needs. Firms typically hold an additional balance, referred to as a *precautionary balance*, just in case transactions needs exceed the transactions balance. But how much to keep as a precaution depends on the degree of the transactions uncertainty—how well the firm can predict the firm's transactions needs. For example, a retail store has a good idea from experience about how much cash to have on hand to meet the typical day's transactions. In addition to what is needed for a typical day, the retail store may keep more cash on hand to meet a higher than usual level of transactions.

In addition to the precautionary balances, firms may keep cash on hand for unexpected future opportunities. Referred to as a *speculative balance*, this is the amount of cash or securities that can be easily turned into cash, above what is needed for transactions and precaution. The speculative balance enables a firm to take advantage of investment opportunities on short notice and to meet extraordinary demands for cash. For example, an automobile manufacturers may need an additional cash cushion to pay its bills in case a wildcat strike closes down a plant.

In addition to the cash balances for transactions, precautionary, and speculative needs, a firm may keep cash in a bank account in the form of a *compensating balance*—a cash balance required by banks in exchange for banking services. By keeping a balance in an account that is noninterest earning or low-interest earning, the firm is effectively compensating the bank for the loans and other services it provides. Some bank loans and bank services require a specified amount or average balance be maintained in an account.

Costs Associated with Cash

There is a cost to holding assets in the form of cash. Because cash does not generate earnings, the cost of holding assets in the form of cash, referred to as the *holding cost*, is an opportunity cost—what the cash could have earned if invested in another asset.

If a firm needs cash, it must either sell an asset or borrow cash. There are transactions costs associated with both. Transactions costs are the fees, commissions, or other costs associated with selling assets or borrowing to get cash; they are analogous to the ordering costs for inventory.

Determining the Investment in Cash

How much cash should a firm hold? For transactions purposes, enough to meet the demands of day-to-day operations. To determine how much is enough transactions purposes, a manager compares the cost of having too much cash to the cost getting cash—in other words, a manager compares the holding cost and transactions cost.

As more cash is held, its holding cost increases. With more cash on hand, the costs of making transactions to meet cash needs for operations declines. That's because with larger cash balances, the firm needs fewer transactions (selling marketable securities or borrowing from a bank) to meet your cash needs.

The manager wants to have on hand the amount of cash that minimizes the sum of the costs of making transactions to get the cash (selling securities or borrowing) and the opportunity cost of holding more cash than we need. The various economic models that can be used for determining the level of cash and when it will be needed. They include the Baumol model and the Miller-Orr model.[1]

We look at the Baumol Model and the Miller-Orr Model to help us decide on the level of cash we need and when we need it.

Cash Management Techniques

Cash management has very simple goals:

- Have enough cash on hand to meet immediate needs, but not too much.
- Get cash from those who owe it to you as soon as possible and pay it out to those you owe as late as possible.

The Baumol and Miller-Orr models help firms manage cash to satisfy the first goal. But the second goal requires methods that speed up incoming cash and slow down outgoing cash. To understand these methods, the manager needs to understand the check clearing process.

The Check Clearing Process

The process of receiving cash from customers involves several time-consuming steps:

---

[1] See Baumol (1952) and Miller and Orr (1966).

- The customer sends the check.
- The check is processed within the firm—so the customer can be credited with paying.
- The check is sent to the firm's bank.
- The bank sends the check through the clearing system.
- The firm is credited for the amount of the check.

Several days may elapse between the time when the firm receives the check and the time when the firm is credited with the amount of the check. During that time, the firm cannot use the funds. The amount of funds tied up in transit and in the banking system is referred to as the *float*. The float occurs because of the time tied up in the mail, in check processing within the firm, and in check processing in the banking system.

The float can be costly to those who are on the receiving end. Suppose on average customers make $1 million in payments each day. If the float is seven days, therefore seven times $1,000,000 = $7,000,000 coming to the firm that cannot be used. If a manager can speed up collections to five days, the manager can reduce the float to $5 million—and use the freed-up $2 million for other things.

The float can be beneficial to the payer. Suppose a manager makes payments to suppliers, on average, $1 million per day. And suppose it takes suppliers five days after they receive the checks to complete the check processing system. The manager has $5 million in float per day. If the manager could slow down the check processing by one day, the manager increases the float to $6 million. That's $1 million more cash available to use each day.

There are several ways we can speed up incoming cash:

- *Lockbox system.* A system where customers send their checks to post office boxes and banks pick up and begin processing these checks immediately.
- *Selection of banks.* Choosing banks that are well connected in the banking system, such as clearinghouse banks or correspondent banks, can speed up the collection of checks.
- *Check processing within the firm.* Speed up processing of checks within the firm so that deposits are made quickly.
- *Electronic collection.* Avoid the use of paper checks, dealing only with electronic entries.
- *Concentration banking.* The selection of a bank or banks that are located near customers, reducing the mail float.

A *clearinghouse* is a location where banks meet to exchange checks drawn on each other, and a *clearinghouse bank* is a participant in a clearinghouse. Clearinghouses may involve local banks or local and other banks. Being a member of a clearinghouse can reducing check clearing time by up to one-half a day relative to clearing checks through the Federal Reserve system. A *correspondent bank* is a bank that has an agreement with a clearinghouse bank to exchange its checks in the clearinghouse. Banks can become correspondents to clearinghouses in other parts of the country, reducing their check clearing time relative to clearing checks through the Federal Reserve system.

In addition, there are several methods you can use to slow up our payment of cash:

- *Controlled disbursements.* Minimizing bank balances by depositing only what is needed to make immediate demands on the account.
- *Remote disbursement.* Paying what is owed with checks drawn on a bank that is not readily accessible to the payee, increasing the check processing float.

Whichever way a manager decides to speed up the receipt of cash or slow down the payment of cash there is a cost. A manager must weigh the benefits with the cost of altering the float.

We will look closely at one speed-up device—the lockbox system—and one slow-down device—controlled disbursements—to see how the float can be altered.

Lockbox System

With a *lockbox system,* a firm's customers send their payments directly to a post office box controlled by the firm's bank. This skips the step where the firm receives and handles the check and paperwork (see Figure 15.1).

FIGURE 15.1 An Example of the Time Line Corresponding to a Lockbox System

The lockbox system may reduce the mail float (due to the placement of the lockboxes near the customer) and changes what was the "firm float" to a "bank float" since the bank now processes the checks received from customers.

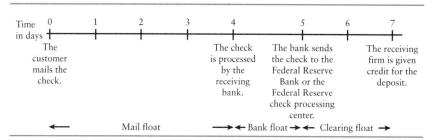

The lockbox system can cut down on the time it takes to process checks in two ways. First, the firm can use post office boxes (and collecting banks) throughout the country, reducing the time a check spends in the mail—reducing the mail float. Second, because the bank processes the checks and paperwork, the lockbox avoids the time the checks spend at the receiving firm—eliminating the time it takes to process checks in the firm.

To see the savings using a lockbox, suppose it can reduce a firm's total float from eight to five days. For every $1 million per year collected through the lockbox system, three days worth of collections ($1,000,000/365 × 3 days = $8,219) freed up for investment during the year. If a manager can earn 5% a year investing in marketable securities, this amounts to an increase in earnings of $8,219 × 0.05 = $411 per $1 million collected. As long as the cost of the lockbox system is less than the cost savings per year, there is a benefit to using it.

We can state the increased earnings from the lockbox system as

> Benefit from lockbox system
>
> = (Collections per day) × (Reduction of float in days)
>
> × (Opportunity cost of funds per year)

To decide whether or not to use such a system involves comparing the benefit obtained from the lockbox system with the lockbox fees charged by the bank.

Controlled Disbursements

If a firm seeks have more cash available for its use, a manager can slow down the payments made by the firm—increasing the float to others. A *controlled disbursement* is an arrangement with a bank to minimize the amount that it holds in bank balances to pay what it owes. Under this system, a manager minimizes the firm's bank balance to only the funds necessary for immediate disbursing. To make this work, the manager needs to work closely with the bank—the bank notifies the manager of checks being cashed on the firm's account and the manager immediately wire the necessary funds.

An extreme disbursement method is referred to as a *zero-balance account* (ZBA). In an ZBA arrangement, the firm keeps no funds in the bank—the manager simply deposit funds as the checks written on the account are presented for payment through the banking system. Some banks will even automatically invest funds in excess of the firm's payments needs into short-term securities—insuring that there are no idle funds.

MARKETABLE SECURITIES

An integral part of cash management is storing excess cash in an asset that earns a return—such as marketable securities. Precautionary and speculative needs for cash can often be satisfied by funds stored in marketable securities, selling them as needs for cash arise. Models of cash management assume that managers stash cash they don't need right away into marketable securities and convert them to cash as needed. In this way, marketable securities are a substitute for cash.

If cash flows of a firm are uneven—perhaps seasonal—the firm can deal with the uneven demands for cash by either borrowing for the short-term or selling marketable securities. If short-term borrowing is not possible or is costly, marketable securities can be used: Buy marketable securities when cash inflows exceed outflows; sell marketable securities when cash inflows are less than outflows. In this way, marketable securities are a temporary investment.

Aside from the uneven cash demands from operations, marketable securities may be a convenient way of storing funds for planned expenditures. If a firm generates cash from operations or from the sale of securities for an investment in the near future, the funds can be kept in marketable securities until needed.

Marketable Securities and Risk

The primary role of marketable securities is to store cash that isn't needed immediately, but may be needed soon. We should therefore consider only marketable securities that provide safety and liquidity. In evaluating safety, we need to look at the risks we accept in investing in securities. The relevant risks for a manager to consider are:

- *Default risk.* The risk that the issuer will not pay interest or principal as promised.
- *Interest rate risk.* The risk that interest rates will change, changing the value of your investment.
- *Liquidity risk.* Also referred to as marketability risk, the risk that the security will not be marketable, at least at its true value, due to the lack of investor interest in the security.

We will discuss these risk further in Chapter 19 where we explain bond portfolio management.

TABLE 15.1   Money Market Securities

Security	Description
Certificates of deposit	Debt issued by banks sold in large denominations. This debt has maturities ranging generally up to one year. Because this debt is issued by banks, but exceeds the amount for deposit guarantees by bank insurance, there is some default risk.
Commercial paper	Debt issued by large corporations that is sold in large denominations and generally matures in 30 days. While the debt is unsecured credit and is issued by corporations, there is some default risk, though this is minimized by the back-up lines of credit at commercial banks.
Eurodollars deposits	Loans and certificates of deposits of non-U.S. banks that are denominated in the U.S. dollar. These debts are generally large denominations with maturities up to six months. Like loans and certificates of U.S. banks, there is some default risk.
Treasury bills	Securities issued by the U.S. Government that have maturities of one month, three months, and six months. These securities are considered default-free and are readily marketable.

Types of Marketable Securities

The marketable securities that satisfy the criteria of safety and liquidity are most likely money market securities. Money market securities are listed and described in Table 15.1.

Some money market securities, such as government securities, have no default risk; the ones that do have very little default risk. Due to the short maturity of money market securities and the fact that they are generally issued by large banks or corporations (who are not likely to get into deep financial trouble in a short time), their default risk is low. Even so, a manager can look at the credit ratings by Moody's, Standard & Poor's, and Fitch for an evaluation of the default risk of any particular money market security.

Money market securities have relatively little interest rate risk. Because these securities are short-term, their values are not as affected by changes in interest rates as, say, a 10-year U.S. Treasury security.

MANAGEMENT OF ACCOUNTS RECEIVABLE

When a company allows customers to pay for goods and services at a later date, it creates accounts receivable. By allowing customers to pay some time after they receive the goods or services, a company is granting credit, which is referred to as trade credit, merchandise credit, or dealer credit. Trade credit is an informal credit arrangement, but, unlike other forms of credit, it is not usually evidenced by notes, but rather is generated spontaneously: Trade credit is granted when a customer buys goods or services.

Reasons for Extending Credit

Companies extend credit to customers to help stimulate sales. Suppose a company offers a product for sale at $20, demanding cash at the time of the sale. And suppose a competitor of the company offers the same product for sale, but allows customers 30 days to pay. Who is going to sell the product? If the product and its price are the same, the competitor, of course. So the benefit of extending credit is the profit from the increased sales.

Extending credit is both a financial and a marketing decision. When a company extends credit to its customers, it does so to encourage sales of its goods and services. The most direct benefit is the profit on the increased sales. If the company has a variable cost margin (that is, variable cost/sales) of 80%, then increasing sales by $100,000 increases the company's profit before taxes by $20,000. Another way of stating this is that the contribution margin (funds available to cover fixed costs) is 20%: For every $1 of sales, 20 cents is available after variable costs.

The benefit of extending credit is the contribution made by the change in sales:

Benefit from extending credit = Contribution margin × Change in sales

If a company has a contribution margin of 25% and liberalizes its credit, resulting in an increase of sales of $5 million, the benefit from liberalizing credit is 25% of $5 million, or $1.25 million.

Costs of Credit

But like any credit, trade credit has a cost. The company granting the credit is forgoing the use of the funds for a period—so there is an opportunity cost associated with giving credit. In addition, there are costs of administering the accounts receivable—keeping track of what is owed. And there is a chance that the customer may not pay what is due when it is due.

The Cost of Discounts

Do companies grant credit at no cost to the customer? No, because as just explained, a company has costs in granting credit. So they generally give credit with an implicit or hidden cost:

- The customer that pays cash on delivery or within a specified time thereafter—called a *discount period*—gets a discount from the invoice price.
- The customer that pays after this discount period pays the full invoice price.

Paying after the discount period is really borrowing. The customer pays the difference between the discounted price and the full invoice price. How much has been borrowed? A customer paying in cash within the discount period pays the discounted price. So what is effectively borrowed is the cash price.

In analyses of *credit terms*, the dollar cost to granting a discount is

Cost of discount = Discount percentage × Credit sales using discount

If a discount is 5% and there are $20 million credit sales using the discount, the cost of the discount is 5% of $20 million, or $1 million.

But wait. Is this the only effect of granting a discount? Only if it is assumed that when the company establishes the discount it does not adjust the full invoice price of their goods. But is this reasonable? Probably not. If management decides to alter the company's credit policy to institute a discount, most likely it will increase the full invoice sufficiently to be compensated for the time value of money and the risk borne when extending credit.

The difference between the cash price and the invoice price is a cost to the customer—and, effectively, a return to the company for this trade credit. Consider a customer that purchases an item for $100, on terms of 2/10, net 30. This means if they pay within 10 days, they receive a 2% discount, paying only $98 (the cash price). If they pay on day 11, they pay $100. Is the seller losing $2 if the customer pays on day 10? Yes and no. We have to assume that the seller would not establish a discount as a means of cutting price. Rather, a company establishes the full invoice price to reflect the profit from selling the item and a return from extending credit. If the customer pays within the discount period, there is a cost to the company—the opportunity cost of not getting the cash at the exact date of the sale but rather some time later. With the terms 2/10 net 30, if the customer pays on the tenth day the seller has just given a 10-day interest-free loan to the customer. This is part of the carrying cost of accounts receivable, which we will discuss shortly.

Suppose the Discount Warehouse revises its credit terms, which had been payment in full in 30 days, and introduces a discount of 2% for accounts paid within 10 days. And suppose Discount's contribution margin is 20%. To analyze the effect of these changes, we have to project the increase in Discount's future sales and how soon Discount's customers will pay.

Let's first assume that Discount does not change its sales prices. And let's also assume that with this change Discount's sales will increase by $100,000 to $1,100,000, with 30% paying within 10 days and the rest paying within 30 days. The benefit from this discount is the increased contribution toward before tax profit of $100,000 × 20% = $20,000. The cost of the discount is the forgone profit of 2% on 30% of the $1.1 million sales, or $6,600.

Now let's assume that Discount changes its sales prices when it institutes the discount so that the profit margin (available to cover the company's fixed costs) after the discount is still 20%:

$$\text{Contribution margin} \times (1 - 0.02) = 20\%$$

$$\text{Contribution margin} = \frac{0.20}{(1 - 0.02)} = 20.48\%$$

If sales increase to $1.1 million, the benefit is the difference in the profit, so the incremental benefit is $24,488. And the cost, in terms of the discounts taken, is 2% of 30% of $1,100,000, or $6,600.

While we have not taken into consideration the other costs involved (such as the carrying cost of the accounts and bad debts), we see that we get a different picture of the benefits and costs of discounts depending on what the company does to the price of its goods and services when the discount is instituted. So what appears to be the "cost" from the discounts does not give us the whole picture, because the company most likely changes its contribution margin at the same time to include compensation for granting credit. In that way, it increases the benefit from the change in the policy.

Other Costs

There are a number of costs of credit in addition to the cost of the discount. These costs include:

- The carrying cost of tying up funds in accounts receivable instead of investing them elsewhere.
- The cost of administering and collecting the accounts.
- The risk of bad debts.

The carrying cost is similar to the holding cost that we looked at for cash balances: the product of the opportunity cost of investing in accounts receivable and the investment in the accounts. The opportunity cost is the return the company could have earned on its next best opportunity. The investment is the amount the company has invested to generate sales. For example, if a product is sold for $100, and its contribution margin is 25%, the company has invested $75 in the sold item (in raw materials, labor, and other variable costs).

Suppose a company liberalizes its credit policy, resulting in an increase in accounts receivable of $1 million. And suppose that this company's contribution margin is 40% (which means its variable cost ratio is 60%). The company's increased investment in accounts receivable is 60% of $1 million, or $600,000. If the company's opportunity cost is 5%, the carrying cost of accounts receivable is

Carrying cost of accounts receivable = 5% of $600,000 = $30,000

We can state the carrying cost more formally as

Carrying cost of accounts receivable
= (Opportunity cost) × (Variable cost ratio) × (Change in accounts receivable)

In addition to the carrying cost, there are costs of administering and collecting accounts. Extending credit involves recordkeeping. Moreover, costs are incurred in personnel and paperwork to keep track of which customers owe what amount. In addition to simply recording these accounts, there are expenses in collecting accounts that are past due. Whether the company collects its own accounts or hires a collection agency to collect these accounts, there are costs involved in making sure that customers pay.

Still another cost of trade credit is unpaid accounts—bad debts. If the company demanded cash for each sale, there would be no unpaid accounts. By allowing customers to pay after the sale, the company is taking on risk that the customer will not pay as promised. And by liberalizing its credit terms (for example, allowing longer to pay) or to whom it extend credit, the company may attract customers who are less able to pay their obligations when promised.

The Implicit Cost of Trade Credit to the Customer

Trade credit is often stated in terms of a rate of discount, a discount period, and a net period when payment in full is due. The *implicit cost of trade credit* to the customer can be calculated by determining first the effective interest cost for the period of credit and then placing this effective cost on an annual basis so that we can compare it with the cost of other forms of credit.

If the credit terms are stated as "2/10, net 30," this means that the customer can take a 2% discount from the invoice price if they pay within 10 days; otherwise, the full price is due within 30 days. If you purchase an item that costs $100, you would either pay $98 within the first 10 days after purchase or the full $100 price if you pay after 10 days. The effective cost of credit is the discount forgone. For a $100 purchase, this is $2. Putting this in percentage terms, you pay 2% of the invoice price to borrow 98% of the invoice price:

Cost of credit = r = 0.02/0.98 = 0.020408 or 2.0408% per credit period

The effective annual cost is calculated by determining the compounded annual cost if this form of financing is done through the year. Assuming that payment is made on the net day (30 days after the sale), the credit period (the difference between the net period and the discount period) is 20 days and there are t = 365/20 = 18.25 such credit periods in a year. The effective annual cost is

$$\text{Effective annual cost} = (1 + r)^t - 1$$

The flipside of this trade credit is that the company granting credit has an effective return on credit of 44.58% per year.

Credit and the Demand for a Company's Goods and Services

When a company decides to grant credit, it must consider the effect on its pricing and its sales. Let's return to the case where a competitor offers credit terms of payment in 30 days and the company does not. While on the surface it may seem that the competitor has an advantage, this may not be. What if the competitor also charges higher prices? Perhaps these prices are just high enough to compensate it for the expected costs of bad debts and the time value of money. Does this mean that the company will increase sales if it extends credit? Most likely, as long as the company does not change its prices, or maybe, if the company does increase prices.

To analyze the effect of extending credit, a company must consider a number of factors:

- The price elasticity of your goods and services. How price sensitive are sales?
- The probability of bad debts. When a company extends credit, how likely is it that some customers may pay late or never pay? How much compensation should the company require to bear this risk?
- When customers are most likely to pay. If the company offers discount terms, will all its customers pay at the end of the discount period? What proportion of its customers will pay within the discount period?

It should be clear that there are many variables to consider, and these variables differ from company to company and industry to industry. An understanding of its market by management and its customers' needs are required in analyzing the effects of a change in credit policy.

Credit and Collection Policies

A company's credit and *collection policies* specify the terms of extending credit, deciding who gets credit, and procedures for collecting delinquent accounts. In deciding what its credit and collection policies will be, management considers the trade-off between the costs of accounts receivable—the opportunity cost of investing in receivables, the cost of administering the receivables, and the cost of delinquent accounts—and the benefits of accounts receivable—the expected increase in profits and the return received from its trade credit.

Credit Policies

Credit terms consist of the maximum amount of credit, the length of period allowed for payment (that is, the net period), and the discount rate and discount period, if any. The purpose of discounts is to attract customers, thereby increasing sales, and to encourage the early payment of accounts, thereby reducing the amount tied up in accounts receivable. Credit terms should somehow balance the marketing needs (increased sales) and the costs of these receivables (the cost of administration of receivables, the risk of bad debts, and the opportunity cost of funds). To design terms to meet its marketing needs, management must consider:

- *Customers' cash flow patterns.* Do its customers have seasonal cash flows? How long is its customers' operating cycle? For example, if a company is a toy manufacturer, its customers (toy retailers) have seasonal cash flow. Management could tailor the terms using seasonal dating, where the discount period begins at the start of the customer's busy season.
- *The terms competitors are offering.*
- *The equitability of credit terms among customers.* Companies must be careful not to discriminate among customers. For example, different terms can be applied to customers with different credit risks, but there must be some basis for classifying them.

Evaluation of Creditworthiness

In evaluating the creditworthiness of its customers, management must take into consideration the four Cs of credit analysis:

1. *Capacity.* Ability of the customer to pay.
2. *Character.* Willingness of the customer to pay debts.
3. *Collateral.* Ability of creditors to collect on bad debts if the customer liquidates its assets.
4. *Conditions.* The sensitivity of the customer's ability to pay to underlying economic and market factors.

Management should use the following sources of information to assess the creditworthiness of customers:

- Prior experience with the customer.
- The credit rating assigned by rating agencies and reports on the customer, such as those of Dun & Bradstreet and TRW.
- Contact with the customer's bank or other creditors.
- Analysis of the customer's financial condition.

In setting *credit policies*, management must consider the cost of these sources, such as fees for credit reports, as well as the costs of personnel and other resources in evaluating the information contained in the credit reports. Often, companies will extend a small amount of credit to a customer to get experience with that customer—to see whether they actually do pay on time.

Collection Policies

Collection policies specify the procedures for collecting delinquent accounts. Collection could start with polite reminders, continuing in progressively severe steps, and ending by placing the account in the hands of a collection agency, a company that specializes in collecting accounts. The following sequence is typical:

1. When an account is a few days overdue, a letter is sent reminding the customer of the amount due and the credit terms.
2. When an account is a month overdue, a telephone call is made reminding the customer of the amount due, the credit terms, and efforts to collect the account by letter.

3. When an account is two months overdue, it is handed over to a collection agency.

In designing the collection procedures, management must keep in mind that aggressive efforts to collect may result in lost future sales. Management also has to consider its customers' circumstances. For example, if the customer is in the midst of a labor strike, management may wish to avoid collection tactics that would be detrimental to its relationship with this particular customer.

Monitoring Accounts Receivable

Management can monitor how well accounts receivable are managed using financial ratios and aging schedules. Financial ratios can be used to get an overall picture of how fast we collect on accounts receivable. Aging schedules, which are breakdowns of the accounts receivable by how long they have been around, helps management get a more detailed picture of its collection efforts.

Management can get an idea of how quickly accounts receivable can be collected by calculating a ratio called the *number of days of credit*. This measure is the ratio of the balance in accounts receivable at a point in time (say, at the end of a year) to the *credit sales per day* (on average, the dollar amount of credit sales during a day):

$$\text{Number of days of credit} = \frac{\text{Accounts receivable}}{\text{Credit sales per day}}$$

where credit sales per day is the ratio of credit sales over a period, divided by the number of business days in that period. For example, averaging over a year,

$$\text{Credit sales per day} = \frac{\text{Credit sales}}{365 \text{ days}}$$

The number of days credit ratio, also referred to as the *average collection period* and *days sales outstanding* (DSO), measures how long, on average, it takes a company to collect its accounts receivable.

Suppose that Whole Loaves, a wholesale bakery, has $1 million of credit sales per year and currently has a balance in accounts receivable of $80,000. Therefore,

$$\text{Credit sales per day} = \frac{\$1,000,000}{365 \text{ days}} = \$2,740 \text{ per day}$$

and

$$\text{Number of days of credit} = \frac{\$80,000}{\$2,740 \text{ per day}} = 29 \text{ days}$$

This means the company has, on average, 29 days' worth of sales that have not been paid for as yet.

Management can use this measure to evaluate the effectiveness of its collection policies, comparing the number of days of credit with the net period allowed in the credit terms. Management can also use this information to help in cash forecasting since it tells how long before each credit sale turns into cash, on average.

But management needs to consider certain factors in applying this measure. For example, if a company's sales are seasonal, which accounts receivable balance does management use? Over what period does management measure credit sales per day? Management must be careful when interpreting this ratio because both the numerator and denominator are influenced by the pattern of sales. For example, management tends to select the end of the company's fiscal year to be the low point of the company's operating cycle. This is when business is slowest, which means the lowest inventory level and, possibly, the lowest receivables. If management evaluates receivables at the company's year-end, it may not get the best measure of collections. It is preferable (though not always possible) for management to look at quarterly or monthly averages of receivables.

Management also monitors receivables using an aging schedule. Preparing an aging schedule allows management to look at all the company's receivables and group them according to how long they were outstanding, such as 1 to 30 days, 31 to 40 days, and so on as in this example:

Number of Days Outstanding	Number of Accounts	Amount Outstanding
1 to 30 days	120	$320,000
31 to 40 days	40	80,000
41 to 50 days	10	18,000
51 to 60 days	5	15,000
Over 60 days	3	3,000

This schedule can represent the receivables according to how many there are in each age group or according to the total dollars the receivables represent in each age group. The higher the number of accounts or the number of dollars in the shortest-term groups, the faster the collection. Looking at a breakdown of accounts receivable in an aging schedule allows management to do the following:

- Estimate the extent of customers' compliance with credit terms.
- Estimate cash inflows from collections in the near future.
- Identify accounts that are most overdue.

Management must keep in mind that the age of receivables may change from month to month if credit sales change. For example, a company's 30- to 60-day-old accounts receivable may increase from June to July simply because credit sales increased from May to June—not because collections of receivables became slower.

Establishing and Changing Credit Policies

The credit decisions involve trade-offs, the profit from the additional sales versus the costs of extending credit, as follows:

Benefits	Costs
Increased profits from increased sales	Opportunity cost of funds
	Administration and collection costs
	Bad debts

It is difficult for management to measure the benefit of extending credit or changing credit terms because there are many variables to consider: If management liberalizes the company's credit policy, extending credit to more customers, do the costs associated with this increased credit change? Most likely. Do they change in a predictable manner? Most likely not, because management will not know the costs associated with these additional sales until it changes the credit policy.

Ideally, management wants to design its company's credit (and collection) policy so that the marginal benefits from extending credit equals its marginal cost of extending credit. At this point, management maximizes owners' wealth. But the benefits and costs are uncertain. The best management can do in forecasting the benefits and costs from its credit and collection policies is to learn from its own experience (make changes and see what happens) or from the experience of others (look at what happens when a competitor changes its policies).

Captive Finance Subsidiaries

Some corporations choose to form a wholly owned subsidiary—a corporation owned by the parent corporation—to provide the credit-granting and collection function of the parent corporation. For example, if you buy a Ford Motor Company car, you can finance your purchase through Ford

Motor Credit Company, a wholly owned subsidiary of Ford. Ford Motor Credit is an example of the kind of company referred to as a *captive finance subsidiary*. Its sole purpose is to finance the customers' purchase of the parent company's products.

These subsidiaries can stimulate sales by providing easy access to loans. For example, Hyundai Motors of America found that customers were having difficulty getting auto loans for their low-priced cars, since loan default rates are typically high for loans on such autos. So Hyundai established its own finance company—Hyundai Motor Finance Company (HMFC)—to finance customers' purchases and increase sales.

Another motive is to separate the credit function from the rest of the company. By operating the credit-granting and collection function as a separate profit center, it is easier to evaluate how well accounts receivable are managed.

Securitization of Accounts Receivable

A strategy to management account receivable that is common today is to securitize receivables. The process of securitization involves selling accounts receivable to a *special purpose vehicle* (SPV), a process we described in Chapter 12. The SPV obtains funds to acquire the accounts receivable from the sale of debt securities, generically referred to as asset-backed securities. The company via securitization removes the accounts receivables from it balance sheet and obtains the funds from the sale to the SPE.

INVENTORY MANAGEMENT

Inventory is the stock of physical goods for eventual sale and consists of raw material, work-in-process, and finished goods available for sale. There are many factors in a decision of how much inventory to have on hand. As with accounts receivable, there is a trade-off between the costs of investing in inventory and the costs of insufficient inventory. There is a cost associated with holding to too much inventory, and there is a cost associated with holding too little inventory.

Reasons for Holding Inventory

There are several reasons for a company to hold inventory. The most obvious is that if a company sells a product, it cannot transact business without inventory. Another obvious reason is that goods cannot be manufactured instantaneously. If a company manufactures goods, it is likely to have some inventory in various stages of production. This is referred to as *work-in-process inventory*.

Management also may want to have some inventory of finished goods in case sales are greater than expected. Or management may want to hold some speculative inventory for dealing with events such as a change in the product or a change in the cost of the raw materials.

Further, some companies hold inventory to satisfy contractual agreements. For example, a retail outlet that is the sole distributor or representative of a product in a region, may be required to carry a specified inventory of goods for sale.

The decision to invest in inventory involves, ultimately, determining the level of inventory such that the marginal benefit (such as providing for transactions and precautionary needs) equal the marginal cost (such as carrying costs). The level of inventory at which the marginal benefits equal the marginal cost is the owners' wealth maximizing level.

Costs Associated with Inventory

There are two types of inventory cost—the cost of holding inventory and the cost of obtaining more inventory.

The *holding cost* for inventory, also referred to as the *carrying cost*, is the cost of keeping inventory—storage, depreciation, and obsolescence—and the opportunity cost of tying up funds in inventory. If management estimates holding cost on a per-unit basis, the holding cost is

Holding cost = (Average quantity) × (Holding cost per unit)

Replenishing its inventory is costly. Management must place orders—by phone, fax, or Internet—and may have to pay shipping charges for each order. These costs make up the ordering cost. Given a cost per order, management can calculate ordering costs as

Ordering cost = (Fixed cost per order) × (Number of orders per period)

The total cost of inventory is the sum of the holding cost and ordering cost:

Total inventory cost = Holding cost + Ordering cost

Let

c = holding or carrying cost, in dollars per unit

Q = quantity ordered
K = cost per transaction
S = total number of units needed during the period

Then,

$Q/2$ = average inventory balance
S/Q = number of orders

Therefore, the total inventory cost is

$$\text{Total inventory cost} = c + Q/2 + K(S/Q)$$

For example, suppose that the ABCD Company has a total demand for 500,000 units during a month. If management orders 50,000 units at a time, that is 10 orders. If it costs the company $100 each time an order is placed, the ordering costs are 10 × $100 = $1,000. If management orders 50,000 units each time it runs out of inventory, then on average there are 25,000 units on hand.

Suppose management estimates that the carrying cost per unit is $0.20. If there are 25,000 units on average, on hand, then there the holding costs are $0.20 × 25,000 or $5,000. Therefore,

$$\text{Total inventory cost} = [\$0.20 \times (50{,}000/2)] + [\$100 \times (500{,}000/50{,}000)]$$
$$= \$6{,}000$$

Next we examine two models of *inventory management* to discover ways to decrease inventory costs while still maintaining adequate inventory on hand.

Models of Inventory Management

There are alternative models for *inventory management*, but the basic idea for all of them is the same: minimize inventory costs. We will look at two—the economic order quantity model and the just-in-time inventory model—to see how they minimize costs.

The Economic Order Quantity Model

The *economic order quantity* (EOQ) model helps management to determine what quantity of inventory to order each time we order so that total inventory costs throughout the period are minimized. The economic order quantity model assumes that:

- Inventory is received instantaneously.
- Inventory is used uniformly over the period.
- Inventory shortages are not desirable.

With these assumptions, companies can minimize the costs of inventory—the sum of the carrying costs and the ordering costs—by ordering a specific amount of inventory, referred to as the *economic order quantity*, each time they run out of inventory.

The economic order quantity is the value of Q in

$$\text{Total cost} = c(Q/2) + K(S/Q)$$

which minimizes the total cost. Invoking a bit of calculus to minimize total costs with respect to Q, $d(\text{total cost})/d(Q)$, it turns out that the economic order quantity, Q^*, is

$$\text{Economic order quantity} = \sqrt{\frac{2(\text{Cost per transaction})(\text{Total demand})}{\text{Carrying cost per unit}}}$$

or

$$Q^* = \sqrt{\frac{2KS}{c}}$$

For example, if, c = \$0.20 per unit, K = \$100 per transaction, and S = 500,000 units, then

$$Q^* = \sqrt{\frac{2(\$100)(500,000)}{\$0.20}} = 22,361 \text{ units}$$

Then, for this order quantity,

$$\text{Total inventory cost} = \text{Holding cost} + \text{Ordering cost}$$
$$= (\$0.20 \times (22,361/2)) + (\$100(500,000/22,361))$$
$$= \$4,472$$

Are costs minimized at this point? Let's check it out by looking at the costs at a couple of other order quantities:

If the Order Quantity Is:	Then, Total Inventory Cost Is:
10,000 units	\$4,500
30,000 units	\$4,667

The costs are lowest at Q = 22,361 units.

We can modify the EOQ model to include factors such as safety stock, lead time, and an allowance for stock-out.

Safety stock is an additional level of inventory intended to enable the company to continue to meet demand in case sales levels turn out to be higher than predicted and in case there are unexpected delays in either receiving raw materials or in producing goods. The level of safety stock depends on the degree of uncertainty in our sales and production and the cost of lost sales (where the cost of lost sales comprises sales lost and the loss of customer goodwill).

For example, a large portion of automobile manufacturers' employees are unionized. A strike in one plant that makes parts can cause a ripple effect throughout the company, shutting down production at not only the striking plant but all others. The employees at one of General Motors' Canadian parts plants struck the firm in the fall of 1996. General Motors had stocked sufficient parts at several U.S. locations and was able to maintain operations at its U.S. plants throughout the three-week strike.

Lead time is the time it takes between placing an order for more inventory and the time when it is received or produced. We can modify the EOQ model so that ordering takes place early enough so that the new inventory arrives just as the existing inventory runs out. If it takes, say, three days to receive inventory, having three days' worth of inventory demand prior to reaching the reorder point is prudent.

The *allowance for stock-out* is the tolerance for a shortage of goods for sale. We can modify the EOQ model to permit shortages—though we risk the loss of sales and customer goodwill.

The EOQ model is useful in pointing out the trade-off between holding and ordering costs. But there are some problems applying it to actual inventory management. One problem is that it does not consider the possibility that inventory may be held in several locations. For example, if a company has many retail outlets and regional warehousing, the model has to be altered to consider order quantities for the company as a whole, each warehouse, and each store. Another problem is that there may be different types of inventory—raw materials, work-in-process, and finished goods—and many different goods, requiring EOQ models for each one. Still another problem is that EOQ is not useful in cases where the demand for inventory is seasonal. Furthermore, EOQ is not readily adapted to cases when quantity discounts available.

Just-in-Time Inventory

Just-in-time (JIT) is a management philosophy that was developed by the Ford Motor Company in the 1920s, but was implemented in a larger scale setting at Toyota Motor Company in the 1950s. The basic philosophy is to minimize the costs associated with holding goods and materials used in production by developing a set of signals to indicate the need for ordering of additional goods and materials.

The goal of JIT is to cut down on the company's need to keep inventory on hand, coordinating the supply of raw materials with the production and marketing of the goods. In JIT, the raw materials are only acquired precisely when they are needed—just in time. The idea of JIT is to have zero inventory or as near zero as possible without adversely affecting production or sales. The goal of this strategy is to cut down on inventory costs by:

1. Holding less inventory, so that there are lower storage costs, lower levels of spoilage, and less risk of obsolescence.
2. Coordinating with suppliers to minimize the cost of reordering inventory.

JIT requires coordination between a company and its suppliers. To make JIT work, management must have timely, reliable delivery of goods and materials. Further, management must have a predictable production process so that it can determine the input needs in advance, which requires a high degree of production automation. In addition, demand must be predictable. If production is constantly modified to suit the demand for a company's product, JIT will not work well or may not work at all.

JIT is a strategy of coordination among suppliers, production, and marketing to minimize the amount of inventory to the point where it is always possible to supply exactly what consumers demand. Supplies and raw materials are delivered only when needed for production. The company produces only those items that are needed for anticipated demand. This requires lots of coordination and falls apart if there is poor quality in any one part of the process—a defective bolt can gum up the works.

JIT works hand in hand with two other management techniques, *total quality control* (TQC) and *employee involvement* (EI). TQC is the principle that quality goods and services be a goal of all efforts of the company—production, accounting, marketing, etc. Part of TQC is recognizing that some personnel of the company are customers of other personnel. For example, the financial manager serves the production management by evaluating the expansion of the production facilities, whereas the accounting staff serves the financial manager, supplying financial data necessary for the financial manager's evaluation of the expansion.

EI is the philosophy that employees at all levels should be involved in the company's decision-making. By participating in decision-making, employees are able to understand and perform their tasks better. Also, employees make significant contributions to the decision-making process due to their unique perspective regarding the decision.

This management strategy of JIT inventory management is similar to the zero-balance account disbursements technique for cash management. Both are based on the idea that management can reduce costs if the company carries a lower balance. And both require coordination and planning to make them work.

JIT has been globally manage inventory. For example, Ford Motor Company allows its suppliers to tap into its inventory management system computer so they can figure out what supplies are needed and when to deliver them to Ford's production plants. This helps Ford's suppliers in their own planning, which benefits Ford through more efficient delivery of the goods it needs.

Other Considerations

The goal of both the economic order quantity and JIT is to minimize the costs of holding and ordering inventory. The EOQ model does this through the quantity of goods ordered that will minimize costs. JIT inventory management does this a bit differently than EOQ, by focusing on the source of these costs and minimizing holding costs.

In addition to the holding and ordering costs, there are other considerations in determining the appropriate level of inventory. One consideration is taxes on inventory. For example, there may be a state tax based on the value of inventory held as of a specified date, say December 31. In that case, management would hold on that date the smallest amount of inventory that would not cause a shortage of goods for its customers.

Another consideration is the possibility of expropriation. If the company is doing business in another country, there may be a risk of that country's government expropriating the company's goods. When doing business in other countries, management must assess the risk of expropriation and, if high, minimize the inventory holdings in that country.

Still another consideration is export-import quotas. For example, if a company produces goods in the United States and sell them in Japan, there may be a limit on the amount Japan will import. Suppose the limit on imports into Japan is 50,000 units per month. If demand in Japan is seasonal—say, 20,000 per month every month except June when the demand shoots up to 200,000 units—the importer in Japan will have to import more than needed for several months to build up inventory for June.

Monitoring Inventory Management

Management can monitor inventory by looking at financial ratios in much the same way it can monitor other current assets such as receivables. The *number of days of inventory* is the ratio of the dollar value of inventory at a point in time to the cost of goods sold per day:

$$\text{Number of days of inventory} = \frac{\text{Inventory}}{\text{Average day's cost of goods sold}}$$

This ratio is an estimate of the number of days' worth of sales the company has on hand. Combined with an estimate of the demand for the company's goods, this ratio helps management in planning production and purchasing of goods. For example, automobile manufacturers keep a close watch on the number of days of autos on car lots. If there are more than is typical, they tend to offer rebates and financing incentives. If there are fewer than is typical, they may step up production.

Another way to monitor inventory is the inventory turnover ratio—the ratio of what a company sells over a period (the cost of goods sold) to what it has on hand at the end of that period (inventory):

$$\text{Inventory turnover} = \frac{\text{Cost of goods sold}}{\text{Inventory}}$$

The inventory turnover ratio tells management, on average, how many times inventory flows through the company—from raw materials to goods sold—during the period. If the typical inventory turnover for a company is, say, five times, that means that the company completes the cycle of investing in inventory and selling it five times in the year. From the above equations, you can see that the inventory turnover is related to the number of days of inventory: The inventory turnover is the result of 365 divided by the number of days of inventory.

If the turnover is above the typical, this may suggest to management that there is a risk of stock-out. If the turnover is less than usual, this may suggest either production is slower (resulting in relatively more work-in-process), or that sales are sluggish and perhaps need a boost from providing sales incentives or discounting prices.

Management must be careful, however, in interpreting these ratios. Because the production and sale of goods may be seasonal—and not always in sync—the value management puts into the calculations may not represent what is actually going on. Most companies select the lowest point in their seasonal pattern of activity as their fiscal year-end. For example, Wal-Mart

Stores ends its fiscal year on January 31 since its peak business period is the Christmas season. For the 2006 fiscal year, the Wal-Mart inventory was:

Quarter End	Inventory (in millions)
April 30, 2007	$31,900
July 31, 2007	32,087
October 31, 2006	38,531
January 31, 2007	35,200

The cost of goods sold for these four quarters was $264,152 million. If management calculates the inventory turnover using January 31, 2007 inventory, Wal-Mart's inventory turnover was 7.50 times. If, on the other hand, the average inventory (averaging the four quarter-end inventories) is used, the inventory turnover was 7.67 times. While both are correct values for inventory turnover, 7.67 times is probably more representative of the company's management of inventory throughout the year.

Also, interpretation of an inventory turnover ratio is not straightforward. Is a higher turnover good or bad? It could be either. A high turnover may mean that the company is using its investment in inventory efficiently. But it might mean that the company is risking a shortage of inventory. Not keeping enough on hand (relative to what is sold) incurs a chance of lost sales and customer goodwill. If Wal-Mart runs out of stock on the "hottest" toys in the Christmas season, one can be sure that customers will shop elsewhere. Using inventory turnover ratios along with measures of profitability can give management a better idea of whether it is getting an adequate return on your investment in inventory.

SUMMARY

The management of current assets involves decisions related to cash, marketable securities, accounts receivable, and inventory. The objective of short-term investments is the same as for long-term investment decisions: Maximize owners' wealth. But since the manager is basing the decision on cash flows received over the short term, the focus is less on the time value of money and more on identifying the costs and benefits associated with decisions.

The common purpose of our decisions related to cash and marketable securities is to minimize the firm's investment in the short-term asset. But in all cases, a manager must have some investment in the asset because the firm will incur costs if it does not have enough of it. A manager needs to strike the right balance between the cost of having and not having the asset. The "right balance" is different for each firm. Each firm must assess its costs of having and not having the asset.

Cash management involves the trade-off between the benefits from having enough cash to meet day-to-day operations and the costs of having cash (e.g., opportunity cost of funds and costs of getting and storing cash). There are economic models that can be used in the management of cash to determine the amount of funds to transfer in and out of cash.

Marketable securities are a store of excess cash. A firm invests funds in marketable securities to have a ready, liquid source of cash. Marketable securities include U.S. Treasury bills, commercial paper, and certificates and deposit.

The purpose of decisions related to accounts receivable is to minimize investment in short-term assets. A company must have some investment in accounts receivable because if management fails to offer competitive credit terms, there will be sales lost to competitors. Receivables management involves a trade-off between the benefits of increased sales and the costs of credit (e.g., the opportunity cost of funds and defaults by credit customers). Credit and collection policies must be formulated by management to consider the benefits arising from increasing sales and the costs associated with extending credit.

The management of current assets requires balancing the cost of having too much tied up in the asset against the benefits of having a sufficient amount of the asset on hand. Though business practices and customs differ among industries, the general idea in the management of receivables is to grant credit to encourage sales and stay competitive, while considering the costs of tying up funds and of possibly incurring bad debts. In the management of inventory, the investment in inventory differs among industries since the nature of the goods for sale dictates in large part the type of inventory required. However, even considering this, companies can manage the amount invested in inventory. The economic order quantity model and the just-in-time management technique can aid management in managing the investment in inventory.

REFERENCES

Baumol, W. J. (1952). The transactions demand for cash: An inventory theoretic approach. *Quarterly Journal of Economics* 66, no. 4: 545–556.

Miller, M. H. and Orr, D. (1966). A model of the demand for money by firms. *Quarterly Journal of Economics* 80, no. 3: 413–435.

CHAPTER 16

Financial Risk Management

All firms face a variety of risks. Scandals such as Enron, WorldCom, Tyco, and Adelphia and tragic events such as 9/11 have reinforced the need of companies to manage risk. Moreover, risk management should not be placed at the end of the agenda for a board meeting as "other business," but be a key agenda item that is discussed regularly at board meetings. In practice, the board can provide only oversight and direction. The responsibility of risk management is often delegated to either (1) the audit, finance, or compliance committee of the company's board of directors; or (2) a risk management officer (typically called the chief risk officer) or a risk management group headed by a risk management officer. Regardless of the structure, to assure effective performance of the risk management process, the committee or group responsible for risk management should have regular interaction with the chief financial officer, internal auditors, general counsel, and managers of business units.

In this chapter we discuss the four key processes in financial risk management: risk identification, risk assessment, risk mitigation, and risk transferring. The process of risk management involves determining which risks to accept, which to neutralize, and which to transfer.

RISK DEFINED

There is no shortage of definitions for *risk*. In everyday parlance, risk is often viewed as something that is negative. But we know that some risks lead to economic gains while others have purely negative consequences. For example, the purchase of a lottery ticket involves an action that results in the risk of the loss equal to the cost of the ticket but potentially has a substantial monetary reward. In contrast, the risk of death or injury from a random shooting is purely a negative consequence.

In the corporate world, accepting risks is necessary to obtain a competitive advantage and generate a profit. In fact, "risk" is derived from the

Italian verb *riscare*, which means "to dare." Corporations "dare to" generate profits by taking advantage of the opportunistic side of risk.[1] The former Delaware Supreme Court Chief Justice Norman Veasey (2000, pp. 26–27) in a decision wrote:

> Potential profit often corresponds to the potential risk. . . . Stockholders' investment interests . . . will be advanced if corporate directors and managers honestly assess risk and reward and accept for the corporation the highest available risk-adjusted returns that are above the firm's cost of capital.

We have already seen various definitions of risk throughout this book and there will be more in later chapters. In the discussion of capital budgeting in Chapter 14, various measures of risk were introduced. However, risk as used at the corporate level has a more general meaning than does its use in capital budgeting. Outreville (1998), for example, distinguishes between the following types of risk that are useful for ultimately managing risks: financial risk, peril, accident, and hazard.

When a corporation is exposed to an event that can cause a shortfall in a targeted financial measure or value, this type of risk is called *financial risk*. The financial measure or value could be earnings per share, return on equity, or cash flows, to name some of the important ones. Financial risks include market risk, credit risk, market liquidity risk, operational risk, and legal risk.

Culp (2006, p. 27) defines perils, accidents, and hazards as follows:

> A peril is a natural, man-made, or economic "situation" that can cause an unexpected loss for a firm, the size of which is usually *not* based on the realization of one or more financial variables. A peril thus is essentially a *non-financial risk*. An accident is a specific negative event arising from a peril that gives rise to a loss, and is usually considered unintentional. A hazard is something that increases the probability of a peril-related loss occurring, whether intentional or not.

Culp (2006, p. 27–28) provides the following types of perils faced by corporations:

- *Production.* Unexpected changes in the demand for products sold, increases in input costs, failures of marketing.

---

[1] While there is a debate by scholars, the Chinese ideogram for "crisis" is a combination of "danger" or "risk" and "opportunity." True or not, motivational speakers and authors of risk management books use this interpretation to emphasize that along with risk comes opportunity.

- *Operational.* Failures in processes, people, or systems.
- *Social.* Adverse changes in social policy (e.g., political incorrectness of a product sold), strained labor relations, changes in fashions and tastes, etc.).
- *Political.* Unexpected changes in government, nationalization of resources, war, and so on.
- *Legal.* Tort and product liability and other liabilities whose exposures are not driven by financial variables.
- *Physical.* Destruction or theft of assets in place, impairment of asset functionality, equipment or mechanical failure, chemical-related perils, energy-related perils, and so on.
- *Environmental.* Flood, fire, windstorm, hailstorm, earthquake, cyclone, and so on.

Examples of hazards that increase the likelihood that there will be a loss for different perils are:

- *Human.* Fatigue, ignorance, carelessness, smoking
- *Environmental.* Weather, noise
- *Mechanical.* Weight, stability, speed
- *Energy.* Electrical, radiation
- *Chemical.* Toxicity, flammability, combustability.

Risks can also be classified as *core risks* and *noncore risks*. The distinction is important in the management of risk. In attempting to generate a return on invested funds that exceeds the risk-free interest rate, a firm must bear risk. The core risks are those risks that the firm is in the business to bear and the term *business risk* is used to describe this risk. In contrast to core risk, risks that are incidental to the operations of a business are referred to as *noncore risks*. To understand the difference, consider the risk associated with the uncertainty about the price of electricity. For a firm that produces and sells electricity, the risk that the price of electricity that it supplies may decline is a core risk. However, for a manufacturing firm that uses electricity to operate its plants, the price risk associated with electricity (i.e., the price increasing) is a noncore risk. Yet changing the circumstances could result in a different classification. For example, suppose that the firm producing and selling electricity is doing so on a fixed-price contract for the next three years. In this case, the price risk associated with electricity is a non-core risk.

Sustainability Risk

In the past, the management of risks that a firm faces has focused on its business and financial risks. The business risks include the sales risk—driven by competition and demand—and operating risks, affected by the structure of operating costs. The financial risks relate to the use of debt in the firm's capital structure.

In the past two decades there has been a broadening of the perception of risk to extend traditional business and financial risks to the complete spectrum of risk that a firm faces that includes social and environmental responsibilities. For example, the social responsibilities of a firm include labor and human rights, working conditions, training, governance, and ethics, whereas the environmental responsibilities include recycling and waste management, oversight, reporting, and resource use. Without effective management of these risks, a business risks the potential damages from boycotts, shareholder actions, lawsuits, and additional regulations.

The concept of sustainability has slowly gained prominence in the past two decades as investors, regulators, and firms grappled with the effects of corporate scandals, catastrophes, and tragedies. Many began to question whether the objective of the firm as shareholder wealth maximization is too simplistic. In other words, the question arises as to whether a firm is valued considering not only its financial performance, but its environmental and social responsibility records as well. There is no definitive empirical evidence that the environmental and social dimensions of a firm affect its value, but there is anecdotal evidence that investors may consider these dimensions.

As the issue of sustainability has grown in prominence, there has also been a surge of measures of firms' sustainability risk, including the Institutional Shareholders Services Sustainability Risk Reports and the Deloitte Sustainability Reporting Scorecard. In addition, indexes, including the Dow Jones Sustainability Indexes (DJSI) and the FTSE4Good indexes, have been created that track the performance of companies focusing on sustainability. Further, many companies are now reporting their sustainability risk and risk management efforts to investors. For example, some companies now report on sustainability using the framework provided by the Global Reporting Initiative (GRI), though others develop their own reporting frameworks. Though GRI and other measures are still evolving, there is increasing pressure for some form of reporting on these risks.

ENTERPRISE RISK MANAGEMENT

The traditional process of risk management focuses on managing the risks of only parts of the business (products, departments, or divisions), ignoring the implications for the value of the firm. The organization of a risk management process focusing on only parts of a business is referred to as a *silo structure*. What is needed is a process that management can employ to effectively handle uncertainty and evaluate how the risks and opportunities that a firm faces can either create, destroy, or preserve a firm's value. This process should allow management to:

- Align the risk appetite and strategies across the firm.
- Improve the quality of the firm's risk-response decisions.
- Identify the risks across the firm.
- Manage the risks across the firm.

This process is referred to as *enterprise risk management* (ERM).

Internal controls provide a mechanism for mitigating risks and increase the likelihood that a firm will achieve its financial objective. As we will explain, ERM goes beyond internal controls in three significant ways. First, when establishing its strategy for the firm, ERM requires that the board consider risks. Second, ERM requires that the board identify what level of risk it is willing to accept. Finally, ERM requires that risk management decisions be made throughout the firm in a manner consistent with the risk policy established.

Definitions of ERM

While corporations and consulting firms may have their own definitions of ERM, the most popular one is that proposed by the Committee of Sponsoring Organizations of the Treadway Commission (COSO). COSO defines ERM as:

> a process, effected by an entity's board of directors, management and other personnel, applied in strategy setting and across the enterprise, designed to identify potential events that may affect the entity, and manage risk to be within its risk appetite, to provide reasonable assurance regarding the achievement of entity objectives.[2]

This definition and the framework for ERM suggested builds on a 1992 study by COSO where it recommended a uniform approach to developing business controls systems and for assessing their effectiveness.[3]

A broader definition of ERM is provided by the Casualty Actuarial Society (CAS), which describes it as:

---

[2] *Internal Control—Integrated Framework Executive Summary*, Committee of Sponsoring Organizations of the Treadway Commission (1992).

[3] *Enterprise Risk Management—Integrated Framework Executive Summary*, Committee of Sponsoring Organizations of the Treadway Commission, (September 2004), p. 8.

the discipline by which an organization in any industry assesses, controls, exploits, finances and monitors risk from all sources for the purposes of increasing the organization's short- and long-term value to its stakeholders.[4]

There are common attributes to both the COSO and CAS definitions of ERM, as well as other definitions that have appeared in the ERM literature. First, ERM is an ongoing process that provides a structured means for reducing the adverse consequences of big surprises due to natural catastrophes, terrorism, changes in the economic, political, and legal environments, tax litigation, failure of the firm's corporate governance, and product and financial market volatility. In fact, Moody's states that the ultimate objective of a firm's risk management organization should be to make sure that there are no major surprises that place the firm in peril.[5] Second, the starting point for an effective ERM system is at the board level. This means that corporate governance is a critical element.

The term *enterprise* can have different meanings in ERM. As the Society of Actuaries (SOA) points out, there are two main definitions.[6] In the first definition "enterprise" has an "Auditing/Process control nuance" in that it is a process that is used in a consistent and effective manner throughout the firm. Within the context of process control, ERM is linked to strategic planning and organizational objectives.

The second definition is in terms of *modern portfolio theory* (MPT). In this theory, formulated by Markowitz (1958) and discussed in Chapter 17, the focus is on the risk of the portfolio and not the individual securities comprising the portfolio. More specifically, it is not the stand-alone risk of an individual security that is relevant but the contribution of that security to portfolio risk. A portfolio manager can use MPT to create efficient portfolios (i.e., portfolios that offer the maximum expected return for a given level of risk). The portfolio manager will select one of these efficient portfolios given the manager's or client's risk appetite. The manager can use derivatives instruments to alter the risk profile of a portfolio and can use risk budgeting to decide how to allocate risk. In the context of ERM, the enterprise is viewed as a "portfolio of risks." It is not stand-alone risk that is key but the risk to the entire firm, a point we made in Chapter 14 when discussing risk within the context of capital budgeting. The risk profile can be altered using derivative instruments as well as other risk transfer products and strategies discussed later in this chapter.

---

[4] *Overview of Enterprise Risk Management by Casualty Actuarial Society* (May 2003).

[5] *Moody's Research Methodology: Risk Management Assessments* (July 2004).

[6] *Enterprise Risk Management Specialty Guide*, Society of Actuaries (May 2006), p. 9.

ERM Process

There is no fixed formula for developing an ERM system, but instead, general principles that are offered as guidance. This is because there is considerable variation in company size, organizational structures (centralized versus decentralized, for example), and types of risk faced in different industries. So, although different internal controls vary from firm to firm, the underlying principles do not. In the literature, there are several proposals for the ERM process.

The four risk objectives of ERM as per the COSO framework are the following:

1. *Strategic.* Supporting the corporation's strategic goals (i.e., high-level goals).
2. *Operations.* Achieving performance goals and taking measures to safeguard against loss through operational efficiency.
3. *Reporting.* Providing reliable financial and operational data and reports internally and externally.
4. *Compliance.* Complying with laws and regulations at all levels (local, state, national, and in other countries where the firm operates).

While there are common risks shared by all firms and there are risks unique to some firms, the building blocks for the ERM process are common to all firms.

Basically, ERM is chiefly concerned with (1) the evaluation of the firm's risk processes and risk controls and (2) the identification and quantification of risk exposures. ERM is broader in its scope than traditional risk management, which focuses on products, departments, or divisions practiced within a silo structure. In ERM, all the risks of a firm are treated as a portfolio of risks and managed on a portfolio or firm level. That is, the risk context is the firm, not individual products, departments, or divisions.

For example, suppose that a firm has a target minimum earnings figure that is established either by its own financial plan or based on Wall Street analysts' consensus earnings. ERM can be used to identify the threats to the firm of hitting that target. Once those risk are identified and prioritized, management can examine the potential shortfall that may occur and decide how to reduce the likelihood that there will be shortfall using some risk transfer strategies.

Themes of ERM

ERM has four themes:

1. Risk control
2. Strategic risk management
3. Catastrophic control
4. Risk management culture[7]

The *risk control* process involves: (1) identifying the risks; (2) evaluating risks; (3) monitoring risks; (4) setting risk limits; (5) avoiding certain risks; (6) offsetting certain risks; (7) transferring risks; and (8) reviewing and evaluating new products.

The process of reflecting risk and risk capital in strategic options from which a corporation can select is called *strategic risk management*. This process involves (1) estimating economic capital; (2) pricing products on a risk-adjusted basis; (3) capital budgeting; and (4) evaluating performance on a risk-adjusted basis.

Extreme events that could threaten the survival of a corporation are referred to as *catastrophic events*. *Catastrophic risk management* involves planning so as to minimize the impact of potential catastrophic events and having in place an early warning system that, if possible, could identify a potential disaster. The process of catastrophic risk management includes (1) trend analysis to identify any patterns suggesting potential emergence of catastrophes; (2) stress testing of the impact of a catastrophe on the financial condition and reputation of the firm; (3) contingency planning for certain scenarios; (4) preparing actions to be taken to effectively communicate with stakeholders and the media when a catastrophe occurs; (5) incorporating the lessons from previous major problems into future plans; and (6) evaluating catastrophic risk transfer alternatives.

The SOA defines *risk management culture* as "the general approach of the firm to dealing with its risks" and the "primary objective is to create a situation where Operational, Strategic and Catastrophic Risk Management take place in an organization without the direct oversight or intervention of the Risk Officer or the Risk Committee."[8] The process of risk management culture includes (1) identification and measurement of all the firm's risks; (2) identification of the best risk management practices; (3) development of supporting documentation that can be used by management; (4) communication with all interested parties; and (5) reinforcement by training employees.

Specifying the Firm's Risk Policy

The implementation of an ERM policy requires that the amount of risk that a firm is willing to accept be specified. Corporations through their board set

---

[7] *Enterprise Risk Management Specialty Guide*, pp. 26–28.
[8] *Enterprise Risk Management Specialty Guide*, p. 28.

the boundaries as to how much risk the firm is prepared to accept. Often in referring to risk, the terms *risk appetite* and *risk tolerance* are used interchangeably. However, there is a difference and COSO distinguishes between the two terms as follows:

> Risk appetite is a higher level statement that considers broadly the levels of risks that management deems acceptable while risk tolerances are more narrow and set the acceptable level of variation around objectives. For instance, a company that says that it . . . does not accept risks that could result in a significant loss of its revenue base is expressing appetite. When the same company says that it does not wish to accept risks that would cause revenue from its top-10 customers to decline by more than 10% it is expressing tolerance. Operating within risk tolerances provides management greater assurance that the company remains within its risk appetite, which, in turn, provides a higher degree of comfort that the company will achieve its objectives.[9]

Basically, the firm's risk appetite is the amount of risk exposure that the board decides the firm is willing to accept/retain. When the risk exposure of the firm exceeds the risk appetite threshold, risk management processes are implemented to return the exposure level back within the accepted range.

Once the risk policy of the firm is agreed on by the board, the firm must communicate it to stakeholders via the management discussion section required in SEC filings (8-K and 10-K), press releases, communications with rating agencies, and investor meetings.

Now that the credit rating services are incorporating ERM measures into the credit rating process, it is more important than ever for management to pay attention to the company's ERM system and to communicate this system to stakeholders.

MANAGING RISKS

A firm's *retention decision* refers to how a firm elects to manage an identified risk. This decision is more than a risk management decision, it is also a capital structure decision. The choices are:

1. Retaining the risk
2. Neutralizing the risk
3. Transferring the risk

---

[9] *Enterprise Risk Management—Integrated Framework Executive Summary*, p. 2.

Of course, each identified risk faced by the firm can be treated in a different way. As will be explained, for each of the three choices—retention, neutralization, and transfer of risk—there are in turn two further decisions as to how they can be handled.

Retained Risk and Risk Finance

The decision by a firm as to which identified risks to retain is based on an economic analysis of the expected benefits versus expected costs associated with bearing that particular risk. The aggregate of all the risks across the firm that it has elected to bear is called its *retained risk*. Because if a retained risk is realized it will adversely impact the firm's earnings, a firm must decide whether a retained risk is to be unfunded or funded.

An *unfunded retained risk* is a retained risk for which potential losses are not financed until they occur. In contrast, a *funded retained risk* is a retained risk for which an appropriate amount is set aside upfront (either as cash or an identified source for raising funds) to absorb the potential loss. For example, with respect to corporate taxes, management may decide to hold as cash reserves all or a portion of the potential adverse outcome of a litigation with tax authorities. This management of retained risk is referred to as *risk finance*.

Risk Neutralization

If a firm elects not to retain an identified risk, it can either neutralize the risk or transfer the risk. *Risk neutralization* is a risk management policy whereby a firm acts on its own to mitigate the outcome of an expected loss from an identified risk without transferring that risk to a third party. This can involve reducing the likelihood of the identified risk occurring or reducing the severity of the loss should the identified risk be realized. Risk neutralization management for some risks may be a natural outcome of the business or financial factors affecting the firm. Here is an example involving a business risk. Suppose that a firm expects returns due to product defects that are projected to result in an annual loss of $30 million to $50 million and this amount is material relative to its profitability. A firm can introduce improved production processes to reduce the upper range of the potential loss.

As an example involving a financial factor, a U.S. multinational firm will typically have cash inflows and outflows in the same currency such as the euro. As a result, there is currency risk—the risk that the currency will moved adversely to the firm's exposure in that currency. But this risk has offsetting tendencies if there are both cash inflows and outflows in the same currency. Assuming the currency is the euro, the cash inflows are exposed to a depreciation of the euro relative to the U.S. dollar; the cash outflows are exposed to an appreciation of the euro relative to the U.S. dollar. If the firm projects future cash inflows over a certain time period of €50 million and a cash outflow over the same period of €40 million, then the firm's net currency exposure is a €10 million cash inflow. That is, €40 million exposure is naturally hedged.

Risk Transfer

For certain identifiable risks, the firm may decide to transfer the risk from shareholders to a third party. This can be done either by entering into a contract with a counterparty willing to take on the risk the firm seeks to transfer, or by embedding that risk in a structured financial transaction, thereby transferring it to bond investors willing to accept that risk. In the next section, we look at the various forms of *risk transfer management*.

RISK TRANSFER

The vehicles or instruments for transferring risk include:

- Traditional insurance
- Derivatives
- Alternative risk transfer
- Structured finance

Structured finance or structured financing involves the creation of non-traditional-type securities with risk/return profiles targeted to certain types of investors. Structured finance includes asset securitization, structured notes, and leasing. Since we discuss these forms of financing in later chapters, we will not examine them here. Instead, below we discuss the first three ways that risk can be transferred.

Traditional Insurance

The oldest form of risk transfer vehicle is insurance, with marine insurance more than likely being the oldest type of insurance policy. An insurance policy is a contract whereby an insurance company agrees to make a payment to the insured if a defined adverse event is triggered. The insured receives the protection by paying a specified amount periodically, called the *insurance premium*.

The contract can be a valued contract or unvalued contract. In a *valued contract*, the policy specifies the agreed value of the property insured.

With the exception of life insurance contracts purchased by firms, valued contracts are not commonly used as a form of risk transfer. There are exceptions, of course, such as an art museum insuring valuable works of art with the amount fixed at the time of negotiation of the contract to avoid needing an appraisal of the artwork after the insured event is triggered.

In an *unvalued contract*, also called a *contract of indemnity*, the value of the insured property is not fixed but while there may be a maximum amount payable, the payment is contingent on the actual amount of the insured's loss resulting from the trigger event. A contract of indemnity is the typical type of contract used in risk transfer.

Commercial and corporate insurance policies cover a wide range of property and acts. They include:

- Property damage
- Liability insurance
  - Employer liability
  - Public liability
  - Product liability
  - Construction liability
  - Directors and officers liability
  - Professional indemnity
- Business interruption
- Contractors all rights
- Marine hull
- Commercial motor and fleet
- Goods in transit

Another type of traditional insurance includes credit insurance and financial guarantees.[10] Credit insurance includes *trade credit insurance* whose purpose is to insure against risk of nonpayment resulting from the nonpayment of a customer due to insolvency and protracted defaults (i.e., nonpayment after a specified period of delinquency). These policies can be customized to cover losses on foreign sales due to political risk, predelivery costs, the nondelivery of prepaid goods, and the failure of another party to honor a letter of credit.

Financial guarantees provide for a payment by an insurer to the policy beneficiary if there is loss on a financial obligation held and that loss is the result of a specified event that causes the default. The financial guarantee can call for a payment equal to the entire amount of the loss or for a partial amount of the loss. A financial guarantee can be either a *pure financial*

---

[10] For an extensive discussion of credit insurance and financial guarantees, see Chapter 10 in Culp (2006).

guarantee or a *financial surety bond*, the distinction being who is the beneficiary of the policy. For a pure financial guarantee, the beneficiary of the policy is the credit protection buyer; for a financial surety bond (also called an *insurance wrap*), the beneficiary is not the credit protection buyer, but a third party. In this case, the credit protection buyer is a corporation that has issued a financial obligation to the third party.

An alternative to credit insurance is a *letter of credit* (LOC) typically issued by a bank. In this arrangement, the bank issuing the LOC is guaranteeing the performance of the corporation that obtained the LOC. Banks charge a fee for the LOC.

Derivatives

There are capital market products available to management to transfer risks that are not readily insurable by an insurance company. Such risks include risks associated with a rise in the price of commodity purchased as an input, a decline in a commodity price of a product the firm sells, a rise in the cost of borrowing funds, and an adverse exchange-rate movement. The capital market instruments that can be used to provide such protection are called *derivative instruments*. These instruments include futures contracts, forward contracts, option contracts, swap agreements, and cap and floor agreements.

There have been shareholder concerns about the use of derivative instruments by firms. This concern arises from major losses resulting from positions in derivative instruments.[11] However, an investigation of the reason for major losses would show that the losses were not due to derivatives per se, but the improper use of them by management that either was ignorant about the risks associated with using derivative instruments or sought to use them in a speculative manner rather than as a means for managing risk.

How a derivative is treated for financial accounting purposes is governed by the rules set forth in FASB No. 133, "Accounting for Derivative Instruments and Hedging Activities," and FASB No. 149, "Amendment of Statement 133 on Derivative Instruments and Hedging Activities." FASB No. 133 requires that all derivatives be recognized by a corporation on its balance sheet as either assets or liabilities and recorded at their fair market value. The treatment of any gain or loss on a derivative instrument depends on whether it is designated as being used for hedging. If a derivative instrument is not designated as being used for hedging purposes, any gain or loss is recognized in earnings for the period.

---

[11] Well-publicized losses in the 1990s include Procter & Gamble's losses related to foreign exchange derivatives, Gibson Greetings' losses related to interest rate swaps, and Pier 1 Imports' losses due to the trading of bond futures and options.

The treatment for a derivative instrument designated as being used for hedging purposes depends on what it is being used to hedge. The three categories of hedging are given below, along with the hedge accounting treatment:

1. When a derivative instrument is designated as hedging exposure to changes in the fair value of an asset or liability or an unrecognized commitment, the hedge is referred to as a *fair value hedge*. For such hedges, any gain or loss is recognized in earnings for the period of change, but offset by the loss or gain on the hedged item attributable to the risk being hedged. Thus, earnings are impacted to the extent to which the hedge fails to achieve offsetting changes in fair value.

2. When a derivative instrument is designated as hedging exposure to variable cash flows of a forecasted transaction, the hedge is referred to as a *cash flow hedge*.[12] For such hedges, intially the effective portion of the derivative's gain or loss is reported as a component of other comprehensive income (outside earnings); subsequently that gain or loss is reclassified into earnings when the forecasted transaction affects earnings. Thus, the ineffective portion of the gain or loss is reported in earnings immediately.

3. When a derivative instrument is designated as hedging exposure to the foreign currency exposure of a net investment in a foreign operation, an unrecognized commitment, an available-for-sale security, or a foreign-currency-denominated forecasted transaction, any gain or loss is reported in other comprehensive income (outside earnings) as part of the cumulative translation adjustment. Fair value hedge accounting treatment is used for a derivative designated as a hedge of the foreign currency exposure of an unrecognized firm commitment or an avail-

---

[12] Here is an example from Berry Plastics Holding Corp. (from S-4 Amendment 12/21/06, p. 544):

> The Company consumes plastic resin during the normal course of production. The fluctuations in the cost of plastic resin can vary the costs of production. As part of its risk management strategy, the Company entered into resin forward hedging transactions constituting approximately 15% of its estimated 2005 resin needs and 10% of its 2006 estimated resin needs based on 2004 volumes prior to the Kerr Acquisition. These contracts obligate the Company to make or receive a monthly payment equal to the difference in the unit cost of resin per the contract and an industry index times the contracted pounds of plastic resin. Such contracts are designated as hedges of a portion of the Company's forecasted purchases through 2006 and are effective in hedging the Company's exposure to changes in resin prices during this period.

able-for-sale security. Cash flow hedge accounting treatment is used for a derivative designated as a hedge of the foreign currency exposure of a foreign-currency-denominated forecasted transaction.

If a corporation wants to apply hedge accounting treatment, when establishing the hedge it is required to specify (1) the methodology that it will employ for assessing how effective the derivative instrument is for hedging; and (2) the measurement approach for determining the ineffective aspect of the hedge. Moreover, the methodology must be consistent with the corporation's approach to managing risk.

In Chapter 6, we discussed derivative instruments.

Alternative Risk Transfer

Alternative risk transfer (ART), also known as *structured insurance*, provides unique ways to transfer the increasingly complex risks faced by corporations that cannot be handled by traditional insurance and has led to the growth in the use of this form of risk transfer. These products combine elements of traditional insurance and capital market instruments to create highly sophisticated risk transfer strategies tailored for a corporate client's specific needs and liability structure that traditional insurance cannot handle. For this reason, ART is sometimes referred to as "insurance-based investment banking." According to a September 2006 report by Conning Research & Consulting, traditional insurance covers roughly 70% of the commercial insurance market in the United States and the balance is provided by ART.[13]

ART includes:

- Insurance-linked notes
- Captives and mutuals
- Finite insurance
- Multiline insurance
- Contingent insurance

We briefly review each of these next.[14]

Insurance-Linked Notes

Insurance-linked notes (ILNs) have been primarily used by life insurers and property and casualty insurers to bypass the conventional reinsurance mar-

---

[13] "Alternative Markets: Structural and Functional Evolution," Conning Research & Consulting, Inc., September 2006.

[14] For a more detailed discussion of ART, see Chapters 22–26 in Culp (2006) and Chapters 4–10 in Banks (2004).

ket and synthetically reinsure against losses by tapping the capital markets. Basically, an ILN is a means for securitizing insurance risk. ILNs can be classified as single-peril and multiperil bonds. The former ILNs are typically referred to as *catatrophe-linked bonds* or simply *cat bonds*. Typically cat bonds are issued through a special-purpose entity.

The first use of cat bonds in corporate risk management by a noninsurance company was by the owner-operator of Tokyo Disneyland, Oriental Land Co. Rather than obtain traditional insurance against earthquake damage for the park, it issued a $200 million cat bond in 1999. Three years later, Vivendi Universal obtained protection for earthquake damage for its studios (Universal Studios) in California by issuing a $175 million cat bond with a maturity of 3.5 years. Moreover, the bond had a lower coupon rate than a similarly rated corporate bond.[15]

While cat bonds have primarily been used for perils such as earthquakes and hurricanes, corporations are using them in other ways. For example, the risk to the lessor (i.e., the owner of the leased equipment) in a leasing transaction is that the value of the leased equipment when the lease terminates (called the residual value) is below its expected value when the lease was negotiated. Toyota Motor Credit Corp., for example, was concerned that the 260,000 1998 motor vehicles (cars and light-duty trucks) it leased to customers would decline in value if the used-car market weakened. To protect itself, Toyota issued a cat bond that insured against a loss in market value of the fleet of leased motor vehicles. As another example, the sponsors of the World Cup, the Fédération Internationale de Football Association (FIFA), issued a $260 million cat bond to protect itself against a (terrorism-related) cancellation of the 2006 event in Germany.

Captives

A parent company, trade association, or a group of companies within an industry can set up a captive insurance company. These entities can be used for financing the retention risk that we described earlier as well as risk transfer. In order to benefit from a captive, a company needs good information to evaluate the risks that are being incurred by the captive and have sufficient financial resources for funding an annual premium that is large enough to justify the costs of setting up and maintaining a captive. In a mutual insurance company the owners of the company are the policyholders. A group of companies can create a mutual insurance company to insure against specific types of risk common to them. Basically, a mutual insurance company is a form of self-insurance.

---

[15] See Mathias (2003).

According to the report by Conning Research & Consulting cited earlier, self-insurance and single-parent captives account for 90% of the ART market.

Finite Insurance

Finite insurance is an insurance policy that sharply limits the amount of the loss that the insurer can realize. The controversy associated with this type of insurance is whether it truly transfers risk from a corporation seeking protection to the insurer. The reason is that typically for this type of policy the corporation seeking protection pays a large premium to the insurer, the amount being sufficient to cover the insurer's expected losses. The premium is then held by an insurer in an interest-bearing account. If at the end of the policy's term the actual losses are less than the premium, the insurer pays the difference to the corporation. However, if the losses exceed the premium, the corporation makes an additional premium payment to the insurer for the difference.

Basically, it has been argued that finite insurance provided a means not for risk management but for earnings management. Public and regulatory awareness of the problem with finite insurance resulted from the SEC enforcement action against Brightpoint Inc. and American International Group (AIG). The SEC charged AIG with accounting fraud because of the insurer's role in devising and selling an "insurance" product that Brightpoint Inc. used to report false and misleading financial statements that concealed $11.9 million in losses that Brightpoint sustained in 1998. Without admitting or denying the SEC's allegations, AIG and Brightpoint agreed to pay a civil penalty of $10 million and $450,000, respectively. In 2007, the director of Brightpoint's risk management was found liable for aiding and abetting Brightpoint's fraud, as well as other violations of securities laws.[16] There were further SEC investigations of other issuers of finite insurance, as well as then–New York Attorney General Eliot Spitzer's investigation of a $500 million finite insurance deal between AIG and General Re.

These actions have made CFOs reluctant to use finite insurance, particularly because there is the risk that such insurance might result in an earnings restatement. According to experts, however, the major concern with finite coverage is not that it may allow earnings manipulation but that it fails to transfer risk.

Experts in ART have argued that there are legitimate uses for finite insurance. Culp, for example, states that finite insurance "leads to a higher quality of earnings than if the firm doesn't reserve for a major loss or just

---

[16] U.S. Securities and Exchange Commission, Litigation Release No. 20185, July 9, 2007.

tries to set money aside internally,"[17] further noting that companies can use finite insurance to shield them from allegations that they are setting up "cookie jar" reserves to inflate future results. A second advantage pointed out by some experts in ART is that the coverage provided by finite insurance can assist companies that are reluctant to purchase traditional insurance to fix the cost of risk exposures that are difficult to quantify over a span of years. Finally, it is argued that finite insurance is particularly useful in "covering severe risks that are outside the core functions of a company."[18]

Multiline Insurance

Multiline insurance offers a tool for integrated risk management by offering one large aggregate limit across several lines of business such as liability, property, and business interruption. The insurer makes a payment if the combined losses on all lines reach a specified amount. The programs usually operate on a multiyear basis. The corporation deals with only one insurer rather than several insurers covering different lines. Moreover, the corporation only has to renew the program every three to five years, thereby reducing the time the chief risk officer must devote to negotiating insurance contracts each year. The flexibility of creating multiline insurance allows an insurer to work with a corporation to obtain tailor-made coverage based on the corporation's needs.

Contingent Insurance

Contingent insurance, more popularly referred to as as contingent cover, is an option granted by an insurance company giving a corporation the right to enter into an insurance contract at some future date. All of the terms of the insurance contract that can be entered into, including the premium that must be paid if the option is exercised, are specified at the time the contingent cover policy is purchased by the corporation. Contingent cover includes premium protection options, contingent cover embedded in existing programs, and contingent insurance-linked notes.[19]

SUMMARY

Financial risk is the exposure of a corporation to an event that can cause a shortfall in a targeted financial measure or value and includes market risk, credit risk, market liquidity risk, operational risk, and legal risk. Risks can

[17] As cited in Katz (2005, p. 2).
[18] Ibid.
[19] See Chapter 26 in Culp (2006).

also be classified as *core risks* and *noncore risks*. Core risks, or business risks, are those risks that the firm is in the business to bear; noncore risks are risks that are incidental to the operations of a business. A more comprehensive view of a firm's risk is the concept of sustainability risk, which encompasses not only the risk associated with economic performance, but also the risks associated with environmental and social issues.

The traditional process of risk management focused on managing the risks of only parts of the business, ignoring the implications for the value of the firm. Enterprise risk management makes it possible for management to align the risk appetite and strategies across the firm, improve the quality of the firm's risk-response decisions, identify the risks across the firm, and manage the risks across the firm. ERM requires that the board consider risks, the board identify what level of risk it is willing to accept, and that risk management decisions be made throughout the firm in a manner consistent with the established risk policy of the firm. There is no fixed formula for developing an ERM system, but instead, general principles that are offered as guidance.

ERM is chiefly concerned with evaluation of the firm's risk processes and risk controls and the identification and quantification of risk exposures. The four themes of ERM are risk control, strategic risk management, catastrophic control, and risk management culture. To implement an ERM system, the amount of risk that a firm is willing to accept must be specified by the board. The risk policy established by the firm must be communicated to stakeholders and rating agencies.

The retention decision refers to how a firm elects to manage an identified risk, with the three choices being risk retention, risk neutralization, and risk transfer. A retained risk can be a funded retained risk or an unfunded retained risk. Risk finance refers to the management of retained risk. Risk neutralization is a risk management policy whereby a firm acts on its own to mitigate the outcome of an expected loss from an identified risk without transferring that risk to a third party. Risk transfer management involves strategies for dealing with identifiable risks that the the firm decides to transfer to a third party. The vehicles or instruments for transferring risk include traditional insurance, derivatives, alternative risk transfer, and structured finance. Structured finance or structured financing involves the creation of nontraditional-type securities with risk-return profiles that target certain types of investors.

Traditional commercial and corporate insurance policies cover a wide range of property and acts. Traditional insurance also includes credit insurance (trade credit insurance) and financial guarantees. Financial guarantees, which can be either a pure financial guarantee (corporation is the beneficiary) or a financial surety bond (third party is the beneficiary), provide for a payment by an insurer to the insured if there is loss on a financial obligation to the insured and that loss is the result of a specified event that causes the default.

Derivatives can be used for risk management transfer. FASB No. 133 specifies the rules for reporting transactions in derivative instruments; there are special rules when the derivative instrument is designated as being used for hedging purposes: fair value hedge accounting and cash flow hedge accounting.

Alternative risk transfer provides unique ways a corporation can transfer complex risks that cannot be handled by traditional insurance by combining elements of traditional insurance and capital market instruments. ART includes insurance-linked notes (one particular type being cat bonds), captives and mutuals, finite insurance, multiline insurance, and contingent insurance.

REFERENCES

Banks, E. (2004). *Alternative Risk Transfer: Integrated Risk Management Through Insurance, Reinsurance and the Capital Markets.* Hoboken, NJ: John Wiley & Sons.

Culp, C. L. (2006). *Structured Finance and Insurance: The ART of Managing Capital and Risk.* Hoboken, NJ: John Wiley & Sons.

Field, A. R. (2007). Rating risk practices. *Treasury & Risk* (December-January).

Katz, D. M. (2005). Finite insurance: Beyond the scandals. *CFO.com* (April 14).

Markowitz, H. M. (1952). Portfolio selection. *Journal of Finance* 7, no. 1: 77–91.

Outreville, J. F. (1998). *Theory and Practice of Insurance.* Boston: Kluwer.

Veasey, N. (2000). The role of the judiciary in corporate law, corporate governance and economics goals. In *Company Law Reform in OECD Countries: A Comparative Outlook of Current Trends* (pp. 26–27). (Paris: Organisation for Economic Co-operation and Development).

PART Four

Investment Management

CHAPTER 17

The Basic Principles of Investment Management

In this chapter, we describe the activities associated with *investment management*. This field of finance is also referred to as *asset management*, *portfolio management*, and *money management*. In the the two chapters that follow, we discuss the management of the two major asset classes: equities and bonds.

THE INVESTMENT MANAGEMENT PROCESS

The *investment management process* involves the following five steps:

Step 1. Setting investment objectives
Step 2. Establishing an investment policy
Step 3. Selecting an investment strategy
Step 4. Selecting the specific assets
Step 5. Measuring and evaluating investment performance

We describe each step in this section.

Step 1. Setting Investment Objectives

Setting investment objectives starts with a thorough analysis of the investment objectives of the entity whose funds are being managed. These entities can be classified as individual investors and institutional investors. Within each of these broad classifications, is a wide range of investment objectives.

The objectives of an individual investor may be to accumulate funds to purchase a home or other major acquisition, to have sufficient funds to be able to retire at a specified age, or to accumulate funds to pay for college tuition for children. An individual investor may engage the services of a financial advisor or consultant in establishing investment objectives.

Institutional investors include:

- Pension funds.
- Depository institutions (commercial banks, savings and loan associations, and credit unions).
- Insurance companies (life companies, property and casualty companies, and health companies).
- Regulated investment companies (mutual funds).
- Hedge funds.
- Endowments and foundations.
- Treasury department of corporations, municipal governments, and government agencies.

Classification of Investment Objectives

We can classify the objectives of institutional investors into the following two broad categories: nonliability driven objectives and liability-driven objectives. As the name indicates, those institutional investors that fall into the first category can manage their assets without regard to satisfying any liabilities. An example of an institutional investor that is not driven by liabilities is a regulated investment company (mutual fund).

The second category includes institutional investors that must meet contractually specified liabilities. A *liability* is a cash outlay that must be made at a specific time to satisfy the contractual terms of an issued obligation. An institutional investor is concerned with both the *amount* and *timing* of liabilities because its assets must produce the cash flow to meet any payments it has promised to make in a timely way. Here are three examples of institutional investors that face liabilities:

- Depository institutions raise funds by a mix of interest-paying deposit and issuance of debt obligations in the financial market. The objective in managing the assets of a depository institution is to earn a return that is greater than the cost of the funds raised.
- Life insurance companies have a wide range of investment-oriented products. One such product is a *guaranteed investment contract* (GIC). For this product, a life insurance company guarantees an interest rate on the funds given it to by a customer. With respect to the GIC account, the investment objective of the asset manager is to earn a return greater than the rate guaranteed.
- There are two types of pension plans offered by sponsors. The sponsor can be a corporation, a state government, or local government. The two types of pension plans that can be sponsored are a defined contribution

or a defined benefit plan. For defined contribution plans, the sponsor need only provide a specified amount for an employee to invest and the employee is responsible for investing those funds. The plan sponsor has no further obligation. However, in the case of a defined benefit plan, the plan sponsor has agreed to make specified payments to the employee after retirement. Thus, the plan sponsor has created a liability against itself and in managing the assets of the pension plan, the asset manager must earn a return adequate to meet those future pension liabilities.

Keep in mind that some institutional investors may have accounts that have both nonliability-driven objectives and liability-driven objectives. For example, a life insurance company may have a GIC account (which as explained above is a liability-driven objective product) and a variable annuity account. With a variable annuity account, an investor makes either a single payment or a series of payment to the life insurance company and in turn the life insurance company (1) invests the payments received and (2) makes payments to the investor at some future date. The payments that the life insurance company makes will depend on the performance of the insurance company's asset manager. While the life insurance company does have a liability, it does not guarantee any specific dollar payment.

Benchmark

Regardless of the type of investment objective, a benchmark is established to evaluate the performance of an asset manager. The determination of a benchmark is in some cases, fairly simple. For example, in the case of a liability-driven objective, the benchmark is typically an interest rate target. In the case of a nonliability-driven objective, the benchmark is typically the asset class in which the assets are invested. One such asset class is large capitalization stocks. There are several benchmarks for that asset class and the client and asset manager will jointly determine the one to use.

It is not always simple to determine the benchmark. A client and the asset manager may decide to develop a customized benchmark.

Step 2. Establishing an Investment Policy

The second step in the investment management process is establishing policy guidelines to satisfy the investment objectives. Setting policy begins with the *asset allocation decision*. That is, a decision must be made as to how the funds to be invested should be distributed among the major asset classes.

There are some institutional investors that make the asset allocation decision based purely on their understanding of the risk-return characteristics of the various asset classes and expected returns. Nevertheless, the asset allocation takes into consideration any investment constraints or restrictions. In the development of an investment policy, the following factors must be considered: client constraints, regulatory constraints, and tax considerations.

Client-Imposed Constraints

Examples of client-imposed constraints would be restrictions that specify the types of securities that a manager may invest and concentration limits on how much or little may be invested in a particular asset class or in a particular issuer. Where the objective is to meet the performance of a particular market or customized benchmark, there may be a restriction as to the degree to which the manager may deviate from some key characteristics of the benchmark.

For example, in this chapter and the next two we discuss certain portfolio risk measures that are used to quantify different types of risk. The three major examples are (1) tracking error risk for any type of asset class; (2) market risk as measured by beta for a common stock portfolio (explained later in this chapter); and (3) duration for a bond portfolio. These portfolio risk measures provide an estimate of the exposure of a portfolio to changes in key factors that affect the portfolio's performance—the market overall in the case of a portfolio's beta and the general level of interest rates in the case of a portfolio's duration.

Typically, a client will not set a specific value for the level of risk exposure. Instead, the client restriction may be in the form of a maximum on the level of the risk exposure or a permissible range for the risk measure relative to the benchmark. For example, a client may restrict the portfolio's duration to be +0.5 or –0.5 of the client-specified benchmark. Thus, if the duration of the client-imposed benchmark is 4, the manager has the discretion of constructing a portfolio with a duration between 3.5 and 4.5.

Regulatory Constraints

There are many types of regulatory constraints. These involve constraints on the asset classes that are permissible and concentration limits on investments. Moreover, in making the asset allocation decision, consideration must be given to any risk-based capital requirements. For depository institutions and insurance companies, the amount of statutory capital—that is, equity—required is related to the quality of the assets in which the institution has invested. For example, for banks there are credit risk-based capital requirements. As another example, for regulated investment management companies, there are restrictions on the amount of leverage that can be used.

Tax Considerations

Tax considerations are important for several reasons. First, certain institutional investors such as pension funds, endowments, and foundations are exempt from federal income taxation. Consequently, the asset classes in which they invest will not be those that are tax-advantaged investments. Second, there are tax factors that must be incorporated into the investment policy. For example, while a pension fund might be tax-exempt, there may be certain assets or the use of some investment vehicles in which it invests whose earnings may be taxed.

Step 3. Selecting a Portfolio Strategy

Selecting a portfolio strategy that is consistent with the investment objectives and investment policy guidelines of the client or institution is the third step in the investment management process. Portfolio strategies can be classified as either active or passive.

An *active portfolio strategy* uses available information and forecasting techniques to seek a better performance than a portfolio that is simply diversified broadly. Essential to all active strategies are expectations about the factors that have been found to influence the performance of an asset class. For example, with active common stock strategies this may include forecasts of future earnings, dividends, or price-earnings ratios. With bond portfolios that are actively managed, expectations may involve forecasts of future interest rates and sector spreads. Active portfolio strategies involving foreign securities may require forecasts of local interest rates and exchange rates.

A *passive portfolio strategy* involves minimal expectational input and, instead, relies on diversification to match the performance of some market index. In effect, a passive strategy assumes that the marketplace will efficiently reflect all available information in the price paid for securities. Between these extremes of active and passive strategies, several strategies have sprung up that have elements of both. For example, the core of a portfolio may be passively managed with the balance actively managed.

A useful way of thinking about active versus passive management is in terms of the following three activities performed by the manager: (1) portfolio construction (deciding on the stocks to buy and sell); (2) trading of securities; and (3) portfolio monitoring. Generally, active managers devote the majority of their time to portfolio construction. In contrast, with passive strategies managers devote less time to this activity.

In the bond area, there are several strategies classified as *structured portfolio strategies* that are a type of liability-driven strategy. A structured portfolio strategy is one in which a portfolio is designed to achieve the performance of some predetermined liabilities that must be paid out. These strategies are frequently used when trying to match the funds received from an investment portfolio to the future liabilities that must be paid.

Given the choice among active and passive management, which should be selected? The answer depends on (1) the client's or money manager's view of how "price-efficient" the market is; (2) the client's risk tolerance; and (3) the nature of the client's liabilities. By marketplace price efficiency, we mean how difficult it would be to earn a greater return than passive management after adjusting for the risk associated with a strategy and the transaction costs associated with implementing that strategy. In our discussion of secondary markets in Chapter 4, we discussed the different forms of market efficiency.

Step 4. Selecting the Specific Assets

Once a portfolio strategy is selected, the next step is to select the specific assets to be included in the portfolio. It is in this phase of the investment management process that the asset manager attempts to construct an *efficient portfolio*. An efficient portfolio is one that provides the greatest expected return for a given level of risk, or equivalently, the lowest risk for a given expected return. In the next section, we will explain what portfolio theory has to say about how efficient portfolios should be constructed.

Step 5. Measuring and Evaluating Performance

The measurement and evaluation of investment performance is the last step in the investment management process. Actually, it is misleading to say that it is the last step because the investment management process is an ongoing process. This step involves measuring the performance of the portfolio and then evaluating that performance relative to some benchmark. We describe this process in more detail at the end this chapter.

THE THEORY OF PORTFOLIO SELECTION

In this section, we present the theory of portfolio selection as formulated by Markowitz (1952). This theory is also referred to as *mean-variance portfolio analysis* or simply *mean-variance analysis*.

Some Basic Concepts

Portfolio theory draws on concepts from two fields: financial economic theory, and probability and statistical theory. This section presents the concepts from financial economic theory we use in portfolio theory. While many of the concepts presented here have a more technical or rigorous definition, the purpose is to keep the explanations simple and intuitive so the reader can appreciate the importance and contribution of these concepts to the development of modern portfolio theory.

Utility Function and Indifference Curves

In life there are many situations where entities (i.e., individuals and firms) face two or more choices. The economic "theory of choice" uses the concept of a utility function to describe the way entities make decisions when faced with a set of choices. A *utility function* assigns a (numeric) value to all possible choices faced by the entity. The higher the value of a particular choice, the greater the utility derived from that choice. The choice that is selected is the one that results in the maximum utility given a set of constraints faced by the entity.

In portfolio theory too, entities are faced with a set of choices. Different portfolios have different levels of expected return and risk. Also, the higher the level of expected return, the larger the risk. Entities are faced with the decision of choosing a portfolio from the set of all possible risk-return combinations where return is a desirable that increases the level of utility, and risk is an undesirable that decreases the level of utility. Therefore, entities obtain different levels of utility from different risk-return combinations. The utility obtained from any possible risk-return combination is expressed by the utility function. Put simply, the utility function expresses the preferences of entities over perceived risk and expected return combinations.

A utility function can be expressed in graphical form by a set of indifference curves. Figure 17.1 shows indifference curves labeled u_1, u_2, and u_3. By convention, the horizontal axis measures risk and the vertical axis measures expected return. Each curve represents a set of portfolios with different combinations of risk and return. All the points on a given indifference curve indicate combinations of risk and expected return that will give the same level of utility to a given investor. For example, on utility curve u_1, there are two points u and u', with u having a higher expected return than u', but also having a higher risk. Because the two points lie on the same indifference curve, the investor has an equal preference for (or is indifferent to) the two points, or, for that matter, any point on the curve. The (positive) slope of an indifference curve reflects the fact that, to obtain the same level of utility, the investor requires a higher expected return in order to accept higher risk.

For the three indifference curves shown in Figure 17.1, the utility the investor receives is greater the further the indifference curve is from the

FIGURE 17.1   Indifference Curves

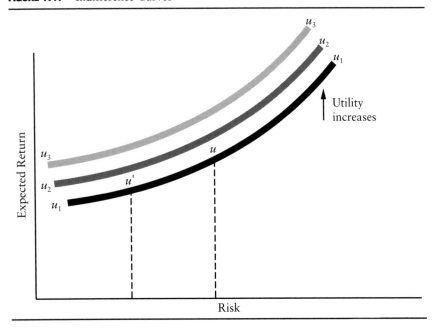

horizontal axis because that curve represents a higher level of return at every level of risk. Thus, for the three indifference curves shown in the exhibit, u_3 has the highest utility and u_1 the lowest.

The Set of Efficient Portfolios and the Optimal Portfolio

Portfolios that provide the largest possible expected return for given levels of risk are called *efficient portfolios*. To construct an efficient portfolio, it is necessary to make some assumption about how investors behave when making investment decisions. One reasonable assumption is that investors are *risk averse*. A risk-averse investor is an investor who, when faced with choosing between two investments with the same expected return but two different risks, prefers the one with the lower risk.

In selecting portfolios, an investor seeks to maximize the expected portfolio return given his tolerance for risk. Alternatively stated, an investor seeks to minimize the risk that he is exposed to given some target expected return. Given a choice from the set of efficient portfolios, an *optimal portfolio* is the one that is most preferred by the investor.

Risky Assets vs. Risk-Free Assets

A risky asset is one for which the return that will be realized in the future is uncertain. For example, an investor who purchases the stock of Microsoft Corporation today with the intention of holding it for some finite time does not know what return will be realized at the end of the holding period. The return will depend on the price of Microsoft's stock at the time of sale and on the dividends that the company pays during the holding period. Thus, Microsoft stock, and indeed the stock of all companies, is a risky asset.

Securities issued by the U.S. government are also risky. For example, an investor who purchases a U.S. government bond that matures in 30 years does not know the return that will be realized if this bond is held for only one year. This is because changes in interest rates in that year will affect the price of the bond one year from now and that will affect the return on the bond over that year.

There are assets, however, for which the return that will be realized in the future is known with certainty today. Such assets are referred to as *risk-free* or *riskless assets*. The risk-free asset is commonly defined as a short-term obligation of the U.S. government. For example, if an investor buys a U.S. government security that matures in one year and plans to hold that security for one year, then there is no uncertainty about the return that will be realized. The investor knows that in one year, the maturity date of the security, the government will pay a specific amount to retire the debt. Notice how this situation differs for the U.S. government security that matures in 30 years. Whereas the one-year and the 30-year securities are obligations of the U.S. government, the former matures in one year so that there is no uncertainty about the return that will be realized. In contrast, while the investor knows what the government will pay at the end of 30 years for the 30-year bond, he does not know what the price of the bond will be one year from now.

Measuring a Portfolio's Expected Return

We are now ready to define and measure the actual and expected return of a risky asset and a portfolio of risky assets.

Measuring Single-Period Portfolio Return

The actual return on a portfolio of assets over some specific time period is a weighted average of the returns on the individual assets in the portfolio, and is straightforward to calculate using the following:

$$R_p = w_1 R_1 + w_2 R_2 + \ldots + w_G R_G \tag{17.1}$$

where

R_p = rate of return on the portfolio over the period

R_g = rate of return on asset g over the period

w_g = weight of asset g in the portfolio (i.e., market value of asset g as a proportion of the market value of the total portfolio) at the beginning of the period

G = number of assets in the portfolio

In shorthand notation, equation (17.1) can be expressed as follows:

$$R_p = \sum_{g=1}^{G} w_g R_i \tag{17.2}$$

Equation (17.2) states that the return on a portfolio (R_p) of G assets is equal to the sum over all of the product of the individual assets' weights in the portfolio and their respective return. The portfolio return R_p is sometimes called the *holding period return* or the *ex post return*.

For example, consider the following portfolio consisting of three assets:

Asset	Market Value at the Beginning of Holding Period	Rate of Return Over Holding Period
1	$6 million	12%
2	8 million	10%
3	11 million	5%

The portfolio's total market value at the beginning of the holding period is $25 million. Therefore,

w_1 = $6 million/$25 million = 0.24, or 24% and R_1 = 12%

w_2 = $8 million/$25 million = 0.32, or 32% and R_2 = 10%

w_3 = $11 million/$25 million = 0.44, or 44% and R_3 = 5%

Notice that the sum of the weights is equal to 1. Substituting into equation (17.1), we get the holding period portfolio return:

$$R_p = 0.24(12\%) + 0.32(10\%) + 0.44(5\%) = 8.28\%$$

Note that since the holding period portfolio return is 8.28%, the growth in the portfolio's value over the holding period is given by ($25 million) × 0.0828 = $2.07 million.

The Expected Return of a Portfolio of Risky Assets

Equation (17.1) shows how to calculate the actual return of a portfolio over some specific time period. In portfolio management, the investor also wants to know the expected (or anticipated) return from a portfolio of risky assets. The expected portfolio return is the weighted average of the expected return of each asset in the portfolio. The weight assigned to the expected return of each asset is the percentage of the market value of the asset to the total market value of the portfolio. That is,

$$E(R_p) = w_1 E(R_1) + w_2 E(R_2) + \ldots + w_G E(R_G) \qquad (17.3)$$

The $E(\ )$ signifies expectations, and $E(R_p)$ is sometimes called the *ex ante* return, or the expected portfolio return over some specific time period.

The expected return, $E(R_i)$, on a risky asset i is calculated as follows. First, a probability distribution for the possible rates of return that can be realized must be specified. A probability distribution is a function that assigns a probability of occurrence to all possible outcomes for a random variable. Given the probability distribution, the expected value of a random variable is simply the weighted average of the possible outcomes, where the weight is the probability associated with the possible outcome.

In our case, the random variable is the uncertain return of asset i. Having specified a probability distribution for the possible rates of return, the expected value of the rate of return for asset i is the weighted average of the possible outcomes. Finally, rather than use the term "expected value of the return of an asset," we simply use the term "expected return." Mathematically, the expected return of asset i is expressed as

$$E(R_i) = p_1 R_1 + p_2 R_2 + \ldots + p_N R_N \qquad (17.4)$$

where

R_n = the nth possible rate of return for asset i
p_n = the probability of attaining the rate of return n for asset i
N = the number of possible outcomes for the rate of return

How do we specify the probability distribution of returns for an asset? We shall see later on in this chapter that in most cases the probability

TABLE 17.1   Probability Distribution for the Rate of Return for Stock XYZ

n	Rate of Return	Probability of Occurrence
1	12%	0.18
2	10	0.24
3	8	0.29
4	4	0.16
5	−4	0.13
Total		1.00

distribution of returns is based on historical returns. Probabilities assigned to different return outcomes that are based on the past performance of an uncertain investment act as a good estimate of the probability distribution. However, for purpose of illustration, assume that an investor is considering an investment, stock XYZ, which has a probability distribution for the rate of return for some time period as given in Table 17.1. The stock has five possible rates of return and the probability distribution specifies the likelihood of occurrence (in a probabilistic sense) for each of the possible outcomes.

Substituting into equation (17.4) we get

$$E(R_{XYZ}) = 0.18(12\%) + 0.24(10\%) + 0.29(8\%) + 0.16(4\%) + 0.13(-4\%)$$
$$= 7\%$$

Thus 7% is the expected return or mean of the probability distribution for the rate of return on stock XYZ.

Measuring Portfolio Risk

The dictionary defines risk as "hazard, peril, exposure to loss or injury." With respect to investments, investors have used a variety of definitions to describe risk. Markowitz (1952) quantified the concept of risk using the well-known statistical measures of variances and covariances. He defined the risk of a portfolio as the sum of the variances of the investments and covariances among the investments. The notion of introducing the covariances among returns of the investments in the portfolio to measure the risk of a portfolio forever changed how the investment community thought about the concept of risk.

Variance and Standard Deviation as a Measure of Risk

The variance of a random variable is a measure of the dispersion or variability of the possible outcomes around the expected value (mean). In the case of an asset's return, the variance is a measure of the dispersion of the possible rate of return outcomes around the expected return.

The equation for the variance of the expected return for asset i, denoted $\sigma^2(R_i)$, is

$$\sigma^2(R_i) = p_1[r_1 - E(R_i)]^2 + p_2[r_2 - E(R_i)]^2 + \ldots + p_N[r_N - E(R_i)]^2$$

or

$$\sigma^2(R_i) = \sum_{i=1}^{N} p_n[r_n - E(R_i)]^2 \qquad (17.5)$$

Using the probability distribution of the return for stock XYZ, we can illustrate the calculation of the variance:

$$\sigma^2(R_{XYZ}) = 0.18(12\% - 7\%)^2 + 0.24(10\% - 7\%)^2$$
$$+0.29(8\% - 7\%)^2 + 0.16(4\% - 7\%)^2 + 0.13(-4\% - 7\%)^2$$
$$= 24.1\%$$

The variance associated with a distribution of returns measures the compactness with which the distribution is clustered around the mean or expected return. Markowitz argued that this compactness or variance is equivalent to the uncertainty or riskiness of the investment. If an asset is riskless, it has an expected return dispersion of zero. In other words, the return (which is also the expected return in this case) is certain, or guaranteed.

Standard Deviation   Since the variance is squared units, it is common to see the variance converted to the standard deviation (σ) by taking the positive square root of the variance:

$$\sigma(R_i) = \sqrt{\sigma^2(R_i)}$$

For stock XYZ, then, the standard deviation is

$$\sigma(R_{XYZ}) = \sqrt{24.1\%} = 4.9\%$$

The variance and standard deviation are conceptually equivalent; that is, the larger the variance or standard deviation, the greater the investment risk.

There are two criticisms of the use of the variance as a measure of risk. The first criticism is that because the variance measures the dispersion of an asset's return around its expected return, it treats both the returns above and below the expected return identically. There has been research in the area of behavioral finance to suggest that investors do not view return outcomes above the expected return in the same way as they view returns below the expected return. Whereas returns above the expected return are considered favorable, outcomes below the expected return are disliked. Because of this, some researchers have argued that measures of risk should not consider the possible return outcomes above the expected return.

Markowitz recognized this limitation and, in fact, suggested a measure of downside risk—the risk of realizing an outcome below the expected return—called the *semivariance*. The semivariance is similar to the variance except that in the calculation no consideration is given to returns above the expected return. However, because of the computational problems with using the semivariance, and the limited resources available to him at the time, Markowitz used the variance in developing portfolio theory.

Today, practitioners use various measures of downside risk. However, regardless of the measure used, the basic principles of portfolio theory developed by Markowitz and set forth in this chapter are still applicable. That is, the choice of the measure of risk may affect the calculation but doesn't invalidate the theory.

The second criticism is that the variance is only one measure of how the returns vary around the expected return. When a probability distribution is not symmetrical around its expected return, a statistical measure of the skewness of a distribution should be used in addition to the variance.[1]

Because expected return and variance are the only two parameters that investors are assumed to consider in making investment decisions, the Markowitz formulation of portfolio theory is often referred to as a "two-parameter model."

Measuring the Portfolio Risk of a Two-Asset Portfolio In equation (17.5), we provide the variance for an individual asset's return. The variance of a portfolio consisting of two assets is a little more difficult to calculate. It depends not only on the variance of the two assets, but also upon how closely the returns of one asset track those of the other asset. The formula is

$$\sigma^2(R_p) = \sigma^2(R_i) + \sigma^2(R_j) + 2w_i w_j \operatorname{cov}(R_i, R_j) \tag{17.6}$$

where

$\operatorname{cov}(R_i, R_j)$ = covariance between the return for assets i and j

In words, equation (17.6) states that the variance of the portfolio return is the sum of the squared weighted variances of the two assets plus two times the weighted covariance between the two assets. We will see that this

---

[1] See Ortobelli et al. (2005).

equation can be generalized to the case where there are more than two assets in the portfolio.

Covariance   Like the variance, the covariance has a precise mathematical translation. Its practical meaning is the degree to which the returns on two assets covary or change together. In fact, the covariance is just a generalized concept of the variance applied to multiple assets. A positive covariance between two assets means that the returns on two assets tend to move or change in the same direction, while a negative covariance means the returns tend to move in opposite directions. The covariance between any two assets i and j is computed using the following formula:

$$\text{cov}(R_i, R_j) = p_1[r_{i1} - E(R_i)][r_{j1} - E(R_j)] + p_2[r_{i2} - E(R_i)][r_{j2} - E(R_j)] \\ + \cdots + p_N[r_{iN} - E(R_i)][r_{jN} - E(R_j)] \quad (17.7)$$

where

r_{in} = the nth possible rate of return for asset i
r_{jn} = the nth possible rate of return for asset j
p_n = the probability of attaining the rate of return n for assets i and j
N = the number of possible outcomes for the rate of return

The covariance between asset i and i is just the variance of asset i.

To illustrate the calculation of the covariance between two assets, we use the two stocks in Table 17.2. The first is stock XYZ from Table 17.1 that we used earlier to illustrate the calculation of the expected return and the standard deviation. The other hypothetical stock is ABC, whose data are shown in Table 17.2. Substituting the data for the two stocks from Table 17.2 into equation (17.7), the covariance between stocks XYZ and ABC is calculated as follows:

$$\text{cov}(R_{XYZ}, R_{ABC}) = 0.18(12\% - 7\%)(21\% - 10\%) \\ + 0.24(10\% - 7\%)(14\% - 10\%) \\ + 0.29(8\% - 7\%)(9\% - 10\%) \\ + 0.16(4\% - 7\%)(4\% - 10\%) \\ + 0.13(-4\% - 7\%)(-3\% - 10\%) \\ = 34$$

Relationship between Covariance and Correlation   The correlation is analogous to the covariance between the expected returns for two assets. Specifically, the correlation between the returns for assets i and j is defined as the covariance of the two assets divided by the product of their standard deviations:

TABLE 17.2 Probability Distribution for the Rate of Return for Asset XYZ and Asset ABC

n	Rate of Return for Asset XYZ	Rate of Return for Asset ABC	Probability of Occurrence
1	12%	21%	0.18
2	10	14	0.24
3	8	9	0.29
4	4	4	0.16
5	−4	−3	0.13
Total			1.00
Expected return	7.0%	10.0%	
Variance	24.1%	53.6%	
Standard deviation	4.9%	7.3%	

$$cor(R_i,R_j) = cov(R_i,R_j)/[\sigma(R_i)\sigma(R_j)] \qquad (17.8)$$

The correlation and the covariance are conceptually equivalent terms. Dividing the covariance between the returns of two assets by the product of their standard deviations results in the correlation between the returns of the two assets. Because the correlation is a standardized number (i.e., it has been corrected for differences in the standard deviation of the returns), the correlation is comparable across different assets. The correlation between the returns for stock XYZ and stock ABC is

$$cor(R_{XYZ},R_{ABC}) = 34/(4.9 \times 7.3) = 0.94$$

The correlation coefficient can have values ranging from +1.0, denoting perfect comovement in the same direction, to −1.0, denoting perfect comovement in the opposite direction. Because the standard deviations are always positive, the correlation can only be negative if the covariance is a negative number. A correlation of zero implies that the returns are uncorrelated. Finally, though causality implies correlation, correlation does not imply causality.

Measuring the Risk of a Portfolio Comprised of More than Two Assets

So far we have defined the risk of a portfolio consisting of two assets. The extension to three assets—i, j, and k—is as follows:

$$\sigma^2(R_p) = w_i^2\sigma^2(R_i) + w_j^2\sigma^2(R_j) + w_k^2\sigma^2(R_k) + 2w_iw_j\,\text{cov}(R_i, R_j)$$
$$+ 2w_iw_k\,\text{cov}(R_i, R_k) + 2w_jw_k\,\text{cov}(R_j, R_k) \tag{17.9}$$

In words, equation (17.9) states that the variance of the portfolio return is the sum of the squared weighted variances of the individual assets plus two times the sum of the weighted pairwise covariances of the assets. In general, for a portfolio with G assets, the portfolio variance is given by

$$\sigma^2(R_p) = \sum_{g=1}^{G}\sum_{h=1}^{G} w_g w_h\,\text{cov}(R_g, R_h) \tag{17.10}$$

In (17.10), the terms for which $h = g$ results in the variances of the G assets, and the terms for which $h \neq g$ results in all possible pairwise covariances amongst the G assets. Therefore, (17.10) is a shorthand notation for the sum of all G variances and the possible covariances amongst the G assets.

Portfolio Diversification

Often one hears investors talking about diversifying their portfolio. An investor who diversifies constructs a portfolio in such a way as to reduce portfolio risk without sacrificing return. This is certainly a goal that investors should seek. However, the question is how to do this in practice.

Some investors would say that including assets across all asset classes could diversify a portfolio. For example, an investor might argue that a portfolio should be diversified by investing in stocks, bonds, and real estate. While that might be reasonable, two questions must be addressed in order to construct a diversified portfolio. First, how much should be invested in each asset class? Should 40% of the portfolio be in stocks, 50% in bonds, and 10% in real estate, or is some other allocation more appropriate? Second, given the allocation, which specific stocks, bonds, and real estate should the investor select?

Some investors who focus only on one asset class such as common stock argue that these portfolios should also be diversified. By this they mean that an investor should not place all funds in the stock of one corporation, but rather should include stocks of many corporations. Here, too, several questions must be answered to construct a diversified portfolio. First, which corporations should be represented in the portfolio? Second, how much of the portfolio should be allocated to the stocks of each corporation?

A major contribution of the theory of portfolio selection is that, by using the concepts discussed above, we can provide a quantitative measure of the diversification of a portfolio, and it is this measure that we can use to achieve the maximum diversification benefits.

The Markowitz diversification strategy is primarily concerned with the degree of covariance between asset returns in a portfolio. Indeed a key contribution of Markowitz diversification is the formulation of an asset's risk in terms of a portfolio of assets, rather than in isolation. Markowitz diversification seeks to combine assets in a portfolio with returns that are less than perfectly positively correlated, in an effort to lower portfolio risk (variance) without sacrificing return. It is the concern for maintaining return while lowering risk through an analysis of the covariance between asset returns, that separates Markowitz diversification from a naive approach to diversification and makes it more effective.

Markowitz diversification and the importance of asset correlations can be illustrated with a simple two-asset portfolio example. To do this, we will first show the general relationship between the risk of a two-asset portfolio and the correlation of returns of the component assets. Then we will look at the effects on portfolio risk of combining assets with different correlations.

Portfolio Risk and Correlation

In our two-asset portfolio, assume that asset C and asset D are available with expected returns and standard deviations as shown:

Asset	$E(R)$	$\sigma(R)$
Asset C	12%	30%
Asset D	18%	40%

If an equal 50% weighting is assigned to both stocks C and D, the expected portfolio return can be calculated as

$$E(R_p) = 0.50(12\%) + 0.50(18\%) = 15\%$$

The variance of the return on the two-stock portfolio from equation (17.6) is

$$\sigma^2(R_p) = w_C^2\sigma^2(R_C) + w_D^2\sigma^2(R_D) + 2w_Cw_D\,\text{cov}(R_C,R_D)$$
$$= (0.5)^2(30\%)^2 + (0.5)^2(40\%)^2 + 2(0.5)(0.5)\,\text{cov}(R_C,R_D)$$

From equation (17.8),

$$\text{cor}(R_C,R_D) = \text{cov}(R_C,R_D)/[\sigma(R_C)\sigma(R_D)]$$

so

$$\text{cov}(R_C,R_D) = \sigma(R_C)\sigma(R_D)\text{cor}(R_C,R_D)$$

Because $\sigma(R_C) = 30\%$ and $\sigma(R_D) = 40\%$, then

$$\text{cov}(R_C, R_D) = (30\%)(40\%) \, \text{cor}(R_C, R_D)$$

Substituting into the expression for $\sigma^2(R_p)$, we get

$$\sigma^2(R_p) = (0.5)^2(30\%)^2 + (0.5)^2(40\%)^2 + 2(0.5)(0.5)(30\%)(40\%) \, \text{cor}(R_C, R_D)$$

Taking the square root of the variance gives

$$\sigma(R_p) = \sqrt{(0.5)^2(30\%)^2 + (0.5)^2(40\%)^2 + 2(0.5)(0.5)(30\%)(40\%)\text{cor}(R_C, R_D)}$$
$$= \sqrt{625 + (600)\text{cor}(R_C, R_D)}$$

The Effect of the Correlation of Asset Returns on Portfolio Risk

How would the risk change for our two-asset portfolio with different correlations between the returns of the component stocks? Let's consider the following three cases for $\text{cor}(R_C, R_D)$: +1.0, 0, and −1.0. Substituting into equation (11) for these three cases of $\text{cor}(R_C, R_D)$, we get:

$\text{cor}(R_C, R_D)$	$E(R_p)$	$\sigma(R_p)$
+1.0	15%	35%
0.0	15	25
−1.0	15	5

As the correlation between the expected returns on stocks C and D decreases from +1.0 to 0.0 to −1.0, the standard deviation of the expected portfolio return also decreases from 35% to 5%. However, the expected portfolio return remains 15% for each case.

This example clearly illustrates the effect of Markowitz diversification. The principle of Markowitz diversification states that as the correlation (covariance) between the returns for assets that are combined in a portfolio decreases, so does the variance (hence the standard deviation) of the return for the portfolio. This is due to the degree of correlation between the expected asset returns.

The good news is that investors can maintain expected portfolio return and lower portfolio risk by combining assets with lower (and preferably negative) correlations. However, the bad news is that very few assets have small to negative correlations with other assets! The problem, then, becomes one of searching among large numbers of assets in an effort to discover the portfolio with the minimum risk at a given level of expected return or, equivalently, the highest expected return at a given level of risk.

The stage is now set for a discussion of efficient portfolios and their construction.

Choosing a Portfolio of Risky Assets

Diversification in the manner suggested by Professor Markowitz leads to the construction of portfolios that have the highest expected return at a given level of risk. Such portfolios are called *efficient portfolios*. In order to construct efficient portfolios, the theory makes some basic assumptions about asset selection behavior by the entities. The assumptions are as follows:

Assumption 1. The only two parameters that affect an investor's decision are the expected return and the variance. (That is, investors make decisions using the two-parameter model formulated by Markowitz.)

Assumption 2. Investors are risk averse. (That is, when faced with two investments with the same expected return but two different risks, investors will prefer the one with the lower risk.)

Assumption 3. All investors seek to achieve the highest expected return at a given level of risk.

Assumption 4. All investors have the same expectations regarding expected return, variance, and covariances for all risky assets. (This is referred to as the *homogeneous expectations assumption.*)

Assumption 5. All investors have a common one-period investment horizon.

Constructing Efficient Portfolios

The technique of constructing efficient portfolios from large groups of stocks requires a massive number of calculations. In a portfolio of G securities, there are $(G^2 - G)/2$ unique covariances to calculate. Hence, for a portfolio of just 50 securities, there are 1,224 covariances that must be calculated. For 100 securities, there are 4,950. Furthermore, in order to solve for the portfolio that minimizes risk for each level of return, a mathematical technique called quadratic programming must be used. A discussion of this technique is beyond the scope of this chapter. However, it is possible to illustrate the general idea of the construction of efficient portfolios by referring again to the simple two-asset portfolio consisting of assets C and D.

Recall that for two assets, C and D, $E(R_C) = 12\%$, $\sigma(R_C) = 30\%$, $E(R_D) = 18\%$, and $\sigma(R_D) = 40\%$. We now further assume that $cor(R_C, R_D) = -0.5$.

Table 17.3 presents the expected portfolio return and standard deviation for five different portfolios made up of varying proportions of C and D.

Feasible and Efficient Portfolios

A *feasible portfolio* is any portfolio that an investor can construct given the assets available. The five portfolios presented in Table 17.3 are all feasible portfolios. The collection of all feasible portfolios is called the *feasible set of portfolios*. With only two assets, the feasible set of portfolios is graphed as a curve that represents those combinations of risk and expected return that are attainable by constructing portfolios from all possible combinations of the two assets.

Figure 17.2 presents the feasible set of portfolios for all combinations of assets C and D. As mentioned earlier, the portfolio mixes listed in Table 17.3 belong to this set and are shown by the points 1 through 5, respectively. Starting from 1 and proceeding to 5, asset C goes from 100% to 0%, while asset D goes from 0% to 100%—therefore, all possible combinations of C and D lie between portfolios 1 and 5, or on the curve labeled 1–5. In the case of two assets, any risk-return combination not lying on this curve is not attainable, since there is no mix of assets C and D that will result in that risk-return combination. Consequently, the curve 1–5 can also be thought of as the feasible set.

In contrast to a feasible portfolio, an *efficient portfolio* is one that gives the highest expected return of all feasible portfolios with the same risk. An efficient portfolio is also said to be a *mean-variance efficient portfolio*. Thus, for each level of risk there is an efficient portfolio. The collection of all efficient portfolios is called the *efficient set*.

TABLE 17.3 Portfolio Expected Returns and Standard Deviations for Five Mixes of Assets C and D
Asset C: $E(R_C) = 12\%$, $\sigma(R_C) = 30\%$
Asset D: $E(R_D) = 18\%$, and $\sigma(R_D) = 40\%$
Correlation between Asset C and D = $cor(R_C, R_D) = -0.5$

Portfolio	Proportion of Asset C	Proportion of Asset D	$E(R_p)$	$\sigma(R_p)$
1	100%	0%	12.0%	30.0%
2	75	25	13.5%	19.5%
3	50	50	15.0%	18.0%
4	25	75	16.5%	27.0%
5	0	100	18.0%	40.0%

FIGURE 17.2   Feasible and Efficient Portfolios for Assets C and D

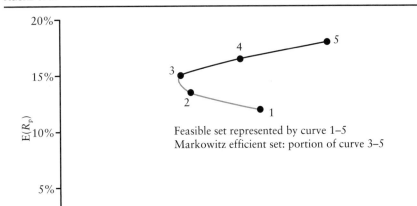

The efficient set for the feasible set presented in Figure 17.2 is differenti-ated by the bold curve section 3–5. Efficient portfolios are the combinations of assets C and D that result in the risk-return combinations on the bold section of the curve. These portfolios offer the highest expected return at a given level of risk. Notice that two of our five portfolio mixes—portfolio 1 with $E(R_p)$ = 12% and $\sigma(R_p)$ = 20% and portfolio 2 with $E(R_p)$ = 13.5% and $\sigma(R_p)$ = 19.5%—are not included in the efficient set. This is because there is at least one portfolio in the efficient set (for example, portfolio 3) that has a higher expected return and lower risk than both of them. We can also see that portfolio 4 has a higher expected return and lower risk than portfolio 1. In fact, the whole curve section 1–3 is not efficient. For any given risk-return combination on this curve section, there is a combination (on the curve section 3–5) that has the same risk and a higher return, or the same return and a lower risk, or both. In other words, for any portfolio that results in the return/risk combination on the curve section 1–3 (excluding portfolio 3), there exists a portfolio that dominates it by having the same return and lower risk, or the same risk and a higher return, or a lower risk and a higher return. For example, portfolio 4 dominates portfolio 1, and portfolio 3 dominates both portfolios 1 and 2.

Figure 17.3 shows the feasible and efficient sets when there are more than two assets. In this case, the feasible set is not a curve, but an area. This is because, unlike the two-asset case, it is possible to create asset portfolios that result in risk/return combinations that not only result in combinations that lie on the curve I–II–III, but all combinations that lie in the shaded area. However, the efficient set is given by the curve II–III. It is easily seen that all the portfolios on the efficient set dominate the portfolios in the shaded area.

The efficient set of portfolios is sometimes called the *efficient frontier* because, graphically, all the efficient portfolios lie on the boundary of the set of feasible portfolios that have the maximum return for a given level of risk. Any risk-return combination above the efficient frontier cannot be achieved, while risk-return combinations of the portfolios that make up the efficient frontier dominate those that lie below the efficient frontier.

Choosing the Optimal Portfolio in the Efficient Set

Now that we have constructed the efficient set of portfolios, the next step is to determine the optimal portfolio.

FIGURE 17.3 Feasible and Efficient Portfolios with More Than Two Assets[a]

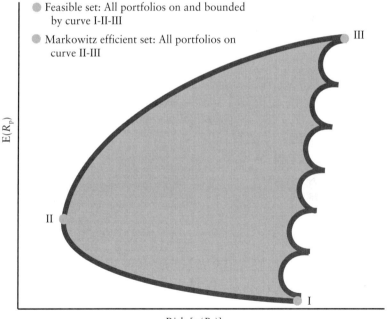

^a The picture is for illustrative purposes only. The actual shape of the feasible region depends on the returns and risks of the assets chosen and the correlation among them.

Because all portfolios on the efficient frontier provide the greatest possible return at their level of risk, an investor or entity will want to hold one of the portfolios on the efficient frontier. Notice that the portfolios on the efficient frontier represent trade-offs in terms of risk and return. Moving from left to right on the efficient frontier, the risk increases, but so does the expected return. The question is which one of those portfolios should an investor hold? The best portfolio to hold of all those on the efficient frontier is the *optimal portfolio*.

Intuitively, the optimal portfolio should depend on the investor's preference over different risk/return trade-offs. As explained earlier, this preference can be expressed in terms of a utility function.

In Figure 17.4, three indifference curves representing a utility function and the efficient frontier are drawn on the same diagram. An indifference

FIGURE 17.4   Selection of the Optimal Portfolio

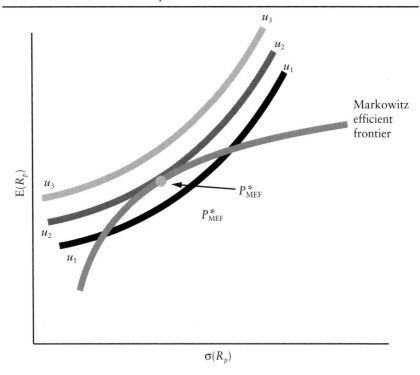

u_1, u_2, u_3 = indifference curves with $u_1 < u_2 < u_3$

P^*_{MEF} = optimal portfolio on Markowitz efficient frontier

curve indicates the combinations of risk and expected return that give the same level of utility. Moreover, the farther the indifference curve from the horizontal axis, the higher the utility.

From Figure 17.4, it is possible to determine the optimal portfolio for the investor with the indifference curves shown. Remember that the investor wants to get to the highest indifference curve achievable given the efficient frontier. Given that requirement, the optimal portfolio is represented by the point where an indifference curve is tangent to the efficient frontier. In Figure 17.4, that is the portfolio P^*_{MEF}. For example, suppose that P^*_{MEF} corresponds to portfolio 4 in Figure 17.2. We know from Table 17.3 that this portfolio is made up of 25% of asset C and 75% of asset D, with an $E(R_p)$ = 16.5% and $\sigma(R_p)$ = 27.0%.

Consequently, for the investor's preferences over risk and return as determined by the shape of the indifference curves represented in Figure 17.4, and expectations for asset C and D inputs (returns and variance-covariance) represented in Table 17.2, portfolio 4 is the optimal portfolio because it maximizes the investor's utility. If this investor had a different preference for expected risk and return, there would have been a different optimal portfolio. For example, Figure 17.5 shows the same efficient frontier but three other indifference curves. In this case, the optimal portfolio is P^{**}_{MEF}, which has a lower expected return and risk than P^*_{MEF} in Figure 17.4. Similarly, if the investor had a different set of input expectations, the optimal portfolio would be different.

At this point in our discussion, a natural question is how to estimate an investor's utility function so that the indifference curves can be determined. Unfortunately, there is little guidance about how to construct one. In general, economists have not been successful in estimating utility functions.

The inability to estimate utility functions does not mean that the theory is flawed. What it does mean is that once an investor constructs the efficient frontier, the investor will subjectively determine which efficient portfolio is appropriate given his or her tolerance to risk.

Index Model's Approximations to the Covariance Structure

The inputs to mean-variance analysis include expected returns, variance of returns, and either covariance or correlation of returns between each pair of securities. For example, an analysis that allows 200 securities as possible candidates for portfolio selection requires 200 expected returns, 200 variances of return, and 19,900 correlations or covariances. An investment team tracking 200 securities may reasonably be expected to summarize their analyses in terms of 200 means and variances, but it is clearly unreasonable for them to produce 19,900 carefully considered correlations or covariances.

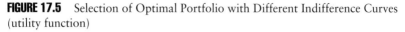

FIGURE 17.5   Selection of Optimal Portfolio with Different Indifference Curves (utility function)

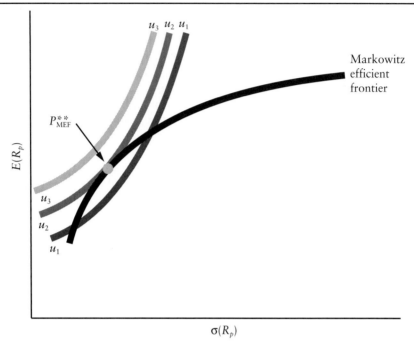

u_1, u_2, u_3 = indifference curves with $u_1 < u_2 < u_3$

P^{**}_{MEF} = optimal portfolio on Markowitz efficient frontier

It was clear to Markowitz that some kind of model of covariance structure was needed for the practical application of normative analysis to large portfolios. He did little more than point out the problem and suggest some possible models of covariance for research.

One model Markowitz proposed to explain the correlation structure among security returns assumed that the return on the ith security depends on an "underlying factor, the general prosperity of the market as expressed by some index." Mathematically, the relationship is expressed as follows (Markowitz, 1959, pp. 96–101):[2]

$$r_i = \alpha_i + \beta_i F + u_i \tag{17.11}$$

---

[2] Note that Markowitz (1959) used the notation I in proposing the model given by equation (17.11).

where

r_i = the return on security i
F = value of some index
u_i = error term

The expected value of u_i is zero and u_i is uncorrelated with F and every other u_i. The parameters α_i and β_i are parameters to be estimated. When measured using regression analysis, β_i is the ratio of the covariance of asset i's return and F to the variance of F.

Markowitz further suggested that the relationship need not be linear and that there could be several underlying factors.

Single-Index Market Model

Sharpe (1963) tested equation (17.11) as an explanation of how security returns tend to go up and down together with general market index, F. For the index in the market model he used a market index for F. Specifically, Sharpe estimated using regression analysis the following model:

$$r_{it} = \alpha_i + \beta_i\, r_{mt} + u_{it} \tag{17.12}$$

where

r_{it} = return on asset i over the period t
r_{mt} = return on the market index over the period t
α_i = a term that represents the nonmarket component of the return on asset i
β_i = the ratio of the covariance of the return of asset i and the return of the market index to the variance of the return of the market index
u_{it} = a zero mean random error term

The model given by equation (17.12) is called the *single-index market model* or simply the *market model*. It is important to note that when Markowitz discussed the possibility of using equation (17.11) to estimate the covariance structure, the index he suggested was not required to be a market index.

Suppose that the Dow Jones Wilshire 5000, a stock market index that we describe in the next chapter, is used to represent the market index, then for a portfolio of G assets regression analysis is used to estimate the values of the βs and αs. The beta of the portfolio (β_p), is simply a weighted average of the computed betas of the individual assets (β_i), where the weights are the percentage of the market value of the individual assets relative to the total market value of the portfolio. That is,

$$\beta_p = \sum_{i=1}^{G} w_i \beta_i$$

So, for example, the beta for a portfolio comprised of the following:

Company	Weight	β
General Electric	20%	1.24
McGraw Hill	25%	0.86
IBM	15%	1.22
General Motors	10%	1.11
Xerox	30%	1.27

would have the following beta:

Portfolio beta = 20%(1.24) + 25%(0.86) + 15%(1.22) + 10%(1.11) + 30%(0.27)
= 1.14

Multi-Index Market Models

Sharpe concluded that equation (17.11) was as complex a covariance as seemed to be needed. This conclusion was supported by research of Cohen and Pogue (1967). King (1966) found strong evidence for industry factors in addition to the marketwide factor. Rosenberg (1974) found other sources of risk beyond a marketwide factor and industry factor.

One alternative approach to full mean-variance analysis is the use of these multi-index or factor models to obtain the covariance structure.

TRACKING ERROR

As explained earlier, the risk of a portfolio can be measured by the standard deviation of portfolio returns. This statistical measure provides a range around the average return of a portfolio within which the actual return over a period is likely to fall with some specific probability. The mean return and standard deviation (or volatility) of a portfolio can be calculated over a period of time.

The standard deviation or volatility of a portfolio or a market index is an absolute number. A portfolio manager or client can also ask what the variation of the return of a portfolio is relative to a specified benchmark.

Such variation is called the portfolio's *tracking error*. More specifically, tracking error measures the dispersion of a portfolio's returns relative to the returns of its benchmark. That is, tracking error is the standard deviation of the portfolio's *active return* where active return is defined as

Active return = Portfolio's actual return − Benchmark's actual return

A portfolio created to match the benchmark (that is, an index fund) that regularly has zero active returns (that is, always matches its benchmark's actual return) would have a tracking error of zero. But a portfolio that is actively managed that takes positions substantially different from the benchmark would likely have large active returns, both positive and negative, and thus could have an annual tracking error of, say, 5% to 10%.

To find the tracking error of a portfolio, it is first necessary to specify the benchmark. The tracking error of a portfolio, as indicated, is its standard deviation relative to the benchmark, not its total standard deviation. Table 17.4 presents the information used to calculate the tracking error for a hypothetical portfolio and benchmark using 30 weekly observations. (The last column in the table shows the calculation of the information ratio, a measure to be described shortly.) The fourth column in the table shows the active return for the week. It is from the data in this column that the tracking error is computed. As reported in the table, the standard deviation of the weekly active returns is 0.54%. This value is then annualized by multiplying by the square root of 52, where 52 representing the number of weeks in a year. This gives a value of 3.89%. If the observations were monthly rather than weekly, the monthly tracking error would be annualized by multiplying by the square root of 12.

Given the tracking error, a range for the possible portfolio's active return and corresponding range for the portfolio can be estimated assuming that the active returns are normally distributed. For example, assume the following:

Benchmark = S&P 500
Expected return on S&P 500 = 20%
Tracking error relative to S&P 500 = 2%

and assuming that the tracking error is normally distributed:

Number of Standard Deviations	Range for Portfolio Active Return	Corresponding Range for Portfolio Return	Probability
1	±2%	18%–22%	67%
2	±4%	16%–24%	95%
3	±6%	14%–26%	99%

TABLE 17.4 Data and Calculation for Active Return, Alpha, and Information Ratio

Week	Weekly Returns (%)		
	Portfolio	Benchmark	Active
1	3.69%	3.72%	–0.02%
2	–0.56	–1.09	0.53
3	–1.41	–1.35	–0.06
4	0.96	0.34	0.62
5	–4.07	–4.00	–0.07
6	1.27	0.91	0.37
7	–0.39	–0.08	–0.31
8	–3.31	–2.76	–0.55
9	2.19	2.11	0.09
10	–0.02	–0.40	0.37
11	–0.46	–0.42	–0.05
12	0.09	0.71	–0.62
13	–1.93	–1.99	0.06
14	–1.91	–2.37	0.46
15	1.89	1.98	–0.09
16	–3.75	–4.33	0.58
17	–3.38	–4.22	0.84
18	0.60	0.62	–0.02
19	–10.81	–11.60	0.79
20	6.63	7.78	–1.15
21	3.52	2.92	0.59
22	1.24	1.89	–0.66
23	–0.63	–1.66	1.03
24	3.04	2.90	0.14
25	–1.73	–1.58	–0.15
26	2.81	3.05	–0.23
27	0.40	1.64	–1.23
28	1.03	1.03	0.01
29	–0.94	–0.95	0.00
30	1.45	1.66	–0.21

Average of active returns = 0.04%; Standard deviation of active returns = 0.54%
Annualizing:
Annual average = Weekly average × 52
Annual variance = Weekly variance × 52
Annual std dev = Weekly std dev × $(52^{0.5})$
Hence, on an annual basis:
Alpha = 1.83% (= 0.04% × 52 = Annualized average of weekly active returns)
Tracking error = 3.89% (= 0.54% × $[52^{0.5}]$ = Annualized std. dev. of weekly active returns)
Information ratio-alpha/Tracking error = 1.83%/3.89% = 0.47

Forward-Looking vs. Backward-Looking Tracking Error

In Table 17.4, the tracking error of the hypothetical portfolio is shown based on the active returns reported. However, the performance shown is the result of the portfolio manager's decisions during those 30 weeks with respect to portfolio positioning. Hence, we can call the tracking error calculated from these trailing active returns a *backward-looking tracking error.* It is also called the *ex post tracking error.*

One problem with a backward-looking tracking error is that it does not reflect the effect of current decisions by the portfolio manager on the future active returns and hence the future tracking error that may be realized. If, for example, the manager significantly changes the portfolio's composition today, then the backward-looking tracking error that is calculated using data from prior periods would not accurately reflect the current portfolio's risks going forward. That is, the backward-looking tracking error will have little predictive value and can be misleading regarding the portfolio's risks going forward.

The portfolio manager needs a forward-looking estimate of tracking error to accurately reflect the portfolio's risk going forward. The way this is done in practice is by using the services of a commercial vendor that has a model, called a *multifactor risk model*, that has defined the risks associated with a benchmark. Statistical analysis of the historical return data of the stocks in the benchmark index are used to obtain the factors and quantify their risks. Using the manager's current portfolio holdings, the portfolio's current exposure to the various factors can be calculated and compared to the benchmark's exposures to the factors. Using the differential factor exposures and the risks of the factors, a *forward-looking tracking error* for the portfolio can be computed. This tracking error is also referred to as the *predicted tracking error* or *ex ante tracking error.*

Each of these estimates has its use. The forward-looking tracking error is useful in risk control and portfolio construction. The manager can immediately see the likely effect on tracking error of any intended change in the portfolio. Thus, the manager can perform a what-if analysis of various portfolio strategies and eliminate those that would result in tracking errors beyond the client's tolerance for risk. The backward-looking tracking error can be useful for assessing actual performance analysis, such as the information ratio discussed later.

MEASURING AND EVALUATING PERFORMANCE

In this section, we see how to evaluate the investment performance of an asset manager. In doing so, we must distinguish between performance measurement and performance evaluation. *Performance measurement* involves the calculation of the return realized by a money manager over some time interval that we call the *evaluation period*. As we will see, several important issues must be addressed in developing a methodology for calculating a portfolio's return.

Performance evaluation is concerned with two issues: (1) determining whether the money manager added value by outperforming the established benchmark; and (2) determining how the money manager achieved the calculated return. For example, as explained in the next chapter, there are several strategies the manager of a stock portfolio can employ. Did the asset manager achieve the return by market timing, buying undervalued stocks, buying low-capitalization stocks, overweighting specific industries, and so on? The decomposition of the performance results to explain the reasons why those results were achieved is called *performance attribution analysis*. Moreover, performance evaluation requires the determination of whether the asset manager achieved superior performance (i.e., added value) by skill or by luck.

Measuring Performance

The starting point for evaluating the performance of an asset manager is measuring return. This might seem quite simple, but several practical issues make the task complex because one must take into account any cash distributions made from a portfolio during the evaluation period.

Alternative Return Measures

The dollar return realized on a portfolio for any evaluation period (i.e., a year, month, or week) is equal to the sum of:

1. The difference between the market value of the portfolio at the end of the evaluation period and the market value at the beginning of the evaluation period.
2. Any distributions made from the portfolio.

It is important that any capital or income distributions from the portfolio to a client or beneficiary of the portfolio be taken into account.

The rate of return, or simply return, expresses the dollar return in terms of the amount of the market value at the beginning of the evaluation period. Thus, the return can be viewed as the amount (expressed as a fraction of the initial portfolio value) that can be withdrawn at the end of the evaluation period while maintaining the initial market value of the portfolio intact.

In equation form, the portfolio's *return* can be expressed as follows:

$$R_P = \frac{MV_1 - MV_0 + D}{MV_0} \tag{17.13}$$

where

R_P = the return on the portfolio

MV_1 = the portfolio market value at the end of the evaluation period

MV_0 = the portfolio market value at the beginning of the evaluation period

D = the cash distributions from the portfolio to the client during the evaluation period

To illustrate the calculation of a return, assume the following information for an external money manager for a pension plan sponsor: The portfolio's market value at the beginning and end of the evaluation period is $25 million and $28 million, respectively, and, during the evaluation period, $1 million is distributed to the plan sponsor from investment income. Therefore,

$$MV_1 = \$28,000,000 \quad MV_0 = \$25,000,000 \quad D = \$1,000,000$$

Then

$$R_P = \frac{\$28,000,000 - \$25,000,000 + \$1,000,000}{\$25,000,000} = 0.16 = 16\%$$

There are three assumptions in measuring return as given by equation (17.13). The first assumption is that cash inflows into the portfolio from dividends and interest that occur during the evaluation period but are not distributed are reinvested in the portfolio. For example, suppose that during the evaluation period, $2 million is received from dividends. This amount is reflected in the market value of the portfolio at the end of the period.

The second assumption is that if there are distributions from the portfolio, they either occur at the end of the evaluation period or are held in the form of cash until the end of the evaluation period. In our example, $1 million is distributed to the plan sponsor. But when did that distribution actually occur? To understand why the timing of the distribution is important, consider two extreme cases: (1) the distribution is made at the end of the evaluation period, as assumed by equation (17.13); and (2) the distribution is made at the beginning of the evaluation period. In the first case, the money manager had the use of the $1 million to invest for the entire evaluation period. By contrast, in the second case, the money manager loses the opportunity to invest the funds until the end of the evaluation period. Consequently, the timing of the distribution will affect the return, but this is not considered in equation (17.13).

The third assumption is that there is no cash paid into the portfolio by the client. For example, suppose that sometime during the evaluation period, the plan sponsor gives an additional $1.5 million to the external money manager to invest. Consequently, the market value of the portfolio at the end of the evaluation period, $28 million in our example, would reflect the contribution of $1.5 million. Equation (17.13) does not reflect that the ending market value of the portfolio is affected by the cash paid in by the sponsor. Moreover, the timing of this cash inflow will affect the calculated return.

Thus, while the return calculation for a portfolio using equation (17.13) can be determined for an evaluation period of any length of time—such as one day, one month, or five years—from a practical point of view, the assumptions of this approach limit its application. The longer the evaluation period, the more likely the assumptions will be violated. For example, it is highly likely that there may be more than one distribution to the client and more than one contribution from the client if the evaluation period is five years. Therefore, a return calculation made over a long period of time, if longer than a few months, would not be very reliable because of the assumption underlying the calculations that all cash payments and inflows are made and received at the end of the period.

Not only does the violation of the assumptions make it difficult to compare the returns of two money managers over some evaluation period, but it is also not useful for evaluating performance over different periods. For example, equation (17.13) will not give reliable information to compare the performance of a one-month evaluation period and a three-year evaluation period. To make such a comparison, the return must be expressed per unit of time, for example, per year.

The way to handle these practical issues is to calculate the return for a short unit of time such as a month or a quarter. We call the return so calculated the *subperiod return*. To get the return for the evaluation period, the subperiod returns are then averaged. So, for example, if the evaluation period is one year, and 12 monthly returns are calculated, the monthly returns are the subperiod returns, and they are averaged to get the one-year return. If a three-year return is sought, and 12 quarterly returns can be calculated, quarterly returns are the subperiod returns, and they are averaged to get the three-year return. The three-year return can then be converted into an annual return by the straightforward procedure described later.

Three methodologies have been used in practice to calculate the average of the subperiod returns:

1. The arithmetic average rate of return.
2. The time-weighted rate of return (also called the *geometric rate of return*).
3. The dollar-weighted return.

Table 17.5 compares these methods side by side.

Arithmetic Average (Mean) Rate of Return

The *arithmetic average (mean) rate of return* is an unweighted average of the subperiod returns. The general formula is

$$R_A = \frac{R_{P1} + R_{P2} + \cdots + R_{PN}}{N} \qquad (17.14)$$

where

R_A = the arithmetic average rate of return
R_{Pk} = the portfolio return for subperiod k as measured by equation (17.1), where $k = 1, \dots, N$
N = the number of subperiods in the evaluation period

For example, if the portfolio returns [as measured by equation (17.13)] were –10%, 20%, and 5% in months July, August, and September, respectively, the arithmetic average monthly return is 5%, as shown below:

TABLE 17.5 Three Methods for Averaging Subperiod Returns

Method	Interpretation	Limitations
Arithmetic average (mean) rate of return	Average value of the withdrawals (expressed as a fraction of the initial portfolio market value) that can be made at the end of each subperiod while keeping the initial portfolio market value intact	Overvalues total return when subperiod returns vary greatly Assumes the maintenance of initial market value
Time-weighted (geometric) rate of return	The compounded rate of growth of the initial portfolio market value during the evaluation period	Assumes all proceeds are reinvested
Dollar-weighted rate of return (internal rate of return)	The interest rate that will make the present value of the sum of the subperiod cash flows (plus the terminal market value) equal to the initial market value of the portfolio	Is affected by client contributions and withdrawals beyond the control of the money manager

$$N = 3 \qquad R_{P1} = -0.10 \qquad R_{P2} = 0.20 \qquad \text{and} \qquad R_{P3} = 0.05$$

$$R_A = \frac{-0.10 + 0.20 + 0.05}{3} = 0.05 = 5\%$$

There is a major problem with using the arithmetic average rate of return. To see this problem, suppose the initial market value of a portfolio is $28 million, and the market values at the end of the next two months are $56 million and $28 million, respectively, and assume that there are no distributions or cash inflows from the client for either month. Then, using equation (17.13), we find the subperiod return for the first month (R_{P1}) is 100%, and the subperiod return for the second month (R_{P2}) is –50%. The arithmetic average rate of return using equation (17.14) is then 25%. Not a bad return! But think about this number. The portfolio's initial market value was $28 million. Its market value at the end of two months is $28 million. The return over this two-month evaluation period is zero. Yet equation (17.14) says it is a whopping 25%.

Thus it is improper to interpret the arithmetic average rate of return as a measure of the average return over an evaluation period. The proper interpretation is as follows: It is the average value of the withdrawals (expressed as a fraction of the initial portfolio market value) that can be made at the end of each subperiod while keeping the initial portfolio market value intact. In our first example above, in which the average monthly return is 5%, the investor must add 10% of the initial portfolio market value at the end of the first month, can withdraw 20% of the initial portfolio market value at the end of the second month, and can withdraw 5% of the initial portfolio market value at the end of the third month. In our second example, the average monthly return of 25% means that 100% of the initial portfolio market value ($28 million) can be withdrawn at the end of the first month, and 50% must be added at the end of the second month.

Time-Weighted Rate of Return

The *time-weighted rate of return* measures the compounded rate of growth of the initial portfolio market value during the evaluation period, assuming that all cash distributions are reinvested in the portfolio. This return is also commonly referred to as the *geometric mean return* because it is computed by taking the geometric average of the portfolio subperiod returns calculated from equation (17.13). The general formula is

$$R_T = [(1 + R_{P1})(1 + R_{P2}) \ldots (1 + R_{PN})]^{1/N} - 1 \qquad (17.15)$$

where R_T is the time-weighted rate of return, and R_{Pk} and N are as defined earlier.

For example, let us assume the portfolio returns were –10%, 20%, and 5% in July, August, and September, as in the first example above. Then the time-weighted rate of return as given by equation (17.15) is

$$R_T = \{[1 + (-0.10)] (1 + 0.20) (1 + 0.05)\}^{1/3} - 1$$
$$= [(0.90) (1.20) (1.05)]^{1/3} - 1 = 0.043$$

Because the time-weighted rate of return is 4.3% per month, $1 invested in the portfolio at the beginning of July would have grown at a rate of 4.3% per month during the three-month evaluation period.

The time-weighted rate of return in the second example is 0%, as expected, as shown below:

$$R_T = \{(1 + 1.00)[1 + (-0.50)\}^{1/2} - 1 = [(2.00)(0.50)]^{1/2} - 1 = 0\%$$

In general, the arithmetic and time-weighted average returns will give different values for the portfolio return over some evaluation period. This is because, in computing the arithmetic average rate of return, the amount invested is assumed to be maintained (through additions or withdrawals) at its initial portfolio market value. The time-weighted return, on the other hand, is the return on a portfolio that varies in size because of the assumption that all proceeds are reinvested.

In general, the arithmetic average rate of return will exceed the time-weighted average rate of return. The exception is in the special situation where all the subperiod returns are the same, in which case the averages are identical. The magnitude of the difference between the two averages is smaller the less the variation in the subperiod returns over the evaluation period. For example, suppose that the evaluation period is four months, and that the four monthly returns are as follows:

$$R_{P1} = 0.04 \qquad R_{P2} = 0.06 \qquad R_{P3} = 0.02 \qquad R_{P4} = -0.02$$

The arithmetic average rate of return is 2.5%, and the time-weighted average rate of return is 2.46%. Not much of a difference. In our earlier example, in which we calculated an average rate of return of 25% but a time-weighted average rate of return of 0%, the large discrepancy is due to the substantial variation in the two monthly returns.

Dollar-Weighted Rate of Return

The *dollar-weighted rate of return* is computed by finding the interest rate that will make the present value of the cash flows from all the subperiods in the evaluation period plus the terminal market value of the portfolio equal to the initial market value of the portfolio. The cash flow for each subperiod reflects the difference between the cash inflows due to investment income (i.e., dividends and interest) and to contributions made by the client to the portfolio and the cash outflows reflecting distributions to the client. Notice that it is not necessary to know the market value of the portfolio for each subperiod to determine the dollar-weighted rate of return.

The dollar-weighted rate of return is simply an internal rate of return calculation, and, hence, it is also called the *internal rate of return*. The general formula for the dollar-weighted return is

$$V_0 = \frac{C_1}{(1+R_D)} + \frac{C_2}{(1+R_D)^2} + \cdots + \frac{C_N + V_N}{(1+R_D)^n} \quad (17.16)$$

where

R_D = the dollar-weighted rate of return
V_0 = the initial market value of the portfolio
V_N = the terminal market value of the portfolio
C_k = the cash flow for the portfolio (cash inflows minus cash outflows) for subperiod k, where $k = 1, 2, ..., N$

For example, consider a portfolio with a market value of $100,000 at the beginning of July, capital withdrawals of $5,000 at the end of months July, August, and September, no cash inflows from the client in any month, and a market value at the end of September of $110,000. Then

$$V_0 = \$100,000 \quad N = 3 \quad C_1 = C_2 = C_3 = \$5,000 \quad V_3 = \$110,000$$

and R_D is the interest rate that satisfies the following equation:

$$\$100,000 = \frac{\$5,000}{(1+R_D)} + \frac{\$5,000}{(1+R_D)^2} + \frac{\$5,000+\$110,000}{(1+R_D)^3}$$

It can be verified that the interest rate that satisfies the above expression is 8.1%. This, then, is the dollar-weighted return.

The dollar-weighted rate of return and the time-weighted rate of return will produce the same result if no withdrawals or contributions occur over the evaluation period and if all investment income is reinvested. The problem with the dollar-weighted rate of return is that it is affected by factors that are beyond the control of the money manager. Specifically, any contributions made by the client or withdrawals that the client requires will affect the calculated return. This makes it difficult to compare the performance of two money managers.

To see this, suppose that a pension plan sponsor engaged two money managers, A and B, giving $10 million to A to manage, and $200 million to B. Suppose that (1) both money managers invest in identical portfolios (that is, the two portfolios have the same securities and are held in the same proportion); (2) for the following two months, the rate of return on the two portfolios is 20% for month 1 and 50% for month 2; and (3) the amount received in investment income is in cash. Also assume that the plan sponsor does not make an additional contribution to the portfolio of either money manager. Under these assumptions, it is clear that the performance of both money managers would be identical. Suppose, however, that the plan sponsor withdraws $4 million from A at the end of month 1. This means that A could not invest the entire amount at the end of month 1 and capture the 50% increase in the portfolio value. A's net cash flow would be as follows: In month 1, the cash flow is $6 million because $2 million is realized in investment income, and $4 million is withdrawn by the plan sponsor. The cash flow in month 2 is $12. The dollar-weighted rate of return is then calculated as follows:

$$\$10 = \frac{\$6}{(1+R_D)} + \frac{\$12}{(1+R_D)^2} \qquad R_D = 43.6\%$$

For B, the cash inflow for month 1 is $40 million ($200 million times 20%), and the portfolio value at the end of month 2 is $360 million ($240 million times 1.5). The dollar-weighted rate of return is

$$\$200 = \frac{\$40}{(1+R_D)} + \frac{\$360}{(1+R_D)^2} \qquad R_D = 44.5\%$$

We therefore find different results for the two money managers we agreed had identical performance. The withdrawal by the plan sponsor and the size of the withdrawal relative to the portfolio value had a significant effect on the calculated return. Notice also that even if the plan sponsor had withdrawn $4 million from B at the beginning of month 2, this would not have had as significant an impact. The problem would also have occurred if we assumed that the return in month 2 is –50%, and that, instead of A realizing a withdrawal of $4 million, the plan sponsor contributed $4 million.

Despite this limitation, the dollar-weighted rate of return does provide information. It indicates information about the growth of the fund that a client will find useful. This growth, however, is not attributable to the performance of the money manager because of contributions and withdrawals.

Annualizing Returns

The evaluation period may be less than or greater than one year. Typically, return measures are reported as an average annual return. This requires the annualization of the subperiod returns. The subperiod returns are usually calculated for a period of less than one year for the reasons described earlier. The subperiod returns are then annualized using the following formula:

$$\text{Annual return} = (1 + \text{Average period return})^{\text{Number of periods in year}} - 1 \quad (17.17)$$

So, for example, suppose the evaluation period is three years, and a monthly period return is calculated. Suppose further that the average monthly return is 2%. Then the annual return would be

$$\text{Annual return} = (1.02)^{12} - 1 = 26.8\%$$

Suppose, instead, that the period used to calculate returns is quarterly, and the average quarterly return is 3%. Then the annual return is

$$\text{Annual return} = (1.03)^{4} - 1 = 12.6\%$$

Evaluating Performance

A performance measure does not answer two questions: (1) How did the asset manager perform after adjusting for the risk associated with the active strategy employed? And (2) how did the asset manager achieve the reported return?

The answers to these two questions are critical in assessing how well or how poorly the asset manager performed relative to some benchmark. In answering the first question, we must draw upon the various measures of risk that we described earlier. We can then judge whether the performance was acceptable in the face of the risk.

The answer to the second question tells us whether the asset manager, in fact, achieved a return by following the anticipated strategy. While a client would expect that any superior return accomplished is a result of a stated strategy, that may not always be the case. For example, suppose a manager solicits funds from a client by claiming he can achieve superior common stock performance by selecting underpriced stocks. Suppose also that this manager does generate a superior return compared with the S&P 500 Index. The client should not be satisfied with this performance until the return realized by the manager is segregated into the various components that generated the return. A client may find that the superior performance is the result of the manager's timing of the market, rather than of his selecting underpriced stocks. In such an instance, the asset manager may have outperformed the S&P 500 (even after adjusting for risk), but not by following the strategy the asset manager told the client he intended to pursue.

Below we briefly describe methodologies for adjusting returns for risk so as (1) to determine whether a superior return was realized and (2) to analyze the actual return of a portfolio to uncover the reasons why a return was realized. We refer to this analysis as performance evaluation. We begin with a discussion of the various benchmarks that can be used to evaluate the performance of an asset manager.

Benchmark Portfolios

To evaluate the performance of an asset manager, a client must specify a benchmark against which the asset manager will be measured when there are nonliability driven objectives, the two types of benchmarks that have been used in practice are market indexes and generic-investment-style indexes. Developed by various consulting firms, a generic-investment-style index measures the various investment styles. The problem with these indexes is that it is often difficult to classify an asset manager by a particular investment style. Below we limit our discussion to market indexes.

Single-Index Performance Evaluation Measures

In the 1960s, several single-index measures were used to evaluate the relative performance of money managers. These measures of performance evaluation did not specify how or why a money manager may have outperformed or underperformed a benchmark. The three measures, or indexes, are the Treynor index, the Sharpe index, and the Jensen index. All three indexes assume that there is a linear relationship between the portfolio's return and the return on some broad-based market index.

In the early studies of asset managers, these measures were used to evaluate the performance of the managers of mutual funds. However, they are of very limited use in the evaluation of asset managers today because of the development of the performance attribution models discussed later.

Treynor Index The *Treynor index* is a measure of the excess return per unit of risk. This measure, developed by Jack Treynor (1965) is defined as the excess return is defined as the difference between the portfolio's return and the risk-free rate of return over the same evaluation period. The risk measure in the

Treynor index is the relative systematic risk as measured by the portfolio's beta. Treynor argues that this is the appropriate risk measure because, in a well-diversified portfolio, the unsystematic risk is close to zero. In equation form, the Treynor index is

$$\frac{\text{Portfolio return} - \text{Risk-free rate}}{\text{Portfolio's beta}}$$

Sharpe Index As with the Treynor index, the *Sharpe index* is a measure of the reward-risk ratio. Introduced by William Sharpe (1966), the numerator of this index is the same as in the Treynor index. The risk of the portfolio is measured by the standard deviation of the portfolio's return. Therefore, the Sharpe index is

$$\frac{\text{Portfolio return} - \text{Risk-free rate}}{\text{Standard deviation of the portfolio's return}}$$

Thus the Sharpe index is a measure of the excess return relative to the total variability of the portfolio. The Sharpe and Treynor indexes will give identical ranking if the portfolios evaluated are well diversified. If they are poorly diversified, the ranking could be quite different.

Jensen Index Proposed by Michael Jensen (1968), the *Jensen index* uses the capital asset pricing model that we described in Chapter 8 to determine whether the money manager outperformed the market index. The empirical analogue of the CAPM is

$$E(R_p) - R_F = \beta_p[E(R_M) - R_F] + e$$

where

$E(R_p)$ = the expected return on the portfolio
R_F = the risk-free rate
β_p = the beta of the portfolio
$E(R_M)$ = expected return on the market
e = random error term

In words,

Excess return = Beta × [Excess return on the market index]
+ Random error term

If the excess return produced by the manager does not exceed the excess return described by this formula, the manager has added nothing. After all, the historical beta of the portfolio represents an expectation of information-free performance; a random portfolio should perform this well. Jensen, then, added a factor to represent the portfolio's performance that diverges from its beta. This *alpha* is a measure of the manager's performance. Using time-series data for the return on the portfolio and the market index, we can estimate the following equation by regression analysis:

$$R_{pt} - R_{Ft} = \alpha_p + \beta_p[R_{Mt} - R_{Ft}] + e_{pt}$$

The intercept term alpha, α_p, in the above equation is the unique return realized by the money manager. That is,

Excess return = Unique return + Beta
× [Excess return on the market index] + Random error term

The Jensen measure is the alpha or unique return that is estimated from the above regression. If the alpha is not statistically different from zero, there is no unique return. A statistically significant alpha that is positive means that the money manager outperformed the market index; a negative value means that the money manager underperformed the market index.

As with the Treynor index, the Jensen measure assumes that the portfolio is fully diversified so that the only risk remaining in the portfolio is systematic risk.

The estimated alpha is sensitive to the beta level of the portfolio. To correct for this, the alpha can be divided by the expected return for the portfolio to reflect its systematic risk.

Information Ratio

Alpha is the average active return over a time period. Since backward-looking tracking error measures the standard deviation of a portfolio's active return, it is different from alpha. A portfolio does not have backward-looking tracking error simply because of outperformance or underperformance. For instance, consider a portfolio that outperforms (or underperforms) its benchmark by exactly 10 basis points every month. This portfolio would have a backward-looking tracking error of zero and a positive (negative) alpha of 10 basis points. In contrast, consider a portfolio that outperforms its benchmark by 10 basis points during half the months and underperforms by

10 basis points during the other months. This portfolio would have a backward-looking tracking error that is positive but an alpha equal to zero.[3]

The information ratio combines alpha and tracking error as follows:

$$\text{Information ratio} = \frac{\text{Alpha}}{\text{Backward-looking tracking error}}$$

The *information ratio* is essentially a reward-to-risk ratio. The reward is the average of the active return, that is, alpha. The risk is the standard deviation of the active return, the tracking error, and, more specifically, backward-looking tracking error. The higher the information ratio, the better the manager performed relative to the risk assumed.

To illustrate the calculation of the information ratio, consider the active returns for the hypothetical portfolio shown in Table 17.4. The weekly average active return is 0.04%. Annualizing the weekly average active return by multiplying by 52 gives an alpha of 1.83%. Since the backward-tracking error is 3.89%, the information ratio is 0.47 (1.83%/3.89%).

Performance Attribution Models

In broad terms, the return performance of a portfolio can be explained by three actions followed by an asset manager. The first is actively managing a portfolio to capitalize on factors that are expected to perform better than other factors. The second is actively managing a portfolio to take advantage of anticipated movements in the market. For example, the manager of a common stock portfolio can increase the portfolio's beta when the market is expected to increase, and decrease it when the market is expected to decline. The third is actively managing the portfolio by buying securities that are believed to be undervalued, and selling (or shorting) securities that are believed to be overvalued.

In the case of a common stock portfolio, we can categorize the sources of return of a portfolio in terms of these three active management strategies. The three sources are referred to as *timing short-term factor trends, market timing,* and *security analysis.* Thus, understanding a managed portfolio's return comes down to answering these four questions:

1. What were the major sources of added value?
2. Was short-term factor timing statistically significant?
3. Was market timing statistically significant?
4. Was security selection statistically significant?

---

[3] Note that in some texts, alpha and tracking error are calculated respectively as the average and the standard deviation of the beta-adjusted active return, instead of the total active return.

Notice that for the last three questions, we must determine whether the result is statistically significant or just a result of luck. For this reason, statistical analysis must be employed.

The methodology for answering these questions is called *performance attribution analysis*. The single indexes discussed above do not help answer these questions. However, there are commercially available models that can be used to do this analysis. We will not describe these models here. Instead, we use an illustration of how these models are used.

Rennie and Cowhey (1989) report the performance of three external money managers for Bell Atlantic (now Verizon Communications).[4] Table 17.6 shows the results for the three money managers since they began managing funds for Bell Atlantic. The values shown in parentheses in Table 17.6 are statistical measures that indicate the probability that the estimated value is statistically different from zero. The value in parentheses is referred to as a *confidence level*. The higher the confidence level, the more likely the estimated value is different from zero and, therefore, performance can be attributed to skill rather than luck.

The active management return represents the difference between the actual portfolio return and the benchmark return. Manager A's active management return is 420 basis points and, thus, seems to have outperformed the benchmark. But was this by investment skill or luck? The confidence level of 99% suggests that it was through investment skill. The lower panel

TABLE 17.6 Performance Attribution Analysis for Three Money Managers of Bell Atlantic

	Manager A		Manager B		Manager C	
Actual return	19.1%		17.0%		12.6%	
Benchmark portfolio	14.9		15.2		12.6	
Active management return	4.2%	(99)	1.8%	(53)	0.0%	(3)
Components of return:						
Market timing	–0.2%	(40)	–0.6%	(64)	–0.5%	(73)
Industry exposure	0.2	(20)	–2.0	(89)	0.3	(34)
Sector emphasis	2.2	(99)	3.9	(99)	0.3	(51)
Security selection	1.9	(84)	0.6	(43)	0.1	(7)
Unreconciled return[a]	0.1		–0.1		–0.2	

( ) denotes confidence level.
[a] Difference between actual management return and sum of components of return.
Source: Adapted from Rennie and Cowhey (1989, p. 37).

---

[4] Bell Atlantic merged with GTE to form Verizon Communications, Inc.

of the table shows how this was achieved. Of the four components of return, two are statistically significant—sector emphasis and security selection. The other two components—market timing and industry exposure—are not statistically significant. This means that either manager A's skills in these two areas did not significantly impact the portfolio's return, or the manager did not emphasize these skills. In fact, this manager's stated investment style is to add value through sector emphasis and security selection and neutralize market timing and industry exposure. The results of the performance attribution analysis are consistent with this investment style.

An analysis of the results of manager B indicates that the manager outperformed the benchmark by 180 basis points. The confidence level, however, is 53%. In most statistical tests, this confidence level would suggest that the 180 basis points is not statistically different from zero. That is, the 180-basis-point active management return can be attributed to luck rather than skill. However, Rennie and Cowhey state that this is an acceptable level of confidence for Bell Atlantic, but that it does provide a warning to the company to carefully monitor this manager's performance for improvement or deterioration. The stated investment style of this manager is to identify undervalued securities. The component return of 60 basis points from security selection with a confidence level of only 43% suggests that this manager is not adding value in this way. This is another warning sign that this manager must be more carefully monitored.

Manager C has to be carefully monitored because this manager did not outperform the benchmark, and none of the component returns are statistically significant. This manager is a candidate for termination. What is the minimum active management return that Bell Atlantic expects from its active equity managers? According to Rennie and Cowhey, it is 1% per year over a 2.5-year investment horizon with a confidence level of at least 70%. Moreover, the component analysis should corroborate what the manager states is the manager's investment style.

SUMMARY

The investment management process involves five steps: (1) setting investment objectives, (2) establishing an investment policy, (3) selecting a portfolio strategy, (4) constructing a portfolio, and (5) evaluating performance. The investment process involves the analysis of the investment objectives of the entity whose funds are being invested. Given the investment objectives, an investor must then establish policy guidelines to satisfy the investment objectives. This phase begins with the decision as to how to allocate funds across the major asset classes and requires a thorough understanding of the risks associated with investing in each asset class. After establishing the investment objectives and the investment policy, the investor must develop a portfolio strategy. Portfolio strategies can be classified as either active or passive. The next step is to construct the portfolio by selecting the specific securities to be included in the portfolio. Periodically, the investor must evaluate the performance of the portfolio and therefore the portfolio strategy. This step begins with the calculation of the investment return and then evaluates that return relative to the portfolio risk.

Developed by Harry Markowitz, modern portfolio theory explains how investors should construct efficient portfolios and select the best or optimal portfolio from among all efficient portfolios. The theory differs from previous approaches to portfolio selection in that Markowitz demonstrated how the key parameters should be measured. These parameters include the risk and the expected return for an individual asset and a portfolio of assets. Moreover, the concept of diversifying a portfolio, the goal of which is to reduce a portfolio's risk without sacrificing expected return, can be cast in terms of these key parameters plus the covariance or correlation between assets. All these parameters are estimated from historical data and draw from concepts in statistics.

A portfolio's expected return is simply a weighted average of the expected return of each asset in the portfolio. The weight assigned to each asset is the market value of the asset in the portfolio relative to the total market value of the portfolio. The risk of an asset is measured by the variance or standard deviation of its return. Unlike the portfolio's expected return, a portfolio's risk is not a simple weighting of the standard deviation of the individual assets in the portfolio. Rather, the portfolio risk is affected by the covariance or correlation between the assets in the portfolio. The lower the correlation, the smaller the portfolio risk.

Markowitz has set forth the theory for the construction of an efficient portfolio, which has come to be called a Markowitz efficient portfolio, a portfolio that has the highest expected return of all feasible portfolios with the same level of risk. The collection of all Markowitz efficient portfolios is called the Markowitz efficient set of portfolios or the Markowitz efficient frontier. The optimal portfolio is the one that maximizes an investor's preferences with respect to return and risk. An investor's preference is described by a utility function that can be represented graphically by a set of indifference curves. The utility function shows how much an investor is willing to trade off between expected return and risk. The optimal portfolio is the one where an indifference curve is tangent to the Markowitz efficient frontier.

Tracking error measures the variation of a portfolio's return relative to its benchmark index. For a portfolio manager, the risk of heavily underperforming the benchmark rises as the tracking error increases. Thus tracking error is an important indicator of portfolio performance and should be monitored frequently.

REFERENCES

Cohen, K. J. and Pogue, G. A. (1967). An empirical evaluation of alternative portfolio selection models. *Journal of Business* 40, no. 2: 166–193.

Jensen, M. C. (1968). The performance of mutual funds in the period 1945–1964. *Journal of Finance* 23, no. 2: 389–416.

King, B. F. (1966). Market and industry factors in stock price behavior. *Journal of Business* 39, 1 (Part 2: Supplement on Security Prices): 139–190.

Leavens, D. H. (1945). Diversification of investments. *Trusts and Estates* 80, no. 5: 469–473.

Markowitz, H. M. (1952). Portfolio selection. *Journal of Finance* 7, no. 1: 77–91

Markowitz, H. M. (1959). *Portfolio Selection: Efficient Diversification of Investments.* Cowles Foundation Monograph 16. New York: John Wiley & Sons.

Ortobelli, S., Rachev, S. T., Stoyanov, S., Fabozzi, F. J., and Biglova, A. (2005). Proper use of risk measures in portfolio theory. *International Journal of Theoretical and Applied Finance* 8, no. 8: 1–27.

Rennie, E. P. and Cowhey, T. J. (1989). The successful use of benchmark portfolios. In Darwin M. Bayston and H. Russell Fogler (eds.) *Improving Portfolio Performance with Quantitative Models* (pp. 32–44). Charlottesville, VA: Institute of Chartered Financial Analysts.

Rosenberg, B. (1974). Extra-market components of covariance in security returns. *Journal of Financial and Quantitative Analysis* 19, no. 2: 23–274.

Sharpe, W. F. (1963). A simplified model for portfolio analysis. *Management Science* 9, no. 2: 277–293.

Sharpe, W. F. (1966). Mutual fund performance. *Journal of Business* 34, no. 1 (Part I): 119–38.

Treynor, J. (1965). How to rate management of investment funds. *Harvard Business Review* 44, no. 1: 63–75.

von Neumann, J. and Morgenstern, O. (1944). *Theory of Games and Economic Behavior.* Princeton, NJ: Princeton University Press.

CHAPTER 18

Equity Portfolio Management

I n this chapter, we provide an overview of equity portfolio management and describe the various strategies pursued by asset managers and the evidence on the performance of such strategies.

STOCK MARKET INDICATORS

Stock market indicators perform a variety of functions, from serving as benchmarks for evaluating the performance of professional money managers to answering the question "How did the market do today?" Thus stock market indicators (indexes or averages) are a part of everyday life. Even though many of the stock market indicators are used interchangeably, it is important to realize that each indicator applies to, and measures, a different facet of the stock market.

Tables 18.1 and 18.2 provide a list of the various stock indexes in the United States. In general, stock market indexes rise and fall in fairly similar patterns. The indexes do not move in exactly the same ways at all times. The differences in movement reflect the different ways in which the indexes are constructed. Three factors enter into that construction:

- The universe of stocks represented by the sample underlying the index.
- The relative weights assigned to the stocks included in the index.
- The method of averaging across all the stocks in the index.

The stocks included in a stock market index must be combined in certain proportions, and each stock must be given a weight. The three main approaches to weighting are (1) weighting by the market capitalization of the stock's company, which is the value of the number of shares multiplied by the price per share; (2) weighting by the price of the stock; and (3) equal weighting for each stock, regardless of its price or its firm's market value. With the exception of the Dow Jones averages and the Value Line Composite Index,

TABLE 18.1   U.S. Stock Market Indexes: Exchange Provided Indexes

New York Stock Exchange (NYSE)

NYSE Composite Index	NYSE World Leaders Index
NYSE U.S. 100 Index	NYSE TMT Index

The American Stock Exchange (Amex)

Amex Composite	Amex Gold Bugs
Amex 20 Stock Index	Amex Industrial Sector Index
Amex Airline Index	Amex LT 20 Index
Amex Basic Industries Sector Index	Amex MS Consumer Index
Amex Biotech Index	Amex MS Cyclical Index
Amex Broker/Dealer Index	Amex MS Healthcare Payer Index
Amex Composite Index	Amex MS Healthcare Products Index
Amex Computer Technology Index	Amex MS Healthcare Providers Index
Amex Consumer Service Sector Index	Amex MS Hi-Tech 35 Index
Amex Consumer Staples Sector Index	Amex MS REIT Index
Amex CSFB Technology Index	Amex Natural Gas Index
Amex Cyclical/Transport Sector Index	Amex Networking Index
Amex Defense Index I	Amex Oil & Gas Index
Amex Disk Drive Index	Amex Stockcar Stocks
Amex Drug Index	Amex Technology Sector Index
Amex Electric Power & Natural Gas	Amex Telecomm Index
Amex Energy Sector Index	Amex Utility Sector Index
Amex Financial Sector Index	Amex Institutional Index

Nasdaq

Nasdaq Composite Index	Nasdaq Bank Index
Nasdaq National Market Composite Index	Nasdaq Computer Index
Nasdaq-100 Index	Nasdaq Health Care Index
Nasdaq-100 Equal Weighted Index	Nasdaq Industrial Index
Nasdaq-100 Technology Sector Index	Nasdaq National Market Industrial
Nasdaq-100 Ex-Tech Sector Index	Index
Nasdaq Financial-100 Index	Nasdaq Insurance Index
Nasdaq Biotechnology Index	Nasdaq Other Finance Index
Nasdaq Biotechnology Equal Weighted	Nasdaq Telecommunications Index
Index	Nasdaq Transportation Index

all the most widely used indexes are market-value weighted and the Value Line Composite Index is a value-weighted index. The Dow Jones Industrial Average (DJIA) is a price-weighted average.

Stock market indicators can be classified into three groups:

- Those produced by stock exchanges based on all stocks traded on the exchanges.

- Those produced by organizations that subjectively select the stocks to be included in indexes.
- Those where stock selection is based on an objective measure, such as the market capitalization of the company.

The first group, exchange-provided indexes, are shown in Table 18.1. The more popular indexes include the New York Stock Exchange Composite Index and, although it is not an exchange, the Nasdaq Composite Index, falls into this category because the index represents all stocks tracked by the Nasdaq system.

Indexes that fall into the second group are shown in Table 18.2. The two most popular stock market indicators in the second group are the Dow Jones Industrial Average and the Standard & Poor's 500 (S&P 500). The DJIA is constructed from 30 of the largest and most widely held U.S. industrial companies. The companies included in the average are those selected by Dow Jones & Company, publisher of the *Wall Street Journal*. The S&P 500 represents stocks chosen from the two major national stock exchanges and the over-the-counter market. The stocks in the index at any given time are determined by a committee of the Standard & Poor's Corporation, which may occasionally add or delete individual stocks or the stocks of entire industry groups. The aim of the committee is to capture present overall stock market conditions as reflected in a broad range of economic indicators. The Value Line Composite Index, produced by Value Line Inc., covers a broad range of widely held and actively traded NYSE, the American Stock Exchange (Amex), and *over-the-counter* (OTC) issues selected by Value Line.

Some indexes represent a broad segment of the stock market while others represent a particular sector such as technology, oil and gas, and financial. In addition, because the notion of an equity investment style (which we discuss later in this chapter) is widely accepted in the investment community, early acceptance of equity-style investing (in the form of growth versus value and small market capitalization versus large capitalization) has led to the creation and proliferation of published *style indexes*. Both the broad and the style indexes are shown in Table 18.2.

In the third group, also shown in Table 18.2, we have the Wilshire indexes produced by Wilshire Associates (Santa Monica, California) and published jointly with Dow Jones and Russell indexes produced by the Frank Russell Company (Tacoma, Washington), a consultant to pension funds and other institutional investors. The criterion for inclusion in each of these indexes is solely a firm's market capitalization. The most comprehensive index is the Wilshire 5000, which actually includes more than 6,700 stocks now, up from 5,000 at its inception. The Wilshire 4500

TABLE 18.2 Nonexchange Indexes

Dow Jones & Co.
Dow Jones Average–30 Industrial	Dow Jones Average–15 Utilities
Dow Jones Average–20 Transportation	

Dow Jones & Co./Wilshire Associates
Dow Jones Wilshire 5000 Total Market Index	Dow Jones Wilshire U.S. Small-Cap Growth Index
The Dow Jones Wilshire 4500 Completion Index	Dow Jones Wilshire U.S. 2500 Index
Dow Jones Wilshire U.S. Large-Cap Index	The Wilshire Large Cap 750 Index
Dow Jones Wilshire U.S. Mid-Cap Index	The Wilshire Mid-Cap 500 Index
Dow Jones Wilshire U.S. Small-Cap Index	The Wilshire Small Cap 1750 Index
Dow Jones Wilshire U.S. Micro-Cap Index	The Wilshire Micro-Cap Index
Dow Jones Wilshire U.S. Large-Cap Value Index	The Wilshire Large Value Index
	The Wilshire Large Growth Index
Dow Jones Wilshire U.S. Large-Cap Growth Index	The Wilshire Mid-Cap Value Index
	The Wilshire Mid-Cap Growth Index
Dow Jones Wilshire U.S. Mid-Cap Value Index	The Wilshire Small Value Index
	The Wilshire Small Growth Index
Dow Jones Wilshire U.S. Mid-Cap Growth Index	The Wilshire All Value Index
	The Wilshire All Growth Index
Dow Jones Wilshire U.S. Small-Cap Value Index	The Wilshire Small Cap 250

Standard & Poor's
S&P Composite 1500 Index	S&P MidCap 400 Index
S&P 100 Index	S&P SmallCap 600 Index
S&P 500 Index	

Frank Russell
Russell–3000 Index	Russell 2000 Value
Russell–2000 Index	Russell 1000 Growth
Russell–1000 Index	Russell 1000 Value
Russell 2000 Growth	Frank Russell–Midcap Index

Value Line
Value Line Composite Index

includes all stocks in the Wilshire 5000 except for those in the S&P 500. Thus shares in the Wilshire 4500 have smaller capitalization than those in the Wilshire 5000. The Russell 3000 encompasses the 3,000 largest companies in terms of their market capitalization. The Russell 1000 is limited to the largest 1,000 of those, and the Russell 2000 has the remaining smaller firms.

TOP-DOWN VS. BOTTOM-UP APPROACHES

An equity manager who pursues an active strategy may follow either a *top-down approach* or *bottom-up approach*. With the top-down approach, an equity manager begins by assessing the macroeconomic environment and forecasting its near-term outlook. Based on this assessment and forecast, an equity manager decides on how much of the portfolio's funds to allocate among the different sectors of the equity market and how much to allocate to cash equivalents (i.e., short-term money market instruments).

The sectors of the equity market can be classified as follows: basic materials, communications, consumer staples, financials, technology, utilities, capital goods, consumer cyclicals, energy, health care, transportation.[1] Industry classifications give a finer breakdown and include, for example, aluminum, paper, international oil, beverages, electric utilities, telephone and telegraph, and so on.

In making the allocation decision, a manager who follows a top-down approach relies on an analysis of the equity market to identify those sectors and industries that will benefit the most on a relative basis from the anticipated economic forecast. Once the amount to be allocated to each sector and industry is made, the manager then looks for the individual stocks to include in the portfolio.

In contrast to the top-down approach, an equity manager who follows a bottom-up approach focuses on the analysis of individual stocks and gives little weight to the significance of economic and market cycles. The primary tool of the manager who pursues a bottom-up approach is fundamental security analysis. We will discuss this tool in the next section. The product of the analysis is a set of potential stocks to purchase that have certain characteristics that the manager views as being attractive. For example, these characteristics can be low price-earnings ratios or small market capitalizations. Three well-known managers who follow a bottom-up approach are Warren Buffett (Berkshire Hathaway, Inc), Dean LeBaron (Batterymarch Financial Management), and Peter Lynch (formerly of Fidelity Magellan Fund).

Within the top-down and bottom-up approaches, there are different strategies pursued by active equity managers. These strategies are often referred to as *equity styles* and will be discussed later in this chapter.

FUNDAMENTAL VS. TECHNICAL ANALYSIS

Also within top-down and bottom-up approaches to active management are two camps as to what information is useful in the selection of stocks and

---

[1] These are the categories used by Standard & Poor's. There is another sector labeled "miscellaneous" that includes stocks that do not fall into any of the other sectors.

the timing of the purchase of stocks. These two camps are the fundamental analysis camp and the technical analysis camp.

Traditional fundamental analysis involves the analysis of a company's operations to assess its economic prospects. The analysis begins with the financial statements of the company in order to investigate the earnings, cash flow, profitability, and debt burden. The fundamental analyst will look at the major product lines, the economic outlook for the products (including existing and potential competitors), and the industries in which the company operates. The results of this analysis will be the growth prospects of earnings. Based on the growth prospects of earnings, a fundamental analyst attempts to determine the fair value of the stock using one or more of the equity valuation models discussed in Chapters 7 and 8. The estimated fair value is then compared to the market price to determine if the stock is fairly priced in the market, cheap (a market price below the estimated fair value), or rich (a market price above the estimated fair value). The father of traditional fundamental analysis is Benjamin Graham, who espoused this analysis in his classic book, *Security Analysis.*[2]

The limitation of traditional fundamental analysis is that it does not quantify the risk factors associated with a stock and how those risk factors affect its valuation. In Chapter 8, we described how risk can be quantified within an asset pricing framework.

Technical analysis ignores company information regarding the economics of the firm. Instead, technical analysis focuses on price and trading volume of individual stocks, groups of stocks, and the overall market resulting from shifting supply and demand. This type of analysis is not only used for the analysis of common stock, but it is also a tool used in the trading of commodities, bonds, and futures contracts. This analysis can be traced back to the seventeenth century, where it was applied in Japan to analyze the trend in the price of rice.[3] The father of modern technical analysis is Charles Dow, a founder of the *Wall Street Journal* and its first editor from July 1889 to December 1902.

In a later section in this chapter, we will discuss some of the strategies that are employed by active managers who follow fundamental analysis and technical analysis. We'll also look at the evidence regarding the performance of these strategies. It is critical to understand, however, that fundamental analysis and technical analysis can be integrated within a strategy. Specifically, a manager can use fundamental analysis to identify stocks that are

---

[2] There have been several editions of this book. The first edition was printed in 1934 and coauthored with Sidney Cottle. A more readily available edition is a coauthored version with David Dodd (Graham, Dodd, and Cottle, 1962).

[3] See Shaw (1998, p. 313).

candidates for purchase or sale, and the manager can employ technical analysis to time the purchase or sale.

POPULAR STOCK MARKET STRATEGIES

Throughout the history of the stock market, there have been numerous strategies suggested about how to "beat the market." At one time, these strategies were debated, and casual observations regarding performance were used to confirm or dispute a strategy. Today, the statistical tool kit of the modern portfolio manager allows a manager to better test whether or not a strategy can consistently outperform the stock market. Basically, this involves testing the efficiency of the stock market. In this section we provide an overview of several popular strategies and then present the empirical evidence. Some of these studies that investigate the strategies described were performed more than 40 years ago.

Strategies Based on Technical Analysis

Various common stock strategies that involve only historical price movement, trading volume, and other technical indicators have been suggested since the beginning of stock trading in the United States, as well as in commodity markets throughout the world. Many of these strategies involve investigating patterns based on historical trading data (past price data and trading volume) to identify the future movement of individual stocks or the market as a whole. Based on the observed patterns, mechanical trading rules indicating when a stock should be bought, sold, or sold short are developed. Thus no consideration is given to any factor other than the specified technical indicators. As we explained earlier, this approach to active management is called technical analysis. Because some of these strategies involve the analysis of charts that plot price and volume movements, investors who follow a technical analysis approach are sometimes called *chartists*. The overlying principle of these strategies is to detect changes in the supply of and demand for a stock and capitalize on the expected changes. The book by Edwards and Magee (1948) is widely acknowledged as the bible of technical analysis.

There is considerable debate on the value of technical analysis. Consider the following quotes from well-known market observers and practitioners:

The central proposition of charting is absolutely false, and investors who follow its precepts will accomplish nothing but increasing substantially the brokerage charges they pay. There has been a remarkable uniformity in the conclusions of studies done on all forms of technical analysis. Not one has consistently outperformed the placebo of a buy-and-hold strategy. (Malkiel, 1996).

The one principal that applies to nearly all these so-called 'technical approaches' is that one should buy *because* a stock or the market has gone up and one should sell *because* it has declined. This is the exact opposite of sound business sense everywhere else, and it is most unlikely that it can lead to lasting success in Wall Street. In our own stock-market experience and observation, extending over 50 years, we have not known a single person who has consistently or lastingly made money by thus 'following the market.' We do not hesitate to declare that this approach is as fallacious as it is popular. (Graham, 1973).

Technical analysts are the witch doctors of our business. By deciphering stock price movement patterns and volume changes, these Merlins believe they can forecast the future. (Gross, 1997).

On the other side of the debate is Mark Hulbert, a columnist for *Forbes* magazine. He takes issue with the statement that there is no support for technical analysis. As evidence, he cites a study by Brock, Lakonishok, and LeBaron (1992). In their empirical tests, they find support for some of the trading strategies based on technical analysis discussed below and conclude that earlier conclusions that technical analysis had no merit were premature. However, several years latter, Sullivan, Timmermann, and White (1999) found that for the best technical analysis strategies reported by Brock, Lakonishok and LeBaron, "there is scant evidence that technical trading rules were of any economic value." More recently, Hsu and Kuan (2005) examined the profitability of almost 40,000 technical trading strategies for the period 1989 to 1992 for four stock indexes that we describe later in this chapter. They found that the performance of trading strategies depended on the maturity of the indexes (i.e., how long the indexes were outstanding). Basically they found that technical trading strategies were significantly profitable when applied to the two relatively immature stock indexes they studied but not when applied to the two mature stock indexes studied.

A comprehensive discussion of all of the empirical studies of technical analysis strategies is beyond the scope of this chapter. In the rest of this section we provide a brief description of four technical-analysis based strategies: Dow theory strategies, simple filter rules strategies, momentum strategies, and market overreaction strategies. But before doing so, let's review such strategies in the context of pricing efficiency. Recall that the weak form of pricing efficiency asserts that an investor cannot generate abnormal returns by merely looking at historical price and volume movements. Thus, if technical analysis strategies can outperform the market, then the market is price-inefficient in the weak form. Another way of viewing this is that if a manager or client believes that the stock market is price-efficient in the weak form, then pursuing a strategy based on technical analysis will not consistently outperform the market after consideration of transaction costs and risk.

It is important to note that some market observers believe that the patterns of stock price behavior are so complex that simple mathematical models are insufficient for detecting historical price patterns and developing models for forecasting future price movements. Thus, while stock prices may appear to change randomly, there may be a pattern, but simple mathematical tools are insufficient for that purpose. Scientists have developed complex mathematical models for detecting patterns from observations of some phenomena that appear to be. Generically, these models are called *nonlinear dynamic models* because the mathematical equations used to detect if there is any structure in a pattern are nonlinear equations and there is a system of such equations. The particular form of nonlinear dynamic models that has been suggested is *chaos theory*. At this stage, the major insight provided by chaos theory is that stock price movements that may appear to be random may, in fact, have a structure that can be used to generate abnormal returns. However, the actual application seems to have fallen far short of the mark.[4]

Dow Theory Strategies

The grandfather of the technical analysis school is Charles Dow. During his tenure as editor of the *Wall Street Journal*, his editorials theorized about the future direction of the stock market. The ideas presented by Dow, which were refined by Hamilton (1922) after Dow's death in 1902, are what we now refer to as the *Dow theory*. This theory rests on two basic assumptions. First, according to Charles Dow, "The averages in their day-to-day fluctuations discount everything known, everything foreseeable, and every condition that can affect the supply of or the demand for corporate securities." This assumption sounds very much like the efficient market theory. But there's more. The second basic assumption is that the stock market moves in trends—up and down—over periods of time. According to Charles Dow, it is possible to identify these stock price trends and predict their future movement. If this is so and an investor can realize abnormal returns, then the stock market is not price-efficient in the weak form.

---

[4] See Scheinkman and LeBaron (1989) and Peters (1991).

According to the Dow theory, there are three types of trends, or market cycles. The primary trend is the long-term movement in the market. These are basically four-year trends in the market. From the primary trend, a trend line showing where the market is heading can be derived. The secondary trend represents short-run departures of stock prices from the trend line. The third trend is short-term fluctuations in the stock prices. Charles Dow believed that upward movements in the stock market were tempered by fallbacks that lost a portion of the previous gain. A *market turn* occurs when the upward movement was not greater than the last gain. In assessing whether or not a gain did in fact occur, he suggested examining the comovements in different stock market indexes such as the Dow Jones Industrial Average and the Dow Jones Transportation Average. One of the averages is selected as the primary index, and the other as the confirming index. If the primary index reaches a high above its previous high, the increase is expected to continue if it is confirmed by the other index also reaching a high above its previous high.

The theory formulated by Dow focused on the longer-term trends of business activity and its impact on the relationship between stock prices of stock averages. While employed as the financial editor of *Forbes* magazine in the early 1930, Schabacker modified the Dow theory to bar charts of individual securities on a short to intermediate time frame, and is the principal architect of many of the chart patterns used by technical analysts today (see Schabacker (1930, 1932, 1934)).

Empirically, it is difficult to test the Dow theory because it is dependent upon identifying turning points. Several studies have attempted to test this theory as formulated by Hamilton. The first was by Cowles (1934) who found that that it simply did not work. However, a study by Glickstein and Wubbels (1983) found support for the Dow theory, the authors concluding that "successful market timing is by no means impossible." Brown, Goetzmann and Kumar (1998) revisited the Cowles study by taking into account risk. More specifically, they used the Sharpe ratio and the Jensen measure that we described in Chapter 17. In contrast to the findings of Cowles, they found support for the Dow theory.

Simple Filter Rules Strategy

The simplest type of technical strategy is to buy and sell on the basis of a predetermined movement in the price of a stock; the rule is basically that if the stock increases by a certain percentage, the stock is purchased and held until the price declines by a certain percentage, at which time the stock is sold. The percentage by which the price must change is called the "filter." Every investor pursuing this technical strategy makes up their own filter.

The original study of the profitability of simple filter rules was performed by more than 40 years ago by Alexander (1961). Adjustments for methodological deficiencies of the Alexander study by Fama and Blume (1966) found that price changes do show persistent trends; however, the trends were too small to exploit after considering transaction costs and other factors that must be taken into account in assessing the strategy. Two subsequent studies by Sweeney (1988, 1990), however, suggest that a short-term technical trading strategy based on past price movements can produce statistically significant risk-adjusted returns after adjusting for the types of transaction costs faced by floor traders and professional equity managers.

Momentum Strategies

Practitioners and researchers alike have identified several ways to successfully predict security returns based on the historical returns. Among these findings, perhaps the most popular ones are those of price momentum and price reversal strategies. The basic idea of a *price momentum strategy* is to buy stocks that have performed well (referred to as "winners") and to sell the stocks that have performed poorly (referred to as "losers") with the hope that the same trend will continue in the near future. In contrast, in a *price reversal strategy* stocks that have historically poor performance are purchased (i.e., losers are purchased) with the hope that they will eventually reverse and outperform in the future and short stocks that that have historically poor performance (i.e., winners are shorted) hoping that they will underperform in the future. Because a price reversal strategy is one in which the performance in the future is expected to be contrary to the historical performance, it is also referred to as a *contrarian strategy*. Basically, the price reversal strategy is the inverse of the price momentum strategy.

Some asset managers are only permitted to buy and not short stocks; these asset managers are referred to as "long-only" managers. As a result, they can only pursue a price momentum strategy in which they buy winners or one in which they sell losers. Asset managers, such as hedge funds manager, that are free to take on both long and short positions can pursue any of the price momentum or reversal strategies. In fact, to create leverage these asset managers can employ a price momentum strategy such that the value of the portfolio of winners is funded by shorting a portfolio of losers. That is, the net investment to the fund is close to zero. Similarly, in price reversal strategy the shorting of the winner portfolio is used to fund the purchase of the loser portfolio.

There is ample evidence supporting price momentum and price reversal strategies. The effect was first documented in the academic literature by Jegadeesh and Titman (1993) for the U.S. stock market and has thereafter been shown to be present in many other international equity markets by Rouwenhorst. The empirical findings show that stocks that outperformed (underperformed) over a horizon of 6 to 12 months will continue to perform well (poorly) on a horizon of 3 to 12 months to follow. Jegadeesh (1990) was the first to identify a short-term (one month) reversal effect and De Bondt and Thaler (1985) a long-term reversal effect. Typical backtests of these strategies have historically earned about 1% per month over the following 12 months. However, there is an empirical question regarding the changing nature of markets that suggests price momentum strategies will not longer produce superior returns. This has been documented by Hwang and Rubesam (2007) who, using data from 1927 to 2005, argued that momentum phenomena disappeared during the 2000–2005 period. Figelman (2007), however, analyzing the S&P 500 Index over the 1970–2004 period, found new evidence of momentum and reversal phenomena previously not described.

Today, many practitioners rely on momentum strategies—both on shorter as well as longer horizons. Short-term strategies tend to capitalize on intraday buy and sell pressures, whereas more intermediate and long-term strategies can be attributed to over- and underreaction of prices relative to their fundamental value as new information becomes available.[5]

Momentum portfolios tend to have high turnover, so transaction and trading costs become an issue. Most studies show that the resulting profits of momentum strategies decrease if transaction costs are taken into account. For example, Korajczyk and Sadka,[6] taking into account the different costs of buying and short-selling stocks, report that depending on the method of measurement and the particular strategy, profits between 17 and 35 basis points per month (after transaction costs) are achievable.

While researchers seem to be in somewhat of an agreement on the robustness and pervasiveness of the momentum phenomenon, the debate is still ongoing on whether the empirical evidence indicates market inefficiency or if it can be explained by rational asset pricing theories.

Let's briefly look at an explanation from behavioral finance theory that provides a foundation for price momentum and reversal strategies. To benefit from favorable news or to reduce the adverse effect of unfavorable news, investors must react quickly to new information. Cognitive psychologists have shed some light on how people react to extreme events. In general, people tend to overreact to extreme events. People tend to react more strongly to recent information; and they tend to heavily discount older information.

The question is, do investors follow the same pattern? That is, do investors overreact to extreme events? The *overreaction hypothesis* in finance suggests that when investors react to unanticipated news that will benefit a

---

[5] See Daniel, Hirshleifer, and Subrahmanyam (1998).
[6] See Korajczyk and Sadka (2004).

company's stock, the price rise will be greater than it should be, given that information, resulting in a subsequent decline in the price of the stock. In contrast, the overreaction to unanticipated news that is expected to adversely affect the economic well-being of a company will force the price down too much, followed by a subsequent correction that will increase the price.

If, in fact, the market does overreact, investors may be able to exploit this to realize positive abnormal returns if they can (1) identify an extreme event and (2) determine when the effect of the overreaction has been impounded in the market price and is ready to reverse. We refer to this theory as the market overreaction hypothesis. Investors who are capable of doing this will pursue the following strategies. When positive news is identified, investors will buy the stock and sell it before the correction to the overreaction. In the case of negative news, investors will short the stock and then buy it back to cover the short position before the correction to the overreaction.

As originally formulated by DeBondt and Thaler (1985), the overreaction hypothesis can be described by two propositions. First, the extreme movement of a stock price will be followed by a movement in the stock price in the opposite direction. This is called the *directional effect*. Second, the more extreme the initial price change (i.e., the greater the overreaction), the more extreme the offsetting reaction (i.e., the greater the price correction). This is called the *magnitude effect*. However, as Bernstein (1985) pointed out, the directional effect and the magnitude effect may simply mean that investors overweight short-term sources of information. To rectify this, Brown and Harlow (1988) added a third proposition, called the *intensity effect*, which states that the shorter the duration of the initial price change, the more extreme the subsequent response will be.

Several empirical studies support the directional effect and the magnitude effect.[7] Brown and Harlow tested for all three effects (directional, magnitude, and intensity) and found that for intermediate and long-term responses to *positive* events, there is only mild evidence that market pricing is inefficient; however, evidence on short-term trading responses to *negative* events is strongly consistent with all three effects. They conclude that "the tendency for the stock market to correct is best regarded as an asymmetric, short-run phenomenon." It is asymmetric because investors appear to overreact to negative, not positive, extreme events.

Strategies Based on Fundamental Analysis

As explained earlier, fundamental analysis involves an economic analysis of a firm with respect to its earnings growth prospects, ability to meet debt

---

[7] See DeBondt and Thaler (1985, 1987), Howe (1986), and Brown and Harlow (1988).

obligations, its competitive environment, and so on. Proponents of semistrong market efficiency argue that strategies based on fundamental analysis will not produce abnormal returns. The reason is simply that there are many analysts undertaking basically the same sort of analysis, with the same publicly available data, so that the price of the stock reflects all the relevant factors that determine value.

The focus of strategies based on fundamental analysis is on the earnings of a company and the expected change in earnings. In fact, a study by Chugh and Meador (1994) found that two of the most important measures used by analysts are short-term and long-term changes in earnings.

Next we describe several popular fundamental-analysis related strategies.

Earnings Surprise Strategies

Studies have found that it is not merely the change in earnings that is important to investors. The reason is that analysts have a consensus forecast of a company's earnings. What might be expected to generate abnormal returns is the extent to which the market's forecast of future earnings differs from actual earnings that are subsequently announced. The divergence between the forecasted earnings by the market and the actual earnings announced is called an *earnings surprise*. When the actual earnings exceed the market's forecast, then this is a *positive earnings surprise;* a *negative earnings surprise* arises when the actual earnings are less than the market's forecast.

There have been numerous studies of earnings surprises.[8] These studies seem to suggest that identifying stocks that may have positive earnings surprises and purchasing them may generate abnormal returns. Of course, the difficulty is identifying such stocks.

Low Price-Earnings Ratio Strategies

The legendary Benjamin Graham proposed a classic investment model in 1949 for the "defensive investor"—one without the time, expertise, or temperament for aggressive investment. The model was updated in each subsequent edition of his book, *The Intelligent Investor.*[9] Some of the basic investment criteria outlined in the 1973 edition are representative of the approach:

1. A company must have paid a dividend in each of the past 20 years.

---

[8] The first of these tests was by Joy, Lizenberger and McEnally (1977).
[9] This model is fully described in Chapter 14 in Graham (1973).

2. Minimum size of a company is $100 million in annual sales for an industrial company and $50 million for a public utility.
3. Positive earnings must have been achieved in each of the past 10 years.
4. Current price should not be more than 1.5 times the latest book value.
5. Market price should not exceed 15 times the average earnings for the past three years.

Graham considered the P/E ratio as a measure of the price paid for value received. He viewed high P/Es with skepticism and as representing a large premium for difficult-to-forecast future earnings growth. Hence, lower-P/E, higher-quality companies were viewed favorably as having less potential for earnings disappointments and the resulting downward revision in price.

A study by Oppenheimer and Schlarbaum (1981) reveals that over the period 1956–1975, significant abnormal returns were obtained by following Graham's strategy, even after allowing for transaction costs. While originally intended for the defensive investor, numerous variations of Graham's low-P/E approach are currently followed by a number of professional investment advisers.[10]

Market-Neutral Long-Short Strategy

An active strategy that seeks to capitalize on the ability of a manager to select stocks is a *market-neutral long-short strategy*. The basic idea of this strategy is as follows. First, a manager analyzes the expected returns of individual stocks within a universe of stocks. Based on this analysis, the manager can classify those stocks as either "high-expected-return stocks" or "low-expected-return stocks." A manager could then do one of the following: (1) purchase only high-expected-return stocks; (2) short low-expected-return stocks; or (3) simultaneously purchase high-expected return stocks and short low-expected-return stocks.

The problem with the first two strategies is that movements in the market in general can have an adverse affect. For example, suppose that a manager selects high-expected-return stocks and that the market declines. Because of the positive correlation between the return on all stocks and the market, the drop in the market will produce a negative return even though the manager may have indeed been able to identify high-expected-return stocks. Similarly, if a manager shorts low-expected return stocks and the market rallies, the portfolio will realize a negative return. This is because a rise in the market means that the manager must cover the short position of each stock at a price higher than the price at which a stock was sold.

---

[10] For a thorough presentation of the low P/E investment strategy, see Dreman (1982).

Let's look at the third alternative—simultaneously purchasing stocks with high expected returns and shorting those stocks with low expected returns. Consider what happens to the long and the short positions when the general market in moves. A drop in the market will hurt the long position but benefit the short position. A market rally will hurt the short position but benefit the long position. Consequently, the long and short positions provide a hedge against each other.

Although the long-short positions provide a hedge against general market movements, the degree to which one position moves relative to the other is not controlled by simply going long the high-expected-return stocks and going short the low-expected-return stocks. That is, the two positions do not neutralize the risk against general market movements. However, the long and short positions can be created with a market exposure that neutralizes any market movement. Specifically, long and short positions can be constructed to have the same beta, and, as a result, the beta of the long-short position is zero. For this reason, this strategy is called a *market-neutral long-short strategy*. If, indeed, a manager is capable of identifying high- and low-expected-return stocks, then neutralizing the portfolio against market movements will produce a positive return whether the market rises or falls.

Here is how a market-neutral long-short portfolio is created. It begins with a list of stocks that fall into the high-expected-return stocks and low-expected-return stocks. One or a combination of the models described is used. (In fact, we classify this strategy as a fundamental analysis strategy because fundamental analysis is used to identify the stocks that fall into the high- and low-expected return stock categories.) The high-expected-return stocks are referred to as "winners" and are those that are candidates to be included in the long portfolio; the low-expected-return stocks are referred to as "losers" and are those that are candidates to be included in the short portfolio.

Suppose a client allocates $10 million to a manager to implement a market-neutral long-short strategy.[11] Suppose that the manager (with the approval of the client) uses the $10 million to buy stocks on margin. As explained later in this chapter, the investor can borrow up to a specified percentage of the market value of the margined stocks, with the percentage determined by the Federal Reserve. Let's assume that the margin requirement is 50%. This means that the manager has $20 million to invest—$10 million in the long position and $10 million in the short position.

When buying securities on margin, the manager must be prepared for a margin call. Therefore, a prudent policy with respect to managing the risk of a margin call is not to invest the entire amount. Instead, a liquidity buffer of about 10% of the equity capital is typically maintained. This amount is

---

[11] This illustration is from is Jacobs and Levy (1997).

invested in a high-quality short-term money market instrument. The portion held in this instrument is said to be held in "cash." In our illustration, since the equity capital is $10 million, $1 million is held in cash, leaving $9 million to be invested in the long position; therefore, $9 million is shorted. The portfolio then looks as follows: $1 million cash, $9 million long, and $9 million short.

Market Anomaly Strategies

While there are managers who are skeptical about technical analysis and fundamental analysis, some managers believe that there are pockets of pricing inefficiency in the stock market. That is, there are some investment strategies that have historically produced statistically significant positive abnormal returns. These market anomalies are referred to as the *small-firm effect*, the *low-price-earnings-ratio effect*, the *neglected-firm effect*, and various *calendar effects*. There is also a strategy that involves following the trading transactions of insiders of a company.

Some of these anomalies are a challenge to the semistrong form of pricing efficiency because they use the financial data of a company. These would include the small-firm effect and the low-price-earnings effect. The calendar effects are a challenge to the weak form of pricing efficiency. Following insider activities with regard to buying and selling the stock of their company is a challenge to both the weak and strong forms of pricing efficiency. The challenge to the former is that, as will be explained below, information on insider activity is publicly available and, in fact, has been suggested as a technical indicator in popular television programs such as *Wall Street Week*. The question is whether "outsiders" can use information about trading activity by insiders to generate abnormal returns. The challenge to the strong form of pricing efficiency is that insiders are viewed as having special information, and, therefore, they may be able to generate abnormal returns using information acquired from their special relationship with the firm.

Small-Firm Effect Strategy

The small-firm effect emerges in several studies that have shown that portfolios of small firms (in terms of total market capitalization) have outperformed the stock market (consisting of both large and small firms).[12] Because of these findings, there has been increased interest in stock market indicators that monitor small-capitalization firms. We describe this more fully when we discuss equity-style management later.

---

[12] See Reinganum (1981) and Banz (1981).

Low-P/E Effect Strategy

Earlier, we discussed Benjamin Graham's strategy for defensive investors based on low price-earnings ratios. The low-price-earnings-ratio effect is supported by several studies showing that portfolios consisting of stocks with a low price-earnings ratio have outperformed portfolios consisting of stocks with a high price-earnings ratio.[13] However, there have been studies that found that after adjusting for transaction costs necessary to rebalance a portfolio as prices and earnings change over time, the superior performance of portfolios of low-price-earnings-ratio stocks no longer holds.[14] An explanation for the presumably superior performance is that stocks trade at low price-earnings ratios because they are temporarily out of favor with market participants. Because fads do change, companies not currently in vogue will rebound at some indeterminate time in the future.[15]

Neglected-Firm Effect

Not all firms receive the same degree of attention from security analysts, and one school of thought is that firms that are neglected by security analysts will outperform firms that are the subject of considerable attention. One study has found that an investment strategy based on changes in the level of attention devoted by security analysts to different stocks may lead to positive abnormal returns.[16] This market anomaly is referred to as the *neglected-firm effect*.

Calendar Effects

While some empirical work focuses on selected firms according to some criteria such as market capitalization, price-earnings ratio, or degree of analysts' attention, the calendar effect looks at the best time to implement strategies. Examples of anomalies are the January effect, month-of-the-year effect, day-of-the-week effect, and holiday effect. It seems from the empirical evidence that there are times when the implementation of a strategy will, on average, provide a superior performance relative to other calendar time periods. However, since it is not possible to predict when such a strategy will work, this again supports the idea that the market is at least weak-form efficient.

---

[13] See Basu (1977).
[14] See Levy and Lerman (1985).
[15] See Dreman (1979).
[16] See Arbel and Stebel (1983).

PASSIVE STRATEGIES

If investors believe that the market is efficient with respect to pricing stocks, then they should accept the implication that attempts to outperform the market cannot be successful systematically, except by luck. This does not mean that investors should shun the stock market, but rather that they should pursue a passive strategy, which is one that does not attempt to outperform the market. Is there an optimal investment strategy for someone who holds this belief in the pricing efficiency of the stock market? Indeed, there is. Its theoretical basis is modern portfolio theory (see Chapter 17) and capital market theory (see Chapter 8). According to modern portfolio theory, the "market" portfolio offers the highest level of return per unit of risk in a market that is price-efficient. A portfolio of financial assets with characteristics similar to those of a portfolio consisting of the entire market (i.e., the market portfolio) will capture the pricing efficiency of the market.

But how can such a passive strategy be implemented? More specifically, what is meant by a "market portfolio," and how should that portfolio be constructed? In theory, the market portfolio consists of all financial assets, not just common stock. The reason is that investors compare all investment opportunities, not just stock, when committing their capital. Therefore, the principles of investing that we accept are based on capital market theory, not stock market theory. When the theory has been followed by those investing in the stock market, the market portfolio has been defined as consisting of a large universe of common stocks. How much of each common stock should be purchased when constructing the market portfolio? The theory states that the chosen portfolio should be an appropriate fraction of the market portfolio; hence, the weighting of each stock in the market portfolio should be based on its relative market capitalization. Thus, if the aggregate market capitalization of all stocks included in the market portfolio is $T, and the market capitalization of one of these stocks is $A, then the fraction of this stock that should be held in the market portfolio is $A/$T.

The passive strategy that we have just described is called *indexing*. Because pension fund sponsors increasingly believe that asset managers have been unable to outperform the stock market, the amount of funds managed using an indexing strategy has increased since the 1980s.

EQUITY-STYLE MANAGEMENT

In the early 1970s, academic studies found that there were categories of stocks that had similar characteristics and performance patterns. Moreover, the returns of these stock categories performed differently than did those of other categories of stocks. That is, the returns of stocks within a category were highly correlated, and the returns between categories of stocks were relatively uncorrelated. The first such study was by Farrell (1975), who called these categories of stocks "clusters." He found that for stocks, there were at least four such categories or clusters—growth, cyclical, stable, and energy. In the later half of the 1970s, other studies suggested that an even simpler categorization by size (as measured by total capitalization) produced different performance patterns.

Practitioners began to view these categories or clusters of stocks with similar performance as a "style" of investing. Some managers, for example, held themselves out as "growth stock managers," and others as "cyclical stock managers." Using size as a basis for categorizing style, some managers became "large-cap" investors, and others "small-cap" investors. ("Cap" is short for market capitalization.) Moreover, there was a commonly held belief that a manager could shift "styles" to enhance return performance.

Today, the notion of an *equity investment style* is widely accepted in the investment community. The acceptance of equity-style investing can also be seen from the proliferation of style indexes published by several vendors and the introduction of futures and options contracts based on some of these style indexes.

Types of Equity Styles

Stocks can be classified by style in many ways. The most common is in terms of one or more measures of "growth" and "value." Within a growth and value style, there is a substyle based on some measure of size. The most plain vanilla classification of styles is as follows:

- Large value
- Large growth
- Small value
- Small growth

The motivation for the value and growth style categories can be explained in terms of the most commonly used measure for classifying stocks as growth or value—the *price-to-book value per share* (P/B) ratio.[17] Earnings growth will increase the book value per share. Assuming no change in the P/B ratio, a stock's price will increase if earnings grow. A manager who is growth oriented is concerned with earnings growth, and seeks those stocks from a universe of stocks that have higher relative earnings growth.

---

[17] Support for the use of this measure is provided by Fama and French (1993).

The growth manager's risks are that growth in earnings will not materialize and/or that the P/B ratio will decline.

For a value manager, concern is with the price component rather than with the future earnings growth. Stocks would be classified as value stocks within a universe of stocks if they are viewed as cheap in terms of their P/B ratio. By cheap, it is meant that the P/B ratio is low relative to the universe of stocks. The expectation of the manager who follows a value style is that the P/B ratio will return to some normal level and, thus, even with book value per share constant, the price will rise. The risk is that the P/B ratio will not increase.

Within the value and growth categories, there are substyles. As mentioned above, one substyle is based on size. The substyles are based on other classifications of the stocks selected.

In the value category, there are three substyles: low price-to-earnings (P/E) ratio, contrarian, and yield.[18] The *low-P/E manager* concentrates on companies trading at low prices relative to their P/E ratio.[19] The P/E ratio can be defined as the current P/E, a normalized P/E, or a discounted future earnings. The *contrarian manager* looks at the book value of a company and focuses on those companies that are selling at low valuation relative to book value. The companies that fall into this category are typically depressed cyclical stocks or companies that have little or no current earnings or dividend yields. The expectation is that the stock is on a cyclical rebound or that the company's earnings will turn around. Both of these occurrences are expected to lead to substantial price appreciation. The most conservative value managers are those who look at companies with above average dividend yields that are expected to be capable of increasing, or at least maintaining, those yields. This style is followed by a manager referred to as a *yield manager*.

Growth managers seek companies with above average growth prospects. In the growth manager style category, there tend to be two major substyles.[20] The first is a growth manager who focuses on high-quality companies with consistent growth. A manager who follows this substyle is referred to as a *consistent growth manager*. The second growth substyle is followed by an *earnings momentum growth manager*. In contrast to a growth manager, an earnings momentum growth manager prefers companies with more volatile, above average growth. Such a manager seeks to buy companies in expectation of an acceleration of earnings.

---

[18] See Christopherson and Williams (1997).
[19] For a discussion of an approach based on low price-earnings, see Schlarbaum (1997).
[20] See Christopherson and Williams (1997).

TYPES OF STOCK MARKET STRUCTURES[21]

There are two overall market structures for trading stocks. The first model is *order-driven*, in which buy and sell orders of public participants who are the holders of the securities establish the prices at which other public participants can trade. These orders can be either *market orders* or *limit orders*. An order-driven market is also referred to as an *auction market*. The second model is *quote-driven*, in which intermediaries, that is market-makers or dealers, quote the prices at which the public participants trade. Market-makers provide a *bid quote* (to buy) and an *offer quote* (to sell) and realize revenues from the spread between these two quotes. Thus market-makers derive a profit from the spread and the turnover of their stocks.

Order-Driven Markets

An order-driven market is also referred to as a *dealer market*. Participants in a *pure order-driven market* are referred to as "naturals" (the natural buyers and sellers). No intermediary participates as a trader in a pure order-driven market. Rather, the investors supply the liquidity themselves. That is, the *natural buyers* are the source of liquidity for the *natural sellers*, and vice versa. The naturals can be either buyers or sellers, each using market or limit orders.

Order-driven markets can be structured in two very different ways: a continuous market and a call auction at a specific point of time. In the *continuous market*, a trade can be made at any moment in continuous time during which a buy order and a sell order meet at a specific time. In this case, trading is a series of bilateral matches. In the *call auction*, orders are batched together for a simultaneous execution in a multilateral trade at a specific point in time. At the time of the call, a market-clearing price is determined; buy orders at this price and higher and sell orders at this price and lower are executed.

Continuous trading is better for customers who need immediacy. On the other hand, for markets with very low trading volume, an intraday call may focus liquidity at one (or a few) times of the day and permit the trades to occur. In addition, very large orders—block trades that will be described later—may be advantaged by the feasibility of continuous trading.

Nonintermediated markets involve only naturals; that is, such markets do not require a third party. A market may not, however, have sufficient liquidity to function without the participation of intermediaries, who are

---

[21] This section and the one to follow (The U.S. Stock Markets: Exchanges and OTC Market) are adapted from Fabozzi and Jones (2008).

third parties in addition to the natural buyers and sellers. This leads to the need for intermediaries and quote-driven markets.

Quote-Driven Markets

Quote-driven markets permit intermediaries to provide liquidity. Intermediaries may be *brokers* (who are *agents* for the naturals); *dealers* or *marketmakers* (who are *principals* in the trade); and *specialist*, as on the New York Stock Exchange (who act as both agents and principals). Dealers are independent, profit-making participants in the process. Dealers operate as principals, not agents. Dealers continually provide bid and offer quotes to buy for or sell from their own accounts and profit from the spread between their bid and offer quotes.

Dealers compete with each other in their bids and offers. Obviously, from the customer's perspective, the "best" market is highest bid and lowest offer among the dealers. This highest bid–lowest offer combination is referred to as the "inside market" or the "top of the book." For example, assume that dealers A, B, and C have the bids and offers (also called *asking prices*) for stock Alpha as shown in the following table:

Dealer	Bid	Offer
A	80.50	81.20
B	80.35	81.10
C	80.20	81.00

The best (highest) bid is by dealer A of 40.50; the best (lowest) offer is by dealer C of 41.00. Therefore, the inside market is 40.50 bid (by A) and 41.00 offer (by C). Note that A's spread is 40.50 bid and 41.20 offer for a spread (or profit margin) of 0.70. A has the highest bid but not the lowest offer. C has the lowest offer but not the highest bid. B has neither the highest bid nor the lowest offer. For a stock in the U.S. market, the highest bid and lowest offer across all markets is called the *national best bid and offer* (NBBO).

Dealers provide value to the transaction process by providing capital for trading and facilitating order handling. With respect to providing capital for trading, they buy and sell for their own accounts at their bid and offer prices, respectively, thereby providing liquidity. With respect to order handling, they provide value in two ways. First, they assist in the price improvement of customer orders, that is, the order is executed within the bid-offer spread. Second, they facilitate the market timing of customer orders to achieve price discovery. Price discovery is a dynamic process that involves customer orders being translated into trades and transaction prices. Because price discovery is not instantaneous, individual participants have an incentive to "market-time" the placement of their orders. Intermediaries may understand the order flow and may assist the customer in this regard. The intermediary may be a person or an electronic system.

The over-the-counter markets are quote-driven markets. The OTC markets began during a time when stocks were bought and sold in banks and the physical certificates were passed over the counter.

A customer may choose to buy or sell to a specific market-maker to whom they wish to direct an order. Directing an order to a specific market is referred to as "preferencing."

Order-Driven vs. Quote-Driven Markets

Overall, nonintermediated, order-driven markets may be less costly due to the absence of profit-seeking dealers. But the markets for many stocks are not inherently sufficiently liquid to operate in this way. For this reason, intermediated, dealer markets are often necessary for inherently less liquid markets. The dealers provide dealer capital, participate in price discovery and facilitate market timing, as discussed above.

Because of the different advantages of these two approaches, many equity markets are now *hybrid markets*. For example, the NYSE is primarily a continuous auction order-driven system based on customer orders but the specialists enhance the liquidity by their market-making to maintain a fair and orderly market. Overall, the NYSE is primarily an auction, order-driven market that has specialists (who often engage in market-making), other floor traders, call markets at the open and close, and upstairs dealers who provide proprietary capital to facilitate block transactions. The NYSE is a hybrid combination of these two models. Another hybrid aspect of the NYSE is that it opens and closes trading with a call auction. The continuous market and call auction market are combined. That makes the NYSE a continuous market during the trading day and a call auction market to open and close the market and to reopen after a stop in trading—and so, again, a hybrid market. Nasdaq (an acronym for National Association of Securities Dealers Automated Quotations System) that will be discussed further later, began as a descendent of the OTC dealer network, and is a dealer quote-driven market. It remains primarily a quote-driven market, but has added some order-driven making it a hybrid market.

An overview of the non-intermediated, auction, order-driven market and the intermediated, dealer, quote driven markets is provided in Figure 18.1.

FIGURE 18.1   Structure of Stock Markets

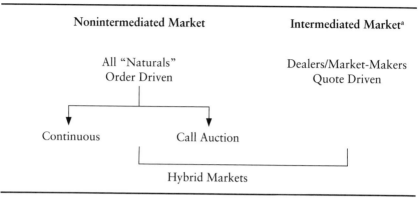

Nonintermediated Market	Intermediated Market[a]
All "Naturals" Order Driven	Dealers/Market-Makers Quote Driven

Continuous   Call Auction

Hybrid Markets

[a] Intermediaries include:
- Dealers/Market-makers(principals)
- Brokers (agents)
- Specialists (operate as both principals and agents)

Source: Jones and Fabozzi (2008).

THE U.S. STOCK MARKETS: EXCHANGES AND OTC MARKETS

An *exchange* is often defined as a market where intermediaries meet to deliver and execute customer orders. This description, however, also applies to many dealer networks. In the United States, an exchange is an institution that performs this function and is registered with the SEC as an exchange. There are also some off-exchange markets that perform this function.

The basis for the federal government regulation of the stock market resides with the SEC. The SEC's authority is primarily based on two important pieces of federal legislation. The first is the Securities Act of 1933 (the "Securities Act"), which covers the primary markets, that is, the new issues of securities. The second is the Securities Act of 1934 (the "Exchange Act"), which covers the secondary markets. The SEC was created by the Exchange Act. In addition to the SEC regulations, the exchanges also play a role in their own regulation through self-regulating organizations (SROs). The SRO of the NYSE has been responsible for the member regulation, enforcement, and arbitration functions of the NYSE. In addition, the NASD has had the SEC authority to set standards for its member firms and standards of conduct for issuing securities and selling securities to the public. The NASD has also monitored the Nasdaq stock market. There have, however, been some overlapping responsibilities of these two SROs and, therefore, some competition between them. As a result, these two SROs merged and in July 2007 were replaced by the single organization, the Financial Industry Regulation Authority (FINRA). This consolidation resulted in all firms dealing with only one rulebook, one set of examiners, and one enforcement staff, thereby reducing costs and inconsistencies. Thus FINRA is the single remaining SRO.

Figure 18.2 provides a general overview of the current construct of the U.S. stock markets. The components of the current U.S. stock market are discussed next.

National Exchanges

There are two national stock exchanges in the United States: the NYSE and the American Stock Exchange (Amex or ASE). As of the first quarter of 2008, the NYSE made a bid to acquire the Amex.

FIGURE 18.2 The "Big Picture" of the U.S Stock Market

I. Stock Exchanges

  A. National Exchanges

    1. New York Stock Exchange Euronext

      a. NYSE Hybrid Market
      b. Arcapelago ("Arca")

    2. American Stock Exchange

  B. Regional Exchanges

    1. Chicago Stock Exchange (CHX)
    2. Philadelphia Stock Exchange (PHLX)
    3. Boston Stock Exchange (BeX)
    4. National Stock Exchange (formerly the Cincinnati Stock Exchange) (NSX)
    5. Pacific Stock Exchange (owned by Arcapelago; in turn owned by the NYSE)

  C. Nasdaq—the OTC Market (technically became an exchange during June 2006)

    1. Nasdaq National Market (NNM)
    2. Small Cap Market

  D. Other OTC Markets

    1. Bulletin Board ("Bullies")
    2. Pink Sheets

  E. Off Exchange Markets /Alternative Electronic Markets

    1. Electronic Communication Networks (ECNs)
    2. Alternative Trading Systems (ATS)

      a. Crossing Networks
      b. Dark Pools

New York Stock Exchange

The trading mechanism of the NYSE (referred to as the "Big Board") has been based on the specialist system. This system is a hybrid of primarily an order-driven market with some quote-driven features. According to this mechanism, each stock is assigned to an individual specialist. Each specialist "specializes" in many stocks but each stock is assigned to only one specialist. Each specialist is located at a "booth" or "post." All orders for a stock are received at this post and the specialist conducts an auction based on these orders to determine the execution price. The orders arrive at the specialists' posts either physically, delivered via firm brokers, or electronically via the Designated Order Turnaround (DOT) system or its successors. In conducting the auction, typically the specialist is an agent, simply matching orders. At times, however, the specialist becomes a principal and trades for itself in the interest of maintaining an "orderly market."

In the next section we describe the different types of orders that can be placed when transacting in stocks and the advantages and disadvantages of each. For now, we briefly describe two types: market order and limit order. A *market order* is an order to be executed at the best price available in the market. A *limit order* is an order where the investor designates a price threshold for the execution of the trade (maximum price to purchase or minimum price to sell). A limit order that is not executable at the time it reaches the market is recorded in a *limit order book* kept by the specialist in their "book" (originally a physical paper book but now an electronic book). These limit orders are executed by the specialist when the market price moves to the limit. The book is open to all the traders on the exchange floor. Overall, the NYSE trading mechanism is an auction-based, order-driven market. This type of trading mechanism is often judged to provide the best price but, on a time basis, often a less rapid execution. Consequently, there is a tradeoff between price and speed.

American Stock Exchange

The American Stock Exchange, like the NYSE, lists stocks from throughout the United States and also international stocks. Amex is therefore a national exchange. Amex is also an auction-type market based on orders. Its specialist system is similar to that of the NYSE. At one time the Amex was the second largest stock market in the United States. However, in recent years this national exchange has lost it market share.

Regional Exchanges

Regional exchanges developed to trade stocks of local firms that listed their shares on the regional exchanges and also to provide alternatives to the national stock exchanges for their listed stocks. Regional stock exchanges now exist in Chicago, Philadelphia, and Boston and have existed in many other U.S. cities. These exchanges have also been specialist-type, auction-based systems. Some of the regional stock exchanges, including Philadelphia and Boston, as well as the Amex have been driven by trading in stock options and index options rather than stock in recent years.

Nasdaq Stock Market: The OTC Market

The Nasdaq, as an electronic exchange, has no physical trading floor, but makes all its trades through a computer and telecommunications system. The exchange is a dealers' market, meaning brokers buy and sell stocks through a market maker rather than from each other. A market-maker deals in a particular stock and holds a certain number of stocks on its own books so that when a broker wants to purchase shares, the broker can purchase them directly from the market maker.

Nasdaq is a dealer system or OTC system where multiple dealers provide quotes (bids and offers) and make trades. There is no specialist system and, therefore, there is no single place where an auction takes place. Nasdaq is essentially a telecommunication network that links thousands of geographically dispersed, market-making participants. Nasdaq is an electronic quotation system that provides price quotations to market participants on Nasdaq listed stocks. Nasdaq is essentially an electronic communication network (ECN) structure which allows multiple market participants to trade through it. Nasdaq allows multiple market participants to trade through its ECN structure, increasing competition.

Since Nasdaq dealers provide their quotes independently, the market has been called "fragmented." So while the NYSE market is an auction/agency, order-based market, the Nasdaq is a *competitive dealer, quote-based system*.

There are two sections of the Nasdaq stock market are the Nasdaq National Market (NNM) and the Small Cap Market (also known as the Nasdaq Capital Market Issues). For a stock to be listed on the NNM, the company must meet certain strict financial criteria. For example, a company must maintain a stock price of at least $1, and the total value of outstanding stocks must be at least $1.1 million and must meet lower requirements for assets and capital. To qualify for listing on the exchange, a company must be registered with the SEC and have at least three market-makers. However the Nasdaq also has a market for smaller companies unable to meet these and other requirements, called the Nasdaq Small Caps Market. Nasdaq will move companies from one market to the other as their eligibility changes.

The NYSE vs. Nasdaq

Fundamentally, the NYSE has been an auction type market that is based on orders (order-driven), while Nasdaq has been a dealer type market based on quotes (quote-driven). For years and decades, debates continued about which system—the NYSE or Nasdaq system—was most competitive and efficient. Those who think the Nasdaq OTC market is superior to the specialist-based NYSE often cite the greater competition from numerous dealers and the greater amount of capital they bring to the trading system. They also argue that specialists are conflicted in balancing their obligation to conduct a fair and orderly market and their need to make a profit.

Proponents of the specialist NYSE market structure argue that the commitment of the dealers in the OTC market to provide a market for shares is weaker than the obligation of the specialists on the exchanges. On the NYSE, specialists are obligated to maintain fair and orderly markets. Failure to fulfill this obligation may result in a loss of specialist status. A dealer in the OTC market is under no such obligation to continue its market-making activity during volatile and uncertain market conditions. Supporters of the specialist system also assert that without a single location for an auction, the OTC markets are fragmented and do not achieve the best trade price.

Another difference of opinion comes from traders who say that the specialist system may arrive at the better price, but take a longer period of time, during which the market price may move against the trader, or at least expose the trader to the risk that it will do so. The OTC market may, on the other hand, lead to a faster execution but not arrive at a better, market-clearing price. Professional traders, in this case, often prefer higher speed over better pricing. Retail investors on the other hand may prefer a better price.

While the NYSE has been an auction type/order driven market, it has adopted many dealer-type features. Similarly, while the Nasdaq has been a dealer-type and quote-driven market, it has adopted many auction-type features. Thus, while distinct differences continue between these two markets, they have converged considerably and are both currently hybrid markets, although with different mixes of order-driven and quote-driven features.

Other OTC Markets

The OTC market is often called a market for "unlisted" stocks. As described previously, there are listing requirements for exchanges. And while technically the Nasdaq has not been an exchange—it was an OTC market—there are also listing requirements for the Nasdaq National Market and the Small Capitalization OTC markets. Nevertheless, exchange-traded stocks are called "listed," and stocks traded on the OTC markets, including Nasdaq, are called "unlisted."

There are three parts to the OTC market: the two under Nasdaq and a third market for truly unlisted stocks that are therefore non-Nasdaq OTC markets. The third non-Nasdaq OTC Market is composed of two parts, the OTC Bulletin Board (OTCBB) and the Pink Sheets.

Thus, technically, both exchanges and the Nasdaq have listing requirements and only the non-Nasdaq OTC markets are nonlisted. However, in common parlance, the exchanges are often called the "listed market," and Nasdaq, by default, referred to as the "unlisted market." As a result, a more useful and practical categorization of the U.S. stock trading mechanisms is as follows.

1. Exchange listed stocks
   a. National Exchanges
   b. Regional Exchanges
2. Nasdaq listed OTC stocks
   a. Nasdaq National Market (NNM)
   b. Nasdaq Small Cap Market (Capital Market Issues)
3. Non-Nasdaq OTC stocks-unlisted
   a. OTC Bulletin Board (OTCBB)
   b. Pink Sheets

There are two categories of non-Nasdaq stocks. The first is the OTC Bulletin Board (OTCBB), also called simply the Bulletin Board or Bulletin (often just the "Bullies"). The OTCBB is a regulated electronic quotation service that displays real time quotes, last sale prices, and volume information in the OTC equity securities. These equity securities are generally securities that are not listed or traded on the Nasdaq or the national stock exchanges. The OTCBB is not part of nor related to the Nasdaq Stock Market.

The second non-Nasdaq OTC market is the Pink Sheets. The Pink Sheets is an electronic quotation system that displays quotes from broker-dealers for many OTC securities. Market markers and other brokers who buy and sell OTC securities can use the Pink Sheets to publish their bid and ask quotation prices. The name "Pink Sheets" comes from the color of paper on which the quotes were historically printed prior to the electronic system. They are currently published today by Pink Sheets LLC, a privately owned company. Pink Sheets LLC is neither a NASD broker-dealer nor registered with the SEC; it is also not a stock exchange.

Off-Exchange Markets/Alternative Electronic Markets

The national and regional exchanges have continued to evolve and, in particular, have become much more electronically oriented. As of early 2008, however, a large volume of U.S. stock trading is done off any of the regulated stock exchanges. There has been significant growth and innovation in this sector of the U.S. stock markets in recent years. The *off-exchange markets* (also called *alternative electronic markets*) have continued to grow rapidly and become much more diverse. In general, these off-exchange markets are divided into two categories: electronic communication networks and alternative trading systems.

Electronic communication networks (ECNs) are essentially off-exchange exchanges. They are direct descendants of (and part of) Nasdaq, not the NYSE. ECNs are privately owned broker-dealers that operate as market participants, initially within the Nasdaq system. They display bids and offers; that is, they provide an open display. They provide institutions and market-makers with an anonymous way to enter orders. Essentially, an ECN is a limit order book that is widely disseminated and open for continuous trading to subscribers who may enter and access orders displayed on the ECN. ECNs offer transparency, anonymity, automated service, and reduced costs, and are therefore effective for handling small orders.

Alternative trading systems (ATS) developed as alternatives to exchanges. It is not necessary in order for two natural parties to conduct a transaction to use an intermediary. That is, the services of a broker or a dealer are not required to execute a trade. The direct trading of stocks between two customers without the use of a broker or an exchange is called an ATS. Broadly, there are two types of ATS, crossing networks, which have functioned for over since the 1980s, and dark pools, which are much more recent.

Crossing networks are electronic venues that do not display quotes but anonymously match large orders. Crossing networks are systems developed to allow institutional investors to cross trades—that is, match buyers and sellers directly—typically via computer. These networks are batch processors that aggregate orders for execution at prespecified times. Crossing networks provide anonymity and reduce cost, and are specifically designed to minimize market impact trading costs. They vary considerably in their approach, including the type of order information that can be entered by the subscriber and the amount of pretrade transparency that is available to participants. The major drawbacks of the crossing networks are (1) that their execution rates tend to be low; and (2) that if they draw too much order flow away from the main market, they can, to their own detriment, undermine the quality of the very prices on which they are basing their trades.

Dark pools fulfill the need for a neutral gathering place and fulfill the traditional role of an exchange. They are private crossing networks in which participants submit orders to cross trades at externally specified prices and therefore provide anonymous sources of liquidity (hence the name "dark"). No quotes are involved—only orders at the externally determined price—and so there is no price discovery. Dark pools are electronic execution systems that do not display quotes but provide transactions at externally provided prices. Both the buyer and seller must submit a willingness to transact at this externally provided price—often the midpoint of the NBBO—to complete a trade. Dark pools are designed to prevent information leakage and offer access to undisclosed liquidity. Unlike open or displayed quotes, dark pools are anonymous and leave no "footprints."

TRADING MECHANICS

Once a strategy is selected and the stocks to be both or sold are determined, the asset management selects the best way to execute the trades. To effectively execute trades, the asset manager must understand trading mechanics. These mechanics involve the types of orders that the asset manager can place to buy or sell stocks and the transaction costs associated with trades. There are special arrangements that have been developed in the market for accommodating trading of institutional investors.

Types of Orders

When an asset manager wants to buy or sell shares of common stock, the price and conditions under which the order is to be executed must be communicated to a broker. The simplest type of order is the *market order*, an order to be executed at the best price available in the market.

The danger of a market order is that an adverse price movement may take place between the time the asset manager places the order and the time the order is executed. To avoid this danger, the investor can place a *limit order* that designates a price threshold for the execution of the trade. A *buy limit order* indicates that the stock may be purchased only at the designated price or lower. A *sell limit order* indicates that the stock may be sold at the designated price or higher. The key disadvantage of a limit order is it offers no guarantee it will be executed at all; the designated price may simply not be obtainable.

The limit order is a *conditional order*: It is executed only if the limit price or a better price can be obtained. Another type of conditional order is the *stop order*, which specifies that the order is not to be executed until the market moves to a designated price, at which time it becomes a market order. A *buy stop order* specifies that the order is not to be executed until the market rises to a designated price, that is, until it trades at or above, or is bid at or above, the designated price. A *sell stop order* specifies that the order is not to be executed until the market price falls below a designated price, that is, until it trades at or below, or is offered at or below, the designated price. A stop order is useful when an asset manager cannot watch the market constantly. Profits can be preserved or losses minimized on a stock position by allowing market movements to trigger a trade. In a sell (buy) stop order, the designated price is lower (higher) than the current market price of the stock. In a sell (buy) limit order, the designated price is higher (lower) than the current market price of the stock.

There are two dangers are associated with stop orders. Stock prices sometimes exhibit abrupt price changes, so the direction of a change in a stock price may be quite temporary, resulting in the premature trading of a stock. Also, once the designated price is reached, the stop order becomes a market order and is subject to the uncertainty of the execution price noted earlier for market orders.

A *stop-limit order*, a hybrid of a stop order and a limit order, is a stop order that designates a price limit. In contrast to the stop order, which becomes a market order if the stop is reached, the stop-limit order becomes a limit order if the stop is reached. The stop-limit order can be used to cushion the market impact of a stop order. An asset manager may limit the possible execution price after the activation of the stop. As with a limit order, the limit price may never be reached after the order is activated, which therefore defeats one purpose of the stop order—to protect a profit or limit a loss.

An asset manager may also enter a *market-if-touched order*. This order becomes a market order if a designated price is reached. A market-if-touched order to buy becomes a market order if the market falls to a given price, while a stop order to buy becomes a market order if the market price rises to a given price. Similarly, a market-if-touched order to sell becomes a market order if the market rises to a specified price, while the stop order to sell becomes a market order if the market falls to a given price. We can think of the stop order as an order designed to get out of an existing position at an acceptable price (without specifying the exact price), and the market-if-touched order as an order designed to get into a position at an acceptable price (also without specifying the exact price).

Orders may be placed to buy or sell at the open or the close of trading for the day. An *opening order* indicates a trade to be executed only in the opening range for the day, and a *closing order* indicates a trade is to be executed only within the closing range for the day. An asset manager may enter orders that contain order cancellation provisions. A *fill-or-kill order* must be executed as soon as it reaches the trading floor or it is immediately canceled. Orders may designate the time period for which the order is effective—a day, week, or month, or perhaps by a given time within the day. An *open order*, or *good until canceled order*, is good until the asset manager specifically terminates the order.

Orders are also classified by their size. One *round lot* is typically 100 shares of a stock. An *odd lot* is defined as less than a round lot.

Short Selling

Short selling involves the sale of a security not owned by the investor at the time of sale. Investors can arrange to have their broker borrow the stock from someone else, and the borrowed stock is delivered to implement the sale. To cover their short position, investors must subsequently purchase the stock and return it to the party that lent the stock.

Let us look at an example of how this is done in the stock market. Suppose that on March 17, 2008 Ms. Karly believes that the common stock of Merck (ticker symbol MRK) is overpriced at $38.30 per share and wants to be in a position to benefit if her assessment is correct. Ms. Karly calls her broker, Mr. James, indicating that she wants to sell 100 shares of MRK. Mr. James will do two things: (1) sell 100 shares of MRK on behalf of Ms. Karly; and (2) arrange to borrow 100 shares of MRK to deliver to the buyer. Suppose that Mr. James is able to sell the stock for $38.30 per share and borrows the stock from Mr. Jordan. The shares borrowed from Mr. Jordan will be delivered to the buyer of the 100 shares. The proceeds from the sale (ignoring commissions) will be $3,830. However, the proceeds do not go to Ms. Karly because she has not given her broker the 100 shares of MRK. Therefore, Ms. Karly is said to be "short 100 shares of MRK."

Now let's suppose one week later the price of MRK stock declines to $35 per share. Ms. Karly may instruct her broker to buy 100 shares of MRK. The cost of buying the shares (once again ignoring commissions) is $1,500. The shares purchased are then delivered to Mr. Jordan, who lent 100 shares of MRK to Ms. Karly. At this point, Ms. Karly has sold 100 shares and bought 100 shares of MRK stock. So, she no longer has any obligation to her broker or to Mr. Jordan; she has "covered" her short position. She is entitled to the funds in her account that were generated by the selling and buying activity. She sold the stock for $3,830 and bought it for $3,500. Therefore, she realizes a profit before commissions of $330. From this amount, commissions are subtracted.

Two more costs will reduce the profit further. First, a fee will be charged by the lender of the stock. We will discuss this fee shortly. Second, if there are any dividends paid by MRK while the stock is borrowed, Ms. Karly must compensate Mr. Jordan for the dividends to which he would have been entitled.

There is a risk. If instead of falling, the price of MRK stock rises, Ms. Karly will realize a loss when she is forced to cover her short position. For example, if the price rises to $43.30, Ms. Karly will lose $500, to which must be added commissions and the cost of borrowing the stock (and possibly dividends).

Margin Transactions

Investors can borrow cash to buy securities and use the securities themselves as collateral. For example, suppose Mr. Zhou has $38,300 to invest and is considering buying MRK at a price of $38.30 per share. With his $38,300 Mr. Zhou can buy 1,000 shares (ignoring commissions). Suppose Mr. Zhou's broker can arrange for him to borrow an additional $38,300 so that Mr. Huang can buy an additional 1,000 shares. Thus, with a $76,600 investment, he can purchase a total of 2,000 shares. The 2,000 shares will be used as collateral for the $38,300 borrowed, and Mr. Zhou will have to pay interest on the amount borrowed.

A transaction in which an investor borrows to buy shares using the shares themselves as collateral is called *buying on margin*. By borrowing funds, an investor creates financial leverage. Note that Mr. Zhou, for a $38,300 investment, realizes the consequences associated with a price change of 2,000 shares of MRK rather than 1,000 shares. He will benefit if the price rises but be worse off if the price falls (compared to borrowing no funds).

To illustrate, we now look at what happens if the price subsequently changes. If the price of MRK stock rises to $47.30 per share, ignoring commissions and the cost of borrowing, Mr. Zhou will realize a profit of $9 per share on 2,000 shares, or $18,000. Had Mr. Zhou not borrowed $38,300 to buy the additional 1,000 shares, his profit would be only $9,000. Suppose, instead, the price of MRK stock decreases to $31.30 per share. Then, by borrowing to buy 1,000 additional shares, Mr. Huang lost $7 per share on 2,000 shares instead of $7 per share on just 1,000 shares.

The funds borrowed to buy the additional stock will be provided by the broker, and the broker gets the money from a bank. The interest rate that banks charge brokers for funds of this purpose is named the *broker call rate* or *call money rate*. The broker charges the borrowing investor the call money rate plus a service charge.

The Securities Exchange Act of 1934 prohibits brokers from lending more than a specified percentage of the market value of the securities. The *initial margin requirement* is the proportion of the total market value of the securities that the investor must pay as an equity share, and the remainder is borrowed from the broker. The Exchange Act gives the Board of Governors of the Federal Reserve (the Fed) the responsibility to set initial margin requirements, which it does under Regulations T and U. The Fed changes margin requirements as an instrument of economic policy. The initial margin requirement for common stock has been below 40%; it was 50% as March 2008. Initial margin requirements vary for stocks and bonds.

The Fed also establishes a *maintenance margin requirement*. This is the minimum proportion of (1) the equity in the investor's margin account to (2) the total market value. If the investor's margin account falls below the minimum maintenance margin (which would happen if the share's price fell), the investor is required to put up additional cash. The investor receives a margin call from the broker specifying the additional cash to be put into the investor's margin account. If the investor fails to put up the additional cash, the broker has the authority to sell the securities for the investor's account. As of March 2008, the maintenance margin requirement was 30%.

Let us illustrate the maintenance margin requirement. Assume an investor buys 200 shares of a stock at $30 per share for $6,000 of stock on 50% margin and the maintenance margin is 30%. By purchasing $6,000 of a stock on 50% margin, the investor must put up $3,000 of cash (or other equity) and so borrows $3,000. The investor, however, must maintain 30% margin. Accordingly, if the stock price declines $21.43 the stock position has a value of $4,286 ($21.43 × 200 shares). With a loan of $3,000, the equity in the account is $1,286 ($4,286 – $3,000), or 30% of the account value ($1,286/$4,000 = 30%). If the price of the stock decreases below $21.43, the investor must deposit more equity to bring the equity level up to 30%.

There are also margin practices for short selling. Consider a similar margin example for a short position. An investor shorts (borrows and sells) 200 shares of a stock at $30 for a total stock value of $6,000. With an initial margin of 50%, the investor must deposit $3,000 (in addition to leaving the $6,000 from the sale in the account). This leaves the investor with a balance of $9,000 (which does not change with the stock price since it is in cash). However, the investor owes 200 shares of the stock at the current market price. Assuming the maintenance margin is 30%, if the stock price rises to $34.62 the 200 shares are worth $6,923 or 30% of the market value of the position ($2,077/$6,923) and additional margin must be posted.

Special Trading Arrangement for Institutional Investors

With the increase in trading by institutional investors, trading arrangements more suitable to these investors developed. Institutional investor needs include trading in large size and trading groups of stocks, both at a low commission and with low market impact (discussed below). These requirements resulted in the evolution of special arrangements for the execution of certain types of orders commonly sought by institutional investors: (1) orders requiring the execution of a trade of a large number of shares of a given stock; and (2) orders requiring the execution of trades in a large number of different stocks as simultaneously as possible. The former types of trades are called *block trades*; the latter are called *program trades*. An example of a block trade would be a mutual fund that seeks to buy 15,000 shares of IBM stock. An example of a program trade would be a pension fund that wants to buy shares of 200 companies at the end of a trading day.

On the New York Stock Exchange, block trades are defined as either trades of at least 10,000 shares of a given stock, or trades of shares with a market value of at least $200,000, whichever is less. In 1961, about nine block trades occurred per day, which accounted for about 3% of the trading volume of the NYSE. By 2007, the number of block trades ranged from about 4,000 to 5,000 per day.

Program trades involve the buying and selling of a large number of names (i.e., companies) simultaneously. Such trades are also called *basket trades* because effectively a "basket" of stock is being traded. The NYSE defines a program trade as any trade involving the purchase or sale of a basket of at least 15 stocks with a total value of $1 million or more.

Transaction and Trading Costs

An important aspect of an investment strategy is controlling the transaction costs necessary to implement the strategy. The measurement of trading costs, although important, is difficult.

Institutional investors have developed computer-automated programs to enter trading orders to minimize the costs associated with trading that we discuss in this section. The use of computer programs for this purpose is known as *algorithmic trading* or *algo*, which is discussed later in this section. Once an asset manager makes a decision to buy or sell a large stock position, the program partitions the trade into several smaller orders so as to minimize transaction costs.[22]

We describe algorithmic trading further later.

Trading costs can be decomposed into two major components: explicit costs and implicit costs. *Explicit trading costs* are the direct costs of trading,

---

[22] Sometimes algorithmic trading is confused with automated trading. The latter employs computer programs to make investment decisions about what to buy or sell. Algorithmic trading is used to determine how to place the order. However, algorithmic trading does not require that the decision of what to buy or sell be made by automated trading.

such as broker commissions, fees, and taxes. *Implicit trading costs* represent such indirect costs as the price impact of the trade and the opportunity costs of failing to execute in a timely manner or at all. Whereas explicit costs are associated with identifiable accounting charges, no such reporting of implicit costs occurs.

Explicit Costs

The main explicit cost is the commission paid to the broker for execution. Commission costs are fully negotiable and vary systematically by broker type and market mechanism.

The commission may depend on both the price per share and the number of shares in the transaction. In addition to commissions, other explicit costs include custodial fees (the fees charged by an institution that holds securities in safekeeping for an investor) and transfer fees (the fees associated with transferring an asset from one owner to another).

Implicit Costs

Implicit trading costs include impact costs, timing costs, and opportunity costs.

The *impact cost* of a transaction is the change in market price due to supply/demand imbalances caused by the presence of the trade. Bid-ask spread estimates, although informative, fail to capture the fact that large trades—those that exceed the number of shares the market-maker is willing to trade at the quoted bid and ask prices—may move prices in the direction of the trade. That is, large trades may increase the price for buy orders and decrease the price for sell orders. The resulting market impact or price impact of the transaction can be thought of as the deviation of the transaction price from the "unperturbed price" that would prevail if the trade did not occur.

The *timing cost* of a trade is measured as the price change between the time the parties to the implementation process assume responsibility for the trade and the time they complete the responsibility. Timing costs occur when orders sit on the trading desk of a buy side firm (e.g., an investment management firm), but are not yet released to the broker because the trader fears that the trade may swamp the market.

The *opportunity cost* of a trade is the "cost" of securities not traded. This cost results from missed or only partially completed trades. These costs are the natural consequence of the release delays. For example, if the price moves too much before the trade can be completed, the asset manager will not make the trade. In practice, this cost is measured on shares not traded based on the difference between the market price at the time of decision and the closing price 30 days later.

Although commissions and impact costs are actual and visible out-of-pocket costs, opportunity costs and timing costs are the costs of forgone opportunities and are invisible. Opportunity costs can arise for two reasons. First, some orders are executed with a delay, during which the price moves against the investor. Second, some orders incur an opportunity cost because they are only partially filled or are not executed at all.

Algorithmic Trading

Traditionally, orders for stock executions have been conducted by traders who execute the trades on a trading desk for a portfolio manager or whomever determines what trades should be executed. Traders are judged to have "market information and savvy" which permits them to conduct the trades at a lower cost and with less market impact than the portfolio manager conducting the trades on a less formal basis themselves.

The effectiveness of these traders is often measured by execution evaluation services and traders are often compensated partially on the basis of their effectiveness. But some observers believe that the traders, in the interest of maximizing their compensation, may have different incentives than the portfolio managers and do not optimize the portfolio manager's objectives—this is referred to as an *agency effect*. In addition, some think that trades could be conducted more efficiently by electronic systems then by human traders.

As a result, due to improved technology and quantitative techniques, and also regulatory changes, electronic trading systems have been developed to supplement or replace human traders and their trading desks—that is, algorithmic trading or, simply, algo.

Algorithmic trading is a relatively recent type of trading technique whereby an overall trade (either buy or sell) is conducted electronically in a series of small transactions instead of one large transaction. Such trades are conducted via computers, which make the decision to trade or not trade depending on whether recent price movements indicate whether the market will be receptive to the intended trade at the moment or, on the other hand, will cause the price to move significantly against the intended price. Algorithmic trading also permits the traders to hide their intentions. Trading may involve small trades on a continuous basis rather than a large trade at a point in time. The algo is often said to leave no "footprint" and is a "soft touch" way of trading.

Algos provide anonymity, which the "visible markets," like exchanges and ECNs, do not. Algos are often described as "hiding in plain view."

The advent and wide use of algos is due primarily to both technology and regulation. The technology element is based on faster and cheaper technological systems to execute via improved quantitative methods. The regulatory element is the adoption of pennies and the approval of the order handling rules which provided for the growth of ECNs by the SEC. The adoption of "pennies," which provides for smaller pricing increments, and technological advancements which provide for low-latency trading have made algorithmic trading more necessary and feasible (*low latency* refers to a short period of time to execute an instruction, i.e., high speed).

The use of algorithmic trading is significant by large traders such as hedge funds and mutual funds. Some traders maintain their own algorithmic trading facilities and others use the systems provided by another organization. Overall, algorithmic trading has the advantages of being scalable, anonymous, transparent, and very fast.

SUMMARY

Stock market indicators can be classified into three groups: (1) those produced by stock exchanges and that include all stocks to be traded on the exchange; (2) those in which a committee subjectively selects the stocks to be included in the index; and (3) those in which the stocks selected are based solely on stocks' market capitalizations.

We outlined a number of active portfolio management strategies. Active portfolio management strategies are characterized by the emphasis on the stock selection process. Traditionally, there are two major types of stock selection approaches, those based on fundamental analysis and those based on technical analysis. Fundamental analysis tries to assess the viability of a firm from a business point of view, looking at financial statements as well as corporate operations. The objective is to identify companies that will produce a solid future stream of cash flows. Technical analysis looks at patterns in prices and returns. Technical analysis is based on the assumption that prices and returns follow discernable patterns.

The underpinning of active portfolio management is the belief that there are market inefficiencies, that is, that there are situations where a stock's price does not fully reflect all available information. Both fundamental and technical analysis attempt to identify situations where the market somehow makes mistakes in the processing information, leading to pricing anomalies. The purpose of equity style management is to identify groups of stocks that are mispriced.

There are two market structures: the order-driven, specialist, floor-based mechanism of the NYSE on the one hand, and the quote-driven, dealer-based, electronic mechanism of Nasdaq on the other. In the real world, however, these two market structures have converged significantly toward hybrid markets. Alternative trading systems have developed to satisfy the needs of institutional market participants.

Different types of orders may be submitted to the stock markets. The most common type is a market order, which means that the order must be filled immediately at the best price. Other types of orders, such as stop and limit orders, are filled only if the market price reaches a price specified in the order.

In buying and selling stock in the secondary market, the brokerage commission is the most obvious type of trading cost and object of competition among broker-dealers for both institutional and retail investors. However, other types of trading costs, such as impact costs and opportunity costs, may be larger than commissions. To accommodate the trading needs of institutional investors who tend to place orders of larger sizes and with a large number of names, special arrangements have evolved such as block trades and program trades.

REFERENCES

Alexander, S. S. (1961). Price movements in speculative markets: Trends or random walks. *Industrial Management Review* 2, no. 2: 7–26.

Banz, R. W. (1981). The relationship between return and market value of stocks. *Journal of Financial Economics* 9, no. 1: 103–126.

Bernstein, P. L. (1985). Does the market overreact?: Discussion. *Journal of Finance* 40, no. 3: 806–808.

Birinyi, L., and Miller, K. (1987). Market breadth: An analysis. Salomon Brothers (September).

Brock, W., Lakonishok, J., and LeBaron, B. (1992). Simple technical trading rules and the stochastic properties of stock returns. *Journal of Finance* 47, no. 5: 1731–1764.

Brown, K. C., and van Harlow, W. (1988). Market overreaction: Magnitude and intensity. *Journal of Portfolio Management* 14, no. 2: 6–13.

Brown, S. J., Goetzmann, W. A., and Kumar, A. (1998). The Dow Theory: William Peter Hamilton's track record reconsidered. *Journal of Finance* 53(4): 1311–1333.

Christopherson, J. A., and Williams, C. N. (1997). Equity style: What it is and why it matters. In T. Daniel Coggin, Frank J. Fabozzi, and Robert D. Arnott (eds.), *The Handbook of Equity Style Management*, 2nd ed. (pp. 9–10). Hoboken, NJ: John Wiley & Sons.

Collins, B. M., and Fabozzi, F. J. (1991). A methodology for measuring transactions costs. *Financial Analysts Journal* 47, no. 2 (March/April): 27–36.

Cootner, P. H. (1962). Stock prices: Random vs. systematic risk. *Industrial Management Review* 3 (Spring): 24–45.

Daniel, K. D., Hirshleifer, D., and Subrahmanyam, A. (1998). Investor psychology and security market under- and overreactions. *Journal of Finance* 53, no. 4: 1839–1885.

DeBondt, W., and Thaler, R. (1985). Does the market overreact? *Journal of Finance* 40, no. 3: 793–805.

DeBondt, W., and Thaler, R. (1987). Further evidence on investor overreaction and stock market seasonality. *Journal of Finance* 42, no. 3: 557–581.

Dreman, D. (1982). *The New Contrarian Investment Strategy*. New York: Random House.

Edwards, R. D., and Magee, J. (1992). *Technical Analysis of Stock Trends*, Boston: John Magee Inc.

Fabozzi, F. J., and Jones, F. J. (2008). The U.S. equity markets. In Frank J. Fabozzi (ed.), *The Handbook of Finance: Volume I* (pp. 125–150). Hoboken, NJ: John Wiley & Sons.

Fama, E. F., and Blume, M. (1966). Filter rules and stock-market trading. *Journal of Business* 39, no. 1: 226–241.

Fama, E. F., and French, K. R. (1993). Common risk factors on stocks and bonds. *Journal of Financial Economics* 33, no. 1: 3–56.

Farrell, J. L., Jr. (1975). Homogenous stock groupings: Implications for portfolio management. *Financial Analysts Journal* 31, no. 3 (May/June): 50–62.

Figelman, I. (2007). Stock return momentum and reversal. *Journal of Portfolio Management* 34, no. 1: 51–69.

Glickstein, D., and Wubbels, R. (1983). Dow theory is alive and well! *Journal of Portfolio Management* 10 (Spring): 28–32.

Graham, B. (1973). *The Intelligent Investor,* 4th rev. ed. New York: Harper & Row.

Graham, B., Dodd, D. L., and Cottle, S. (1962). *Security Analysis*, 4th ed. New York: McGraw-Hill.

Gross, W. (1997). *Everything You've Heard About Investing Is Wrong!* New York: Crown.

Hamilton, W. P. (1922). *The Stock Market Barometer*, New York: Harper & Brothers.

Hwang, S., and Rubesam, A. (2007). The disappearance of momentum. Working paper, Cass Business School, City University, London.

Jacobs, Bruce I., and Levy, Kenneth N. (1997). The long and short on long-short. *Journal of Investing* 6, no. 1 (Spring): 78–88.

James, F. E. (1969). Monthly moving averages—An Effective Investment Tool? *Journal of Financial and Quantitative Analysis* 4, no. 3: 315–326.

Jegadeesh, N. (1990). Evidence of predictable behavior of security returns. *Journal of Finance* 45, no. 3: 881–898.

Jegadeesh, N., and Titman, S. (1993). Returns to buying winners and selling losers: Implications for stock market efficiency. *Journal of Finance* 48, no. 1: 65–91.

Jensen, M. C. (1967). Random walks: A comment. *Financial Analysts Journal* 23 (November/December): 77–78.

Jensen, M. C., and Bennington, G. (1970). Random walks and technical theories: Some additional evidence. *Journal of Finance* 25, no. 2: 469–482.

Korajczyk, R. A., and Sadka, R. (2004). Are momentum profits robust to trading costs? *Journal of Finance* 59, no. 2: 1039–1082.

Levy, R. (1966). Conceptual foundations of technical analysis. *Financial Analysts Journal* 22 (July–August): 83–89.

Malkiel, B. G. (1996). *A Random Walk Down Street,* 6th ed. New York: W. W. Norton.

O'Higgins, M. (1992). *Beating the Dow,* New York: Harper Perennial.

Oppenheimer, H. R., and Schlarbaum, G. G. (1981). Investing with Ben Graham: An *ex ante* test of the efficient market hypothesis. *Journal of Financial and Quantitative Analysis* 16, no. 3: 341–360.

Peters, E. E. (1991). *Chaos and Order in the Capital Markets: A New View of Cycles, Prices, and Market Volatility.* New York: John Wiley & Sons.

Reinganum, M. R. (1981). Misspecification of capital asset pricing: Empirical anomalies based on earnings yields and market values. *Journal of Financial Economics* 9, no. 1: 19–46.

Rouwenhorst, K. G. (1998). International momentum strategies. *Journal of Finance* 53, no. 1: 267–283.

Schabacker, R. W. (1930a). *Stock Market Theory and Practice.* New York: B. C. Forbes.

Schabacker, R. W. (1932 [1997]). *Technical Analysis and Stock Market Profits.* New York: Pitman.

Schabacker, R. W. (1934). *Stock Market Profits.* New York: B. C. Forbes.

Scheinkman, J., and LeBaron, B. (1989). Nonlinear dynamics and stock returns. *Journal of Business* 62 (July): 311–337.

Schlarbaum, G. G. (1997). Value-based equity strategies. In T. Daniel Coggin, Frank J. Fabozzi, and Robert D. Arnott (eds.), *The Handbook of Equity Style Management*, 2nd ed. (pp. 133–150). Hoboken, NJ: John Wiley & Sons.

Shaw, A. R. (1988). Market timing and technical analysis. In Summer N. Levine (ed.), *The Financial Analyst's Handbook* (pp. 944–988). Homewood, IL: Dow Jones–Irwin.

Sweeney, R. J. (1988). Some new filter rule tests: Methods and results. *Journal of Financial and Quantitative Analysis* 23, no. 3: 285–300.

Sweeney, R. J. (1990). Evidence on short-term trading strategies. *Journal of Portfolio Management* 17, no. 1: 20–26.

Van Horne, J. C., and Parker, G. (1967). The random walk theory: An empirical test. *Financial Analysts Journal* 23 (November/December): 87–92.

CHAPTER 19

Bond Portfolio Management

Bonds are debt instruments that are issued by a wide range of entities throughout the world. Unlike the investor in common stock who hopes to share in the good fortunes of a corporation, through increased dividends and price appreciation in the stock's price, an investor in a bond has agreed to accept a fixed contractual interest rate. The features that may be included in a bond affect its performance when market interest rates and their risk characteristics change.

In this chapter, we explain the types of bonds, their investment characteristics, the types of risks to which investors are exposed and how some risks can be quantified, and bond portfolio strategies. The valuation of a bond, just like the valuation of any financial asset, is explained in Chapter 7.

SECTORS OF THE BOND MARKET

The U.S. bond market is the largest bond market in the world. There are many ways to classify the bond markets. One way is in terms of the taxability of the interest at the federal income tax level. In the United States, most securities issued by state and local governments and by entities that they establish, referred to as *municipal bonds* or *municipal securities*, are exempt from federal income taxation. While there are reasons why some issuers of municipal bonds will issue taxable bonds, the municipal bond market is generally viewed as the market for tax-exempt securities. As such, the primary attraction to investors is this tax feature.

The largest part of the market is the taxable market. There are various ways to describe this sector. Investment banking firms that have developed bond market indexes use various classifications. The most popular indexes are those published by Lehman Brothers (purchased in 2008 by Barclays), in the group of indexes Lehman Brothers publishes, and the one followed most closely by investors, is the U.S. Aggregate Index. That index contains the six sectors shown in Table 19.1 along with the percentage of each sector

TABLE 19.1   Sectors of the Lehman Brothers U.S. Aggregate Index

Sector	Percent of Market Value (as of September 26, 2008)
Treasury	22%
Agency	10%
Credit	23%
Mortgage Pass-through	39%
Commercial Mortgage–Backed Securities	5%
Asset-Backed Securities	1%

Source: Data obtained from Lehman Brothers, *Global Relative Value*, Fixed Income Research, September 29, 2008, p. 4.

in terms of market value as of September 26, 2008. We describe each sector in this section.

Another way of classifying bond markets is in terms of the *global bond market*. One starts by partitioning a given country's bond market into a national bond market and an international bond market. In turn, a country's national bond market can be divided into a domestic bond market and a foreign bond market with the distinction being the domicile of the issuer. The *domestic bond market* is the market where bond issues of entities domiciled within that country are issued and then traded; the *foreign bond market* is the market where bond issues of nondomiciled entities of that country are issued and then subsequently traded within the country. Each country has a nickname for foreign bonds. For example, in the United States, "Yankee bonds" are bonds issued by non-U.S. entities and then traded in the U.S. market. In the United Kingdom, foreign bonds are called "bulldog bonds." The *international bond market*, also referred to as *offshore bond market*, are bond issues issued and then traded outside of the country and not regulated by the country. One extremely important sector of the international bond market is the market for bond issues that were underwritten by an international syndicate, issued simultaneously to investors in a number of countries, and issued outside of the jurisdiction of any single country. This market is popularly referred to as the *Eurobond market* and the bonds are called *Eurobonds*. Unfortunately, the name is misleading. The currency in which Eurobonds are denominated can be any currency, not just euros. In fact, Eurobonds are classified according to the denomination of the currency (e.g., Eurodollar bonds and Euroyen bonds). Nor are Eurobonds traded in just Europe. *Global bonds* from the perspective of a country are bonds that are not only traded in that country's foreign bond market but also in the Eurobond market.

Treasury Securities

The securities issued by the U.S. Department of the Treasury (U.S. Treasury hereafter) are called *Treasury securities, Treasuries,* or *U.S. government bonds.* Because they are backed by the full faith and credit of the U.S. government, market participants throughout the world view them as having no credit risk. Hence, the interest rates on Treasury securities are the benchmark default-free interest rates.

Types of Treasury Securities

There are two types of marketable Treasury securities issued: fixed principal securities and inflation-indexed securities. The securities are issued via a regularly scheduled auction process.

Fixed Principal Securities The U.S. Treasury issues two types of *fixed principal securities*: discount securities and coupon securities. Discount securities are called *Treasury bills*; coupon securities are called *Treasury notes* and *Treasury bonds.*

Treasury bills are issued at a discount to par value, have no coupon rate, and mature at face value. Generally, Treasury bills can be issued with a maturity of up to two years. The U.S. Treasury typically issues only certain maturities. As of mid-2008, the practice of the U.S. Treasury is to issue Treasury bills with maturities of 4 weeks, 13 weeks, 26 weeks, and 6 months. At one time, the U.S. Treasury issued a one-year Treasury bill. As discount securities, Treasury bills do not pay coupon interest. Instead, Treasury bills are issued at a discount from their face value; the return to the investor is the difference between the face value and the purchase price.

The U.S. Treasury issues securities with initial maturities of two years or more as coupon securities. Coupon securities are issued at approximately par and, in the case of fixed principal securities, mature at par value. They are not callable. *Treasury notes* are coupon securities issued with original maturities of more than two years but no more than 10 years. As of year-end 2007, the U.S. Treasury issues a 2-year note, a 5-year note, and a 10-year. At one time the U.S. Treasury issued a 3-year notes and 7-year notes. Treasuries with original maturities greater than 10 years are called *Treasury bonds.* As of mid-2008, the U.S. Treasury issues a 30-year bond.

Treasury Inflation-Protected Securities The U.S. Treasury issues coupon securities that provide inflation protection and are popularly referred to as *Treasury inflation-protected securities* (TIPS). They do so by having the principal increase or decrease based on the rate of inflation such that when the security matures, the investor receives the greater of the principal adjusted for inflation or the original principal. As of mid-2008, the U.S. Treasury issues a 5-year TIPS, a 10-year TIPS, and a 20-year TIPS.

TIPS work as follows. The coupon rate on an issue is set at a fixed rate, the rate being determined via the auction process just like fixed principal Treasury securities. The coupon rate is referred to as the *real rate* because it is the rate that the investor ultimately earns above the inflation rate. The inflation index used for measuring the inflation rate is the nonseasonally-adjusted U.S. City Average All Items Consumer Price Index for All Urban Consumers (CPI-U).

The adjustment for inflation is as follows: The principal that the U.S. Treasury will base both the dollar amount of the coupon payment and the maturity value on is adjusted semiannually. This is called the *inflation-adjusted principal*. For example, suppose that the coupon rate for a TIPS is 3.5% and the annual inflation rate is 3%. Suppose further that an investor purchases, on January 1, $100,000 par value (principal) of this issue. The semiannual inflation rate is 1.5% (3% divided by 2). The inflation-adjusted principal at the end of the first six-month period is found by multiplying the original par value by one plus the semiannual inflation rate. In our example, the inflation-adjusted principal at the end of the first six-month period is $101,500. It is this inflation-adjusted principal that is the basis for computing the coupon interest for the first six-month period. The coupon payment is then 1.75% (one-half the real rate of 3.5%) multiplied by the inflation-adjusted principal at the coupon payment date ($101,500).The coupon payment is therefore $1,776.25.

Let's look at the next six months. The inflation-adjusted principal at the beginning of the period is $101,500. Suppose that the semiannual inflation rate for the second six-month period is 1%.Then the inflation-adjusted principal at the end of the second six-month period is the inflation-adjusted principal at the beginning of the six-month period ($101,500) increased by the semiannual inflation rate (1%). The adjustment to the principal is $1,015 (1% times $101,500). So, the inflation-adjusted principal at the end of the second six-month period (December 31 in our example) is $102,515 ($101,500 + $1,015). The coupon interest that will be paid to the investor at the second coupon payment date is found by multiplying the inflation-adjusted principal on the coupon payment date ($102,515) by one-half the real rate (that is, one-half of 3.5%). That is, the coupon payment will be $1,794.01.

As can be seen, part of the adjustment for inflation comes from the coupon payment since it is based on the inflation-adjusted principal. Because of the possibility of disinflation (that is, price declines), the inflation-adjusted principal at maturity may turn out to be less than the original par value.

However, the Treasury has structured TIPS so that they are redeemed at the greater of the inflation-adjusted principal and the original par value.

Stripped Treasury Securities

The U.S. Treasury does not issue zero-coupon notes or bonds. However, because of the demand for zero-coupon instruments with no credit risk, the private sector has created such securities using a process called *coupon stripping*.

To illustrate the process, suppose that $2 billion of a 10-year fixed principal Treasury note with a coupon rate of 5% is purchased by a dealer firm to create zero-coupon Treasury securities. The cash flow from this Treasury note is 20 semiannual payments of $50 million each ($2 billion times 0.05 divided by 2) and the repayment of principal of $2 billion 10 years from now. As there are 21 different payments to be made by the U.S. Treasury for this note, a security representing a single payment claim on each payment is issued, which is effectively a zero-coupon Treasury security. The amount of the maturity value or a security backed by a particular payment, whether coupon or principal, depends on the amount of the payment to be made by the U.S. Treasury on the underlying Treasury note. In our example, 20 zero-coupon Treasury securities each have a maturity value of $50 million, and one zero-coupon Treasury security, backed by the principal, has a maturity value of $2 billion. The maturity dates for the zero-coupon Treasury securities coincide with the corresponding payment dates by the U.S. Treasury.

Zero-coupon Treasury securities are created as part of the U.S. Treasury's Separate Trading of Registered Interest and Principal of Securities (STRIPS) program to facilitate the stripping of designated Treasury securities.

Federal Agency Securities

Federal agency securities can be classified by the type of issuer—federally related institutions and government-sponsored enterprises. Federal agencies that provide credit for certain sectors of the credit marker issue two types of securities: debentures and mortgage- and asset-backed securities. We review the former securities here and the latter later in this chapter.

Federally Related Institutions

Federally related institutions are arms of the federal government and generally do not issue securities directly in them marketplace. Federally related institutions include the Export-Import Bank of the United States, the Tennessee Valley Authority, the Commodity Credit Corporation, the Farmers

Housing Administration, the General Services Administration, the Government National Mortgage Association, the Maritime Administration, the Private Export Funding Corporation, the Rural Electrification Administration, the Rural Telephone Bank, the Small Business Administration, and the Washington Metropolitan Area Transit Authority.

With the exception of securities of the Tennessee Valley Authority and the Private Export Funding Corporation, the securities are backed by the full faith and credit of the U.S. government. The federally related institution that has issued securities in recent years is the Tennessee Valley Authority (TVA).

Government-Sponsored Enterprises

Government-sponsored enterprises (GSEs) are privately owned, publicly chartered entities. They were created by Congress to reduce the cost of capital for certain borrowing sectors of the economy deemed to be important enough to warrant assistance. GSEs issue securities directly in the marketplace. The market for these securities, while smaller than that of Treasury securities, has in recent years become an active and important sector of the bond market.

There are five GSEs that currently issue debentures: Freddie Mac, Fannie Mae, Federal Home Loan Bank System, Federal Farm Credit System and the Federal Agricultural Mortgage Corporation. Fannie Mae, Freddie Mac, and Federal Home Loan Bank are responsible for providing credit to the housing sectors. The Federal Agricultural Mortgage Corporation provides the same function for agricultural mortgage loans. The Federal Farm Credit Bank System is responsible for the credit market in the agricultural sector of the economy.

With the exception of the securities issued by the Farm Credit Financial Assistance Corporation, GSE securities are not backed by the full faith and credit of the U.S. government, as is the case with Treasury securities. Consequently, investors purchasing GSEs are exposed to credit risk. The yield spread between these securities and Treasury securities of comparable maturity reflects differences in perceived credit risk and liquidity. The spread attributable to credit risk reflects any financial difficulty faced by the issuing GSEs and the likelihood that the federal government will allow the GSE to default on its outstanding obligations.

Corporate Bonds

Corporations issue in public markets several types of debt obligations that provide intermediate to long-term financing. Debt instruments that are publicly issued include corporate bonds and asset-backed securities. Here our focus is on the general characteristics of corporate bonds. Asset-backed securities fall into another sector of the bond market that we describe below.

A corporate bond can be secured or unsecured. By secured debt it is meant that some form of collateral is pledged to ensure repayment of the debt. Debt can be secured by many different assets. For example, a debt issue can be secured by a first-priority lien on substantially all of the issuer's real property, machinery, and equipment, and by a second priority lien on its inventory, accounts receivables, and intangibles. *Collateral trust debentures,* bonds, and notes are secured by financial assets such as cash, receivables, other notes, debentures, or bonds, and not by real property. Unsecured debt, like secured debt, comes in several different layers or levels of claim against the corporation's assets. But in the case of unsecured debt, the nomenclature attached to the debt issues sounds less substantial. For example, "general and refunding mortgage bonds" may sound more important than "subordinated debentures," even though both are basically second claims on the issuing corporation. In addition to the normal debentures and notes, there are junior issues representing the secondary and tertiary levels of the capital structure. The difference in a high-grade issuer may be considered insignificant as long as the issuer maintains its quality. But in cases of financial distress, the junior issues usually fare worse than the senior issues. Only in cases of very well-protected junior issues will investors come out whole—in which case, so would the holders of senior indebtedness.

A key investment attribute of corporate bonds is their credit risk that we cover later in this chapter when we describe the various dimensions of credit risk and the credit ratings assigned to corporate bonds and the factors considered by rating agencies (Moody's Investor Service, Standard & Poor's, and Fitch Ratings) in credit ratings. Based on credit ratings, the corporate bond market is classified into two major sectors: investment-grade corporate sector and noninvestment-grade corporate sector.

Residential Mortgage-Backed Securities

Mortgage-backed securities (MBS) are securities whose cash flows are backed by the interest and principal payments made on a pool of mortgage loans. *Residential mortgage-backed securities* (RMBS) are constructed by aggregating large numbers of similar residential mortgage loans into mortgage pools. Residential mortgage loans are loans backed by one- to four-family properties. The RMBS market is divided into two general sectors. The first sector consists of RMBS issued by the Governmental National Mortgage Association (Ginnie Mae) and the two GSEs, Fannie Mae and Freddie Mac. This sector is referred to as the "agency MBS" market. Although the securities issued by Ginnie Mae carry the full faith and credit of the U.S. government, those issued by the two GSEs do not. Despite this, the MBS issued by Fannie Mae and Freddie Mac are viewed as having little credit risk. The other sector of the RMBS market consists of the nonagency MBS market. This sector includes RMBS issued by private entities such as commercial banks, securities houses, and mortgage banks. As subsector in the nonagency MBS market is RMBS backed by borrowers with blemished or impaired credit ratings and is referred to as the subprime mortgage market.

In broad-based bond market indexes, the RMBS sector is referred to as the "mortgage sector" and includes only agency MBS. The nonagency MBS sector is included as part of the asset-backed securities sector described below.

The basic agency MBS is an *agency mortgage pass-through security*. The cash flow from a mortgage pool is the aggregate of the interest, regularly schedule principal payment (i.e., amortization), and prepayments made by the borrowers. Prepayments are payments made in excess of the borrower's regularly scheduled principal payment. The most common reason for a borrower to make a prepayment is pay off a mortgage to take advantage of lower mortgage rates available in the market. For a mortgage pass-through security, the cash flow from the underlying mortgage pool is passed through to the certificate holders on a pro rata basis after deducting certain fees. For example, if there are X certificates issued that are backed by a mortgage pool and $Y is the cash flow from the pool after deducting fees, then each certificate holder receives a cash flow of $Y/X.

From agency mortgage pass-through securities, dealer firms have created several types of agency mortgage derivative securities. These include agency collateralized debt obligations and stripped MBS. This is done by reallocating the cash flow of the mortgage pool based on a set of priority rules. This process of allocating cash flows is referred to as "tranching" the cash flow. By doing so, dealer firms can create RMBS that are more appealing to a wide range of institutional investors throughout the world. Basically, agency mortgage derivative securities alter the exposure of agency mortgage pass-through securities to interest rate and the risk of prepayments. That is, the bond classes that are created have different exposure to these two risks than the mortgage pass-through security from which they were created.

In the mortgage sector of the broad-based bond market indexes, agency mortgage derivative securities are not included. That is, the mortgage sector includes only agency mortgage pass-through securities.

Commercial MBS

A commercial real estate loan is secured by a commercial real estate property. The major property types of commercial properties include multifamily properties, apartment buildings, office buildings, industrial properties (including warehouses), shopping centers, hotels, and health care facilities (e.g., senior housing care facilities). The principal and interest on the loan are generally paid from cash flows generated by the property. Real estate borrowers, or sponsors, will take out loans to purchase properties, refinance existing debt, or add on to an existing loan. Unlike residential mortgage loans, commercial mortgage loans have contractual provisions that significantly reduce the risk that the borrower will be prepay a loan prior to the stated maturity date.

Commercial mortgage-backed securities (CMBS) are backed by a pool of commercial mortgage loans. The loan pool is carved up into a number of rated bond classes by the process of tranching as with agency mortgage derivative securities, and principal and interest payments received from the underlying loans are used to pay principal and interest to the bond classes sequentially by seniority. Any credit losses experienced by the underlying loan pool are absorbed, in order, by the most junior bond classes. In tranching the cash flow in the case of agency mortgage derivative securities, the process results in bond classes with different exposure to interest rate and prepayment risk. In the case of CMBS, tranching results in bond classes that have different exposure to credit risk of the underlying pool. In addition, typically the senior bond classes in a CMBS structure are tranched to create bonds with different exposure to interest rate risk.

Asset-Backed Securities

Asset-backed securities (ABS) are debt instruments that are backed by a pool of loans or receivables. There is considerable diversity in the types of assets that have been securitized. These assets can be classified as residential mortgage assets and nonmortgage assets. The former includes nonagency RMBS. The largest sectors in the ABS market backed by nonmortgage assets are credit card receivable–backed securities, automobile loan–backed securities, rate reduction bonds (issued by utilities), student loan–backed securities, and Small Business Adminstration loan–backed securities.

ABS are created using the tranching technology to redirect the cash flows from the underlying loan pool to different bond classes so as to create bond classes with different exposures to credit risk and interest rate and prepayment risk.

Municipal Bonds

Issuers of *municipal bonds* include municipalities, counties, towns and townships, school districts, and special service system districts. Included in the category of municipalities are cities, villages, boroughs, and incorporated towns that received a special state charter. Counties are geographical subdivisions of states whose functions are law enforcement, judicial administration, and construction and maintenance of roads. As with counties, towns and townships are geographical subdivisions of states and perform similar functions as counties. A special purpose service system district, or simply special district, is a political subdivision created to foster economic development or related services to a geographical area. Special districts provide public utility services (water, sewers, and drainage) and fire protection services. Public agencies or instrumentalities include authorities and commissions. The number of municipal bond issuers is remarkable: more than 60,000. Even more noteworthy is the number of different issues: more than 1.3 million.

There are both tax-exempt and taxable municipal securities. "Tax-exempt" means that interest on a municipal security is exempt from federal income taxation. The tax exemption of municipal securities applies to interest income, not capital gains. Most municipal securities that have been issued are tax-exempt. Municipal securities are commonly referred to as tax-exempt securities, although taxable municipal securities have been issued and are traded in the market. Municipalities issue *taxable municipal bonds* to finance projects (such as a sports stadium) that do not qualify for financing with tax-exempt bonds. The most common types of taxable municipal bonds are *industrial revenue bonds* and *economic development bonds.*

There are basically two types of municipal security structures: tax-backed debt and revenue bonds. *Tax-backed debt obligations* are secured by some form of tax revenue. The broadest type of tax-backed debt obligation is the general obligation debt. General obligation pledges include unlimited and limited tax general obligation debt. The stronger form is the unlimited tax general obligation debt because it is secured by the issuer's unlimited taxing power (corporate and individual income taxes, sales taxes, and property taxes) and is said to be secured by the full faith and credit of the issuer. A limited tax general obligation debt is a limited tax pledge because for such debt there is a statutory ceiling on the tax rates that may be levied to service the issuer's debt.

Revenue bonds are the second basic type of security structure found in the municipal bond market. These bonds are issued for enterprise financings that are secured by the revenues generated by the completed projects themselves, or for general public-purpose financings in which the issuers pledge to the bondholders the tax and revenue resources that were previously part of the general fund. Examples of revenue bonds are utility revenue bonds, transportation revenue bonds, housing revenue bonds, higher education revenue bonds, health care revenue bonds, and seaport revenue bonds.

Municipal bonds can be credit enhanced by an unconditional guarantee of a commercial insurance company. These bonds are called *insured municipal bonds.* The insurance cannot be canceled and typically is in place for the term of the bond. The insurance provides for the insurance company writing the policy to make payments to the bondholders of any principal or coupon interest that is due on a stated maturity date but that has not been paid by the bond issuer.

FEATURES OF BONDS

In this section we will describe the basic features of bonds: maturity, par value, coupon rate, accrued interest, provision for paying off a bond, and options granted to bondholders.

Maturity

Unlike common stock that has a perpetual life, bonds have a date in which they mature. The number of years over which the issuer has promised to meet the conditions of the obligation is referred to as the *term to maturity.* The *maturity* of a bond refers to the date that the debt will cease to exist, at which time the issuer will redeem the bond by paying the amount borrowed. The maturity date of a bond is always identified when describing a bond. For example, a description of a bond might state "due 12/15/2025."

The practice in the bond market is to refer to the "term to maturity" of a bond as simply its "maturity" or "term." Despite sounding like a fixed date in which the bond matures, there are provisions that may be included in the indenture that grants either the issuer or bondholder the right to alter a bond's term to maturity. These provisions, which will be described later in this chapter, include call provision, put provision, conversion provision, and an accelerated sinking fund provision.

The maturity of a debt instrument is used to describe two sectors of the market. Debt instruments with a maturity of one year or less are referred to as *money market instruments* and trading in the *money market.* What we typically refer to as the "bond market" is debt instruments with a maturity greater than one year. The bond market is then categorized further based on the debt instrument's term to maturity: short term, intermediate term, and long term. The classification is somewhat arbitrary and varies amongst market participants. A common classification is that short-term bonds have a maturity of from one to five years, intermediate-term bonds have a maturity from 5 to 12 years, and long-term bonds have a maturity that exceeds 12 years. Generally, bonds with a maturity between one and five years are considered short term. Bonds with a maturity between 5 and 12 years are viewed as intermediate-term, and long-term bonds are those with a maturity of more than 12 years.

Typically, the maturity of a bond does not exceed 30 years. There are of course expectations. For example, Walt Disney Co. issued 100-year bonds in July 1993 and the Tennessee Valley Authority issued 50-year bonds in December 1993.

The term to maturity of a bond is important for two reasons in addition to indicating the time period over which the bondholder can expect to receive interest payments and the number of years before the principal will be paid in full. The first reason is that the yield on a bond depends on it. At any given point in time, the relationship between the yield and maturity of a bond (called the *yield curve*) indicates how bondholders are compensated for investing in bonds with different maturities. The second reason is that the price of a bond will fluctuate over its life as interest rates in the market change. The degree of price volatility of a bond is dependent on its maturity. More specifically, all other factors constant, the longer the maturity of a bond, the greater the price volatility resulting from a change in interest rates.

Par Value

The *par value* of a bond is the amount that the issuer agrees to repay the bondholder by the maturity date. This amount is also referred to as the *principal, face value, redemption value*, or *maturity value*.

Because bonds can have a different par value, the practice is to quote the price of a bond as a percentage of its par value. A value of 100 means 100% of par value. So, for example, if a bond has a par value of $1,000 and is selling for $850, this bond would be said to be selling at 85. If a bond with a par value of $100,000 is selling for $106,000, the bond is said to be selling for 106.

Coupon Rate

The annual interest rate that the issuer agrees to pay each year is called the *coupon rate*. The annual amount of the interest payment made to bondholders during the term of the bond is called the *coupon* and is determined by multiplying the coupon rate by the par value of the bond. For example, a bond with a 6% coupon rate and a par value of $1,000 will pay annual interest of $60.

When describing a bond issue, the coupon rate is indicated along with the maturity date. For example, the expression "5.5s of 2/15/2024" means a bond with a 5.5% coupon rate maturing on 2/15/2024.

For bonds issued in the United States, the usual practice is for the issuer to pay the coupon in two semiannual installments. Mortgage-backed securities and asset-backed securities typically pay interest monthly. For bonds issued in some markets outside the United States, coupon payments are made only once per year.

In addition to indicating the coupon payments that the investor should expect to receive over the term of the bond, the coupon rate also affects the bond's price sensitivity to changes in market interest rates. All other factors constant, the higher the coupon rate, the less the price will change in response to a change in market interest rates.

There are securities that have a coupon rate that increases over time according to a specified schedule. These securities are called *step-up notes* because the coupon rate "steps up" over time. For example, a five-year step-up note might have a coupon rate that is 5% for the first two years and 6% for the last three years. Or, the step-up note could call for a 5% coupon rate for the first two years, 5.5% for the third and fourth years, and 6% for the fifth year. When there is only one change (or step up), as in our first example, the issue is referred to as a single step-up note. When there is more than one increase, as in our second example, the issue is referred to as a *multiple step-up note*.

Not all bonds make periodic coupon payments. *Zero-coupon bonds* as the name indicates do not make periodic coupon payments. Instead, the holder of a zero-coupon bond realizes interest at the maturity date. The aggregate interest earned is the difference between the maturity value and the purchase price. For example, if an investor purchases a zero-coupon bond for 63, the aggregate interest at the maturity date is 37, the difference between the par value (100) and the price paid (63). The reason why certain investors like zero-coupon bonds is that they eliminated one of the risks that we will discuss later, reinvestment risk. The disadvantage of a zero-coupon bonds is that the accrued interest earned each year is taxed despite the fact that no actual cash payment is made.

There are issues whose coupon payment is deferred for a specified number of years. That is, there is no coupon payment for the deferred period and then a lump sum payment at some specified date and coupon payments until maturity. These securities are referred to as *deferred interest securities*.

A coupon-bearing security need not have a fixed interest rate over the term of the bond. There are bonds that have an interest rate that is variable. There bonds are referred to as *floating rate securities*. In fact, another way to classify bond markets is the *fixed rate bond market* and the *floating rate bond market*. Floating rate securities appeal to institutional investors such as depository institutions (banks, savings and loan associations, and credit unions) because it provides a better match against their funding costs, which are typically floating rate debt. We discussed these securities in Chapter 12.

Accrued Interest

In the United States, coupon interest is typically paid semiannually for government bonds, corporate, agency, and municipal bonds. In some countries, interest is paid annually. For mortgage-backed and asset-backed securities, interest is usually paid monthly. The coupon interest payment is made to the bondholder of record. Thus, if an investor sells a bond between coupon payments and the buyer holds it until the next coupon payment, the entire coupon interest earned for the period will be paid to the buyer of the bond since the buyer will be the holder of record. The seller of the bond gives up the interest from the time of the last coupon payment to the time until the bond is sold. The amount of interest over this period that will be received by the buyer even though it was earned by the seller is called *accrued interest*.

In the United States and in many countries, the bond buyer must compensate the bond seller for the accrued interest. The amount that the buyer pays the seller is the agreed upon price for the bond plus accrued interest. This amount is called the *full price*. The agreed upon bond price without accrued interest is called the *clean price*.

There are exceptions to the rule that the bond buyer must pay the bond seller accrued interest. The most important exception is when the issuer has not fulfilled its promise to make the periodic payments. In this case, the issuer is said to be in default. In such instances, the bond's price is sold without accrued interest and is said to be *traded flat*.

Provisions for Paying off Bonds

The issuer of a bond agrees to repay the principal by the stated maturity date. The issuer can agree to repay the entire amount borrowed in one lump sum payment at the maturity date. That is, the issuer is not required to make any principal repayments prior to the maturity date. Such bonds are said to have a *bullet maturity*.

There are bond issues that consist of a series of blocks of securities maturing in sequence. The blocks of securities are said to be *serial bonds*. The coupon rate for each block can be different. One type of corporate bond in which there are serial bonds is an equipment trust certificate. Municipal bonds are often issued as serial bond.

Bonds backed by pools of loans (mortgage-backed securities and asset-backed securities) often have a schedule of principal repayments. Such bonds are said to be *amortizing securities*. For many loans, the payments are structured so that when the last loan payment is made, the entire amount owed is fully paid off. Another example of an amortizing feature is a bond that has a *sinking fund provision*. This provision for repayment of a bond may be designed to liquidate all of an issue by the maturity date, or it may be arranged to repay only a part of the total by the maturity date.

Many issues have a call provision granting the issuer an option to retire all or part of the issue prior to the stated maturity date. Some issues specify that the issuer must retire a predetermined amount of the issue periodically. Various types of call provisions are discussed next.

Call and Refunding Provisions

An issuer generally wants the right to retire a bond issue prior to the stated maturity date because it recognizes that at some time in the future the general level of interest rates may fall sufficiently below the issue's coupon rate so that redeeming the issue and replacing it with another issue with a lower coupon rate would be economically beneficial. This right is a disadvantage to the bondholder because proceeds received must be reinvested at a lower interest rate. As a result, an issuer who wants to include this right as part of a bond offering must compensate the bondholder when the issue is sold by offering a higher coupon rate, or equivalently, accepting a lower price than if the right is not included.

The right of the issuer to retire the issue prior to the stated maturity date is referred to as a *call option*. If an issuer exercises this right, the issuer is said to "call the bond." The price that the issuer must pay to retire the issue is referred to as the call price. Typically, there is not one call price but a call schedule that sets forth a call price based on when the issuer can exercise the call option.

When a bond is issued, typically the issuer may not call the bond for a number of years. That is, the issue is said to have a *deferred call*. The date at which the bond may first be called is referred to as the *first call date*. However, not all issues have a deferred call. If a bond issue does not have any protection against early call, then it is said to be a currently callable issue. But most new bond issues, even if currently callable, usually have some restrictions against certain types of early redemption. The most common restriction is that prohibiting the refunding of the bonds for a certain number of years. *Refunding* a bond issue means redeeming bonds with funds obtained through the sale of a new bond issue.

Generally, the call schedule is such that the call price at the first call date is a premium over the par value and scaled down to the par value over time. The date at which the issue is first callable at par value is referred to as the *first par call date*. However, not all issues have a call schedule in which the call price starts out as a premium over par. There are issues where the call price at the first call date and subsequent call dates is par value. In such cases, the first call date is the same as the first par call date. Call protection is much more absolute than refunding protection. While there may be certain exceptions to absolute or complete call protection in some cases, it still provides greater assurance against premature and unwanted redemption than does refunding protection. Refunding prohibition merely prevents redemption only from certain sources of funds, namely the proceeds of other debt issues sold at a lower cost of money. The bondholder is only protected if interest rates decline and the borrower can obtain lower-cost money to pay off the debt.

The call prices in a call schedule are referred to as the regular or general redemption prices. There are also special redemption prices for debt redeemed through the sinking fund and through other provisions, and the proceeds from the confiscation of property through the right of eminent domain.

Prepayments

For amortizing securities backed by loans and that have a schedule of principal repayments, individual borrowers typically have the option to pay off all or part of their loan prior to the scheduled date. Any principal repayment prior to the scheduled date is called a *prepayment*. The right of borrowers to prepay is called the *prepayment option.*

Basically, the prepayment option is the same as a call option. However, unlike a call option, there is not a call price that depends on when the borrower pays off the issue. Typically, the price at which a loan is prepaid is at par value.

Sinking Fund Provision

A *sinking fund provision* included in a bond indenture requires the issuer to retire a specified portion of an issue each year. Usually, the periodic payments required for sinking fund purposes will be the same for each period. A few indentures might permit variable periodic payments, where payments change according to certain prescribed conditions set forth in the indenture. The alleged purpose of the sinking fund provision is to reduce credit risk. This kind of provision for repayment of debt may be designed to liquidate all of a bond issue by the maturity date, or it may be arranged to pay only a part of the total by the end of the term. If only a part is paid, the remainder is called a *balloon maturity.* Many indentures include a provision that grants the issuer the option to retire more than the amount stipulated for sinking fund retirement. This is referred to as an *accelerated sinking fund provision.*

To satisfy the sinking fund requirement, an issuer is typically granted one of following choices: (1) make a cash payment of the face amount of the bonds to be retired to the trustee, who then calls the bonds for redemption using a lottery; or (2) deliver to the trustee bonds purchased in the open market that have a total par value equal to the amount that must be retired. If the bonds are retired using the first method, interest payments stop at the redemption date.

Usually the sinking fund call price is the par value if the bonds were originally sold at par. When issued at a price in excess of par, the call price generally starts at the issuance price and scales down to par as the issue approaches maturity.

There is a difference between the amortizing feature for a bond with a sinking fund provision, and the regularly scheduled principal repayment for a mortgage-backed and an asset-backed security. The owner of a mortgage-backed security or an asset-backed security knows that, assuming no default, there will be principal repayments. In contrast, the owner of a bond with a sinking fund provision is not assured that his or her particular holding will be called to satisfy the sinking fund requirement.

Options Granted to Bondholders

A provision in the indenture could grant either the bondholder or the issuer an option to take some action against the other party. The most common type of option embedded in a bond is the call option discussed earlier. This option is granted to the issuer. There are two options that can be granted to the bondholder: the right to put the issue and the right to convert the issue.

An issue with a put provision grants the bondholder the right to sell the issue (i.e., force the issuer to redeem the issue) at a specified price on designated dates. The specified price is called the put price. Typically, a bond is putable at par value if it is issued at or close to par value. For a zero-coupon bond, the put price is below par. The advantage of the put provision to the bondholder is that if after the issue date market rates rise above the issue's coupon rate, the bondholder can force the issuer to redeem the bond at the put price and then reinvest the proceeds at the prevailing higher rate.

A *convertible bond* is an issue giving the bondholder the right to exchange the bond for a specified number of shares of common stock. Such a feature allows the bondholder to take advantage of favorable movements in the price of the issuer's common stock. An *exchangeable bond* allows the bondholder to exchange the issue for a specified number of shares of common stock of a corporation different from the issuer of the bond.

Currency Denomination

The payments that the issuer makes to the bondholder can be in any currency. For bonds issued in the United States, the issuer typically makes both coupon payments and principal repayments in U.S. dollars. However, there is nothing that forces the issuer to make payments in U.S. dollars. The indenture can specify that the issuer may make payments in some other specified currency. For example, payments may be made in euros or yen.

An issue in which payments to bondholders are in U.S. dollars is called a *dollar-denominated issue*. A *nondollar-denominated issue* is one in which payments are not denominated in U.S. dollars. There are some issues whose coupon payments are in one currency and whose principal payment is in another currency. An issue with this characteristic is called a *dual-currency issue*.

Some issues allow either the issuer or the bondholder the right to select the currency in which a payment will be paid. This option effectively gives the party with the right to choose the currency the opportunity to benefit from a favorable exchange rate movement.

YIELD MEASURES

When purchasing a bond, an investor expects to receive a dollar return from one or more of the following sources:

1. The coupon interest payments made by the issuer.
2. Any capital gain (or capital loss—a negative dollar return) when the security matures, is called, or is sold.
3. Income from reinvestment of the interim cash flows.

Any yield measure that purports to measure the potential return from a bond should consider all three sources of return described earlier.

The most obvious source of return is the periodic coupon interest payments. For zero-coupon instruments, the return from this source is zero, although the investor is effectively receiving interest by purchasing a security below its par value and realizing interest at the maturity date when the investor receives the par value.

When the proceeds received when a bond matures, is called, or is sold are greater than the purchase price, a capital gain results. For a bond held to maturity, there will be a capital gain if the bond is purchased below its par value. A bond purchased below its par value is said to be purchased at a discount. For example, a bond purchased for $94.17 with a par value of $100 will generate a capital gain of $5.83 ($100 – $94.17) if held to maturity. For a callable bond, a capital gain results if the price at which the bond is called (i.e., the call price) is greater than the purchase price. For example, if the bond in our previous example is callable and subsequently called at $100.5, a capital gain of $6.33 ($100.5 − $94.17) will be realized. If the same bond is sold prior to its maturity or before it is called, a capital gain will result if the proceeds exceed the purchase price. So, if our hypothetical bond is sold prior to the maturity date for $103, the capital gain would be $8.83 ($103 − $94.17).

A capital loss is generated when the proceeds received when a bond matures, is called, or is sold are less then the purchase price. For a bond held to maturity, there will be a capital loss if the bond is purchased for more than its par value. A bond purchased for more than its par value is said to be purchased at a premium. For example, a bond purchased for $102.5 with a par value of $100 will generate a capital loss of $2.5 ($102.5 − $100) if held to maturity. For a callable bond, a capital loss results if the price at which the bond is called is less than the purchase price. For example, if the bond in our previous example is callable and subsequently called at $100.5, a capital loss of $2 ($102.5 − $100.5) will be realized. If the same bond is sold prior to its maturity or before it is called, a capital loss will result if the sale price is less than the purchase price. So, if our hypothetical bond is sold prior to the maturity date for $98.5, the capital loss would be $4 ($102.5 − $98.5).

With the exception of zero-coupon instruments, bonds make periodic payments of interest that can be reinvested until the security is removed from the portfolio. There are also instruments in which there are periodic principal repayments that can be reinvested until the security is removed from the portfolio. Repayment of principal prior to the maturity date occurs for amortizing instruments such as mortgage-backed securities and asset-backed securities. The interest earned from reinvesting the interim cash flows (interest and principal payments) until the security is removed from the portfolio is called reinvestment income.

There are several yield measures cited in the bond market. These include current yield, yield to maturity, yield to call, yield to put, yield to worst, and cash flow yield. Next we explain how each measure is calculated and its limitations.

Current Yield

The *current yield* relates the annual dollar coupon interest to the market price. The formula for the current yield is

$$\text{Current yield} = \frac{\text{Annual dollar coupon interest}}{\text{Price}}$$

For example, the current yield for a 7% 8-year bond whose price is $94.17 is 7.43% as shown:

Annual dollar coupon interest = 0.07 × $100 = $7
Price = $94.17

$$\text{Current yield} = \frac{\$7}{\$94.17} = 0.0743 = 7.43\%$$

The current yield will be greater than the coupon rate when the bond sells at a discount; the reverse is true for a bond selling at a premium. For a bond selling at par, the current yield will be equal to the coupon rate.

The drawback of the current yield is that it considers only the coupon interest and no other source that will impact an investor's return. No consideration is given to the capital gain that the investor will realize when a bond is purchased at a discount and held to maturity; nor is there any recognition of the capital loss that the investor will realize if a bond purchased at a premium is held to maturity.

Yield to Maturity

The most popular measure of yield in the bond market is the *yield to maturity*. The yield to maturity is the interest rate that will make the present value of the cash flows from a bond equal to its market price plus accrued interest. To find the yield to maturity, we first determine the cash flows. Then an iterative procedure is used to find the interest rate that will make the present value of the cash flows equal to the market price plus accrued interest. In the illustrations presented below, we assume that the next coupon payment will be six months from now so that there is no accrued interest.

To illustrate, consider a 7% 8-year bond selling for $94.17. The cash flows for this bond are (1) 16 payments every six months of $3.50 and (2) a payment 16 six-month periods from now of $100. The present value using various discount (interest) rates is:

Interest rate	3.5%	3.6%	3.7%	3.8%	3.9%	4.0%
Present value	100.00	98.80	97.62	96.45	95.30	94.17

When a 4.0% interest rate is used, the present value of the cash flows is equal to $94.17, which is the price of the bond. Hence, 4.0% is the semiannual yield to maturity.

The market convention adopted is to double the semiannual yield and call that the yield to maturity. Therefore, the yield to maturity for the above bond is 8% (2 times 4.0%). The yield to maturity computed using this convention-doubling the semiannual yield-is called a *bond-equivalent yield*.

The following relationships between the price of a bond, coupon rate, current yield, and yield to maturity hold:

Bond Selling at	Relationship
Par	Coupon rate = Current yield = Yield to maturity
Discount	Coupon rate < Current yield < Yield to maturity
Premium	Coupon rate > Current yield > Yield to maturity

The yield to maturity considers not only the coupon income, but also any capital gain or loss that the investor will realize by holding the bond to maturity. The yield to maturity also considers the timing of the cash flows. It does consider reinvestment income; however, it assumes that the coupon payments can be reinvested at an interest rate equal to the yield to maturity. So, if the yield to maturity for a bond is 8%, for example, to earn that yield the coupon payments must be reinvested at an interest rate equal to 8%. The following illustration clearly demonstrates this point.

Suppose an investor has $94.17 and places the funds in a certificate of deposit that pays 4% every six months for eight years or 8% per year (on a bond-equivalent basis). At the end of eight years, the $94.17 investment will grow to $176.38. Instead, suppose an investor buys the following bond: a 7% eight-year bond selling for $94.17. The yield to maturity for this bond is 8%. The investor would expect that at the end of eight years, the total dollars from the investment will be $176.38.

Let's look at what the investor will receive. There will be 16 semiannual interest payments of $3.50, which will total $56. When the bond matures, the investor will receive $100. Thus, the total dollars that the investor will receive is $156 by holding the bond to maturity. But this is less than the $176.38 necessary to produce a yield of 8% on a bond-equivalent basis by $20.38 ($176.38 minus $156). How is this deficiency supposed to be made up? If the investor reinvests the coupon payments at a semiannual interest rate of 4% (or 8% annual rate on a bond-equivalent basis), then the interest earned on the coupon payments will be $20.38. Consequently, of the $82.21 total dollar return ($176.38 minus $94.17) necessary to produce a yield of 8%, about 25% ($20.38 divided by $82.21) must be generated by reinvesting the coupon payments.

Clearly, the investor will only realize the yield to maturity that is stated at the time of purchase if (1) the coupon payments can be reinvested at the yield to maturity; and (2) the bond is held to maturity. With respect to the first assumption, the risk that an investor faces is that future interest rates will be less than the yield to maturity at the time the bond is purchased. This risk is referred to as reinvestment risk—a risk we explain later in this chapter. If the bond is not held to maturity, it may have to be sold for less than its purchase price, resulting in a return that is less than the yield to maturity. The risk that a bond will have to be sold at a loss is referred to as interest rate risk as explained later in this chapter.

There are two characteristics of a bond that determine the degree of reinvestment risk. First, for a given yield to maturity and a given coupon rate, the longer the maturity the more the bond's total dollar return is dependent on reinvestment income to realize the yield to maturity at the time of purchase (i.e., the greater the reinvestment risk). The implication is that the yield to maturity measure for long-term coupon bonds tells little about the potential yield that an investor may realize if the bond is held to maturity. For long-term bonds in high interest rate environments, the reinvestment income component may be as high as 70% of the bond's potential total dollar return.

The second characteristic that determines the degree of reinvestment risk is the coupon rate. For a given maturity and a given yield to maturity, the higher the coupon rate, the more dependent the bond's total dollar return will be on the reinvestment of the coupon payments in order to produce the yield to maturity at the time of purchase. This means that holding maturity and yield to maturity constant, premium bonds will be more dependent on reinvestment income than bonds selling at par. In contrast, discount bonds will be less dependent on reinvestment income than bonds selling at par. For zero-coupons bonds, none of the bond's total dollar return is dependent on reinvestment income. So, a zero-coupon bond has no reinvestment risk if held to maturity.

Yield to Call

When a bond is callable, the practice has been to calculate a *yield to call* as well as a yield to maturity. As explained earlier, a callable bond may have a call schedule. The yield to call assumes that the issuer will call the bond at some assumed call date and the call price is then the call price specified in the call schedule.

Typically, investors calculate a yield to first call or yield to next call, a yield to first par call, and yield to refunding. The *yield to first call* is computed for an issue that is not currently callable, while the *yield to next call* is computed for an issue that is currently callable. *Yield to refunding* is used when bonds are currently callable but have some restrictions on the source of funds used to buy back the debt when a call is exercised. The refunding date is the first date the bond can be called using lower-cost debt.

The procedure for calculating any yield to call measure is the same as for any yield calculation: Determine the interest rate that will make the present value of the expected cash flows equal to the price plus accrued interest. In the case of yield to first call, the expected cash flows are the coupon payments to the first call date and the call price. For the yield to first par call, the expected cash flows are the coupon payments to the first date at which the issuer can call the bond at par and the par value. For the yield to refunding, the expected cash flows are the coupon payments to the first refunding date and the call price at the first refunding date.

To illustrate the computation, consider a 7% eight-year bond with a maturity value of $100 selling for $106.36. Suppose that the first call date is three years from now and the call price is $103. The cash flows for this bond if it is called in three years are (1) six coupon payments of $3.50 and (2) $103 in six six-month periods from now. The process for finding the yield to first call is the same as for finding the yield to maturity. It can be shown that a semiannual interest rate of 2.8% makes the present value of the cash flows equal to the price is 2.8%. Therefore, the yield to first call on a bond-equivalent basis is 5.6%.

Let's take a closer look at the yield to call as a measure of the potential return of a security. The yield to call does consider all three sources of potential return from owning a bond. However, as in the case of the yield to maturity, it assumes that all cash flows can be reinvested at the yield to call until the assumed call date. As we just demonstrated, this assumption may be inappropriate. Moreover, the yield to call assumes that (1) the investor will hold the bond to the assumed call date; and (2) the issuer will call the bond on that date.

These assumptions underlying the yield to call are often unrealistic. They do not take into account how an investor will reinvest the proceeds if the issue is called. For example, consider two bonds, M and N. Suppose that the yield to maturity for bond M, a five-year noncallable bond, is 7.5%, while for bond N the yield to call, assuming the bond will be called in three years, is 7.8%. Which bond is better for an investor with a five-year investment horizon? It's not possible to tell for the yields cited. If the investor intends to hold the bond for five years and the issuer calls bond N after three years, the total dollars that will be available at the end of five years will depend on the interest rate that can be earned from investing funds from the call date to the end of the investment horizon.

Yield to Put

When a bond is putable, the yield to the first put date is calculated. The yield to put is the interest rate that will make the present value of the cash flows to the first put date equal to the price plus accrued interest. As with all yield measures (except the current yield), yield to put assumes that any interim coupon payments can be reinvested at the yield calculated. Moreover, the yield to put assumes that the bond will be put on the first put date.

Yield to Worst

A yield can be calculated for every possible call date and put date. In addition, a yield to maturity can be calculated. The lowest of all these possible yields is called the yield to worst. For example, suppose that there are only four possible call dates for a callable bond and that a yield to call assuming each possible call date is 6%, 6.2%, 5.8%, and 5.7%, and that the yield to maturity is 7.5%. Then the yield to worst is the minimum of these values, 5.7% in our example.

The yield to worst measure holds little meaning as a measure of potential return.

Cash Flow Yield

Mortgage-backed securities and asset-backed securities are backed by a pool of loans. The cash flows for these securities include principal repayment as well as interest. The complication that arises is that the individual borrowers whose loans make up the pool typically can prepay their loan in whole or in part prior to the scheduled principal repayment date. Because of prepayment, and in order to project the cash flows, it is necessary to make an assumption about the rate at which prepayments will occur. This rate is called the *prepayment rate* or *prepayment speed.*

Given the cash flows based on the assumed prepayment rate, a yield can be calculated. The yield is the interest rate that will make the present value of the projected cash flows equal to the price plus accrued interest. A yield calculated is commonly referred to as a *cash flow yield.*

Typically, the cash flows for mortgage-backed and asset-backed securities are monthly. Therefore the interest rate that will make the present value of the projected principal repayment and interest payments equal to the market price plus accrued interest is a monthly rate. The bond-equivalent yield is found by calculating the effective six-month interest rate and then doubling it. That is

Cash flow yield on a bond-equivalent basis (if monthly pay)
$$= 2[(1 + \text{Monthly yield})^6 - 1]$$

For example, if the monthly yield is 0.5%, then

Cash flow yield on a bond-equivalent basis = $2[(1.005)^6 - 1] = 6.08\%$

As noted, the yield to maturity has two shortcomings as a measure of a bond's potential return: (1) it is assumed that the coupon payments can be reinvested at a rate equal to the yield to maturity; and (2) it is assumed that the bond is held to maturity. These shortcomings are equally present in application of the cash flow yield measure: (1) the projected cash flows are assumed to be reinvested at the cash flow yield; and (2) the mortgage-backed or asset-backed security is assumed to be held until the final payoff of all the loans based on some prepayment assumption. The importance of reinvestment risk—the risk that the cash flows will be reinvested at a rate less than the cash flow yield—is particularly important for mortgage-backed and asset-backed securities since payments are typically monthly and include principal repayments (scheduled and prepayments), as well as interest. Moreover, the cash flow yield is dependent on realization of the projected cash flows according to some prepayment rate. If actual prepayments differ significantly from the prepayment rate assumed, the cash flow yield will not be realized.

RISKS ASSOCIATED WITH INVESTING IN BONDS

Bonds expose an investor to one or more of the following risks: (1) interest rate risk; (2) call and prepayment risk; (3) credit risk; (4) liquidity risk; (5) exchange rate or currency risk; and (6) inflation or purchasing power risk.

Interest Rate Risk

The price of a typical bond will change in the opposite direction from a change in interest rates. That is, when interest rates rise, a bond's price will fall; when interest rates fall, a bond's price will rise. For example, consider a 6% 20-year bond. If the yield investors require to buy this bond is 6%, the price of this bond would be $100. However, if the required yield increased to 6.5%, the price of this bond would decline to $94.4479. Thus, for a 50 basis point increase in yield, the bond's price declines by 5.55%. If, instead, the yield declines from 6% to 5.5%, the bond's price will rise by 6.02% to $106.0195.

The reason for this inverse relationship between price and changes in interest rates or changes in market yields is as follows. Suppose investor X purchases our hypothetical 6% coupon 20-year bond at par value ($100). The yield for this bond is 6%. Suppose that immediately after the purchase of this bond two things happen. First, market interest rates rise to 6.50%

so that if an investor wants to buy a similar 20-year bond a 6.50% coupon rate would have to be paid by the bond issuer in order to offer the bond at par value. Second, suppose investor X wants to sell the bond. In attempting to sell the bond, investor X would not find an investor who would be willing to pay par value for a bond with a coupon rate of 6%. The reason is that any investor who wanted to purchase this bond could obtain a similar 20-year bond with a coupon rate 50 basis points higher, 6.5%. What can the investor do? The investor cannot force the issuer to change the coupon rate to 6.5%. Nor can the investor force the issuer to shorten the maturity of the bond to a point where a new investor would be willing to accept a 6% coupon rate. The only thing that the investor can do is adjust the price of the bond so that at the new price the buyer would realize a yield of 6.5%. This means that the price would have to be adjusted down to a price below par value. The new price must be $94.4469. While we assumed in our illustration an initial price of par value, the principle holds for any purchase price. Regardless of the price that an investor pays for a bond, an increase in market interest rates will result in a decline in a bond's price.

Suppose, instead of a rise in market interest rates to 6.5%, they decline to 5.5%. Investors would be more than happy to purchase the 6% coupon 20-year bond for par value. However, investor X realizes that the market is only offering investors the opportunity to buy a similar bond at par value with a coupon rate of 5.5%. Consequently, investor X will increase the price of the bond until it offers a yield of 5.5%. That price is $106.0195.

Since the price of a bond fluctuates with market interest rates, the risk that an investor faces is that the price of a bond held in a portfolio will decline if market interest rates rise. This risk is referred to as *interest rate risk* and is by far the major risk faced by investors in the bond market.

Bond Features that Affect Interest Rate Risk

The degree of sensitivity of a bond's price to changes in market interest rates depends on various characteristics of the issue, such as maturity and coupon rate. Consider first maturity. All other factors constant, the longer the maturity, the greater the bond's price sensitivity to changes in interest rates. For example, we know that for a 6% 20-year bond selling to yield 6%, a rise in the yield required by investors to 6.5% will cause the bond's price to decline from $100 to $94.4479, a 5.55% price decline. For a 6% five-year bond selling to yield 6%, the price is $100. A rise in the yield required by investors from 6% to 6.5% would decrease the price to $97.8944. The decline in the bond's price is only 2.11%.

Now let's turn to the coupon rate. A property of a bond is that all other factors constant, the lower the coupon rate, the greater the bond's price sensitivity to changes in interest rates. For example, consider a 9% 20-year bond selling to yield 6%. The price of this bond would be $112.7953. If the yield required by investors increases by 50 basis points to 6.5%, the price of this bond would fall by 2.01% to $110.5280. This decline is less than the 5.55% decline for the 6% 20-year bond selling to yield 6%. An implication is that zero-coupon bonds have greater price sensitivity to interest rate changes than same-maturity bonds bearing a coupon rate and trading at the same yield.

Because of default or credit risk (discussed later), different bonds trade at different yields, even if they have the same coupon rate and maturity. How, then, holding other factors constant, does the level of interest rates affect a bond's price sensitivity to changes in interest rates? As it turns out, the higher the level of interest rates that a bond trades at, the lower the price sensitivity.

To see this, we can compare a 6% 20-year bond initially selling at a yield of 6%, and a 6% 20-year bond initially selling at a yield of 10%. The former is initially at a price of $100, and the latter carries a price of $65.68. Now, if the yield on both bonds increases by 100 basis points, the first bond trades down by 10.68 points ($10.68/$100 = 10.68%.) After the assumed increase in yield, the second bond will trade at a price of $59.88, for a price decline of only 5.80 points (or $5.80/$65.68 = 8.83%). Thus, we see that the bond that trades at a lower yield is more volatile in both percentage price change and absolute price change, as long as the other bond characteristics are the same. An implication of this is that, for a given change in interest rates, price sensitivity is lower when the level of interest rates in the market is high, and price sensitivity is higher when the level of interest rates is low.

We can summarize these three characteristics that affect the bond's price sensitivity to changes in market interest rates as follows:

> *Characteristic 1.* For a given maturity and initial yield, the lower the coupon rate the greater the bond's price sensitivity to changes in market interest rates.
>
> *Characteristic 2.* For a given coupon rate and initial yield, the longer the maturity of a bond the greater the bond's price sensitivity to changes in market interest rates.
>
> *Characteristic 3.* For a given coupon rate and maturity, the lower the level of interest rates the greater the bond's price sensitivity to changes in market interest rates.

A bond's price sensitivity bond will also depend on any options embedded in the issue. This is explained next when we discuss call risk.

Interest Rate Risk for Floating Rate Securities

The change in the price of a fixed rate coupon bond when market interest rates change is due to the fact that the bond's coupon rate differs from the prevailing market interest rate. For a floating rate security, the coupon rate is reset periodically based on the prevailing value for the reference rate plus the contractually specified index spread. The index spread is set for the life of the security. The price of a floating rate security will fluctuate depending on the following three factors.

First, the longer the time to the next coupon reset date, the greater the potential price fluctuation. For example, consider a floating rate security whose coupon resets every six months and the coupon formula is six-month LIBOR plus 20 basis points. Suppose that on the coupon reset date six-month LIBOR is 5.8%. If the next day after the coupon is reset, six-month LIBOR rises to 6.1%, this means that this security is offering a six-month coupon rate that is less than the prevailing six-month rate for the remaining six months. The price of the security must decline to reflect this. Suppose instead that the coupon resets every month at one-month LIBOR and that this rate rises right after a coupon rate is reset. Then, while the investor would be realizing a sub-market one-month coupon rate, it is for only a month. The price decline will be less than for the security that resets every six months.

The second reason why a floating rate security's price will fluctuate is that the index spread that investors want in the market changes. For example, consider once again the security whose coupon reset formula is six-month LIBOR plus 20 basis point. If market conditions change such that investors want an index spread of 30 basis points rather than 20 basis points, this security would be offering a coupon rate that is 10 basis points below the market rate. As a result, the security's price will decline.

Finally, as noted earlier, a floating rate security may have a cap. Once the coupon rate as specified by the coupon reset formula rises above the cap rate, the security offers a below market coupon rate and its price will decline. In fact, once the cap is reached, the security's price will react much the same way to changes in market interest rates as that of a fixed rate coupon security.

Call and Prepayment Risk

As explained earlier, a bond may include a provision that allows the issuer to retire or call all or part of the issue before the maturity date. From the investor's perspective, there are three disadvantages to call provisions. First, the cash flow pattern of a callable bond is not known with certainty. Second, because the issuer will call the bonds when interest rates have dropped, the investor is exposed to reinvestment risk; that is, the investor will have to reinvest the proceeds when the bond is called at relatively lower interest rates. Finally, the capital appreciation potential of a bond will be reduced because the price of a callable bond may not rise much above the price at which the issuer will call the bond. Because of these disadvantages faced by the investor, a callable bond is said to expose the investor to call risk. The same disadvantages apply to bonds that can prepay. In this case the risk is referred to as *prepayment risk.*

Credit Risk

While investors commonly refer to *credit risk* as if it is one dimensional, there are actually three forms of this risk. *Credit default risk* is the risk that the issuer will fail to satisfy the terms of the obligation with respect to the timely payment of interest and repayment of the amount borrowed. To gauge credit default risk, investors rely on analysis performed by nationally recognized statistical rating organizations that perform credit analysis of issues and issuers and express their conclusions in the form of a credit rating. *Credit spread risk* is the loss or underperformance of an issue or issues due to an increase in the credit spread. *Downgrade risk* is the risk that an issue or issuer will be downgraded, resulting in an increase in the credit spread.

Credit Default Risk

The prospectus or offer document for an issue provides investors with information about the issuer so that credit analysis can be performed on the issuer before the bonds are placed. Credit assessments take time, however, and also require the specialist skills of credit analysts. Large institutional investors do, in fact, employ such specialists to carry out credit analysis; however, often it is too costly and time consuming to assess every issuer in the bond market. Therefore, investors commonly rely on credit ratings.

A *credit rating* is a formal opinion given by a company referred to as a *rating agency* of the credit default risk faced by investing in a particular issue of debt securities. For long-term debt obligations, a credit rating is a forward-looking assessment of the probability of default and the relative magnitude of the loss should a default occur. For short-term debt obligations, a credit rating is a forward-looking assessment of the probability of default.

The nationally recognized rating agencies include Moody's Investors Service, Standard & Poor's, and Fitch Ratings. On receipt of a formal request, the rating agencies will carry out a rating exercise on a specific issue of debt capital. The request for a rating comes from the organization planning the issuance of bonds. Although ratings are provided for the benefit of investors, the issuer must bear the cost. However, it is in the issuer's interest to request a rating as it raises the profile of the bonds, and investors may refuse to buy a bond that is not accompanied by a recognized rating.

Although the rating exercise involves credit analysis of the issuer, the rating is applied to a specific debt issue. This means that, in theory, the credit rating is applied not to an organization itself, but to specific debt securities that the organization has issued or is planning to issue. In practice, it is common for the market to refer to the creditworthiness of organizations themselves in terms of the rating of their debt. A highly rated company, for example, may be referred to as a "triple-A-rated" company, although it is the company's debt issues that are rated as triple A.

The rating systems of the rating agencies use similar symbols. Separate categories are used by each rating agency for short-term debt (with original maturity of 12 months or less) and long-term debt (over one year original maturity). Table 19.2 shows the long-term debt ratings. In all rating systems, the term "high grade"means low credit risk or, conversely, high probability of future payments. The highest-grade bonds are designated by Moody's by the letters Aaa, and by the others as AAA. The next highest grade is designated as Aa by Moody's, and by the others as AA; for the third grade, all rating agencies use A. The next three grades are Baa (Moody's) or BBB, Ba (Moody's) or BB, and B, respectively. There are also C grades. Standard and Poor's (S&P) and Fitch use plus or minus signs to provide a narrower credit quality breakdown within each class. Moody's uses 1, 2, or 3 for the same purpose. Bonds rated triple A (AAA or Aaa) are said to be "prime"; double A (AA or Aa) are of "high quality"; single A issues are called "upper medium grade"; and triple B are "medium grade." Lower-rated bonds are said to have "speculative" elements or be "distinctly speculative."

Bond issues that are assigned a rating in the top four categories are referred to as *investment-grade bonds*. Bond issues that carry a rating below the top four categories are referred to as *noninvestment-grade bonds* or more popularly as *high-yield bonds* or *junk bonds*. Thus, the bond market can be divided into two sectors: the *investment grade sector* and the *noninvestment-grade sector*. *Distressed debt* is a subcategory of noninvestment-grade bonds. These bonds may be in bankruptcy proceedings, may be in default of coupon payments, or may be in some other form of distress.

Credit Spread Risk

The credit spread is the premium over the government or risk-free rate required by the market for taking on a certain assumed credit exposure. In the United States, the benchmark is yield on comparable-maturity Treasury securities. The higher the credit rating, the smaller the credit spread to the benchmark yield. Credit spread risk is the risk of financial loss resulting

TABLE 19.2 Summary of Long-Term Bond Rating Systems and Symbols

Fitch	Moody's	S&P	Summary Description
Investment Grade			
AAA	Aaa	AAA	Gilt edged, prime, maximum safety, lowest risk, and when sovereign borrower considered "default-free"
AA+	Aa1	AA+	
AA	Aa2	AA	High-grade, high-credit quality
AA–	Aa3	AA–	
A+	A1	A+	
A	A2	A	Upper-medium grade
A–	A3	A–	
BBB+	Baa1	BBB+	
BBB	Baa2	BBB	Lower-medium grade
BBB–	Baa3	BBB–	
Speculative Grade			
BB+	Ba1	BB+	
BB	Ba2	BB	Low grade; speculative
BB–	Ba3	BB–	
B+	B1		
B	B	B	Highly speculative
B–	B3		
Predominantly Speculative, Substantial Risk or in Default			
CCC+		CCC+	
CCC	Caa	CCC	Substantial risk, in poor standing
CC	Ca	CC	May be in default, very speculative
C	C	C	Extremely speculative
		CI	Income bonds—no interest being paid
DDD			
DD Default			
D		D	

from changes in the level of credit spreads. Changes in credit spreads affect the value of the portfolio and can lead to underperformance relative to a benchmark for portfolio managers. A measure of how a credit-risky bond's price will change if the credit spread sought by the market changes is called "spread duration" and is explained later in this chapter.

Downgrade Risk

As explained earlier, market participants gauge the credit default risk of an issue by looking at the credit ratings assigned to issues by the rating agencies. Once a credit rating is assigned to a debt obligation, a rating agency monitors the credit quality of the issuer and can reassign a different credit rating. An improvement in the credit quality of an issue or issuer is rewarded with a better credit rating, referred to as an *upgrade*; a deterioration in the credit rating of an issue or issuer is penalized by the assignment of an inferior credit rating, referred to as a *downgrade*. The actual or anticipated downgrading of an issue or issuer increases the credit spread and results in a decline in the price of the issue or the issuer's bonds. This risk is referred to as *downgrade risk* and is closely related to credit spread risk. A rating agency may announce in advance that it is reviewing a particular credit rating, and may go further and state that the review is a precursor to a possible downgrade or upgrade. This announcement is referred to as putting the issue under *credit watch*.

Occasionally, the ability of an issuer to make interest and principal payments changes seriously and unexpectedly because of an unforeseen event. This can include any number of idiosyncratic events that are specific to the corporation or to an industry, including a natural or industrial accident, a regulatory change, a takeover or corporate restructuring, or even corporate fraud. This risk is referred to generically as *event risk* and will result in a downgrading of the issuer by the rating agencies. Because the price of the entity's securities will typically change dramatically or jump in price, this risk is sometimes referred to as *jump risk*.

The rating agencies periodically publish, in the form of a table, information about how issues that they have rated change over time. This table is called a *rating transition matrix*, *rating migration table*, or *rating transition table*. The table is useful for investors to assess the likelihood of a ratings change, based on experiences of rated securities. A rating migration table is available for different lengths of time.

Liquidity Risk

When an investor wants to sell a bond prior to the maturity date, he or she is concerned whether the price that can be obtained from dealers is close to the true value of the issue. For example, if recent trades in the market for a particular issue have been between 97.25 and 97.75 and market conditions have not changed, an investor would expect to sell the bond somewhere in the 97.25 to 97.75 area.

Liquidity risk is the risk that the investor will have to sell a bond below its true value where the true value is indicated by recent transactions. The primary measure of liquidity is the size of the spread between the bid price (the price at which a dealer is willing to buy a security) and the ask price (the price at which a dealer is willing to sell a security). The wider the bid-ask spread, the greater the liquidity risk.

A liquid market can generally be defined by "small bid-ask spreads, which do not materially increase for large transactions" (Gerber, 1997, p. 278). Bid-ask spreads, and therefore liquidity risk, change over time.

For investors who plan to hold a bond until maturity and need not mark a position to market, liquidity risk is not a major concern. An institutional investor that plans to hold an issue to maturity but is periodically marked to market is concerned with liquidity risk. By marking a position to market, it is meant that the security is revalued in the portfolio based on its current market price. For example, mutual funds are required to mark to market at the end of each day the holdings in their portfolio in order to compute the *net asset value* (NAV). While other institutional investors may not mark to market as frequently as mutual funds, they are marked to market when reports are periodically sent to clients or the board of directors or trustees.

Exchange Rate or Currency Risk

A nondollar-denominated bond (i.e., a bond whose payments occur in a foreign currency) has unknown U.S. dollar cash flows. The dollar cash flows are dependent on the exchange rate at the time the payments are received. For example, suppose an investor purchases a bond whose payments are in euros. If the euro depreciates relative to the U.S. dollar, then fewer dollars will be received. The risk of this occurring is referred to as *exchange rate risk* or *currency risk*. Of course, should the euro appreciate relative to the U.S. dollar, the investor will benefit by receiving more dollars.

Inflation or Purchasing Power Risk

Inflation risk or purchasing power risk arises because of the variation in the value of cash flows from a security due to inflation, as measured in terms of purchasing power. For example, if an investor purchases a bond with a coupon rate of 7%, but the rate of inflation is 8%, the purchasing power of the cash flow has declined. For all but floating rate securities, an investor is exposed to inflation risk because the interest rate the issuer promises to make is fixed for the life of the issue. To the extent that interest rates reflect the expected inflation rate, floating rate securities have a lower level of inflation risk.

MEASURING INTEREST RATE RISK

An investor or a portfolio manager can measure the exposure to interest rate changes of a position by revaluing that position based on various interest rate scenarios. However, the typical way in which interest rate risk is measured is by approximating the impact of a change in interest rates on a bond or a bond portfolio. The first approximation is referred to as *duration*. In general, duration is a measure of the sensitivity of a security's value to a change in the market yield of the security. To improve upon this approximation, a second measure is estimated and is referred to as convexity. There are different types of duration measures: duration, dollar duration, modified duration, Macaulay duration, effective duration, effective duration, option-adjusted duration, portfolio duration, contribution to portfolio duration, spread duration, index duration. The duration and convexity estimates require a good valuation model. We will discuss valuation models later.

As noted earlier, the two characteristics of a bond that affect its interest rate risk are it coupon r ate and its maturity. In addition, the level of interest rates affects a bond's exposure to changes in interest rates. However, to effectively control a portfolio's exposure to interest rate risk, it is necessary to quantify this risk. The most popular measure of interest rate risk is duration. A portfolio manager or risk manager who wants to reduce exposure to interest rates, will reduce the duration of a position. In the extreme case where a portfolio manager wants to eliminate interest rate risk (i.e., hedge interest rate risk), a position will be altered to have a duration of zero.

In this section, we explain how duration is estimated for bonds and portfolios. There are different types of duration measures for individual bonds and portfolios. We also explain the limitations of duration. We then discuss how the duration measure can be improved by using a measure called convexity.

Duration

The most obvious way to measure the price sensitivity as a percentage of the security's current price to changes in interest rates is to change rates (i.e., "shock" rates) by a small number of basis points and calculate how a security's value will change as a percentage of the current price. The name popularly used to refer to the approximate percentage price change is duration. The following formula can be used to estimate the duration of a security:

$$\text{Duration} = \frac{P_- - P_+}{2P_0(\Delta y)} \tag{19.1}$$

where

Δy = the change (or shock) in interest rates (in decimal form)

P_0 = the current price of the bond

P_- = the estimated price of the bond if interest rates are decreased by the change in interest rates

P_+ = the estimated price of the bond if interest rates are increased by the change in interest rates

Throughout this chapter, when we use "change in interest rate" and "change in yield" interchangeably.

It is important to understand that the two values in the numerator of equation (19.1) are the estimated values if interest rates change obtained from a valuation model. Consequently, the duration measure is only as good as the valuation model employed to obtain the estimated values in equation (19.1). The more difficult it is to estimate the value a bond, the less confidence an investor or portfolio manager may have in the estimated duration. We will see that the duration of a portfolio is nothing more than a market-weighted average of the duration of the bonds comprising the portfolio. Hence, a portfolio's duration is sensitive to the estimated duration of the individual bonds.

To illustrate the duration calculation, consider the following option-free bond: a 6% coupon five-year bond trading at par value to yield 6%. The current price is $100. Suppose the yield is changed by 50 basis points. Thus, Δy = 0.005 and P_0 = $100. This is simple bond to value if interest rates or yield is changed. If the yield is decreased to 5.5%, the price of this bond would be $102.1600. If the yield is increased to 6.5%, the value of this bond would be $97.8944. That is, P_- = $102.1600 and P_+ = $97.8944. Substituting into equation (19.1), we obtain

$$\text{Duration} = \frac{\$102.1600 - \$97.8944}{2(\$100)(0.005)} = 4.27$$

There are various ways in that practitioners have interpreted what the duration of a bond is. We believe the most useful way to think about a bond's duration is as the approximate percentage change in the bond's price for a 100 basis point change in interest rates. Thus a bond with a duration of say

5 will change by approximately 5% for a 100 basis point change in interest rates (i.e., if the yield required for this bond changes by approximately 100 basis points). For a 50 basis point change in interest rates, the bond's price will change by approximately 2.5%; for a 25 basis point change in interest rates, 1.25%, and so on.

Dollar Duration

In estimating the sensitivity of the price of bond to changes in interest rates, we looked at the percentage price change. However, for two bonds with the same duration but trading at different prices, the dollar price change will not be the same. To see this, suppose that we have two bonds, B_1 and B_2, that both have a duration of 5. Suppose further that the current price of B_1 and B_2 are $100 and $90, respectively. A 100 basis point change for both bonds will change the price by approximately 5%. This means a price change of $5 (5% times $100) for B_1 and a price change of $4.5 (5% times $90) for B_2.

The dollar price change of a bond can be measured by multiplying duration by the full dollar price and the number of basis points (in decimal form) and is called the dollar duration. That is,

Dollar duration = Duration × Dollar price × Change in rates in decimal

The dollar duration for a 100 basis point change in rates is

$$\text{Dollar duration} = \text{Duration} \times \text{Dollar price} \times 0.01 \qquad (19.2)$$

So, for bonds B_1 and B_2, the dollar duration for a 100 basis point change in rates is

For bond B_1: Dollar duration = 5 × $100 × 0.01 = $5.0
For bond B_2: Dollar duration = 5 × $90 × 0.01 = $4.5

Knowing the dollar duration allows a portfolio manager to neutralize the risk of bond position. For example, consider a position in bond B_2. If a trader wants to eliminate the interest rate risk exposure of this bond (i.e., hedge the exposure), the trader will look for a position in another financial instrument(s) (for example, an interest rate derivative described in Chapter 5) whose value will change in the opposite direction to bond B_2's price by an amount equal to $4.5. So if the trader has a long position in B_2, the position will decline in value by $4.5 for a 100 basis point increase in interest rates. To hedge this risk exposure, the trader can take a position in another financial instrument whose value increases by \$4.5 if interest rates increase by 100 basis points.

The dollar duration can also be computed without having to know a bond's duration. This is done by simply looking at the average price change for a bond when interest rates are increased and decreased by the same number of basis points. This can be done easily for interest rate derivatives. For example, the dollar duration for an interest rate futures contract and an interest rate swap can be computed by changing interest rates and determining how the price of the derivative changes on average. This is important because when trying to control the interest rate risk of a position, a portfolio manager or risk manager will employ interest rate derivatives.

Dollar duration is related to another measure often cited for measuring interest rate risk exposure: the *dollar value of an 01* (DV01). This measure, also referred to as the *basis point value* (BPV), or the *price value of a basis point* (PV01), is the average price change for a 1 basis change in interest rates.

Modified Duration, Macaulay Duration, and Effective Duration

A popular form of duration that is used by practitioners is modified duration. *Modified duration* is the approximate percentage change in a bond's price for a 100 basis point change in interest rates, assuming that the bond's cash flows do not change when interest rates change. What this means is that in calculating the values used in the numerator of the duration formula, the cash flows used to calculate the current price are assumed. Therefore, the change in the bond's value when interest rates change by a small number of basis points is due solely to discounting at the new yield level.

Modified duration is related to another measure commonly cited in the bond market: *Macaulay duration*. The formula for this measure, first used by Frederick Macaulay (1938), is rarely used in practice so it will not be produced here. For a bond that pays coupon interest semiannually, modified duration is related to Macaulay duration as follows:

$$\text{Modified duration} = \text{Macaulay duration}/(1 + \text{yield}/2)$$

where yield is the bond's yield to maturity in decimal form. Practically speaking, there is very little difference in the computed values for modified duration and Macaulay duration.

The assumption that the cash flows will not change when interest rates change makes sense for option-free bonds because the payments by the issuer are not altered when interest rates change. This is not the case for callable bond, putable bonds, bonds with accelerated sinking fund options, mortgage-backed securities, and certain types of asset-backed securities (i.e., mortgage related securities). For these securities, a change in interest rates may alter the expected cash flows.

The price-yield relationship for callable bonds and prepayable securites is shown in Figure 19.1. As market rates (yields) decline, investors become concerned that they will decline further so that the issuer or homeowner will benefit from calling the bond. The precise yield level where investors begin to view the issue likely to be called may not be known, but we do know that there is some level. In Figure 19.1, at yield levels below y^*, the price-yield relationship for the callable bond departs from the price-yield relationship for the option-free bond. If, for example, the market yield is such that an option-free bond would be selling for $109, but since it is callable would be called at $104, investors would not pay $109. If they did, and the bond is called, investors would receive $104 (the call price) for a bond they purchased for $109. Notice that for a range of yields below y^*, there is price compression (i.e., there is limited price appreciation as yields decline). The portion of the callable bond price-yield relationship below y^* is said to be *negatively convex.*

Negative convexity means that the price appreciation will be less than the price depreciation for a large change in yield of a given number of basis points. In contrast, a bond that is option-free exhibits positive convexity. This means that the price appreciation will be greater than the price depreciation for a large change in yield.

FIGURE 19.1   Price-Yield Relationship for an Option-Free Bond and a Callable Bond

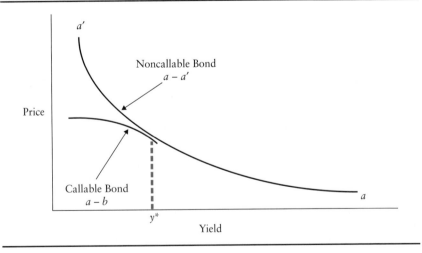

For bonds with embedded options, there are valuation models that take into account how changes in interest rates will affect cash flows that we will describe in the next section. When the values used in the numerator of equation (19.1) are obtained from a valuation model that takes into account both the discounting at different interest rates and how the cash flows can change, the resulting duration is referred to as *effective duration* or *option-adjusted duration*.

Spread Duration for Fixed Rate Bonds

Duration is a measure of the change in the value of a bond when rates change. The interest rate that is assumed to shift is the Treasury rate. However, for non-Treasury securities, the yield is equal to the Treasury yield plus a spread to the Treasury yield curve. The price of a bond exposed to credit risk can change even though Treasury yields are unchanged because the spread required by the market changes. A measure of how a non-Treasury issue's price will change if the spread sought by the market changes is called *spread duration*. For example, a spread duration of 2.2 for a security means that if the Treasury rate is unchanged but spreads change by 100 basis points, the security's price will change by approximately 2.2%.

Duration of a Floating Rate Security

The price of a fixed rate coupon bond fluctuates in the market because the prevailing market interest rate is different from the issue's coupon rate. For a floating rate security, the coupon rate resets periodically to a rate that should be close to the prevailing market interest rate. The coupon reset formula for a floating rate security is the reference rate plus the quoted margin.

Assuming that the quoted margin the market requires over the reference rate does not change, the greater the reset frequency, the smaller the duration because the coupon rate adjusts to the market rate and therefore the price stays near par value. When the coupon reset date is close, the duration is close to zero. If the quoted margin that the market requires changes, then a floating rate security can trade at a premium or discount to maturity value even at a coupon reset date.

Two measures are used to estimate the sensitivity of a floater to each component of the coupon reset formula: the reference rate and the spread. *Index duration* is a measure of the price sensitivity of a floater to changes in the reference rate (i.e., index) holding the spread constant. *Spread duration* measures a floater's price sensitivity to a change in the spread, assuming that the reference rate is unchanged. Note that "spread duration" is also used for fixed rate bonds as described earlier. The context in which the term is used should make it clear whether spread duration is for a fixed rate bond or a floating rate bond.

Portfolio Duration

Portfolio duration can be obtained by calculating the weighted average of the duration of the bonds in the portfolio. The weight is the proportion of the portfolio that a security comprises. Mathematically, portfolio duration can be calculated as follows:

$$\text{Portfolio duration} = w_1 D_1 + w_2 D_2 + \dots + w_N D_N \qquad (19.3)$$

where

w_i = market value of bond i/market value of the portfolio
D_i = duration of bond i
N = number of bonds in the portfolio

To illustrate this calculation, consider the $240,220,000 10-bond portfolio shown in Table 19.3. The table shows the market value of each bond, the percentage that each bond is of the portfolio, and the duration of each bond. The fifth column gives the product of the weight and the duration. The last row in that column shows the portfolio duration as given by equation (19.3): 5.21.

A portfolio duration of 5.21 means that for a 100 basis point change in the yield for all 10 bonds, the market value of the portfolio will change by approximately 5.21%. But keep in mind that the yield on all 10 bonds must change by 100 basis points for the duration measure to be most useful.

The assumption that all interest rates must change by the same number of basis points is a critical assumption, and its importance cannot be over-emphasized. Market practitioners refer to this as the *parallel yield curve shift assumption*.

Portfolio duration can also be computed by using dollar duration as given by equation (19.2). This is done by computing the dollar duration for each bond in the portfolio. The sixth column of Table 19.3 gives the dollar duration for each bond in the portfolio. The portfolio duration as shown in the last row of the sixth column of the table is $12,522,888. This means that for a 100 basis point change in interest rates, the change in the portfolio's value will be approximately $12,522,888. Since the market value of the portfolio is $240,220,000, this means that the percentage change in the value of the portfolio for a 100 basis point change in interest rates is 5.21% ($12,522,888/$240,220,000). Since duration is the approximate percentage

TABLE 19.3 Calculation of Portfolio Duration and Contribution to Portfolio Duration

Bond	Market Value ($)	Percent of Portfolio	Duration	Duration × Percent of Portfolio = Contribution to Portfolio Duration	Dollar Duration ($)
1	10,000,000	4.1629	4.70	0.20	470,000
2	18,500,000	7.7013	3.60	0.28	666,000
3	14,550,000	6.0569	6.25	0.38	909,375
4	26,080,000	10.8567	5.42	0.59	1,413,536
5	24,780,000	10.3155	2.15	0.22	532,770
6	35,100,000	14.6116	3.25	0.47	1,140,750
7	15,360,000	6.3941	6.88	0.44	1,056,768
8	26,420,000	10.9983	6.50	0.71	1,717,300
9	40,000,000	16.6514	4.75	0.79	1,900,000
10	29,430,000	12.2513	9.23	1.13	2,716,389
Port.	240,220,000	100.0000		5.21	12,522,888

change in value for a 100 basis point change in interest rates, we can see that the portfolio duration is 5.21%, the same duration obtained from using equation (19.3).

To appreciate why it is helpful to know the portfolio dollar duration, suppose that the portfolio manager wants to change the current duration of 5.21 for the 10-bond portfolio to a duration of 4. What this means is that the portfolio manager wants a dollar duration for of 4% of $240,220,000 or $9,608,800. But the current portfolio duration is $12,522,888. To get the portfolio to 4, the portfolio manager must get rid of $2,914,088 ($12,522,888 – $9,608,800). To do this, the portfolio manager, if authorized to use interest rate derivatives), will take a position in one or more derivatives whose dollar duration is –$2,914,088.

Contribution to Portfolio Duration

Portfolio managers commonly assess their exposure to an issue in terms of the percentage of that issue in the portfolio. A better measure of exposure of an individual issue to changes in interest rates is in terms of its *contribution to portfolio duration*. This is found by multiplying the percentage that the individual issue is of the portfolio by the duration of the individual issue. That is,

Contribution to portfolio duration

$$= \frac{\text{Market value of issue}}{\text{Market value of portfolio}} \times \text{Duration of issue} \qquad (19.4)$$

Notice the contribution to portfolio duration is simply the individual components in portfolio duration formula given by equation (19.3). In Table 19.3, the contribution to portfolio duration for each bond is shown in the fifth column.

While we shown how to compute the contribution to portfolio duration for each bond in a portfolio, the same formula can be used to determine the contribution to portfolio duration for each bond sector represented in a portfolio.

The contribution to the spread duration of a portfolio can also be computed using spread duration of an issue in equation (19.4).

BOND INDEXES

In the previous chapter, we discussed the role of stock market indexes. The same applies to bond indexes. The wide range of bond market indexes available can be classified as broad-based market indexes and specialized market indexes. The three broad-based market indexes most commonly used by institutional investors are the Lehman Brothers Aggregate Index, the Salomon Brothers Broad Investment-Grade Bond Index, and the Merrill Lynch Domestic Market Index. The sectors bond market sectors covered by these three indexes are the same as those described in Table 19.1

The specialized market indexes focus on only one sector of the bond market or a subsector of the bond market. Indexes on sectors of the market are published by the three investment banking firms that produce the broad-based market indexes. The index providers have created family of indexes. Some of these indexes are simply sub-indexes of the broad-based bond index. For example, Lehman publishes the following indexes: Lehman Treasury Index, Lehman Government-Related Index, Lehman Credit Index, Lehman Corporate Index, Lehman MBS Index, and Lehman Asset Backed Securities (ABS) Index. Firms that do not produce one of the three broad-based market indexes may provide specialized indexes. For example, Credit Suisse published a convertible bond index and a high-yield bond index.

Although we have focused on the broad-based bond indexes that include only U.S. securities, there are more global bond indexes. For example, Lehman publishes the following indexes: Lehman Global Aggregate Index, Lehman Global Treasury Index, Lehman Global Investment-Grade/

High-Yield Credit Index, Lehman Global High-Yield Credit Index, and Lehman Securitized Index.

In the municipal bond market there are several indexes commonly used by institutional investors that are those produced by Lehman Brothers. This firm's broad-based index is the Lehman Municipal Bond Index. As of early 2008, there were 42,689 issues in this index. The index is divided into subindexes or sectors that are also published. Lehman also publishes a High-Yield Municipal Index and enhanced state specific indexes.

Asset managers in consultation with their clients have been moving in the direction of *customized benchmarks*. A customized benchmark is a benchmark that is designed to meet a client's requirements and long-term objectives.

ACTIVE BOND PORTFOLIO STRATEGIES

In this section, we describe bond portfolio strategies. As with active equity portfolio strategies described in the previous chapter, bond portfolio strategies can be classified as active and passive strategies. In addition, there are structured bond portfolio strategies that are used by institutional investors with liability-driven objectives.

Active bond portfolio strategies can be classified into four categories:

- Interest rate expectations strategies.
- Yield curve strategies.
- Yield spread strategies.
- Individual security selection strategies.

Interest Rate Expectations Strategies

An asset manager who believes that he or she can accurately forecast the future level of interest rates will alter the portfolio's sensitivity to interest rate changes. But how is a portfolio's sensitivity to interest rate changes measured? Recall that duration is a measure of interest rate risk and that duration can be calculated for an individual bond, a bond portfolio, or a bond trading position. An *interest rate expectations strategy* involves increasing a portfolio's duration if interest rates are expected to fall, and reducing duration if interest rates are expected to rise. For those asset managers whose benchmark is a bond index, this means increasing the portfolio duration relative to the benchmark index if interest rates are expected to fall, and reducing it if interest rates are expected to rise. The degree to which the duration of the managed portfolio is permitted to diverge from that of the benchmark index may be limited by the client

A portfolio's duration may be altered by swapping (or exchanging) bonds in the portfolio for new bonds that will achieve the target portfolio duration. Such swaps are commonly referred to as *rate anticipation swaps*. Alternatively, a more efficient means for altering the duration of a bond portfolio is to use interest rate futures or swaps contracts as explained in the next chapter.

The key to this active strategy is, of course, an ability to forecast the direction of future interest rates. The academic literature, however, does not support the view that interest rates can be forecast so that risk-adjusted excess returns can be consistently realized. It is doubtful whether betting on future interest rates will provide a consistently superior return.

Yield Curve Strategies

The yield curve for U.S. Treasury securities shows the relationship between their maturities and yields. The shape of this yield curve changes over time. *Yield curve strategies* involve positioning a portfolio to capitalize on expected changes in the shape of the Treasury yield curve. Here we will describe the different ways in which the Treasury yield curve has shifted, the different types of yield curve strategies, and the usefulness of duration as a measure of the price sensitivity of a bond or portfolio when the yield curve shifts.

Types of Shifts in the Yield Curve and Impact on Historical Returns

A shift in the yield curve refers to the relative change in the yield for each Treasury maturity. A parallel shift in the yield curve refers to a shift in which the change in the yield on all maturities is the same. A nonparallel shift in the yield curve means that the yield for each maturity does not change by the same number of basis points.

Historically, two types of nonparallel yield curve shifts have been observed: a twist in the slope of the yield curve and a change in the humpedness of the yield curve. All these shifts are graphically portrayed in Figure 19.2. A twist in the slope of the yield curve refers to a flattening or steepening of the yield curve. In practice, the slope of the yield curve is measured by the spread between some long-term Treasury yield and some short-term Treasury yield. For example, some practitioners refer to the slope as the difference between the 30-year Treasury yield and the 1-year Treasury yield. Regardless of how it is defined, a *flattening of the yield curve* means that the yield spread between the yield on a long-term and a short-term Treasury has decreased; a *steepening of the yield curve* means that the yield spread between a long-term and a short-term Treasury has increased. The other type of nonparallel shift, a change in the humpedness of the yield curve, is referred to as a *butterfly shift*.

There have been several empirical studies that have investigated the importance of changes in the shape of the yield on the performance (i.e., total return) of Treasury securities. These studies consistently find that parallel shifts and twists in the yield curve are responsible for from 90% to 93% of Treasury returns, while 4% to 6% of the returns is attributable to butterfly shifts, and the balance to unexplained factor shifts. These findings suggest that yield curve strategies require a forecast of the direction of the shift and a forecast of the type of twist.

Types of Yield Curve Strategies

In portfolio strategies that seek to capitalize on expectations based on short-term movements in yields, the dominant source of return is the change in the price of the securities in the portfolio. This means that the maturity of the securities in the portfolio will have an important impact on the portfolio's return. For example, a total return over a 1-year investment horizon for a portfolio consisting of securities all maturing in 1 year will not be sensitive to changes in how the yield curve shifts 1 year from now. In contrast, the total return over a 1-year investment horizon for a portfolio consisting of securities all maturing in 30 years will be sensitive to how the yield curve shifts because, 1 year from now, the value of the portfolio will depend on the yield offered on 29-year securities. As we know from our earlier discussion, long-maturity bonds have substantial price volatility when yields change.

A portfolio consisting of equal proportions of securities maturing in 1 year and securities maturing in 30 years will have quite a different total return over a 1-year investment horizon than the two portfolios we previously described when the yield curve shifts. The price of the 1-year securities in the portfolio will not be sensitive to how the 1-year yield has changed, but the price of the 30-year securities will be highly sensitive to how long-term yields have changed. The key point is that for short-term investment horizons, the spacing of the maturity of bonds in the portfolio will have a significant impact on the total return.

Consequently, yield curve strategies involve positioning a portfolio with respect to the yield curve strategies: (1) bullet strategies, (2) barbell strategies, and (3) ladder strategies. Each of these strategies is depicted in Figure 19.3.

In a *bullet strategy*, the portfolio is constructed so that the maturities of the securities in the portfolio are highly concentrated at one point on the yield curve. In a *barbell strategy*, the maturities of the securities included in the portfolio are concentrated at two extreme maturities. Actually, in practice, when asset managers refer to a barbell strategy, it is relative to a bullet strategy. For example, a bullet strategy might be to create a portfolio with maturities concentrated around 10 years, while a corresponding barbell strategy might be a portfolio with 5-year and 20-year maturities. In a *ladder strategy*, the portfolio is constructed to have approximately equal amounts of each maturity. So, for example, a portfolio might have equal amounts of securities with one year to maturity, two years to maturity, and so on.

Each of these strategies will result in a different performance when the yield curve shifts. The actual performance will depend on both the type of shift and the magnitude of the shift. Thus, no general statements can be made about the optimal yield curve strategy. The framework for analyzing a yield curve strategy will be discussed later.

Duration and Yield Curve Shifts

Let's reconsider the concept of duration and its role in approximating the price volatility of a bond portfolio when the yield curve shifts. Earlier we explained how duration is a measure of the sensitivity of the price of a bond or the value of a bond portfolio to changes in market yields. For example, a portfolio with a duration of 4 means that if market yields increase by 100 basis points, the portfolio will change by approximately 4%.

In explaining the limitations of duration, we indicated that an assumption is made about how market yields change. Specifically, if a portfolio of bonds consists of 5-year bonds, 10-year bonds, and 20-year bonds, and the portfolio's duration is 4, what market yield is assumed to change when we say that this portfolio will change in value by 4% if yields change by 100 basis points? Is it the 5-year yield, 10-year yield, or 20-year yield? In fact, the assumption made when using duration as a measure of how the value of a portfolio will change if market yields change is that the yield on *all* maturities will change by the same number of basis points. Thus, if our three-bond portfolio has a duration of 4, the statement that the portfolio's value will change by 4% for a 100-basis-point change in yields actually should be stated as follows: The portfolio's value will change by 4% if the yields on 5-year bonds, 10-year bonds, and 20-year bonds all change by 100 basis points. That is, it is assumed that there is a parallel yield curve shift.

There several measures that have been developed to estimate a bond portfolio's exposure to nonparallel shifts in the yield curve. The most popular one is *rate duration*. Basically, rate duration is an estimate of how the yield curve will change if the interest rate for one maturity sector changes and all other interest rates are unchanged. For example, a 10-year rate duration of say 2 means that if the 10-year Treasury rate changes by 100 basis points and all other rates remain unchanged, the portfolio will change by roughly 2%. In practice, asset managers focus on certain "key" maturity sectors when they look at rate duration. The set of these rate durations are referred to as *key rate durations*.

Yield Spread Strategies

Yield spread strategies involve positioning a portfolio to capitalize on expected changes in yield spreads between sectors of the bond market. Swaps that involve exchanging one bond for another when the manager believes (1) that the prevailing yield spread between the two bonds in the market is out of line with the bonds' historical yield spread; and (2) that the yield spread will realign by the end of the investment horizon are called *intermarket spread swaps*.

One of the most common yield spread strategies in the bond market involves changes in corporate credit spreads. Credit spreads change because of expected changes in economic prospects. Credit spreads between Treasury and non-Treasury issues widen in a declining or contracting economy and narrow during economic expansion. The economic rationale is that in a declining or contracting economy, corporations experience a decline in revenue and reduced cash flows, making it difficult for corporate issuers to service their contractual debt obligations. To induce investors to hold non-Treasury securities of lower-quality issuers, the yield spread relative to Treasury securities must widen. The converse is that during economic expansion and brisk economic activity, revenue and cash flows pick up, increasing the likelihood that corporate issuers will have the capacity to service their contractual debt obligations.

Individual Security Selection Strategies

There are several active strategies that money managers pursue to identify mispriced securities. The most common strategy identifies an issue as undervalued because either (1) its yield is higher than that of comparably rated issues; or (2) its yield is expected to decline (and price therefore rise) because credit analysis indicates that its rating will improve.

A swap in which an asset money manager exchanges one bond for another bond that is similar in terms of coupon, maturity, and credit quality, but offers a higher yield, is called a *substitution swap*. This swap depends on a capital market imperfection. Such situations sometimes exist in the bond market because of temporary market imbalances and the fragmented nature of the non-Treasury bond market. The risk the asset manager faces in making a substitution swap is that the bond purchased may not be truly identical to the bond for which it is exchanged. Moreover, typically bonds will have similar but not identical maturities and coupons. This could lead to difference in the price movement of the bonds when interest rates change that is not captured by duration.

An active strategy used in the mortgage-backed securities market is to identify individual issues of pass-throughs, *collateralized mortgage obligations* (CMO), CMO bond classes, or stripped MBSs that are mispriced, given the assumed prepayment speed to price the security. Another active strategy commonly used in the mortgage-backed securities market is to create a package of securities that will have a better return profile for a wide range of interest rate and yield curve scenarios than similar-duration securities available in the market. Because of the fragmented nature of the mortgage-backed securities market and the complexity of the structures, such opportunities are not unusual

PASSIVE BOND PORTFOLIO STRATEGIES

Passive bond portfolio strategies are often referred to as *structured bond portfolio strategies*. Such strategies seek to match the performance of a predetermined benchmark. There are two types of structured bond portfolio strategies: bond indexing and liability-driven strategies. In a bond indexing strategy, the benchmark is a bond index. Liability-driven strategies are formulated to satisfy liability objective with the client's liabilities serving as the benchmark for portfolio performance.

Bond Indexing

Bond indexing involves s designing a portfolio so that its performance will match the performance of some bond index. There are several reasons why investors have turned to bond indexing. First, there is empirical evidence that suggests that historically the overall performance of active bond managers has been poor. Second is the reduced advisory management and custodial fees charged for an indexed portfolio compared with the fees for active management.

Critics of indexing point out that although an indexing strategy matches the performance of some index, the performance of that index does not necessarily represent optimal performance. Moreover, matching an index does not mean that the manager will satisfy a client's return-requirement objective. For example, if the objective of a life insurance company or a pension fund is to have sufficient funds to satisfy a predetermined liability, indexing only reduces the likelihood that performance will not be materially worse than the index. The index's return is not necessarily related to the sponsor's liability. Finally, matching an index means that a money manager is restricted to the sectors of the bond market that are in the index, even though there may be attractive opportunities in market sectors excluded from the index. While the broad-based bond market indexes typically include agency pass-through securities, other mortgage-backed securities such as agency CMOs and nonagency MBS are generally not included. Yet it is in these fairly new markets that attractive returns to enhance performance may be available.

Once the decision is made to pursue a bond indexing strategy and the index (broad-based bond market index, specialized market index, or customized benchmark) has been selected, the next step is to construct a portfolio that will track the index. One approach in constructing the indexed portfolio is for the asset manager to purchase all the issues in the index according to their weight in the benchmark index. However, substantial underperformance will result from the transaction costs (and other fees) associated with purchasing all the issues and reinvesting cash flow (maturing principal and coupon interest). A broad-based market index could include over 4,000 issues in the corporate bond area alone, so large transaction costs may make this approach impractical. In addition, some issues in the index may not be available at the prices used in constructing the index. Instead of purchasing all issues in the index, the asset manager may purchase just a sample of issues. While this approach reduces transaction costs, it increases the mismatch of the portfolio with index and thereby increases the likelihood of performance different from the index.

Generally speaking, the fewer the number of issues used to replicate the index, the smaller the deviation of the indexed portfolio relative to the index due to transaction costs, but the greater the risk of the deviation due to the mismatch of the characteristics of the indexed portfolio and the index. In contrast, the more issues purchased to replicate the index, the greater the risk of deviation attributable to transaction costs, and the smaller the risk of deviation due to the mismatch of the indexed portfolio and the index. Obviously, then, there is a trade-off between the risk of deviation and the number of issues used to construct the indexed portfolio.

There are three methodologies for designing a portfolio to replicate an index: (1) the stratified sampling, or cell, approach; (2) the optimization approach; and (3) the variance minimization approach. These methodologies are described in Fabozzi (2008).

An indexer faces several logistical problems in constructing an indexed bond portfolio. First of all, the prices for each issue used by the organization that publishes the index may not be the execution prices available to the indexer. In fact, they may be materially different from the prices offered by some dealers. In addition, the prices used by organizations reporting the value of indexes are based on bid prices. Dealer ask prices, however, are the ones that the asset manager would have to transact at when constructing or rebalancing the indexed portfolio. So a bias exists between the performance of the index and the indexed portfolio that is equal to the bid-ask spread.

Furthermore, there are logistical problems unique to certain sectors in the bond market. Consider first the corporate bond market. There are typically about 4,000 issues in the corporate bond sector of a broad-based index. Because of the illiquidity of this sector of the bond market, not only may the prices used by the organization that publishes the index be unreliable, but also many of the issues may not even be available. Next, consider the mortgage-backed securities market. There are over 800,000 agency pass-through issues. The organizations that publish indexes lump all these issues into a few hundred generic issues. The indexer is then faced with the difficult task of finding pass-through securities with the same risk–return profiles of these hypothetical issues.

Finally, recall that the total return depends on the reinvestment rate available on coupon interest. If the organization publishing the index regularly overestimates the reinvestment rate, then the indexed portfolio could underperform the index by 10 to 15 basis points a year.

Structured Bond Portfolio Strategies

Liability-driven strategies fall into two categories. The first is when the liability is a single liability. In this case an *immunization strategy* is employed. An immunization strategy is designed so that as interest rates change, interest rate risk and reinvestment risk will offset each other in such a way that the minimum accumulated value sought by the investor (or minimum rate of return) becomes the target accumulated value (or target yield). An immunization strategy requires that an asset manager create a bond portfolio with a duration equal to the investment horizon (i.e., the scheduled due date for the liability). That is, it is a duration-matching strategy.

The second is when there is a stream of future liabilities that must be satisfied. In this case, the most commonly used strategy is a *cash flow matching strategy*. This strategy, also referred to as dedicated portfolio strategy, does not impose any duration requirement. The strategy can be summarized as follows. A bond is selected with a maturity that matches the last liability stream. An amount of principal plus final coupon equal to the amount of the last liability stream is then invested in this bond. The remaining elements of the liability stream are then reduced by the coupon payments on this bond, and another bond is chosen for the new, reduced amount of the next-to-last liability. Going backward in time, this cash flow matching process is continued until all liabilities have been matched by the payment of the securities in the portfolio.

SUMMARY

Basically, a bond is a financial obligation of an entity (the issuer) who promises to pay a specified sum of money at specified future dates. The investment features of a bond include maturity, par value, coupon rate, provisions for paying off a bond issue, and any embedded options.

The sources of return from holding a bond to maturity are the coupon interest payments, any capital gain or loss, and reinvestment income. Reinvestment income is the interest income generated by reinvesting coupon interest payments and any principal repayments from the time of receipt to the bond's maturity. The current yield relates the annual dollar coupon interest to the market price and fails to recognize any capital gain or loss and reinvestment income. The yield to maturity is the interest rate that will make the present value of the cash flows from a bond equal to the price plus accrued interest. This yield measure will only be realized if the interim cash flows can be reinvested at the yield to maturity and the bond is held to maturity. The yield to call is the interest rate that will make the present value of the expected cash flows to the assumed call date equal to the price plus accrued interest. Yield measures for callable bonds include yield to first call, yield to next call, yield to first par call, and yield to refunding. The yield to worst is the lowest yield from among all possible yield to calls, yield to puts, and the yield to maturity. For mortgage-backed and asset-backed securities, the cash flow yield based on some prepayment rate is the interest rate that equates the present value of the projected principal and interest payments to the price plus accrued interest. The cash flow yield assumes that all cash flows (principal payments and interest payments) can be reinvested at the calculated yield and that the prepayment rate will be realized over the security's life.

Bonds expose an investor to various risks. The price of a bond changes inversely with a change in market interest rates. Interest rate risk refers to the adverse price movement of a bond as a result of a change in market interest rates; for the owner of a bond it is the risk that interest rates will rise. The coupon rate and maturity of a bond affect its price sensitivity to changes in market interest rate. Call risk and prepayment risk refer to the risk that a security will be paid off before the scheduled principal repayment date. From an investor's perspective, the disadvantages to call and prepayment provisions are (1) the cash flow pattern is uncertain; (2) reinvestment risk because proceeds received will have to be reinvested at a relatively lower interest rate; and (3) the capital appreciation potential of a bond will be reduced. Credit risk consists of three types of risk: default risk, credit spread risk, and downgrade risk. Default risk is gauged by the ratings assigned by the nationally recognized statistical rating organizations (rating agencies).

Liquidity risk depends on the ease with which an issue can be sold at or near its true value and is primarily gauged by the bid-ask spread quoted by a dealer. From the perspective of a U.S. investor, exchange rate risk is the risk that a currency in which a security is denominated will depreciate relative to the U.S. dollar. Inflation risk or purchasing power risk arises because of the variation in the value of cash flows from a security due to inflation.

The duration of a bond measures the approximate percentage price change for a 100 basis point change in interest rates. Important analytical interest rate risk measures in managing a portfolio are portfolio duration, key rate duration, and contribution to portfolio duration.

As with equity portfolio management strategies, there are active and passive bond portfolio strategies. There are four general types of active bond portfolio strategies: interest rate expectations strategies, yield curve strategies, yield spread strategies, and individual security selection strategies. Passive strategies include bond indexing and liability-driven strategies. Bond indexing is more difficult to implement in the bond area than in the equity area for a variety of reasons. Liability-driven strategies include single period immunization in attempting to satisfy a single period liability and a cash flow matching strategy to satisfy multiple-period liabilities.

REFERENCES

Fabozzi, F. J. (1999). *Duration, Convexity, and Other Bond Risk Measures*. Hoboken, NJ: John Wiley & Sons.

Fabozzi, F. J. (2002). *Fixed Income Securities*. Hoboken, NJ: John Wiley & Sons.

Fabozzi, F. J. (ed.) (2005). *Handbook of Fixed Income Securities*, 7th ed. New York: McGraw Hill.

Fabozzi, F. J. (2008). *Bond Markets, Analysis, and Strategies*, 7th ed. Upper Saddle River, NJ: Prentice Hall.

Fabozzi, F. J., Bhattacharya, A. K., and Berliner W. S. (2007). *Mortgage-Backed Securities: Products, Structuring, and Analytical Techniques*. Hoboken, NJ: John Wiley & Sons.

Fabozzi, F. J. and Mann, S. V. (2001). *Floating Rate Securities*. Hoboken, NJ: John Wiley & Sons.

Gerber, R. I. (1997). A user's guide to buy-side bond trading. In F. J. Fabozzi (ed.), *Managing Fixed Income Portfolios* (pp. 277–290). Hoboken, NJ: John Wiley & Sons.

Wilson, R. W. and Fabozzi, F. J. (1996). *Corporate Bonds: Structures and Analysis*. Hoboken, NJ: John Wiley & Sons.

CHAPTER 20

Use of Stock Index Futures and Treasury Futures Contracts in Portfolio Management

In the previous two chapters, we explained the management of equity and bond portfolios. Our attention was on the implementation of investment strategies by buying or selling individual securities. Without futures, asset managers would have only one trading location to alter portfolio positions when they get new information that is expected to influence the value of assets they manage—the *cash market*, also called the *spot market*. If adverse economic news is received, asset managers can reduce their price risk exposure to that asset by selling the asset. The opposite is true if the new information is expected to impact the value of that asset favorably: An asset manager would increase price risk exposure to that asset, buying additional quantities of that asset.

There are, of course, transaction costs associated with altering exposure to an asset—explicit costs (commissions) and hidden or execution costs (bid-ask spreads and market impact costs), which we discussed in Chapter 18. The futures market is an alternative market that asset managers can use to alter their risk exposure to an asset when new information is acquired. But which market—cash or futures—should the money manager employ to alter a position quickly on the receipt of new information? The answer is simple: the one that more efficiently achieves the investment objective of the asset manager. The factors to consider are liquidity, transaction costs, speed of execution, and leverage potential.

Typically, it is easier and less costly to alter a portfolio position using futures than using the cash market. The speed at which orders can be executed also often gives the advantage to the futures market. The advantage is also on the side of the futures market when it comes to the amount of money that must be put up in a transaction (i.e., leverage). Margin requirements for transactions in stocks and bonds are considerably higher than in the futures market.

For many types of strategies employed in investment management, there may be a more efficient way to implement an investment strategy: buying or selling futures contracts. Futures and swaps make it possible for asset managers to alter the market exposure of a stock portfolio or implement a strategy economically and quickly, thereby reducing transaction costs.

In this chapter, we see how futures contracts are used by asset managers. We described these derivative instruments in Chapter 6, as well as the pricing of futures and forward contracts. Here we will describe two futures contracts that are used in equity and bond futures contracts used in asset management: stock index futures and Treasury bond and note futurds contracts. In addition, we explain how the basic futures pricing model explained in Chapter 6 has to be modified to allow for the nuances of equity and bond futures. In the next chapter, we discuss how options are used in investment management.

It should be noted that the purpose here is only to give the reader a feel for the contracts and how they are used. In practice, there are wide range of futures and swap contracts that are used in addition to stock index futures and Treasury bond and note futures contracts. The most important contract is that of interest rate swaps, which are used by asset managers in managing the risk of a bond portfolio, as well as by corporate managers in managing funding costs.

USING STOCK INDEX FUTURES IN EQUITY PORTFOLIO MANAGEMENT

We begin with the use of equity derivatives in equity portfolio management. While there are both future contracts on stock indexes and individual stocks, the most commonly used futures are on the former. Therefore, we focus only on stock index futures.

Basic Features of Stock Index Futures

The underlying for a stock index futures contract can be a broad-based stock market index or a narrow-based index. Examples of broad-based stock market indexes that are the underlying for a futures contract are the S&P 500, S&P Midcap 400, Dow Jones Industrial Average, Nasdaq 100 Index, NYSE Composite Index, and the Russell 2000 Index.

A narrow-based stock index futures contract is one based on a subsector or components of a broad-based stock index containing groups of stocks or a specialized sector developed by a bank. For example, Dow Jones MicroSector Indexes are traded on OneChicago. There are 15 sectors in the index.

The dollar value of a stock index futures contract is the product of the futures price and a "multiple" that is specified for the futures contract. That is,

Dollar value of a stock index futures contract = Futures price × Multiple

For example, suppose that the futures price for the S&P 500 is 1,410. The multiple for the S&P 500 futures contract is $250. Therefore, the dollar value of the S&P 500 futures contract would be $352,500 (= 1,410 × $250). If an investor buys an S&P 500 futures contract at 1,410 and sells it at 1,430, the investor realizes a profit of 20 times $250, or $5,000. If the futures contract is sold instead for 1,360, the investor will realize a loss of 50 times $250, or $12,500.

Stock index futures contracts are cash settlement contracts. This means that at the settlement date, cash will be exchanged to settle the contract. For example, if an investor buys an S&P 500 futures contract at 1,410 and the futures settlement price is 1,430, settlement would be as follows. The investor has agreed to buy the S&P 500 for 1,410 times $250, or $352,500. The S&P 500 value at the settlement date is 1430 times $250, or $357,500. The seller of this futures contract must pay the investor $5,000 ($357,500 − $352,500). Had the futures price at the settlement date been 1360 instead of 1,430, the dollar value of the S&P 500 futures contract would be $340,000. In this case, the investor must pay the seller of the contract $12,500 ($352,500 − $340,000). (Of course, in practice, the parties would be realizing any gains or losses at the end of each trading day as their positions are marked to the market.)

Clearly, an investor who wants to short the entire market or a sector will use stock index futures contracts. The costs of a transaction are small relative to shorting the individuals stocks comprising the stock index or attempting to construct a portfolio that replicates the stock index with minimal tracking error.

Pricing of Stock Index Futures

In Chapter 6, we demonstrated that the theoretical futures price is determined using arbitrage arguments. The equation for the theoretical futures price is reproduced as follows:

Theoretical futures price = Cash market price + (Cash market price)
× (Financing cost − Cash yield)

In Chapter 6, we said that the model had to be refined to allow for the nuances of institutional constraints and contract specifications of specific contracts. The refinement is necessary because of the assumptions underlying the derivative of the general pricing model just given. Some of the refinements such as short selling and transaction costs, were discussed in Chapter 6. The two of particular interest for stock index futures are the interim cash flows for the underlying and the deliverable being a basket of stocks rather than a single asset.

As explained in Chapter 6, in the derivation of a basic pricing model, it is assumed that no interim cash flows arise because of changes in futures prices (that is, there is no variation margin). For a stock index, there are interim cash flows. In fact, there are many cash flows that are dependent upon the dividend dates of the component companies. To correctly price a stock index future contract, it is necessary to incorporate the interim dividend payments. Yet the dividend rate and the pattern of dividend payments are not known with certainty. Consequently, they must be projected from the historical dividend payments of the companies in the index. Once the dividend payments are projected, they can be incorporated into the pricing model. The only problem is that the value of the dividend payments at the settlement date will depend on the interest rate at which the dividend payments can be reinvested from the time they are projected to be received until the settlement date. The lower the dividend, and the closer the dividend payments to the settlement date of the futures contract, the less important the reinvestment income is in determining the futures price.

Now let's look at the issue of having a basket of assets to deliver. The problem in arbitraging stock index futures contracts is that it may be too expensive to buy or sell every stock included in the stock index. Instead, a portfolio containing a smaller number of stocks may be constructed to track the basket or index (which means having price movements that are very similar to changes in the stock index. Nonetheless, the two arbitrage strategies involve a tracking portfolio rather than a single asset for the underlying, and the strategies are no longer risk-free because of the risk that the tracking portfolio will not precisely replicate the performance of the stock index. For this reason, the market price of futures contracts based on a stock index is likely to diverge from the theoretical price and have wider bands (i.e., lower and upper theoretical futures price that cannot be exploited).

Applications for Stock Index Futures

Now that we know what stock index futures are and how they are priced, we can look at how they can be used by institutional investors. Prior to the development of stock index futures, an investor who wanted to speculate on the future course of stock prices had to buy or short individual stocks. Now, however, the stock index can be bought or sold in the futures market. But making speculation easier for investors is not the main function of stock index futures contracts. The other strategies discussed below show how institutional investors can effectively use stock index futures to meet investment objectives.

Controlling the Risk of a Stock Portfolio

An asset manager who wishes to alter exposure to the market can do so by revising the portfolio's beta. This can be done by rebalancing the portfolio with stocks that will produce the target beta, but there are transaction costs associated with rebalancing a portfolio. Because of the leverage inherent in futures contracts, asset managers can use stock index futures to achieve a target beta at a considerably lower cost. Buying stock index futures will increase a portfolio's beta, and selling will reduce it.

Hedging against Adverse Stock Price Movements

The major economic function of futures markets is to transfer price risk from hedgers to speculators. *Hedging* is the employment of futures contracts as a substitute for a transaction to be made in the cash market. If the cash and futures markets move together, any loss realized by the hedger on one position (whether cash or futures) will be offset by a profit on the other position. When the profit and loss are equal, the hedge is called a *perfect hedge.*

Short Hedge and Long Hedge   A *short hedge* is used by a hedger to protect against a decline in the future cash price of the underlying. To execute a short hedge, the hedger sells a futures contract. Consequently, a short hedge is also referred to as a *sell hedge.* By establishing a short hedge, the hedger has fixed the future cash price and transferred the price risk of ownership to the buyer of the contract.

As an example of an asset manager who would use a short hedge, consider a pension fund manager who knows that the beneficiaries of the fund must be paid a total of $3 million four months from now. This will necessitate liquidating a portion of the fund's common stock portfolio in order to satisfy these payments. If the value of the shares that she intends to liquidate decline in value four months from now, a larger portion of the portfolio will have to be liquidated. The easiest way to handle this situation is for the money manager to sell the needed amount of stocks and invest the proceeds in a Treasury bill that matures in four months. However, suppose that for some reason, the money manager is constrained from making the sale today.

The pension fund manager can use a short hedge to lock in the value of the stocks that will be liquidated.

A *long hedge* is undertaken to protect against rising prices of future intended purchases. In a long hedge, the hedger buys a futures contract, so this hedge is also referred to as a *buy hedge*. As an example, consider once again a pension fund manager. This time, suppose that the manager expects a substantial contribution from the plan sponsor four months from now, and that the contributions will be invested in common stock of various companies. The pension fund manager expects the market price of the stocks in which he will invest the contributions to be higher in four months and, therefore, takes the risk that he will have to pay a higher price for the stocks. The manager can use a long hedge to effectively lock in a future price for these stocks now.

Return on a Hedged Position Hedging is a special case of controlling a stock portfolio's exposure to adverse price changes. In a hedge, the objective is to alter a current or anticipated stock portfolio position so that its beta is zero. A portfolio with a beta of zero should generate a risk-free interest rate. This is consistent with the capital asset pricing model discussed in Chapter 8. Thus, in a perfect hedge, the return will be equal to the risk-free interest rate. More specifically, it will be the risk-free interest rate corresponding to a maturity equal to the number of days until settlement of the futures contract.

Therefore, say, a portfolio that is identical to the S&P 500 (i.e., an S&P 500 index fund) is fully hedged by selling an S&P 500 futures contract with 60 days to settlement, which is priced at its theoretical value. The return on this hedged position will be the 60-day risk-free return. Notice what has been done. If a manager wanted to temporarily eliminate all exposure to the S&P 500, she could sell all the stocks and, with the funds received, invest in a Treasury bill. By using a futures contract, the manager can eliminate exposure to the S&P 500 by hedging, and the hedged position will earn the same return as that on a Treasury bill. The manager thereby saves on the transaction costs associated with selling a stock portfolio. Moreover, when the manager wants to get back into the stock market, rather than having to incur the transaction costs associated with buying stocks, she simply removes the hedge by buying an identical number of stock index futures contracts.

Cross Hedging In practice, hedging is not a simple exercise. When hedging with stock index futures, a perfect hedge can be obtained only if the return on the portfolio being hedged is identical to the return on the futures contract.

The effectiveness of a hedged stock portfolio is determined by:

1. The relationship between the cash portfolio and the index underlying the futures contract.
2. The relationship between the cash price and futures price when a hedge is placed and when it is lifted (liquidated).

Recall that the difference between the cash price and the futures price is the basis. It is only at the settlement that the basis is known with certainty. As explained earlier, at the settlement date, the basis is zero. If a hedge is lifted at the settlement date, the basis is therefore known. However, if the hedge is lifted at any other time, the basis is not known in advance. The uncertainty about the basis at the time a hedge is to be lifted is called *basis risk*. Consequently, *hedging involves the substitution of basis risk for price risk*.

A stock index futures contract has a stock index as its underlying. Since the portfolio that an asset manager seeks to hedge will typically have different characteristics from the underlying stock index, there will be a difference in return pattern of the portfolio being hedged and the futures contract. This practice—hedging with a futures contract that is different from the underlying being hedged—is called *cross hedging*. In the commodity futures markets, this occurs, for example, when a farmer who grows okra hedges that crop by using corn futures contracts because there are no exchange-traded contracts in which okra is the underlying. In the stock market, an asset manager who wishes to hedge a stock portfolio must choose the stock index, or combination of stock indexes, that best (but imperfectly) tracks the portfolio.

Consequently, cross hedging adds another dimension to basis risk because the portfolio does not track the return on the stock index perfectly. Mispricing of a stock index futures contract is a major portion of basis risk and is largely random.

The foregoing points about hedging will be made clearer in the illustrations that follows.

Hedge Ratio To implement a hedging strategy, it is necessary to determine not only which stock index futures contract to use, but also how many of the contracts to take a position in (i.e., how many to sell in a short hedge and buy in a long hedge). The number of contracts depends on the relative return volatility of the portfolio to be hedged and the return volatility of the futures contract. The hedge ratio is the ratio of volatility of the portfolio to be hedged and the return volatility of the futures contract.

It is tempting to use the portfolio's beta as a hedge ratio because it is an indicator of the sensitivity of a portfolio's return to the stock index return. It appears, then, to be an ideal way to adjust for the sensitivity of the return of the portfolio to be hedged. However, applying beta relative to a stock index as a sensitivity adjustment to a stock index futures contract assumes that the index and the futures contract have the same volatility. If futures were always to sell at their fair price, this would be a reasonable assumption. However, mispricing is an extra element of volatility in a stock index futures contract. Since the futures contract is more volatile than the underlying index, using a portfolio beta as a sensitivity adjustment would result in a portfolio being overhedged.

The most accurate sensitivity adjustment would be the beta of a portfolio relative to the futures contract. It can be shown that the beta of a portfolio relative to a futures contract is equivalent to the product of the portfolio relative to the underlying index and the beta of the index relative to the futures contract.[1] The beta in each case is estimated using regression analysis in which the data are historical returns for the portfolio to be hedged, the stock index, and the stock index futures contract.

The regression estimated is

$$r_P = a_P + B_{PI}r_I + e_P$$

where

r_P = the return on the portfolio to be hedged
r_I = the return on the stock index
B_{PI} = the beta of the portfolio relative to the stock index
a_P = the intercept of the relationship
e_P = the error term

and

$$r_I = a_I + B_{IF}\, r_F + e_I$$

where

r_F = the return on the stock index futures contract
B_{IF} = the beta of the stock index relative to the stock index futures contract
a_I = the intercept of the relationship
e_I = the error term

Given B_{PI} and B_{IF}, the minimum risk hedge ratio can then be expressed as

$$\text{Hedge ratio} = B_{PI} \times B_{IF}$$

---

[1] See Peters (1987).

The coefficient of determination of the regression (i.e., R-squared) will indicate how good the estimated relationship is and thereby allow the asset manager to assess the likelihood of success of the proposed hedge.

The number of contracts needed can be calculated using the following three steps after B_{PI} and B_{IF} are estimated:

Step 1. Determine the equivalent market index units of the market by dividing the market value of the portfolio to be hedged by the current index price of the futures contract:

$$\text{Equivalent market index units} = \frac{\text{Market value of the portfolio to be hedged}}{\text{Current index value of the futures contract}}$$

Step 2. Multiply the equivalent market index units by the hedge ratio to obtain the beta-adjusted equivalent market index units:

Beta-adjusted equivalent market index units
= Hedge ratio × Equivalent market index units

or

Beta-adjusted equivalent market index units
= BPI × BIF × Equivalent market index units

Step 3. Divide the beta-adjusted equivalent units by the multiple specified by the stock index futures contract:

$$\text{Number of contracts} = \frac{\text{Beta-adjusted equivalent market index units}}{\text{Multiple of the contract}}$$

We use two examples to illustrate the implementation of a hedge and the risks associated with hedging that are adapted from Fabozzi and Peters (1989). While the illustration is over 20 years old, it still brings out the major points discussed in this chapter.

In our first illustration, consider a portfolio manager on July 1, 1986, who is managing a $100 million portfolio that is identical to the S&P 500. The manager wants to hedge against a possible market decline. More specifically, the manager wants to hedge the portfolio until August 31, 1986. To hedge against an adverse market move during the period July 1, 1986, to August 31, 1986, the portfolio manager decides to enter into a short hedge by selling the S&P 500 futures contracts that settled in September 1986. On July 1, 1986, the September 1986 futures contract was selling for 253.95.

Since the portfolio to be hedged is identical to the S&P 500, the beta of the portfolio relative to the index (BPI) is, of course, 1. The beta relative to the futures contract (BIF) was estimated to be 0.745. Therefore, the number of contracts needed to hedge the $100 million portfolio is computed as follows:

Step 1.

$$\text{Equivalent market index units} = \frac{\$100,000,000}{253.95} = \$393,778$$

Step 2.

$$\text{Beta-adjusted equivalent market index units} = 1 \times 0.745 \times \$393,778$$
$$= \$293,365$$

Step 3. The multiple for the S&P 500 contract is 500. Therefore,

$$\text{Number of contracts to be sold} = \frac{\$293,365}{\$500} = 587$$

This means that the futures position was equal to $74,534,325 (587 × $500 × 253.95). On August 31, 1986, the hedge was removed. The portfolio that mirrored the S&P 500 had lost $6,796,540. At the time the hedge was lifted, the September 1986 S&P 500 contract was selling at 233.15. Since the contract was sold on July 1, 1986, for 253.95 and bought back on August 31, 1986, for 233.15, there was a gain of 20.8 index units per contract. For the 587 contracts, the gain was $6,104,800 (20.8 × $500 × 587). This results in a small loss of $691,740 ($6,104,800 gain on the futures position and $6,796,540 loss on the portfolio). The total transaction costs for the futures position would have been less than $12,000. Remember, had the asset manager not hedged the position, the loss would have been $6,796,540.

Let's analyze this hedge to see not only why it was successful but also why it was not a perfect hedge. As explained earlier, in hedging, basis risk is substituted for price risk. Consider the basis risk in this hedge. At the time the hedge was placed, the cash index was at 252.04, and the futures contract was selling at 253.95. The basis was equal to −1.91 index units (the cash index of 252.04 minus the futures price of 253.95). At the same time, it was calculated that, based on the cost of carry, the theoretical basis was −1.26 index units. That is, the fair value for this futures contract at the time the hedge was placed should have been 253.3. Thus, the futures contract was mispriced by 0.65 index unit.

When the hedge was removed at the close of August 31, 1986, the cash index stood at 234.91, and the futures contract at 233.15. Thus, the basis changed from –1.91 index units at the time the hedge was initiated to –1.76 index units (234.91 – 233.15) when the hedge was lifted. The basis had changed by 3.67 index units (1.91 + 1.76) alone, or $1,835 per contract (3.67 times the multiple of $500). This means that the basis alone returned $1,077,145 for the 587 contracts ($1,835 × 587). The index dropped 17.13 index units, for a gain of $8,565 per contract, or $5,027,655. Thus, the futures position returned $1,077,145 due to the change in the basis risk, and $5,027,655 due to the change in the index. Combined, this comes out to be the $6,104,800 gain in the futures position.

We examined basis risk in our illustration. Because we were hedging a portfolio that was constructed to replicate the S&P 500 index using the S&P 500 futures contract, there was no cross-hedging risk. However, most portfolios are not matched to the S&P 500. Consequently, cross-hedging risk results because the estimated beta for the price behavior of the portfolio may not behave as predicted by B_{PI}. To illustrate this situation, suppose that a money manager owned all the stocks in the Dow Jones Industrial Average on July 1, 1986. The market value of the portfolio held was $100 million. Also assume that the portfolio manager wanted to hedge the position against a decline in stock prices from July 1, 1986, to August 31, 1986, using the September 1986 S&P 500 futures contract. Since the S&P 500 futures September contract is used here to hedge a portfolio of Dow Jones Industrials to August 31, 1986, this is a cross hedge.

Information about the S&P 500 cash index and futures contract when the hedge was placed on July 1, 1986, and when it was removed on August 31, 1986, was given in the previous illustration. The beta of the index relative to the futures contract (B_{IF}) was 0.745. The Dow Jones Index in a regression analysis was found to have a beta relative to the S&P 500 of 1.05 (with an R-squared of 93%). We follow the three steps enumerated above to obtain the number of contracts to sell:

Step 1.

$$\text{Equivalent market index units} = \frac{\$100,000,000}{253.95} = \$393,778$$

Step 2.

$$\text{Beta-adjusted equivalent market index units} = 1.05 \times 0.745 \times \$393,778$$
$$= \$308,033$$

Step 3. The multiple for the S&P 500 contract is 500. Therefore,

$$\text{Number of contracts to be sold} = \frac{\$308,033}{500} = 616$$

During the period of the hedge, the Dow Jones Index actually lost $7,350,000. This meant a loss of 7.35% on the portfolio consisting of the Dow Jones stocks. Since 616 S&P 500 futures contracts were sold and the gain per contract was 20.58 points, the gain from the futures position was $6,338,640 ($20.58 × 616 × 500) from the futures position. This means that the hedged position resulted in a loss of $1,011,360, or equivalently, a return of −1.01%.

We already analyzed why this was not a perfect hedge. In the previous illustration, we explained how changes in the basis affected the outcome. Let's look at how the relationship between the Dow Jones and the S&P 500 Index affected the outcome. As stated in the previous illustration, the S&P 500 over this same period declined in value by 6.8%. With the beta of the portfolio relative to the S&P 500 Index (1.05), the expected decline in the value of the portfolio based on the movement in the S&P 500 was 7.14% (1.05 × 6.8%). Had this actually occurred, the Dow Jones portfolio would have lost only $7,140,000 rather than $7,350,000, and the net loss from the hedge would have been $801,360, or −0.8%. Thus, there is a difference of a $210,000 loss due to the Dow Jones performing differently than predicted by beta.

Constructing an Indexed Portfolio

As we explained in Chapter 18, some institutional equity funds are indexed to some broad-based stock market index. There are management fees and transaction costs associated with creating a portfolio to replicate a stock index that has been targeted to be matched. The higher these costs, the greater the divergence between the performance of the indexed portfolio and the target index. Moreover, because a fund manager creating an indexed portfolio will not purchase all the stocks that make up the index, the indexed portfolio is exposed to tracking error risk. Instead of using the cash market to construct an indexed portfolio, the manager can use stock index futures.

Let's illustrate how and under what circumstances stock index funds can be used to create an indexed portfolio. If stock index futures are priced according to their theoretical value, a portfolio consisting of a long position in stock index futures and Treasury bills will produce the same portfolio return as that of the underlying cash index. To see this, suppose that an index fund manager wishes to index a $90 million portfolio using the S&P 500 as the target index. Also assume the following:

1. The S&P 500 at the time was 1200.
2. The S&P 500 futures index with six months to settlement is currently selling for 1212.
3. The expected dividend yield for the S&P 500 for the next six months is 2%.
4. Six-month Treasury bills are currently yielding 3%.

The theoretical futures price is found using the formula presented earlier:

Cash market price + Cash market price × (Financing cost – Dividend yield)

Because the financing cost is 3% and the dividend yield is 2%, the theoretical futures price is

$$1200 + 1200 \times (0.03 - 0.02) = 1212$$

and, therefore, the futures price in the market is equal to the theoretical futures price.

Consider two strategies that the index fund manager may choose to pursue:

Strategy 1. Purchase $90 million of stocks in such a way as to replicate the performance of the S&P 500.

Strategy 2. Buy 600 S&P 500 futures contracts with settlement six months from now at 1212, and invest $90 million in six-month Treasury bills.[2]

How will the two strategies perform under various scenarios for the S&P 500 value when the contract settles six months from now? Let's investigate three scenarios:

Scenario 1. The S&P 500 increases to 1320 (an increase of 10%).

Scenario 2. The S&P 500 remains at 1200.

Scenario 3. The S&P500 declines to 1080 (a decrease of 10%).

---

[2] There are two points to note here. First, this illustration ignores margin requirements. The Treasury bills can be used for initial margin. Second, 600 contracts are selected in this strategy because with the current market index at 1200 and a multiple of $500, the cash value of 600 contracts is $90 million.

At settlement, the futures price converges to the value of the index. Table 20.1 shows the value of the portfolio for both strategies for each of the three scenarios. As can be seen, for a given scenario, the performance of the two strategies is identical.

This result should not be surprising because a futures contract can be replicated by buying the instrument underlying the futures contract with borrowed funds. In the case of indexing, we are replicating the underlying instrument by buying the futures contract and investing in Treasury bills. Therefore, if stock index futures contracts are properly priced, index fund managers can use stock index futures to create an index fund.

Several points should be noted. First, in strategy 1, the ability of the portfolio to replicate the S&P 500 depends on how well the portfolio is constructed to track the index. On the other hand, assuming that the expected dividends are realized and that the futures contract is fairly priced, the futures–Treasury bill portfolio (strategy 2) will mirror the performance of the S&P 500 exactly. Thus tracking error is reduced.

Second, the cost of transacting is less for strategy 2. For example, if the cost of one S&P 500 futures is $15, then the transaction costs for strategy 2 would be only $9,000 for a $90 million fund. This would be considerably less than the transaction costs associated with the acquisition and maintenance of a broadly diversified stock portfolio designed to replicate the S&P 500. In addition, for a large fund that wishes to index, the market impact cost is lessened by using stock index futures rather than using the cash market to create an index.

The third point is that custodial costs are obviously less for an index fund created using stock index futures. The fourth point is that the performance of the synthetically created index fund will depend on variation margin.

In synthetically creating an index fund, we assumed that the futures contract was fairly priced. Suppose, instead, that the stock index futures price is less than the theoretical futures price (i.e., the futures contracts are cheap). If that situation occurs, the index fund manager can enhance the indexed portfolio's return by buying the futures and buying Treasury bills. That is, the return on the futures–Treasury bill portfolio will be greater than that on the underlying index when the position is held to the settlement date.

To see this, suppose that in our previous illustration, the current futures price is 1204 instead of 1200, so that the futures contract is cheap (undervalued). The futures position for the three scenarios in Table 20.1 would be $600,000 greater (2 index units × $500 × 600 contracts). Therefore, the value of the portfolio and the dollar return for all three scenarios will be greater by $600,000 by buying the futures contract and Treasury bills rather than buying the stocks directly.

TABLE 20.1 Comparison of Portfolio Value from Purchasing Stocks to Replicate an Index and a Futures/Treasury Bill Strategy when the Futures Contract is Fairly Priced

Assumptions:
1. Amount to be invested = $90 million
2. Current value of S&P 500 = 1200
3. Current value of S&P futures contract = 1212
4. Expected dividend yield = 2%
5. Yield on Treasury bills = 3%
6. Number of S&P 500 contracts to be purchased = 600

Strategy 1. Direct Purchase of Stocks

	Index Value at Settlement		
	1320	1200	1080
Change in index value	10%	0%	–10%
Market value of portfolio that mirrors the index	$99,000,000	$90,000,000	$81,000,000
Dividends (0.02 × $90,000,000)	$1,800,000	$1,800,000	$1,800,000
Value of portfolio	$100,800,000	$91,800,000	$82,800,000
Dollar return	$1,080,000	$180,000	$(720,000)

Strategy 2. Futures/T-Bill Portfolio

	Index Value at Settlement[a]		
	1320	1200	1080
Gain /loss for 600 contracts			
(600 $500 × gain/ per contract)	$8,100,000	–$9,000,000	–$9,990,000
Value of Treasury bills ($90,000,000 × 1.03)	$92,700,000	$92,700,000	$92,700,000
Value of portfolio	$100,800,000	$91,800,000	$82,800,000
Dollar return	$1,080,000	$180,000	$(720,000)

[a] Because of convergence of cash and futures price, the S&P 500 cash index and stock index futures price will be the same.

Alternatively, if the futures contract is expensive based on its theoretical price, an index fund manager who owns stock index futures and Treasury bills will swap that portfolio for the stocks in the index. An index fund manager who swaps between the futures–Treasury bills portfolio and a stock portfolio based on the value of the futures contract relative to the cash market index is attempting to enhance the portfolio's return. This strategy, referred to as a *stock replacement strategy*, is one of several strategies used to attempt to enhance the return of an indexed portfolio.

Transaction costs can be reduced measurably by using a return enhancement strategy. Whenever the difference between the actual basis and the theoretical basis exceeds the market impact of a transaction, the aggressive manager should consider replacing stocks with futures or vice versa. Once the strategy has been put into effect, several subsequent scenarios may unfold. For example, consider an index manager who has a portfolio of stock index futures and Treasury bills. First, should the futures contract become sufficiently rich relative to stocks, the futures position is sold and the stocks repurchased, with program trading used to execute the buy orders. Second, should the futures contract remain at fair value, the position is held until expiration, when the futures settle at the cash index value and stocks are repurchased at the market at close. Should an index manager own a portfolio of stocks and the futures contract becomes cheap relative to stocks, then the manager will sell the stocks and buy the stock index futures contracts.

USING TREASURY BOND AND NOTE FUTURES CONTRACTS IN BOND PORTFOLIO MANAGEMENT

Basic Features of Treasury Bond and Note Futures Contracts

The Treasury bond and note futures contracts and traded on the Chicago Board of Trade (CBOT). The underlying instrument for this contract is $100,000 par value of a hypothetical 20-year coupon bond. This hypothetical bond's coupon rate is called the *notional coupon*. Suppose that the notional coupon is 6%. There are three Treasury note futures contracts: 10-year, 5-year, and 2-year. All three contracts are modeled after the Treasury bond futures contract and are traded on the CBOT. The underlying instrument for the 10-year Treasury note contract is $100,000 par value of a hypothetical 10-year 6% Treasury note. Treasury futures contracts trade with March, June, September, and December settlement months. The futures price is quoted in terms of par being 100. Since the bond and notes futures contract are similar, for the remainder of our discussion we will focus on the bond futures contract.

We have been referring to the underlying instrument as a hypothetical Treasury bond. While some interest rate futures contracts can only be settled in cash, the seller (the short) of a Treasury bond futures contract who chooses to make delivery rather than liquidate his or her position by buying back the contract prior to the settlement date must deliver some Treasury bond. This begs the question "which Treasury bond"? The CBOT allows the seller to deliver one of several Treasury bonds that the CBOT specifies are acceptable for delivery. A trader who is short a particular bond is always concerned with the risk of being unable to obtain sufficient securities to cover their position.

The set of all bonds that meet the delivery requirements for a particular contract is called the *deliverable basket*. The CBOT makes its determination of the Treasury issues that are acceptable for delivery from all outstanding Treasury issues that have at least 15 years to maturity from the first day of the delivery month. For settlement purposes, the CBOT specifies that a given issue's term to maturity is calculated in complete three month increments (that is, complete quarters). For example, the actual maturity of the issue is 15 years and five months would be rounded down to a maturity of 15 years and one quarter (three months). Moreover, all bonds delivered by the seller must be of the same issue.

It is important to keep in mind that while the underlying Treasury bond for this contract is a hypothetical issue and therefore cannot itself be delivered into the futures contract, the bond futures contract is not a cash settlement contract. The only way to close out a Treasury bond futures contract is to either initiate an offsetting futures position or to deliver a Treasury issue from the deliverable basket.

The delivery process for the Treasury bond futures contract is innovative and has served as a model for government bond futures contracts traded on various exchanges throughout the world. On the settlement date, the seller of the futures contract (the short) is required to deliver the buyer (the long) $100,000 par value of a 6% 20-year Treasury bond. As noted, no such bond exists, so the seller must choose a bond from the deliverable basket to deliver to the long. Suppose the seller selects a 5% coupon, 20-year Treasury bond to settle the futures contract. Since the coupon of this bond is less than the notional coupon of 6%, this would be unacceptable to the buyer who contracted to receive a 6% coupon, 20-year bond with a par value of $100,000. Alternatively, suppose the seller is compelled to deliver a 7% coupon, 20-year bond. Since the coupon of this bond is greater than the notional coupon of 6%, the seller would find this unacceptable. In summary, how do we adjust for the fact that bonds in the deliverable basket have coupons and maturities that differ from the notional coupon of 6%?

To make delivery equitable to both parties, the CBOT uses conversion factors for adjusting the price of each Treasury issue that can be delivered to satisfy the Treasury bond futures contract. Given the conversion factor for an issue and the futures price, the adjusted price is found by multiplying the conversion factor by the futures price. The adjusted price is called the *converted price*. That is,

Converted price = Contract size × Futures settlement price
× Conversion factor

For example, suppose the settlement price of a Treasury bond futures contract is 110 and the issue selected by short has a conversion factor of 1.25. Given the contract size is $100,000, the converted price is

$$\$100,000 \times 1.10 \times 1.25 = \$137,500$$

The price that the buyer must pay the seller when a Treasury bond is delivered is called the *invoice price*. Intuitively, the invoice price should be the futures settlement price plus accrued interest. However, as just noted, the seller can choose any Treasury issue from the deliverable basket. To make delivery fair to both parties, the invoice price must be adjusted using the conversion factor of the actual Treasury issue delivered. The invoice price is

Invoice price = Contract size × Futures settlement price
× Conversion factor + Accrued interest

In selecting the issue to be delivered, the short will select from all the deliverable issues the one that will give the largest rate of return from a *cash-and-carry trade*. A cash-and-carry-trade is one in which a cash bond that is acceptable for delivery is purchased with borrowed funds and simultaneously the Treasury bond futures contract is sold. The bond purchased can be delivered to satisfy the short futures position. Thus, by buying the Treasury issue that is acceptable for delivery and selling the futures, an investor has effectively sold the bond at the delivery price (that is, the converted price).

A rate of return can be calculated for this trade. This rate of return is referred to as the *implied repo rate*. Once the implied repo rate is calculated for each bond in the deliverable basket, the issue selected will be the one that has the highest implied repo rate (that is, the issue that gives the maximum return in a cash-and-carry trade). The issue with the highest return is referred to as the cheapest-to-deliver issue. This issue plays a key role in the pricing of a Treasury futures contract.[3]

In addition to the choice of which acceptable Treasury issue to deliver—sometimes referred to as the *quality option* or *swap option*—the short has at

---

[3] While a particular Treasury bond may be the cheapest to deliver today, changes in interest rates, for example, may cause some other issue to be the cheapest to deliver at a future date. A sensitivity analysis can be performed to determine how a change in yield affects the cheapest to deliver bond. In particular, the sensitivity analysis identifies which bond in the deliverable basket is cheapest to deliver following various shocks to the yield curve.

least two more options granted under CBOT delivery guidelines. The short is permitted to decide when in the delivery month, delivery actually will take place. This is called the *timing option*. The other option is the right of the short to give notice of intent to deliver up to 8:00 P.M. Chicago time after the closing of the exchange (3:15 P.M. Chicago time) on the date when the futures settlement price has been fixed. This option is referred to as the *wildcard option*. The quality option, the timing option, and the wildcard option (in sum referred to as the *delivery options*), mean that the long position can never be sure which Treasury bond issue will be delivered or when it will be delivered. These three delivery options are summarized as follows:

Delivery Option	Description
Quality or swap option	Choice of which acceptable Treasury issue to deliver
Timing option	Choice of when in delivery month to deliver
Wild card option	Choice to deliver after the closing price of the futures contract is determined

Pricing of Treasury Bond and Note Futures Contracts

Once again, let's look at how the specifics of a futures contract necessitate the refinement of the theoretical futures pricing model. The two assumptions that require a refinement of the model are the assumptions regarding no interim cash flows and the deliverable asset and the settlement date are known.

With respect to interim cash flows, for a Treasury futures contract the underlying is a Treasury note or a Treasury bond. Unlike a stock index futures contract, the timing of the interest payments that will be made by the U.S. Department of the Treasury for a given issue that is acceptable as deliverable for a contract is known with certainty and can be incorporated into the pricing model. However, the reinvestment interest that can be earned from the payment dates to the settlement of the contract is unknown and depends on prevailing interest rates at each payment date.

Now let's look at the implications regarding a known deliverable and known settlement date. Neither assumption is consistent with the delivery rules for some futures contracts. For U.S. Treasury note and bond futures contracts, for example, the contract specifies that any one of several Treasury issues that is acceptable for delivery can be delivered to satisfy the contract. Such issues are referred to as *deliverable issues*. The selection of which deliverable issue to deliver is an option granted to the party who is short the contract (that is, the seller). Hence, the party that is long the contract (that is, the buyer of the contract) does not know the specific Treasury issue that will be delivered. However, market participants can determine the *cheapest-to-deliver* issue from the issues that are acceptable for delivery. It is this issue that is used in obtaining the theoretical futures price. The net effect of the short's option to select the issue to deliver to satisfy the contract is that it reduces the theoretical future price by an amount equal to the value of the delivery option granted to the short.

Moreover, unlike other futures contract, the Treasury bond and note contracts do not have a delivery date. Instead, there is a delivery month. The short has the right to select when in the delivery month to make delivery. The effect of this option granted to the short is once again to reduce the theoretical futures price. More specifically,

Theoretical futures price adjusted for delivery options

= Cash market price + (Cash market price) × (Financing cost − Cash yield)

− Value of the delivery options granted to the short

Bond Portfolio Management Applications

There are various ways an asset money manager can use interest rate futures contracts in addition to speculating on the movement of interest rates.

Controlling the Interest Rate Risk of a Portfolio

Asset managers can use interest rate futures to alter the interest rate sensitivity, or duration, of a portfolio. Those with strong expectations about the direction of the future course of interest rates will adjust the duration of their portfolios so as to capitalize on their expectations. Specifically, a money manager who expects rates to increase will shorten duration; a money manager who expects interest rates to decrease will lengthen duration. While money managers can use cash market instruments to alter the durations of their portfolios, using futures contracts provides a quicker and less expensive means for doing so (on either a temporary or permanent basis).

A formula to approximate the number of futures contracts necessary to adjust the portfolio duration to a new level is

$$\frac{\left(\begin{array}{c}\text{Target portfolio} \\ \text{duration}\end{array} - \begin{array}{c}\text{Current portfolio} \\ \text{duration}\end{array}\right) \times \text{Market value of the portfolio}}{\text{Dollar duration of the futures contract}}$$

The dollar duration of the futures contract is the dollar price sensitivity of the futures contract to a change in interest rates.

Notice that if the asset manager wishes to increase the portfolio's current duration, the numerator of the formula is positive. This means that futures contracts will be purchased. That is, buying futures increases the duration of the portfolio. The opposite is true if the objective is to shorten the portfolio's current duration: The numerator of the formula is negative and this means that futures must be sold. So selling futures contracts reduces the portfolio's duration.

Hedging

Hedging is a special case of risk control where the target duration sought is zero. If cash and futures prices move together, any loss realized by the hedger from one position (whether cash or futures) will be offset by a profit on the other position. When the net profit or loss from the positions is exactly as anticipated, the hedge is referred to as a perfect hedge.

In practice, hedging is not that simple as noted earlier for stock index futures. In bond portfolio management, typically the bond to be hedged is not identical to the bond underlying the futures contract and, therefore, there is cross hedging. This may result in substantial basis risk.

Conceptually, cross hedging is somewhat more complicated than hedging deliverable securities because it involves two relationships. In the case of bond futures contracts, the first relationship is between the cheapest-to-deliver issue and the futures contract. The second relationship in the case of bond futures contracts is the relationship between the security to be hedged and the cheapest-to-deliver issue.

The key to minimizing risk in a cross hedge is to choose the right hedge ratio. The hedge ratio depends on volatility weighting, or weighting by relative changes in value. The purpose of a hedge is to use gains or losses from a futures position to offset any difference between the target sale price and the actual sale price of the asset.

Accordingly, the hedge ratio is chosen with the intention of matching the volatility (that is, the dollar change) of the Treasury bond futures contract to the volatility of the asset. Consequently, the hedge ratio for a bond is given by

$$\text{Hedge ratio} = \frac{\text{Volatility of bond to be hedged}}{\text{Volatility of Treasury bond futures contract}}$$

For hedging purposes we are concerned with volatility in absolute dollar terms. To calculate the dollar volatility of a bond, one must know the precise time that volatility is to be calculated (because volatility generally declines as a bond seasons), as well as the price or yield at which to calculate volatility (because higher yields generally reduce dollar volatility for a given yield change). The relevant point in the life of the bond for calculating volatility is the point at which the hedge will be lifted. Volatility at any other point is essentially irrelevant because the goal is to lock in a price or rate only on that particular day. Similarly, the relevant yield at which to calculate volatility initially is the target yield. Consequently, the "volatility of bond to be hedged" referred to in the equation for the hedge ratio is the price value of a basis point for the bond on the date the hedge is expected to be delivered.

We will use an illustration to show how to calculate the hedge ratio and then verify that it will do an effective job in hedging a bond position.[4] We will assume that on December 24, 2007, a bond portfolio manager wants to hedge a position in Procter & Gamble (P&G) 5.55% of 3/5/2037 that he anticipates selling on March 31, 2008. The par value of the P&G bonds is $10 million. The portfolio manager decides that he will use the March 2008 Treasury bond futures to hedge the bond position which he can settle on March 31, 2008. Because the portfolio manager is trying to protect against a decline in the value of the P&G bonds between December 24, 2007, and the anticipated sale date, he will short (sell) a number of March 2008 Treasury bond futures contracts. Because the bond to be hedged is a corporate bond and the hedging instrument is a Treasury bond futures contract, this is an example of a cross hedge.

On December 24, 2007, the P&G bond was selling at 97.127 and offering a yield of 5.754%. Since the par value of the P&G bond held in the portfolio is $10 million, this means that the market value of the bond is $9,712,700 (97.127 × $10,000,000). The price of the March 2008 Treasury bond futures contract on December 24, 2007, was 114.375. The portfolio manager determines that the Treasury 6.25s of 8/15/2023 issue was the cheapest-to-deliver issue for the March 2008 Treasury bond futures contract. The price of this Treasury issue is 117.719 (a yield of 4.643%) and the conversion factor for this Treasury issue is 1.0246. The yield spread between the P&G bond and the cheapest-to-deliver issue was 111.1 basis points (5.754% − 4.643%). To simplify the analysis, the portfolio manager assumes that this 111.1 yield spread will remain the same over the period the bond is hedged.

What target price is the portfolio manager seeking to lock in for the P&G bonds? One might think it is the current market price of the P&G bonds, 97.127. However, that is not correct. The target price is determined by the March 2008 Treasury bond futures contract that is being shorted. Some calculations are required to determine the target price. We begin by determining the target price for the CTD issue. Given the conversion factor for the CTD issue (1.0246) and the futures price for the March 2007 con-

---

[4] We thank Peter Ru of Morgan Stanley for providing this illustration.

tract (114.375), the target price for the CTD issue is found by multiplying these two values. that is, the target price for the CTD issue is 117.1886. But there is a target yield for the CTD issue that corresponds to the price of 117.1886. For the Treasury 6.25s of August 15, 2023, issue, the yield if the price is 117.1886 on March 31, 2008 (the settlement date), is 4.670%. Therefore, the target yield for the CTD issue is 4.670%.

Given the target for yield for the CTD issue of 4.670%, the portfolio manager can calculate the target yield for the P&G bond. Here the portfolio manager makes use of the assumption that yield spread between the P&G bond and the CTD issue remains at 111.1 basis points. For the target yield for the CTD issue of 4.670%, the portfolio manager adds the 111.1 basis point spread, giving a target yield for the P&G bond of 5.781%. The final step to estimate the target price for the P&G bond as of March 31, 2008, is to determine the price for the P&G bond on the settlement date given a target yield of 5.781%. This is a straightforward calculation given the coupon and maturity date of the P&G bond. The target price is 96.788. For a $10 million par value holding of the P&G bond, the target market value that the portfolio manager seeks is $9,678,000.

To calculate the hedge ratio, the portfolio manager needs to know the volatility of the March 2008 Treasury bond futures contract. Fortunately, knowing the volatility of the bond to be hedged relative to the cheapest-to-deliver issue and the volatility of the cheapest-to-deliver bond relative to the futures contract, we can modify the hedge ratio as follows:

$$\text{Hedge ratio} = \frac{\text{Volatility of bond to be hedged}}{\text{Volatility of CTD issue}}$$
$$\times \frac{\text{Volatility of CTD bond}}{\text{Volatility of Treasury bond futures contract}}$$

The second ratio above can be shown to equal the conversion factor for the CTD issue. Assuming a fixed yield spread between the bond to be hedged and the CTD issue, the equation can be rewritten as

$$\text{Hedge ratio} = \frac{\text{PVBP of bond to be hedged}}{\text{PVBP of CTD issue}} \times \text{Conversion factor for CTD issue}$$

where PVBP is equal to the price value of a basis point. As explained in the previous chapter, the PVBP is computed by changing the yield of a bond by one basis point and determining the change in the bond's price. It is a measure of price volatility to interest rate changes and related to duration.

The portfolio manager can calculate the PVBP of the P&G bond and the CTD issue from the target yield and the target price for the bonds at the settlement date. For the CTD issue, it is 0.1207 and for the P&G bond it is 0.1363. Substituting these two values plus the conversion factor for the CTD issue (1.0246) into the previous equation, we get

$$\text{Hedge ratio} = \frac{0.1363}{0.1207} \times 1.0246 = 1.157$$

Given the hedge ratio, the number of contracts that must be short is determined as

$$\text{Number of contracts} = \text{Hedge ratio} \times \frac{\text{Par value to be hedged}}{\text{Par value of the futures contract}}$$

Because the amount to be hedged is $10 million and each Treasury bond futures contract is for $100,000 par value, this means that the number of futures contracts that must be sold is

$$\text{Number of contracts} = \text{Hedge ratio} \times \frac{\$10,000,000}{\$100,000}$$
$$= 1.157 \times 100 = 116 \text{ contracts (rounded)}$$

Table 20.2 shows that if the simplifying assumptions that were made in this illustration to calculate the hedge ratio are satisfied, a futures hedge wherein 116 futures contracts are shorted very nearly locks in the target market value of $9,696,000 for $10 million par value of the P&G bond. There are refinements that can be made to the hedging procedure to improve this hedge.[5] However, these are unimportant for a basic understanding of hedging with Treasury bond futures contracts.

USING STOCK INDEX FUTURES AND TREASURY BOND FUTURES TO IMPLEMENT AN ASSET ALLOCATION DECISION

As explained in Chapter 17, one of the major steps is the allocation of funds among major asset classes. As the asset allocation of a client changes, it is necessary to shift funds among the asset classes. Funds can be shifted in one of two ways. The most obvious is by buying or selling the amount specified in the asset mix in the cash market. The costs associated with shifting funds in this manner are the transaction costs with respect to commissions, bid-ask spreads, and market impact. Moreover, there will be a disruption of the activities of the asset managers who are managing funds for each asset class. For example, a pension sponsor typically engages certain assets managers for managing equity funds, and different ones for managing bond funds.

---

[5] See Fabozzi (2006).

TABLE 20.2 Hedge of the $10 Million Par Value of Procter & Gamble 5.55% Expiring March 5, 2003, with March 2008 Treasury Bond Futures Contract with Settlement on March 31, 2008

Actual Sale Price of P&G Bond	Yield at Sale	Yield of Treasury[a]	Price of Treasury	Futures Price[b]	Gain (loss) on 116 contracts	Effective Sale Price[c]
8,000,000	7.204%	6.093%	101.544	99.106	1,771,194	9,771,194
8,200,000	7.010%	5.899%	103.508	101.023	1,548,862	9,748,862
8,400,000	6.824%	5.713%	105.438	102.907	1,330,323	9,730,323
8,600,000	6.645%	5.534%	107.341	104.764	1,114,875	9,714,875
8,800,000	6.472%	5.361%	109.224	106.601	901,748	9,701,748
9,000,000	6.306%	5.195%	111.071	108.404	692,606	9,692,606
9,200,000	6.144%	5.033%	112.914	110.203	484,008	9,684,008
9,400,000	5.989%	4.878%	114.714	111.960	280,164	9,680,164
9,600,000	5.838%	4.727%	116.504	113.707	77,476	9,677,476
9,800,000	5.691%	4.580%	118.282	115.442	(123,809)	9,676,191
10,000,000	5.550%	4.439%	120.021	117.139	(320,633)	9,679,367
10,200,000	5.412%	4.301%	121.755	118.831	(516,925)	9,683,075
10,400,000	5.278%	4.167%	123.469	120.505	(711,032)	9,688,968
10,600,000	5.149%	4.038%	125.149	122.144	(901,256)	9,698,744
10,800,000	5.022%	3.911%	126.832	123.787	(1,091,785)	9,708,215
11,000,000	4.899%	3.788%	128.490	125.405	(1,279,473)	9,720,527
11,200,000	4.780%	3.669%	130.120	126.996	(1,464,047)	9,735,953
11,400,000	4.663%	3.552%	131.749	128.586	(1,648,452)	9,751,548
11,600,000	4.550%	3.439%	133.347	130.145	(1,829,358)	9,770,642

[a] By assumption, the yield on the CTD issue (6.25% of August 15, 2003) is 111.1 basis points lower than the yield on the P&G bond.
[b] By convergence, the futures price equals the price of the CTD issue divided by 1.0246 (the conversion factor).
[c] Transaction costs and the financing of margin flows are ignored.

An asset allocation decision requiring the reallocation of funds will necessitate the withdrawal of funds from some asset managers and the placement of funds with others. If the shift is temporary, there will be a subsequent revision of the asset allocation, further disrupting the activities of the asset managers.

An alternative approach is to use the futures market to change an exposure to an asset class. As we explained earlier in this chapter, buying futures contracts increases exposure to the asset class underlying the futures contract, while selling futures contracts reduces it. For the major asset classes, equities and bonds, a client can use stock index futures and Treasury bond futures to alter the asset mix. The advantages shows of using financial futures contracts over transacting in the cash market for each asset class are (1) transaction costs are lower; (2) execution is faster in the futures market; (3) market impact costs are avoided or reduced because the plan sponsor has more time to buy and sell securities in the cash market; and (4) activities of the asset managers employed by the pension sponsor are not disrupted. A strategy of using futures for asset allocation by pension sponsors to avoid disrupting the activities of asset managers is sometimes referred to as an *overlay strategy*.

SUMMARY

In this chapter, we described stock index futures and Treasury bond futures contracts and how they can be employed in portfolio management. We also explained how the basic model for determining the theoretical futures price of a stock index futures contract and Treasury bond futures contract must be adjusted given the contract specifications. In addition to their use in managing a portfolio of equities and bonds, stock index futures and Treasury bond futures can be employed in an overlay strategy by a pension plan sponsor to implement an asset allocation decision

REFERENCES

Fabozzi, F. J. (2006). *Bond Markets, Analysis, and Strategies*. Upper Saddle River, NJ: Prentice Hall.

Fabozzi, F. J., and E. Peters (1989). Hedging with stock index futures. In F.J. Fabozzi and G.M. Kipnis (eds.), *The Handbook of Stock Index Futures and Options*. (pp. 188–222). Homewood, IL: Richard D. Irwin.

Peters, E. (1987). Equity portfolios: Components of risk and return. *Advances in Futures and Options Research*, 1B: 75–92.

CHAPTER 21

Use of Options in Portfolio Management

In Chapter 6, we described the basic feature of options, their risk-return characteristics, and the basic option positions. Options provide portfolio managers with another derivative tool to manage risk and to achieve the desired investment objective. As with futures contracts described in the previous chapter, options can be used to modify the risk characteristics of an investment portfolio, to enhance the expected return of a portfolio, and to reduce transaction costs associated with managing a portfolio.

Options can be classified as *listed options* (also called *exchange-traded options*) and *over-the-counter options*. A couple of advantages of listed options are that they provide accurate and consistent information about pricing and virtually eliminate counterparty risk. Moreover, because of these characteristics and the standardization of products, listed options often have low transaction costs and moderate to high liquidity. The issue of transaction costs and liquidity can play an important role in the decision to use derivatives as part of the investment process. However, there has been an explosion in OTC options, which suggests that portfolio managers find these products serve an important investment purpose.

As we did in the previous chapter, we begin our discussion of the use of options in equity portfolio management and then turn to bond portfolio management. We describe the types of listed options and OTC options.

USING STOCK OPTIONS AND INDEX OPTIONS IN EQUITY PORTFOLIO MANAGEMENT

Basic Features of Listed Equity Options

Listed options can be classified into four groups: (1) stock options, (2) index options, (3) Long-Term Equity Anticipation Securities™, and (4) FLexible EXchange Options™. We describe each in this section.

Stock Options

Stock options refer to listed options on individual stocks. The underlying is 100 shares of the designated stock. All listed stock options in the United States may be exercised any time before the expiration date; that is, they are American-style options. Option contracts for a given stock are based on expiration dates that fit on a cycle, typically nine months for a stock; for stock options the cycles are two near-term months plus two additional months from the January, February, or March quarterly cycles. Common cycles include January-April-July-October (JAJO) expiring options, February-May-August-November (FMAN) expiring options, and March-June-September-December (MJSD) expiring options.

Index Options

Index options are options where the underlying is a stock index rather than an individual stock. An index call option gives the option buyer the right to buy the underlying stock index, while a put option gives the option buyer the right to sell the underlying stock index. Unlike stock options where a stock can be delivered if the option is exercised by the option holder, it would be extremely complicated to settle an index option by delivering all the stocks that constitute the index. Instead, as with stock index futures, index options are cash settlement contracts. This means that if the option is exercised by the option holder, the option writer pays cash to the option buyer. There is no delivery of any stocks.

Index options include industry options, sector options, and style options. The most liquid index options are those on the S&P 100 index (OEX) and the S&P 500 index (SPX). Both trade on the Chicago Board Options Exchange (CBOE). Index options can be American or European style. The S&P 500 index option contract is European, while the OEX is American. Both index option contracts have specific standardized features and contract terms. Moreover, both have short expiration cycles, which are the four near-term months.

The dollar value of the stock index underlying an index option is equal to the current cash index value multiplied by the contract's multiple. That is,

Dollar value of the underlying index = Cash index value × Multiple

For example, suppose the cash index value for the S&P 500 is 1410. Since the contract multiple is $100, the dollar value of the SPX is $141,000 (= 1410 × $100).

For a stock option, the price at which the buyer of the option can buy or sell the stock is the strike price. For an index option, the strike index is the index value at which the buyer of the option can buy or sell the underlying stock index. The strike index is converted into a dollar value by multiplying the strike index by the multiple for the contract. For example, if the strike index is 1400, the dollar value is $140,000 (= 1400 × $100). If an investor purchases a call option on the SPX with a strike index of 1400, and exercises the option when the index value is 1410, the investor has the right to purchase the index for $140,000 when the market value of the index is $141,000. The buyer of the call option would then receive $1,000 from the option writer.

Long-Term Equity Anticipation Securities™ and FLexible EXchange Options™

Long-Term Equity Anticipation Securities™ (LEAPS) and FLexible EXchange Options™ (FLEX) are options that essentially modify an existing feature of either a stock option or an index option. For example, as noted above, stock option and index option contracts have short expiration cycles. LEAPS are designed to offer options with longer maturities. These contracts are available on individual stocks and some indexes. Stock option LEAPS are comparable to standard stock options except the maturities can range up to 39 months from the origination date. Index options LEAPS differ in size compared with standard index options having a multiplier of 10 rather than 100.

FLEX options allow users to specify the terms of the option contract for either a stock option or an index option. The process for entering into a FLEX option agreement is well documented by the Chicago Board Options Exchange, where these options trade. The value of FLEX options is the ability to customize the terms of the contract along four dimensions: underlying, strike price, expiration date, and settlement style. Moreover, the exchange provides a secondary market to offset or alter positions and an independent daily marking of prices. The development of the FLEX option is a response to the growing OTC market. The exchanges seek to make the FLEX option attractive by providing price discovery[1] through a competitive auction market, an active secondary market, daily price valuations, and the virtual elimination of counterparty risk. The FLEX option represents a link between listed options and OTC products.

Risk and Return Characteristics of Listed Options

In Chapter 6 we explained and illustrated the risk and return characteristics of the four basic option positions:

---

[1] *Price discovery* is the valuation of an asset that reflects all currently available information, including the value of the underlying.

- Buying a call option (long a call option)
- Selling a call option (short a call option)
- Buying a put option (long a put option)
- Selling a put option (short a put option)

More complicated positions are explained later in this chapter.

Buying calls or selling puts allows the investor to gain if the price of the underlying rises. Buying calls gives the investor unlimited upside potential, but limits the loss to the option price. Selling puts limits the profit to the option price, but provides no protection if the price of the underlying falls, with the maximum loss occurring if the price of the underlying falls to zero.

Buying puts and selling calls allows the investor to gain if the price of the underlying falls. Buying puts gives the investor upside potential, with the maximum profit realized if the price of the underlying declines to zero. However, the loss is limited to the option price. Selling calls limits the profit to the option price, but provides no protection if the stock price rises, with the maximum loss being theoretically unlimited.

In Chapter 6, our illustrations of the four option positions did not address the time value of money. Specifically, the buyer of an option must pay the seller the option price at the time the option is purchased. Therefore, the buyer must finance the purchase price of the option or, assuming the option's purchase price does not have to be borrowed, the buyer loses the income that can be earned by investing the amount of the option price until the option is sold or exercised. In contrast, assuming the seller does not have to use the option price as margin for the short position or can use an interest-earning asset as security, the seller has the opportunity to earn income from the proceeds of the option sale.

The time value of money changes the profit/loss profile of the option positions. The break-even price for the buyer and the seller of an option will not be the same as in our illustrations in Chapter 6. The break-even price for the underlying stock at the expiration date is higher for the buyer of the option; for the seller, it is lower.

Our comparisons of the option position with positions in the underlying stock also ignore the time value of money. We did not consider the fact that the underlying stock may pay dividends. The buyer of a call option is not entitled to any dividends paid by the corporation. The buyer of the underlying stock, however, would receive any interim cash flows and would have the opportunity to reinvest them. A complete comparison of the long call option position and the long position in the underlying stock must take into account the additional dollars gained from reinvesting any dividends. Moreover, any effect on the price of the underlying stock as a result of the distribution of cash must also be considered. This occurs, for example, when as a result of a dividend payment, the stock declines in price.

Later in this chapter, when we discuss strategies with options, we are more thorough by considering the cost of borrowing, the lending rate that reflects the opportunity to invest funds short term, and the dividends from the underlying stock or stock index or coupon interest payments from bonds.

Use of Listed Equity Options in Portfolio Management

Investors can use the listed options market to address a range of investment problems. In this section, we consider the use of calls, puts, and combinations in the context of the investment process, which could involve (1) risk management, (2) cost management, or (3) return enhancement.

Recall from our discussion in Chapter 6 that the distinction between options versus futures contracts is that the former have nonlinear payouts that will fundamentally alter the risk profile of an existing portfolio. The following basic strategies can be used to establish a hedged position in an individual stock or a replicating portfolio.

Risk Management Strategies

Risk management in the context of equity portfolio management focuses on price risk. Consequently, the strategies discussed in this section in some way address the risk of a price decline or a loss due to adverse price movement. Options can be used to create asymmetric risk exposures across all or part of the core equity portfolio. This allows the investor to hedge downside risk at a fixed cost with a specific limit to losses should the market turn down. The basic risk management objective is to create the optimal risk exposure and to achieve the target rate of return. Options can help accomplish this by reducing risk exposure. The various risk management strategies will also affect the expected rate of return on the position unless some form of inefficiency is involved. This may involve the current mix of risk and return or be the result of the use of options. Below we discuss two risk management strategies: protective put and collar.[2] We also provide a detailed illustration of these two strategies later in this chapter, when we demonstrate how they are applied to bond portfolio management.

Protective Put   Protective put strategies are valuable to portfolio manager who currently hold a long position in the underlying security or investors

---

[2] Other risk management strategies are discussed in Chapter 3 of Collins and Fabozzi (1999).

who desire upside exposure and downside protection. The motivation is either to hedge some or all of the total risk. Index put options hedge mostly market risk, while equity put options hedge the total risk associated with a specific stock. This allows portfolio managers to use protective put strategies for separating tactical and strategic strategies. Consider, for example, a portfolio manager who is concerned about exogenous or nonfinancial events increasing the level of risk in the marketplace. Furthermore, assume the portfolio manager is satisfied with the core portfolio holdings and the strategic mix. Put options could be employed as a tactical risk reduction strategy designed to preserve capital and still maintain strategic targets for portfolio returns.

For this reason, a portfolio manager concerned about downside risk is a candidate for a protective put strategy. Nonetheless, protective put strategies may not be suitable for all portfolio managers. The value of protective put strategies, however, is that they provide the investor with the ability to invest in volatile stocks with a degree of desired insurance and unlimited profit potential over the life of the strategy.

The protective put involves the purchase of a put option combined with a long stock position. This is the equivalent of a position in a call option on the stock combined with the purchase of risk-free discount bond. In fact, the combined position yields the well-known call option payout pattern. The put option is comparable to an insurance policy written against the long stock position. The option price is the cost of the insurance premium and the amount the option is out-of-the-money is the deductible. Just as in the case of insurance, the deductible is inversely related to the insurance premium. The deductible is reduced as the strike price increases, which makes the put option more in-the-money or less out-of-the-money. The higher strike price causes the put price to increase and makes the insurance policy more expensive.

The profitability of the strategy from inception to termination can be expressed as follows:

$$\text{Profit} = N_s(S_T - S_t) + N_p[\text{Max}(0, K - S_T) - \text{Put}]$$

where

N_s = number of shares of the stock

N_p = number of put options

S_T = price of stock at termination date (time T)

S_t = price of stock at time t

K = strike price

Put = put price

The profitability of the protective put strategy is the sum of the profit from the long stock position and the put option. If held to expiration, the minimum payout is the strike price (K) and the maximum is the stock price (S_T). If the stock price is below the strike price of the put option, the investor exercises the option and sells the stock to the option writer for K. If we assume that the number of shares $N_s = + N_p$, the number of options, then the loss would amount to

$$\text{Profit} = S_T - S_t + K - S_t - \text{Put} = K - S_t - \text{Put}$$

Notice that the price of the stock at the termination date does not enter into the profit equation.

For example, if the original stock price was \$100 (S_t), the strike price \$95 (K), the closing stock price \$80 (S_T), and the put premium (Put) \$4, then the profit would equal the following:

$$\text{Profit} = \$95 - \$100 - \$4 = -\$9$$

The portfolio manager would have realized a loss of \$20 without the hedge. If, on the other hand, the stock closed up \$20, then the profit would look like this:

$$\text{Profit} = S_T - S_t + \$100 - \text{Put} = \$120 - \$100 - \$4 = \$16$$

The cost of the insurance is 4% in percentage terms and is manifest as a loss of upside potential. If we add transaction costs, the shortfall is increased slightly. The maximum loss, however, is the sum of the put premium and the difference between the strike price and the original stock price, which is the amount of the deductible. The problem arises when the portfolio manager is measured against a benchmark and the cost of what amounted to an unused insurance policy causes the portfolio to underperform the benchmark. Equity managers can use stock selection, market timing, and the prudent use of options to reduce the cost of insurance. The break-even stock price is given by the sum of the original stock price and the put price. In this example, break-even is \$104, which is the stock price necessary to recover the put premium. The put premium is never really recovered because of the performance lag. This lag falls in significance as the return increases.

A graphical depiction of the protective put strategy is provided in Figure 21.1. The figure shows the individual long stock and long put positions and the combined impact, which is essentially a long call option. The maximum loss is the put premium plus the out-of-the-money amount, which is the insurance premium plus the deductible.

FIGURE 21.1 Protective Put Strategy

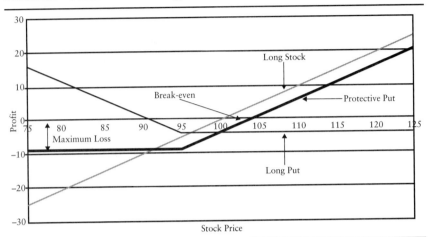

Collar An alternative to a protective put is a collar. The strategy consists of a long stock, a long put, and a short call. By varying the strike prices, a range of trade-offs among downside protection, costs, and upside potential is possible. When the long put is completely financed by the short call position, the strategy is referred to as a *zero-cost collar*.

Collars are designed for investors who currently hold a long equity position and want to achieve a level of risk reduction. The put exercise price establishes a floor and the call exercise price a ceiling. The resulting payout pattern is shown in Figure 21.2. The figure includes the components of the strategy and the combined position. This is an example of a near zero-cost collar. In order to pay for the put option, a call option was written with a strike price of $110. Selling this call option pays for the put premium, but caps the upside to 10.23%. The floor completes the collar and limits downside losses to the out-of-the money amount of the put option. In order to provide full insurance, an at-the-money put option would cost slightly above 6%, which would be paid for by limiting upside potential returns to 5%. Portfolio managers can determine the appropriate trade-offs and protection consistent with their objectives.

The profit equation for a collar is simply the sum of a long stock position, a long put, and a short call. That is,

$$\text{Profit} = N_s(S_T - S_t) + N_p[\text{Max}(0, K_p - S_T) - \text{Put}] - N_c[\text{Max}(0, S_T - K_c + \text{Call}]$$

where K_p and K_c are the strike price of the put and call, respectively, and Call is the price of the call option.

FIGURE 21.2 Protective Put Strategy

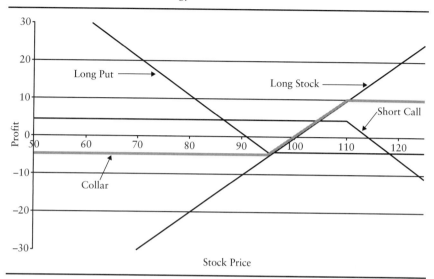

Management Strategies

Options can be used to manage the cost of maintaining an equity portfolio in a number of ways. Among the strategies are the use of short put and short call positions to serve as a substitute for a limit order in the cash market. Cash-secured put strategies can be used to purchase stocks at the target price, while covered calls or overwrites can be used to sell stocks at the target price. The target price is the one consistent with the portfolio manager's valuation or technical models and the price intended to produce the desired rate of return.

Choices also exist for a variety of strategies derived from put/call parity relationships that was explained in Chapter 6. There is always an alternative method of creating a position.[3]

Return Enhancement Strategies

Options can be used for return enhancement. Here we describe the most popular return enhance strategy: covered call strategy. Other return enhancement strategies include covered combination strategy and volatility valuation strategy.[4]

---

[3] Cost management strategies are discussed in Chapter 3 of Collins and Fabozzi (1999).

[4] These strategies are described in Collins and Fabozzi (1999).

Covered Call There are many variations of what is popularly referred to as a covered call strategy. If the portfolio manager owns the stock and writes a call on that stock, the strategy has been referred to as an *overwrite strategy*. If the strategy is implemented all at once (i.e., buy the stock and sell the call option), it is referred to as a *buy-write strategy*. The essence of the covered call is to trade price appreciation for income. The strategy is appropriate for slightly bullish investors who don't expect much out of the stock and want to produce additional income. These are investors who are willing either to limit upside appreciation for limited downside protection or to manage the costs of selling the underlying stock. The primary motive is to generate additional income from owning the stock.

Although the call premium provides some limited downside protection, this is not an insurance strategy because it has significant downside risk. Consequently, investors should proceed with caution when considering a covered call strategy.

A covered call is less risky than buying the stock because the call premium lowers the break-even recovery price. The strategy behaves like a long stock position when the stock price is below the strike price. On the other hand, the strategy is insensitive to stock prices above the strike price and is therefore capped on the upside. The maximum profit is given by the call premium and the out-the-money amount of the call option.

The payout pattern diagram is presented in Figure 21.3, which includes the long stock, short call, and covered call positions.

FIGURE 21.3   Covered Call Strategy

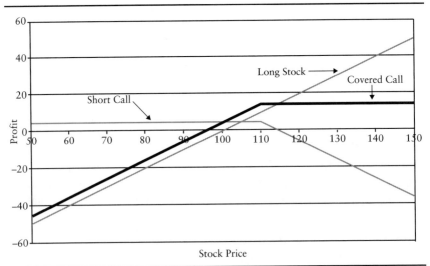

Basics of Features of OTC Equity Options

OTC options can be classified as first-generation and second-generation options. The latter are called *exotic options*. We describe each type of OTC option in this section.

First-Generation OTC Options

The basic type of first-generation OTC options either relaxed or extended the standardized structure of an existing listed option or created an option on stocks, stock baskets, or stock indexes without listed options or futures. OTC options were therefore first used to modify one or more of the features of listed options: the strike price, maturity, size, exercise type (American or European), and delivery mechanism. The terms were tailored to the specific needs of the investor. For example, the strike price can be any level, the maturity date at any time, the contract of any size, the exercise type American or European, the underlying can be a stock, a stock portfolio, or an equity index or a foreign equity index, and the settlement can be physical, in cash or a combination.

An example of how OTC options can differ from listed options is exemplified by an Asian option. Listed options are either European or American in structure relating to the timing of exercise. Flex options are listed options that go beyond standard European or American styles. One example is to provide a capped structure. Asian options are options with a payout that is dependent on the average price of the spot price over the life of the option. Due to the averaging process involved, the volatility of the spot price is reduced. The lower the expected volatility for the underlying, the lower the price of the option. Therefore, Asian options are cheaper than similar European or American options.

The first generation of OTC equity options offered flexible solutions to investment situations that listed options did not. For example, hedging strategies using the OTC equity market allow portfolio managers to achieve customized total risk protection for a specific time horizon. The first generation of OTC equity options allow investors to fine-tune their traditional equity investment strategies through customizing strike prices, and maturities, and choosing any underlying equity security or portfolio of securities.

Exotics: Second-Generation OTC Options

The second generation of OTC equity options includes a set of products that have more complex payoff characteristics than standard American or European call and put options. These second-generation options are sometimes referred to as *exotic options* and are essentially options with specific rules that govern the payoff. Exotic option structures can be created on a stand-alone basis or as part of a broader financing package such as an attachment to a bond issue.

Some OTC option structures are path dependent, which means that the value of the option to some extent depends on the price pattern of the underlying asset over the life of the option. In fact, the survival of some options, such as barrier options, depends on this price pattern. Other examples of path-dependent options include Asian options, lookback options, and reset options. Another group of OTC option structures has properties similar to step functions; they have fixed singular payoffs when a particular condition is met. Examples of this include digital or binary options and contingent options. A third group of options is classified as multivariate because the payoff is related to more than one underlying asset. Examples of this group include a general category of rainbow options such as spread options and basket options.

Competitive market makers offer portfolio managers a broad range of derivative products that satisfy their specific investment needs needs. The fastest growing portion of this market pertaining to equities involves products with option-like characteristics on major stock indexes or stock portfolios. It is derived from investor demand for long-dated European options and for options with more complex option structures. The real attractiveness of this market is that there is virtually no limit to the types of payouts.

In this section, we now review a few selective OTC product structures that can be used as management tools for equity portfolio management. (We have already reviewed one such option, Asian options.) However, don't look for details here.[5]

Barrier Options   A *barrier option* is a path-dependent option whose value and survival depends on the path or price pattern of the underlying asset over the life of the option. Moreover, the survival of the option is dependent on whether a "barrier" or predetermined price is crossed by the price of the underlying asset. *Knock-out* and *knock-in options* are examples of barrier options. A knock-out option goes out of existence or does not survive when the barrier price is reached or exceeded. A knock-in option, however, comes into existence when a barrier is reached or exceeded. The option can be a call or a put and the barrier can be below or above the current underlying asset value. In practice, when a knockout option is terminated, a rebate is given to the holder of the option. Conversely, if a knock-in option comes into existence, a rebate is paid to the option writer.

---

[5] A more detailed description of these options is provided in Nelken (1996) and Francis, Toy, and Whittaker (1995).

Barrier options can be structured as European, American or Bermudan with regard to when they may be exercised.

Compound Options   A *compound option* is an option written against another option. In other words, the underlying asset of a compound option is an option itself. There are 16 different types of compound options based on the exercise provisions of both the option and the underlying option, and whether each is a call or a put. For that reason, a call on a put would allow the holder of the call option to purchase a put option. The call could be a European type and the underlying put could be an American type. Compound options are an alternative way of paying a premium upfront for the right to purchase an option at a later date should the need arise.

Rainbow Options   The most common rainbow option is the option to exchange one asset for another, which is another name for a spread option or an overperformance option. These options are structured to yield a payoff that depends on the relative performance of one asset versus another. An at-the-money call structure would pay off if there is a positive return differential between the two assets. For example, a call spread option on the relative returns of two stocks, A and B, would pay off if the returns to stock A were sufficiently above the returns to stock B over the investment horizon to pay for the cost of the option. The intrinsic value of the option is the difference between the returns since inception of the contract. The usefulness of this contract is that it can pay off even when equity prices are declining.

Lookback Options   A *lookback option* is one that allows the holder to buy or sell the underlying asset at the most favorable price attained over the life of the contract. This is the price that maximizes the value of the option at expiration. For lookback call options with fixed strike prices, this means using the highest price over that time and for a put option it means using the lowest price. For lookback options with floating strike prices, which are the most common, the opposite holds true.

Chooser Options   A *chooser option* is also called an *as-you-like-it option* or a *pay-now-choose-later option*. It is initiated as neither a call nor a put but contains a provision that allows the holder to designate within some prescribed period whether the option will become a call or a put. There are two important types of chooser options: simple chooser and complex chooser. In the case of a simple chooser structure, the call and put alternatives have the same strike price and time to expiration. This is not the case for complex choosers, which can have a call and put alternatives that vary in both strike price and expiration.

Basket Options   A *basket option* is an option structured against a portfolio or basket of assets, which may include a group of stocks or may include multiple asset classes. For equity baskets, the stocks are selected on the basis of a criterion such as industry group, risk characteristic or other factor that represents the investor's objective. This is comparable to an index option where the price of the option on an equity index is less than the average price of the options on each individual stock that makes up the index. Basket options are particularly appropriate for investors with equity portfolios that do no resemble the indexes that underlie listed index option contracts. These options are suitable for an investor wishing to use options with an underlying asset that exactly reflects their current portfolio holdings.

Binary Options   A *binary option* makes an inherent gamble that pays off if the price of the underlying asset is above or below a particular price at expiration of the option. Binary options are like gambles that pay something when you win and nothing when you lose. The payment can be cash or the asset or nothing. Binary options are also called *digital options* or *all-or-nothing options* or *cash-or-nothing options*. These options can be structured to pay out only if the spot price is higher than the strike price at expiration or if the spot price exceeds the strike price at any time during the life of the option. The magnitude of the price move of the underlying is irrelevant because the payout is all or nothing.

Use of Exotic Equity Options

Before a portfolio manager decides to use exotic options, it is important to understand the impact that a specific exotic structure will have on the risk-reward profile of the current investment and the cost of implementing the strategy. For example, a lookback option that guarantees the optimal exercise value of the option seems very attractive. However, due to the expense of such an option, the portfolio manager may not be better off than simply purchasing the underlying security. The cost therefore becomes an important consideration in evaluating the impact of using exotics.

In order to accomplish this, investors need to understand the nature of the exotic derivative in question, including the pricing dynamics, the risks, and the expected benefits. Moreover, a complete understanding of what could go wrong is necessary including the potential costs, the tax implications, and the impact on the portfolio's performance. Consider, for example, a situation where the investor chooses a put option with a barrier structure that is designed to knock out at some level above the current price. If the barrier is hit suddenly and the put option is "knocked out," the risk is that the market reverses just as suddenly leaving the investor unprotected. It is crucial, then, that the investor understand that the cost saving of a barrier option compared to a standard put option has a risk component.

Despite the potential applications, the use of exotic options brings a new element into the portfolio management process. The use of exotics ought to be carefully considered and should provide a degree of precision to satisfy the investment objective that can only be achieved with an OTC exotic structure. Investment objectives that can be met with equal efficiency, using methods that don't involve options, need not require the use of exotic options. Nonetheless, OTC options do provide investors with opportunities to fine-tune their risk-reward profiles by providing flexible product structures that meet very specific investor requirements.

Options have risk management, returns management, and cost management applications. The addition of exotics can only add to these applications. We can sum this up by saying that the value of these products is the means they provide in meeting objectives with greater flexibility and efficiency. However, it must be emphasized that exotic structures are not appropriate in all situations. On the one hand, there are some portfolio managers who are eager to use the latest derivative product whether they need to or not; on the other hand, there are portfolio managers who fear derivatives and will not use them regardless of whether it would facilitate meeting their financial objectives. It is crucial to evaluate the investor's investment objectives in terms of risk and return and how these objectives can be efficiently met. When risk management needs can be met using listed markets, it may be prudent to do so. However, for investors with specific needs that cannot be met by the listed market, a derivatives process ought to be developed and a set of criteria established that can be used as guidelines for determining whether or not an exotic structure makes sense.

USING INTEREST RATE OPTIONS IN BOND PORTFOLIO MANAGEMENT

Interest rate options can be written on a fixed income security or an interest rate futures contract. The former options are called *options on physicals* and the latter are called *futures options*. The most liquid exchange-traded options on a fixed income security is an option on Treasury bonds traded on the Chicago Board of Trade. For reasons to be explained later, options on interest rate futures have been far more popular than options on physicals. However, portfolio managers have made increasingly greater use of OTC options. As with OTC options on stock indexes, typically they are purchased by institutional investors that want to hedge the risk associated with a specific security or index. Besides options on fixed income securities, there are OTC options on the shape of the yield curve or the yield spread between two securities. A discussion of these OTC options is beyond the scope of this chapter.

Exchange-Traded Futures Options

A futures option gives the buyer the right to buy from or sell to the writer a designated futures contract at the strike price at any time during the life of the option. If the futures option is a call option, the buyer has the right to purchase one designated futures contract at the strike price. That is, the buyer has the right to acquire a long futures position in the designated futures contract. If the buyer exercises the call option, the writer acquires a corresponding short position in the futures contract.

A put option on a futures contract grants the buyer the right to sell one designated futures contract to the writer at the strike price. That is, the option buyer has the right to acquire a short position in the designated futures contract. If the put option is exercised, the writer acquires a corresponding long position in the designated futures contract. Table 21.1 summarizes these positions. There are futures options on all the Treasury bond futures contracts that we discussed in the previous chapter.

The CBOT's Treasury bond futures contracts have delivery months of March, June, September, and December. In the previous chapter, we described the delivery process and the choices granted to the short. As with stock index futures contracts, there are *flexible Treasury futures options*. These futures options allow counterparties to customize options within certain limits. Specifically, the strike price, expiration date, and type of exercise (American or European) can be customized subject to CBOT constraints.

TABLE 21.1 Call and Put Futures Options

Type	Buyer Has the Right to ...	If Exercised, the Seller Has a ...	If Exercised, the Seller Pays the Buyer ...
Call	Purchase one futures at the strike price	A short futures position	Current futures price – Strike price
Put	Sell one futures at the strike price	A long futures position	Strike price – Current futures price

Mechanics of Trading Futures Options

Because the parties to the futures option will realize a position in a futures contract when the option is exercised, the question is, "What will the futures price be?" That is, at what price will the long be required to pay for the instrument underlying the futures contract, and at what price will the short be required to sell the instrument underlying the futures contract.

Upon exercise, the futures price for the futures contract will be set equal to the strike price. The position of the two parties is then immediately marked to market in terms of the then-current futures price. The futures position of the two parties will then be at the prevailing futures price. At the same time, the option buyer will receive from the option seller the economic benefit from exercising. In the case of a call futures option, the option writer must pay to the buyer of the option the difference between the current futures price and the strike price. In the case of a put futures option, the option writer must pay the option buyer the difference between the strike price and the current futures price.

For example, suppose an investor buys a call option on some futures contract in which the strike price is 85. Assume also that the futures price is 95 and that the buyer exercises the call option. Upon exercise, the call buyer is given a long position in the futures contract at 85, and the call writer is assigned the corresponding short position in the futures contract at 85. The futures positions of the buyer and the writer are immediately marked to market by the exchange. Because the prevailing futures price is 95 and the strike price is 85, the long futures position (the position of the call buyer) realizes a gain of 10, while the short futures position (the position of the call writer) realizes a loss of 10. The call writer pays the exchange 10, and the call buyer receives 10 from the exchange. The call buyer, who now has a long futures position at 95, can either liquidate the futures position at 95 or maintain a long futures position. If the former course of action is taken, the call buyer sells a futures contract at the prevailing futures price of 95. There is no gain or loss from liquidating the position. Overall, the call buyer realizes a gain of 10. The call buyer who elects to hold the long futures position will face the same risk and reward of holding such a position, but still realizes a gain of 10 from the exercise of the call option.

Suppose, instead, that the futures option is a put rather than a call, and the current futures price is 60 rather than 95. If the buyer of this put option exercises it, the buyer would have a short position in the futures contract at 85; the option writer would have a long position in the futures contract at 85. The exchange then marks the position to market at the then-current futures price of 60, resulting in a gain to the put buyer of 25, and a loss to the put writer of the same amount. The put buyer, who now has a short futures position at 60, can either liquidate the short futures position by buying a futures contract at the prevailing futures price of 60 or maintain the short futures position. In either case, the put buyer realizes a gain of 25 from exercising the put option.

Reasons for the Popularity of Futures Options

There are three reasons why futures options on Treasuries are preferred to options on physicals as the options vehicle of choice for institutional investors.[6] First, unlike options on Treasury securities, options on Treasury futures do not require payments for accrued interest to be made. Consequently, when a futures option is exercised, the call buyer and the put writer need not compensate the other party for accrued interest. Second, futures options are believed to be "cleaner" instruments because of the reduced likelihood of delivery squeezes. Market participants who must deliver a Treasury security are concerned that at the time of delivery, the Treasury to be delivered will be in short supply, resulting in a higher price to acquire the security. Because the deliverable supply of futures contracts is more than adequate for futures options currently traded, there is no concern about a delivery squeeze. Finally, in order to price any option, it is imperative to know at all times the price of the underlying instrument. In the bond market, current prices are not as easily available as price information on the futures contract. The reason is that Treasury securities trade in the OTC market, and, consequently, there is less price information compared to Treasury futures which are traded on an exchange.

Applications to Bond Portfolio Management

In our explanation of how to use options in equity portfolio management, we explained that they can be used in risk management and return enhancement. We do not repeat an explanation of the applications here. Instead, we illustrate how futures options can be used for hedging and return enhancement. More specifically, we demonstrate a protective put strategy (a risk management application) and a covered call writing strategy (a return enhancement application). As will be seen, the applications are complicated by the fact that the option is not an option on a physical but a futures option.

Protective Put Buying Strategy with Futures Options

Buying puts on Treasury futures options is one of the easiest ways to purchase protection against rising rates. As explained earlier in this chapter, this strat-

---

[6] The reasons are given by Goodman (1985, pp, 13–14).

egy is called a protective put buying strategy. To illustrate this strategy, we use a Procter & Gamble (P&G) bond to demonstrate the protective put buying strategy with Treasury bond futures for hedging. We can also compare hedging with Treasury bond futures provided in the previous chapter with hedging with Treasury futures options.

Let's assume that the portfolio manager owns $10 million par value of the P&G 5.55% expiring March 5, 2037, and used Treasury bond futures to lock in a sale price for those bonds on a futures delivery date. The P&G bond was selling at a yield of 5.74%. The specific contract used for hedging was the Treasury bond futures contract with settlement in March 2008. The *cheapest-to-deliver* (CTD) issue for the Treasury bond futures contract was the Treasury 6.25% August 15, 2023, selling to yield 4.643%.

Now we want to show how the portfolio manager could have used Treasury bond futures options instead of Treasury bond futures to protect against rising rates. In this illustration, we assume that the portfolio manager uses a put option on the March 2008 Treasury bond futures contract. The put options for this contract expire on February 22, 2008. For simplicity, we assumed that this yield spread would remain at 111.1 basis points.

To hedge the portfolio manager must determine the minimum price for the P&G bond. In the illustration it is assumed that the minimum price is 96.219 per bond or $9,621,900 for $10 million of par value. Thus, 96.219 becomes the target price for the P&G bond. However, the problem is that the portfolio manager is not purchasing an option on the P&G bond but a put option on a Treasury bond futures contract. Therefore, the hedging process requires that the portfolio manager must determine the strike price for a put option on a Treasury bond futures contract that is equivalent to a strike price of 96.219 for the P&G bond.

The process involves several steps. These steps are shown in Figure 21.4. Because the minimum price is 96.219 (Box 1) for the P&G bond, this means that the portfolio manager is seeking to establish a maximum yield of 5.821%. We know this because given the price, coupon, and maturity of the bond, the yield can easily be computed. This gets us to Box 2 in Figure 21.4. Now we have to make use of the assumption that the yield spread between the P&G bond and the CTD issue is 111.1 basis points. By subtracting this yield spread from the maximum yield of 5.821%, we get the maximum yield for the CTD issue of 4.710%. This gets us to Box 3 in Figure 21.4.

Now we move on to Box 4 in the figure. Given the yield of 4.710% for the CTD issue, the minimum price can be determined. Because the CTD issue is the Treasury 6.25% expiring August 15, 2023, a 4.710% yield means a target price for that issue is 116.8044. The corresponding futures price is found by dividing the price of the CTD issue by the conversion factor.[7] This

---

[7] The conversion factor was explained in the previous chapter.

FIGURE 21.4   Calculating Equivalent Strike Prices and Yields for Hedging with Futures Options

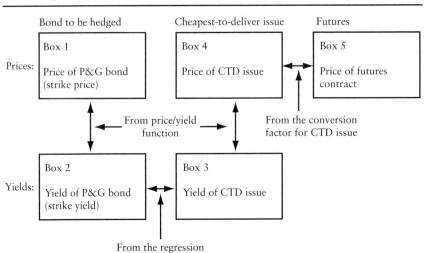

gets us to Box 5 in the figure. The conversion factor for the CTD issue is 1.0246. Therefore, the futures price is about 114.373 (116.8044 divided by 1.0246). Now the portfolio manager must look to the options market to determine what strike prices are available because there are a limited number of strike prices. In this illustration, we will assume that the strike price available to the portfolio manager is a strike price of 114 for a put option on a Treasury bond futures contract. This means that a put option on a Treasury bond futures contract with a strike price of 114 is roughly equivalent to a put option on the P&G bond with a strike price of 96.219.

The steps identified in Figure 21.4 and described above are always necessary to identify the appropriate strike price on a put futures option. The process involves simply (1) the relationship between price and yield; (2) the assumed relationship between the yield spread between the hedged bonds and the CTD issue; and (3) the conversion factor for the CTD issue. As with hedging with futures illustrated in the previous chapter, the success of the hedging strategy will depend on (1) whether the CTD issue changes and (2) the yield spread between the hedged bonds and the CTD issue.

The hedge ratio is determined using the same equation provided in the previous chapter because we will assume a constant yield spread between the bond to be hedged and CTD issue. To compute the hedge ratio, the portfolio manager must calculate the price values of a basis point at the option expiration date (assumed to be February 22, 2008) and at the yields corresponding to the futures strike price of 114 (4.710% yield for the CTD issue and 5.821% for the P&G bond). The price value of a basis point per $100 par value for the P&G bond and the CTD issue were 0.1353 and 0.1208, respectively. This results in a hedge ratio of 1.148 for the options hedge, or 1.15 with rounding. Because the par value of the futures option is $100,000 and the par value to be protected is $10,000, 115 put options on the Treasury bond futures contract should be purchased. At the time of the hedge, December 24, 2007, the price quote for this put option was 1.972. This means the dollar cost of each option is $197.2. Since 115 contracts would have to be purchased, the total cost of the put options (ignoring commissions) would be $22,678.

To create a table for the protective put hedge, we can use some of the numbers from Table 20.2 in Chapter 20. The first column in Table 21.2 repeats the numbers in the first column of Table 20.2 in the previous chapter; the second column in Table 21.2 reproduces the futures price from the fifth column Table 20.2 in the previous chapter. The rest of the columns in Table 20.2 are computed. The value of the put options shown in the third column of the table is easy to calculate because the value of each option at expiration is the strike price of the futures option (114) minus the futures price (or zero if that difference is negative). The difference is then multiplied by $1,000. Let's see why by looking at the first row that corresponds to a future price of 99.139. Since the strike price for the put option is 114, the value of the put option is 14.861 (114.000 – 99.139) per $100 of par value. Because the par value for the Treasury bond futures contract is $100,00, the 14.861 must be multiplied by $1,000. Thus the value of the contract is 14.861 times $1,000 or $14,861. For the 115 contracts purchased for this strategy, the total value is $1,709,015. The value of the 115 put options shown the third column of $1,709,040 differs by $25 due to rounding in earlier calculation.

The next-to-the-last column of Table 21.2 shows the cost of the 115 put options. The effective sale price for the P&G bond can then be computed. It is equal to the sum of the actual market price for the P&G bond and the value of the 115 put options at expiration, reduced by the cost of the 115 put options. The effective sale price is shown in the last column of the table. This effective sale price is never less than $9,601,824. Recall that we established a minimum price of $9,621,900. This minimum effective sale price is something that can be calculated prior to the implementation of the hedge. Note that as prices decline, the effective sale price actually exceeds the projected effective minimum sale price by a small amount. This is due only to rounding and the fact that the hedge ratio is left unaltered, although the relative price values of a basis point that go into the hedge ratio calculation

TABLE 21.2 Hedge of the $10 million Par Value of Procter & Gamble 5.55% Expiring March 5, 20037, Using a Protective Put Options Strategy

Actual Sale Price of P&G Bonds	Futures Price[a]	Value of 115 Put Options[b]	Cost of 115 Put Options	Effective Sale Price[c]
8,000,000	99.139	1,709,040	22,678	9,686,362
8,200,000	101.054	1,488,827	22,678	9,666,149
8,400,000	102.946	1,271,207	22,678	9,648,529
8,600,000	104.812	1,056,651	22,678	9,633,973
8,800,000	106.647	845,619	22,678	9,622,941
9,000,000	108.469	636,036	22,678	9,613,358
9,200,000	110.265	429,516	22,678	9,606,838
9,400,000	112.042	225,118	22,678	9,602,440
9,600,000	113.787	24,502	22,678	9,601,824
9,800,000	115.519	0	22,678	9,777,322
10,000,000	117.237	0	22,678	9,977,322
10,200,000	118.938	0	22,678	10,177,322
10,400,000	120.608	0	22,678	10,377,322
10,600,000	122.269	0	22,678	10,577,322
10,800,000	123.908	0	22,678	10,777,322
11,000,000	125.522	0	22,678	10,977,322
11,200,000	127.135	0	22,678	11,177,322
11,400,000	128.721	0	22,678	11,377,322
11,600,000	130.303	0	22,678	11,577,322

[a] These numbers are approximate because futures trade in even 32nds.
[b] From 115 × $1,000 × Max[(114 − Futures price), 0].
[c] Does not include transaction costs or the financing of the options position.

change as yields change. As prices increase, however, the effective sale price of the P&G bond increases as well. Unlike the futures hedge shown in Table 20.2 in the previous chapter, the protective put buying strategy protects the portfolio manager if rates rise but allows the portfolio manager to profit if rates fall.

Table 21.3 compares the hedging strategy involving shorting Treasury bond futures with that of the protective put buying strategy.

TABLE 21.3 Comparison of Hedging with Treasury Bond Futures and Protective Put Buying Strategy

Actual Sale Price of P&G Bonds	Effective Sale Price with Futures Hedge	Effective Sale Price with Protective Puts
8,000,000	9,767,401	9,686,362
8,200,000	9,745,273	9,666,149
8,400,000	9,725,761	9,648,529
8,600,000	9,709,339	9,633,973
8,800,000	9,696,472	9,622,941
9,000,000	9,685,066	9,613,358
9,200,000	9,676,751	9,606,838
9,400,000	9,670,575	9,602,440
9,600,000	9,668,215	9,601,824
9,800,000	9,667,281	9,777,322
10,000,000	9,668,034	9,977,322
10,200,000	9,670,700	10,177,322
10,400,000	9,676,990	10,377,322
10,600,000	9,684,253	10,577,322
10,800,000	9,694,165	10,777,322
11,000,000	9,706,975	10,977,322
11,200,000	9,719,797	11,177,322
11,400,000	9,735,913	11,377,322
11,600,000	9,752,347	11,577,322

Covered Call Writing Strategy

To see how covered call writing with futures options works, we assume that the portfolio manager owns the P&G bond used in our previous illustration. With futures selling around 114.375, a futures call option with a strike price of a 120 might be appropriate. The price for the March call options with a strike of 120 expiring on February 22, 2008, was 0.512. As before, it is assumed that the P&G bond will remain at a 111.11 basis point spread off the CTD issue. The number of options contracts sold will be the same, 115.

Table 21.4 shows the results of the covered call writing strategy given these assumptions. To calculate the effective sale price of the bonds in the covered call writing strategy, the premium received from the sale of the call options is added to the actual sale price of the bonds, and the liability

TABLE 21.4   Hedge of the $10 million Par Value, Procter & Gamble 5.55% March 5, 20037, Using a Cover Call Writing Strategy

Actual Sale Price of P&G Bonds	Futures Price[a]	Liability of 115 Call Options[b]	Premium of 115 Call Options	Effective Sale Price[c]
8,000,000	99.139	0	5,888	8,005,888
8,200,000	101.054	0	5,888	8,205,888
8,400,000	102.946	0	5,888	8,405,888
8,600,000	104.812	0	5,888	8,605,888
8,800,000	106.647	0	5,888	8,805,888
9,000,000	108.469	0	5,888	9,005,888
9,200,000	110.265	0	5,888	9,205,888
9,400,000	112.042	0	5,888	9,405,888
9,600,000	113.787	0	5,888	9,605,888
9,800,000	115.519	0	5,888	9,805,888
10,000,000	117.237	0	5,888	10,005,888
10,200,000	118.938	0	5,888	10,205,888
10,400,000	120.608	69,902	5,888	10,335,986
10,600,000	122.269	260,978	5,888	10,344,910
10,800,000	123.908	449,427	5,888	10,356,461
11,000,000	125.522	635,003	5,888	10,370,885
11,200,000	127.135	820,568	5,888	10,385,320
11,400,000	128.721	1,002,866	5,888	10,403,022
11,600,000	130.303	1,184,850	5,888	10,421,038

[a] These numbers are approximate because futures trade in even 32nds.
[b] From $115 \times \$1,000 \times \text{Max}[(\text{Futures price} - 120), 0]$.
[c] Does not include transaction costs or the financing of the options position.

associated with the short call position is subtracted from the actual sale price. The liability associated with each call is the futures price minus the strike price of 120 (or zero if this difference is negative), all multiplied by $1,000.The middle column of Table 21.4 is just this value multiplied by 115, the number of options sold.

Just as the minimum effective sale price could be calculated beforehand for the protective put strategy, the maximum effective sale price can be calculated beforehand for the covered call writing strategy. The maximum effective sale price will be the price of the P&G bond corresponding to the strike price of the call option sold, plus the premium received. In this case the strike price on the futures call option was 120. A futures price of 120 corresponds to a price of 122.9520 (from 120 times the conversion factor of 1.0246), and a corresponding yield of 4.126% for the CTD issue. The equivalent yield for the P&G bond is 111.11 basis points higher, or 5.3271%, for a corresponding price of 103.273. Adding on the premium received, 0.512, the final maximum effective sale price will be about 103.785 or $10,378,500. As Table 21.4 shows, if the P&G bond does trade at 111.1 basis points over the CTD issue as assumed, the maximum effective sale price for the P&G bond is, in fact, slightly more than that amount. The discrepancies shown in the table are due to rounding and the fact that the position is not adjusted even though the relative price values of a basis point change as yields change.

SUMMARY

In this chapter we explained how options can be used in portfolio management. Options permit investors to mold the shape of the return distribution to meet investment objectives better. Options can be used to control portfolio risk and to enhance portfolio returns.

Equity options include options on common stock and options on stock indexes. The underlying stock market index may be a broad-based index or a narrow-based index. Interest rate options include options on bonds (physical optons) and options on interest rate futures contracts (futures options). In bond portfolio manager, futures options are the preferred exchange-traded vehicle for implementing investment strategies.

APPENDIX: PRICING MODELS ON OPTIONS ON PHYSICALS AND FUTURES OPTIONS

In the appendix to Chapter 6, we discussed the Black-Scholes option pricing model. Here, we provide an overview of pricing models for options on physicals and futures options. In general, these options are much more complex than options on stocks or stock indexes because of the need to take into consideration the term structure of interest rates.

Black-Scholes Model for Valuing Options on Treasury Securities

As explained in the appendix to Chapter 6, by imposing certain assumptions and using arbitrage arguments, the Black-Scholes model computes the fair (or theoretical) price of a European call option on a nondividend-paying stock. Let's see if we can use the same model to price an option on a Treasury bond. Because the basic Black-Scholes model is for a noncash-paying security, let's apply it to a Treasury strip (i.e., zero-coupon Treasury) with three years to maturity. Assume the following values:

Strike price[8] = $88.00
Time remaining to expiration = 2 years
Current price= $83.96
Expected price volatility_standard deviation = 10%
Risk-free rate = 6%

In terms of the values in the Black-Scholes formula presented in the appendix to Chapter 6:

S = $83.96
K = 88.00
t = 2
s = 0.10
r = 0.06

Substituting these values into the Black-Scholes formula produces a price of $8.12. There is no reason to suspect that this estimated value is unreasonable. However, let's change the problem slightly. Instead of a strike price of $88, let's make the strike price for the call option on this Treasury strip $100.25. Substituting the new strike price into the Black-Scholes formulas give a value of $2.79. Since the Black-Scholes model tells us that this call option has a fair value of $2.79, is there any reason to believe this is unreasonable? Well, consider that this is a call option on a Treasury strip that will never have a value greater than its maturity value of $100 (it makes no coupon payments). Consequently, a call option with a strike price of $100.25 must have a value of zero. Yet the Black-Scholes model tells us that the value is $2.79! In fact, with a higher volatility assumption, the model would give an even greater value for the call option.

The reason for obtaining an unrealistic value for this option is the underlying assumptions of the model. There are three assumptions underlying the Black-Scholes model that limit its use in pricing options on Treasury securities. First, the probability distribution for the prices assumed by the Black-Scholes model permits some probability—no matter how small—that the price can take on any positive value. But in the case of a Treasury strip, the price cannot take on a value above $100. In the case of a Treasury coupon bond, we know that the price cannot exceed the sum of the coupon pay-

---

[8] Note the current price is $83.96, which is the present value of the maturity value of $100 discounted at 6% (i.e., $100/(1.06)^3).

ments plus the maturity value. Thus, unlike stock prices, Treasury prices have a maximum value. So any probability distribution for prices assumed by an option pricing model that permits Treasury prices to be higher than the maximum value could generate nonsensical option prices. The Black-Scholes model does allow Treasury prices to exceed the maximum bond value.

The second assumption of the Black-Scholes model is that the short-term interest rate is constant over the life of the option. Yet the price of a Treasury security will change as interest rates change. A change in the short-term interest rate changes the rates along the yield curve. Therefore, to assume that the short-term rate will be constant is inappropriate for Treasury options.

The third assumption is that the variance of prices is constant over the life of the option. Recall from Chapter 19 that as a bond moves closer to maturity, its price volatility declines. Therefore, the assumption that price variance is constant over the life of a Treasury option is inappropriate.

Black Model for Treasury Futures Options

The most commonly used model for futures options is the one developed by Black (see Black, 1976). The Black model was initially developed for valuing European options on forward contracts. There are two problems with this model. First, the Black model does not overcome the problems just identified for the Black-Scholes model. Failing to recognize the yield curve means that there will not be a consistency between pricing Treasury futures and options on Treasury futures. Second, the Black model was developed for pricing European options on futures contracts. Treasury futures options, however, are American options. The second problem can be overcome. The Black model was extended by Barone-Adesi and Whaley (1987) to American options on futures contracts. This is the model used by the CBOT to settle the flexible Treasury futures options. However, this model was also developed for equities and is subject to the first problem noted above. Despite its limitations, the Black model is the most popular option pricing model for options on Treasury futures

REFERENCES

Barone-Adesi, G., and Whaley, R. E. (1987). Efficient analytic approximation of American option values. *Journal of Finance* 42, no. 2: 301–320.

Black, F. (1976). The pricing of commodity contracts. *Journal of Financial Economics* 3 (March): 161–179.

Francis, J. C., Toy, W., and Whittaker, G. (1995). *The Handbook of Equity Derivatives*. Burr Ridge, IL: Irwin Professional Publishing.

Goodman, L. S. (1985) Introduction to debt options. In F. J. Fabozzi (ed.). *Winning the Interest Rate Game: A Guide to Debt Options* (pp. 3–24). Chicago: Probus.

Nelken, I. (ed.) (1996). *The Handbook of Exotic Options.* Burr Ridge, IL: Irwin.